# Database Concepts
## International Edition

Fifth Edition

# David M. Kroenke

# David J. Auer
Western Washington University

Boston   Columbus   Indianapolis   New York   San Francisco   Upper Saddle River
Amsterdam   Cape Town   Dubai   London   Madrid   Milan   Munich   Paris   Montreal   Toronto
Delhi   Mexico City   Sao Paulo   Sydney   Hong Kong   Seoul   Singapore   Taipei   Tokyo

**Editorial Director:** Sally Yagan
**Editor in Chief:** Eric Svendsen
**Executive Editor:** Bob Horan
**Editorial Project Manager:** Kelly Loftus
**Director of Marketing:** Patrice Lumumba
  Jones
**Senior Marketing Manager:** Anne Fahlgren
**Marketing Assistant:** Melinda Jensen
**Senior Managing Editor:** Judy Leale
**Production Project Manager:** Kelly Warsak
**Senior Operations Supervisor:** Arnold Vila
**Operations Specialist:** Ilene Kahn
**Senior Art Director:** Janet Slowik
**Creative Director:** Christy Mahon
**Sr. Art Director/Design Supervisor:**
  Janet Slowik

**Cover Designer:** Jodi Notowitz
**Manager, Visual Research:** Karen Sanatar
**Manager, Rights and Permissions:**
  Hessa Albader
**Media Director:** Lisa Rinaldi
**Lead Media Project Manager:** Denise
  Vaughn
**Full-Service Project Management:** Jennifer
  Welsch/BookMasters, Inc.
**Composition:** Integra Software Services
**Printer/Binder:** Courier/Kendallville
**Cover Printer:** Lehigh-Phoenix
  Color/Hagerstown
**Text Font:** 10/12, Simoncini Garamond

Microsoft® and Windows® are registered trademarks of the Microsoft Corporation in the U.S.A. and other countries. Screen shots and icons reprinted with permission from the Microsoft Corporation. This book is not sponsored or endorsed by or affiliated with the Microsoft Corporation.

MySQL®, the MySQL GUI Tools® (MySQL Query Brower® and MySQL Administrator®), the MySQL Command Line Client®, the MySQL Workbench®, and the MySQL Connector/ODBC® are registered trademarks of Sun Microsystems, Inc./Oracle Corporation. Screenshots and icons reprinted with permission of Oracle Corporation. This book is not sponsored or endorsed by or affiliated with Oracle Corporation.

Eclipse® and The Eclipse PHP Development Tools (PDT) Project® are trademarks of the Eclipse Foundation, Inc. The Eclipse platform is copyright Eclipse copyright holders and others, 2000, 2007. Screenshots reprinted under the terms of the Eclipse Public License v1.0 available at www.eclipse.org/legal/epl-v10.html. This book is not sponsored or endorsed by or affiliated with the Eclipse Foundation, Inc.

PHP is copyright The PHP Group 1999–2008, and is used under the terms of the PHP Public License v3.01 available at http://www.php.net/license/3_01.txt. This book is not sponsored or endorsed by or affiliated with The PHP Group.

This is a special edition of an established title widely used by colleges and universities throughout the world. Pearson published this exclusive edition for the benefit of students outside the United States and Canada. If you purchased this book within the United States or Canada you should be aware that it has been imported without the approval of the Publisher or the Author.

Many of the designations by manufacturers and seller to distinguish their products are claimed as trademarks. Where those designations appear in this book, and the publisher was aware of a trademark claim, the designations have been printed in initial caps or all caps.

10 9 8 7 6 5 4 3 2 1
ISBN 10:    0-13-208847-9
ISBN 13: 978-0-13-208847-3

# Brief Contents

## ONLINE APPENDICES: SEE PAGE 467 FOR INSTRUCTIONS

# Contents

# Preface

Colin Johnson is a production supervisor for a small manufacturer in Seattle. Several years ago, Colin wanted to build a database to keep track of components in product packages. At the time, he was using a spreadsheet to perform this task, but he could not get the reports he needed from the spreadsheet. Colin had heard about Microsoft Access, and he tried to use it to solve his problem. After several days of frustration, he bought several popular Microsoft Access books and attempted to learn from them. Ultimately, he gave up and hired a consultant who built an application that more or less met his needs. Over time, Colin wanted to change his application, but he did not dare try.

Colin was a successful businessperson who was highly motivated to achieve his goals. A seasoned Windows user, he had been able to teach himself how to use Microsoft Excel, Microsoft PowerPoint, and a number of production-oriented application packages. He was flummoxed at his inability to use Microsoft Access to solve his problem. "I'm sure I could do it, but I just don't have any more time to invest," he thought. This story is especially remarkable because it has occurred tens of thousands of times over the past decade, to many other people.

Microsoft, Oracle, IBM, and other database management system (DBMS) vendors are aware of such scenarios and have invested millions of dollars in creating better graphical interfaces, hundreds of multipanel wizards, and many sample applications. Unfortunately, such efforts treat the symptoms and not the root of the problem. In fact, most users have no clear idea what the wizards are doing on their behalf. As soon as these users require changes to database structure or to components such as forms and queries, they drown in a sea of complexity for which they are unprepared. With little understanding of the underlying fundamentals, these users grab at any straw that appears to lead in the direction they want. The consequence is poorly designed databases and applications that fail to meet the users' requirements.

Why can people like Colin learn to use a word processor or a spreadsheet product yet fail when trying to learn to use a DBMS product? First, the underlying database concepts are unnatural to most people. Whereas everyone knows what paragraphs and margins are, no one knows what a relation is. Second, it seems as though using a DBMS product ought to be easier than it is. "All I want to do is keep track of something. Why is it so hard?" people ask. Without knowledge of the relational model, breaking a sales invoice into five separate tables before storing the data is mystifying to business users.

This book is intended to help people like Colin understand, create and use databases in a DBMS product, whether they are individuals who found this book in a bookstore or students using this book as their textbook in a class.

## NEW TO THIS EDITION

Students and other readers of this book will benefit from new content and features in this edition. These include:

> The use of Microsoft Access 2010 to demonstrate and reinforce principles of database creation and use. This book has been revised to update all references to Microsoft Access and other Microsoft Office products (for example, Microsoft Excel) to the recently released Microsoft Office 2010 versions.

> The updating of the book to reflect the use of Microsoft SQL Server 2008/2008 R2 Express edition. Although most of the topics covered are backward compatible with Microsoft SQL Server 2005 Express Edition, all material in the book now uses SQL Server 2008 in conjunction with Office 2010 exclusively.

> The updating of the book to reflect the use of the MySQL Workbench as the sole database development tool for MySQL 5.1. The MySQL GUI Tools utilities used in *Database Concepts,* 4th edition, were declared "end of life" by MySQL on December 18, 2009. The MySQL Workbench 5.2.x now integrates the functionality of the MySQL GUI Tools bundle and is used throughout *Database Concepts,* 5th edition.

> The use of the Microsoft Windows 7 operating system as the workstation operating system discussed and illustrated in text. The previous edition used the Windows XP and Windows Vista operating systems, and *Database Concepts,* 5th edition, has been updated to the current Microsoft workstation OS.

> The addition of online Appendix C, "Getting Started in Systems Analysis and Design." This new material provides an introduction to systems analysis and design concepts for students or readers who have not had a course on this material. It presents basic methods used to gather the input material needed for data modeling, which is discussed in Chapter 4, and puts database development into the context of application development.

> The addition of online Appendix D, "Getting Started with Microsoft Visio 2010." This new material provides an introduction to the use of Microsoft Visio 2010 for data modeling, which is discussed in Chapter 4, and database design, which is discussed in Chapter 5.

> The addition of online Appendix E, "Getting Started with Web Servers, PHP and the Eclipse PDT." This new material provides an introduction to the installation and use of the Microsoft IIS Web server, PHP, and the Eclipse PDT IDE used for Web database application development, which is discussed in Chapter 7.

## THE NEED FOR ESSENTIAL CONCEPTS

With today's technology, it is impossible to utilize a DBMS successfully without first learning fundamental concepts. After years of developing databases with business users, we believe that the following database concepts are essential:

> Fundamentals of the relational model
> Structured Query Language (SQL)
> Data modeling
> Database design
> Database administration

And because of the increasing use of the Internet, the World Wide Web, and commonly available analysis tools, two more essential concepts need to be added to the list:

> Web database processing
> Business intelligence (BI) systems

Users like Colin—and students who will accept jobs similar to his—need not learn these topics to the same depth as future information systems professionals. Consequently, this textbook presents only essential concepts—those that are necessary for users like Colin who want to create and use small databases. Many of the discussions in this book are rewritten and simplified explanations of topics that you will find fully discussed in David M. Kroenke and David J. Auer's *Database Processing: Fundamentals, Design, and*

*Implementation*.[1] However, in creating the material for this text, we have endeavored to ensure that the discussions remain accurate and do not mislead. Nothing here will need to be unlearned if students take more advanced database courses.

# TEACHING CONCEPTS INDEPENDENT OF DBMS PRODUCTS

This book does not assume that students will use any particular DBMS product. The book does illustrate database concepts with Microsoft Access, SQL Server Express edition, and MySQL so that students can use these products as tools and actually try out the material, but all the concepts are presented in a DBMS-agnostic manner. When students learn the material this way, they come to understand that the fundamentals pertain to any database, from the smallest Microsoft Access database to the largest Microsoft Database or DB2 database. Moreover, this approach avoids a common pitfall. When concepts and products are taught at the same time, students frequently confound concepts with product features and functions. For example, consider referential integrity constraints. When taught from a conceptual standpoint, students learn that there are times when the values of a column in one table must always be present as values of a column in a second table. Students also learn how this constraint arises in the context of relationship definition and how either the DBMS or the application must enforce this constraint. If taught in the context of a DBMS—say in the context of Microsoft Access—students will only learn that in some cases you check a check box, and in other cases you do not. The danger is that the underlying concept will be lost in the product feature.

All this is not to say that a DBMS should not be used in this class. On the contrary, students can best master these concepts by applying them using a commercial DBMS product. This edition of the book was written to include enough basic information about Microsoft Access, SQL Server Express edition, and MySQL so that you can use these products in your class without the need for a second book or other materials. Microsoft Access is covered in some depth because of its popularity as a personal database and its inclusion in the Microsoft Office Professional suite of applications. However, if you want to cover a particular DBMS in depth or use a DBMS product not discussed in the book, you need to supplement this book with another text or additional materials. Prentice Hall provides a number of books for Microsoft Access 2010 and other DBMS products, and many of them can be packaged with this text.

# THE ACCESS WORKBENCH

This new edition of the text continues using "The Access Workbench," a feature first introduced in the third edition. Because Microsoft Access is widely used in introductory database classes, we feel it is important to include specific information on using Microsoft Access. Each chapter has an accompanying section of "The Access Workbench," which illustrates the chapter's concepts and techniques using Microsoft Access. "The Access Workbench" topics start with creating a database and a single table in Chapter 1 and move through various topics, finishing with Web database processing against a Microsoft Access database in Chapter 7 and using Microsoft Access (together with Microsoft Excel) to produce PivotTable OLAP reports in Chapter 8. This material is not intended to provide comprehensive coverage of Microsoft Access, but all the necessary basic Microsoft Access topics are covered so that your students can learn to effectively build and use Microsoft Access databases.

---

[1]David M. Kroenke and David J. Auer, *Database Processing: Fundamentals, Design, and Implementation*, 11th edition (Upper Saddle River, NJ: Pearson/Prentice Hall, 2010).

## KEY TERMS, REVIEW QUESTIONS, EXERCISES, AND PROJECTS

Because it is important for students to apply the concepts they learn, each chapter concludes with sets of key terms (new to this edition), review questions, exercises (including exercises tied to "The Access Workbench"), and three projects that run throughout the book. Students should know the meaning of each of the key terms and be able to answer the review questions if they have read and understood the chapter material. Each of the exercises requires students to apply the chapter concepts to a small problem or task.

The first of the projects, Garden Glory, concerns the development and use of a database for a partnership that provides gardening and yard maintenance services to individuals and organizations. The second project, James River Jewelry, addresses the need for a database to support a frequent-buyer program for a retail store. The third project, Queen Anne Curiosity Shop, concerns the sales and inventory needs of a retail business. These three projects appear in all of the book's chapters. In each instance, students are asked to apply the project concepts from the chapter. Instructors will find more information on the use of these projects in the instructor's manual and can obtain databases and data from the password-protected instructor's portion of this book's Web site (**www.pearsonhighered. com/kroenke**).

## SOFTWARE USED IN THE BOOK

Just as we have treated our discussions in a DBMS-agnostic way, whenever possible, we have selected software to be as operating system independent as possible. It is amazing how much excellent software is available online. Many major DBMS vendors provide free versions of their premier products (for example, Microsoft's SQL Server Express edition, Oracle Corporation's Oracle Database and MySQL). Web editors and integrated development environments (IDEs) are also available (for example, Eclipse, NetBeans, and Visual Studio Express edition). PHP, considered the fourth most commonly used programming language, is downloadable for use with many operating systems and Web servers.

So although the examples in this book were created using a Microsoft operating system, SQL Server 2008/2008 R2 Express edition, Microsoft Access 2010, Microsoft Excel 2010, and the IIS Web Server, most of them could just as easily be accomplished using Linux, MySQL Server Community edition, OpenOffice.org Base, OpenOffice.org Calc, and the Apache Web server. Some software products used in the book, such as PHP and Eclipse, are available for multiple operating systems.

Over the past 30-plus years, we have found the development of databases and database applications to be an enjoyable and rewarding activity. We believe that the number, size, and importance of databases will increase in the future and that the field will achieve even greater prominence. It is our hope that the concepts, knowledge, and techniques presented in this book will help students to participate successfully in database projects now and for many years to come.

## CHANGES FROM THE FOURTH EDITION

The most significant change in this edition is the coverage of Microsoft Access 2010 in the text and in all sections of "The Access Workbench." With the arrival of Microsoft Office 2010, we have updated this text to reflect the changes in that product. And, of course, we have also updated information on all the other products in the book. In particular, Windows 7 is now the operating system used to illustrate the applications shown in this book, and the MySQL Workbench is now the GUI used for MySQL database development.

We have kept and improved several features introduced in earlier editions of the book:

> The use of "The Access Workbench" sections in each chapter to provide coverage of Microsoft Access fundamentals
> Introductions to the use of Microsoft SQL Server 2008 R2 Express Edition (Appendix A, available online) and Oracle MySQL Community Server 5.1 (Appendix B, available online)
> The use of fully developed data sets for the three example databases that run throughout various portions of the book—Wedgewood Pacific Corporation, Heather Sweeney Designs, and Wallingford Motors
> The use of the PHP scripting language and the Eclipse IDE in the Web database processing topics
> Extended coverage of XML
> Extended coverage of business intelligence (BI) systems
> Coverage of the dimensional database model

In this edition, we continue to use the more effective discussion of normalization added in an earlier edition. We have presented a prescriptive procedure for normalizing relations through the use of a four-step process. This approach not only makes the normalization task easier, it also makes normalization principles easier to understand. Therefore, this approach has been retained in this edition. For instructors who want a bit more detail on normal forms, short definitions of most normal forms are included in Chapter 5.

## BOOK OVERVIEW

This textbook consists of eight chapters and five appendixes (all of which are readily available online at **www.pearsonhighered.com/kroenke**). Chapter 1 explains why databases are used, what their components are, and how they are developed. Students will learn the purpose of databases and their applications, as well as how databases differ from and improve on lists in spreadsheets. Chapter 2 introduces the relational model and defines basic relational terminology. It also introduces the fundamental ideas that underlie normalization and describe the normalization process.

Chapter 3 presents fundamental SQL statements. Basic SQL statements for data definition are described, as are SQL SELECT and data modification statements. No attempt is made to present advanced SQL statements; only the essential statements are described. Chapter 3A adds coverage of SQL views.

The next two chapters consider database design. Chapter 4 addresses data modeling, using the entity-relationship (E-R) model. This chapter describes the need for data modeling, introduces basic E-R terms and concepts, and presents a short case application (Heather Sweeney Designs) of E-R modeling. Chapter 5 describes database design and explains the essentials of normalization. The data model from the case example in Chapter 4 is transformed into a relational design in Chapter 5.

The last three chapters consider database management and the uses of databases in applications. Chapter 6 provides an overview of database administration. The case example database is built as a functioning database, and it serves as the example for a discussion of the need for database administration. The chapter surveys concurrency control, security, and backup and recovery techniques. Database administration is an important topic because it applies to all databases, even personal, single-user databases. In fact, in some ways this topic is more important for those smaller databases because no professional database administrator is present to ensure that critical tasks are performed. Chapter 6 also provides a discussion of distributed databases and object-relational databases.

Chapter 7 introduces the use of Web-based database processing, including a discussion of Open Database Connectivity (ODBC) and the use of the PHP scripting language. It also discusses the emergence and basic concepts of Extensible Markup Language (XML).

Chapter 8 discusses business intelligence (BI) systems and the data warehouse architectures that support them. It also discusses dimensional databases. The chapter also walks through how to build a dimensional database for Heather Sweeney Designs and then use it to produce a PivotTable Online Analytical Processing (OLAP) report.

Appendix A provides a short introduction to SQL Server 2008 R2 Express Edition, and Appendix B provides a similar introduction for MySQL 5.1. Microsoft Access is covered in "The Access Workbench" sections included in each chapter. Appendix C provides an introduction to systems analysis and design, and can be used to provide context for Chapter 4 (data modeling) and Chapter 5 (database design)—although in this book we focus on databases, databases are used in applications, and Appendix C describes the application development process in more detail. Appendix D is a short introduction to Microsoft Visio 2010, which can be used as a tool for data modeling (Chapter 4) and database design (Chapter 5). Another useful database design tool is the MySQL Workbench, and this use of the MySQL Workbench is discussed in Appendix B. Finally, Appendix E provides detailed support for Chapter 7 by giving detailed instructions on getting the Microsoft IIS Web server, PHP and the Eclipse PHP Development Tools (PDT) up and running.

## KEEPING CURRENT IN A RAPIDLY CHANGING WORLD

In order to keep *Database Concepts* up-to-date between editions, we post updates on the book's Web site, at **www.pearsonhighered.com/kroenke**, as needed. For example, after Microsoft Office 2007 was released, we posted Microsoft Access 2007 material so that instructors using Microsoft Access 2007 in their classes would have the needed versions of "The Access Workbench" sections and PowerPoint slides. Instructor resources and student materials are also available on the site, so be sure to check it from time to time.

## ACKNOWLEDGMENTS

We would like to thank the following reviewers for their insightful and helpful comments:

Edward Chan, Midlands Tech College
Rashmi Malhotra, St. Joseph's University
Tina Ostrander, Highline Community College
Darlene Ringhand, University of Rio Grande
Diane Wolfe, Oklahoma State University
Guoying Zhang, Midwestern State University

We would like to thank Bob Horan, our editor, Kelly Loftus, our assistant editor, and Kelly Warsak, our production editor, for their professionalism, insight, support and assistant in the development of this project. We would also like to thank Don Nilson for his detailed comments on the final manuscript. Finally, David Kroenke would like to thank his wife, Lynda, and David Auer would like to thank his wife, Donna, for their love, encouragement and patience while this project was being completed.

**David Kroenke**
**Seattle, Washington**
**David Auer**
**Bellingham, Washington**

# About the Authors

**David M. Kroenke** entered the computing profession as a summer intern at the RAND Corporation in 1967. Since then, his career has spanned education, industry, consulting, and publishing.

He has taught at the University of Washington, Colorado State University, and Seattle University. Over the years, he has led dozens of teaching seminars for college professors. In 1991 the International Association of Information Systems named him Computer Educator of the Year.

In industry, Kroenke has worked for the U.S. Air Force and Boeing Computer Services, and he was a principal in the start up of three companies. He was also vice president of product marketing and development for the Microrim Corporation and was chief technologist for the database division of Wall Data, Inc. He is the father of the semantic object data model. Kroenke's consulting clients include IBM Corporation, Microsoft, Computer Sciences Corporation, and numerous other companies and organizations.

His text *Database Processing: Fundamentals, Design, and Implementation*, first published in 1977, is now in its 11th edition. He introduced *Database Concepts* (now in the 5th edition that you are reading) in 2003. Kroenke has published many other textbooks, including the classic *Business Computer Systems* (1981). Recently, he has authored *Experiencing MIS* (3rd edition), *MIS Essentials* (2nd Edition), and *Using MIS* (4th edition).

An avid sailor, Kroenke also wrote *Know Your Boat: The Guide to Everything That Makes Your Boat Work*. Kroenke lives in Seattle, Washington. He is married and has two children and three grandchildren.

Since 1994, **David J. Auer** has been the director of Information Systems and Technology Services at Western Washington University's College of Business and Economics (CBE) and a lecturer in CBE's Department of Decision Sciences. Since 1981, he has taught CBE courses in quantitative methods, production and operations management, statistics, finance, and management information systems. Besides managing CBE's computer, network, and other technology resources, he also teaches management information systems courses. He has taught the Principles of Management Information Systems and Business Database Development courses, and he was responsible for developing CBE's network infrastructure courses, including Computer Hardware and Operating Systems, Telecommunications, and Network Administration. He has coauthored several MIS-related textbooks.

Auer holds a bachelor's degree in English literature from the University of Washington, a bachelor's degree in mathematics and economics from Western Washington University, a master's degree in economics from Western Washington University, and a master's degree in counseling psychology from Western Washington University. He served as a commissioned officer in the U.S. Air Force, and he has also worked as an organizational development specialist and therapist for an employee assistance program (EAP).

Auer and his wife, Donna, live in Bellingham, Washington. He has two children and five grandchildren.

# PART I

# Database Fundamentals

Part I introduces fundamental concepts and techniques of relational database management. Chapter 1 explains database technology, discusses why databases are used, and describes the components of a database system. Chapter 2 introduces the relational model and defines key relational database terms. It also presents basic principles of relational database design. Chapter 3 presents Structured Query Language, an international standard for creating and processing relational databases.

After you have learned these fundamental database concepts, we will focus on database modeling, design, and implementation in Part II. Finally, we will discuss database management, Web database applications, and business intelligence (BI) systems in Part III.

# CHAPTER 1

# Getting Started

**Chapter Objectives**

> Identify the purpose and scope of this book

> Know the potential problems with lists

> Understand the reasons for using a database

> Understand how using related tables helps you avoid the problems of using lists

> Know the components of a database system

> Learn the elements of a database

> Learn the purpose of a database management system (DBMS)

> Understand the functions of a database application

Knowledge of database technology increases in importance every day. Databases are used everywhere: They are key components of e-commerce and other Web-based applications. They lay at the heart of organization-wide operational and decision support applications. Databases are also used by thousands of work groups and millions of individuals. Estimates of the number of active databases in the world today exceed 10 million.

The purpose of this book is to teach you the essential database concepts, technology, and techniques that you need to begin a career as a database developer. This book does not teach everything of importance in database technology, but it will give you sufficient background to be able to create your own personal databases and to participate as a member of a team in the development of larger, more complicated databases. You will also be able to ask the right questions to learn more on your own.

In this first chapter, we investigate the reasons for using a database. We begin by describing the problems that can occur when using lists. Using a series of examples, we illustrate how using sets of related tables helps you to avoid those problems. Next, we describe the components of a database system and explain the elements of a database, the purpose of the database management system (DBMS), and the functions of a database application.

# WHY USE A DATABASE?

A database is used to help people keep track of things. You might wonder why we need a special term (and course) for such technology when a simple **list** could serve the same purpose. Many people do keep track of things by using lists, and sometimes such lists are valuable. In other cases, however, simple lists lead to data inconsistencies and other problems.

In this section, we examine several different lists and show some of these problems. As you will see, we can solve the problems by splitting lists into tables of data. Such tables are the key components of a database. A majority of this text concerns the design of such tables and techniques for manipulating the data they contain.

## Problems with Lists

Figure 1-1 shows a simple list of student data, named the Student List,[1] stored in a spreadsheet. The Student List is a very simple list, and for such a list a spreadsheet works quite well. Even if the list is long, you can sort it alphabetically by last name, first name, or email address to find any entry you want. You can change the data values, add data for a new student, or delete student data. With a list like the Student List in Figure 1-1, none of these actions is problematic, and a database is unnecessary. Keeping this list in a spreadsheet is just fine.

Suppose, however, we change the Student List by adding adviser data, as shown in Figure 1-2. You can still sort the new Student with Adviser List in a number of ways to find an entry, but making changes to this list causes **modification problems**. Suppose, for example, that you want to delete the data for the student Chip Marino. As shown in Figure 1-3, if you delete the seventh row you not only remove Chip Marino's data, you also remove the fact that there is an adviser named Tran and that Professor Tran's email address is Ken.Tran@ourcamus.edu.

Similarly, updating a value in this list can have unintended consequences. If, for example, you change AdviserEmail in the eighth row, you will have inconsistent data. After the change, the fifth row indicates one email address for professor Taing, and the eighth row indicates a different email address for the same professor. Or is it the same professor? From this list, we cannot tell if there is one professor Taing with two inconsistent email addresses or whether there are two professors named Taing with different email addresses. By making this update, we add confusion and uncertainty to the list.

Finally, what do we do if we want to add data for a professor who has no advisees? For example, Professor Greene has no advisees, but we still want to record his or her email address. As shown in Figure 1-3, we must insert a row with incomplete values, called **null**

---

**FIGURE 1-1**

The Student List in a Spreadsheet

| | A | B | C |
|---|---|---|---|
| 1 | LastName | FirstName | Email |
| 2 | Andrews | Matthew | Matthew.Andrews@ourcampus.edu |
| 3 | Brisbon | Lisa | Lisa.Brisbon@ourcampus.edu |
| 4 | Fischer | Douglas | Douglas.Fischer@ourcampus.edu |
| 5 | Hwang | Terry | Terry.Hwang@ourcampus.edu |
| 6 | Lai | Tzu | Tzu.Lai@ourcampus.edu |
| 7 | Marino | Chip | Chip.Marino@ourcampus.edu |
| 8 | Thompson | James | James.Thompson@ourcampus.edu |

---

**FIGURE 1-2**

The Student with Advisor List

| | A | B | C | D | E |
|---|---|---|---|---|---|
| 1 | LastName | FirstName | Email | AdviserLastName | AdviserEmail |
| 2 | Andrews | Matthew | Matthew.Andrews@ourcampus.edu | Baker | Linda.Baker@ourcampus.edu |
| 3 | Brisbon | Lisa | Lisa.Brisbon@ourcampus.edu | Valdez | Richard.Valdez@ourcampus.edu |
| 4 | Fischer | Douglas | Douglas.Fischer@ourcampus.edu | Baker | Linda.Baker@ourcampus.edu |
| 5 | Hwang | Terry | Terry.Hwang@ourcampus.edu | Taing | Susan.Taing@ourcampus.edu |
| 6 | Lai | Tzu | Tzu.Lai@ourcampus.edu | Valdez | Richard.Valdez@ourcampus.edu |
| 7 | Marino | Chip | Chip.Marino@ourcampus.edu | Tran | Ken.Tran@ourcampus.edu |
| 8 | Thompson | James | James.Thompson@ourcampus.edu | Taing | Susan.Taing@ourcampus.edu |

---

[1]In order to easily identify and reference the lists being discussed, we capitalize the first letter of each word in the list names in this chapter. Similarly, we capitalize the names of the database tables associated with the lists.

FIGURE 1-3

**Modification Problems in the Student with Adviser List**

values, in the database field. As you will learn in the next chapter, null values are always problematic, and we want to avoid them whenever possible.

Now, what exactly happened in these two examples? We had a simple list with three columns, added two more columns to it, and thereby created several problems. The problem is not just that the list has five columns instead of three. The Student with Residence List in Figure 1-4 has five columns, yet it suffers from none of the problems of the Student with Adviser List in Figure 1-3.

In the Student with Residence List in Figure 1-4, we can delete the data for student Chip Marino and lose only data for that student. No unintended consequences occur. Similarly, we can change the value of Residence for student Tzu Lai without introducing any inconsistency. Finally, we can add data for student Garret Ingram and not have any null values.

An essential difference exists between the Student with Adviser List in Figure 1-3 and the Student with Residence List in Figure 1-4. Looking at those two figures, can you determine the difference? The essential difference is that the Student with Residence List in Figure 1-4 is all about a *single thing*: All the data in that list concern *students*. In contrast, the Student with Adviser List in Figure 1-3 is about *two things*: Some of the data concern *students*, and some of the data concern *advisers*. In general, whenever a list has data about two or more different things modification problems will result.

To reinforce this idea, examine the Student with Adviser and Department List in Figure 1-5. This list has data about three different things: *students*, *advisers*, and *departments*. As you can see in the figure, the problems with inserting, updating, and deleting data just get worse. A change in the value of AdviserLastName, for example, might necessitate a change in only AdviserEmail, or it might require a change in AdviserEmail, Department, and AdminLastName. As you can imagine, if this list is long—for example, if it has thousands of rows—and if several people process it, it will be a mess in a very short time.

FIGURE 1-4

**The Student with Residence List**

| | A | B | C | D | E |
|---|---|---|---|---|---|
| 1 | LastName | FirstName | Email | Phone | Residence |
| 2 | Andrews | Matthew | Matthew.Andrews@ourcampus.edu | 301-555-2225 | 123 15th St Apt 21 |
| 3 | Brisbon | Lisa | Lisa.Brisbon@ourcampus.edu | 301-555-2241 | Dorsett Room 201 |
| 4 | Fischer | Douglas | Douglas.Fischer@ourcampus.edu | 301-555-2257 | McKinley Room 109 |
| 5 | Hwang | Terry | Terry.Hwang@ourcampus.edu | 301-555-2229 | McKinley Room 208 |
| 6 | Ingram | Garrett | Garett.Ingram@ourcampus.edu | 301-555-2223 | Dorsett Room 218 |
| 7 | Lai | Tzu | Tzu.Lai@ourcampus.edu | 301-555-2231 | McKinley Room 115 |
| 8 | Marino | Chip | Chip.Marino@ourcampus.edu | 301-555-2243 | 234 16th St Apt 32 |
| 9 | Thompson | James | James.Thompson@ourcampus.edu | 301-555-2245 | 345 17th St Apt 43 |

Inserted row— data OK

Changed row—no inconsistent data

Deleted row—no data loss

FIGURE 1-5

The Student with Adviser and Department List

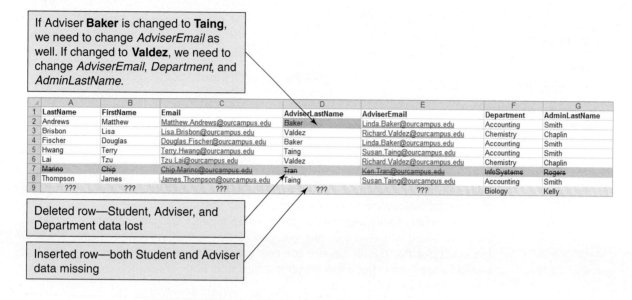

If Adviser **Baker** is changed to **Taing**, we need to change *AdviserEmail* as well. If changed to **Valdez**, we need to change *AdviserEmail*, *Department*, and *AdminLastName*.

| | A | B | C | D | E | F | G |
|---|---|---|---|---|---|---|---|
| 1 | LastName | FirstName | Email | AdviserLastName | AdviserEmail | Department | AdminLastName |
| 2 | Andrews | Matthew | Matthew.Andrews@ourcampus.edu | Baker | Linda.Baker@ourcampus.edu | Accounting | Smith |
| 3 | Brisbon | Lisa | Lisa.Brisbon@ourcampus.edu | Valdez | Richard.Valdez@ourcampus.edu | Chemistry | Chaplin |
| 4 | Fischer | Douglas | Douglas.Fischer@ourcampus.edu | Baker | Linda.Baker@ourcampus.edu | Accounting | Smith |
| 5 | Hwang | Terry | Terry.Hwang@ourcampus.edu | Taing | Susan.Taing@ourcampus.edu | Accounting | Smith |
| 6 | Lai | Tzu | Tzu.Lai@ourcampus.edu | Valdez | Richard.Valdez@ourcampus.edu | Chemistry | Chaplin |
| 7 | Marino | Chip | Chip.Marino@ourcampus.edu | Tran | Ken.Tran@ourcampus.edu | InfoSystems | Rogers |
| 8 | Thompson | James | James.Thompson@ourcampus.edu | Taing | Susan.Taing@ourcampus.edu | Accounting | Smith |
| 9 | ??? | ??? | ??? | ??? | ??? | Biology | Kelly |

Deleted row—Student, Adviser, and Department data lost

Inserted row—both Student and Adviser data missing

## Using Relational Database Tables

The problems of using lists were first identified in the 1960s, and a number of different techniques were developed to solve them. Over time, a methodology called the **relational model** emerged as the leading solution, and today almost every commercial database is based on the relational model. We will examine the relational model in detail in Chapter 2. Here, however, we introduce the basic ideas of the relational model by showing how it solves the modification problems of lists.

Remember your eighth-grade English teacher? He or she said that a paragraph should have a single theme. If you have a paragraph with more than one theme, you need to break it up into two or more paragraphs, each with a *single theme.* That idea is the foundation of the design of relational databases. A **relational database** contains a collection of separate tables. A **table** holds data about one and only one theme in most circumstances. If a table has two or more themes, we break it up into two or more tables.

> **B T W**
>
> A table and a *spreadsheet* (also known as a *worksheet*) are very similar in that you can think of both as having rows, columns, and cells. The details that define a table as something different from a spreadsheet are discussed in Chapter 2. For now, the main differences you see are that tables have column names instead of identifying letters (for example, *Name* instead of *A*) and that the rows are not necessarily numbered.

**A Relational Design for the Student with Adviser List** The Student with Adviser List in Figure 1-2 has two themes: *students* and *advisers*. If we put this data into a relational database, we place the student data in one table named STUDENT and the adviser data in a second table named ADVISER.

> ## B T W
>
> In this book, table names appear in all capital, or uppercase, letters (STUDENT, ADVISER). Column names have initial capitals (Phone, Address), and where column names consist of more than one word the initial letter of each word is capitalized (LastName, AdviserEmail).

We still want to show which students have which advisers, however, so we leave AdviserLastName in the ADVISER table. As shown in Figure 1-6, the values of AdviserLastName now let us link rows in the two tables to each other.

Now consider possible modifications to these tables. As you saw in the last section, three basic **modification actions** are possible: **insert**, **update**, and **delete**. To evaluate a design, we need to consider each of these three actions. As shown in Figure 1-7, we can insert, update, and delete in these tables with no modification problems.

## FIGURE 1-6

The ADVISER and STUDENT Tables

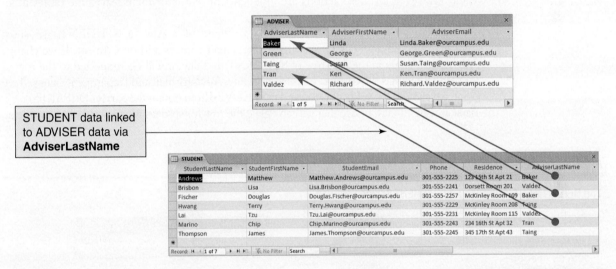

STUDENT data linked to ADVISER data via **AdviserLastName**

## FIGURE 1-7

Modifying the ADVISER and STUDENT Tables

Changed data—data remains consistent

Inserted data—no STUDENT data required

Deleted data—no ADVISER data lost

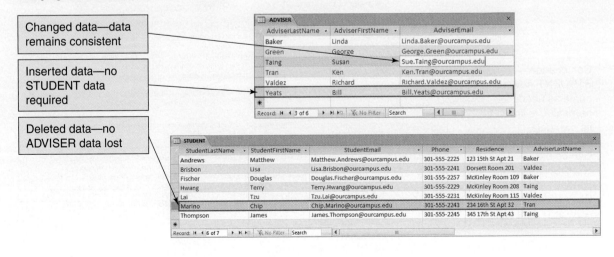

For example, we can insert the data for Professor Yeats by just adding his or her data to the ADVISER table. No student references Professor Yeats, but this is not a problem. Perhaps a student will have Yeats as an adviser in the future. We can also update data values without unintended consequences. The email address for Professor Taing can be changed to Sue.Taing@ourcampus.edu, and no inconsistent data will result because Professor Taing's email address is stored just once in the ADVISER table. Finally, we can delete data without associated consequences. For example, if we delete the data for student Marino from the STUDENT table, we lose no adviser data.

**A Relational Design for the Student with Adviser and Department List**   We can use a similar strategy to develop a relational database for the Student with Adviser and Department List shown in Figure 1-5. This list has three themes: *students*, *advisers*, and *departments*. Accordingly, we create three tables, one for each of these three themes, as shown in Figure 1-8.

As illustrated in Figure 1-8, we can use AdviserLastName and Department to link the tables. Also, as shown in this figure, this set of tables does not have any modification problems. We can insert new data without creating null values, we can modify data without creating inconsistencies, and we can delete data without unintended consequences. Notice in particular that when we add a new row to DEPARTMENT we can add rows in ADVISER, if we want, and we can add rows in STUDENT for each of the new rows in ADVISER, if we want. However, all these actions are independent. None of them leaves the tables in an inconsistent state.

Similarly, when we modify AdviserLastName of a row in STUDENT, we automatically pick up adviser's correct first name, email address and department. If we change AdviserLastName in the first row of STUDENT to Taing, it will be connected to the row in ADVISER that has the correct AdviserFirstName, AdviserEmail and Department values. If we want, we can use the value of Department in ADVISER to obtain the correct DEPARTMENT data, as well. Finally, notice that we can delete the row for student Marino without a problem.

---

**FIGURE 1-8**

**The DEPARTMENT, ADVISER, and STUDENT Tables**

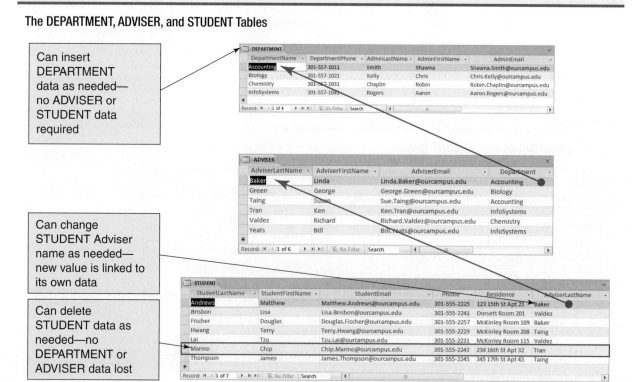

Can insert DEPARTMENT data as needed— no ADVISER or STUDENT data required

Can change STUDENT Adviser name as needed— new value is linked to its own data

Can delete STUDENT data as needed—no DEPARTMENT or ADVISER data lost

As an aside, the design in Figure 1-8 has removed the problems that occur when modifying a list, but it has also introduced a new problem. Specifically, what would happen if we deleted the first row in ADVISER? Students Andrews and Fischer would have an invalid value of AdviserLastName because Baker would no longer exist in the ADVISER table. To prevent this problem, we can design the database so that a deletion of a row is not allowed if other rows depend on it, or we can design it so that the dependent rows are deleted, as well. We are skipping way ahead here; however, we will discuss such issues in later chapters.

**A Relational Design for Art Course Enrollments**   To fix in your mind the ideas we have been examining, consider the Art Course List in Figure 1-9, which is used by an art school that offers art courses to the public. This list has modification problems. For example, suppose we change the value of CourseDate in the first row. This change might mean that the date for the course is changing, in which case the CourseDate values should be changed in other rows, as well. Alternatively, this change could mean that a new Advanced Pastels (Adv Pastels) course is being offered. Either is a possibility.

As with the previous examples, we can remove the problems and ambiguities by creating a separate table for each theme. However, in this case the themes are more difficult to determine. Clearly, one of the themes is *customer* and another one is *art course.* However, a third theme exists that is more difficult to bring to light. The customer has paid a certain amount toward a course. The amount paid is not a property of the customer because it varies depending on which course the customer is taking. For example, customer Ariel Johnson paid $250 for the Advanced Pastels (Adv Pastels) course and $350 for the Intermediate Pastels (Int Pastels) course. Similarly, the amount paid is not a property of the course, because it varies with which customer has taken the course. Therefore, the third theme of this list must concern the *enrollment* of a particular student in a particular class. Figure 1-10 shows a design of three tables that correspond to these three themes.

Notice that this design assigns an **ID column** named CustomerNumber that assigns a unique identifying number to each row of CUSTOMER; this is necessary because some customers might have the same name. Another ID column named CourseNumber has also been added to COURSE. This is necessary because some courses have the same name. Finally, notice that the rows of the ENROLLMENT table show the amount paid by a particular customer for a particular course and that the ID columns CustomerNumber and CourseNumber are used as linking columns to the other tables.

**A Relational Design for Parts and Prices**   Now let's consider a more complicated example. Figure 1-11 shows a spreadsheet that holds the Project Equipment List used by a housing contractor named Carbon River Construction to keep track of the parts that it buys for various construction projects.

Suppose your job is to maintain this list, and your boss tells you that customer Elizabeth Barnaby changed her phone number. How many changes would you need to make to this spreadsheet? For the data in Figure 1-11, you would need to make this change 10 times. Now suppose the spreadsheet has 5,000 rows. How many changes might you need

---

**FIGURE 1-9**

**The Art Course List with Problematic Changes**

| | A | B | C | D | E | F | G |
|---|---|---|---|---|---|---|---|
| 1 | CustomerLastName | CustomerFirstName | Phone | CourseDate | AmountPaid | Course | Fee |
| 2 | Johnson | Ariel | 206-567-1234 | 10/1/2011 | $250.00 | Adv Pastels | $500.00 |
| 3 | Green | Robin | 425-678-8765 | 9/15/2011 | $350.00 | Beg Oils | $350.00 |
| 4 | Jackson | Charles | 360-789-3456 | 10/1/2011 | $500.00 | Adv Pastels | $500.00 |
| 5 | Johnson | Ariel | 206-567-1234 | 3/15/2011 | $350.00 | Int Pastels | $350.00 |
| 6 | Pearson | Jeffery | 206-567-2345 | 10/1/2011 | $500.00 | Adv Pastels | $500.00 |
| 7 | Sears | Miguel | 360-789-4567 | 9/15/2011 | $350.00 | Beg Oils | $350.00 |
| 8 | Kyle | Leah | 425-678-7654 | 11/15/2011 | $250.00 | Adv Pastels | $500.00 |
| 9 | Myers | Lynda | 360-789-5678 | 10/15/2011 | $0.00 | Beg Oils | $350.00 |

How to enter the fee for a new course?

Consequences of changing this date?

Consequences of deleting this row?

FIGURE 1-10

The Art Course Tables

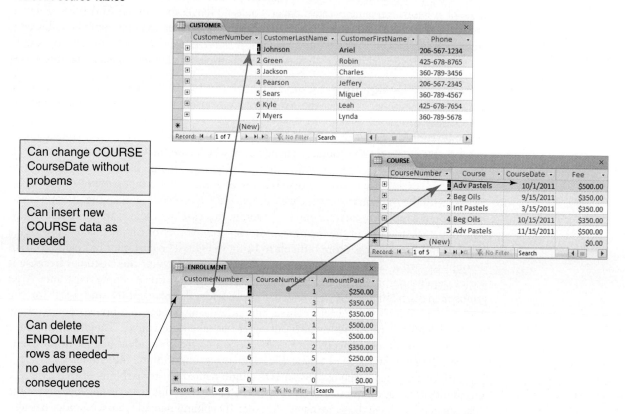

Can change COURSE CourseDate without probems

Can insert new COURSE data as needed

Can delete ENROLLMENT rows as needed— no adverse consequences

to make? The answer could be dozens, and you need to worry not only about the time this will take but also about the possibility of errors—you might miss her name in a row or two.

Consider a second problem with this list. In this business, each supplier agrees to a particular discount for all parts it supplies. For example, in Figure 1-11 the supplier NW Electrical has agreed to a 25-percent discount. With this list, every time you enter a new part quotation, you must enter the supplier of that part, along with the correct discount. If dozens or hundreds of suppliers are used, there is a chance that you will sometimes enter

FIGURE 1-11

The Project Equipment List as a Spreadsheet

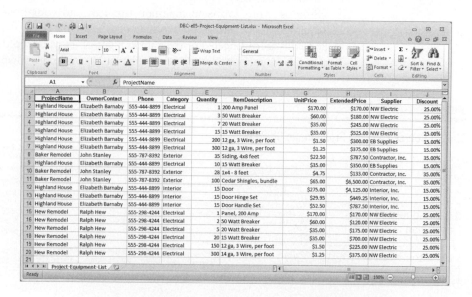

the wrong discount. If you do, the list will have more than one discount for one supplier—a situation that is incorrect and confusing.

Now consider what happens when you enter data correctly but inconsistently. The first row has a part named 200 Amp panel, whereas the 15th row has a part named Panel, 200 Amp. Are these two parts the same item, or are they different? It turns out that they are the same item, but they were named differently.

A fourth problem concerns partial data. Suppose you know that a supplier offers a 20-percent discount, but Carbon River has not yet ordered from the supplier. Where do you record the 20-percent discount?

Just as we did for the previous examples, we can fix the Project Equipment List by breaking it up into separate tables. Because this list is more complicated, we need to use more tables. When we analyze the Project Equipment List, we find data about four themes: *projects*, *items*, *price quotations*, and *suppliers*. Accordingly, we create a database with four tables and relate those four tables using linking values, as before. Figure 1-12 shows our four tables and their relationships.

In Figure 1-12, note that the QUOTE table holds a unique quote identifier (QuoteID), a quantity, a unit price, an extended price (which is equal to [quantity * unit price]), and three ID columns as linking values: ProjectID for PROJECT, ItemNumber for ITEM, and SupplierID for SUPPLIER.

Now if Elizabeth Barnaby changes her phone number we need to make that change only once—in the PROJECT table. Similarly, we need to record a supplier discount only once—in the SUPPLIER table.

## Processing Relational Tables

By now, you may have a burning question: It may be fine to tear the lists up into pieces in order to eliminate processing problems, but what if the users want to view their data in the format of the original list? With the data separated into different tables, the users will have

## FIGURE 1-12

**The Project Equipment Tables**

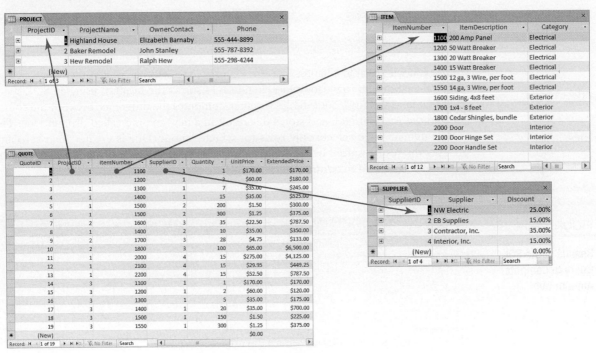

**FIGURE 1-13**

Results of the SQL
Query to Re-create
the Art Course List

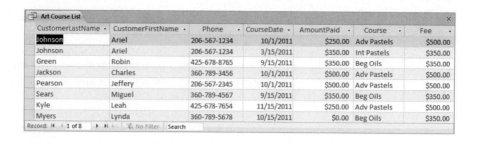

to jump from one table to another to find the information they want, and this jumping around will become tedious.

This is an important question and one that many people addressed in the 1970s and 1980s. Several approaches were invented for combining, querying, and processing sets of tables. Over time, one of those approaches, a language called **Structured Query Language (SQL)**, emerged as the leading technique for data definition and manipulation. Today, SQL is an international standard. Using SQL, you can reconstruct lists from their underlying tables; you can query for specific data conditions; you can perform computations on data in tables; and you can insert, update, and delete data.

**Processing Tables by Using SQL**   You will learn how to code SQL statements in Chapter 3. However, to give you an idea of the structure of such statements, let's look at an SQL statement that joins the three tables in Figure 1-10 to produce the original Art Course List. Do not worry about understanding the syntax of this statement, just realize that it produces the result shown in Figure 1-13, which contains all the Art Course List data (although in a slightly different row order[2]).

```
SELECT    CUSTOMER.CustomerLastName,
          CUSTOMER.CustomerFirstName, CUSTOMER.Phone,
          COURSE.CourseDate, ENROLLMENT.AmountPaid,
          COURSE.Course, COURSE.Fee
FROM      CUSTOMER, ENROLLMENT, COURSE
WHERE     CUSTOMER.CustomerNumber = ENROLLMENT.CustomerNumber
AND       COURSE.CourseNumber = ENROLLMENT.CourseNumber;
```

As you will learn in Chapter 3, it is also possible to select rows, to order them, and to make calculations on row data values. Figure 1-14 shows the result of using an SQL statement that joins the Art Course tables together, computes the difference between the course Fee and the AmountPaid, and stores this result in a new column called AmountDue. The SQL statement then selects only rows for which AmountDue is greater than zero and presents the results sorted by CustomerName. Compare the data in Figure 1-13 with the results in Figure 1-14 to ensure that the results are correct.

**FIGURE 1-14**

Results of the SQL
Query to Compute
Amount Due

| CustomerLastName | CustomerFirstName | Phone | Course | CourseDate | Fee | AmountPaid | AmountDue |
| --- | --- | --- | --- | --- | --- | --- | --- |
| Johnson | Ariel | 206-567-1234 | Adv Pastels | 10/1/2011 | $500.00 | $250.00 | $250.00 |
| Kyle | Leah | 425-678-7654 | Adv Pastels | 11/15/2011 | $500.00 | $250.00 | $250.00 |
| Myers | Lynda | 360-789-5678 | Beg Oils | 10/15/2011 | $350.00 | $0.00 | $350.00 |

Record: 1 of 3 — No Filter — Search

---

[2]We will discuss how to sort data to control the row order in Chapter 3.

# WHAT IS A DATABASE SYSTEM?

As shown in Figure 1-15, a database system consists of the four components: users, the database application, the database management system (DBMS), and the database.

Starting from the right of Figure 1-15, the **database** is a collection of related tables and other structures. The **database management system (DBMS)** is a computer program used to create, process, and administer the database. The DBMS receives requests encoded in SQL and translates those requests into actions on the database. The DBMS is a large, complicated program that is licensed from a software vendor; companies almost never write their own DBMS programs.

A **database application** is a set of one or more computer programs that serves as an intermediary between the user and the DBMS. Application programs read or modify database data by sending SQL statements to the DBMS. Application programs also present data to users in the format of forms and reports. Application programs can be acquired from software vendors, and they are also frequently written in-house. The knowledge you gain from this text will help you write database applications.

**Users**, the fourth component of a database system, employ a database application to keep track of things. They use forms to read, enter, and query data, and they produce reports.

Of these components, we will consider the database, the DBMS, and database applications in more detail.

## The Database

In the most general case, a database is defined as a self-describing collection of related records. For all relational databases (almost all databases today, and the only type considered in this book), this definition can be modified to indicate that a database is a self-describing collection of related tables.

The two key terms in this definition are **self-describing** and **related tables**. You already have a good idea of what we mean by *related tables.* One example of related tables consists of the ADVISER and STUDENT tables, which are related by the common column AdviserName. We will build on this idea of relationships further in the next chapter.

*Self-describing* means that a description of the structure of the database is contained within the database itself. Because this is so, the contents of a database can always be determined just by looking inside the database itself. It is not necessary to look anywhere else. This situation is akin to that at a library, where you can tell what is in the library by examining the catalog that resides within the library.

Data about the structure of a database are called **metadata**. Examples of metadata are the names of tables, the names of columns and the tables to which they belong, properties of tables and columns, and so forth.

All DBMS products provide a set of tools for displaying the structure of their databases. For example, Figure 1-16 shows a diagram produced by Microsoft Access that displays the relationships between the Art Course database tables shown in Figure 1-10. Other tools describe the structure of the tables and other components.

**FIGURE 1-15**

Components of a Database System

Users

**FIGURE 1-17**

Database Contents

- User data
- Metadata
- Indexes and other overhead data
- Application metadata

The contents of a database are illustrated in Figure 1-17. A database has user data and metadata, as just described. A database also has indexes and other structures that exist to improve database performance, and we will discuss such structures in later chapters. Finally, some databases contain application metadata; these are data that describe application elements, such as forms and reports. For example, Microsoft Access carries application metadata as part of its databases.

## The DBMS

The purpose of a DBMS is to create, process, and administer databases. A DBMS is a large, complicated product that is almost always licensed from a software vendor. One DBMS product is Microsoft Access. Other commercial DBMS products are Oracle and MySQL, both from Oracle; DB2, from IBM; and SQL Server, from Microsoft. Dozens of other DBMS products exist, but these five have the lion's share of the market.

Figure 1-18 lists the functions of a DBMS. A DBMS is used to create a database and to create tables and other supporting structures inside that database. As an example of the latter, suppose that we have an EMPLOYEE table with 10,000 rows and that this table includes a column, DepartmentName, that records the name of the department in which an employee works. Furthermore, suppose that we frequently need to access employee data by

**FIGURE 1-18**

Functions of a DBMS

- Create database
- Create tables
- Create supporting structures (e.g., indexes)
- Read database data
- Modify (insert, update, or delete) database data
- Maintain database structures
- Enforce rules
- Control concurrency
- Provide security
- Perform backup and recovery

DepartmentName. Because this is a large database, searching through the table to find, for example, all employees in the accounting department would take a long time. To improve performance, we can create an index (akin to the index at the back of a book) for DepartmentName to show which employees are in which departments. Such an index is an example of a supporting structure that is created and maintained by a DBMS.

The next two functions of a DBMS are to read and modify database data. To do this, a DBMS receives SQL and other requests and transforms those requests into actions on the database files. Another DBMS function is to maintain all the database structures. For example, from time to time it might be necessary to change the format of a table or another supporting structure. Developers use a DBMS to make such changes.

With most DBMS products, it is possible to declare rules about data values and have a DBMS enforce them. For example, in the Art Course database tables in Figure 1-10, what would happen if a user mistakenly entered a value of 9 for CustomerID in the ENROLLMENT table? No such customer exists, so such a value would cause numerous errors. To prevent this situation, it is possible to tell the DBMS that any value of CustomerID in the ENROLLMENT table must already be a value of CustomerID in the CUSTOMER table. If no such value exists, the insert or update request should be disallowed. The DBMS then enforces these rules, which are called **referential integrity constraints**.

The last three functions of a DBMS listed in Figure 1-18 have to do with database administration. A DBMS controls **concurrency** by ensuring that one user's work does not inappropriately interfere with another user's work. This important (and complicated) function is discussed in Chapter 6. Also, a DBMS contains a security system that is used to ensure that only authorized users perform authorized actions on the database. For example, users can be prevented from seeing certain data. Similarly, users' actions can be confined to making only certain types of data changes on specified data.

Finally, a DBMS provides facilities for backing up database data and recovering it from backups, when necessary. The database, as a centralized repository of data, is a valuable organizational asset. Consider, for example, the value of a book database to a company such as Amazon.com. Because the database is so important, steps need to be taken to ensure that no data will be lost in the event of errors, hardware or software problems, or natural or human catastrophes.

**Application Programs**  Figure 1-19 lists the functions of database applications. First, an application program creates and processes forms. Figure 1-20 shows a typical form for entering and processing customer data for the Art Course application.

Notice that this form hides the structure of the underlying tables from the user. By comparing the tables and data in Figure 1-10 to the form in Figure 1-20, we can see that data from the CUSTOMER table appear at the top of the form, whereas data from the ENROLLMENT and the COURSE tables are combined and presented in a tabular section labeled Course Enrollment Data.

The goal of this form, like that for all data entry forms, is to present the data in a format that is useful for the users, regardless of the underlying table structure. Behind the form, the application processes the database in accordance with the users' actions. The application generates an SQL statement to insert, update, or delete data for any of the three tables that underlie this form.

The second function of application programs is to process user queries. The application program first generates a query request and sends it to the DBMS. Results are then formatted and returned to the user. Figure 1-21 illustrates this process in a query of the Art Course database in Figure 1-10.

**FIGURE 1-19**

Functions of
Application Programs

- Create and process forms
- Process user queries
- Create and process reports
- Execute application logic
- Control application

FIGURE 1-20

Example Data Entry
Form

**Customer Data Entry Form**

| | |
|---|---|
| CustomerNumber | 1 |
| CustomerLastName | Johnson |
| CustomerFirstName | Ariel |
| Phone | 206-567-1234 |

Course Enrollment Data

| Course | CourseDate | Fee | AmountPaid | AmountDue |
|---|---|---|---|---|
| Int Pastels | 3/15/2011 | $350.00 | $350.00 | $0.00 |
| Adv Pastels | 10/1/2011 | $500.00 | $250.00 | $250.00 |

Record: 1 of 2 ▶ ▶▶ No Filter Search

Record: 1 of 7 ▶ ▶▶ No Filter Search

FIGURE 1-21

Example Query

Enter Parameter Value

Enter part of course name:

pas

OK Cancel

**(a) Query Parameter Form**

**Course Parameter Query**

| CustomerLastName | CustomerFirstName | Course | CourseDate | Fee | AmountPaid | Amount Due |
|---|---|---|---|---|---|---|
| Jackson | Charles | Adv Pastels | 10/1/2011 | $500.00 | $500.00 | $0.00 |
| Johnson | Ariel | Int Pastels | 3/15/2011 | $350.00 | $350.00 | $0.00 |
| Johnson | Ariel | Adv Pastels | 10/1/2011 | $500.00 | $250.00 | $250.00 |
| Kyle | Leah | Adv Pastels | 11/15/2011 | $500.00 | $250.00 | $250.00 |
| Pearson | Jeffery | Adv Pastels | 10/1/2011 | $500.00 | $500.00 | $0.00 |

Record: 1 of 5 ▶ ▶▶ No Filter Search

**(b) Query Results**

In Figure 1-21(a), the application obtains the name or part of a name of a course. Here, the user has entered the characters *pas.* When the user clicks OK, the application constructs an SQL query statement to search the database for any course containing these characters. The result of this SQL query is shown in Figure 1-21(b). In this particular case, the application queried for the relevant course and then joined the ENROLLMENT and CUSTOMER data to the qualifying COURSE rows. Observe that the only rows shown are those with a course name that includes the characters *pas.*

The third function of an application is to create and process reports. This function is somewhat similar to the second because the application program first queries the DBMS for data (again using SQL). The application then formats the query results as a report. Figure 1-22 shows a report that displays all the Art Course database enrollment data in order by course. Notice that the report, like the form in Figure 1-20, is structured according to the users' needs and not according to the underlying table structure.

In addition to generating forms, queries, and reports, the application program takes other actions to update the database in accordance with application-specific logic. For example, suppose a user using an order entry application requests 10 units of a particular item. Suppose further that when the application program queries the database (via the DBMS) it finds that only eight units are in stock. What should happen? It depends on the logic of that particular application. Perhaps no units should be removed from inventory, and the user should be notified, or perhaps the eight units should be removed and two more placed on back order. Perhaps some other action should be taken. Whatever the case, it is the job of the application program to execute the appropriate logic.

**FIGURE 1-22**

Example Report

**Course Enrollment Report**

| Course | CourseDate | CustomerLastName | CustomerFirstName | Phone | Fee | AmountPaid | AmountDue |
|---|---|---|---|---|---|---|---|
| **Adv Pastels** | | | | | | | |
| | 10/1/2011 | | | | | | |
| | | Jackson | Charles | 360-789-3456 | $500.00 | $500.00 | $0.00 |
| | | Johnson | Ariel | 206-567-1234 | $500.00 | $250.00 | $250.00 |
| | | Pearson | Jeffery | 206-567-2345 | $500.00 | $500.00 | $0.00 |
| | 11/15/2011 | | | | | | |
| | | Kyle | Leah | 425-678-7654 | $500.00 | $250.00 | $250.00 |
| **Beg Oils** | | | | | | | |
| | 9/15/2011 | | | | | | |
| | | Green | Robin | 425-678-8765 | $350.00 | $350.00 | $0.00 |
| | | Sears | Miguel | 360-789-4567 | $350.00 | $350.00 | $0.00 |
| | 10/15/2011 | | | | | | |
| | | Myers | Lynda | 360-789-5678 | $350.00 | $0.00 | $350.00 |
| **Int Pastels** | | | | | | | |
| | 3/15/2011 | | | | | | |
| | | Johnson | Ariel | 206-567-1234 | $350.00 | $350.00 | $0.00 |

Finally, the last function of application programs listed in Figure 1-19 is to control the application. This is done in two ways. First, the application needs to be written so that only logical options are presented to the user. For example, the application may generate a menu with user choices. In this case, the application needs to ensure that only appropriate choices are available. Second, the application needs to control data activities with the DBMS. The application might direct the DBMS, for example, to make a certain set of data changes as a unit. The application might tell the DBMS to either make all these changes or none of them. You will learn about such control topics in Chapter 6.

## Personal Versus Enterprise-Class Database Systems

Database technology can be used in a wide array of applications. On one end of the spectrum, a researcher might use database technology to track the results of experiments performed in a lab. Such a database might include only a few tables, and each table would have, at most, several hundred rows. The researcher would be the only user of this application. This is a typical use of a **personal database system**.

At the other end of the spectrum, some enormous databases support international organizations. Such databases have hundreds of tables with millions of rows of data and support thousands of concurrent users. These databases are in use 24 hours a day, 7 days a week. Just making a backup of such a database is a difficult task. These databases are typical uses of **enterprise-class database systems**.

Figure 1-23 shows the four components of a personal database application. As you can see from this figure, Microsoft Access (and other personal DBMS products) takes on the role of both the database application and the DBMS. Microsoft designed Microsoft Access this way to make it easier for people to build personal database systems. Using

**FIGURE 1-23**

Personal Database Systems

User

Database application

Database management system (DBMS)

Database

**Microsoft Access or other personal DBMS**

**FIGURE 1-24**

SQL Generated by a Microsoft Access Query

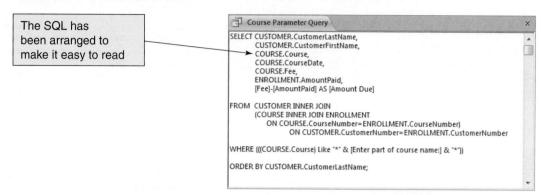

The SQL has been arranged to make it easy to read

```
Course Parameter Query                                              ×

SELECT CUSTOMER.CustomerLastName,
       CUSTOMER.CustomerFirstName,
       COURSE.Course,
       COURSE.CourseDate,
       COURSE.Fee,
       ENROLLMENT.AmountPaid,
       [Fee]-[AmountPaid] AS [Amount Due]

FROM  CUSTOMER INNER JOIN
      (COURSE INNER JOIN ENROLLMENT
           ON COURSE.CourseNumber=ENROLLMENT.CourseNumber)
                ON CUSTOMER.CustomerNumber=ENROLLMENT.CustomerNumber

WHERE (((COURSE.Course) Like "*" & [Enter part of course name:] & "*"))

ORDER BY CUSTOMER.CustomerLastName;
```

Microsoft Access, you can switch between DBMS functions and application functions and never know the difference.

By designing Microsoft Access this way, Microsoft has hidden many aspects of database processing. For example, behind the scenes Microsoft Access uses SQL just as all other relational DBMS products do. You have to look hard, however, to find it. Figure 1-24 shows the SQL that Microsoft Access used for the query in Figure 1-21. As you examine this figure, you might be thinking, "I'm just as glad they hid it—it looks complicated and hard." In fact, it looks harder than it is, but we will leave that topic for Chapter 3.

The problem with database technology being hidden (and with using lots of *wizards* to accomplish database design tasks) is that you do not understand what is being done on your behalf. As soon as you need to perform some function that the Microsoft Access team did not anticipate, you are lost. Therefore, to be even an average database developer you have to learn what is behind the scenes.

Furthermore, such products are useful only for personal database applications. When you want to develop larger database systems, you need to learn all the hidden technology. For example, Figure 1-25 shows an enterprise-class database system that has three different applications, each of which has many users. The storage of the database itself is spread over many different disks—perhaps even over different specialized computers known as *database servers.*

**FIGURE 1-25**

Enterprise-Class Database System

Notice that in Figure 1-25 the applications are written in three different languages: Java, C#, and a blend of HTML and ASP.NET. These applications call on an industrial-strength DBMS product to manage the database. No wizards or simple design tools are available to develop a system like this; instead, the developer writes program code using standard tools, such as those in integrated development environments. To write such code, you need to know SQL and other data access standards.

Although hidden technology and complexity are good in the beginning, business requirements will soon take you to the brink of your knowledge, and then you will need to know more. To be a part of a team that creates such a database application, you will need to know everything in this book. Over time, you will need to learn more.

## THE ACCESS WORKBENCH

### Section 1

### Getting Started with Microsoft Access

"The Access Workbench" is designed to reinforce the concepts you learn in each chapter. In addition, you will learn many Microsoft Access skills by following along on your computer. In this chapter's section of "The Access Workbench," we will review some database basics from Chapter 1 as we walk through the basic steps necessary to build and use Microsoft Access database applications.

As discussed in this chapter, Microsoft Access is a personal database that combines a DBMS with an application generator. The DBMS performs the standard DBMS functions of database creation, processing, and administration, and the application generator adds the abilities to create and store forms, reports, queries, and other application-related functions. In this section, we will work with only one table in a database; in Chapter 2's section of "The Access Workbench," you will expand this to include two or more tables.

We will begin by creating a Microsoft Access database to store the database tables and the application forms, reports, and queries. In this section, we will work with basic forms and reports. Microsoft Access queries are discussed in Chapter 3's section of "The Access Workbench."

### The Wallingford Motors Customer Relations Management System

Our Microsoft Access database will be used by a car dealership named Wallingford Motors, which is located in the Wallingford district of Seattle, Washington. Wallingford Motors is the dealer for a new line of hybrid cars named Gaea.[3] Instead of using only a gasoline or diesel engine, hybrid cars are powered by a combination of energy sources, such as gasoline and electricity. Gaea produces the following four models:

1. **SUHi**       The sport-utility hybrid (Gaea's answer to the SUV)
2. **HiLuxury**   A luxury-class four-door sedan hybrid
3. **HiStandard** A basic four-door sedan hybrid
4. **HiElectra**  A variant of the HiStandard that uses a higher proportion of electrical power

Interest in hybrid cars—and specifically in the Gaea product line—is increasing. The sales staff at Wallingford Motors needs a way to track its customer contacts.

---

[3]Gaea, or Gaia, was the Greek goddess of the Earth [see **http://en.wikipedia.org/wiki/Gaia_(mythology)**]. For more information on hybrid cars, see **www.hybridcars.com**.

*(Continued)*

Therefore, our database application will be a simple example of what is known as a **customer relationship management (CRM) system**. A CRM is used (among other uses) by sales staff to track current, past, and potential customers as well as the sales staff's contacts with these customers. We will start out with a personal CRM used by one salesperson and expand it into a companywide CRM in later sections.[4]

### Creating a Microsoft Access Database

We will name our Microsoft Access application and its associated database **WMCRM**. Our first step is to create a new Microsoft Access database.

#### Creating the Microsoft Access Database WMCRM

1. Select **Start | All Programs | Microsoft Office | Microsoft Access 2010.** The Microsoft Access window appears, as shown in Figure AW-1-1. Note that the Microsoft Access window is immediately displayed with the **Backstage view** (which is controlled by the **File command tab**) open, and the New tab selected. Associated with the New tab is a page displaying Microsoft Access database templates available to the user. The Blank Database template selected and the details of that template are displayed in the template details pane on the right of the screen.

   - **NOTE:** The menu commands, icon location, and file locations used in "The Access Workbench" are those found when using Microsoft Access 2010 in the Microsoft Windows 7 operating system. If you are using the Microsoft Windows Vista or Microsoft XP operating systems, the exact operating system

---

### FIGURE AW-1-1

**The Microsoft Access 2010 Window**

---

terminology may vary somewhat, but these variations will not change the required actions.

- **NOTE:** Microsoft Access 2010 is used in these sections, and the wording of the steps and appearance of the screenshots reflect its use. If you have a different version of Microsoft Access, there will be some differences in the step details and in what you see onscreen. However, the basic functionality is the same, and you can complete "The Access Workbench" operations using any version of Microsoft Access.

- **NOTE:** By default, in Windows 7 the database will be created in the *My Documents* folder in the *Documents* library folder. The *Documents* library folder contains both a *My Documents* folder and a *Public Documents* folder.

2. Type in the database name **WMCRM.accdb** in the File Name text box, and then click the **Create** button.

- **NOTE:** If you clicked the Open button to browse to a different file location, use the File New Database dialog box to create the new database file. Once you have browsed to the correct folder, type the database name in the File Name text box of the File New Database dialog box, and then click the OK button to create the new database.

3. The new database appears, as shown in Figure AW-1-2. The Microsoft Access window itself is now named **WMCRM: Database (Access 2007)—Microsoft Access** to include the database name.

- **NOTE:** The reference to Microsoft Access 2007 in the window name indicates that the database is stored as an \*.*accdb* file, which is the Microsoft Access database file format introduced with Microsoft Access 2007. Prior versions of Microsoft Access used the \*.*mdb* file format. Microsoft Access 2010 does not

---

**FIGURE AW-1-2**

**The New Microsoft Access Database**

The database name **WMCRM : Database (Access 2007)**

The Document Window using the tabbed documents interface

The **Close** button

*(Continued)*

introduce a new database file format, but continues to use the Microsoft Access 2007 *.accdb* file format.

4. Note that because this is a new database Microsoft Access has assumed that you will want to immediately create a new table. Therefore, a new table named **Table1** is displayed in Datasheet view in the document window. We do *not* want this table open at this time, so click the **Close** document button shown in Figure AW-1-2.

5. The Microsoft Access 2010 window with the new database appears, as shown in Figure AW-1-3. You can see most of the features of the Microsoft Office Fluent user interface in this window.

### The Microsoft Office Fluent User Interface

Microsoft Access 2010 uses the **Microsoft Office Fluent user interface** found in most (but not all) of the Microsoft Office 2007 and Office 2010 applications. The major features of the interface can be seen in Figure AW-1-3. To illustrate its use, we will modify some of the default settings of the Microsoft Access database window.

### *The Quick Access Toolbar*

First, we will modify the Quick Access Toolbar shown in Figure AW-1-3 to include a Quick Print button and a Print Preview button.

### *Modifying the Microsoft Access Quick Access Toolbar*

1. Click the **Customize Quick Access Toolbar** drop-down button shown in Figure AW-1-4. The Customize Quick Access Toolbar drop-down list appears as shown in Figure AW-1-4.

---

**FIGURE AW-1-3**

The Microsoft Office Fluent User Interface

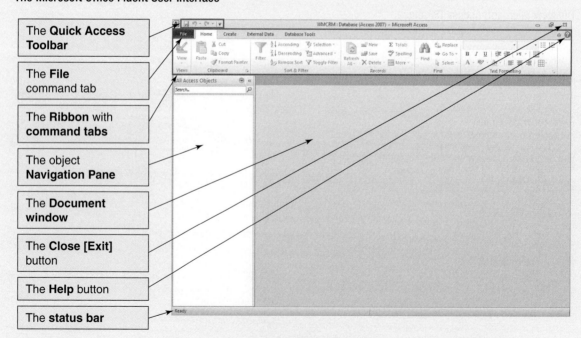

## FIGURE AW-1-4

The Quick Access Toolbar

The **Quick Access Toolbar**

The **Customize Quick Access Toolbar** drop-down button

The **Customize Quick Access Toolbar drop-down list**—click an item to add it to the toolbar

2. Click **Quick Print**. The Quick Print button is added to the Quick Access Toolbar.
3. Click the **Customize Quick Access Toolbar** drop-down button. The Customize Quick Access Toolbar drop-down list appears.
4. Click **Print Preview**. The Print Preview button is added to the Quick Access Toolbar.
5. The added buttons are visible in the figures shown later in this section of "The Access Workbench," such as Figure AW-1-5.

### Database Objects and the Navigation Pane

Microsoft uses the term **object** as a general name for the various parts of a Microsoft Access database. Thus, a *table* is an object, a *report* is an object, a *form* is an object, and so on. Microsoft Access objects are displayed in the Microsoft Access **Navigation Pane**, as shown in Figure AW-1-3. However, because you have not created any objects in the WMCRM database, the Navigation Pane is currently empty.

The Navigation Pane is currently labeled as *All Access Objects*, which is what we want to see displayed. We can, however, select exactly which objects will be displayed by using the **Navigation Pane drop-down list**. As shown in Figure AW-1-5, the Navigation Pane drop-down list is controlled by the **Navigation Pane drop-down list button**. Figure AW-1-6 shows the empty Navigation Pane, and the **Shutter Bar Open/Close button**. We can hide the Navigation Pane if we want to by clicking the Shutter Bar Open/Close button, which is displayed as a left-facing double chevron button on the upper-right corner of the Navigation Pane in Figure AW-1-6. If we click the button, the Navigation Pane shrinks to a small band labeled *Navigation Pane* on the right side of the Microsoft Access 2010 window. The band will then display the Shutter Bar Open/Close button as a right-facing double chevron button that we can click to restore the Navigation Pane when we want to use it again.

### Closing a Database and Exiting Microsoft Access

The *Close* button shown in Figure AW-1-3 is actually a *close and exit button*. You can click it to close the active database and then exit Microsoft Access. Note that Microsoft Access actively saves most changes to a database, and it prompts you with *Save* command requests when they are needed. For example, when you close a table with modified column widths

*(Continued)*

**FIGURE AW-1-5**

The Navigation Pane Drop-Down List

The **Quick Print** button

The **Print Preview** button

The **Navigation Pane** drop-down list button

The **All Access Objects** drop-down list

**FIGURE AW-1-6**

The Empty Navigation Pane

Use the **Shutter Bar Open/Close** button to hide or display the Navigation Pane

The Navigation Pane is empty because we have not created any objects for this database

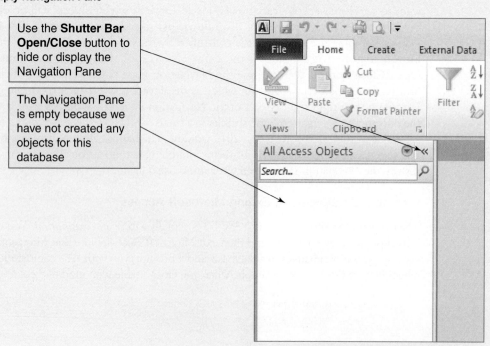

Microsoft Access asks if you want to save the changes in the table layout. Therefore, you do not need to save Microsoft Access databases the way you save Microsoft Word documents and Microsoft Excel workbooks. You can simply close a database, knowing that Microsoft Access has already saved all critical changes since you opened it.

### Closing a Database and Exiting Microsoft Access

1. Click the **Close** button. The database closes, and you exit Microsoft Access.

Instead of clicking the Close button, you can simultaneously close the database and exit Microsoft Access by clicking the **File** command tab, and then clicking the **Exit** command. To close just the database while leaving Microsoft Access open, select the **File** command tab, and then click the **Close Database** command.

## Opening an Existing Microsoft Access Database

Earlier in this section of "The Access Workbench" we created a new Microsoft Access database for the Wallingford Motors CRM (WMCRM.accdb), modified some Microsoft Access settings, and closed the database and exited Microsoft Access. Before we can continue building this database, we need to start Microsoft Access and open the WMCRM.accdb database.

When we open an existing database, Microsoft Access 2010 (like Microsoft Access 2007 before it) gives us the option of using Microsoft Access security options to shut down certain Microsoft Access 2010 features in a database to protect ourselves against harm not only from viruses but from other possible problems. Unfortunately, the Microsoft Access 2010 security options also shut down significant and needed operational features of Microsoft Access. Therefore, we will normally enable the features that the Microsoft Access 2010 security warning warns us about when we open an existing database.

### Opening a Recently Opened Microsoft Access Database

1. Open Microsoft Access 2010 by selecting **Start | All Programs | Microsoft Office | Microsoft Access 2010**. Microsoft Access 2010 is displayed with the Backstage view open and New tab selected, as previously shown in Figure AW-1-1.
2. Click the **Recent** tab in the Backstage view to display the Recent page, as shown in Figure AW-1-7. Note that the database file WMCRM.accdb is listed in both the **Recent Documents** pane and in the **quick access list**.
3. Note that if the database has been used very recently, it will always be available in the Backstage view's quick access list regardless of whether the Recent tab page is displayed. Otherwise, we will need to click the Recent tab to see it. At this point, however, we can open the database by clicking on *either* entry. Because the Recent tab page is open, click the **WMCRM.accdb** file name in the **Recent Databases** area to open the database.
4. A **Security Warning** bar appears with the database, as shown in Figure AW-1-8.
5. At this point, we have the option of clicking the Security Warning bar's **Click for more details** link, which will display a detailed version of the warning together with security options. However, for our purposes in this text, we simply need to enable the active content, so click the **Enable Content** button.
   - ■ **NOTE:** At some point, you should select the **Click for more details** link and explore the available security settings.

*(Continued)*

---

**FIGURE AW-1-7**

The Backstage View Recent

The **WMCRM.accdb** database in Recent Databases

The **WMCRM.accdb** database in the quick access list

The **Recent** tab

This setting controls how many databases are shown in the quick access list

---

**FIGURE AW-1-8**

The Security Warning Bar

The **Security Warning** bar

The **Click for more details** link

Click the **Enable Content** button

---

■ **NOTE:** In Microsoft Access 2007, the Security Warning bar appeared every time the database was reopened (although from in a *nontrusted location*—see the Chapter 6 section of "The Access Workbench" for a discussion of *trusted locations*). In Microsoft Access 2010, the Security Warning bar is only displayed the first time you reopen a database, and your choice of options is remembered from that point on.

### Creating a Microsoft Access Database Table

At this point, the database will be used by one salesperson, so we need only two tables in the WMCRM database—CUSTOMER and CONTACT. We will create the CUSTOMER table first. The CUSTOMER table will contain the columns and characteristics shown in the table in Figure AW-1-9. The column characteristics are type, key, required, and remarks.

**FIGURE AW-1-9**

Database Column Characteristics for the CUSTOMER Table

| Column Name | Type | Key | Required | Remarks |
|---|---|---|---|---|
| CustomerID | AutoNumber | Primary Key | Yes | Surrogate Key |
| LastName | Text (25) | No | Yes | |
| FirstName | Text (25) | No | Yes | |
| Address | Text (35) | No | No | |
| City | Text (35) | No | No | |
| State | Text (2) | No | No | |
| ZIP | Text (10) | No | No | |
| Phone | Text (12) | No | Yes | |
| Fax | Text (12) | No | No | |
| Email | Text (100) | No | No | |

**Type** refers to the kind of data the column will store. Some possible Microsoft Access data types are shown in Figure AW-1-10. For CUSTOMER, most data are stored as **text** data (also commonly called **character** data), which means we can enter strings of letters, numbers, and symbols (a space is considered a symbol). The number behind the word *Text* indicates how many characters can be stored in the column. For example, customer last names may be up to 25 characters long. The only **number**, or **numeric**, data column in the CUSTOMER table is CustomerID, which is listed as **AutoNumber**. This indicates that Microsoft Access will automatically provide a sequential number for this column for each new customer that is added to the table.

**Key** refers to table identification functions assigned to a column. These are described in detail in Chapter 2. At this point, you simply need to know that a **primary**

**FIGURE AW-1-10**

Microsoft Access 2010 Data Types

| Name | Type of Data | Size |
|---|---|---|
| Text | Characters and numbers | Maximum 255 characters |
| Memo | Large text | Maximum 65,535 characters |
| Number | Numeric data | Varies with Number type |
| Date/Time | Dates and times from the year 100 to the year 9999 | Stored as 8-byte double-precision integers |
| Currency | Numbers with decimal places | One to four decimal places |
| AutoNumber | A unique sequential number | Incremented by one each time |
| Yes/No | Fields that can contain only two values | Yes/No, On/Off, True/False, etc. |
| OLE Object | An object embedded in or linked to a Microsoft Access table | Maximum 1 GB |
| Hyperlink | A hyperlink address | Maximum 2,048 characters in each of three parts of the hyperlink address |
| Attachment | Any supported type of file may be attached to a record | Independent of Microsoft Access |
| Calculated | Results of a calculation based on data in other cells | Varies depending on values used in calculation |
| Lookup Wizard . . . | A list of possible data values located in a value list | Varies depending on the values in the value list |

*(Continued)*

**key** is a column value used to identify each row; therefore, the values in this column must be unique. This is the reason for using the AutoNumber data type, which automatically assigns a unique number to each row in the table as it is created.

**Required** refers to whether the column must have a data value. If it must, a value must be present in the column. If not, the column may be blank. Note that because CustomerID is a primary key used to identify each row it *must* have a value.

**Remarks** contains comments about the column or how it is used. For CUSTOMER, the only comment is that CustomerID is a **surrogate key**. Surrogate keys are discussed in Chapter 2. At this point, you simply need to know that surrogate keys are usually computer-generated unique numbers used to identify rows in a table (that is, a primary key). This is done by using the Microsoft Access AutoNumber data type.

### Creating the CUSTOMER Table

1. Click the **Create** command tab to display the **Create** command groups.
2. Click the **Table Design** button, as shown in Figure AW-1-11.
3. The **Table1** tabbed document window is displayed in **Design** view, as shown in Figure AW-1-12. Note that along with the **Table1** window a contextual tab grouping named **Table Tools** is displayed and that this tab grouping adds a new command tab named **Design** to the set of command tabs displayed.
   - **NOTE:** It seems like now would be a good time to name the new table CUSTOMER. With Microsoft Access, however, you do not name a table until you save it the first time, and you cannot save a table until you have at least one column defined. So, we will define the columns, and then we will save and name the table. If you want, save the table after you have defined just one column. This will close the table, so you will have to reopen it to define the remaining columns.
4. In the **Field Name** column text box of the first line, type the column name **CustomerID** and then press the **Tab** key to move to the **Data Type** column. (You can also click the Data Type column to select it.)
   - **NOTE:** The terms *column* and *field* are considered synonyms in database work. The term *attribute* is also considered to be equivalent to these two words.
5. Select the **AutoNumber** data type for CustomerID from the **Data Type** drop-down list, as shown in Figure AW-1-13.
6. If you like, an optional comment may be stored in the Description column. To do so, move to the Description column by pressing the **Tab** key or clicking in the **Description** text box. Type the text **Surrogate key for CUSTOMER** and then press the **Tab** key to move to the next row. The **Table1** tabbed document window now looks as shown in Figure AW-1-14.

---

**FIGURE AW-1-11**

**The Table Design Button**

The **Create** tab

The **Table Design** button

The tool tip for the button shows that a new table object will be created

## FIGURE AW-1-12

### The Table1 Tabbed Document Window

The **Table Tools** contextual command tab is displayed along with the set of command tabs that comprise Table Tools

The **Design** command tab and its command groups are displayed

The **Table1** tabbed document window in Design view

■ **NOTE:** The Remarks column in the set of database column characteristics shown in Figure AW-1-9 is *not* the same as the table Description column shown in Figure AW-1-14. Be careful not to confuse them. The Remarks column is used to record technical data, such as facts about table keys and data default values

## FIGURE AW-1-13

### Selecting the Data Type

The **Data Type** drop-down list arrow

The **Data Type** drop-down list

Select **AutoNumber**

*(Continued)*

---

**FIGURE AW-1-14**

The Completed CustomerID Column

The completed **CustomerID** column definition

that are necessary for building the table structure. The Description column is used to describe to the user the data stored in that field so that the user understands the field's intended use.

7. The other columns of the CUSTOMER table are created using the sequence described in steps 4 through 6.

■ **NOTE:** See Figure AW-1-17 for the Description entries.

8. To set the number of characters in text columns, edit the **Data Type Field Size** property text box, as shown in Figure AW-1-15. The default value for Field Size is 255, which is also the maximum value for a text field.

9. To make a column required, click anywhere in the column **Data Type Required** property text box to display the **Required** property drop-down list arrow button, then click the button to display the Required property drop-down list, as shown in Figure AW-1-16, and then select **Yes** from the Required property drop-down list. The default is No (not required), and Yes must be selected to make the column required.[5]

Now we need to set a primary key for the CUSTOMER table. According to Figure AW-1-9, we need to use the CustomerID column as the primary key for this table.

*Setting the CUSTOMER Table Primary Key*

1. Move the mouse pointer to the **row selector column** of the row containing the CustomerID properties, as shown in Figure AW-1-17, and click to select the row.

2. Click the **Primary Key** button in the Tools group of the Design tab, as shown in Figure AW-1-18. CustomerID is selected as the primary key for the CUSTOMER table.

---

[5]Microsoft Access has an additional Data Type property named Allow Zero Length. This property confounds the settings necessary to truly match the SQL constraint NOT NULL discussed in Chapter 3. However, the discussion of Allow Zero Length is beyond the scope of this book. See the Microsoft Access Help system for more information.

**FIGURE AW-1-15**

Editing the Text Field Size

Edit this number to set the number of characters

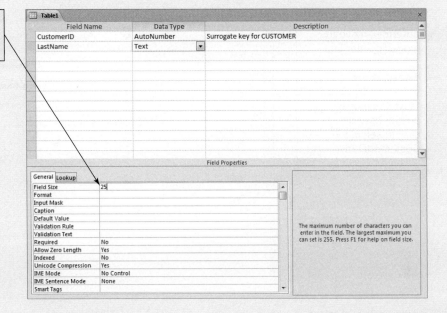

**FIGURE AW-1-16**

Setting the Column Required Property Value

Click anywhere in the Required text box to display the arrow—the **Required property** drop-down list arrow

Select **Yes** from the Required property drop-down list

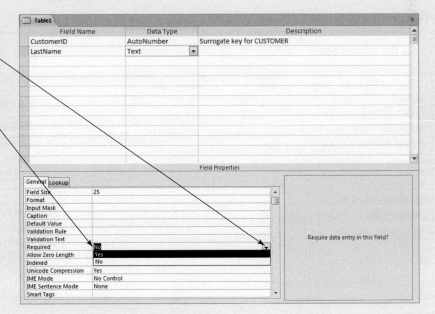

(Continued)

## FIGURE AW-1-17

### Selecting the CustomerID Row

We have finished building the CUSTOMER table. Now we need to name, save, and close the table.

### Naming, Saving, and Closing the CUSTOMER Table

1.  To name and save the CUSTOMER table, click the **Save** button in the Quick Access Toolbar. The **Save As** dialog box appears, as shown in Figure AW-1-19.

## FIGURE AW-1-18

### Setting the Primary Key

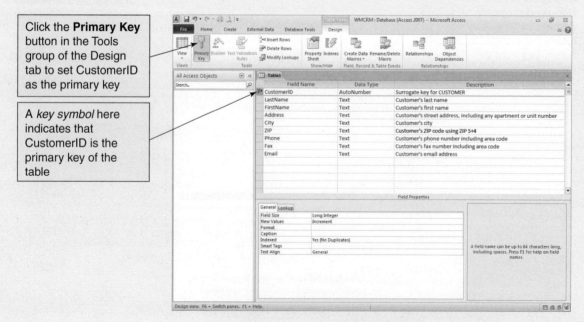

## FIGURE AW-1-19

### Naming and Saving the CUSTOMER Table

Click the **Save** button in the Quick Access Toolbar to display the **Save As** dialog box

Type the table name **CUSTOMER** in the Table Name text box

The **OK** button

2. Type the table name **CUSTOMER** into the **Save As** dialog box's Table Name text box and then click **OK**. The table is named and saved. The table name CUSTOMER now appears on the document tab, and the CUSTOMER table object is displayed in the Navigation Pane, as shown in Figure AW-1-20.
3. To close the CUSTOMER table, click the **Close** button in the upper-right corner of the tabbed documents window, as shown in Figure AW-1-20. After the table is closed, the CUSTOMER table object remains displayed in the Navigation Pane, as shown in Figure AW-1-21.

### Inserting Data into Tables—The Datasheet View

There are three commonly used methods for adding data to a table. First, we can use a table as a **datasheet**, which is visually similar to and works like a Microsoft Excel worksheet.

## FIGURE AW-1-20

### The Named CUSTOMER Table

The table object CUSTOMER is displayed in the Navigation Pane

The table is now named CUSTOMER *and* the table name appears on the document tab

Click the **Close** button to close the CUSTOMER table

*(Continued)*

---

**FIGURE AW-1-21**

The CUSTOMER Table Object

The table object CUSTOMER is displayed in the Navigation Pane

When we do this, the table is in **Datasheet view**, and we enter the data cell by cell. Second, we can build a **data entry form** for the table and then use the form to add data. Third, we can use SQL to insert data. This section covers the first two of these methods; we will use the SQL method in Chapter 3's section of "The Access Workbench."

In Microsoft Access 2010, we can also use Datasheet view to create and modify table characteristics. When we open a table in Datasheet view, the Table Tools contextual tab includes a Datasheet command tab and ribbon with tools to do this. We do *not* recommend this; it is better to use Design view, as previously discussed in this section, for creating and modifying table structures.

However, at this point we do not need to modify the table structure—we simply need to put some data into the CUSTOMER table. Figure AW-1-22 shows some data for Wallingford Motors customers.

### Adding Data to the CUSTOMER Table in Datasheet View

1. In the Navigation Pane, double-click the **CUSTOMER** table object. The CUSTOMER table window appears in a tabbed document window in Datasheet view, as shown in Figure AW-1-23. Note that some columns on the right side of the datasheet do not appear in the window, but you can access them by scrolling or minimizing the Navigation Pane.

---

**FIGURE AW-1-22**

CUSTOMER Data

| LastName | FirstName | Address | City | State | Zip |
|---|---|---|---|---|---|
| Griffey | Ben | 5678 25th NE | Seattle | WA | 98178 |
| Christman | Jessica | 3456 36th SW | Seattle | WA | 98189 |
| Christman | Rob | 4567 47th NW | Seattle | WA | 98167 |
| Hayes | Judy | 234 Highland Place | Edmonds | WA | 98210 |

| LastName | FirstName | Phone | Fax | Email |
|---|---|---|---|---|
| Griffey | Ben | 206-456-2345 | | Ben.Griffey@somewhere.com |
| Christman | Jessica | 206-467-3456 | | Jessica.Christman@somewhere.com |
| Christman | Rob | 206-478-4567 | 206-478-9998 | Rob.Christman@somewhere.com |
| Hayes | Judy | 425-354-8765 | | Judy.Hayes@somewhere.com |

**FIGURE AW-1-23**

The CUSTOMER Table in Datasheet View

The **Table Tools** tab

If you need to switch between Datasheet view and Design view, use the **Design View** button

The **Shutter Bar Open/Close** button

The **CUSTOMER** tabbed document window with the table in Datasheet view

■ **NOTE:** As in a worksheet, the intersection of a row and column in a datasheet is called a *cell.*

2. Click the **Shutter Bar Open/Close** button to collapse the Navigation Pane. This makes more of the CUSTOMER datasheet visible, as shown in Figure AW-1-24.

3. Click the **CUSTOMER** document tab to select the CUSTOMER table in Datasheet view.

**FIGURE AW-1-24**

The Collapsed Navigation Pane

The **Shutter Bar Open/Close** button

The collapsed **Navigation Pane**

The **CUSTOMER** tabbed document window with the table in Datasheet view

*(Continued)*

4. Click the cell in the CustomerID column with the phrase **(New)** in it to select that cell in the new row of the CUSTOMER datasheet.
5. Press the **Tab** key to move to the LastName cell in the new row of the CUSTOMER datasheet. For customer Ben Griffey, type **Griffey** in the LastName cell. Note that as soon as you do this the AutoNumber function puts the number 1 in the CustomerID cell and a new row is added to the datasheet, as shown in Figure AW-1-25.
6. Using the **Tab** key to move from one column to another in the CUSTOMER datasheet, enter the rest of the data values for Ben Griffey.
7. The final result is shown in Figure AW-1-26. Note that the width of the Email column was expanded using the mouse to move the border of the column—just as you would in a Microsoft Excel worksheet.
   - **NOTE:** If you make a mistake and need to return to a cell, click the cell to select it, and you go into Edit mode. Alternatively, you can use **Shift-Tab** to move to the right in the datasheet and then press **F2** to edit the contents of the cell.
   - **NOTE:** Remember that LastName, FirstName, and Phone *require* a data value. You will not be able to move to another row or close the table window until you have a value in each of these cells.
   - **NOTE:** Figure AW-1-26 shows a column labeled *Click to Add* to the right of the Email column. This is a table tool in Datasheet view that you can use to create or modify table structures. We do not recommend using these tools—we prefer to use Design view instead!
8. Use the **Tab** key to move to the next row of the CUSTOMER datasheet and enter the data for Jessica Christman, as shown in Figure AW-1-27.

---

### FIGURE AW-1-25

**Entering Data Values for Ben Griffey**

This row has been autonumbered as CustomerID 1

A new, blank row is added to the datasheet

---

### FIGURE AW-1-26

**The Completed Row of Data Values**

Column widths can be adjusted by using the mouse to drag the column border to the desired width

## FIGURE AW-1-27

### The Completed CUSTOMER Datasheet

Many column widths had to be adjusted to get all the data to show in one window—use the mouse to drag the column borders to the desired widths

Click the **Close** button to close the CUSTOMER datasheet

9. Adjust the datasheet column widths so that you can see the contents of the datasheet in one screen. The final result is shown in Figure AW-1-27.
10. Click the **Close** button in the upper-right corner of the document window to close the CUSTOMER datasheet. A dialog box appears that asks if you want to save the changes you made to the layout (column widths). Click the **Yes** button.
11. Click the **Shutter Bar Open/Close** button to expand the Navigation Pane. This makes the objects in the Navigation Pane visible.

## Modifying Data in Tables—The Datasheet View

After entering data into a table, you can modify or change the data by editing the data values in the Datasheet view. To illustrate this, we will temporarily change Jessica Christman's phone number to 206-467-9876.

### *Modifying Data in the CUSTOMER Table in Datasheet View*

1. In the Navigation Pane, double-click the **CUSTOMER** table object. The CUSTOMER table window appears in a tabbed document window in Datasheet view.
2. Click the **Shutter Bar Open/Close** button to collapse the Navigation Pane.
3. Click the **cell** that contains Jessica Christman's phone number to select it. Microsoft Access automatically puts the cell into Edit mode.
   - **NOTE:** If you instead use the **Tab** key (or **Shift-Tab** to move to the left in the datasheet) to select the cell, press the **F2** key to edit the contents of the cell.
4. Change the phone number to **206-467-9876**.
   - **NOTE:** Remember that Phone has a field size of 12 characters. You have to delete characters before you can enter new ones.
5. Press the **Enter** key or otherwise move to another cell to complete the edit. The CUSTOMER datasheet appears as shown in Figure AW-1-28.
6. Because we really do not want to change Jessica Christman's phone number, edit the Phone value back to its original value of **206-467-3456**. Complete the edit and click the **Save** button on the Quick Access Toolbar to save the changes.
7. Click the **Close** button in the upper-right corner of the document window to close the CUSTOMER datasheet.
8. Click the **Shutter Bar Open/Close** button to expand the Navigation Pane.

*(Continued)*

The Modified CUSTOMER Datasheet

The phone number has been modified

### Deleting Rows in Tables—The Datasheet View

After the data have been entered into a table, you can delete an entire row in Datasheet view. To illustrate this, we will temporarily delete Jessica Christman's data.

*Deleting a Row in the CUSTOMER Table in Datasheet View*

1. In the Navigation Pane, double-click the **CUSTOMER** table object. The CUSTOMER table window appears in a tabbed document window in Datasheet view.
2. Click the **Shutter Bar Open/Close** button to collapse the Navigation Pane.
3. Right-click the **row selector cell** on the left side of the CUSTOMER datasheet for the row that contains Jessica Christman's data. This selects the entire row and displays a shortcut menu, as shown in Figure AW-1-29.
   - ■ **NOTE:** The terms *row* and *record* are synonymous in database usage.
4. Click the **Delete Record** command in the shortcut menu. As shown in Figure AW-1-30, a Microsoft Access dialog box appears, warning you that you are about to permanently delete the record.
   - ■ **NOTE:** As also shown in Figure AW-1-30, Microsoft Access 2010 with default settings performs the visual trick of actually removing the row! However, the row is not permanently deleted until you click the **Yes** button in the Microsoft Access dialog box. If you click the **No** button, the row reappears.

Deleting a Row in the CUSTOMER Datasheet

Click a cell in this column to select an entire row—a left-click will simply select the row, whereas a right-click will select the row and display a shortcut menu

The **Delete Record** command in the shortcut menu

**FIGURE AW-1-30**

**The Microsoft Access Deletion Warning Dialog Box**

The row with Jessica Christman's data has already been visually removed!

Click the **Yes** button to actually delete the row

**FIGURE AW-1-31**

**The New CustomerID Number**

The row with the reentered Jessica Christman data now has a CustomerID of 3—AutoNumber numbers are sequential and are used only once!

5.  Click the **Yes** button to complete the deletion of the row.
    ▪  **NOTE:** Alternatively, you can delete the row by clicking the **row selector cell** and then pressing the **Delete** key. The same Microsoft Access dialog box shown in Figure AW-1-30 then appears.
6.  Because we do not want to really lose Jessica Christman's data at this point, add a new row to the CUSTOMER datasheet that contains Jessica's data. As shown in Figure AW-1-31, the CustomerID number for Jessica Christman is now 3 instead of 2. In an autonumbered column, each number is used only once.
7.  Click the **Close** button in the upper-right corner of the document window to close the CUSTOMER datasheet.
8.  Click the **Shutter Bar Open/Close** button to expand the Navigation Pane.

### Inserting Data into Tables—Using a Form

Now, we will create and use a **form** to insert data into a table. A form provides a visual reference for entering data in the various data columns, and Microsoft Access has a form generator as part of its application generator functions. We could build a form manually in Form Design view, but instead we can take the easy route and use the **Form Wizard**, which will take us through a step-by-step process to create the form we want.

*(Continued)*

### Creating a Data Entry Form for the CUSTOMER Table

1. Click the **Create** command tab to display the Create command tab and its command groups, as shown in Figure AW-1-32.
2. Click the **Form Wizard** button shown in Figure AW-1-32. The Form Wizard appears, as shown in Figure AW-1-33.
3. The CUSTOMER table is already selected as the basis for the form, so we only have to select which columns we want to include on the form. We can choose columns one at a time by highlighting a column name and clicking the right-facing single chevron button. Or we can choose all the columns at once by clicking the right-facing double chevron button. We want to add all the columns in this case, so click the **right-facing double chevron** button to add all the columns and then click the **Next** button.
   - ■ **NOTE:** In a real-world situation, we might not want to display the CustomerID value. In that case, we would deselect it by highlighting it and clicking the left-facing single chevron button.
4. When asked, "What layout would you like for your form?" click the **Next** button to select the default Columnar layout.
5. When asked, "What title do you want for your form?" type the form title **WMCRM Customer Data Form** into the text box and then click the **Finish** button. As shown in

---

**FIGURE AW-1-32**

The Create Command Tab and Form Wizard Button

The **Create** command tab

The **Form Wizard** button

The **Forms** command group

---

**FIGURE AW-1-33**

The Form Wizard

The **Form Wizard**

The CUSTOMER table is already selected

The **right-facing single chevron** button

Click the **right-facing double chevron** button to select all of the fields in the table

The **Next** button

## FIGURE AW-1-34

### The Completed WMCRM Customer Data Form

The **WMCRM Customer Data Form** tabbed document window

The **Forms** section of the Navigation Pane

The **WMCRM Customer Data Form** object

The **New Record** button

Figure AW-1-34, the completed form appears in a tabbed document window and a WMCRM Customer Data Form object is added to the Navigation Pane.

■ **NOTE:** The WMCRM Customer Data Form is properly constructed and sized for our needs. Sometimes, however, we might need to make adjustments to the form design. We can make form design changes by switching to form Design view. To switch to form Design view, click the **Design View** button in the View gallery.

Now that we have the form we need, we can use the form to add some data to the CUSTOMER table.

### *Inserting Data into the CUSTOMER Table Using a Form*

1. Click the **New Record** button. A blank form appears.
2. Click the **LastName** text box to select it. Enter the data for Rob Christman shown in Figure AW-1-22. You can either use the **Tab** key to move from text box to text box, or you can click the text box you want to edit.
3. When you are done entering the data for Rob Christman, enter the data for Judy Hayes shown in Figure AW-1-22. After you have entered the data for Judy Hayes, your form will look as shown in Figure AW-1-35.
4. Click the **Close** button in the upper-right corner of the document window to close the WMCRM Customer Data Form.

### Modifying Data and Deleting Records—Using a Form

Just as we can modify data and delete rows in Datasheet view, we can edit data and delete records by using a form. Editing data is simple: Move to the record you want to edit by using the **record navigation buttons** (First Record, Previous Record, etc.) shown

*(Continued)*

## FIGURE AW-1-35

**The WMCRM Customer Data Form for Customer Judy Hayes**

in Figure AW-1-35, click the appropriate field text box, and then edit the contents. Deleting a record is also simple: Move to the record you want to edit by using the record navigation buttons and then click the *Delete Record* button in the Delete drop-down list of the Records group of the Home command tab, as shown in Figure AW-1-36. However, you will not use these capabilities at this time.

## FIGURE AW-1-36

**The Delete Record Button**

### Creating Single-Table Microsoft Access Reports

One common function of an application is to generate printed reports. Microsoft Access 2010 has a report generator as part of its application generator functions. Just as with forms, we could build a form manually, or we can take the easy route and use the **Report Wizard.**

#### *Creating a Report for the CUSTOMER Table*

1. Click the **Create** command tab to display the Create command groups, as shown in Figure AW-1-37.
2. Click the **Report Wizard** button shown in Figure AW-1-37. The Report Wizard appears, as shown in Figure AW-1-38.
3. The CUSTOMER table is already selected as the basis for the report, so we only have to select which columns we want on the form. Just as with the Form Wizard, we can choose columns one at a time by highlighting the column name and clicking the

## FIGURE AW-1-37

The Create Command Tab and Report Wizard Button

## FIGURE AW-1-38

The Report Wizard

*(Continued)*

right-facing single chevron button. We can also choose all the columns at once by clicking the right-facing double chevron button. In this case, we want to use only the columns **LastName**, **FirstName**, **Phone**, **Fax**, and **Email**. Click each column name in the Available Fields list to select it and then click the **right-facing single chevron** button to move each column to Selected Fields. The completed selection looks as shown in Figure AW-1-39.

■  **NOTE:** You can select only one column at a time. The usual technique of selecting more than one column name at a time by pressing and holding the **Ctrl** key while clicking each additional column name does *not* work in this case.

4.  Click the **Next** button.

5.  Microsoft Access now asks, "Do you want to add any grouping levels?" Grouping can be useful in complex reports, but we do not need any groupings for this simple report that lists customers. Instead, we can use the default nongrouped column listing, so click the **Next** button.

6.  As shown in Figure AW-1-40, we are now asked, "What sort order do you want for your records?" The most useful sorting order in this case is by last name, with sorting by first name for identical last names. For both sorts, we want an *ascending* sort (from A to Z). Click the **sort field 1** drop-down list arrow and select **LastName**. Leave the sort order button set to **Ascending**.

7.  Click the **sort field 2** drop-down list arrow and select **FirstName**, leave the sort order button set to **Ascending**, and click the **Next** button.

8.  We are now asked, "How would you like to lay out your report?" We will use the default setting of **tabular layout**, but click the **Landscape orientation** radio button to change the report orientation to landscape. Click the **Next** button.

9.  Finally, when we are asked, "What title do you want for your report?" we edit the report title to read **Wallingford Motors Customer Report**. Leave the **Preview the report** radio button selected. Click the **Finish** button. As shown in Figure AW-1-41, the completed report appears in a tabbed document window, a Reports section has been added to the Navigation Pane, and the Wallingford Motors Customer Report object appears in this section.

10.  Click the **Close** button in the upper-right corner of the document window.

---

### FIGURE AW-1-39

The Completed Column Selection

The **Selected Fields** list

The **Next** button

**FIGURE AW-1-40**

Choosing the Sort Order

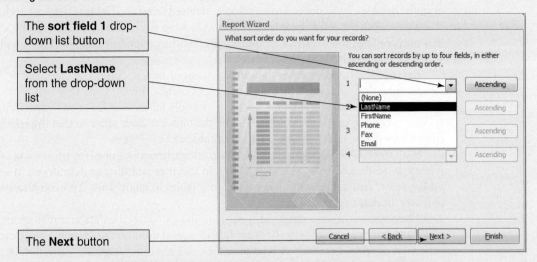

The **sort field 1** drop-down list button

Select **LastName** from the drop-down list

The **Next** button

## Closing a Database and Exiting Microsoft Access 2010

We have finished all the work we need to do in this chapter's "The Access Workbench." We have learned how to create a database; how to build database tables, forms, and reports; and how to populate a table with data by using Datasheet view and a form. We finish by closing the database and Microsoft Access.

### Closing the WMCRM Database and Exiting Microsoft Access 2010

1. To close WMCRM: Database and exit Microsoft Access 2010, click the **Close** button in the upper-right corner of the Microsoft Access 2010 window.

**FIGURE AW-1-41**

The Finished Report

The **Wallingford Motors Customer Report** print preview window

The **Reports** section of the Navigation Pane

The **Wallingford Motors Customer Report** object

The report is sorted by LastName and then FirstName

The **Close** button

## SUMMARY

The importance of database processing increases every day because databases are used in information systems everywhere—and increasingly so. The purpose of this book is to teach you essential database concepts and to help you get started using and learning database technology.

The purpose of a database is to help people keep track of things. Lists can be used for this purpose, but if a list involves more than one theme modification problems will occur when data are inserted, updated, or deleted.

Relational databases store data in the form of tables. Almost always, the tables are designed so that each table stores data about a single theme. Lists that involve multiple themes need to be broken up and stored in multiple tables, one for each theme. When this is done, a column needs to be added to link the tables to each other so that the relationship from a row in one table to a row in another table can be shown.

Structured Query Language (SQL) is an international language for processing tables in relational databases. You can use SQL to join together and display data stored in separate tables, create new tables, and query data from tables in many ways. You can also use SQL to insert, update and delete data.

The components of a database system are the database, the database management system (DBMS), one or more database applications, and users. A database is a self-describing collection of related records. A relational database is a self-describing collection of related tables. A database is self-describing because it contains a description of its contents within itself, which is known as metadata. Tables are related by storing linking values of a common column. The contents of a database are user data; metadata; supporting structures, such as indexes; and sometimes application metadata.

A database management system (DBMS) is a large, complicated program used to create, process, and administer a database. DBMS products are almost always licensed from software vendors. Specific functions of a DBMS are summarized in Figure 1-18.

The functions of database applications are to create and process forms, to process user queries, and to create and process reports. Application programs also execute specific application logic and control the application. Users provide data and data changes and read data in forms, queries, and reports.

DBMS products for personal database systems provide functionality for application development and database management. They hide considerable complexity, but at a cost: Requirements unanticipated by DBMS features cannot be readily implemented. Enterprise-class database systems include multiple applications that might be written in multiple languages. These systems may support hundreds or thousands of users.

## KEY TERMS

| | | |
|---|---|---|
| concurrency | insert | related tables |
| database | list | relational database |
| database application | metadata | relational model |
| database management system (DBMS) | modification action | self-describing |
| | modification problem | Structured Query Language (SQL) |
| delete | null value | table |
| enterprise-class database system | personal database system | update |
| ID column | referential integrity constraint | user |

## REVIEW QUESTIONS

**1.1** What is the purpose of this book?

**1.2** Why is the study of database technology important?

**1.3** Describe the purpose of a database.

**FIGURE 1-26**

The Veterinary Office List—Version One

| | A | B | C | D | E | F | G | H |
|---|---|---|---|---|---|---|---|---|
| 1 | PetName | PetType | PetBreed | PetDOB | OwnerLastName | OwnerFirstName | OwnerPhone | OwnerEmail |
| 2 | King | Dog | Std. Poodle | 27-Feb-10 | Downs | Marsha | 201-823-5467 | Marsha.Downs@somewhere.com |
| 3 | Teddy | Cat | Cashmier | 01-Feb-09 | James | Richard | 201-735-9812 | Richard.James@somewhere.com |
| 4 | Fido | Dog | Std. Poodle | 17-Jul-11 | Downs | Marsha | 201-823-5467 | Marsha.Downs@somewhere.com |
| 5 | AJ | Dog | Collie Mix | 05-May-11 | Frier | Liz | 201-823-6578 | Liz.Frier@somewhere.com |
| 6 | Cedro | Cat | Unknown | 06-Jun-06 | James | Richard | 201-735-9812 | Richard.James@somewhere.com |
| 7 | Woolley | Cat | Unknown | ??? | James | Richard | 201-735-9812 | Richard.James@somewhere.com |
| 8 | Buster | Dog | Border Collie | 11-Dec-05 | Trent | Miles | 201-634-7865 | Miles.Trent@somewhere.com |

**1.4** What is a modification problem? What are the three possible types of modification problems?

**1.5** Figure 1-26 shows a list that is used by a veterinary office. Describe three modification problems that are likely to occur when using this list.

**1.6** Name the two themes in the list in Figure 1-26.

**1.7** What is an ID column?

**1.8** Break the list in Figure 1-26 into two tables, each with data for a single theme. Assume that owners have a unique phone number but that pets have no unique column. Create an ID column for pets like the one created for customers and courses for the Art Course database tables in Figure 1-10.

**1.9** Show how the tables you created for question 1.8 solve the problems you described in question 1.5.

**1.10** What does SQL stand for, and what purpose does it serve?

**1.11** Another version of the list used by the veterinary office is shown in Figure 1-27. How many themes does this list have? What are they?

**1.12** Break the list in Figure 1-27 into tables, each with a single theme. Create ID columns as you think necessary.

**1.13** Show how the tables you created for question 1.12 solve the three problems of lists identified in this chapter.

**1.14** Define the term *database.*

**1.15** Name the four components of a database system.

**1.16** Describe in your own words and illustrate with tables how relationships are represented in a relational database.

**1.17** Why do you think it is important for a database to be self-describing?

**1.18** List the components of a database.

**1.19** Define the term *metadata.*

**1.20** What are application metadata?

**1.21** Describe the use of an index.

**1.22** What is the purpose of a DBMS?

**1.23** List the specific functions of a DBMS.

**1.24** Explain the difference between a DBMS and a database.

**1.25** Define the term *referential integrity constraint.* Give an example of a referential integrity constraint for the tables you created for question 1.8.

**1.26** List the functions of a database application.

**FIGURE 1-27**

The Veterinary Office List—Version Two

| | A | B | C | D | E | F | G | H | I | J | K |
|---|---|---|---|---|---|---|---|---|---|---|---|
| 1 | PetName | PetType | PetBreed | PetDOB | OwnerLastName | OwnerFirstName | OwnerPhone | OwnerEmail | Service | Date | Charge |
| 2 | King | Dog | Std. Poodle | 27-Feb-10 | Downs | Marsha | 201-823-5467 | Marsha.Downs@somewhere.com | Ear Infection | 17-Aug-11 | $ 65.00 |
| 3 | Teddy | Cat | Cashmier | 01-Feb-09 | James | Richard | 201-735-9812 | Richard.James@somewhere.com | Nail Clip | 05-Sep-11 | $ 27.50 |
| 4 | Filo | Dog | Std. Poodle | 17-Jul-11 | Downs | Marsha | 201-823-5467 | Marsha.Downs@somewhere.com | | | |
| 5 | AJ | Dog | Collie Mix | 05-May-11 | Frier | Liz | 201-823-6578 | Liz.Frier@somewhere.com | One year shots | 05-May-11 | $ 42.50 |
| 6 | Cedro | Cat | Unknown | 06-Jun-06 | James | Richard | 201-735-9812 | Richard.James@somewhere.com | Nail Clip | 05-Sep-11 | $ 27.50 |
| 7 | Woolley | Cat | Unknown | ??? | James | Richard | 201-735-9812 | Richard.James@somewhere.com | Skin Infection | 03-Oct-11 | $ 35.00 |
| 8 | Buster | Dog | Border Collie | 11-Dec-05 | Trent | Miles | 201-634-7865 | Miles.Trent@somewhere.com | Laceration Repa | 05-Oct-11 | $ 127.00 |

**1.27** Explain the differences between a personal database system and an enterprise-class database system.

**1.28** Summarize the differences between the database systems in Figures 1-23 and 1-25.

**1.29** What is the advantage of hiding complexity from the user of a DBMS? What is the disadvantage?

## EXERCISES

The following spreadsheets form a set of named spreadsheets with the indicated column headings. Use these spreadsheets to answer exercises 1.30 through 1.32.

**A.** Name of spreadsheet: EQUIPMENT
Column headings:
Number, Description, AcquisitionDate, AcquisitionPrice

**B.** Name of spreadsheet: COMPANY
Column headings:
Name, IndustryCode, Gross Sales, OfficerName, OfficerTitle

**C.** Name of spreadsheet: COMPANY
Column headings:
Name, IndustryCode, Gross Sales, NameOfPresident

**D.** Name of spreadsheet: COMPUTER
Column headings:
SerialNumber, Make, Model, DiskType, DiskCapacity

**E.** Name of spreadsheet: PERSON
Column headings:
Name, DateOfHire, DeptName, DeptManager, ProjectID, NumHours, ProjectManager

**1.30** For each of the spreadsheets provided, indicate the number of themes you think the spreadsheet includes and give an appropriate name for each theme. For some of them, the answer may depend on the assumptions you make. In these cases, state your assumptions.

**1.31** For any spreadsheet that has more than one theme, show at least one modification problem that will occur when inserting, updating, or deleting data.

**1.32** For any spreadsheet that has more than one theme, break up the columns into tables such that each table has a single theme. Add ID columns if necessary, and add a linking column (or columns) to maintain the relationship between the themes.

## ACCESS WORKBENCH KEY TERMS

AutoNumber (data type)
character (data type)
customer relationship management (CRM) system
data entry form
datasheet
Datasheet view
File command tab
File Menu
form
Form Wizard

key
Microsoft Office Button
Microsoft Office Fluent user interface
Navigation Pane
Navigation Pane drop-down list
Navigation Pane drop-down list button
number (data type)
numeric (data type)

object
primary key
record navigation buttons
remarks
Report Wizard
required
Shutter Bar Open/Close button
surrogate key
text (data type)
type

## ACCESS WORKBENCH EXERCISES

**AW.1.1** The Wedgewood Pacific Corporation (WPC), founded in 1957 in Seattle, Washington, has grown into an internationally recognized organization. The company is located in two buildings. One building houses the Administration, Accounting, Finance, and Human Resources departments, and the second houses the Production, Marketing, and Information Systems departments. The company database contains data about employees; departments; projects; assets, such as computer equipment; and other aspects of company operations.

**A.** Create a Microsoft Access database named WPC in a Microsoft Access file named WPC.accdb.

**B.** Figure 1-28 shows the column characteristics for the WPC EMPLOYEE table. Using the column characteristics, create the EMPLOYEE table in the WPC database.

**C.** Figure 1-29 shows the data for the WPC EMPLOYEE table. Using Datasheet view, enter the data for the first three rows of data in the EMPLOYEE table shown in Figure 1-29 into your EMPLOYEE table.

### FIGURE 1-28

Database Column Characteristics for the EMPLOYEE Table

**EMPLOYEE**

| Column Name | Type | Key | Required | Remarks |
| --- | --- | --- | --- | --- |
| EmployeeNumber | AutoNumber | Primary Key | Yes | Surrogate Key |
| FirstName | Text (25) | No | Yes | |
| LastName | Text (25) | No | Yes | |
| Department | Text (35) | No | Yes | |
| Phone | Text (12) | No | No | |
| Email | Text (100) | No | Yes | |

### FIGURE 1-29

Wedgewood Pacific Corporation EMPLOYEE Data

| Employee Number | FirstName | LastName | Department | Phone | Email |
| --- | --- | --- | --- | --- | --- |
| [AutoNumber] | Mary | Jacobs | Administration | 360-285-8110 | Mary.Jacobs@WPC.com |
| [AutoNumber] | Rosalie | Jackson | Administration | 360-285-8120 | Rosalie.Jackson@WPC.com |
| [AutoNumber] | Richard | Bandalone | Legal | 360-285-8210 | Richard.Bandalone@WPC.com |
| [AutoNumber] | Tom | Caruthers | Accounting | 360-285-8310 | Tom.Caruthers@WPC.com |
| [AutoNumber] | Heather | Jones | Accounting | 360-285-8320 | Heather.Jones@WPC.com |
| [AutoNumber] | Mary | Abernathy | Finance | 360-285-8410 | Mary.Abernathy@WPC.com |
| [AutoNumber] | George | Smith | Human Resources | 360-285-8510 | George.Smith@WPC.com |
| [AutoNumber] | Tom | Jackson | Production | 360-287-8610 | Tom.Jackson@WPC.com |
| [AutoNumber] | George | Jones | Production | 360-287-8620 | George.Jones@WPC.com |
| [AutoNumber] | Ken | Numoto | Marketing | 360-287-8710 | Ken.Numoto@WPC.com |
| [AutoNumber] | James | Nestor | InfoSystems | | James.Nestor@WPC.com |
| [AutoNumber] | Rick | Brown | InfoSystems | 360-287-8820 | Rick.Brown@WPC.com |

    **D.** Create a data input form for the EMPLOYEE table and name it WPC Employee Data Form. Make any adjustments necessary to the form so that all data display properly. Use this form to enter the rest of the data in the EMPLOYEE table shown in Figure 1-29 into your EMPLOYEE table.

    **E.** Create a report named Wedgewood Pacific Corporation Employee Report that presents the data contained in your EMPLOYEE table sorted first by employee last name and second by employee first name. Make any adjustments necessary to the report so that all headings and data display properly. Print a copy of this report.

 ## GARDEN GLORY PROJECT QUESTIONS

Garden Glory is a partnership that provides gardening and yard maintenance services to individuals and organizations. Garden Glory is owned by two partners, who employ two office administrators and a number of full- and part-time gardeners. Garden Glory will provide one-time garden services, but it specializes in ongoing service and maintenance. Many of its customers have multiple buildings, apartments, and rental houses that require gardening and lawn maintenance services.

    **A.** Create a sample list of owners and properties. Your list will be similar in structure to that in Figure 1-26, but it will concern owners and properties rather than owners and pets. Your list should include, at the minimum, owner name, phone, and billing address, as well as property name, type, and address.

    **B.** Describe modification problems that are likely to occur if Garden Glory attempts to maintain the list in a spreadsheet.

    **C.** Split the list into tables such that each has only one theme. Create appropriate ID columns. Use a linking column to represent the relationship between a property and an owner. Demonstrate that the modification problems you identified in B have been eliminated.

    **D.** Create a sample list of owners, properties, and services. Your list will be similar to that in Figure 1-27. Your list should include the data items from part A as well as the date, description, and amount charged for each service.

    **E.** Illustrate modification problems that are likely to occur if Garden Glory attempts to maintain the list from part D in a spreadsheet.

    **F.** Split the list from part D into tables such that each has only one theme. Create appropriate ID columns. Use linking columns to represent relationships. Demonstrate that the modification problems you identified in part E have been eliminated.

 ## JAMES RIVER JEWELRY PROJECT QUESTIONS

James River Jewelry is a small jewelry shop that specializes in hard-to-find Asian jewelry. It has a small but loyal clientele, and it wants to further increase customer loyalty by creating a frequent buyer program. In this program, after every 10 purchases, a customer will receive a credit equal to 50 percent of the sum of his or her 10 most recent purchases.

    **A.** Create a sample list of customers and purchases and a second list of customers and credits. Your lists should include customer data you think would be important to

James River, along with typical purchase data. Credit data should include the date of the credit, the total amount of the 10 purchases used as the basis of the credit, and the credit amount.

**B.** Describe modification problems that are likely to occur if James River attempts to maintain the lists in a spreadsheet.

**C.** Split the lists into tables that each have only a single theme. Create appropriate ID columns. Use one ID to represent the relationship between a purchase and a customer and use another ID to represent the relationship between a credit and a customer.

**D.** Attempt to combine the two lists you created in part A into a single list. What problems occur as you try to do this? Look closely at Figure 1-27. An essential difference exists between a list of the three themes *customer*, *purchase*, and *credit* and a list of the three themes *PetName*, *Owner*, and *Service* in Figure 1-27. What do you think is that difference?

**E.** Change the tables from part C so that the purchase list has not only the ID of Customer but also the ID of Credit. Compare this arrangement to the tables in your answer to question 1.12. What is the essential difference between these two designs?

## THE QUEEN ANNE CURIOSITY SHOP PROJECT QUESTIONS

The Queen Anne Curiosity Shop sells both antiques and current-production household items that complement or are useful with the antiques. For example, the store sells antique dining room tables and new tablecloths. The antiques are purchased from both individuals and wholesalers, and the new items are purchased from distributors. The store's customers include individuals, owners of bed-and-breakfast operations, and local interior designers who work with both individuals and small businesses. The antiques are unique, although some multiple items, such as dining room chairs, may be available as a set (sets are never broken). The new items are not unique, and an item may be reordered if it is out of stock. New items are also available in various sizes and colors (for example, a particular style of tablecloth may be available in several sizes and in a variety of colors).

**A.** Create a sample list of purchased inventory items and vendors and create a second list of customers and sales. Your first list should include inventory data, such as a description, manufacturer and model (if available), item cost, and vendor identification and contact data you think should be recorded. Your second list should include customer data you think would be important to The Queen Anne Curiosity Shop, along with typical sales data.

**B.** Describe problems that are likely to occur when inserting, updating, and deleting data in these spreadsheets.

**C.** Attempt to combine the two lists you created in part A into a single list. What problems occur as you try to do this?

**D.** Split the spreadsheets you created in part A into tables with only one theme each. Create appropriate ID columns.

**E.** Explain how the tables in your answer to part D will eliminate the problems you identified in part B.

**F.** What is the relationship between the tables you created from the first spreadsheet and the tables you created from the second spreadsheet? If your set of tables does not already contain this relationship, how will you add it into your set of tables?

# CHAPTER 2

# The Relational Model

## Chapter Objectives

> Learn the conceptual foundation of the relational model

> Understand how relations differ from nonrelational tables

> Learn basic relational terminology

> Learn the meaning and importance of keys, foreign keys, and related terminology

> Understand how foreign keys represent relationships

> Learn the purpose and use of surrogate keys

> Learn the meaning of functional dependencies

> Learn to apply a process for normalizing relations

This chapter explains the relational model, the single most important standard in database processing today. This model, which was developed and published in 1970 by Edgar Frank Codd, commonly referred to as E. F. Codd,[1] then an employee at IBM, was founded on the theory of relational algebra. The model has since found widespread practical application, and today it is used for the design and implementation of almost every commercial database worldwide. This chapter describes the conceptual foundation of this model.

---

[1]E. F. Codd, "A Relational Model of Data for Large Shared Databanks," *Communications of the ACM* (June 1970): 377–387.

# RELATIONS

Chapter 1 states that databases help people keep track of things and that relational DBMS products store data in the form of tables. Here we need to clarify and refine those statements. First, the formal name for a "thing" that is being tracked is **entity**, which is defined as something of importance to the user that needs to be represented in the database. Further, it is not entirely correct to say that DBMS products store data in tables. DBMS products store data in the form of relations, which are a special type of table. Specifically, a **relation** is a two-dimensional **table** consisting of **rows** and **columns** that has the following characteristics:

- Each row of the table holds data that pertain to some entity or a portion of some entity.
- Each column of the table contains data that represent an attribute of the entity. For example, in an EMPLOYEE relation each row would contain data about a particular employee and each column would contain data that represented an attribute of that employee, such as LastName, Phone, or EmailAddress.
- The cells of the table must hold a single value, and thus no repeating elements are allowed in a cell.
- All the entries in any column must be of the same kind. For example, if the third column in the first row of a table contains EmployeeNumber, then the third column in all other rows must contain EmployeeNumber as well.
- Each column must have a unique name, but the order of the columns in the table is unimportant.
- The order of the rows is unimportant.
- No two rows in the table may hold identical data values.

The characteristics of a relation are summarized in Figure 2-1.

## A Sample Relation and Two Nonrelations

Figure 2-2 shows a sample EMPLOYEE table. Consider this table in light of the characteristics discussed earlier. First, each row is about an EMPLOYEE entity, and each column represents an attribute of employees, so those two conditions are met. Each cell has only one value, and all entries in a column are of the same kind. Column names are unique, and we could change the order of either the columns or the rows and not lose any information. Finally, no two rows are identical. Because this table meets all requirements of the definition of *relation*, we can classify it as a relation.

**FIGURE 2-1**

Characteristics of a Relation

- Rows contain data about an entity
- Columns contain data about attributes of the entity
- Cells of the table hold a single value
- All entries in a column are of the same kind
- Each column has a unique name
- The order of the columns is unimportant
- The order of the rows is unimportant
- No two rows may be identical

**FIGURE 2-2**

Sample EMPLOYEE Relation

| EmployeeNumber | FirstName | LastName | Department | Email | Phone |
|---|---|---|---|---|---|
| 100 | Jerry | Johnson | Accounting | JJ@somewhere.com | 834-1101 |
| 200 | Mary | Abernathy | Finance | MA@somewhere.com | 834-2101 |
| 300 | Liz | Smathers | Finance | LS@somewhere.com | 834-2102 |
| 400 | Tom | Caruthers | Accounting | TC@somewhere.com | 834-1102 |
| 500 | Tom | Jackson | Production | TJ@somewhere.com | 834-4101 |
| 600 | Eleanore | Caldera | Legal | EC@somewhere.com | 834-3101 |
| 700 | Richard | Bandalone | Legal | RB@somewhere.com | 834-3102 |

FIGURE 2-3

Nonrelational Table—
Multiple Entries per
Cell

FIGURE 2-3

Nonrelational Table—
Multiple Entries per
Cell

| EmployeeNumber | FirstName | LastName | Department | Email | Phone |
|---|---|---|---|---|---|
| 100 | Jerry | Johnson | Accounting | JJ@somewhere.com | 834-1101 |
| 200 | Mary | Abernathy | Finance | MA@somewhere.com | 834-2101 |
| 300 | Liz | Smathers | Finance | LS@somewhere.com | 834-2102 |
| 400 | Tom | Caruthers | Accounting | TC@somewhere.com | 834-1102, 834-1191, 834-1192 |
| 500 | Tom | Jackson | Production | TJ@somewhere.com | 834-4101 |
| 600 | Eleanore | Caldera | Legal | EC@somewhere.com | 834-3101 |
| 700 | Richard | Bandalone | Legal | RB@somewhere.com | 834-3102, 834-3191 |

FIGURE 2-4

Nonrelational Table—
Order of Rows
Matters and Kind of
Column Entries
Differs in Email

| EmployeeNumber | FirstName | LastName | Department | Email | Phone |
|---|---|---|---|---|---|
| 100 | Jerry | Johnson | Accounting | JJ@somewhere.com | 834-1101 |
| 200 | Mary | Abernathy | Finance | MA@somewhere.com | 834-2101 |
| 300 | Liz | Smathers | Finance | LS@somewhere.com | 834-2102 |
| 400 | Tom | Caruthers | Accounting | TC@somewhere.com | 834-1102 |
| | | | | Fax: | 834-9911 |
| | | | | Home: | 723-8765 |
| 500 | Tom | Jackson | Production | TJ@somewhere.com | 834-4101 |
| 600 | Eleanore | Caldera | Legal | EC@somewhere.com | 834-3101 |
| | | | | Fax: | 834-9912 |
| | | | | Home: | 723-7654 |
| 700 | Richard | Bandalone | Legal | RB@somewhere.com | 834-3102 |

Now consider the tables shown in Figures 2-3 and 2-4. Neither of these tables is a relation. The EMPLOYEE table in Figure 2-3 is not a relation because the Phone column has cells with multiple entries. For example, Tom Caruthers has three values for phone, and Richard Bandalone has two values. Multiple entries per cell are not permitted in a relation.

The table in Figure 2-4 is not a relation for two reasons. First, the order of the rows is important. Because the row under Tom Caruthers contains his fax number, we may lose track of the correspondence between his name and his fax number if we rearrange the rows. The second reason this table is not a relation is that not all values in the Email column are of the same kind. Some of the values are email addresses, and others are types of phone numbers.

Although each cell can have only one value, that value can vary in length. Figure 2-5 shows the table from Figure 2-2 with an additional variable-length Comment attribute. Even though a comment can be lengthy and varies in length from row to row, there is still only one comment per cell. Thus, the table in Figure 2-5 is a relation.

## A Note on Presenting Relation Structures

Throughout this book, when we write out the relation structure of a relation that we are discussing, we use the following format:

RELATION_NAME (Column01, Column02, . . . , LastColumn)

FIGURE 2-5

Relation with
Variable-Length
Column Values

| EmployeeNumber | FirstName | LastName | Department | Email | Phone | Comment |
|---|---|---|---|---|---|---|
| 100 | Jerry | Johnson | Accounting | JJ@somewhere.com | 834-1101 | Joined the Accounting Department March after completing his MBA. Will take the CPA exam this fall. |
| 200 | Mary | Abernathy | Finance | MA@somewhere.com | 834-2101 | |
| 300 | Liz | Smathers | Finance | LS@somewhere.com | 834-2102 | |
| 400 | Tom | Caruthers | Accounting | TC@somewhere.com | 834-1102 | |
| 500 | Tom | Jackson | Production | TJ@somewhere.com | 834-4101 | |
| 600 | Eleanore | Caldera | Legal | EC@somewhere.com | 834-3101 | |
| 700 | Richard | Bandalone | Legal | RB@somewhere.com | 834-3102 | Is a full-time consultant to legal on a retainer basis. |

The relation name is written first, and it is written in all capital (uppercase) letters (for example, EMPLOYEE). If the relation name is a combination of two or more words, we join the words with an underscore (for example, EMPLOYEE_PROJECT_ASSIGNMENT). Column names are contained in parentheses and are written with an initial capital letter followed by lowercase letters (for example, Department). If the column name is a combination of two or more words, the first letter of each word is capitalized (for example, EmployeeNumber and LastName). Thus, the EMPLOYEE relation shown in Figure 2-2 would be written as:

EMPLOYEE (EmployeeNumber, FirstName, LastName, Department, Email, Phone)

> **B T W**
>
> Relation structures, such as the one shown earlier, are part of a database schema. A **database schema** is the design on which a database and its associated applications are built.

## A Note on Terminology

In the database world, people generally use the terms *table* and *relation* interchangeably. Accordingly, from now on this book does the same. Thus, any time we use the term *table* we mean a table that meets the characteristics required for a relation. Keep in mind, however, that, strictly speaking, some tables are not relations.

Sometimes, especially in traditional data processing, people use the term **file** instead of *table*. When they do so, they use the term **record** for *row* and the term **field** for *column*. To further confound the issue, database theoreticians sometimes use yet another set of terms: Although they do call a table a *relation*, they call a *row* a **tuple** (rhymes with *couple*) and a *column* an **attribute**. These three sets of terminology are summarized in Figure 2-6.

To make matters even more confusing, people often mix up these sets of terms. It is not unusual to hear someone refer to a relation that has rows and fields. As long as you know what is intended, this mixing of terms is not important.

We should discuss one other source of confusion. According to Figure 2-1, a table that has duplicate rows is not a relation. However, in practice this condition is often ignored. Particularly when manipulating relations with a DBMS, we may end up with a table that has duplicate rows. To make that table a relation, we should eliminate the duplicates. On a large table, however, checking for duplication can be time-consuming. Therefore, the default behavior for DBMS products is not to check for duplicate rows. Hence, in practice, tables might exist with duplicate rows that are still called relations. You will see examples of this situation in the next chapter.

**FIGURE 2-6**

**Equivalent Sets of Terms**

| Table | Row | Column |
|---|---|---|
| File | Record | Field |
| Relation | Tuple | Attribute |

# TYPES OF KEYS

A **key** is one or more columns of a relation that is used to identify a row. A key can be **unique** or **nonunique**. For example, for the EMPLOYEE relation in Figure 2-2 EmployeeNumber is a *unique key* because a value of EmployeeNumber identifies a unique row. Thus, a query to display all employees having an EmployeeNumber of 200 will produce a single row. In contrast, Department is a *nonunique key*. It is a key because it is used to identify a row, but it is nonunique because a value of Department potentially identifies more than one row. Thus, a query to display all rows having a Department value of Accounting will produce several rows.

From the data in Figure 2-2, it appears that EmployeeNumber, LastName, and Email are all unique identifiers. However, to decide whether this is true database developers must do more than examine sample data. Instead, they must ask the users or other subject-matter experts whether a certain column is unique. The column LastName is an example where this is important. It might turn out that the sample data just happen to have unique values for LastName. The users, however, might say that LastName is not always unique.

## Composite Keys

A key that contains two or more attributes is called a **composite key**. For example, suppose that we are looking for a unique key for the EMPLOYEE relation, and the users say that although LastName is not unique, the combination of LastName and Department is unique. Thus, for some reason the users know that two people with the same last name will never work in the same department. Two Johnsons, for example, will never work in accounting. If that is the case, then the combination LastName, Department is a unique composite key.

Alternatively, the users may know that the combination (LastName, Department) is not unique but that the combination (FirstName, LastName, Department) is unique. The latter combination, then, is a composite key with three attributes.

**B T W**

Composite keys, like one-column keys, can be unique or nonunique.

## Candidate and Primary Keys

**Candidate keys** are keys that uniquely identify each row in a relation. Candidate keys can be single-column keys or they can be composite keys. The **primary key** is the candidate key that is chosen as the key that the DBMS will use to uniquely identify each row in a relation. For example, suppose that we have the following EMPLOYEE relation:

EMPLOYEE (EmployeeNumber, FirstName, LastName, Department, Email, Phone)

The users tell us that EmployeeNumber is a unique key, that Email is a unique key, and that the composite key (FirstName, LastName, DepartmentName) is a unique key. Therefore, we have three candidate keys. When designing the database, we choose one of the candidate keys to be the primary key. In this case, for example, we use EmployeeNumber as the primary key.

> **B T W**
>
> It may help you to understand why the unique keys that could be used as the main identifier for the relation are referred to as candidate keys if you think of them as the "candidates" in the running to be elected "primary key" — but remember that only one candidate will win the election.

The primary key is important not only because it can be used to identify unique rows, but also because it can be used to represent rows in relationships. Although we did not indicate it in Figure 1-10 in Chapter 1, CustomerID was the primary key of CUSTOMER. As such, we used CustomerID to represent the relationship between CUSTOMER and ENROLLMENT by placing CustomerID as a column in the ENROLLMENT table to create the link between the two tables. In addition, many DBMS products use values of the primary key to organize storage for the relation. They also build indexes and other special structures for fast retrieval of rows using primary key values.

In this book, we indicate primary keys by underlining them. Because EmployeeNumber is the primary key of EMPLOYEE, we write the EMPLOYEE relation as:

EMPLOYEE (<u>EmployeeNumber</u>, FirstName, LastName, Department, Email, Phone)

Each DBMS program has its own way of creating and indicating a primary key. In Chapter 1's section of "The Access Workbench," we briefly discussed primary keys and explained how to set a primary key in Microsoft Access 2010. Figure 2-7 shows the CUSTOMER

---

**FIGURE 2-7**

Defining a Primary Key in Microsoft Access 2010

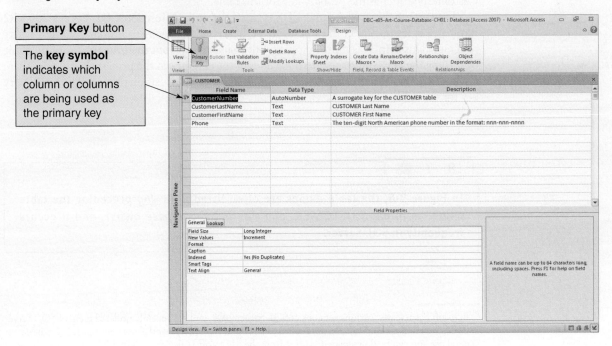

**Primary Key** button

The **key symbol** indicates which column or columns are being used as the primary key

**FIGURE 2-8**

Defining a Primary Key in SQL Server 2008

table from the Art Course database in Figure 1-10 in the Microsoft Access table Design view. In table Design view, we can spot the primary key of the table by finding the key symbol next to the names of the columns in the primary key. In this case, a key symbol is located next to CustomerNumber, which means that the developer has defined CustomerNumber as the primary key for this table.

Figure 2-8 shows the same CUSTOMER table in Microsoft SQL Server 2008 R2 Express,[2] as it appears in the Microsoft SQL Server Management Studio graphical utility program. This display is more complex, but again we can spot the primary key of the table by finding the key symbol next to the names of the columns in the primary key. Again, there is a key symbol next to CustomerNumber, indicating that CustomerNumber is the primary key for this table.

In Figure 2-8, the table names are often listed with *dbo* preceding the table name, as in dbo.CUSTOMER. dbo stands for *database owner*, and it occurs frequently in SQL Server.

---

[2]Microsoft has released various versions of SQL Server 2008, and has recently updated them to SQL Server 2008 R2 (for Release 2). SQL Server 2008 R2 Express is the least powerful version, but it is intended for general use and can be downloaded for free from the Microsoft SQL Server 2008 R2 Express home page at **www.microsoft.com/express/Database/**. For more information, see the online Appendix A—Getting Started with Microsoft SQL Server 2008 R2 Express Edition.

## FIGURE 2-9

Defining a Primary Key in MySQL 5.1

The **key symbol** indicates which column or columns are being used as the primary key

Figure 2-9 shows the same CUSTOMER table in Oracles's MySQL,[3] as seen in the MySQL Workbench graphical utility program. This display is more complex than Microsoft Access, but we can spot the primary key of the table by finding the key symbol next to the name(s) of the primary key column(s) in the Column Name list. Again, there is a key symbol next to CustomerNumber, indicating that CustomerNumber is the primary key for this table.

A common method of specifying primary keys is to use SQL, which we briefly introduced in Chapter 1. We will see how SQL is used to designate primary keys in the next chapter.

## Surrogate Keys

A **surrogate key** is a column with a unique, DBMS-assigned identifier that has been added to a table to be the primary key. The unique values of the surrogate key are assigned by the DBMS each time a row is created, and the values never change.

An ideal primary key is short, numeric, and never changes. Sometimes one column in a table will meet these requirements or come close to them. For example, EmployeeNumber in the EMPLOYEE relation should work very well as a primary key. But in other tables, the

[3]On February 26, 2008, Sun Microsystems completed its acquisition of MySQL from MySQL AB. On April 29, 2009, Oracle Corporation made an offer to buy Sun Microsystems, and on January 27, 2010, Oracle completed its acquisition of Sun Microsystems. For more details, see **www.oracle.com/us/sun/index.htm**. This makes Oracle the owner of both Oracle Database 11g and the MySQL DBMS. As of this writing, MySQL 5.1 is the latest production version of the popular MySQL DBMS, and a beta release, MySQL 5.5, is available. The free MySQL Server Community Edition and the MySQL Workbench (be sure to download the MySQL Workbench 5.2 version, which, as this book goes to press, is available as a release candidate version) can be downloaded from the MySQL Web site, at **www.mysql.com/downloads/**. Like SQL Server 2008, MySQL is an enterprise-class DBMS and, as such, is much more complex than Microsoft Access. Also like SQL Server 2008, MySQL does not include application development tools, such as form and report generators. For more information, see online Appendix B—Getting Started with Oracle MySQL Community Server 5.1.

primary key does not come close to being ideal. For example, consider the relation PROPERTY:

PROPERTY(Street, City, State, ZIP, OwnerID)

The primary key of PROPERTY is (Street, City, State, ZIP), which is long and nonnumeric (although it probably will not change). This is not an ideal primary key. In cases like this, the database designer will add a surrogate key, such as PropertyID:

PROPERTY(PropertyID, Street, City, State, ZIP, OwnerID)

Surrogate keys are short, numeric, and never change—they are ideal primary keys. Because the values of the surrogate primary key will have no meaning to users, they are often hidden on forms and reports.

Surrogate keys have been used in the databases we have already discussed. For example, in the Art Course database shown in Figure 1-10 we added the surrogate keys CustomerNumber to the CUSTOMER table and CourseNumber to the COURSE table.

Most DBMS products have a facility for automatically generating key values. In Figure 2-7, we can see how surrogate keys are defined with Microsoft Access 2010. In Microsoft Access, Data Type is set to AutoNumber. With this specification, Microsoft Access assigns a value of 1 to CustomerNumber for the first row of CUSTOMER, a value of 2 to CustomerNumber for the second row, and so forth.

Enterprise-class DBMS products, such as Microsoft's SQL Server, offer more capability. For example, with SQL Server, the developer can specify the starting value of the surrogate key as well as the amount by which to increment the key for each new row. Figure 2-8 shows how this is done for the definition of the surrogate key CustomerNumber for the CUSTOMER table. In the Column Properties window, which is below the dbo.CUSTOMER table column details window, there is a set of **identity** specifications that have been set to indicate to SQL Server that a surrogate key column exists. The **is identity** value for CustomerNumber is set to Yes to make CustomerNumber a surrogate key. The starting value of the surrogate key is called the **identity seed**. For CustomerNumber, it is set to 1. Furthermore, the amount that is added to each key value to create the next key value is called the **identity increment**. In this example, it is set to 1. These settings mean that when the user creates the first row of the CUSTOMER table, SQL Server will give the value 1 to CustomerNumber. When the second row of CUSTOMER is created, SQL Server will give the value 2 to CustomerNumber, and so forth.

MySQL uses the **AUTO_INCREMENT** function to automatically assign surrogate key numbers. In AUTO_INCREMENT, the starting value can be any value (the default is 1), but the increment will always be 1. Figure 2-9 shows that CustomerNumber is a surrogate key for CUSTOMER that uses AUTO_INCREMENT (AI) to set the value of the column.

## Foreign Keys and Referential Integrity

As described in Chapter 1, we place values from one relation into a second relation to represent a relationship. The values we use are the primary key values (including composite primary key values, when necessary) of the first relation. When we do this, the attribute in the second relation that holds these values is referred to as a **foreign key**. For example, in the Art Course database shown in Figure 1-10 we represent the relationship between customers and the art courses they are taking by placing CustomerNumber, the primary key of CUSTOMER, into the ENROLLMENT relation. In this case, CustomerID in ENROLLMENT is referred to as a foreign key. This term is used because CustomerNumber is the primary key of a relation that is foreign to the table in which it resides.

Consider the following two relations, where besides the EMPLOYEE relation we now have a DEPARTMENT relation to hold data about departments:

EMPLOYEE (<u>EmployeeNumber</u>, FirstName, LastName, Department, Email, Phone)

and:

DEPARTMENT (<u>DepartmentName</u>, BudgetCode, OfficeNumber, DepartmentPhone)

where EmployeeNumber and DepartmentName are the primary keys of EMPLOYEE and DEPARTMENT, respectively.

Now suppose that Department in EMPLOYEE contains the names of the departments in which employees work and that DepartmentName in DEPARTMENT also contains these names. In this case, Department in EMPLOYEE is said to be a foreign key to DEPARTMENT. In this book, we denote foreign keys by displaying them in italics. Thus, we would write these two relation descriptions as follows:

EMPLOYEE (<u>EmployeeNumber</u>, FirstName, LastName, *Department*, Email, Phone)

and:

DEPARTMENT (<u>DepartmentName</u>, BudgetCode, OfficeNumber, DepartmentPhone)

Note that it is not necessary for the primary key and the foreign key to have the same column name. The only requirement is that they have the same set of values.

In most cases, it is important to ensure that every value of a foreign key matches a value of the primary key. In the previous example, the value of Department in every row of EMPLOYEE should match a value of DepartmentName in DEPARTMENT. If this is the case (and it usually is), then we declare the following rule:

Department in EMPLOYEE must exist in DepartmentName in DEPARTMENT

Such a rule is called a **referential integrity constraint**. Whenever you see a foreign key, you should always look for an associated referential integrity constraint.

Consider the Art Course database shown in Figure 1-10. The structure of this database is:

CUSTOMER (<u>CustomerNumber</u>, CustomerLastName, CustomerFirstName, Phone)
COURSE (<u>CourseNumber</u>, Course, CourseDate, Fee)
ENROLLMENT (*<u>CustomerNumber</u>, <u>CourseNumber</u>*, AmountPaid)

The ENROLLMENT table has a composite primary key of (CustomerNumber, CourseNumber), where CustomerNumber is a foreign key linking to CUSTOMER and CourseNumber is a foreign key linking to COURSE. Therefore, two referential integrity constraints are required:

CustomerNumber in ENROLLMENT must exist in CustomerNumber in CUSTOMER

and:

CourseNumber in ENROLLMENT must exist in CourseNumber in COURSE

Just as DBMS products have a means of specifying primary keys, they also have a way to set up foreign key referential integrity constraints. We discuss the details of setting up

**FIGURE 2-10**

Enforcing Referential Integrity in Microsoft Access 2010

The relationship is between CUSTOMER and ENROLLMENT—the foreign key CustomerNumber in ENROLLMENT references the primary key CustomerNumber in CUSTOMER

Use this check box to enforce referential integrity in this relationship

referential integrity constraints in this chapter's section of "The Access Workbench." Figure 2-10 shows the tables from the Art Course database in Figure 1-10 in the Microsoft Access Relationships window and with the Edit Relationships dialog box showing the details of the relationship between CUSTOMER and ENROLLMENT. Notice that the Enforce Referential Integrity check box is checked, so the referential integrity constraint between CustomerNumber in ENROLLMENT (the foreign key) and CustomerNumber in CUSTOMER (the primary key) is being enforced.

Figure 2-11 shows the same foreign key relationship between CUSTOMER and ENROLLMENT in the Microsoft SQL Server Management Studio program. Again, this display is more complex, but notice that the property Table Designer: Enforce Foreign Key Constraint is set to Yes. This means that the referential integrity constraint between CustomerNumber in ENROLLMENT (the foreign key) and CustomerNumber in CUSTOMER (the primary key) is being enforced.

Figure 2-12 shows foreign keys in MySQL. Here the Foreign Keys tab in the MySQL Workbench utility displays the properties of each foreign key.

Just as SQL can be used to specify primary keys, it can also be used to set referential integrity constraints. We will look at how to use SQL to do this in the next chapter.

## THE PROBLEM OF NULL VALUES

Before we leave the discussion of relations and the relationships between them, we need to discuss a subtle but important topic: null values. A **null value** is a missing value in a cell in a relation. Consider the following relation, which is used to track finished goods for an apparel manufacturer:

ITEM (<u>ItemNumber</u>, ItemName, Color, Quantity)

## FIGURE 2-11

### Enforcing Referential Integrity in SQL Server 2008

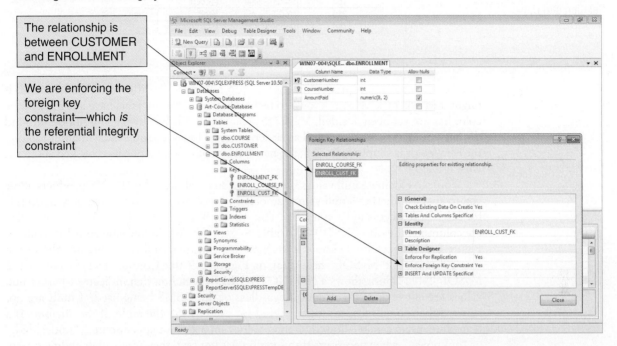

The relationship is between CUSTOMER and ENROLLMENT

We are enforcing the foreign key constraint—which *is* the referential integrity constraint

Figure 2-13 shows sample data for this table. Notice that in the last row of data—the row with ItemNumber 400 and ItemName Spring Hat—there is no value for Color. The problem with null values is that they are ambiguous; we do not know how to interpret them because three possible meanings can be construed. First, it might mean that no

## FIGURE 2-12

### Enforcing Referential Integrity in MySQL 5.1

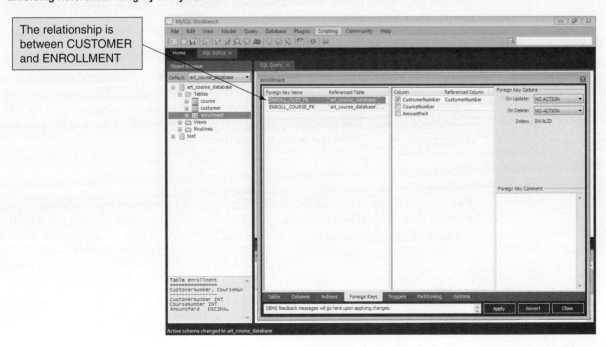

The relationship is between CUSTOMER and ENROLLMENT

**FIGURE 2-13**

Sample ITEM
Relation and Data

| ItemNumber | ItemName | Color | Quantity |
|---|---|---|---|
| 110 | Small T-Shirt | Red | 15 |
| 120 | Small T-Shirt | Blue | 5 |
| 150 | Small T-Shirt | Green | 7 |
| 210 | Med T-Shirt | Red | 8 |
| 400 | Spring Hat | | 5 |

value of Color is appropriate; Spring Hats do not come in different colors. Second, it might mean that the value is known to be blank; that is, Spring Hats have a color, but the color has not yet been decided. Maybe the color is established by placing ribbons around the hats, but this is not done until an order arrives. Finally, the null value might mean that the hats' color is simply unknown; the hats have a color, but no one has checked yet to see what it is.

You can eliminate null values by requiring an attribute value. DBMS products allow you to specify whether a null value can occur in a column. We discussed how to do this for Microsoft Access in Chapter 1's "The Access Workbench." For SQL Server, notice the column in the dbo.CUSTOMER table column details window labeled Allow Nulls in Figure 2-8. A check box without a checkmark means that null values are not allowed in this column. For MySQL, note that in Figure 2-9 the Column Details tab in the MySQL Table Editor shows a NN (NOT NULL) check box that indicates whether null values are allowed in the column. Regardless of the DBMS being used, if nulls are not allowed then some value must be entered for each row in the table. If the attribute is a text value, users can be allowed to enter values such as "not appropriate," "undecided," or "unknown," when necessary. If the attribute is not text, then some other coding system can be developed.

For now, be aware that null values can occur and that they always carry some ambiguity. The next chapter will show another, possibly more serious, problem of null values.

## FUNCTIONAL DEPENDENCIES AND NORMALIZATION

This section introduces some of the concepts used for relational database design; these concepts are used in the next several chapters and expanded in scope in Chapter 5. This book presents only the essentials. To learn more, you should consult other, more comprehensive references.[4]

### Functional Dependencies

To get started, let us take a short excursion into the world of algebra. Suppose you are buying boxes of cookies, and someone tells you that each box costs $5. Knowing this fact, you can compute the cost of several boxes with the formula:

CookieCost = NumberOfBoxes × $5

A more general way to express the relationship between CookieCost and NumberOfBoxes is to say that CookieCost depends upon NumberOfBoxes. Such a statement tells the character of the relationship of CookieCost and NumberOfBoxes, even though it doesn't

---

[4]See David M. Kroenke and David J. Auer, *Database Processing: Fundamentals, Design, and Implementation*, 11th edition (Upper Saddle River, NJ: Prentice Hall, 2010); and C. J. Date, *An Introduction to Database Systems*, 8th edition (Boston: Addison-Wesley, 2004).

give the formula. More formally, we can say that CookieCost is **functionally dependent** on NumberOfBoxes. Such a statement, which is called a **functional dependency,** can be written as follows:

$$NumberOfBoxes \rightarrow CookieCost$$

This expression says that NumberOfBoxes determines CookieCost. The variable on the left, NumberOfBoxes, is called the **determinant**.

Using another example, we can compute the extended price of a part order by multiplying the quantity of the item by its unit price:

$$ExtendedPrice = Quantity \times UnitPrice$$

In this case, we would say that ExtendedPrice is functionally dependent on Quantity and UnitPrice, or:

$$(Quantity, UnitPrice) \rightarrow ExtendedPrice$$

The composite (Quantity, UnitPrice) is the determinant of ExtendedPrice.

Now, let us expand these ideas. Suppose you know that a sack contains either red, blue, or yellow objects. Further suppose you know that the red objects weigh 5 pounds each, the blue objects weigh 5 pounds each, and the yellow objects weigh 7 pounds each. If a friend looks into the sack, sees an object, and tells you the color of the object, you can tell the weight of the object. We can formalize this in the same way as in the previous example:

$$ObjectColor \rightarrow Weight$$

Thus, we can say that Weight is functionally dependent on ObjectColor and that ObjectColor determines Weight. The relationship here does not involve an equation, but this functional dependency is still true. Given a value for ObjectColor, you can determine the object's weight.

In addition, if we know that the red objects are balls, the blue objects are cubes, and the yellow objects are cubes, then:

$$ObjectColor \rightarrow Shape$$

Thus, ObjectColor also determines Shape. We can put these two together and state:

$$ObjectColor \rightarrow (Weight, Shape)$$

Thus, ObjectColor determines Weight and Shape.

Another way to represent these facts is to put them into a table, as shown in Figure 2-14. Note that this table meets all the conditions in our definition of a relation, as listed in Figure 2-1, so we can refer to it as a relation. If we call it the OBJECT relation and use ObjectColor as the primary key, we can write this relation as:

$$OBJECT (\underline{ObjectColor}, Weight, Shape)$$

**FIGURE 2-14**

**Sample OBJECT Relation and Data**

| ObjectColor | Weight | Shape |
|-------------|--------|-------|
| Red | 5 | Ball |
| Blue | 5 | Cube |
| Yellow | 7 | Cube |

Now, you may be thinking that we have just performed some trick or sleight of hand to arrive at a relation, but one can make the argument that the only reason for having relations is to store instances of functional dependencies. Consider a relation such as the CUSTOMER relation from the Art Course database in Figure 1-10:

CUSTOMER (CustomerNumber, CustomerLastName, CustomerFirstName, Phone)

Here, we are simply storing facts that express the following functional dependency:

CustomerNumber → (CustomerLastName, CustomerFirstName, Phone)

## Primary and Candidate Keys Revisited

Now that we have discussed the concept of functional dependency, we can now define primary and candidate keys more formally. Specifically, a primary key of a relation can be defined as "one or more attributes that functionally determine all the other attributes of the relation." The same definition holds for candidate keys, as well.

Recall the EMPLOYEE relation from Figure 2-2 (shown without primary or foreign keys indicated):

EMPLOYEE (EmployeeNumber, FirstName, LastName, Department, Email, Phone)

As previously discussed, based on information from users, this relation has three candidate keys: EmployeeNumber, Email, and the composite (FirstName, LastName, Department). Because this is so, we can state the following:

EmployeeNumber → (FirstName, LastName, Department, Email, Phone)

Equivalently, if we are given a value for EmployeeNumber, we can determine FirstName, LastName, Department, Email, and Phone. Similarly, we can state that:

Email → (EmployeeNumber, FirstName, LastName, Department, Phone)

That is, if we are given a value for Email, we can determine EmployeeNumber, FirstName, LastName, Department, and Phone. Finally, we also can state that:

(FirstName, LastName, Department) → (EmployeeNumber, Email, Phone)

This means that if we are given values of FirstName, LastName, and Department, we can determine EmployeeNumber, Email, and Phone.

These three functional dependencies express the reason the three candidate keys are candidate keys. When we choose a primary key from the candidate keys, we are choosing which functional dependency we want to define as the one that is most meaningful or important to us.

## Normalization

The concepts of functional dependencies and determinants can be used to help in the design of relations. Recalling the concept from Chapter 1 that a table or relation should have only one theme, we can define **normalization** as the process of breaking a table or relation with more than one theme into a set of tables such that each has only one theme. Normalization is a complex topic, and it consumes one or more chapters of more theoretically oriented database books. Here, we reduce this topic to a few ideas that capture the essence of the process, and we expand this discussion in Chapter 5. After that, if you are interested in the topic, you should consult the references mentioned earlier for more information.

The problem that normalization addresses is as follows: A table can meet all the characteristics listed in Figure 2-1 and still have the modification problems we identified for lists in Chapter 1. Specifically, consider the following ADVISER_LIST relation:

ADVISER_LIST (AdviserID, AdviserName, Department, Phone, Office,
    StudentNumber, StudentName)

What is the primary key of this relation? Given the definitions of candidate key and primary key, it has to be an attribute that determines all the other attributes. The only attribute that has this characteristic is StudentNumber. Given a value of StudentNumber, we can determine the values of all the other attributes:

StudentNumber → (AdviserID, AdviserName, Department, Phone, Office,
    StudentName)

We can then write this relation as follows:

ADVISER_LIST (AdviserID, AdviserName, Department, Phone, Office,
    <u>StudentNumber</u>, StudentName)

However, this table has modification problems. Specifically, an adviser's data are repeated many times in the table, once for each advisee. This means that updates to adviser data might need to be made multiple times. If, for example, an adviser changes offices, that change will need to be completed in all the rows for the person's advisees. If an adviser has 20 advisees, that change will need to be entered 20 times.

Another modification problem can occur when we delete a student from this list. If we delete a student who is the only advisee for an adviser, we will delete not only the student's data but also the adviser's data. Thus, we will unintentionally lose facts about two entities while attempting to delete one.

If you look closely at this relation, you will see a functional dependency that involves the adviser's data. Specifically:

AdviserID → (AdviserName, Department, Phone, Office)

Now, we can state the problem with this relation more accurately—in terms of functional dependencies. Specifically, this relation is poorly formed because it has a functional dependency that does not involve the primary key. Stated differently, AdviserID is a determinant of a functional dependency, but it is not a candidate key and thus cannot be the primary key under any circumstances.

## Relational Design Principles

From the discussion so far, we can formulate the following design principles for what we can call a **well-formed relation**:

1. For a relation to be considered well formed, every determinant must be a candidate key.
2. Any relation that is not well formed should be broken into two or more relations that are well formed.

These two principles are the heart of normalization—the process of examining relations and modifying them to make them well formed. This process is called normalization because you can categorize the problems to which relations are susceptible into different types called *normal forms*.

There are many defined normal forms. Technically, our well-formed relations are those that are said to be in **Boyce-Codd Normal Form (BCNF)**. For example, any relation that has the characteristics listed in Figure 2-1 is called a relation in **first normal form (1NF)**. Besides first normal form and Boyce-Codd normal form, other normal forms exist, such as second, third, fourth, fifth, and domain/key normal form. We further describe normal forms in Chapter 5.

However, if we simply follow the aforementioned design principles we will avoid almost all the problems associated with non-normalized tables. In some rare instances, these principles do not address the problems that arise (see questions 2.40 and 2.41 in the Exercises section), but if you follow these principles, you will be safe most of the time.

## The Normalization Process

We can apply the principles just described to formulate the following **normalization process** for normalizing relations:

1. Identify all the candidate keys of the relation.
2. Identify all the functional dependencies in the relation.
3. Examine the determinants of the functional dependencies. If any determinant is not a candidate key, the relation is not well formed. In this case:
   a. Place the columns of the functional dependency in a new relation of their own.
   b. Make the determinant of the functional dependency the primary key of the new relation.
   c. Leave a copy of the determinant as a foreign key in the original relation.
   d. Create a referential integrity constraint between the original relation and the new relation.
4. Repeat step 3 as many times as necessary until every determinant of every relation is a candidate key.

To understand this process, consider the following relation:

PRESCRIPTION (PrescriptionNumber, Date, Drug, Dosage, CustomerName, CustomerPhone, CustomerEmail)

Sample data for the PRESCRIPTION relation are shown in Figure 2-15.

**Step 1 of the Normalization Process**    According to the normalization process, we first identify all candidate keys. PrescriptionNumber clearly determines Date, Drug, and Dosage. If we assume that a prescription is for only one person, then it also determines CustomerName CustomerPhone, and CustomerEmail. By law, prescriptions must be for only one person, so PrescriptionNumber is a candidate key.

---

**FIGURE 2-15**

Sample PRESCRIPTION Relation and Data

| PrescriptionNumber | Date | Drug | Dosage | CustomerName | CustomerPhone | CustomerEmail |
|---|---|---|---|---|---|---|
| P10001 | 10/17/2011 | DrugA | 10mg | Smith, Alvin | 575-523-2233 | ASmith@somewhere.com |
| P10003 | 10/17/2011 | DrugB | 35mg | Rhodes, Jeff | 575-645-3455 | JRhodes@somewhere.com |
| P10004 | 10/17/2011 | DrugA | 20mg | Smith, Sarah | 575-523-2233 | SSmith@somewhere.com |
| P10007 | 10/18/2011 | DrugC | 20mg | Frye, Michael | 575-645-4566 | MFrye@somewhere.com |
| P10010 | 10/18/2011 | DrugB | 30mg | Rhodes, Jeff | 575-645-3455 | JRhodes@somewhere.com |

Does this relation have other candidate keys? Date, Drug, and Dosage do not determine PrescriptionNumber because many prescriptions can be written on a given date, many prescriptions can be written for a given drug, and many prescriptions can be written for a given dosage.

What about customer columns? If a customer had only one prescription, then we could say that some identifying customer column—for example, CustomerEmail—would determine the prescription data. However, people can have more than one prescription, so this assumption is invalid.

Given this analysis, the only candidate key of PRESCRIPTION is PrescriptionNumber.

**Step 2 of the Normalization Process**   In step 2 of the normalization process, we now identify all functional dependencies. PrescriptionNumber determines all the other attributes, as just described. If a drug had only one dosage, then we could state that:

Drug → Dosage

But this is not true because some drugs have several dosages. Therefore, Drug is not a determinant. Furthermore, Dosage is not a determinant because the same dosage can be given for many different drugs.

However, examining the customer columns, we do find a functional dependency:

CustomerEmail → (CustomerName, CustomerPhone)

To know whether functional dependency is true for a particular application, we need to look beyond the sample data in Figure 2-15 and ask the users. For example, it is possible that some customers share the same email address, and it is also possible that some customers do not have email. For now, we can assume that the users say that CustomerEmail is a determinant of the customer attributes.

**Step 3 of the Normalization Process**   In step 3 of the normalization process, we ask whether there is a determinant that is *not* a candidate key. In this example, CustomerEmail is a determinant and not a candidate key. Therefore, PRESCRIPTION has normalization problems and is not well formed. According to step 3, we split the functional dependency into a relation of its own:

CUSTOMER (CustomerName, CustomerPhone, <u>CustomerEmail</u>)

We make the determinant of the functional dependency, CustomerEmail, the primary key of the new relation.

We leave a copy of CustomerEmail in the original relation as a foreign key. Thus, PRESCRIPTION is now:

PRESCRIPTION (<u>PrescriptionNumber</u>, Date, Drug, Dosage, *CustomerEmail*)

Finally, we create the referential integrity constraint:

CustomerEmail in PRESCRIPTION must exist in CustomerEmail in CUSTOMER

At this point, if we move through the three steps, we find that neither of these relations has a determinant that is not a candidate key, and we can say that the two relations are now normalized. Figure 2-16 shows the result for the sample data.

**FIGURE 2-16**

Normalized
Prescription
Customer Relations
and Data

| CustomerName | CustomerPhone | CustomerEmail |
|---|---|---|
| Smith, Alvin | 575-523-2233 | ASmith@somewhere.com |
| Rhodes, Jeff | 575-645-3455 | JRhodes@somewhere.com |
| Frye, Michael | 575-645-4566 | MFrye@somewhere.com |
| Smith, Sarah | 575-523-2233 | SSmith@somewhere.com |

| PrescriptionNumber | Date | Drug | Dosage | CustomerEmail |
|---|---|---|---|---|
| P10001 | 10/17/2011 | DrugA | 10mg | ASmith@somewhere.com |
| P10003 | 10/17/2011 | DrugB | 35mg | JRhodes@somewhere.com |
| P10004 | 10/17/2011 | DrugA | 20mg | SSmith@somewhere.com |
| P10007 | 10/18/2011 | DrugC | 20mg | MFrye@somewhere.com |
| P10010 | 10/18/2011 | DrugB | 30mg | JRhodes@somewhere.com |

**FIGURE 2-17**

Sample STU_DORM
Relation and Data

| StudentNumber | LastName | FirstName | DormName | DormCost |
|---|---|---|---|---|
| 100 | Smith | Terry | Stephens | 3,500.00 |
| 200 | Johnson | Jeff | Alexander | 3,800.00 |
| 300 | Abernathy | Susan | Horan | 4,000.00 |
| 400 | Smith | Susan | Alexander | 3,800.00 |
| 500 | Wilcox | John | Stephens | 3,500.00 |
| 600 | Webber | Carl | Horan | 4,000.00 |
| 700 | Simon | Carol | Stephens | 3,500.00 |

## Normalization Examples

We now illustrate the use of the normalization process with four examples.

**Normalization Example 1** The relation in Figure 2-17 shows a table of student residence data named STU_DORM. The first step in normalizing it is to identify all candidate keys. Because StudentNumber determines each of the other columns, it is a candidate key. LastName cannot be a candidate key because two students have the last name Smith. None of the other columns can be an identifier either, so StudentNumber is the only candidate key.

Next, in step 2, we look for the functional dependencies in the relation. Besides those for StudentNumber, a functional dependency appears to exist between DormName and DormCost. Again, we would need to check this out with the users. In this case, assume that the functional dependency:

DormName → DormCost

is true and assume that our interview with the users indicates that no other functional dependencies exist.

In step 3, we now ask if any determinants exist that are not candidate keys. In this example, DormName is a determinant, but it is not a candidate key. Therefore, this relation is not well formed and has normalization problems.

To fix those problems, we place the columns of the functional dependency (DormName, DormCost) into a relation of their own and call that relation DORM. We make the determinant of the functional dependency the primary key. Thus, DormName is the primary key of DORM. We leave the determinant DormName as a foreign key in STU_DORM. Finally, we find the appropriate referential integrity constraint. The result is:

STU_DORM (StudentNumber, LastName, FirstName, *DormName*)
DORM (DormName, DormCost)

with the constraint:

DormName in STU_DORM must exist in DormName in DORM

The data for these relations appear as shown in Figure 2-18.

**FIGURE 2-18**

Normalized Student
Residence Relations
and Data

| StudentNumber | LastName | FirstName | DormName |
|---|---|---|---|
| 100 | Smith | Terry | Stephens |
| 200 | Johnson | Jeff | Alexander |
| 300 | Abernathy | Susan | Horan |
| 400 | Smith | Susan | Alexander |
| 500 | Wilcox | John | Stephens |
| 600 | Webber | Carl | Horan |
| 700 | Simon | Carol | Stephens |

| DormName | DormCost |
|---|---|
| Alexander | 3,800.00 |
| Horan | 4,000.00 |
| Stephens | 3,500.00 |

**FIGURE 2-19**

Sample EMPLOYEE
Relation and Data

| EmployeeNumber | LastName | Department | Email | DeptPhone |
|---|---|---|---|---|
| 100 | Johnson | Accounting | JJ@somewhere.com | 834-1100 |
| 200 | Abernathy | Finance | MA@somewhere.com | 834-2100 |
| 300 | Smathers | Finance | LS@somewhere.com | 834-2100 |
| 400 | Caruthers | Accounting | TC@somewhere.com | 834-1100 |
| 500 | Jackson | Production | TJ@somewhere.com | 834-4100 |
| 600 | Caldera | Legal | EC@somewhere.com | 834-3100 |
| 700 | Bandalone | Legal | RB@somewhere.com | 834-3100 |

**Normalization Example 2** Now consider the EMPLOYEE table in Figure 2-19. First, we identify the candidate keys in EMPLOYEE. From the data, it appears that EmployeeNumber and Email each identify all the other attributes. Hence, they are candidate keys (again, with the proviso that we cannot depend on sample data to show all cases; we must verify this assumption with the users).

In step 2, we identify other functional dependencies. From the data, it appears that the only other functional dependency is:

Department → DeptPhone

Assuming that this is true, then according to step 3 we have a determinant, Department, that is not a candidate key. Thus, EMPLOYEE has normalization problems.

To fix those problems, we place the columns in the functional dependency in a table of their own and make the determinant the primary key of the new table. We leave the determinant as a foreign key in the original table. The result is the two tables:

EMPLOYEE (EmployeeNumber, LastName, Email, *Department*)
DEPARTMENT (Department, DeptPhone)

with the referential integrity constraint:

Department in EMPLOYEE must exist in Department in DEPARTMENT

The result for the sample data is shown in Figure 2-20.

**Normalization Example 3** Now consider the MEETING table in Figure 2-21. We begin by looking for candidate keys. No column by itself can be a candidate key. Attorney determines different sets of data, so it cannot be a determinant. The same is true for

**FIGURE 2-20**

Normalized
EMPLOYEE and
DEPARTMENT
Relations and Data

| EmployeeNumber | LastName | Department | Email |
|---|---|---|---|
| 100 | Johnson | Accounting | JJ@somewhere.com |
| 200 | Abernathy | Finance | MA@somewhere.com |
| 300 | Smathers | Finance | LS@somewhere.com |
| 400 | Caruthers | Accounting | TC@somewhere.com |
| 500 | Jackson | Production | TJ@somewhere.com |
| 600 | Caldera | Legal | EC@somewhere.com |
| 700 | Bandalone | Legal | RB@somewhere.com |

| Department | DeptPhone |
|---|---|
| Accounting | 834-1100 |
| Finance | 834-2100 |
| Legal | 834-3100 |
| Production | 834-4100 |

| Attorney | ClientNumber | ClientName | MeetingDate | Duration |
|---|---|---|---|---|
| Boxer | 1000 | ABC, Inc | 11/5/2011 | 2.00 |
| Boxer | 2000 | XYZ Partners | 11/5/2011 | 5.50 |
| James | 1000 | ABC, Inc | 11/7/2011 | 3.00 |
| Boxer | 1000 | ABC, Inc | 11/9/2011 | 4.00 |
| Wu | 3000 | Malcomb Zoe | 11/11/2011 | 7.00 |

ClientNumber, ClientName, and MeetingDate. In the sample data, the only column that does not determine different sets of data is Duration, but this uniqueness is accidental. It is easy to imagine that two or more meetings would have the same duration.

The next step is to look for combinations of columns that can be candidate keys. (Attorney, ClientNumber) is one combination, but the values (Boxer, 1000) determine two different sets of data. They cannot be a candidate key. The combination (Attorney, ClientName) fails for the same reason. The only combinations that can be candidate keys of this relation are (Attorney, ClientNumber, MeetingDate) and (Attorney, ClientName, MeetingDate).

Let us consider those possibilities further. The name of the relation is MEETING, and we are asking whether (Attorney, ClientNumber, MeetingDate) or (Attorney, ClientName, MeetingDate) can be a candidate key. Do these combinations make sense as identifiers of a meeting? They do unless more than one meeting of the same attorney and client occurs on the same day. In that case, we need to add a new column, MeetingTime, to the relation and make this new column part of the candidate key. In this example, we assume that this is not the case and that (Attorney, ClientNumber, MeetingDate) and (Attorney, ClientName, MeetingDate) are the candidate keys.

The second step is to identify other functional dependencies. Here, two exist:

ClientNumber → ClientName

and:

ClientName → ClientNumber

Each of these determinants is part of one of the candidate keys. For example, ClientNumber is part of (Attorney, ClientNumber, MeetingDate). However, being part of a candidate key is not enough. The determinant must be the same as the entire candidate key. Thus, the MEETING table is not well formed and has normalization problems.

When you are not certain whether normalization problems exist, consider the three modification operations discussed in Chapter 1: insert, update, and delete. Do problems exist with any of them? For example, in Figure 2-21 if you change ClientName in the first row to ABC, Limited, do inconsistencies arise in the data? The answer is yes because ClientNumber 1000 would have two different names in the table. This and any of the other problems that were identified in Chapter 1 when inserting, updating, or deleting data are sure signs that the table has normalization problems.

To fix the normalization problems, we create a new table, CLIENT, with columns ClientNumber and ClientName. Both of these columns are determinants; thus, either can be the primary key of the new table. However, whichever one is selected as the primary key also should be made the foreign key in MEETING. Thus, two correct designs are possible. First, we can use:

MEETING (Attorney, *ClientNumber*, MeetingDate, Duration)
CLIENT (ClientNumber, ClientName)

with the referential integrity constraint:

ClientNumber in MEETING must exist in ClientNumber in CLIENT

FIGURE 2-22

Normalized MEETING
and CLIENT Relations
and Data

| Attorney | ClientNumber | MeetingDate | Duration |
|---|---|---|---|
| Boxer | 1000 | 11/5/2011 | 2.00 |
| Boxer | 2000 | 11/5/2011 | 5.50 |
| James | 1000 | 11/7/2011 | 3.00 |
| Boxer | 1000 | 11/9/2011 | 4.00 |
| Wu | 3000 | 11/11/2011 | 7.00 |

| ClientNumber | ClientName |
|---|---|
| 1000 | ABC, Inc |
| 2000 | XYZ Partners |
| 3000 | Malcomb Zoe |

Second, we can use:

MEETING (<u>Attorney</u>, *<u>ClientName</u>*, <u>MeetingDate</u>, Duration)
CLIENT (ClientNumber, <u>ClientName</u>)

with the referential integrity constraint:

ClientName in MEETING must exist in ClientName in CLIENT

Data for the first design are shown in Figure 2-22.

Notice in these two designs that either the attribute ClientNumber or ClientName is both a foreign key and also part of the primary key of MEETING. This illustrates that foreign keys can be part of a composite primary key.

Note that when two attributes, such as ClientNumber and ClientName, each determine one another they are **synonyms**. They both must appear in a relation to establish their equivalent values. Given that equivalency, the two columns are interchangeable; one can take the place of the other in any other relation. All things being equal, however, the administration of the database will be simpler if one of the two is used consistently as a foreign key. This policy is just a convenience, however, and not a logical requirement for the design.

**Normalization Example 4**   For our last example, let us consider a relation that involves student data. Specifically:

GRADE (ClassName, Section, Term, Grade, StudentNumber, StudentName,
   Professor, Department, ProfessorEmail)

Given the confused set of columns in this table, it does not seem well formed, and it appears that the table will have normalization problems. We can use the normalization process to find what they are and to remove them.

First, what are the candidate keys of this relation? No column by itself is a candidate key. One way to approach this is to realize that a grade is a combination of a class and a student. In this table, which columns identify classes and students? A particular class is identified by (ClassName, Section, Term), and a student is identified by StudentNumber. Possibly, then, a candidate key for this relation is:

(ClassName, Section, Term, StudentNumber)

This statement is equivalent to saying:

(ClassName, Section, Term, StudentNumber) → (Grade, StudentName, Professor,
   Department, ProfessorEmail)

This is a true statement as long as only one professor teaches a class section. For now, we will make that assumption and consider the alternate case later. If only one professor teaches a section, then (ClassName, Section, Term, StudentNumber) is the one and only candidate key.

Second, what are the additional functional dependencies? One involves student data, and another involves professor data, specifically:

StudentNumber → StudentName

and:

Professor → ProfessorEmail

We also need to ask if Professor determines Department. It will if a professor teaches in only one department. In that case, we have

Professor → (Department, ProfessorEmail)

Otherwise, Department must remain in the GRADE relation.

If we assume that professors teach in just one department, we have:

StudentNumber → StudentName

and:

Professor → (Department, ProfessorEmail)

If we examine the GRADE relation a bit further, however, we can find one other functional dependency. If only one professor teaches a class section, then:

(ClassName, Section, Term) → Professor

Thus, according to step 3 of the normalization process, GRADE has normalization problems because the determinants StudentNumber, Professor, and (ClassName, Section, Term) are not candidate keys. Therefore, we form a table for each of these functional dependencies. As a result, we have a STUDENT table, PROFESSOR table, and a CLASS_PROFESSOR table. After forming these tables, we then take the appropriate columns out of GRADE and put them into a new version of the GRADE table, which we will name GRADE_1. We now have the following design:

STUDENT (<u>StudentNumber</u>, StudentName)
PROFESSOR (<u>Professor</u>, Department, ProfessorEmail)
CLASS_PROFESSOR (<u>ClassName</u>, <u>Section</u>, <u>Term</u>, *Professor*)
GRADE_1(*<u>ClassName</u>*, *<u>Section</u>*, *<u>Term</u>*, Grade, *<u>StudentNumber</u>*)

with the referential integrity constraints:

StudentNumber in GRADE_1 must exist in StudentNumber in STUDENT
Professor in CLASS_PROFESSOR must exist in Professor in PROFESSOR
(ClassName, Section, Term) in GRADE_1 must exist in (ClassName, Section, Term) of CLASS_PROFESSOR

Next, consider what happens if more than one professor teaches a section of a class. In that case, the only change is to make Professor part of the primary key of CLASS_PROFESSOR. Thus, the new relation is:

CLASS_PROFESSOR_1 (<u>ClassName</u>, <u>Section</u>, <u>Term</u>, *<u>Professor</u>*)

Class sections that have more than one professor will have multiple rows in this table—one row for each of the professors.

> **B T W**
>
> In the interest of full disclosure, if professors can teach more than one class, then GRADE has what is called a **multivalued dependency**. We do not discuss such dependencies in this book. If you want to learn about them, see one of the more advanced texts mentioned in the footnote on page 80 and also see exercises 2.40 and 2.41.

This example shows how normalization problems can become more complicated than simple examples might indicate. For large commercial applications that potentially involve hundreds of tables, such problems can sometimes consume days or weeks of design time.

# THE ACCESS WORKBENCH

## Section 2

### Working with Multiple Tables in Microsoft Access

In Chapter 1's "The Access Workbench," we learned how to create Microsoft Access 2010 databases, tables, forms, and reports. However, we were limited to working with only one table. In this section, we will:

- See examples of the modification problems discussed in Chapters 1 and 2
- Work with multiple tables

We will continue to use the WMCRM database we created in Chapter 1's section of "The Access Workbench." At this point, you have created and populated (which means you have inserted the data into) the CONTACT table. Figure AW-2-1 shows the contacts that have been made with each customer. Note that there is no customer with CustomerID 2—this is because we deleted and reentered the data for Jessica Christman.

### FIGURE AW-2-1

#### CONTACT Data

| CustomerID | Date | Type | Remarks |
|---|---|---|---|
| 1 | 7/7/2010 | Phone | General interest in a Gaea. |
| 1 | 7/7/2010 | Email | Sent general information. |
| 1 | 7/12/2010 | Phone | Set up an appointment. |
| 1 | 7/14/2010 | Meeting | Bought a HiStandard. |
| 3 | 7/19/2010 | Phone | Interested in a SUHi, set up an appointment. |
| 1 | 7/21/2010 | Email | Sent a standard follow-up message. |
| 4 | 7/27/2010 | Phone | Interested in a HiStandard, set up an appointment. |
| 3 | 7/27/2010 | Meeting | Bought a SUHi. |
| 4 | 8/2/2010 | Meeting | Talked up to a HiLuxury. Customer bought one. |
| 3 | 8/3/2010 | Email | Sent a standard follow-up message. |
| 4 | 8/10/2010 | Email | Sent a standard follow-up message. |
| 5 | 8/15/2010 | Phone | General interest in a Gaea. |

*(Continued)*

### Possible Modification Problems in the WMCRM Database

We know from the topics covered in this chapter that we really need a separate table to store the CONTACT data, but in order to illustrate the modification problems discussed in Chapter 1 let us combine it in one table with the data already in CUSTOMER. This table is available in the file WMCRM-Combined-Data.accdb, which is available at the Web site for this book (**www.pearsonhighered.com/kroenke**). We will use this database to see modification problems in non-normalized tables and then build the correctly normalized tables in the actual WMCRM database.

We will need to start Microsoft Access 2010, open the WMCRM-Combined-Data.accdb file, and take a look at the WMCRM-Combined-Data database.

#### *Opening an Existing Microsoft Access Database*

1. Select **Start | All Programs | Microsoft Office | Microsoft Access 2010**. The Microsoft Access 2010 window appears with the Backstage view displayed as shown in Figure AW-2-2.
    - **NOTE:** The menu command or icon location used to start Microsoft Access 2010 may vary, depending on the operating system you are using and how Microsoft Office is installed on the computer you are using.
2. Click the **Open** button to display the Open dialog box as shown in Figure AW-2-3.
3. Browse to the **WMCRM-Combined-Data.accdb** file, click the file name to highlight it, and then click the **Open** button.
4. The **Security Warning** bar appears with the database. Click the Security Warning bar's **Enable Content** button to select this option.
5. In the Navigation Pane, double-click the **CUSTOMER_CONTACT** table object to open it.
6. Click the **Shutter Bar Open/Close** button to minimize the Navigation Pane.
7. The CUSTOMER_CONTACT table appears in Datasheet view, as shown in Figure AW-2-4. Note that there is one line for each contact, which has resulted in

---

**FIGURE AW-2-2**

The Microsoft Access 2010 Backstage View

Click the Backstage view **Open** button

## FIGURE AW-2-3

### The Open Dialog Box

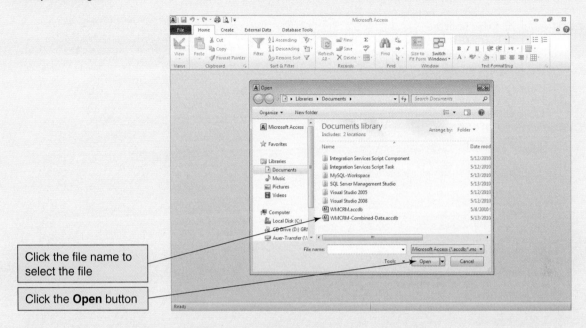

Click the file name to select the file

Click the **Open** button

the duplication of basic customer data. For example, there are five sets of basic data for Ben Griffey.

8. Close the CUSTOMER_CONTACT table by clicking the document window's **Close** button.
9. Click the **Shutter Bar Open/Close** button to expand the Navigation Pane.
10. In the Navigation Pane, double-click the **Customer Contact Data Input Form** object to open it. The Customer Contact Data Input Form appears, as shown in Figure AW-2-5. Note that the form displays all the data for one record in the CUSTOMER_CONTACT table.
11. Close the Customer Contact Data Input Form by clicking the document window's **Close** button.
12. In the Navigation Pane, double-click the report **Wallingford Motors Customer Contact Report** to open it.

## FIGURE AW-2-4

### The CUSTOMER_CONTACT Table

*(Continued)*

**FIGURE AW-2-5**

The Customer Contact Data Input Form

All fields from the CUSTOMER_CONTACT table appear on the form

Form browsing buttons

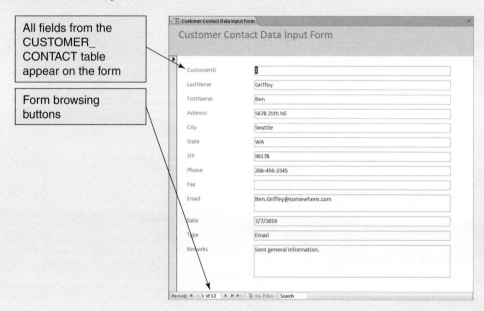

13. Click the **Shutter Bar Open/Close** button to minimize the Navigation Pane.
14. The Wallingford Motors Customer Contact Report appears, as shown in Figure AW-2-6. Note that the form displays the data for all contacts in the CUSTOMER_CONTACT table, sorted by CustomerNumber and Date. For example, all the contact data for Ben Griffey (who has a CustomerID of 1) is grouped at the beginning of the report.
15. Close the Wallingford Motors Customer Contact Report by clicking the document window's **Close** button.
16. Click the **Shutter Bar Open/Close** button to expand the Navigation Pane.

Now, assume that Ben Griffey has changed his email address from Ben.Griffey@ somewhere.com to Ben.Griffey@elsewhere.com. In a well-formed relation, we would have

**FIGURE AW-2-6**

The Wallingford Motors Customer Contact Report

Contact data for each customer are grouped together and sorted by date to make this change only once, but a quick examination of Figures AW-2-4 through AW-2-6 shows that Ben Griffey's email address appears in multiple records. We therefore have to change it in every record to avoid update problems. Unfortunately, it is easy to miss one or more records, especially in large tables.

### *Updating Ben Griffey's Email Address*

1. In the Navigation Pane, double-click the **Customer Contact Data Input Form** object to open it. Because Ben Griffey is the customer in the first record, his data is already in the form.
2. Edit the **Email** address to read *Ben.Griffey@elsewhere.com*, as shown in Figure AW-2-7.
3. Click the **Next Record** button to move to the next record in the table. Again, the record shows Ben Griffey's data, so again edit the **Email** address to read *Ben.Griffey@elsewhere.com.*
4. Click the **Next Record** button to move to the next record in the table. For the third time, the record shows Ben Griffey's data, so again edit the **Email** address to read *Ben.Griffey@elsewhere.com.*
5. Click the **Next Record** button to move to the next record in the table. For the fourth time, the record shows Ben Griffey's data, so again edit the **Email** address to read *Ben.Griffey@elsewhere.com.*
6. Click the **Next Record** button to move to the next record in the table. Finally, another customer's data (the data for Jessica Christman's contact on 7/19/2010) appears in the form, so we assume that we have made all the necessary updates to the database records.
7. Close the Customer Contact Data Input form by clicking the document window's **Close** button.
8. In the Navigation Pane, double-click the report **Wallingford Motors Customer Contact Report** to open it.
9. Click the **Shutter Bar Open/Close** button to minimize the Navigation Pane.

---

### FIGURE AW-2-7

**The Customer Contact Data Input Form with the Updated Email Address**

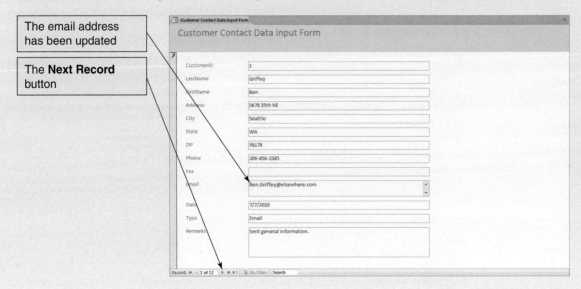

The email address has been updated

The **Next Record** button

*(Continued)*

---

**FIGURE AW-2-8**

The Updated Wallingford Motors Customer Contact Report

A modification problem has occurred. Not all records were updated with the new email address, and the database records are now inconsistent

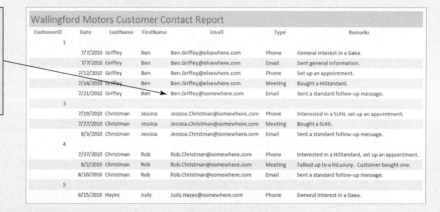

10. The Wallingford Motors Customer Contact Report now looks as shown in Figure AW-2-8. Note that the email addresses shown for Ben Griffey are inconsistent—we missed one record when we updated the table, and now we have inconsistent data. A modification error—in this case an update error—has occurred.
11. Close the Wallingford Motors Customer Contact Report by clicking the document window's **Close** button.
12. Click the **Shutter Bar Open/Close** button to expand the Navigation Pane.

This simple example shows how easily modification problems can occur in tables that are not normalized. With a set of well-formed, normalized tables, this problem would not have occurred.

### Closing the WMCRM-Combined-Data Database

1. Click the **Close** button to close the database and exit Microsoft Access.

### Working with Multiple Tables

The table structure for the CUSTOMER_CONTACT table in the WMCRM-Combined-Data database is:

CUSTOMER_CONTACT (<u>CustomerID</u>, LastName, FirstName, Address, City, State, ZIP, Phone, Fax, Email, <u>Date</u>, <u>Type</u>, <u>Remarks</u>)

Applying the normalization process discussed in this chapter, we will have the following set of tables:

CUSTOMER (<u>CustomerID</u>, LastName, FirstName, Address, City, State, ZIP, Phone, Fax, Email)
CONTACT (<u>ContactID</u>, *CustomerID*, ContactDate, ContactType, Remarks)

with the referential integrity constraint:

CustomerID in CONTACT must exist in CustomerID in CUSTOMER

Note that we have modified a couple of modifications of the column names in the CONTACT table—we are using ContactDate instead of Date and ContactType instead of Type. We will discuss the reason for this later in this section. Our task now is to build and populate the CONTACT table and then to establish the relationship and referential integrity constraint between the two tables.

First, we need to create and populate (insert data into) the CONTACT table, which will contain the columns and column characteristics shown in the table in Figure AW-2-9.[5] The CustomerID column appears again in CONTACT, this time designated as a foreign key. As discussed in this chapter, the term *foreign key* designates this column as the link to the CUSTOMER table. The value in the CustomerID column of CONTACT tells which customer was contacted. All we have to do is look up the value of CustomerID in the CUSTOMER table.

Note that when we build the CONTACT table, there is no "foreign key" setting. We will set up the database relationship between CUSTOMER and CONTACT after we have finished building the CONTACT table.

Note the following:

- Some new data types are being used—Number, Date/Time, and Memo.
- CustomerID must be set as a Number data type and specifically as a Long Integer data type to match the data type Microsoft Access creates for the AutoNumber data type in the CUSTOMER table.
- The Type column has only four allowed values—Phone, Fax, Email, and Meeting. For now, we can simply input only these data values. You will learn how to enforce the data restriction for this column in Chapter 3.

### Creating the CONTACT Table

1. Select **Start | All Programs | Microsoft Office | Microsoft Access 2010**. The Microsoft Access 2010 window appears.
2. In the quick access list of database files, click **WMCRM.accdb**. The database file opens in Microsoft Access.
3. Click the **Create** command tab.
4. Click the **Table Design** button.
5. The Table1 tabbed document window is displayed in Design view. Note that along with the Table1 window a contextual tab named Table Tools is displayed and that this tab adds a new command tab and ribbon, named Design, to the set of command tabs displayed.

---

### FIGURE AW-2-9

Database Column Characteristics for the CONTACT Table

| Column Name | Type | Key | Required | Remarks |
|---|---|---|---|---|
| ContactID | AutoNumber | Primary Key | Yes | Surrogate Key |
| CustomerID | Number | Foreign Key | Yes | Long Integer |
| ContactDate | Date/Time | No | Yes | Short Date |
| ContactType | Text (10) | No | Yes | Allowed values are Phone, Fax, Email, and Meeting |
| Remarks | Memo | No | No | |

---

[5]Although we are using it for simplicity in this example, a column, such as Remarks, can cause problems in a database. For a complete discussion, see David M. Kroenke and David J. Auer, *Database Processing: Fundamentals, Design, and Implementation*, 11th edition (Upper Saddle River, NJ: Prentice Hall, 2010).

*(Continued)*

6. Using the steps we followed to create the CUSTOMER table in Chapter 1's section of "The Access Workbench," begin to create the CONTACT table. The following steps detail only new information that you need to know to complete the CONTACT table.

   ■ **NOTE:** When creating the CONTACT table, be sure to enter appropriate comments in the Description column.

7. When creating the CustomerID column, set the data type to **Number**. Note that the default Field Size setting for Number is Long Integer, so no change is necessary. Be sure to set the Required property to **Yes**.

8. After creating the ContactID column, set it as the primary key of the table.

9. When creating the ContactDate column, start by using the column name *Date*. As soon as you enter the column name and try to move to the Data Type column, Microsoft Access displays a dialog box, warning you that Date is a reserved word, as shown in Figure AW-2-10. Click the **Cancel** button, and change the column name to ContactDate.

   ■ **NOTE:** Normally, you should avoid reserved words such as Date and Time. Generally, column names such as ContactDate are preferred, both to avoid reserved words and to clarify exactly which date you're referring to, and that is why we changed the column names in the CONTACT table.

10. When creating the ContactDate column, set the data type to **Date/Time** and set the format to **Short Date**, as shown in Figure AW-2-11. Be sure to set the Required property to **Yes**.

11. To name and save the CONTACT table, click the **Save** button in the Quick Access Toolbar.

12. Type the table name **CONTACT** into the Save As dialog box text box, and then click the **OK** button. The table is named and saved, and it now appears with the table name CONTACT.

13. To close the CONTACT table, click the **Close** button in the upper-right corner of the tabbed document window. The CONTACT table now appears as a table object in the Navigation Pane.

---

**FIGURE AW-2-10**

**The Reserved Word Warning**

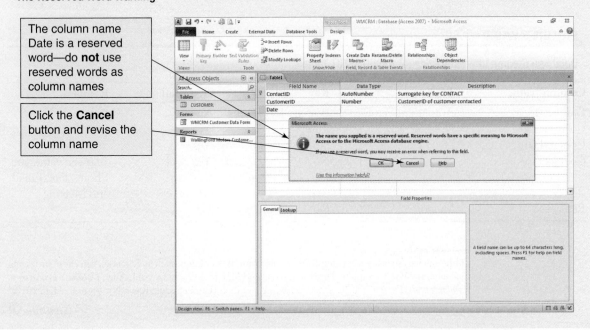

## FIGURE AW-2-11

**Setting the Date Format**

Select the **Short Date** date format from the drop-down list

## Creating Relationships Between Tables

In Microsoft Access, you build relationships between tables by using the **Relationships window**, which you access by using the Tools | Relationships command. After a relationship is created in the Relationships window, referential integrity constraints are set in the **Edit Relationships dialog box** within that window by using the **Enforce Referential Integrity check box**.

### *Creating the Relationship Between the CUSTOMER and CONTACT Tables*

1. Click the **Database Tools** command tab to display the Database Tools command groups, as shown in Figure AW-2-12.
2. Click the **Relationships** button in the Show/Hide group. As shown in Figure AW-2-13, the Relationships tabbed document window appears, together with the Show Table

## FIGURE AW-2-12

**The Database Tools Command Tab**

The **Database Tools** command tab

The **Relationships** button

The **Relationships** command group

*(Continued)*

**FIGURE AW-2-13**

**The Relationships Window**

The **Relationship Tools** contextual command tab

The **Design** command tab

The **Relationships** tabbed document window

The **Show Table** dialog box

Select a table name, then click the **Add** button to add the table to the Relationships window

dialog box. Note that along with the Relationships window, a contextual tab named Relationship Tools is displayed and that this tab adds a new command tab named Design to the set of command tabs displayed.

3. In the Show Table dialog box, the CONTACT table is already selected. Click the **Add** button to add CONTACT to the Relationships window.
4. In the Show Table dialog box, click the **CUSTOMER** table to select it. Click the **Add** button to add CUSTOMER to the Relationships window.
5. In the Show Table dialog box, click the **Close** button to close the dialog box.
6. Rearrange and resize the table objects in the Relationships window using standard Windows drag-and-drop techniques. Rearrange the CUSTOMER and CONTACT table objects until they appear as shown in Figure AW-2-14. Now we are ready to create the relationship between the tables.

**FIGURE AW-2-14**

**The Table Objects in the Relationships Window**

The table objects have been enlarged and rearranged into the arrangement shown here

Click, drag, and drop the **CUSTOMER CustomerID** field onto the **CONTACT CustomerID** field

## FIGURE AW-2-15

### The Edit Relationships Dialog Box

The **Edit Relationships** dialog box

Click the **Enforce Referential Integrity** check box and then click the **Create** button to create the relationship

- **NOTE:** A formal description of how to create a relationship between two tables is "In the Relationships window, drag a primary key column and drop it on top of the corresponding foreign key column." It is easier to understand this after you have actually done it.

7. Click and hold the column name **CustomerID in the CUSTOMER table** and then drag it over the **column name CustomerID in the CONTACT table**. The Edit Relationships dialog box appears, as shown in Figure AW-2-15.

- **NOTE:** In CUSTOMER, CustomerID is the primary key, and in CONTACT CustomerID is the foreign key.

8. Click the **Enforce Referential Integrity check box**.

9. Click the **Create** button to create the relationship between CUSTOMER and CONTACT. The relationship between the tables now appears in the Relationships window, as shown in Figure AW-2-16.

## FIGURE AW-2-16

### The Completed Relationship

The new relationship now appears in the Relationships window diagram—note that the line connects the related fields

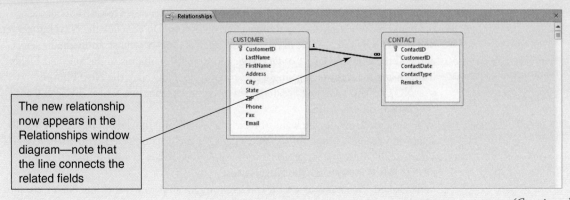

*(Continued)*

### Data in the CONTACT Table

10. To close the Relationships window, click the **Close** button in the upper-right corner of the document window. A Microsoft Access warning dialog box appears, asking whether you want to save changes to the layout of relationships. Click the **Yes** button to save the changes and close the window.

At this point, we need to add data on customer contacts to the CONTACT table. Using the CONTACT table in Datasheet view, as discussed earlier, we enter the data shown in Figure AW-2-1 into the CONTACT table. Note that there is no customer with CustomerID 2—this is because we deleted and reentered the data for Jessica Christman in Chapter 1's section of "The Access Workbench." Also note that because referential integrity is enabled, we cannot enter a CustomerID that does not already exist in the CUSTOMER table. The CONTACT table with the data inserted looks as shown in Figure AW-2-17. Be sure to close the table after the data have been entered.

### Using a Form That Includes Two Tables

In Chapter 1's section of "The Access Workbench," we created a data entry form for the CUSTOMER table. Now we will create a Microsoft Access form that will let us work with the combined data from both tables.

#### Creating a Form for Both the CUSTOMER and CONTACT Tables

1. Click the **Create** command tab.
2. Click the **Form Wizard** button in the Forms command group. The Form Wizard appears.
3. Select the **CUSTOMER** table in the Tables/Queries drop-down list. To add all the columns, click the **right-facing double chevron** button. Do *not* click the **Next** button yet.
4. Select the **CONTACT** table in the Tables/Queries drop-down list. Individually select and add the **ContactDate, ContactType**, and **Remarks** columns to the Selected Fields list by using the **right-facing single chevron** button. Now click the **Next** button.
   - ■ **NOTE:** You have just created a set of columns from two tables that you want to appear on one form.
5. When asked "How do you want to view your data?" use the default **by CUSTOMER** selection because we want to see all contacts for each customer. Also use the selected **Forms with subforms** option to treat the CONTACT data as a subform within the CUSTOMER form. Click the **Next** button.
6. When asked "What layout would you like for your subform?" click the **Next** button to use the default Datasheet layout.

7. When asked "What titles do you want for your form?" type the form title **WMCRM Customer Contacts Form** in the Form: text box, and type the form title **Contact Data** in the Subform: text box. Click the **Finish** button. The completed form appears.
8. Click the **Shutter Bar Open/Close** button to minimize the Navigation Pane. The completed form is displayed as shown in Figure AW-2-18.
9. Click the **Shutter Bar Open/Close button** to expand the Navigation Pane.
10. Close the form window.

## Creating a Report That Includes Data from Two Tables

In this section, we will create a report that includes data from two or more tables. This Microsoft Access report will let us use the combined data from both the CUSTOMER and CONTACT tables.

### Creating a Report for Both the CUSTOMER and CONTACT Tables

1. Click the **Create** tab.
2. Click the **Report Wizard** button to display the Report Wizard.
3. Select the **CUSTOMER** table in the Tables/Queries drop-down list. One by one, click **LastName, FirstName, Phone, Fax**, and **Email** to select each one, and then click the **right-facing single chevron** button to add each column to the Selected Fields list. Do *not* click the **Next** button yet.
4. Select the **CONTACT** table in the Tables/Queries drop-down list. Individually select and add the **ContactDate, ContactType**, and **Remarks** columns to the

---

**FIGURE AW-2-18**

The Completed Form for CUSTOMER and CONTACT Data

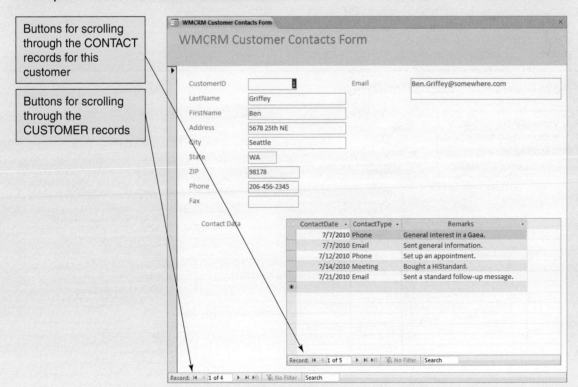

*(Continued)*

Selected Fields list by clicking the **right-facing single chevron** button. Now click the **Next** button.

5. When asked "How do you want to view your data?" click the **Next** button to use the default **by CUSTOMER** selection (in order to see all contacts for each customer).

6. When asked "Do you want to add any grouping levels?" click the **Next** button to use the default nongrouped column listing.

7. We are now asked "What sort order do you want for detail records?" This is the sort order for the CONTACT information. The most useful sorting order is by date, in ascending order. Click the **sort field 1** drop-down list arrow and select **ContactDate**. Leave the sort order button set to **Ascending**. Click the **Next** button.

8. We are now asked "How would you like to lay out your report?" We will use the default setting of stepped layout, but click the **Landscape orientation** radio button to change the report orientation to landscape. Then click the **Next** button.

9. When asked "What title do you want for your report?" edit the report title to read **Wallingford Motors Customer Contacts Report**. Leave the **Preview the report** radio button selected. Click the **Finish** button. The completed report is displayed in Print Preview mode.

10. Click the **Close Print Preview** button to close Print Preview.

11. Click the **Home** command tab.

12. Click the **Shutter Bar Open/Close** button to minimize the Navigation Pane. The completed report is displayed as shown in Figure AW-2-19.

13. Although this may not be the best layout for the report, the Microsoft Access Form Wizard has created a useable report with all columns correctly sized to display the information (if there are any columns that are not correctly displayed use the Layout view in the view gallery to make minor adjustments—this tool can be used to make basic adjustments by simply clicking on the report section you want to change). We will discuss how to use report Design view to modify reports in Chapter 5's section of "The Access Workbench."

**FIGURE AW-2-19**

**The Wallingford Motors Customer Contact Report**

**View** gallery arrow button—use this button to access Layout view if needed

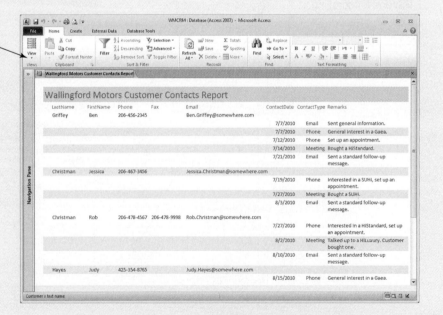

14. Click the **Shutter Bar Open/Close** button to expand the Navigation Pane.
15. Click the document window's **Close** button to close the report window.

### Closing the Database and Exiting Microsoft Access

We have finished the work we need to do in this chapter's "The Access Workbench." As usual, we finish by closing the database and Microsoft Access.

#### Closing the WMCRM Database and Exiting Microsoft Access

1. To close the WMCRM database and exit Microsoft Access 2010, click the **Close** button in the upper-right corner of the Microsoft Access 2010 window.

## SUMMARY

The relational model is the most important standard in database processing today. It was first published by E. F. Codd in 1970. Today, it is used for the design and implementation of almost every commercial database.

An entity is something of importance to a user that needs to be represented in a database. A relation is a two-dimensional table that has the characteristics listed in Figure 2-1. In this book, and in the database world in general, the term *table* is used synonymously with the term *relation*. Three sets of terminology are used for relational structures. The terms *table, row,* and *column* are used most commonly, but *file, record,* and *field* are sometimes used in traditional data processing. Theorists also use the terms *relation, tuple,* and *attribute* for the same three constructs. Sometimes these terms are mixed and matched. Strictly speaking, a relation may not have duplicate rows; however, sometimes this condition is relaxed because eliminating duplicates can be a time-consuming process.

A key is one or more columns of a relation that is used to identify a row. A unique key identifies a single row; a nonunique key identifies several rows. A composite key is a key that has two or more attributes. A relation has one primary key, which must be a unique key. A relation may also have additional unique keys, called candidate keys. A primary key is used to represent the table in relationships, and many DBMS products use values of the primary key to organize table storage. In addition, an index normally is constructed to provide fast access via primary key values. An ideal primary key is short, numeric, and never changes.

A surrogate key is a unique numeric value that is appended to a relation to serve as the primary key. Surrogate key values have no meaning to the user and are normally hidden on forms, queries, and reports.

A foreign key is an attribute that is placed in a relation to represent a relationship. A foreign key is the primary key of a table that is different from (foreign to) the table in which it is placed. Primary and foreign keys may have different names, but they must use the same sets of values. A referential integrity constraint specifies that the values of a foreign key be present in the primary key.

A null value occurs when no value has been given to an attribute. The problem with a null value is that its meaning is ambiguous. It can mean that no value is appropriate, that a value is appropriate but has not yet been chosen, or that a value is appropriate and has been chosen but is unknown to the user. It is possible to eliminate null values by requiring attribute values. (Another problem with null values will be discussed in the next chapter.)

A functional dependency occurs when the value of one attribute (or set of attributes) determines the value of a second attribute (or set of attributes). The attribute on the left side of a functional dependency is called the determinant. One way to view the purpose of a relation is to say that the relation exists to store instances of functional dependencies. Another way to define a primary (and candidate) key is to say that such a key is an attribute that functionally determines all the other attributes in a relation.

Normalization is the process of evaluating a relation and, when necessary, breaking the relation into two or more relations that are better designed and said to be well formed. According to normalization theory, a relation is poorly structured if it has a functional dependency that does not involve the primary key. Specifically, in a well-formed relation, every determinant is a candidate key.

A process for normalizing relations is shown on page 84. According to this process, relations that have normalization problems are divided into two or more relations that do not have such problems. Foreign keys are established between the old and new relations, and referential integrity constraints are created.

## KEY TERMS

| | | |
|---|---|---|
| attribute | foreign key | null value |
| AUTO_INCREMENT | functional dependency | primary key |
| Boyce-Codd Normal Form | functionally dependent | record |
| candidate key | identity | referential integrity constraint |
| column | identity increment | relation |
| composite key | identity seed | row |
| database schema | is identity | surrogate key |
| determinant | key | synonyms |
| entity | multivalued dependency | table |
| field | nonunique key | tuple |
| file | normalization | unique key |
| first normal form (1NF) | normalization process | well-formed relation |

## REVIEW QUESTIONS

**2.1** Define the term *entity* and give an example of an entity.

**2.2** Why is the relational model important?

**2.3** List the characteristics a table must have to be considered a relation.

**2.4** Give an example of a relation (other than one in this chapter).

**2.5** Give an example of a table that is not a relation (other than one from this chapter).

**2.6** Under what circumstances can an attribute of a relation be of variable length?

**2.7** Under what circumstances can a relation have duplicate rows?

**2.8** Explain the use of the terms *relation, tuple*, and *attribute*.

**2.9** Explain the use of the terms *file, record*, and *field*.

**2.10** Define the term *unique key* and give an example.

**2.11** Define the term *nonunique key* and give an example.

**2.12** Give an example of a relation with a unique composite key.

**2.13** Describe four uses of a primary key.

**2.14** Explain the difference between a primary key and a candidate key.

**2.15** What is a *surrogate key*, and under what circumstances would you use one?

**2.16** How do surrogate keys obtain their values?

**2.17** Why are the values of surrogate keys normally hidden from users on forms, queries, and reports?

**2.18** Explain the term *foreign key* and give an example.

**2.19** Explain how primary keys and foreign keys are denoted in this book.

**2.20** Define the term *referential integrity constraint* and give an example of one.

**2.21**  Define the terms *functional dependency* and *determinant*, using an example not in this book.

**2.22**  Explain three possible interpretations of a null value.

**2.23**  Give an example of a null value (other than one from this chapter) and explain each of the three possible interpretations for that value.

**2.24**  In the following equation, name the functional dependency and identify the determinant(s):

Area = Length × Width

**2.25**  Explain the meaning of the following expression:

A → (B, C)

Given this expression, tell if it is also true that:

A → B

and:

A → C

**2.26**  Explain the meaning of the following expression:

(D, E) → F

Given this expression, tell if it is also true that:

D → F

and:

E → F

**2.27**  Explain the differences in your answers to questions 2.25 and 2.26.

**2.28**  Define the term *primary key* in terms of functional dependencies.

**2.29**  If you assume that a relation has no duplicate data, how do you know there is always at least one primary key?

**2.30**  How does your answer to question 2.29 change if you allow a relation to have duplicate data?

**2.31**  In your own words, describe the nature and purpose of the normalization process.

**2.32**  Examine the data in the Veterinary Office List—Version One in Figure 1-26 (see page 63) and state assumptions about functional dependencies in that table. What is the danger of making such conclusions on the basis of sample data?

**2.33**  Describe a modification problem that occurs when changing data in the relation in question 2.32 and a second modification problem that occurs when deleting data in this relation.

**2.34**  Using the assumptions you stated in your answer to question 2.32, what are the determinants of this relation? What attribute(s) can be the primary key of this relation?

**2.35**  Examine the data in the Veterinary Office List—Version Two in Figure 1-27 (see page 63) and state assumptions about functional dependencies in that table.

**2.36**  Explain a modification problem that occurs when changing data in the relation in question 2.35 and a second modification problem that occurs when deleting data in this relation.

**2.37**  Using the assumptions you stated in your answer to question 2.35, what are the determinants of this relation? What attribute(s) can be the primary key of this relation?

## EXERCISES

**2.38** Apply the normalization process to the Veterinary Office List—Version One relation shown in Figure 1-26 to develop a set of normalized relations. Show the results of each of the steps in the normalization process.

**2.39** Apply the normalization process to the Veterinary Office List—Version Two relation shown in Figure 1-27 to develop a set of normalized relations. Show the results of each of the steps in the normalization process.

**2.40** Consider the following relation:

STUDENT(StudentNumber, StudentName, SiblingName, Major)

Assume that the values of SiblingName are the names of all of a given student's brothers and sisters; also assume that students have at most one major.

**A.** Show an example of this relation for two students, one of whom has three siblings and the other of whom has only two siblings.

**B.** List the candidate keys in this relation.

**C.** State the functional dependencies in this relation.

**D.** Explain why this relation does not meet the relational design criteria set out in this chapter (that is, why this is not a well-formed relation).

**E.** Divide this relation into a set of relations that meet the relational design criteria (that is, that are well formed).

**2.41** Alter question 2.40 to allow students to have multiple majors. In this case, the relational structure is:

STUDENT(StudentNumber, StudentName, SiblingName, Major)

**A.** Show an example of this relation for two students, one of whom has three siblings and the other of whom has one sibling. Assume that each student has a single major.

**B.** Show the data changes necessary to add a second major for only the first student.

**C.** Based on your answer to part B, show the data changes necessary to add a second major for the second student.

**D.** Explain the differences in your answers to parts B and C. Comment on the desirability of this situation.

**E.** Divide this relation into a set of well-formed relations.

**2.42** The text states that you can argue that "the only reason for having relations is to store instances of functional dependencies." Explain, in your own words, what this means.

## ACCESS WORKBENCH KEY TERMS

Enforce Referential Integrity      Edit Relationships dialog box      Relationships window
   check box

## ACCESS WORKBENCH EXERCISES

**AW.2.1**  In the "Access Workbench Exercises" in Chapter 1, we created a database for the Wedgewood Pacific Corporation (WPC) of Seattle, Washington, and created and populated the EMPLOYEE table. In this exercise, we will build the rest of the tables needed for the database, create the referential integrity constraints between them, and populate them.

The full set of normalized tables for the WPC database is as follows:

DEPARTMENT (<u>DepartmentName</u>, BudgetCode, OfficeNumber, Phone)
EMPLOYEE (<u>EmployeeNumber</u>, FirstName, LastName, *Department*, Phone, Email)
PROJECT (<u>ProjectID</u>, ProjectName, *Department*, MaxHours, StartDate, EndDate)
ASSIGNMENT (<u>*ProjectID*</u>, <u>*EmployeeNumber*</u>, HoursWorked)

The primary key of DEPARTMENT is DepartmentName, the primary key of EMPLOYEE is EmployeeNumber, and the primary key of PROJECT is ProjectID. Note that the EMPLOYEE table is the same as the table we have created, except that Department is now a foreign key. In EMPLOYEE and PROJECT, Department is a foreign key that references DepartmentName in DEPARTMENT. Note that a foreign key does not need to have the same name as the primary key to which it refers. The primary key of ASSIGNMENT is the composite (ProjectID, EmployeeNumber). ProjectID is also a foreign key that references ProjectID in PROJECT, and EmployeeNumber is a foreign key that references EmployeeNumber in EMPLOYEE.

The referential integrity constraints are:

Department in EMPLOYEE must exist in DepartmentName in DEPARTMENT
Department in PROJECT must exist in DepartmentName in DEPARTMENT
ProjectID in ASSIGNMENT must exist in ProjectID in PROJECT
EmployeeNumber in ASSIGNMENT must exist in EmployeeNumber in EMPLOYEE

A. Figure 2-23 shows the column characteristics for the WPC DEPARTMENT table. Using the column characteristics, create the DEPARTMENT table in the WPC.accdb database.

B. For the DEPARTMENT table, create a data input form named WPC Department Data Form. Make any necessary adjustments to the form so that

**FIGURE 2-23**

Column Characteristics for the DEPARTMENT Table

| Column Name | Type | Key | Required | Remarks |
|---|---|---|---|---|
| DepartmentName | Text (35) | Primary Key | Yes | |
| BudgetCode | Text (30) | No | Yes | |
| OfficeNumber | Text (15) | No | Yes | |
| Phone | Text (12) | No | Yes | |

*(Continued)*

**FIGURE 2-24**

**WPC DEPARTMENT Data**

| DepartmentName | BudgetCode | OfficeNumber | Phone |
|---|---|---|---|
| Administration | BC-100-10 | BLDG01-300 | 360-285-8100 |
| Legal | BC-200-10 | BLDG01-200 | 360-285-8200 |
| Accounting | BC-300-10 | BLDG01-100 | 360-285-8300 |
| Finance | BC-400-10 | BLDG01-140 | 360-285-8400 |
| Human Resources | BC-500-10 | BLDG01-180 | 360-285-8500 |
| Production | BC-600-10 | BLDG02-100 | 360-287-8600 |
| Marketing | BC-700-10 | BLDG02-200 | 360-287-8700 |
| InfoSystems | BC-800-10 | BLDG02-270 | 360-287-8800 |

all data display properly. Use this form to enter into your DEPARTMENT table the data in the DEPARTMENT table shown in Figure 2-24.

**C.** Create the relationship and referential integrity constraint between DEPARTMENT and EMPLOYEE. Enable enforcing of referential integrity and enable cascading of data updates, but do *not* enable cascading of deletions.

**D.** Figure 2-25 shows the column characteristics for the WPC PROJECT table. Using the column characteristics, create the PROJECT table in the WPC.accdb database.

**E.** Create the relationship and referential integrity constraint between DEPARTMENT and PROJECT. Enable enforcing of referential integrity and enable cascading of data updates, but do *not* enable cascading of deletions.

**F.** For the PROJECT table, create a data input form named WPC Project Data Form. Make any necessary adjustments to the form so that all data display properly. Use this form to enter into your PROJECT table the data in the PROJECT table shown in Figure 2-26.

**G.** When creating and populating the DEPARTMENT table, the data were entered into the table before the referential integrity constraint with EMPLOYEE was created, but when creating and populating the PROJECT

**FIGURE 2-25**

**Column Characteristics for the PROJECT Table**

| Column Name | Type | Key | Required | Remarks |
|---|---|---|---|---|
| ProjectID | Number | Primary Key | Yes | Long Integer |
| ProjectName | Text (50) | No | Yes | |
| Department | Text (35) | Foreign Key | Yes | |
| MaxHours | Number | No | Yes | Double, fixed, 2 decimal places |
| StartDate | Date/Time | No | No | Medium date |
| EndDate | Date/Time | No | No | Medium date |

---

**FIGURE 2-26**

**WPC PROJECT Data**

| ProjectID | ProjectName | Department | MaxHours | StartDate | EndDate |
|-----------|-------------|------------|----------|-----------|---------|
| 1000 | 2010 Q3 Product Plan | Marketing | 135.00 | 10-MAY-10 | 15-JUN-10 |
| 1100 | 2010 Q3 Portfolio Analysis | Finance | 120.00 | 05-JUL-10 | 25-JUL-10 |
| 1200 | 2010 Q3 Tax Preparation | Accounting | 145.00 | 10-AUG-10 | 15-OCT-10 |
| 1300 | 2010 Q4 Product Plan | Marketing | 150.00 | 10-AUG-10 | 15-SEP-10 |
| 1400 | 2010 Q4 Portfolio Analysis | Finance | 140.00 | 05-OCT-10 | NULL |

table the referential integrity constraint was created before the data were entered. Why did the order of the steps differ? Which order is normally the correct order to use?

H. Figure 2-27 shows the column characteristics for the WPC ASSIGNMENT table. Using the column characteristics, create the ASSIGNMENT table in the WPC.accdb database.

I. Create the relationship and referential integrity constraint between ASSIGN-MENT and PROJECT and between ASSIGNMENT and EMPLOYEE. When creating both relations, enable enforcing of referential integrity, but do *not* enable cascading of data updates or cascading of data from deleted records.

J. For the ASSIGNMENT table, create a data input form named WPC Assignment Data Form. Make any necessary adjustments to the form so that all data display properly. Use this form to enter into your ASSIGNMENT table the data in the ASSIGNMENT table shown in Figure 2-28.

K. When creating the relationships between the database tables, we allowed the cascading of data changes between some tables but not between others. (*Cascading* means that changes to data in one table are also made to the other table in the relationship.) The value of a primary key changes in this case, and that change is then made in the values of the matching foreign key. Why did we enable cascading of related field values between (1) DEPARTMENT and EMPLOYEE and (2) DEPARTMENT and PROJECT but not for (3) EMPLOYEE and ASSIGNMENT and (4) PROJECT and ASSIGNMENT?

---

**FIGURE 2-27**

**Column Characteristics for the ASSIGNMENT Table**

| Column Name | Type | Key | Required | Remarks |
|-------------|------|-----|----------|---------|
| ProjectID | Number | Primary Key, Foreign Key | Yes | Long Integer |
| EmployeeNumber | Number | Primary Key, Foreign Key | Yes | Long Integer |
| HoursWorked | Number | No | No | Double, fixed, 1 decimal places |

*(Continued)*

### FIGURE 2-28

**WPC ASSIGNMENT Data**

| ProjectID | Employee Number | HoursWorked |
|---|---|---|
| 1000 | 1 | 30.0 |
| 1000 | 8 | 75.0 |
| 1000 | 10 | 55.0 |
| 1100 | 4 | 40.0 |
| 1100 | 6 | 45.0 |
| 1200 | 1 | 25.0 |
| 1200 | 2 | 20.0 |
| 1200 | 4 | 45.0 |
| 1200 | 5 | 40.0 |
| 1300 | 1 | 35.0 |
| 1300 | 8 | 80.0 |
| 1300 | 10 | 50.0 |
| 1400 | 4 | 15.0 |
| 1400 | 5 | 10.0 |
| 1400 | 6 | 27.5 |

L.   For both the DEPARTMENT and EMPLOYEE tables, create a data input form named WPC Department Employee Data Form. This form should show all the employees in each department.

M.   Create a report named Wedgewood Pacific Corporation Department Employee Report that presents the data contained in your DEPARTMENT and EMPLOYEE tables. The report should group employees by department. Print out a copy of this report.

## GARDEN GLORY PROJECT QUESTIONS

Figure 2-29 shows data that Garden Glory collects about properties and services.

A.   Using these data, state assumptions about functional dependencies among the columns of data. Justify your assumptions on the basis of these sample data and also on the basis of what you know about service businesses.

### FIGURE 2-29

**Sample Data for Garden Glory**

| PropertyName | PropertyType | Street | City | ZIP | ServiceDate | Description | Amount |
|---|---|---|---|---|---|---|---|
| Eastlake Building | Office | 123 Eastlake | Seattle | 98119 | 5/5/2010 | Lawn Mow | $    42.50 |
| Elm St Apts | Apartment | 4 East Elm | Lynnwood | 98223 | 5/8/2010 | Lawn Mow | $  123.50 |
| Jefferson Hill | Office | 42 West 7th St | Bellevue | 98040 | 5/8/2010 | Garden Service | $    53.00 |
| Eastlake Building | Office | 123 Eastlake | Seattle | 98119 | 5/10/2010 | Lawn Mow | $    42.50 |
| Eastlake Building | Office | 123 Eastlake | Seattle | 98119 | 5/12/2010 | Lawn Mow | $    42.50 |
| Elm St Apts | Apartment | 4 East Elm | Lynnwood | 98223 | 5/15/2010 | Lawn Mow | $  123.50 |
| Eastlake Building | Office | 123 Eastlake | Seattle | 98119 | 5/19/2010 | Lawn Mow | $    42.50 |

B. Given your assumptions in part A, comment on the appropriateness of the following designs:

1. PROPERTY (<u>PropertyName</u>, PropertyType, Street, City, Zip, ServiceDate, Description, Amount)

2. PROPERTY (PropertyName, PropertyType, Street, City, Zip, <u>ServiceDate</u>, Description, Amount)

3. PROPERTY (<u>PropertyName</u>, PropertyType, Street, City, Zip, <u>ServiceDate</u>, Description, Amount)

4. PROPERTY (<u>PropertyID</u>, PropertyName, PropertyType, Street, City, Zip, ServiceDate, Description, Amount)

5. PROPERTY (<u>PropertyID</u>, PropertyName, PropertyType, Street, City, Zip, <u>ServiceDate</u>, Description, Amount)

6. PROPERTY (<u>PropertyID</u>, PropertyName, PropertyType, Street, City, Zip, *ServiceDate*)

   and:

   SERVICE (<u>ServiceDate</u>, Description, Amount)

7. PROPERTY (<u>PropertyID</u>, PropertyName, PropertyType, Street, City, Zip, ServiceDate)

   and:

   SERVICE (<u>ServiceID</u>, *ServiceDate*, Description, Amount)

8. PROPERTY (<u>PropertyID</u>, PropertyName, PropertyType, Street, City, Zip, *Service*)

   and:

   SERVICE (<u>ServiceID</u>, ServiceDate, Description, Amount, *PropertyID*)

9. PROPERTY (<u>PropertyID</u>, PropertyName, PropertyType, Street, City, Zip)

   and:

   SERVICE (<u>ServiceID</u>, ServiceDate, Description, Amount, *PropertyID*)

C. Suppose Garden Glory decides to add the following table:

SERVICE-FEE (PropertyID, ServiceID, Description, Amount)

Add this table to what you consider to be the best design in your answer to part B. Modify the tables from part B as necessary to minimize the amount of data duplication. Will this design work for the data in Figure 2-29? If not, modify the design so that this data will work. State the assumptions implied by this design.

 **JAMES RIVER JEWELRY PROJECT QUESTIONS**

Figure 2-30 shows data that James River Jewelry collects for its frequent buyer program.

A. Using these data, state assumptions about functional dependencies among the columns of data. Justify your assumptions on the basis of these sample data and also on the basis of what you know about retail sales.

B. Given your assumptions in part A, comment on the appropriateness of the following designs:

1. CUSTOMER (<u>Name</u>, Phone, Email, InvoiceNumber, InvoiceDate, PreTaxAmount)

**FIGURE 2-30**

Sample Data for James River

| Name | Phone | Email | InvoiceNumber | InvoiceDate | PreTaxAmount |
|------|-------|-------|---------------|-------------|--------------|
| Elizabeth Stanley | 555-236-7789 | Elizabeth.Stanley@somewhere.com | 1000 | 5/5/2010 | $ 155.00 |
| Fred Price | 555-236-0091 | Fred.Price@somewhere.com | 1010 | 5/7/2010 | $ 203.00 |
| Linda Becky | 555-236-0392 | Linda.Becky@somewhere.com | 1020 | 5/11/2010 | $ 75.00 |
| Pamela Birch | 555-236-4493 | Pamela.Birch@somewhere.com | 1030 | 5/15/2010 | $ 67.00 |
| Ricardo Romez | 555-236-3334 | Ricardo.Romez@somewhere.com | 1040 | 5/15/2010 | $ 330.00 |
| Elizabeth Stanley | 555-236-7789 | Elizabeth.Stanley@somewhere.com | 1050 | 5/16/2010 | $ 25.00 |
| Linda Becky | 555-236-0392 | Linda.Becky@somewhere.com | 1060 | 5/16/2010 | $ 45.00 |
| Elizabeth Stanley | 555-236-7789 | Elizabeth.Stanley@somewhere.com | 1070 | 5/18/2010 | $ 445.00 |
| Samantha Jackson | 555-236-1095 | Samantha.Jackson@somewhere.com | 1080 | 5/19/2010 | $ 72.00 |

2. CUSTOMER (Name, Phone, Email, <u>InvoiceNumber</u>, InvoiceDate, PreTaxAmount)

3. CUSTOMER (Name, Phone, <u>Email</u>, InvoiceNumber, InvoiceDate, PreTaxAmount)

4. CUSTOMER (<u>CustomerID</u>, Name, Phone, Email, InvoiceNumber, InvoiceDate, PreTaxAmount)

5. CUSTOMER (<u>Name</u>, Phone, Email)

   and:

   PURCHASE (<u>InvoiceNumber</u>, InvoiceDate, PreTaxAmount)

6. CUSTOMER (Name, Phone, <u>Email</u>)

   and:

   PURCHASE (<u>InvoiceNumber</u>, InvoiceDate, PreTaxAmount, *Email*)

7. CUSTOMER (Name, <u>Email</u>)

   and:

   PURCHASE (<u>InvoiceNumber</u>, Phone, InvoiceDate, PreTaxAmount, *Email*)

C. Modify what you consider to be the best design in part B to include a column called AwardPurchaseAmount. The purpose of this column is to keep a balance of the customers' purchases for award purposes. Assume that returns will be recorded, with invoices having a negative PreTaxAmount.

D. Add a new AWARD table to your answer to part C. Assume that the new table will hold data concerning the date and amount of an award that is given after a customer has purchased 10 items. Ensure that your new table has appropriate primary and foreign keys.

 ## THE QUEEN ANNE CURIOSITY SHOP PROJECT QUESTIONS

Figure 2-31 shows typical sales data for the Queen Anne Curiosity Shop, and Figure 2-32 shows typical purchase data.

A. Using these data, state assumptions about functional dependencies among the columns of data. Justify your assumptions on the basis of these sample data and also on the basis of what you know about retail sales.

B. Given your assumptions in part A, comment on the appropriateness of the following designs:

1. CUSTOMER (<u>LastName</u>, FirstName, Phone, Email, InvoiceDate, InvoiceItem, Price, Tax, Total)

FIGURE 2-31

Sample Sales Data for The Queen Anne Curiosity Shop

| LastName | FirstName | Phone | InvoiceDate | InvoiceItem | Price | Tax | Total |
|----------|-----------|-------|-------------|-------------|-------|-----|-------|
| Shire | Robert | 206-524-2433 | 14-Dec-10 | Antique Desk | 3,000.00 | 249.00 | 3,249.00 |
| Shire | Robert | 206-524-2433 | 14-Dec-10 | Antique Desk Chair | 500.00 | 41.50 | 541.50 |
| Goodyear | Katherine | 206-524-3544 | 15-Dec-10 | Dining Table Linens | 1,000.00 | 83.00 | 1,083.00 |
| Bancroft | Chris | 425-635-9788 | 15-Dec-10 | Candles | 50.00 | 4.15 | 54.15 |
| Griffith | John | 206-524-4655 | 23-Dec-10 | Candles | 45.00 | 3.74 | 48.74 |
| Shire | Robert | 206-524-2433 | 5-Jan-11 | Desk Lamp | 250.00 | 20.75 | 270.75 |
| Tierney | Doris | 425-635-8677 | 10-Jan-11 | Dining Table Linens | 750.00 | 62.25 | 812.25 |
| Anderson | Donna | 360-538-7566 | 12-Jan-11 | Book Shelf | 250.00 | 20.75 | 270.75 |
| Goodyear | Katherine | 206-524-3544 | 15-Jan-11 | Antique Chair | 1,250.00 | 103.75 | 1,353.75 |
| Goodyear | Katherine | 206-524-3544 | 15-Jan-11 | Antique Chair | 1,750.00 | 145.25 | 1,895.25 |
| Tierney | Doris | 425-635-8677 | 25-Jan-11 | Antique Candle Holders | 350.00 | 29.05 | 379.05 |

2. CUSTOMER (<u>LastName</u>, <u>FirstName</u>, Phone, Email, InvoiceDate, InvoiceItem, Price, Tax, Total)

3. CUSTOMER (LastName, FirstName, <u>Phone</u>, Email, InvoiceDate, InvoiceItem, Price, Tax, Total)

4. CUSTOMER (<u>LastName</u>, <u>FirstName</u>, Phone, Email, <u>InvoiceDate</u>, InvoiceItem, Price, Tax, Total)

5. CUSTOMER (<u>LastName</u>, <u>FirstName</u>, Phone, Email, InvoiceDate, <u>InvoiceItem</u>, Price, Tax, Total)

6. CUSTOMER (<u>LastName</u>, <u>FirstName</u>, Phone, Email)

and:

SALE (<u>InvoiceDate</u>, InvoiceItem, Price, Tax, Total)

7. CUSTOMER (<u>LastName</u>, <u>FirstName</u>, Phone, Email, *InvoiceDate*)

and:

SALE (<u>InvoiceDate</u>, InvoiceItem, Price, Tax, Total)

FIGURE 2-32

Sample Purchase Data for The Queen Anne Curiosity Shop

| PurchaseItem | PurchasePrice | PurchaseDate | Vendor | Phone |
|--------------|---------------|--------------|--------|-------|
| Antique Desk | 1,800.00 | 7-Nov-10 | European Specialties | 206-325-7866 |
| Antique Desk | 1,750.00 | 7-Nov-10 | European Specialties | 206-325-7866 |
| Antique Candle Holders | 210.00 | 7-Nov-10 | European Specialties | 206-325-7866 |
| Antique Candle Holders | 200.00 | 7-Nov-10 | European Specialties | 206-325-7866 |
| Dining Table Linens | 600.00 | 14-Nov-10 | Linens and Things | 206-325-6755 |
| Candles | 30.00 | 14-Nov-10 | Linens and Things | 206-325-6755 |
| Desk Lamp | 150.00 | 14-Nov-10 | Lamps and Lighting | 206-325-8977 |
| Floor Lamp | 300.00 | 14-Nov-10 | Lamps and Lighting | 206-325-8977 |
| Dining Table Linens | 450.00 | 21-Nov-10 | Linens and Things | 206-325-6755 |
| Candles | 27.00 | 21-Nov-10 | Linens and Things | 206-325-6755 |
| Book Shelf | 150.00 | 21-Nov-10 | Harrison, Denise | 425-746-4322 |
| Antique Desk | 1,000.00 | 28-Nov-10 | Lee, Andrew | 425-746-5433 |
| Antique Desk Chair | 300.00 | 28-Nov-10 | Lee, Andrew | 425-746-5433 |
| Antique Chair | 750.00 | 28-Nov-10 | New York Brokerage | 206-325-9088 |
| Antique Chair | 1,050.00 | 28-Nov-10 | New York Brokerage | 206-325-9088 |

      **8.** CUSTOMER (<u>LastName</u>, <u>FirstName</u>, Phone, Email, *InvoiceDate, InvoiceItem*)

      and:

      SALE (<u>InvoiceDate</u>, <u>Item</u>, Price, Tax, Total)

**C.** Modify what you consider to be the best design in part B to include surrogate ID columns called CustomerID and SaleID. How does this improve the design?

**D.** Modify the design in part C by breaking SALE into two relations named SALE and SALE_ITEM. Modify columns and add additional columns as you think necessary. How does this improve the design?

**E.** Given your assumptions, comment on the appropriateness of the following designs:

      **1.** PURCHASE (<u>PurchaseItem</u>, PurchasePrice, PurchaseDate, Vendor, Phone)

      **2.** PURCHASE (<u>PurchaseItem</u>, <u>PurchasePrice</u>, PurchaseDate, Vendor, Phone)

      **3.** PURCHASE (<u>PurchaseItem</u>, PurchasePrice, <u>PurchaseDate</u>, Vendor, Phone)

      **4.** PURCHASE (<u>PurchaseItem</u>, PurchasePrice, PurchaseDate, <u>Vendor</u>, Phone)

      **5.** PURCHASE (<u>PurchaseItem</u>, PurchasePrice, <u>PurchaseDate</u>)

      and:

      VENDOR (<u>Vendor</u>, Phone)

      **6.** PURCHASE (<u>PurchaseItem</u>, PurchasePrice, <u>PurchaseDate</u>,Vendor)

      and:

      VENDOR (<u>Vendor</u>, Phone)

      **7.** PURCHASE (<u>PurchaseItem</u>, PurchasePrice, <u>PurchaseDate</u>, *Vendor*)

      and:

      VENDOR (<u>Vendor</u>, Phone)

**F.** Modify what you consider to be the best design in part E to include surrogate ID columns called PurchaseID and VendorID. How does this improve the design?

**G.** The relations in your design from part D and part F are not connected. Modify the database design so that sales data and purchase data are related.

# CHAPTER 3

# Structured Query Language

**Chapter Objectives**

> Learn basic SQL statements for creating database structures
> Learn basic SQL statements for adding data to a database
> Learn basic SQL SELECT statements and options for processing a single table
> Learn basic SQL SELECT statements for processing multiple tables with subqueries
> Learn basic SQL SELECT statements for processing multiple tables with joins
> Learn basic SQL statements for modifying and deleting data from a database
> Learn basic SQL statements for modifying and deleting database tables and constraints

This chapter describes and discusses **Structured Query Language (SQL)**. SQL is not a complete programming language; rather, it is a **data sublanguage**. SQL consists only of constructs for defining and processing a database. To obtain a full programming language, SQL statements must be embedded in scripting languages, such as VBScript, or in programming languages, such as Java or C#. SQL statements also can be submitted interactively, using a DBMS-supplied command prompt.

SQL was developed by the IBM Corporation in the late 1970s, and successive versions were endorsed as national standards by the **American National Standards Institute (ANSI)** in 1986, 1989, and 1992. The 1992 version is sometimes referred to as SQL-92 or sometimes ANSI-92 SQL. In 1999, SQL:1999 (also referred to as SQL3), which incorporated some object-oriented concepts, was released. This was followed by the release of SQL:2003 in 2003 and SQL:2006 in 2006 and SQL:2008 in 2008, which added and then extended SQL support for **Extensible Markup Language (XML)**. (XML is discussed in Chapter 7.) Our discussion here focuses on common language features that have been in SQL since SQL-92, and some discussion of the SQL XML features is included in Chapter 7.

SQL is text oriented. It was developed long before graphical user interfaces and requires only a text processor. Today, Microsoft Access, SQL Server, Oracle Database, MySQL, and other DBMS products provide graphic tools for performing many of the tasks that are performed using SQL. However, the key phrase in that last sentence is *many of*. You cannot do everything with graphic tools that you can do with SQL. Furthermore, you must use SQL to generate SQL statements dynamically in program code.

You will learn how to use SQL with Microsoft Access in this chapter's "The Access Workbench." Microsoft Access uses SQL but hides it behind the scenes, presenting a variant of the **Query by Example (QBE)** graphic interface for general use. Although knowledge of SQL is not a requirement for using Microsoft Access, you will be a stronger and more effective Microsoft Access developer if you know SQL.

SQL commands can be broken into several major categories, two of which are of immediate interest for us: a **data definition language (DDL)**, which is used to define database structures, and a **data manipulation language (DML)**, which is used to query and modify database data.[1] In this chapter, we discuss each of these in turn.

## AN EXAMPLE DATABASE

In this chapter, we use an example database that has the following four relations:

DEPARTMENT (<u>DepartmentName</u>, BudgetCode, OfficeNumber, Phone)
EMPLOYEE (<u>EmployeeNumber</u>, FirstName, LastName, *Department*, Phone, Email)
PROJECT (<u>ProjectID</u>, ProjectName, *Department*, MaxHours, StartDate, EndDate)
ASSIGNMENT (<u>*ProjectID*</u>, <u>*EmployeeNumber*</u>, HoursWorked)

The primary key of DEPARTMENT is DepartmentName, the primary key of EMPLOYEE is EmployeeNumber, and the primary key of PROJECT is ProjectID. In EMPLOYEE and PROJECT, Department is a foreign key that references DepartmentName in DEPART-MENT. Remember that a foreign key does not need to have the same name as the primary key to which it refers. The primary key of ASSIGNMENT is the composite (ProjectID, EmployeeNumber). ProjectID is also a foreign key that references ProjectID in PROJECT, and EmployeeNumber is a foreign key that references EmployeeNumber in EMPLOYEE.

The referential integrity constraints are:

Department in EMPLOYEE must exist in DepartmentName in DEPARTMENT
Department in PROJECT must exist in DepartmentName in DEPARTMENT
ProjectID in ASSIGNMENT must exist in ProjectID in PROJECT
EmployeeNumber in ASSIGNMENT must exist in EmployeeNumber in EMPLOYEE

The database column characteristics for these tables are shown in Figure 3-1, and sample data for these relations are shown in Figure 3-2.

In this database, each row of DEPARTMENT is potentially related to many rows of EMPLOYEE and PROJECT. Similarly, each row of PROJECT is potentially related to many rows of ASSIGNMENT, and each row of EMPLOYEE is potentially related to many rows of ASSIGNMENT.

Finally, assume the following rules, which are called **business rules**:

• If an EMPLOYEE row is to be deleted and that row is connected to any ASSIGNMENT, the EMPLOYEE row deletion will be disallowed.
• If a PROJECT row is deleted, then all the ASSIGNMENT rows that are connected to the deleted PROJECT row will also be deleted.

---

[1]Queries by themselves are sometimes considered to be another major category of SQL commands, but we do not make that distinction in this book. For more details, see the Wikipedia article on SQL at **http://en.wikipedia.org/wiki/SQL**.

**FIGURE 3-1**

Database Column Characteristics

| Column Name | Type | Key | Required | Remarks |
|---|---|---|---|---|
| DepartmentName | Text (35) | Primary Key | Yes | |
| BudgetCode | Text (30) | No | Yes | |
| OfficeNumber | Text (15) | No | Yes | |
| Phone | Text (12) | No | Yes | |

**(a) DEPARTMENT Table**

| Column Name | Type | Key | Required | Remarks |
|---|---|---|---|---|
| EmployeeNumber | AutoNumber | Primary Key | Yes | Surrogate Key |
| FirstName | Text (25) | No | Yes | |
| LastName | Text (25) | No | Yes | |
| Department | Text (35) | Foreign Key | Yes | |
| Phone | Text (12) | No | No | |
| Email | Text (100) | No | Yes | |

**(b) EMPLOYEE Table**

| Column Name | Type | Key | Required | Remarks |
|---|---|---|---|---|
| ProjectID | Number | Primary Key | Yes | Long Integer |
| ProjectName | Text (50) | No | Yes | |
| Department | Text (35) | Foreign Key | Yes | |
| MaxHours | Number | No | Yes | Double |
| StartDate | Date/Time | No | No | |
| EndDate | Date/Time | No | No | |

**(c) PROJECT Table**

| Column Name | Type | Key | Required | Remarks |
|---|---|---|---|---|
| ProjectID | Number | Primary Key, Foreign Key | Yes | Long Integer |
| EmployeeNumber | Number | Primary Key, Foreign Key | Yes | Long Integer |
| HoursWorked | Number | No | No | Double |

**(d) ASSIGNMENT Table**

The business sense of these rules is as follows:

- If an EMPLOYEE row is deleted (for example, if the employee is transferred), then someone must take over that employee's assignments. Thus, the application needs someone to reassign assignments before deleting the employee row.
- If a PROJECT row is deleted, then the project has been canceled, and it is unnecessary to maintain records of assignments to that project.

These rules are typical business rules. You will learn more about such rules in Chapter 5.

FIGURE 3-2

Sample Data

| DepartmentName | BudgetCode | OfficeNumber | Phone |
|---|---|---|---|
| Administration | BC-100-10 | BLDG01-300 | 360-285-8100 |
| Legal | BC-200-10 | BLDG01-200 | 360-285-8200 |
| Accounting | BC-300-10 | BLDG01-100 | 360-285-8300 |
| Finance | BC-400-10 | BLDG01-140 | 360-285-8400 |
| Human Resources | BC-500-10 | BLDG01-180 | 360-285-8500 |
| Production | BC-600-10 | BLDG02-100 | 360-287-8600 |
| Marketing | BC-700-10 | BLDG02-200 | 360-287-8700 |
| InfoSystems | BC-800-10 | BLDG02-270 | 360-287-8800 |

(a) DEPARTMENT Table

| Employee Number | FirstName | LastName | Department | Phone | Email |
|---|---|---|---|---|---|
| 1 | Mary | Jacobs | Administration | 360-285-8110 | Mary.Jacobs@WPC.com |
| 2 | Rosalie | Jackson | Administration | 360-285-8120 | Rosalie.Jackson@WPC.com |
| 3 | Richard | Bandalone | Legal | 360-285-8210 | Richard.Bandalone@WPC.com |
| 4 | Tom | Caruthers | Accounting | 360-285-8310 | Tom.Caruthers@WPC.com |
| 5 | Heather | Jones | Accounting | 360-285-8320 | Heather.Jones@WPC.com |
| 6 | Mary | Abernathy | Finance | 360-285-8410 | Mary.Abernathy@WPC.com |
| 7 | George | Smith | Human Resources | 360-285-8510 | George.Smith@WPC.com |
| 8 | Tom | Jackson | Production | 360-287-8610 | Tom.Jackson@WPC.com |
| 9 | George | Jones | Production | 360-287-8620 | George.Jones@WPC.com |
| 10 | Ken | Numoto | Marketing | 360-287-8710 | Ken.Numoto@WPC.com |
| 11 | James | Nestor | InfoSystems | | James.Nestor@WPC.com |
| 12 | Rick | Brown | InfoSystems | 360-287-8820 | Rick.Brown@WPC.com |

(b) EMPLOYEE Table

| ProjectID | ProjectName | Department | MaxHours | StartDate | EndDate |
|---|---|---|---|---|---|
| 1000 | 2010 Q3 Product Plan | Marketing | 135.00 | 10-MAY-10 | 15-JUN-10 |
| 1100 | 2010 Q3 Portfolio Analysis | Finance | 120.00 | 05-JUL-10 | 25-JUL-10 |
| 1200 | 2010 Q3 Tax Preparation | Accounting | 145.00 | 10-AUG-10 | 15-OCT-10 |
| 1300 | 2010 Q4 Product Plan | Marketing | 150.00 | 10-AUG-10 | 15-SEP-10 |
| 1400 | 2010 Q4 Portfolio Analysis | Finance | 140.00 | 05-OCT-10 | |

(c) PROJECT Table

| ProjectID | EmployeeNumber | HoursWorked |
|---|---|---|
| 1000 | 1 | 30.0 |
| 1000 | 8 | 75.0 |
| 1000 | 10 | 55.0 |
| 1100 | 4 | 40.0 |
| 1100 | 6 | 45.0 |
| 1200 | 1 | 25.0 |
| 1200 | 2 | 20.0 |
| 1200 | 4 | 45.0 |
| 1200 | 5 | 40.0 |
| 1300 | 1 | 35.0 |
| 1300 | 8 | 80.0 |
| 1300 | 10 | 50.0 |
| 1400 | 4 | 15.0 |
| 1400 | 5 | 10.0 |
| 1400 | 6 | 27.5 |

(d) ASSIGNMENT Table

### "Does Not Work with Microsoft Access ANSI-89 SQL"

If you have completed the end-of-chapter "Access Workbench Exercises" for Chapters 1 and 2, you will recognize the database we are using in this chapter as the Wedgewood Pacific Corporation database from those exercises. You can use that database to try out the SQL commands in this chapter. However, be warned that not all standard SQL syntax works in Microsoft Access.

As mentioned previously, our discussion of SQL is based on SQL features present in SQL standards since the ANSI SQL-92 standard (which Microsoft refers to as ANSI-92 SQL). Unfortunately, Microsoft Access defaults to the earlier SQL-89 version—Microsoft calls it ANSI-89 SQL or Microsoft Jet SQL (after the Microsoft Jet DBMS used by Microsoft Access). ANSI-89 SQL differs significantly from SQL-92; therefore, some features of the SQL-92 language will not work in Microsoft Access.

Microsoft Access 2010 (and the earlier Microsoft Access 2003 and 2007 versions) does contain a setting that allows you to use SQL-92 instead of the default ANSI-89 SQL. Microsoft included this option to allow Microsoft Access tools such as forms and reports to be used in application development for Microsoft SQL Server, which supports newer SQL standards. To set the option, after you have opened Microsoft Access 2010, click the **File** command tab and then click the **Options** command to open the Access Options dialog box. In the Access Options dialog box, click the **Object Designers** button to display the Microsoft Access Options Object Designers page, as shown in Figure 3-3.

As shown in Figure 3-3, **The SQL Server Compatible Syntax (ANSI 92)** options control which version of SQL is used in a Microsoft Access 2010 database. If you check the **This database** check box, you will use SQL-92 syntax in the current database (if you open Microsoft Access without opening a database, this option is grayed out and not available). Or, you can check the **Default for new databases** check box to make SQL-92 syntax the default for all new databases you create.

---

**FIGURE 3-3**

The Microsoft Access 2010 Options Object Designers Page

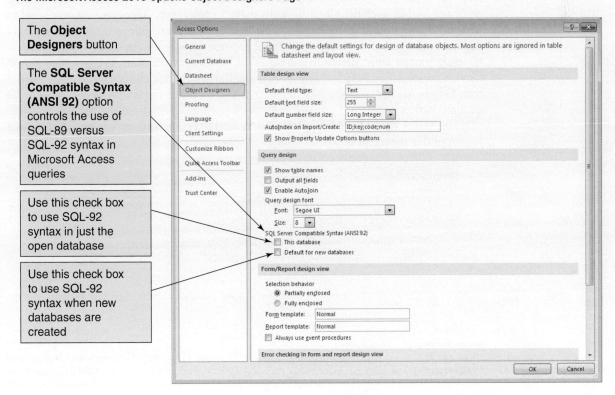

Unfortunately, very few Microsoft Access users or organizations using Microsoft Access are likely to set the Microsoft Access SQL version to the SQL-92 option, and, in this chapter, we assume that Microsoft Access is running in the default ANSI-89 SQL mode. One advantage of doing so is that it will help you understand the limitations of Microsoft Access ANSI-89 SQL and how to cope with them.

In the discussion that follows, we use "Does Not Work with Microsoft Access ANSI-89 SQL" boxes to identify SQL commands and clauses that do not work in Microsoft Access ANSI-89 SQL. We also identify any workarounds that are available. Remember that the one *permanent* workaround is to choose to use the SQL-92 syntax option in the databases you create!

---

**B T W**

Different DBMS products implement SQL in slightly different ways. The SQL statements in this chapter run on Microsoft SQL Server (SQL Server 2008 Express was used to obtain the output shown in this chapter) and also run on Microsoft Access with exceptions, as noted. If you are running the SQL statements on a different DBMS, you may need to make adjustments; consult the documentation for the DBMS you are using.

---

## SQL FOR DATA DEFINITION

The SQL DDL is used to create and alter database structures, such as tables, and to insert, modify, and delete data in the tables.

Before creating tables, you must create a database. Although there is an SQL statement for creating a database, most developers use graphic tools to create databases. The tools are DBMS specific. Creating a database in Microsoft Access is demonstrated in Chapter 1's section of "The Access Workbench." For instructions on how to create a database in Microsoft SQL Server 2008 R2 Express edition, see the online Appendix A—Getting Started with Microsoft Server 2008 R2 Express Edition. For instructions on how to create a database in MySQL 5.1, see the online Appendix B—Getting Started with Oracle MySQL Community Server 5.1. For all other DBMS products, consult the documentation.[2]

The SQL **CREATE TABLE statement** is used to create table structures. The essential format of this statement is:

```
CREATE TABLE NewTableName (
      three-part column definition,
      three-part column definition,
      three-part column definition,
      optional table constraints
      . . .
      );
```

---

[2]Also see David M. Kroenke and David J. Auer, *Database Processing: Fundamentals, Design, and Implementation*, 11th edition (Upper Saddle River, NJ: Prentice Hall, 2010), Chapter 10 for information on creating databases in SQL Server 2008, Chapter 10A for information on creating databases in Oracle Database 11g, and Chapter 10B for information on creating databases in MySQL Server 5.1.

The parts of the three-part column definition are the column name, the column data type, and, optionally, a constraint on column values. Thus, we can restate the CREATE TABLE format as:

```
CREATE TABLE NewTableName (
     ColumnName DataType OptionalConstraint,
     ColumnName DataType OptionalConstraint,
     ColumnName DataType OptionalConstraint,
     optional table constraints
     . . .
     );
```

The column constraints we consider in this text are **PRIMARY KEY**, **NOT NULL**, **NULL**, and **UNIQUE**. In addition to these, there is also a **CHECK** column constraint, which is discussed with the ALTER statement at the end of this chapter. Finally, the **DEFAULT keyword** (DEFAULT may or may not be considered a column constraint depending upon the DBMS—we will treat it as a keyword in this book) can be used to set initial values.

---

**Does Not Work with Microsoft Access ANSI-89 SQL**

Microsoft Access ANSI-89 SQL does not support the UNIQUE and CHECK column constraints, nor the DEFAULT keyword (Microsoft Access documentation treats DEFAULT as a keyword rather than as a constraint).

**Solution:** Equivalent constraints and initial values can be set in the table Design view. See the discussion in this chapter's section of "The Access Workbench."

---

Consider the SQL CREATE TABLE statements for the DEPARTMENT and EMPLOYEE tables shown in Figure 3-4.

The EMPLOYEE column EmployeeNumber has an Integer (abbreviated Int) data type and has a PRIMARY KEY column constraint. The next column, FirstName, uses a Character (signified by Char) data type and is 25 characters in length. The column constraint NOT NULL indicates that a value must be supplied when a new row is created. The fifth column, Phone, uses a Char(12) data type (to store separators between the area code, prefix, and number) with a column constraint of NULL. NULL indicates that null values are allowed, which means that a row can be created without a value for this column.

The fourth column, Department, uses the Char(35) data type, a NOT NULL column constraint, and the DEFAULT keyword to set the department value to the human resources department if no department value is entered when a new row is created.

The sixth and final column, Email, uses the VarChar(100) data type and the NOT NULL and UNIQUE column constraints. VarChar means a variable-length character data type. Thus, Email contains character data values that vary in length from row to row, and the maximum length of an Email address value is 100 characters. However, if an Email address value has only 14 characters, then only 14 characters will be stored.

As implied by the existence of VarChar, Char values are of fixed length. The Char(25) definition for FirstName means that 25 characters will be stored for every value of FirstName, regardless of the length of the value entered. FirstNames will be padded with blanks to fill the 25 spaces when necessary.

You might wonder, given the apparent advantage of VarChar, why it is not used all the time. The reason is that extra processing is required for VarChar columns. A few extra bytes are required to store the length of the value, and the DBMS must go to some trouble to arrange variable-length values in memory and on disk. Vendors of DBMS products usually provide guidelines for when to use which type, and you should check the documentation for your specific DBMS product for more information.

---

**FIGURE 3-4**

---

SQL CREATE TABLE Statements

```
CREATE   TABLE DEPARTMENT(
        DepartmentName   Char(35)      PRIMARY KEY
        BudgetCode       Char(30)      NOT NULL,
        OfficeNumber     Char(15)      NOT NULL,
        Phone            Char(12)      NOT NULL
        );


CREATE   TABLE EMPLOYEE(
        EmployeeNumber   Int           PRIMARY KEY,
        FirstName        Char(25)      NOT NULL,
        LastName         Char(25)      NOT NULL,
        Department       Char(35)      NOT NULL DEFAULT 'Human Resources',
        Phone            Char(12)      NULL,
        Email            VarChar(100)  NOT NULL UNIQUE
        );


CREATE   TABLE PROJECT (
        ProjectID        Int           PRIMARY KEY,
        ProjectName      Char(50)      NOT NULL,
        Department       Char(35)      NOT NULL,
        MaxHours         Numeric(8,2)  NOT NULL DEFAULT 100,
        StartDate        DateTime      NULL,
        EndDate          DateTime      NULL
        );
```

The UNIQUE column constraint for Email means that there cannot be any duplicated values in the Email column. This ensures that each person has a different email address.

In the PROJECT table, the MaxHours column uses the Numeric(8, 2) data type. This means that MaxHours values consist of eight decimal numbers, with two numbers assumed to the right of the decimal point. The decimal point is not stored and does not count as one of the eight. Thus, the DBMS would display the stored value 12345 as 123.45. The DEFAULT keyword is used, and DEFAULT 100 means that when a new row is created, if no value is provided for MaxHours, the DBMS is to provide the value 100.00. Note that the input value does not assume that the last two numbers are to the right of the decimal place.

---

### Does Not Work with Microsoft Access ANSI-89 SQL

Although Microsoft Access supports a Number data type, it does not support the (m,n) extension to specify the number of digits and the number of digits to the right of the decimal place.

Solution: You can set these values in the table Design View after the column is created. See the discussion in this chapter's section of "The Access Workbench."

---

Also in the PROJECT table, the StartDate column uses the DateTime data type. This means that StartDate values will consist of dates (and, actually, with this data type, you could also specify a time if you wished). Various DBMS products handle date and time values in different ways, and, again, you should consult the documentation for your specific DBMS product. According to the SQL standard and as shown in Figure 3-4, every SQL statement should end with a semicolon. Although some DBMS products do not require the semicolon, it is good practice to learn to provide it. Also, as a matter of style, we place the ending parenthesis and the semicolon on a line of its own. This style blocks out the table definitions for easy reading.

The four data types shown in Figure 3-4 are the basic SQL data types, but DBMS vendors have added others to their products. Figures 3-5(a), 3-5(b), and 3-5(c) show some of the data types allowed by SQL Server 2008, Oracle Database 11g, and MySQL 5.1, respectively.

---

**B T W**

Even when Microsoft Access reads standard SQL, the results of running an SQL statement may be a bit different in Microsoft Access. For example, Microsoft Access reads SQL statements containing both Char and VarChar data types, but converts both these data types to a fixed Text data type in the Microsoft Access database.

---

## Defining Primary Keys with Table Constraints

Although primary keys can be defined as shown Figure 3-4, we prefer to define primary keys using a table constraint. Table constraints are identified by the **CONSTRAINT keyword** and can be used to implement various constraints. Consider the CREATE TABLE statements shown in Figure 3-6, which shows how to define the primary keys of tables by using a table constraint.

First, the columns of the table are defined as usual, except that the column that will be the primary key must be given the column constraint NOT NULL. After the table columns are defined, a table constraint, identified by the word CONSTRAINT, is used to create the primary key. Every table constraint has a name followed by the definition of the constraint. Note that in the DEPARTMENT table, the DepartmentName column is now labeled as NOT NULL, and a CONSTRAINT clause has been added at the end of the table definition. The constraint is named DEPARTMENT_PK, and it is defined by the keywords PRIMARY KEY(DepartmentName). The constraint name is selected by the developer, and the only naming restriction is that the constraint name must be unique in the database. Usually a standard naming convention is used. In this text, we name primary key constraints using the name of the table followed by an underscore and the letters: *PK* (TABLENAME_PK).

Defining primary keys using table constraints offers three advantages. First, it is required for defining composite keys because the PRIMARY KEY column constraint cannot be used on more than one column. It is not possible to declare the primary key of the ASSIGNMENT table using the technique in Figure 3-4, but Figure 3-6 (which now includes the ASSIGNMENT table) illustrates the declaration of the primary key ASSIGNMENT_PK as PRIMARY KEY(ProjectID, EmployeeNumber). The second advantage is that by using table constraints you can choose the name of the constraint that defines the primary key. Controlling the name of the constraint has advantages for administering the database, as you will see later, when we discuss the DROP statement.

Finally, using a table constraint to define the primary key allows us to easily define surrogate keys in some DBMS products. Notice that in Figure 3-6, the EmployeeNumber column definition in EMPLOYEE and the ProjectID column definition in PROJECT now include the **IDENTITY (M,N) phrase**. This illustrates how surrogate keys are defined in Microsoft SQL Server. The keyword IDENTITY indicates that this is a surrogate key that will start at value M for the first row created and increase by increment N as each additional row is created. Thus, EmployeeNumber will start with the number 1 and increase by an increment of 1 (that is, 1, 2, 3, 4, 5, . . . ). ProjectID will start with the number 1000 and increase by 100 (that is, 1000, 1100, 1200, . . . ). The exact techniques used to define surrogate key sequences vary extensively from DBMS to DBMS, so consult the documentation for your specific product.

**FIGURE 3-5**

Common Data Types

| Data Type | Description |
| --- | --- |
| Binary | Binary, length 0 to 8,000 bytes. |
| Char | Character, length 0 to 8,000 bytes. |
| Datetime | 8-byte datetime. Range from January 1, 1753, through December 31, 9999, with an accuracy of three-hundredths of a second. |
| Image | Variable-length binary data. Maximum length 2,147,483,647 bytes. |
| Integer | 4-byte integer. Range from –2,147,483,648 through 2,147,483,647. |
| Money | 8-byte money. Range from –922,337,203,685,477.5808 through +922,337,203,685,477.5807, with accuracy to a ten-thousandth of a monetary unit. |
| Numeric | Decimal—can set precision and scale. Range $-10_{38} + 1$ through $10_{38} - 1$. |
| Smalldatetime | 4-byte datetime. Range from January 1, 1990, through June 6, 2079, with an accuracy of one minute. |
| Smallint | 2-byte integer. Range from –32,768 through 32,767. |
| Smallmoney | 4-byte money. Range from –214,748.3648 through +214,748.3647, with accuracy to a ten-thousandth of a monetary unit. |
| Text | Variable-length text, maximum length 2,147,483,648 characters. |
| Tinyint | 1-byte integer. Range from 0 through 255. |
| Varchar | Variable-length character, length 0 to 8,000 bytes. |

**(a) Common SQL Server 2008 Data Types**

| Data Type | Description |
| --- | --- |
| BLOB | Binary large object. Up to 4 gigabytes in length. |
| CHAR(n) | Fixed length character field of length *n*. Maximum 2,000 characters. |
| DATE | 7-byte field containing both date and time. |
| INTEGER | Whole number of length 38. |
| NUMBER(n,d) | Numeric field of length *n*, *d* places to the right of the decimal. |
| VARCHAR(n) or VARCHAR2(n) | Variable-length character field up to *n* characters long. Maximum value of *n* = 4,000. |

**(b) Common Oracle Database 11g Data Types**

| Numeric Data Type | Description |
| --- | --- |
| BIT (M) | M = 1 to 64 |
| TINYINT | –128 to 127 |
| TINYINT UNSIGNED | 0 to 255 |
| BOOLEAN | 0 = FALSE; 1 = TRUE |
| SMALLINT | –32768 to 32767 |
| SMALLINT UNSIGNED | 0 to 65535 |
| MEDIUMINT | –8388608 to 8388607 |
| MEDIUMINT UNSIGNED | 0 to 16777215 |
| INT or INTEGER | –2147483648 to 2147483647 |
| INT UNSIGNED or INTEGER UNSIGNED | 0 to 4294967295 |

**FIGURE 3-5** *(Continued)*

| Numeric Data Type | Description |
|---|---|
| BIGINT | −9223372036854775808 to 9223372036854775807 |
| BIGINT UNSIGNED | 0 to 18446740737095516155 |
| FLOAT (P) | P = Precision = 0 to 24 |
| FLOAT (M, D) | Small (single-precision) floating point number: |
| | M = Display width, |
| | D = Number of significant digits |
| DOUBLE (M, B) | Normal (double-precision) floating point number: |
| | M = display width, |
| | B = Precision = (25 to 53) |
| DEC (M[,D]) or | Fixed-point number: |
| DECIMAL (M[,D]) or | M = Total number of digits, |
| FIXED (M[,D]) | D = Number of decimals |

| Date and Time Data Types | Description |
|---|---|
| DATE | YYYY-MM-DD |
| | 1000-01-01 to 9999-12-31 |
| DATETIME | YYYY-MM-DD HH:MM:SS |
| | 1000-01-01 00:00:00 to |
| | 9999-12-31 23:59:59 |
| TIMESTAMP | See documentation |
| TIME | HH:MM:SS |
| | 00:00:00 to 23:59:59 |
| YEAR (M) | M = 2 or 4 (default) |
| | IF 2 = 1970 to 2069 (70 to 60) |
| | IF 4 = 1901 to 2155 |

| String Data Types | Description |
|---|---|
| CHAR (M) | M = 0 to 255 |
| VARCHAR (M) | M = 1 to 255 |
| BLOB (M) | BLOB = binary large object |
| | Maximum 65535 characters |
| TEXT (M) | Maximum 65535 characters |
| TINYBLOB | See documentation |
| MEDIUMBLOB | See documentation |
| LONGBLOB | See documentation |
| TINYTEXT | See documentation |
| MEDIUMTEXT | See documentation |
| LONGTEXT | See documentation |
| ENUM ('value1', 'value2',…) | An enumeration. Only one value, but chosen from list. |
| | See documentation |
| SET ('value1', 'value2',…) | A set. Zero or more values, all chosen from list. |
| | See documentation |

(c) Common MySQL 5.1 Data Types

**FIGURE 3-6**

Creating Primary Keys with Table Constraints

```
CREATE   TABLE DEPARTMENT(
        DepartmentName    Char(35)        NOT NULL,
        BudgetCode        Char(30)        NOT NULL,
        OfficeNumber      Char(15)        NOT NULL,
        Phone             Char(12)        NOT NULL,
        CONSTRAINT        DEPARTMENT_PK   PRIMARY KEY(DepartmentName)
        );

CREATE   TABLE EMPLOYEE(
        EmployeeNumber    Int             NOT NULL IDENTITY (1, 1),
        FirstName         Char(25)        NOT NULL,
        LastName          Char(25)        NOT NULL,
        Department        Char(35)        NOT NULL DEFAULT 'Human Resources',
        Phone             Char(12)        NULL,
        Email             VarChar(100)    NOT NULL UNIQUE,
        CONSTRAINT        EMPLOYEE_PK     PRIMARY KEY(EmployeeNumber)
        );

CREATE   TABLE PROJECT (
        ProjectID         Int             NOT NULL IDENTITY (1000, 100),
        ProjectName       Char(50)        NOT NULL,
        Department        Char(35)        NOT NULL,
        MaxHours          Numeric(8,2)    NOT NULL DEFAULT 100,
        StartDate         DateTime        NULL,
        EndDate           DateTime        NULL,
        CONSTRAINT        PROJECT_PK      PRIMARY KEY(ProjectID)
        );

CREATE   TABLE ASSIGNMENT (
        ProjectID         Int             NOT NULL,
        EmployeeNumber    Int             NOT NULL,
        HoursWorked       Numeric(6,2)    NULL,
        CONSTRAINT        ASSIGNMENT_PK   PRIMARY KEY(ProjectID, EmployeeNumber)
        );
```

---

**Does Not Work with Microsoft Access ANSI-89 SQL**

Although Microsoft Access does support an AutoNumber data type, it *always* starts at 1 and increments by 1. Further, AutoNumber *cannot* be used as an SQL data type.

Solution: Set AutoNumber data type manually after the table is created. Any other numbering system must be supported manually or by application code.

---

## Defining Foreign Keys with the Table Constraints

You may have noticed that none of the tables in Figure 3-4 or Figure 3-6 include any foreign key columns. You can also use table constraints to define foreign keys and their associated referential integrity constraints. Figure 3-7 shows the final SQL code for our tables, complete with the foreign key constraints.

EMPLOYEE has a table constraint named EMP_DEPART_FK that defines the foreign key relationship between the Department column in EMPLOYEE and the DepartmentName column in DEPARTMENT.

**FIGURE 3-7**

Creating Foreign Keys with Table Constraints

```
CREATE   TABLE DEPARTMENT(
       DepartmentName   Char(35)        NOT NULL,
       BudgetCode       Char(30)        NOT NULL,
       OfficeNumber     Char(15)        NOT NULL,
       Phone            Char(12)        NOT NULL,
       CONSTRAINT       DEPARTMENT_PK   PRIMARY KEY(DepartmentName)
       );

CREATE   TABLE EMPLOYEE(
       EmployeeNumber   Int             NOT NULL IDENTITY (1, 1),
       FirstName        Char(25)        NOT NULL,
       LastName         Char(25)        NOT NULL,
       Department       Char(35)        NOT NULL DEFAULT 'Human Resources',
       Phone            Char(12)        NULL,
       Email            VarChar(100)    NOT NULL UNIQUE,
       CONSTRAINT       EMPLOYEE_PK     PRIMARY KEY(EmployeeNumber),
       CONSTRAINT       EMP_DEPART_FK   FOREIGN KEY(Department)
                            REFERENCES DEPARTMENT(DepartmentName)
                                ON UPDATE CASCADE
       );

CREATE   TABLE PROJECT (
       ProjectID        Int             NOT NULL IDENTITY (1000, 100),
       ProjectName      Char(50)        NOT NULL,
       Department       Char(35)        NOT NULL,
       MaxHours         Numeric(8,2)    NOT NULL DEFAULT 100,
       StartDate        DateTime        NULL,
       EndDate          DateTime        NULL,
       CONSTRAINT       PROJECT_PK      PRIMARY KEY(ProjectID),
       CONSTRAINT       PROJ_DEPART_FK  FOREIGN KEY(Department)
                            REFERENCES DEPARTMENT(DepartmentName)
                                ON UPDATE CASCADE
       );

CREATE   TABLE ASSIGNMENT (
       ProjectID        Int             NOT NULL,
       EmployeeNumber   Int             NOT NULL,
       HoursWorked      Numeric(6,2)    NULL,
       CONSTRAINT       ASSIGNMENT_PK   PRIMARY KEY(ProjectID, EmployeeNumber),
       CONSTRAINT       ASSIGN_PROJ_FK  FOREIGN KEY(ProjectID)
                            REFERENCES PROJECT (ProjectID)
                                ON UPDATE NO ACTION
                                ON DELETE CASCADE,
       CONSTRAINT       ASSIGN_EMP_FK   FOREIGN KEY(EmployeeNumber)
                            REFERENCES EMPLOYEE (EmployeeNumber)
                                ON UPDATE NO ACTION
                                ON DELETE NO ACTION
       );
```

Notice the phrase ON UPDATE CASCADE. The **ON UPDATE phrase** shows what action should be taken if a value of the primary key DepartmentName in DEPARTMENT changes. The **CASCADE keyword** means that the same change should be made to the related Department column in EMPLOYEE. This means that if a department name *Marketing* is changed to *Sales and Marketing*, then the foreign key values should be updated to reflect this change. Because DepartmentName is not a surrogate key, the values could be changed, and setting ON UPDATE CASCADE is reasonable.

The PROJECT table has a similar foreign key relationship with DEPARTMENT, and the same logic applies, except that here there will be two types of projects: completed and in-process. The business rules dealing with this situation are explored in the end-of-chapter exercises.

The ASSIGNMENT table has two foreign key constraints: one to EMPLOYEE and one to PROJECT. The first one defines the constraint ASSIGN_PROJ_FK (the name is up to the developer, as long as it is unique) that specifies that ProjectID in ASSIGN-MENT references the ProjectID column in PROJECT. Here the ON UPDATE phrase is set to **NO ACTION**. Recall that ProjectID is a surrogate key, and thus will never change. In this situation, it is not necessary to cascade updates to the referenced primary key.

Notice that there is also an **ON DELETE phrase**, which shows what action should be taken if a row in PROJECT is deleted. Here the phrase ON DELETE CASCADE means that when a PROJECT row is deleted, all rows in ASSIGNMENT that are connected to the deleted row in PROJECT also should be deleted. Thus, when a PROJECT row is deleted, all ASSIGNMENT rows for that PROJECT row will be deleted as well. This action implements the second business rule on page 118.

The second foreign key table constraint defines the foreign key constraint ASSIGN_EMP_FK. This constraint indicates that the EmployeeNumber column references the EmployeeNumber column of EMPLOYEE. Again, the referenced primary key is a surrogate key, so ON CASCADE NO ACTION is appropriate for this constraint. The phrase ON DELETE NO ACTION indicates to the DBMS that no EMPLOYEE row deletion should be allowed if that row is connected to an ASSIGNMENT row. This declaration implements the first business rule on page 118.

Because ON DELETE NO ACTION is the default, you can omit the ON DELETE expression, and the declaration will default to no action. However, specifying it makes better documentation.[3]

Table constraints can be used for purposes other than creating primary and foreign keys. One of the most important purposes is to define constraints on data values, and we will explore defining CHECK constraints in the end-of-chapter exercises. As always, see the documentation for your DBMS for more information on this topic.

---

### Does Not Work with Microsoft Access ANSI-89 SQL

**Microsoft Access does completely support foreign key CONSTRAINT phrases. Although the basic referential integrity constraint can be created using SQL, the ON UPDATE and ON DELETE clauses are not supported.**

**Solution: ON UPDATE and ON DELETE actions can be set manually after the relationship is created. See the discussion in this chapter's section of "The Access Workbench."**

---

## Submitting SQL to the DBMS

After you have developed a text file with SQL statements like those in Figures 3-4, 3-6, and 3-7, you can submit them to the DBMS. The means by which you do this varies from DBMS to DBMS. With SQL Server 2008 R2, you can type them into a query window in

---

[3]You may be wondering why we do not use the ON DELETE phrase with the foreign key constraints between DEPARTMENT and EMPLOYEE and between DEPARTMENT and PROJECT. After all, there will probably be business rules defining what should be done with employees and projects if a department is deleted. However, enforcing those rules will be more complex than simply using an ON DELETE statement and is beyond the scope of this book. For a full discussion, see David M. Kroenke and David J. Auer, *Database Processing: Fundamentals, Design, and Implementation*, 11th edition (Upper Saddle River, NJ: Prentice Hall, 2010), Chapter 6.

**FIGURE 3-8**

Processing the CREATE TABLE Statements Using SQL Server 2008

The SQL script in the tabbed script window

The objects representing the tables created by the script are shown in the expanded Tables folder—*dbo* stands for *database owner*

Messages are shown here—either that the commands were successful or appropriate error messages

the Microsoft SQL Server Management Studio, or you can enter them via Visual Studio.NET. Oracle Database 11g and MySQL 5.1 use similar techniques. How to do this in Microsoft Access is discussed in this chapter's section of "The Access Workbench."

Figure 3-8 shows the Microsoft SQL Server Management Studio window after the SQL statements in Figure 3-7 have been entered and processed in SQL Server Express Edition. The SQL code itself appears in a query window on the upper right, and the message "Command(s) completed successfully" in the Messages window on the lower right indicates that the SQL statements were processed correctly. The object icons representing the tables can be seen in the Object Explorer window on the left, where the name of each table is prefixed with *dbo*, which SQL Server uses for *database owner*.

Figure 3-9 shows the MySQL Workbench window after the SQL statements in Figure 3-7 [slightly modified to conform to MySQL syntax (see the online Appendix B—Getting Started with Oracle MySQL Community Server 5.1) and note the AUTO_INCREMENT keyword instead of IDENTITY (1, 1)] have been processed in MySQL. The SQL code appears in the SQL Statements window on the right, and the object icons representing the newly created tables can be seen in the Object Explorer window on the left.

---

### Does Not Work with Microsoft Access ANSI-89 SQL

Unlike SQL Server 2008 R2, Oracle Database 11g, and My SQL 5.1, Microsoft Access does not support SQL scripts.

**Solution:** You can still create tables by using the SQL CREATE command and insert data by using the SQL INSERT command (discussed later in this chapter), but you must do so one command at a time. See the discussion in this chapter's section of "The Access Workbench."

---

**FIGURE 3-9**

Processing the CREATE TABLE Statements Using MySQL 5.1

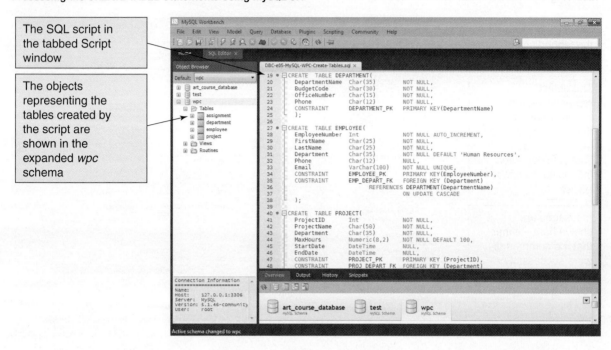

**FIGURE 3-10**

Database Diagram in the Microsoft SQL Server Management Studio

Some DBMS products can create database diagrams that show the tables and relationships in a database. We have already used the Microsoft Access Relationships window (in Chapter 2's section of "The Access Workbench"). For SQL Server 2008 R2, Figure 3-10 shows the WPC database structure in Microsoft SQL Server Management Studio.

## SQL FOR INSERTING RELATIONAL DATA

The SQL DML is used to query databases and to modify data in the tables. In this section, we discuss how to use SQL to insert data into a database, how to query the data, and how to change and delete the data.

The three possible data modification operations are insert, update, and delete. Because we need to populate our database tables, we discuss how to insert data at this time. We will wait until later in the chapter, after we've discussed some other useful SQL syntax, to consider updating and deleting data.

### Inserting Data

Data can be added to a relation by using the SQL **INSERT statement**. This statement has two forms, depending on whether data are supplied for all of the columns.

We will put the data shown in Figure 3-2(a) into the DEPARTMENT table. If the data for all columns are supplied, such as for the administration department, then the following INSERT can be used:

```
INSERT INTO DEPARTMENT VALUES('Administration',
      'BC-100-10', 'BLDG01-300', '360-285-8100');
```

If the DBMS is providing a surrogate key, then the primary key value does not need to be specified.

The data shown in Figure 3-2(c) will be put in the PROJECT table. Because ProjectID is a surrogate key—specified as IDENTITY (1000, 100) in SQL Server—the same type of INSERT statement can be used when data are supplied for all other columns. For example, to insert the data for the 2008 Q3 Product Plan, the following INSERT can be used:

```
INSERT INTO PROJECT VALUES('2010 Q3 Product Plan',
      'Marketing', 135.00, '10-MAY-10', '15-JUN-10');
```

Note that numbers such as Integer and Numeric values are not enclosed in single quotes, but Char, VarChar, and DateTime values are.

---

**B T W**

SQL is very fussy about single quotes. It wants the plain, nondirectional quotes found in basic text editors. The fancy directional quotes produced by many word processors will produce errors. For example, the data value '2010 Q3 Product Plan' is correctly stated, but '2010 Q3 Product Plan' is not. Do you see the difference?

---

If data for some columns are missing, then the names of the columns for which data are provided must be listed. For example, consider the 2010 Q4 Portfolio Analysis project, which does not have an EndDate value. The correct INSERT statement for this data is:

```
INSERT INTO PROJECT
   (ProjectName, Department, MaxHours, StartDate)
      VALUES('2010 Q4 Portfolio Analysis', 'Finance',
      140.00, '05-OCT-10');
```

A NULL value will be inserted for EndDate.

Let us consider three points regarding the second version of the INSERT command. First, the order of the column names must match the order of the values. In the preceding example, the order of the column names is Name, Department, MaxHours, StartDate, so the order of the values must also be Name, Department, MaxHours, StartDate.

Second, although the order of the data must match the order of the column names, the order of the column names does not have to match the order of the columns in the table. For example, the following INSERT, where Department is placed at the beginning of the column list, would also work:

```
INSERT INTO PROJECT
    (Department, ProjectName, MaxHours, StartDate)
        VALUES('Finance', '2010 Q4 Portfolio Analysis',
        140.00, '05-OCT-10');
```

Finally, for the INSERT to work, values for all NOT NULL columns must be provided. You can omit EndDate only because this column is defined as NULL.

Figure 3-11 shows the SQL INSERT statements needed to populate the WPC database tables created by the SQL CREATE TABLE statements in Figure 3-7. Note that the order in which the tables are populated does matter because of the foreign key referential integrity constraints.

---

**B T W**

Oracle Database and MySQL handle surrogate keys in their own unique ways. Oracle Database uses sequences (see the Oracle Database documentation), and MySQL treats the AUTO_INCREMENT value as a missing value so that you have to list all the other column names (see the MySQL documentation).

---

## SQL FOR RELATIONAL QUERIES

After the tables have been defined and populated, you can use SQL DML to query data in many ways. You can also use it to change and delete data, but the SQL statements for these activities will be easier to learn if we begin with the query statements. In the following discussion, assume that the sample data shown in Figure 3-2 have been entered into the database.

### The SQL SELECT/FROM/WHERE Framework

The basic **SQL SELECT/FROM/WHERE framework** for querying a single table in a database uses the SQL SELECT command with FROM and WHERE clauses:

```
SELECT      ColumnNames
FROM        TableName
WHERE       SomeConditionExists;
```

We will use and expand this framework as we work through examples in the following sections. All the examples use the data in Figure 3-2 as the basis for the results of the queries.

### Reading Specified Columns from a Single Table

The following SQL statement queries (reads) three of the six columns of the PROJECT table:

```
SELECT      ProjectName, Department, MaxHours
FROM        PROJECT;
```

FIGURE 3-11

SQL INSERT Statements

```
/*****    DEPARTMENT DATA    ***************************************************/

INSERT INTO DEPARTMENT VALUES(
      'Administration', 'BC-100-10', 'BLDG01-300', '360-285-8100');
INSERT INTO DEPARTMENT VALUES(
      'Legal', 'BC-200-10', 'BLDG01-200', '360-285-8200');
INSERT INTO DEPARTMENT VALUES(
      'Accounting', 'BC-300-10', 'BLDG01-100', '360-285-8300');
INSERT INTO DEPARTMENT VALUES(
      'Finance', 'BC-400-10', 'BLDG01-140', '360-285-8400');
INSERT INTO DEPARTMENT VALUES(
      'Human Resources', 'BC-500-10', 'BLDG01-180', '360-285-8500');
INSERT INTO DEPARTMENT VALUES(
      'Production', 'BC-600-10', 'BLDG02-100', '360-287-8600');
INSERT INTO DEPARTMENT VALUES(
      'Marketing', 'BC-700-10', 'BLDG02-200', '360-287-8700');
INSERT INTO DEPARTMENT VALUES(
      'InfoSystems', 'BC-800-10', 'BLDG02-270', '360-287-8800');


/*****    EMPLOYEE DATA    *****************************************************/

INSERT INTO EMPLOYEE VALUES(
      'Mary', 'Jacobs', 'Administration', '360-285-8110',
      'Mary.Jacobs@WPC.com');
INSERT INTO EMPLOYEE VALUES(
      'Rosalie', 'Jackson', 'Administration', '360-285-8120',
      'Rosalie.Jackson@WPC.com');
INSERT INTO EMPLOYEE VALUES(
      'Richard', 'Bandalone', 'Legal', '360-285-8210',
      'Richard.Bandalone@WPC.com');
INSERT INTO EMPLOYEE VALUES(
      'Tom', 'Caruthers', 'Accounting', '360-285-8310',
      'Tom.Caruthers@WPC.com');
INSERT INTO EMPLOYEE VALUES(
      'Heather', 'Jones', 'Accounting', '360-285-8320',
      'Heather.Jones@WPC.com');
INSERT INTO EMPLOYEE VALUES(
      'Mary', 'Abernathy', 'Finance', '360-285-8410',
      'Mary.Abernathy@WPC.com');
INSERT INTO EMPLOYEE VALUES(
      'George', 'Smith', 'Human Resources', '360-285-8510',
      'George.Smith@WPC.com');
INSERT INTO EMPLOYEE VALUES(
      'Tom', 'Jackson', 'Production', '360-287-8610',
      'Tom.Jackson@WPC.com');
INSERT INTO EMPLOYEE VALUES(
      'George', 'Jones', 'Production', '360-287-8620',
      'George.Jones@WPC.com');
INSERT INTO EMPLOYEE VALUES(
      'Ken', 'Numoto', 'Marketing', '360-287-8710',
      'Ken.Numoto@WPC.com');
```

*(Continued)*

FIGURE 3-11   *(Continued)*

```
INSERT INTO EMPLOYEE(FirstName, LastName, Department, Email)
     VALUES(
     'James', 'Nestor', 'InfoSystems',
     'James.Nestor@WPC.com');
INSERT INTO EMPLOYEE VALUES(
     'Rick', 'Brown', 'InfoSystems', '360-287-8820',
     'Rick.Brown@WPC.com');


/*****   PROJECT DATA   ***********************************************/

INSERT INTO PROJECT VALUES(
     '2010 Q3 Product Plan', 'Marketing', 135.00, '10-MAY-10', '15-JUN-10');
INSERT INTO PROJECT VALUES(
     '2010 Q3 Portfolio Analysis', 'Finance', 120.00, '05-JUL-10',
     '25-JUL-10');
INSERT INTO PROJECT VALUES(
     '2010 Q3 Tax Preparation', 'Accounting', 145.00, '10-AUG-10',
     '15-OCT-10');
INSERT INTO PROJECT VALUES(
     '2010 Q4 Product Plan', 'Marketing', 150.00, '10-AUG-10', '15-SEP-10');
INSERT INTO PROJECT (ProjectName, Department, MaxHours, StartDate)
     VALUES(
     '2010 Q4 Portfolio Analysis', 'Finance', 140.00, '05-OCT-10');


/*****   ASSIGNMENT DATA   ***********************************************/

INSERT INTO ASSIGNMENT VALUES(1000, 1, 30.0);
INSERT INTO ASSIGNMENT VALUES(1000, 8, 75.0);
INSERT INTO ASSIGNMENT VALUES(1000, 10, 55.0);
INSERT INTO ASSIGNMENT VALUES(1100, 4, 40.0);
INSERT INTO ASSIGNMENT VALUES(1100, 6, 45.0);
INSERT INTO ASSIGNMENT VALUES(1200, 1, 25.0);
INSERT INTO ASSIGNMENT VALUES(1200, 2, 20.0);
INSERT INTO ASSIGNMENT VALUES(1200, 4, 45.0);
INSERT INTO ASSIGNMENT VALUES(1200, 5, 40.0);
INSERT INTO ASSIGNMENT VALUES(1300, 1, 35.0);
INSERT INTO ASSIGNMENT VALUES(1300, 8, 80.0);
INSERT INTO ASSIGNMENT VALUES(1300, 10, 50.0);
INSERT INTO ASSIGNMENT VALUES(1400, 4, 15.0);
INSERT INTO ASSIGNMENT VALUES(1400, 5, 10.0);
INSERT INTO ASSIGNMENT VALUES(1400, 6, 27.5);
```

Notice that the names of the columns to be queried follow the keyword SELECT, and the name of the relation to use follows the keyword FROM. The result of this statement is:

| | ProjectName | Department | MaxHours |
|---|---|---|---|
| 1 | 2010 Q3 Product Plan | Marketing | 135.00 |
| 2 | 2010 Q3 Portfolio Analysis | Finance | 120.00 |
| 3 | 2010 Q3 Tax Preparation | Accounting | 145.00 |
| 4 | 2010 Q4 Product Plan | Marketing | 150.00 |
| 5 | 2010 Q4 Portfolio Analysis | Finance | 140.00 |

To show you how the results look in actual DBMS management tools, Figure 3-12 shows the query as executed in SQL Server, and Figure 3-13 shows the query as executed in

**FIGURE 3-12**

SQL Query Results in the Microsoft SQL Server Management Studio

**FIGURE 3-13**

SQL Query Results in the MySQL Workbench

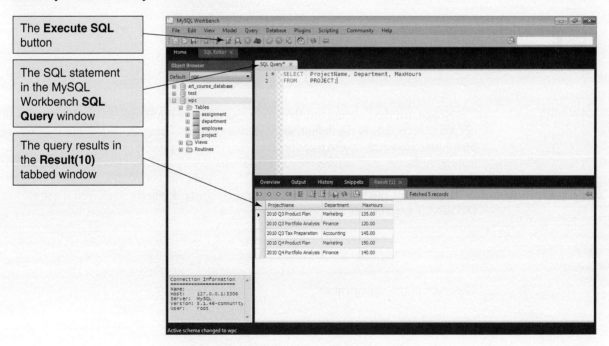

MySQL (the full name of the **Execute SQL** button is actually the **Execute SQL Script in Connecter Server** button, but we will use the short form in this text)

The result of an SQL SELECT statement is a relation. This is always true for SELECT statements. They start with one or more relations, manipulate them in some way, and then produce a relation. Even if the result of the manipulation is a single number, that number is considered to be a relation with one row and one column.

The order of the column names after the keyword SELECT determines the order of the columns in the resulting table. Thus, if you change the order of columns in the previous SELECT statement to:

```
SELECT      ProjectName, MaxHours, Department
FROM        PROJECT;
```

The result will be:

| | ProjectName | MaxHours | Department |
|---|---|---|---|
| 1 | 2010 Q3 Product Plan | 135.00 | Marketing |
| 2 | 2010 Q3 Portfolio Analysis | 120.00 | Finance |
| 3 | 2010 Q3 Tax Preparation | 145.00 | Accounting |
| 4 | 2010 Q4 Product Plan | 150.00 | Marketing |
| 5 | 2010 Q4 Portfolio Analysis | 140.00 | Finance |

The next SQL statement obtains only the Department column from the PROJECT table:

```
SELECT      Department
FROM        PROJECT;
```

The result is:

| | Department |
|---|---|
| 1 | Marketing |
| 2 | Finance |
| 3 | Accounting |
| 4 | Marketing |
| 5 | Finance |

Notice that the first and fourth rows of this table are duplicates, as are the second and last rows. According to the definition of *relation* given in Chapter 2, such duplicate rows are prohibited. However, as also mentioned in Chapter 2, the process of checking for and eliminating duplicate rows is time-consuming. Therefore, by default, DBMS products do not check for duplication. Thus, in practice, duplicate rows can occur.

If you want the DBMS to check for and eliminate duplicate rows, you must use the **DISTINCT keyword**, as follows:

```
SELECT      DISTINCT Department
FROM        PROJECT;
```

The result of this statement is:

| | Department |
|---|---|
| 1 | Accounting |
| 2 | Finance |
| 3 | Marketing |

The duplicate rows have been eliminated, as desired.

## Reading Specified Rows from a Single Table

In the previous SQL statements, we selected certain columns for all rows of a table. SQL statements can also be used for the reverse; that is, they can be used to select all the columns for certain rows. The rows to be selected are specified by using the SQL WHERE clause. For example, the following SQL statement will obtain all the columns of the PROJECT table for projects sponsored by the finance department:

```
SELECT      ProjectID, ProjectName, Department, MaxHours,
            StartDate, EndDate
FROM        PROJECT
WHERE       Department = 'Finance';
```

The result is:

|   | ProjectID | ProjectName | Department | MaxHours | StartDate | EndDate |
|---|-----------|-------------|------------|----------|-----------|---------|
| 1 | 1100 | 2010 Q3 Portfolio Analysis | Finance | 120.00 | 2010-07-05 ... | 2010-07-25 ... |
| 2 | 1400 | 2010 Q4 Portfolio Analysis | Finance | 140.00 | 2010-10-05 ... | NULL |

> **B T W**
>
> The specific treatment of date and time values varies widely among DBMS products. Note that we input the StartDate for ProjectID 1100 as 05-JUL-10 (DD-MMM-YY), but the output above shows it as 2010-07-05 (YYYY-MM-DD). In fact, the StartDate value above is actually 2010-07-05 00:00:00:0000—a combination of the input date and time. (Because we did not input a time, it shows up as all zeros.) Because we do not care about the time, it is not displayed in the results in this book, but it may show up in actual DBMS output. As always, see the documentation for your DBMS product.

A second way to specify all the columns of a table is to use an asterisk (*) after the keyword SELECT. The following SQL statement is equivalent to the previous one:

```
SELECT      *
FROM        PROJECT
WHERE       Department = 'Finance';
```

The result is a table of all the columns of PROJECT for rows that have a Department value of Finance:

|   | ProjectID | ProjectName | Department | MaxHours | StartDate | EndDate |
|---|-----------|-------------|------------|----------|-----------|---------|
| 1 | 1100 | 2010 Q3 Portfolio Analysis | Finance | 120.00 | 2010-07-05 ... | 2010-07-25 ... |
| 2 | 1400 | 2010 Q4 Portfolio Analysis | Finance | 140.00 | 2010-10-05 ... | NULL |

As previously stated, the pattern SELECT/FROM/WHERE is the fundamental pattern of SQL SELECT statements. Many different conditions can be placed in a WHERE clause. For example, the query:

```
SELECT      *
FROM        PROJECT
WHERE       MaxHours > 135;
```

selects all columns from PROJECT where the value of the MaxHours column is greater than 135. The result is:

| | ProjectID | ProjectName | Department | MaxHours | StartDate | EndDate |
|---|---|---|---|---|---|---|
| 1 | 1200 | 2010 Q3 Tax Preparation | Accounting | 145.00 | 2010-08-10 ... | 2010-10-15 ... |
| 2 | 1300 | 2010 Q4 Product Plan | Marketing | 150.00 | 2010-08-10 ... | 2010-09-15 ... |
| 3 | 1400 | 2010 Q4 Portfolio Analysis | Finance | 140.00 | 2010-10-05 ... | NULL |

Notice that when the column data type is Char or VarChar the comparison values must be placed in single quotes. If the column is Integer or Numeric, no quotes are necessary. Thus, you use the notation Department = 'Finance' for a WHERE condition of the Char column Department, but you use the notation MaxHours = 100 for the Numeric column MaxHours.

Values placed in quotation marks may be case sensitive depending upon the DBMS being used. For example, *WHERE Department = 'Finance'* and *WHERE Department = 'FINANCE'* may not be the same. Be sure to check the documentation for the DBMS you are using.

You can place more than one condition in a WHERE clause by using the AND keyword. If the **AND keyword** is used, only rows meeting *all* the conditions will be selected. For example, the following query determines which projects are sponsored by the Finance department *and* are allocated a maximum number of hours greater than 135:

```
SELECT     *
FROM       PROJECT
WHERE      Department = 'Finance' AND MaxHours > 135;
```

The result of this query is:

| | ProjectID | ProjectName | Department | MaxHours | StartDate | EndDate |
|---|---|---|---|---|---|---|
| 1 | 1400 | 2010 Q4 Portfolio Analysis | Finance | 140.00 | 2010-10-05 ... | NULL |

## Reading Specified Columns and Specified Rows from a Single Table

You can combine the techniques just shown to select some columns and some rows from a table. For example, to obtain only the FirstName, LastName, Phone, and Department values of employees in the accounting department, you use:

```
SELECT     FirstName, LastName, Phone, Department
FROM       EMPLOYEE
WHERE      Department = 'Accounting';
```

The result is:

| | FirstName | LastName | Phone | Department |
|---|---|---|---|---|
| 1 | Tom | Caruthers | 360-285-8310 | Accounting |
| 2 | Heather | Jones | 360-285-8320 | Accounting |

You can combine two or more conditions in the WHERE clause by using the AND keyword and the OR keyword. As previously stated, if the AND keyword is used, then only rows meeting *all* the conditions will be selected. However, if the **OR keyword** is used, then rows that meet *any* of the conditions will be selected.

For example, the following query uses the AND keyword to ask for employees that work in accounting *and* have the phone number 360-285-8310:

```
SELECT     FirstName, LastName, Phone, Department
FROM       EMPLOYEE
WHERE      Department = 'Accounting'
   AND     Phone = '360-285-8310';
```

The result is:

| | First Name | Last Name | Phone | Department |
|---|---|---|---|---|
| 1 | Tom | Caruthers | 360-285-8310 | Accounting |

In contrast, this query uses the OR keyword to ask for employees that work in accounting *or* have the phone number 360-285-8410:

```
SELECT     FirstName, LastName, Phone, Department
FROM       EMPLOYEE
WHERE      Department = 'Accounting'
   OR      Phone = '360-285-8410';
```

The result is:

| | First Name | Last Name | Phone | Department |
|---|---|---|---|---|
| 1 | Tom | Caruthers | 360-285-8310 | Accounting |
| 2 | Heather | Jones | 360-285-8320 | Accounting |
| 3 | Mary | Abernathy | 360-285-8410 | Finance |

**B T W**

When using a date in the WHERE clause, you can usually enclose it in single quotes just as you would a character string. However, in Microsoft Access 2010, you must enclose dates with the # symbol. For example:

```
SELECT     *
FROM       PROJECT
WHERE      StartDate = #05/10/10#;
```

Another use of the WHERE clause is to specify that a column should have one of a set of values by using the **IN keyword**, as follows:

```
SELECT     FirstName, LastName, Phone, Department
FROM       EMPLOYEE
WHERE      Department IN ('Accounting', 'Finance', 'Marketing');
```

In this query, a row will be displayed if it has a Department value equal to Accounting, Finance, or Marketing. The result is:

| | First Name | Last Name | Phone | Department |
|---|---|---|---|---|
| 1 | Tom | Caruthers | 360-285-8310 | Accounting |
| 2 | Heather | Jones | 360-285-8320 | Accounting |
| 3 | Mary | Abernathy | 360-285-8410 | Finance |
| 4 | Ken | Numoto | 360-287-8710 | Marketing |

To select rows that do not have a Department value with any of these, you would use the **NOT keyword** in the **NOT IN phrase**, as follows:

```
SELECT     FirstName, LastName, Phone, Department
FROM       EMPLOYEE
WHERE      Department NOT IN ('Accounting', 'Finance',
           'Marketing');
```

The result of this query is:

| | First Name | Last Name | Phone | Department |
|---|---|---|---|---|
| 1 | Mary | Jacobs | 360-285-8110 | Administration |
| 2 | Rosalie | Jackson | 360-285-8120 | Administration |
| 3 | Richard | Bandalone | 360-285-8210 | Legal |
| 4 | George | Smith | 360-285-8510 | Human Resources |
| 5 | Tom | Jackson | 360-287-8610 | Production |
| 6 | George | Jones | 360-287-8620 | Production |
| 7 | James | Nestor | NULL | Info Systems |
| 8 | Rick | Brown | 360-287-8820 | Info Systems |

Notice the essential difference between IN and NOT IN. When using IN, the column may equal *any* of the values in the list. When using NOT IN, the column must not be equal to *all* the values in the list.

## Ranges, Wildcards, and Nulls in WHERE Clauses

WHERE clauses can refer to ranges of values and partial values. The BETWEEN keyword is used for ranges of values. For example, the statement:

```
SELECT     FirstName, LastName, Phone, Department
FROM       EMPLOYEE
WHERE      EmployeeNumber BETWEEN 2 AND 5;
```

will produce the following result:

| | First Name | Last Name | Phone | Department |
|---|---|---|---|---|
| 1 | Rosalie | Jackson | 360-285-8120 | Administration |
| 2 | Richard | Bandalone | 360-285-8210 | Legal |
| 3 | Tom | Caruthers | 360-285-8310 | Accounting |
| 4 | Heather | Jones | 360-285-8320 | Accounting |

FIGURE 3-14

SQL Comparison Operators

| Operator | Indicates |
|---|---|
| = | Equal to |
| > | Greater than |
| < | Less than |
| >= | Greater than or equal to |
| <= | Less than or equal to |
| <> | Not equal to |

This statement is equivalent to the following query, which uses the SQL **comparison operators** >= (greater than or equal to) and <= (less than or equal to):

```
SELECT    FirstName, LastName, Phone, Department
FROM      EMPLOYEE
WHERE     EmployeeNumber >= 2
   AND    EmployeeNumber <= 5;
```

Thus, the end values of BETWEEN (here 2 and 5) are included in the selected range. The set of SQL comparison operators is shown in Figure 3-14. You can use any of them when creating WHERE clauses.

The **LIKE keyword** is used in SQL expressions to select partial values. It is used with **wildcard characters**, which represent unknown characters in a pattern. The SQL wildcard characters are the **underscore symbol** (_), which represents a single, unspecified character, and the **percent sign** (%), which is used to represent a series of one or more unspecified characters.

In the following query, LIKE is used with the underscore symbol to find values that fit a pattern:

```
SELECT    *
FROM      PROJECT
WHERE     ProjectName LIKE '2010 Q_ Portfolio Analysis';
```

The underscore means that any character can occur in the spot occupied by the underscore. The result of this statement is:

| | ProjectID | ProjectName | Department | MaxHours | StartDate | EndDate |
|---|---|---|---|---|---|---|
| 1 | 1100 | 2010 Q3 Portfolio Analysis | Finance | 120.00 | 2010-07-05 ... | 2010-07-25 ... |
| 2 | 1400 | 2010 Q4 Portfolio Analysis | Finance | 140.00 | 2010-10-05 ... | NULL |

One underscore is used for each unknown character. To find all employees who have a Phone value that begins with 360-287-, you can use four underscores to represent any last four digits, as follows:

```
SELECT    *
FROM      EMPLOYEE
WHERE     Phone LIKE '360-287-____';
```

The result is:

| | EmployeeNumber | FirstName | LastName | Department | Phone | Email |
|---|---|---|---|---|---|---|
| 1 | 8 | Tom | Jackson | Production | 360-287-8610 | Tom.Jackson@WPC.com |
| 2 | 9 | George | Jones | Production | 360-287-8620 | George.Jones@WPC.com |
| 3 | 10 | Ken | Numoto | Marketing | 360-287-8710 | Ken.Numoto@WPC.com |
| 4 | 12 | Rick | Brown | InfoSystems | 360-287-8820 | Rick.Brown@WPC.com |

Because the percent sign represents one or more unknown characters, another way to write the query for employees who have a phone number that starts with *360-287-* is:

```
SELECT      *
FROM        EMPLOYEE
WHERE       Phone LIKE '360-287-%';
```

The result is the same as in the previous example:

| | EmployeeNumber | FirstName | LastName | Department | Phone | Email |
|---|---|---|---|---|---|---|
| 1 | 8 | Tom | Jackson | Production | 360-287-8610 | Tom.Jackson@WPC.com |
| 2 | 9 | George | Jones | Production | 360-287-8620 | George.Jones@WPC.com |
| 3 | 10 | Ken | Numoto | Marketing | 360-287-8710 | Ken.Numoto@WPC.com |
| 4 | 12 | Rick | Brown | InfoSystems | 360-287-8820 | Rick.Brown@WPC.com |

If you want to find all the employees who work in departments that end in *ing*, you can use the % character as follows:

```
SELECT      *
FROM        EMPLOYEE
WHERE       Department LIKE '%ing';
```

The result is:

| | EmployeeNumber | FirstName | LastName | Department | Phone | Email |
|---|---|---|---|---|---|---|
| 1 | 4 | Tom | Caruthers | Accounting | 360-285-8310 | Tom.Caruthers@WPC.com |
| 2 | 5 | Heather | Jones | Accounting | 360-285-8320 | Heather.Jones@WPC.com |
| 3 | 10 | Ken | Numoto | Marketing | 360-287-8710 | Ken.Numoto@WPC.com |

---

**B T W**

The NOT keyword, which we used previously as part of the NOT IN phrase, can also be used with LIKE to form the **NOT LIKE** phrase. For example, if you want to find all the employees who work in departments that do *not* end in *ing*, you can use the following SQL query:

```
SELECT   *
FROM     EMPLOYEE
WHERE    Department NOT LIKE '%ing';
```

---

### Does Not Work with Microsoft Access ANSI-89 SQL

Microsoft Access ANSI-89 SQL uses wildcards but not the SQL-92 standard wildcards. Microsoft Access uses a **question mark (?)** instead of an underscore to represent single characters and an **asterisk (*)** instead of a percent sign (%) to represent multiple characters. These symbols have their roots in the MS-DOS operating system, where they appeared as equivalent wildcard characters.

Furthermore, Microsoft Access can sometimes be fussy about stored trailing spaces in a text field. You may have problems with a WHERE clause like this:

```
WHERE      ProjectName LIKE '2010 Q? Portfolio Analysis';
```

But the clause will work if you use a trailing asterisk (*), which allows for the trailing spaces:

```
WHERE      ProjectName LIKE '2010 Q? Portfolio Analysis*';
```

**Solution:** Use the appropriate Microsoft Access wildcard characters, and include a trailing asterisk (*) if needed.

---

Another useful SQL keyword is the **IS NULL keyword**, which can be used in a WHERE clause to search for null values. The following SQL will find the names and departments of all employees who have a null value for Phone:

```
SELECT     FirstName, LastName, Phone, Department
FROM       EMPLOYEE
WHERE      Phone IS NULL;
```

The result of this query is:

| | First Name | Last Name | Phone | Department |
|---|---|---|---|---|
| 1 | James | Nestor | NULL | Info Systems |

---

### B T W

The NOT keyword can also be used with IS NULL to form the **IS NOT NULL phrase.** For example, if you want to find all the employees who *do* have phone numbers, you can use the following SQL query:

```
SELECT     FirstName, LastName, Phone, Department
FROM       EMPLOYEE
WHERE      Phone IS NOT NULL;
```

## Sorting the Results of a Query

The order of rows in the result of a SELECT statement is somewhat arbitrary. If this is undesirable, we can use the **ORDER BY clause** to sort the rows. For example, the following will display the names, phone numbers, and departments of all employees, sorted by Department:

```
SELECT     FirstName, LastName, Phone, Department
FROM       EMPLOYEE
ORDER BY   Department;
```

The result is:

|    | First Name | Last Name | Phone | Department |
|----|-----------|-----------|-------|------------|
| 1  | Tom | Caruthers | 360-285-8310 | Accounting |
| 2  | Heather | Jones | 360-285-8320 | Accounting |
| 3  | Mary | Jacobs | 360-285-8110 | Administration |
| 4  | Rosalie | Jackson | 360-285-8120 | Administration |
| 5  | Mary | Abernathy | 360-285-8410 | Finance |
| 6  | George | Smith | 360-285-8510 | Human Resources |
| 7  | James | Nestor | NULL | Info Systems |
| 8  | Rick | Brown | 360-287-8820 | Info Systems |
| 9  | Richard | Bandalone | 360-285-8210 | Legal |
| 10 | Ken | Numoto | 360-287-8710 | Marketing |
| 11 | Tom | Jackson | 360-287-8610 | Production |
| 12 | George | Jones | 360-287-8620 | Production |

By default, SQL sorts in ascending order. The **ASC keyword** and **DESC keyword** can be used to specify ascending and descending order when necessary. Thus, to sort employees in descending order by Department, use:

```
SELECT     FirstName, LastName, Phone, Department
FROM       EMPLOYEE
ORDER BY   Department DESC;
```

The result is:

|    | First Name | Last Name | Phone | Department |
|----|-----------|-----------|-------|------------|
| 1  | Tom | Jackson | 360-287-8610 | Production |
| 2  | George | Jones | 360-287-8620 | Production |
| 3  | Ken | Numoto | 360-287-8710 | Marketing |
| 4  | Richard | Bandalone | 360-285-8210 | Legal |
| 5  | James | Nestor | NULL | Info Systems |
| 6  | Rick | Brown | 360-287-8820 | Info Systems |
| 7  | George | Smith | 360-285-8510 | Human Resources |
| 8  | Mary | Abernathy | 360-285-8410 | Finance |
| 9  | Mary | Jacobs | 360-285-8110 | Administration |
| 10 | Rosalie | Jackson | 360-285-8120 | Administration |
| 11 | Tom | Caruthers | 360-285-8310 | Accounting |
| 12 | Heather | Jones | 360-285-8320 | Accounting |

Two or more columns can be used for sorting purposes. To sort the employee names and departments first in descending value of Department and then within Department by ascending value of LastName, you specify:

```
SELECT     FirstName, LastName, Phone, Department
FROM       EMPLOYEE
ORDER BY   Department DESC, LastName ASC;
```

The result is:

| | FirstName | LastName | Phone | Department |
|---|---|---|---|---|
| 1 | Tom | Jackson | 360-287-8610 | Production |
| 2 | George | Jones | 360-287-8620 | Production |
| 3 | Ken | Numoto | 360-287-8710 | Marketing |
| 4 | Richard | Bandalone | 360-285-8210 | Legal |
| 5 | Rick | Brown | 360-287-8820 | InfoSystems |
| 6 | James | Nestor | NULL | InfoSystems |
| 7 | George | Smith | 360-285-8510 | Human Resources |
| 8 | Mary | Abernathy | 360-285-8410 | Finance |
| 9 | Rosalie | Jackson | 360-285-8120 | Administration |
| 10 | Mary | Jacobs | 360-285-8110 | Administration |
| 11 | Tom | Caruthers | 360-285-8310 | Accounting |
| 12 | Heather | Jones | 360-285-8320 | Accounting |

## SQL Built-in Functions and Calculations

SQL allows you to calculate values based on the data in the tables. You can use arithmetic formulas, and you can also use **SQL built-in functions**. SQL includes five built-in functions: **COUNT**, **SUM**, **AVG**, **MAX**, and **MIN**. These functions operate on the results of a SELECT statement. COUNT works regardless of column data type, but SUM, AVG, MAX, and MIN operate only on integer, numeric, and other number-oriented columns.

COUNT and SUM sound similar but are different. COUNT counts the number of rows in the result, whereas SUM totals the set of values of a numeric column. Thus, the following SQL statement counts the number of rows in the PROJECT table:

```
SELECT     COUNT(*)
FROM       PROJECT;
```

The result of this statement is the following relation:

As stated earlier, the result of an SQL SELECT statement is always a relation. If, as is the case here, the result is a single number, that number is considered to be a relation that has only a single row and a single column.

Note that the result shown above has no column name. You can assign a column name to the result by using the **AS keyword**:

```
SELECT     COUNT(*) AS NumberOfProjects
FROM       PROJECT;
```

Now the resulting number is identified by the column title:

| | NumberOfProjects |
|---|---|
| 1 | 5 |

Consider the following two SELECT statements:

```
SELECT      COUNT(Department) AS NumberOfDepartments
FROM        PROJECT;
```

and:

```
SELECT      COUNT(DISTINCT Department) AS NumberOfDepartments
FROM        PROJECT;
```

The result of the first statement is the relation:

| | NumberOfDepartments |
|---|---|
| 1 | 5 |

and the result of the second statement is:

| | NumberOfDepartments |
|---|---|
| 1 | 3 |

The difference in answers occurs because duplicate rows were eliminated in the count of the departments in the second SELECT.

---

### Does Not Work with Microsoft Access ANSI-89 SQL

Microsoft Access does not support the DISTINCT keyword as part of the COUNT expression. Although the SQL command with COUNT (Department) will work, the SQL command with COUNT (DISTINCT Department) will fail.

**Solution:** Use an SQL subquery structure (discussed later in this chapter) with the DISTINCT keyword in the subquery itself. This SQL query works:

```
SELECT      COUNT(*) AS NumberOfDepartments
FROM        (SELECT      DISTINCT Department
             FROM        PROJECT) AS DEPT;
```

Note that this query is a bit different from the other queries using subqueries we show in this text because this subquery is in the FROM clause instead of (as you will see) the WHERE clause. Basically, this subquery builds a new temporary table named DEPT containing only distinct Department values, and the query counts the number of those values.

---

The following is another example of built-in functions:

```
SELECT      MIN(MaxHours) AS MinimumMaxHours,
            MAX(MaxHours) AS MaximumMaxHours,
            SUM(MaxHours) AS TotalMaxHours
FROM        PROJECT
WHERE       ProjectID <= 1200;
```

The result is:

| | MinmumMaxHours | MaximumMaxHours | TotalMaxHours |
|---|---|---|---|
| 1 | 120.00 | 145.00 | 400.00 |

Standard mathematical calculations can also be done in SQL. For example, suppose that all employees at Wedgewood Pacific Corporation are paid $18.50 per hour. Given that each project has a MaxHours value, you might want to calculate a *maximum project cost* value for each project that is equal to MaxHours multiplied by the hour wage rate. You can calculate the needed numbers by using the following query:

```
SELECT    ProjectID, ProjectName, MaxHours,
          (18.50 * MaxHours) AS MaxProjectCost
FROM      PROJECT;
```

The result of the query, which now shows the maximum project cost for each project, is:

| | ProjectID | ProjectName | MaxHours | MaxProjectCost |
|---|---|---|---|---|
| 1 | 1000 | 2010 Q3 Product Plan | 135.00 | 2497.5000 |
| 2 | 1100 | 2010 Q3 Portfolio Analysis | 120.00 | 2220.0000 |
| 3 | 1200 | 2010 Q3 Tax Preparation | 145.00 | 2682.5000 |
| 4 | 1300 | 2010 Q4 Product Plan | 150.00 | 2775.0000 |
| 5 | 1400 | 2010 Q4 Portfolio Analysis | 140.00 | 2590.0000 |

Note that column names cannot be mixed with built-in functions, except in certain uses of the SQL GROUP BY clause, as discussed in the next section. Thus, the following is not allowed:

```
SELECT    MaxHours, SUM(MaxHours)
FROM      PROJECT
WHERE     ProjectID <= 1200;
```

SQL Server returns the following error message if you attempt to run this query:

```
Msg 8120, Level 16, State 1, Line 1
Column 'PROJECT.MaxHours' is invalid in the select list because
it is not contained in either an aggregate function or the GROUP BY clause.
```

Also, DBMS products vary in the ways in which built-in functions can be used. Generally, built-in functions cannot be used in WHERE clauses. Thus, a WHERE clause such as the following is not normally allowed:

```
SELECT    ProjectID, MaxHours
FROM      PROJECT
WHERE     MaxHours < AVG(MaxHours);
```

SQL Server returns the following error message if you attempt to run this query:

```
Msg 8120, Level 16, State 1, Line 1
Column 'PROJECT.MaxHours' is invalid in the select list because
it is not contained in either an aggregate function or the GROUP BY clause.
```

## Built-in Functions and Grouping

In SQL, you can use the **GROUP BY clause** to group rows by common values. This increases the utility of built-in functions because you can apply them to groups of rows. For example, the following statement counts the number of employees in each department:

```
SELECT     Department, Count(*) AS NumberOfEmployees
FROM       EMPLOYEE
GROUP BY   Department;
```

The result is:

| | Department | NumberOfEmployees |
|---|---|---|
| 1 | Accounting | 2 |
| 2 | Administration | 2 |
| 3 | Finance | 1 |
| 4 | Human Resources | 1 |
| 5 | InfoSystems | 2 |
| 6 | Legal | 1 |
| 7 | Marketing | 1 |
| 8 | Production | 2 |

The GROUP BY keyword tells the DBMS to sort the table by the named column and then to apply the built-in function to groups of rows that have the same value for the named column. When GROUP BY is used, the name of the grouping column and built-in functions may appear in the SELECT clause. This is the *only* time that a column name and a built-in function can appear together.

We can further restrict the results by using the **HAVING clause** to apply conditions to the groups that are formed. For example, if you want to consider only groups with more than two members, you could specify:

```
SELECT     Department, Count(*) AS NumberOfEmployees
FROM       EMPLOYEE
GROUP BY   Department
HAVING     COUNT(*) > 1;
```

The result of this SQL statement is:

| | Department | NumberOfEmployees |
|---|---|---|
| 1 | Accounting | 2 |
| 2 | Administration | 2 |
| 3 | InfoSystems | 2 |
| 4 | Production | 2 |

It is possible to add WHERE clauses when using GROUP BY. However, an ambiguity results when this is done. If the WHERE condition is applied before the groups are formed, we obtain one result. If, however, the WHERE condition is applied after the groups are formed, we get a different result. To resolve this ambiguity, the SQL standard specifies that when WHERE and GROUP BY occur together, the WHERE condition will be applied first. For example, consider the following query:

```
SELECT     Department, Count(*) AS NumberOfEmployees
FROM       EMPLOYEE
WHERE      EmployeeNumber <= 6
GROUP BY   Department
HAVING     COUNT(*) > 1;
```

In this expression, first the WHERE clause is applied to select employees with an EmployeeNumber less than or equal to 6. Then the groups are formed. Finally, the HAVING condition is applied. The result is:

| | Department | NumberOfEmployees |
|---|---|---|
| 1 | Accounting | 2 |
| 2 | Administration | 2 |

## Querying Multiple Tables with Subqueries

The queries considered so far have involved data from a single table. However, at times, more than one table must be processed to obtain the desired information. For example, suppose we want to know the names of all employees who have worked more than 40 hours on any single assignment. The names of employees are stored in the EMPLOYEE table, but the hours they have worked are stored in the ASSIGNMENT table.

If we knew that employees with EmployeeNumber 8 and 10 have worked more than 50 hours on an assignment (which is true), we could obtain their names with the following expression:

```
SELECT     FirstName, LastName
FROM       EMPLOYEE
WHERE      EmployeeNumber IN (8, 10);
```

The result is:

| | FirstName | LastName |
|---|---|---|
| 1 | Tom | Jackson |
| 2 | Ken | Numoto |

But according to the problem description, we are not given the employee numbers. We can, however, obtain the appropriate employee numbers with the following query:

```
SELECT     DISTINCT EmployeeNumber
FROM       ASSIGNMENT
WHERE      HoursWorked > 50;
```

The result is:

| | EmployeeNumber |
|---|---|
| 1 | 8 |
| 2 | 10 |

Now, we can combine these two SQL statements by using a **subquery**, as follows:

```
SELECT      FirstName, LastName
FROM        EMPLOYEE
WHERE       EmployeeNumber IN
            (SELECT    DISTINCT EmployeeNumber
             FROM      ASSIGNMENT
             WHERE     HoursWorked > 50);
```

The result of this expression is:

| | FirstName | LastName |
|---|---|---|
| 1 | Tom | Jackson |
| 2 | Ken | Numoto |

These are indeed the names of the employees who have worked more than 50 hours on any single assignment.

Subqueries can be extended to include three, four, or even more levels. Suppose, for example, that you need to know the names of employees who have worked more than 40 hours on an assignment sponsored by the accounting department. You can obtain the project IDs of projects sponsored by accounting with:

```
SELECT      ProjectID
FROM        PROJECT
WHERE       Department = 'Accounting';
```

The result is:

| | ProjectID |
|---|---|
| 1 | 1200 |

You can obtain the employee numbers of employees working more than 40 hours on those projects with:

```
SELECT      DISTINCT EmployeeNumber
FROM        ASSIGNMENT
WHERE       HoursWorked > 40
    AND     ProjectID IN
            (SELECT    ProjectID
             FROM      PROJECT
             WHERE     Department = 'Accounting');
```

The result is:

| | EmployeeNumber |
|---|---|
| 1 | 4 |

Finally, you can obtain the names of the employees in the preceding SQL statement with:

```
SELECT      FirstName, LastName
FROM        EMPLOYEE
WHERE       EmployeeNumber IN
            (SELECT   DISTINCT EmployeeNumber
             FROM     ASSIGNMENT
             WHERE    HoursWorked > 40
                AND   ProjectID IN
                      (SELECT     ProjectID
                       FROM       PROJECT
                       WHERE      Department = 'Accounting'));
```

The final result is:

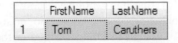

## Querying Multiple Tables with Joins

Subqueries are effective for processing multiple tables, as long as the results come from a single table. If, however, we need to display data from two or more tables, subqueries do not work. We need to use a **join operation** instead.

The basic idea of a join is to form a new relation by connecting the contents of two or more other relations. Consider the following example:

```
SELECT      FirstName, LastName, HoursWorked
FROM        EMPLOYEE, ASSIGNMENT
WHERE       EMPLOYEE.EmployeeNumber =
            ASSIGNMENT.EmployeeNumber;
```

The function of this statement is to create a new table having the two columns ProjectName and HoursWorked. Those columns are to be taken from the EMPLOYEE and ASSIGNMENT tables, under the condition that EmployeeNumber in EMPLOYEE (written in the format *TABLENAME.ColumnName* as EMPLOYEE.EmployeeNumber) equals EmployeeNumber in ASSIGNMENT (written as ASSIGNMENT.Employee-Number). Whenever there is ambiguity about which table the column data are coming from, the column name is always preceded with the table name in the format *TABLENAME.ColumnName*.

---

**B T W**

This ambiguity about which table the column data are coming from often happens (as in this case) because the primary key and foreign key column names are the same, but it can happen in other situations. For example, both EMPLOYEE and DEPARTMENT have a Phone column, but Phone is not a primary key or foreign key in either table. If we wanted to list employees with both their own phone number and their department phone number, we would have to qualify the field names as EMPLOYEE.Phone and DEPARTMENT.Phone.

You can think of the join operation working as follows. Start with the first row in EMPLOYEE. Using the value of EmployeeNumber in this first row [1 for the data in Figure 3-2(b)], examine the rows in ASSIGNMENT. When you find a row in ASSIGNMENT where EmployeeNumber is also equal to 1, join FirstName and LastName of the first row of EMPLOYEE with HoursWorked from the row you just found in ASSIGNMENT.

For the data in Figure 3-2(c), the first row of ASSIGNMENT has EmployeeNumber equal to 1, so you join FirstName and LastName from the first row of EMPLOYEE with HoursWorked from the first row in ASSIGNMENT to form the first row of the join. The result is:

| | FirstName | LastName | HoursWorked |
|---|---|---|---|
| 1 | Mary | Jacobs | 30.00 |

Now, still using the EmployeeNumber value of 1, look for a second row in ASSIGNMENT that has EmployeeNumber equal to 1. For our data, the sixth row of ASSIGNMENT has such a value. So, join FirstName and LastName from the first row of EMPLOYEE to HoursWorked in the sixth row of ASSIGNMENT to obtain the second row of the join, as follows:

| | FirstName | LastName | HoursWorked |
|---|---|---|---|
| 1 | Mary | Jacobs | 30.00 |
| 2 | Mary | Jacobs | 25.00 |

Continue in this way, looking for matches for the EmployeeNumber value of 1. There is one more in the 10th row, and you would add the data for that match to obtain the result:

| | FirstName | LastName | HoursWorked |
|---|---|---|---|
| 1 | Mary | Jacobs | 30.00 |
| 2 | Mary | Jacobs | 25.00 |
| 3 | Mary | Jacobs | 35.00 |

At this point, no more EmployeeNumber values of 1 appear in the sample data, so now you move to the second row of EMPLOYEE, obtain the new value of EmployeeNumber (2), and begin searching for matches for it in the rows of ASSIGNMENT. In this case, the seventh row has such a match, so you add FirstName, LastName, and HoursWorked to the result to obtain:

| | FirstName | LastName | HoursWorked |
|---|---|---|---|
| 1 | Mary | Jacobs | 30.00 |
| 2 | Mary | Jacobs | 25.00 |
| 3 | Mary | Jacobs | 35.00 |
| 4 | Rosalie | Jackson | 20.00 |

You continue until all rows of EMPLOYEE have been examined. The final result is:

| | FirstName | LastName | HoursWorked |
|---|---|---|---|
| 1 | Mary | Jacobs | 30.00 |
| 2 | Mary | Jacobs | 25.00 |
| 3 | Mary | Jacobs | 35.00 |
| 4 | Rosalie | Jackson | 20.00 |
| 5 | Tom | Caruthers | 40.00 |
| 6 | Tom | Caruthers | 45.00 |
| 7 | Tom | Caruthers | 15.00 |
| 8 | Heather | Jones | 40.00 |
| 9 | Heather | Jones | 10.00 |
| 10 | Mary | Abernathy | 45.00 |
| 11 | Mary | Abernathy | 27.50 |
| 12 | Tom | Jackson | 75.00 |
| 13 | Tom | Jackson | 80.00 |
| 14 | Ken | Numoto | 55.00 |
| 15 | Ken | Numoto | 50.00 |

Actually, that is the theoretical result. But remember that row order in an SQL query can be arbitrary. To ensure that you get the above result, you need to add an ORDER BY clause to the query:

```
SELECT     FirstName, LastName, HoursWorked
FROM       EMPLOYEE, ASSIGNMENT
WHERE      EMPLOYEE.EmployeeNumber =
             ASSIGNMENT.EmployeeNumber
ORDER BY   EMPLOYEE.EmployeeNumber, ProjectID;
```

The actual result when the original query is run in SQL Server is:

| | FirstName | LastName | HoursWorked |
|---|---|---|---|
| 1 | Mary | Jacobs | 30.00 |
| 2 | Tom | Jackson | 75.00 |
| 3 | Ken | Numoto | 55.00 |
| 4 | Tom | Caruthers | 40.00 |
| 5 | Mary | Abernathy | 45.00 |
| 6 | Mary | Jacobs | 25.00 |
| 7 | Rosalie | Jackson | 20.00 |
| 8 | Tom | Caruthers | 45.00 |
| 9 | Heather | Jones | 40.00 |
| 10 | Mary | Jacobs | 35.00 |
| 11 | Tom | Jackson | 80.00 |
| 12 | Ken | Numoto | 50.00 |
| 13 | Tom | Caruthers | 15.00 |
| 14 | Heather | Jones | 10.00 |
| 15 | Mary | Abernathy | 27.50 |

The data results are the same, but the row order is definitely different!

A join is just another table, so all the earlier SQL SELECT commands are available for use. We could, for example, group the rows of the join by employee and sum the hours they worked. The following is the SQL for such a query:

```
SELECT     FirstName, LastName,
           SUM(HoursWorked) AS TotalHoursWorked
FROM       EMPLOYEE AS E, ASSIGNMENT AS A
WHERE      E.EmployeeNumber = A.EmployeeNumber
GROUP BY   LastName, FirstName;
```

Note another use for the AS keyword, which is now used to assign aliases to table names so that we can use these aliases in the WHERE clause. This makes it much easier to write queries with long table names. The result of this query is:

|   | First Name | Last Name | Total Hours Worked |
|---|------------|-----------|--------------------|
| 1 | Heather | Jones | 50.00 |
| 2 | Ken | Numoto | 105.00 |
| 3 | Mary | Abernathy | 72.50 |
| 4 | Mary | Jacobs | 90.00 |
| 5 | Rosalie | Jackson | 20.00 |
| 6 | Tom | Caruthers | 100.00 |
| 7 | Tom | Jackson | 155.00 |

Or, we could apply a WHERE clause during the process of creating the join as follows:

```
SELECT     FirstName, LastName, HoursWorked
FROM       EMPLOYEE AS E, ASSIGNMENT AS A
WHERE      E.EmployeeNumber = A.EmployeeNumber
           AND HoursWorked > 50;
```

The result of this join is:

|   | First Name | Last Name | Hours Worked |
|---|------------|-----------|--------------|
| 1 | Tom | Jackson | 75.00 |
| 2 | Ken | Numoto | 55.00 |
| 3 | Tom | Jackson | 80.00 |

Now, suppose we want to join PROJECT to EMPLOYEE and ASSIGNMENT to show the names of the projects that the employees worked on. We can use the same SQL statement structure as before, except for one complication—now you have to use two WHERE phrases combined by an AND to join the three tables:

```
SELECT    ProjectName, FirstName, LastName, HoursWorked
FROM      EMPLOYEE AS E, PROJECT AS P, ASSIGNMENT AS A
WHERE     E.EmployeeNumber = A.EmployeeNumber
   AND    P.ProjectID = A.ProjectID
ORDER BY  P.ProjectID, A.EmployeeNumber;
```

The result of this query is:

| | ProjectName | FirstName | LastName | HoursWorked |
|---|---|---|---|---|
| 1 | 2010 Q3 Product Plan | Mary | Jacobs | 30.00 |
| 2 | 2010 Q3 Product Plan | Tom | Jackson | 75.00 |
| 3 | 2010 Q3 Product Plan | Ken | Numoto | 55.00 |
| 4 | 2010 Q3 Portfolio Analysis | Tom | Caruthers | 40.00 |
| 5 | 2010 Q3 Portfolio Analysis | Mary | Abernathy | 45.00 |
| 6 | 2010 Q3 Tax Preparation | Mary | Jacobs | 25.00 |
| 7 | 2010 Q3 Tax Preparation | Rosalie | Jackson | 20.00 |
| 8 | 2010 Q3 Tax Preparation | Tom | Caruthers | 45.00 |
| 9 | 2010 Q3 Tax Preparation | Heather | Jones | 40.00 |
| 10 | 2010 Q4 Product Plan | Mary | Jacobs | 35.00 |
| 11 | 2010 Q4 Product Plan | Tom | Jackson | 80.00 |
| 12 | 2010 Q4 Product Plan | Ken | Numoto | 50.00 |
| 13 | 2010 Q4 Portfolio Analysis | Tom | Caruthers | 15.00 |
| 14 | 2010 Q4 Portfolio Analysis | Heather | Jones | 10.00 |
| 15 | 2010 Q4 Portfolio Analysis | Mary | Abernathy | 27.50 |

## The SQL JOIN . . . ON Syntax

An alternative join syntax is the **JOIN . . . ON syntax**. Consider our original query example, which uses a join (with the ORDER BY clause for sorting the results):

```
SELECT    FirstName, LastName, HoursWorked
FROM      EMPLOYEE, ASSIGNMENT
WHERE     EMPLOYEE.EmployeeNumber =
            ASSIGNMENT.EmployeeNumber
ORDER BY  EMPLOYEE.EmployeeNumber, ProjectID;
```

Using the JOIN . . . ON syntax, this query would be written as:

```
SELECT    FirstName, LastName, HoursWorked
FROM      EMPLOYEE JOIN ASSIGNMENT
          ON   EMPLOYEE.EmployeeNumber =
                 ASSIGNMENT.EmployeeNumber
ORDER BY  EMPLOYEE.EmployeeNumber, ProjectID;
```

The result of the query, as you would expect, is:

| | First Name | Last Name | Hours Worked |
|---|---|---|---|
| 1 | Mary | Jacobs | 30.00 |
| 2 | Mary | Jacobs | 25.00 |
| 3 | Mary | Jacobs | 35.00 |
| 4 | Rosalie | Jackson | 20.00 |
| 5 | Tom | Caruthers | 40.00 |
| 6 | Tom | Caruthers | 45.00 |
| 7 | Tom | Caruthers | 15.00 |
| 8 | Heather | Jones | 40.00 |
| 9 | Heather | Jones | 10.00 |
| 10 | Mary | Abernathy | 45.00 |
| 11 | Mary | Abernathy | 27.50 |
| 12 | Tom | Jackson | 75.00 |
| 13 | Tom | Jackson | 80.00 |
| 14 | Ken | Numoto | 55.00 |
| 15 | Ken | Numoto | 50.00 |

We can also use the JOIN . . . ON syntax for joins of more than two tables. Here is the previous query to combine data for EMPLOYEE, PROJECT, and ASSIGNMENT rewritten using the JOIN . . . ON style:

```
SELECT     ProjectName, FirstName, LastName, HoursWorked
FROM       EMPLOYEE AS E JOIN ASSIGNMENT AS A
           ON    E.EmployeeNumber = A.EmployeeNumber
                 JOIN PROJECT AS P
                     ON    A.ProjectID = P.ProjectID
ORDER BY   P.ProjectID, A.EmployeeNumber;
```

The result, as you would expect, is the same as we obtained with the previous query:

| | Project Name | First Name | Last Name | Hours Worked |
|---|---|---|---|---|
| 1 | 2010 Q3 Product Plan | Mary | Jacobs | 30.00 |
| 2 | 2010 Q3 Product Plan | Tom | Jackson | 75.00 |
| 3 | 2010 Q3 Product Plan | Ken | Numoto | 55.00 |
| 4 | 2010 Q3 Portfolio Analysis | Tom | Caruthers | 40.00 |
| 5 | 2010 Q3 Portfolio Analysis | Mary | Abernathy | 45.00 |
| 6 | 2010 Q3 Tax Preparation | Mary | Jacobs | 25.00 |
| 7 | 2010 Q3 Tax Preparation | Rosalie | Jackson | 20.00 |
| 8 | 2010 Q3 Tax Preparation | Tom | Caruthers | 45.00 |
| 9 | 2010 Q3 Tax Preparation | Heather | Jones | 40.00 |
| 10 | 2010 Q4 Product Plan | Mary | Jacobs | 35.00 |
| 11 | 2010 Q4 Product Plan | Tom | Jackson | 80.00 |
| 12 | 2010 Q4 Product Plan | Ken | Numoto | 50.00 |
| 13 | 2010 Q4 Portfolio Analysis | Tom | Caruthers | 15.00 |
| 14 | 2010 Q4 Portfolio Analysis | Heather | Jones | 10.00 |
| 15 | 2010 Q4 Portfolio Analysis | Mary | Abernathy | 27.50 |

---

### Does Not Work with Microsoft Access ANSI-89 SQL

Microsoft Access supports the JOIN . . . ON syntax only with a keyword specifying a standard (INNER) or nonstandard (OUTER) JOIN. OUTER joins are discussed next.

**Solution:** The Microsoft Access JOIN . . . ON queries run when written with the INNER keyword as:

```
SELECT      FirstName, LastName, HoursWorked
FROM        EMPLOYEE INNER JOIN ASSIGNMENT
            ON   EMPLOYEE.EmployeeNumber =
                 ASSIGNMENT.EmployeeNumber
ORDER BY    EMPLOYEE.EmployeeNumber, ProjectID;
```

Further, Microsoft Access requires that the joins be grouped using parentheses when three or more tables are joined:

```
SELECT      ProjectName, FirstName, LastName,
            HoursWorked
FROM        (EMPLOYEE AS E INNER JOIN ASSIGNMENT AS A
            ON   E.EmployeeNumber = A.EmployeeNumber)
                 INNER JOIN PROJECT AS P
                    ON   A.ProjectID = P.ProjectID
ORDER BY    P.ProjectID, A.EmployeeNumber;
```

---

Let us add a new project, the 2010 Q4 Tax Preparation project run by accounting, to the PROJECT table as follows:

```
INSERT INTO PROJECT
   (ProjectName, Department, MaxHours, StartDate)
      VALUES('2010 Q4 Tax Preparation', 'Accounting',
      175.00, '10-DEC-10');
```

To see the updated PROJECT table, we use the query:

```
SELECT * FROM PROJECT;
```

The results are:

| | ProjectID | ProjectName | Department | MaxHours | StartDate | EndDate |
|---|---|---|---|---|---|---|
| 1 | 1000 | 2010 Q3 Product Plan | Marketing | 135.00 | 2010-05-10 ... | 2010-06-15 ... |
| 2 | 1100 | 2010 Q3 Portfolio Analysis | Finance | 120.00 | 2010-07-05 ... | 2010-07-25 ... |
| 3 | 1200 | 2010 Q3 Tax Preparation | Accounting | 145.00 | 2010-08-10 ... | 2010-10-15 ... |
| 4 | 1300 | 2010 Q4 Product Plan | Marketing | 150.00 | 2010-08-10 ... | 2010-09-15 ... |
| 5 | 1400 | 2010 Q4 Portfolio Analysis | Finance | 140.00 | 2010-10-05 ... | NULL |
| 6 | 1500 | 2010 Q4 Tax Preparation | Accounting | 175.00 | 2010-12-10 ... | NULL |

Now, with the new project added to PROJECT, we'll rerun the previous query on EMPLOYEE, ASSIGNMENT, and PROJECT:

```
SELECT     ProjectName, FirstName, LastName, HoursWorked
FROM       EMPLOYEE AS E JOIN ASSIGNMENT AS A
           ON   E.EmployeeNumber = A.EmployeeNumber
                JOIN PROJECT AS P
                   ON   A.ProjectID = P.ProjectID
ORDER BY   P.ProjectID, A.EmployeeNumber;
```

The results are:

| | ProjectName | FirstName | LastName | HoursWorked |
|---|---|---|---|---|
| 1 | 2010 Q3 Product Plan | Mary | Jacobs | 30.00 |
| 2 | 2010 Q3 Product Plan | Tom | Jackson | 75.00 |
| 3 | 2010 Q3 Product Plan | Ken | Numoto | 55.00 |
| 4 | 2010 Q3 Portfolio Analysis | Tom | Caruthers | 40.00 |
| 5 | 2010 Q3 Portfolio Analysis | Mary | Abernathy | 45.00 |
| 6 | 2010 Q3 Tax Preparation | Mary | Jacobs | 25.00 |
| 7 | 2010 Q3 Tax Preparation | Rosalie | Jackson | 20.00 |
| 8 | 2010 Q3 Tax Preparation | Tom | Caruthers | 45.00 |
| 9 | 2010 Q3 Tax Preparation | Heather | Jones | 40.00 |
| 10 | 2010 Q4 Product Plan | Mary | Jacobs | 35.00 |
| 11 | 2010 Q4 Product Plan | Tom | Jackson | 80.00 |
| 12 | 2010 Q4 Product Plan | Ken | Numoto | 50.00 |
| 13 | 2010 Q4 Portfolio Analysis | Tom | Caruthers | 15.00 |
| 14 | 2010 Q4 Portfolio Analysis | Heather | Jones | 10.00 |
| 15 | 2010 Q4 Portfolio Analysis | Mary | Abernathy | 27.50 |

The results shown here are correct, but a surprising result occurs. What happened to the new 2010 Q4 Tax Preparation project? The answer is that it does not appear in the join results because its ProjectID value of 1500 had no match in the ASSIGNMENT table. Nothing is wrong with this result; you just need to be aware that unmatched rows do not appear in the result of a join.

## Outer Joins

You saw in the last query in the previous section that data can be lost (or at least appear to be lost) when you perform a join. In particular, if a row has a value that does not match the WHERE clause condition, that row will not be included in the join result. The 2010 Q4 Tax Preparation project did not appear in the previous join because no row in ASSIGNMENT matched its ProjectID value. This kind of loss is not always desirable, so a special type of join, called an **outer join**, was created to avoid it.

Outer joins are not part of the SQL-92 specification, but most DBMS products today support them. The specific syntax for the outer join, however, varies by DBMS product.

---
**B T W**

The original join operation discussed earlier is sometimes referred to as an **equijoin** or **inner join**.

---

Consider the following example and notice the use of the JOIN . . . ON syntax—the **LEFT keyword** is simply added to the SQL query:

```
SELECT    ProjectName, EmployeeNumber, HoursWorked
FROM      PROJECT LEFT JOIN ASSIGNMENT
          ON PROJECT.ProjectID = ASSIGNMENT.ProjectID;
```

The purpose of this join is to append rows of PROJECT to those of ASSIGNMENT, as described previously, except that if any row in the table on the *left side* of the FROM clause (in this case, PROJECT) has no match it is included in the results anyway. The result of this query is:

|    | ProjectName | EmployeeNumber | HoursWorked |
|----|-------------|----------------|-------------|
| 1  | 2010 Q3 Product Plan | 1 | 30.00 |
| 2  | 2010 Q3 Product Plan | 8 | 75.00 |
| 3  | 2010 Q3 Product Plan | 10 | 55.00 |
| 4  | 2010 Q3 Portfolio Analysis | 4 | 40.00 |
| 5  | 2010 Q3 Portfolio Analysis | 6 | 45.00 |
| 6  | 2010 Q3 Tax Preparation | 1 | 25.00 |
| 7  | 2010 Q3 Tax Preparation | 2 | 20.00 |
| 8  | 2010 Q3 Tax Preparation | 4 | 45.00 |
| 9  | 2010 Q3 Tax Preparation | 5 | 40.00 |
| 10 | 2010 Q4 Product Plan | 1 | 35.00 |
| 11 | 2010 Q4 Product Plan | 8 | 80.00 |
| 12 | 2010 Q4 Product Plan | 10 | 50.00 |
| 13 | 2010 Q4 Portfolio Analysis | 4 | 15.00 |
| 14 | 2010 Q4 Portfolio Analysis | 5 | 10.00 |
| 15 | 2010 Q4 Portfolio Analysis | 6 | 27.50 |
| 16 | 2010 Q4 Tax Preparation | NULL | NULL |

Notice that the last row of this table appends a null value to the 2008 Q4 Tax Preparation project.

Right outer joins operate similarly, except that the **RIGHT keyword** is used, and rows in the table on the right-hand side of the FROM clause are included. For example, you could join all three tables together with the following right outer join:

```
SELECT    ProjectName, HoursWorked, FirstName, LastName
FROM      (PROJECT AS P JOIN ASSIGNMENT AS A
          ON P.ProjectID = A.ProjectID)
               RIGHT JOIN EMPLOYEE AS E
                    ON A.EmployeeNumber = E.EmployeeNumber
ORDER BY  P.ProjectID, A.EmployeeNumber;
```

The result of this join, which now shows not only the employees assigned to projects but also those employees who are *not* assigned to any projects, is:

| | ProjectName | HoursWorked | FirstName | LastName |
|---|---|---|---|---|
| 1 | NULL | NULL | Richard | Bandalone |
| 2 | NULL | NULL | George | Smith |
| 3 | NULL | NULL | George | Jones |
| 4 | NULL | NULL | James | Nestor |
| 5 | NULL | NULL | Rick | Brown |
| 6 | 2010 Q3 Product Plan | 30.00 | Mary | Jacobs |
| 7 | 2010 Q3 Product Plan | 75.00 | Tom | Jackson |
| 8 | 2010 Q3 Product Plan | 55.00 | Ken | Numoto |
| 9 | 2010 Q3 Portfolio Analysis | 40.00 | Tom | Caruthers |
| 10 | 2010 Q3 Portfolio Analysis | 45.00 | Mary | Abernathy |
| 11 | 2010 Q3 Tax Preparation | 25.00 | Mary | Jacobs |
| 12 | 2010 Q3 Tax Preparation | 20.00 | Rosalie | Jackson |
| 13 | 2010 Q3 Tax Preparation | 45.00 | Tom | Caruthers |
| 14 | 2010 Q3 Tax Preparation | 40.00 | Heather | Jones |
| 15 | 2010 Q4 Product Plan | 35.00 | Mary | Jacobs |
| 16 | 2010 Q4 Product Plan | 80.00 | Tom | Jackson |
| 17 | 2010 Q4 Product Plan | 50.00 | Ken | Numoto |
| 18 | 2010 Q4 Portfolio Analysis | 15.00 | Tom | Caruthers |
| 19 | 2010 Q4 Portfolio Analysis | 10.00 | Heather | Jones |
| 20 | 2010 Q4 Portfolio Analysis | 27.50 | Mary | Abernathy |

---

### Does Not Work with Microsoft Access ANSI-89 SQL

**Even with the following syntax, which is what has worked before in Microsoft Access:**

```
SELECT      ProjectName, HoursWorked, FirstName,
            LastName
FROM        (PROJECT AS P INNER JOIN ASSIGNMENT AS A
            ON P.ProjectID = A.ProjectID)
                RIGHT JOIN EMPLOYEE AS E
                    ON A.EmployeeNumber =
                       E.EmployeeNumber
ORDER BY    P.ProjectID, A.EmployeeNumber;
```

the error message *Join expression not supported* is returned when the query is run.

**Solution:** Build an equivalent query or set of queries using the Microsoft Access Query by Example (QBE). Query by Example (QBE) is discussed in this chapter's section of "The Access Workbench."

# SQL FOR RELATIONAL DATA MODIFICATION AND DELETION

The SQL DDL contains commands for the three possible data modification operations: insert, modify, and delete. We have already discussed inserting data, and now we consider modifying and deleting data.

## Modifying Data

You can modify the values of existing data by using the SQL **UPDATE . . . SET command**. However, this is a powerful command that needs to be used with care. Consider the EMPLOYEE table. We can see the current data in the table by using the command:

```
SELECT * FROM EMPLOYEE;
```

The current data in the EMPLOYEE table looks like this:

| | EmployeeNumber | FirstName | LastName | Department | Phone | Email |
|---|---|---|---|---|---|---|
| 1 | 1 | Mary | Jacobs | Administration | 360-285-8110 | Mary.Jacobs@WPC.com |
| 2 | 2 | Rosalie | Jackson | Administration | 360-285-8120 | Rosalie.Jackson@WPC.com |
| 3 | 3 | Richard | Bandalone | Legal | 360-285-8210 | Richard.Bandalone@WPC.com |
| 4 | 4 | Tom | Caruthers | Accounting | 360-285-8310 | Tom.Caruthers@WPC.com |
| 5 | 5 | Heather | Jones | Accounting | 360-285-8320 | Heather.Jones@WPC.com |
| 6 | 6 | Mary | Abernathy | Finance | 360-285-8410 | Mary.Abernathy@WPC.com |
| 7 | 7 | George | Smith | Human Resources | 360-285-8510 | George.Smith@WPC.com |
| 8 | 8 | Tom | Jackson | Production | 360-287-8610 | Tom.Jackson@WPC.com |
| 9 | 9 | George | Jones | Production | 360-287-8620 | George.Jones@WPC.com |
| 10 | 10 | Ken | Numoto | Marketing | 360-287-8710 | Ken.Numoto@WPC.com |
| 11 | 11 | James | Nestor | InfoSystems | NULL | James.Nestor@WPC.com |
| 12 | 12 | Rick | Brown | InfoSystems | 360-287-8820 | Rick.Brown@WPC.com |

Note that James Nestor (EmployeeNumber = 11) has a NULL value for his phone number. Suppose that he has just gotten a phone with phone number 360-287-8810. We can change the value of the Phone column for his data row by using the UPDATE . . . SET statement, as shown in the following SQL command:

```
UPDATE    EMPLOYEE
SET       Phone = '360-287-8810'
WHERE     EmployeeNumber = 11;
```

To see the result, we repeat the command:

```
SELECT * FROM EMPLOYEE;
```

The revised data in the EMPLOYEE table with the new phone number now looks like this:

| | EmployeeNumber | FirstName | LastName | Department | Phone | Email |
|---|---|---|---|---|---|---|
| 1 | 1 | Mary | Jacobs | Administration | 360-285-8110 | Mary.Jacobs@WPC.com |
| 2 | 2 | Rosalie | Jackson | Administration | 360-285-8120 | Rosalie.Jackson@WPC.com |
| 3 | 3 | Richard | Bandalone | Legal | 360-285-8210 | Richard.Bandalone@WPC.com |
| 4 | 4 | Tom | Caruthers | Accounting | 360-285-8310 | Tom.Caruthers@WPC.com |
| 5 | 5 | Heather | Jones | Accounting | 360-285-8320 | Heather.Jones@WPC.com |
| 6 | 6 | Mary | Abernathy | Finance | 360-285-8410 | Mary.Abernathy@WPC.com |
| 7 | 7 | George | Smith | Human Resources | 360-285-8510 | George.Smith@WPC.com |
| 8 | 8 | Tom | Jackson | Production | 360-287-8610 | Tom.Jackson@WPC.com |
| 9 | 9 | George | Jones | Production | 360-287-8620 | George.Jones@WPC.com |
| 10 | 10 | Ken | Numoto | Marketing | 360-287-8710 | Ken.Numoto@WPC.com |
| 11 | 11 | James | Nestor | InfoSystems | 360-287-8810 | James.Nestor@WPC.com |
| 12 | 12 | Rick | Brown | InfoSystems | 360-287-8820 | Rick.Brown@WPC.com |

Now consider why this command is dangerous. Suppose that while intending to make this update we make an error and forget to include the WHERE clause. Thus, we submit the following to the DBMS:

```
UPDATE     EMPLOYEE
SET        Phone = '360-287-8810';
```

After this command has executed, we can again use a SELECT command to display the contents of the EMPLOYEE relation:

```
SELECT * FROM EMPLOYEE;
```

The EMPLOYEE relation will appear as follows:

| | EmployeeNumber | FirstName | LastName | Department | Phone | Email |
|---|---|---|---|---|---|---|
| 1 | 1 | Mary | Jacobs | Administration | 360-287-8810 | Mary.Jacobs@WPC.com |
| 2 | 2 | Rosalie | Jackson | Administration | 360-287-8810 | Rosalie.Jackson@WPC.com |
| 3 | 3 | Richard | Bandalone | Legal | 360-287-8810 | Richard.Bandalone@WPC.com |
| 4 | 4 | Tom | Caruthers | Accounting | 360-287-8810 | Tom.Caruthers@WPC.com |
| 5 | 5 | Heather | Jones | Accounting | 360-287-8810 | Heather.Jones@WPC.com |
| 6 | 6 | Mary | Abernathy | Finance | 360-287-8810 | Mary.Abernathy@WPC.com |
| 7 | 7 | George | Smith | Human Resources | 360-287-8810 | George.Smith@WPC.com |
| 8 | 8 | Tom | Jackson | Production | 360-287-8810 | Tom.Jackson@WPC.com |
| 9 | 9 | George | Jones | Production | 360-287-8810 | George.Jones@WPC.com |
| 10 | 10 | Ken | Numoto | Marketing | 360-287-8810 | Ken.Numoto@WPC.com |
| 11 | 11 | James | Nestor | InfoSystems | 360-287-8810 | James.Nestor@WPC.com |
| 12 | 12 | Rick | Brown | InfoSystems | 360-287-8810 | Rick.Brown@WPC.com |

This is clearly not what we intended to do. If you did this at a new job where there are 10,000 rows in the EMPLOYEE table, you would experience a sinking feeling in the pit of your stomach and make plans to update your résumé. The message here: UPDATE is powerful and easy to use, but it is also capable of causing disasters.

The UPDATE command can modify more than one column value at a time, as shown in the following statement. For example, if Heather Jones (EmployeeNumber = 5) is transferred to the finance department from accounting and given a new finance phone number, you can use the following command to update her data:

```
UPDATE      EMPLOYEE
SET         Department = 'Finance', Phone = '360-285-8420'
WHERE       EmployeeNumber = 5;
```

This command changes the values of Phone and Department for the indicated employee. You can use a SELECT command to see the results:

```
SELECT      *
FROM        EMPLOYEE
WHERE       EmployeeNumber = 5;
```

The results are as follows:

| | EmployeeNumber | FirstName | LastName | Department | Phone | Email |
|---|---|---|---|---|---|---|
| 1 | 5 | Heather | Jones | Finance | 360-285-8420 | Heather.Jones@WPC.com |

## Deleting Data

You can eliminate rows with the SQL **DELETE command**. However, the same warnings pertain to DELETE as to UPDATE. DELETE is deceptively simple to use and easy to apply in unintended ways. The following, for example, deletes all projects sponsored by the marketing department:

```
DELETE
FROM        PROJECT
WHERE       Department = 'Marketing';
```

Given that we created an ON DELETE CASCADE referential integrity constraint, this DELETE operation not only removes PROJECT rows, it also removes any related ASSIGNMENT rows. For the WPC data in Figure 3-2, this DELETE operation removes the projects with ProjectID 1000 (2010 Q3 Product Plan) and 1300 (2010 Q3 Product Plan), and six rows (rows 1, 2, and 3 for ProjectID 1000, and rows 10, 11, and 12 for ProjectID 1300) of the ASSIGNMENT table.

As with UPDATE, if you forget to include the WHERE clause, disaster ensues. For example, the SQL code:

```
DELETE
FROM        PROJECT;
```

deletes *all* the rows in PROJECT (and because of the ON DELETE CASCADE constraint, *all* the ASSIGNMENT rows as well). This truly would be a disaster!

Observe how the referential integrity constraint differs with the EMPLOYEE table. Here, if we try to process the command:

```
DELETE
FROM        EMPLOYEE
WHERE       EmployeeNumber = 1;
```

the DELETE operation fails because rows in ASSIGNMENT depend on the EmployeeNumber value of 1 in EMPLOYEE. If you want to delete the row for this employee, you must first reassign or delete his or her rows in ASSIGNMENT.

## SQL FOR TABLE AND CONSTRAINT MODIFICATION AND DELETION

There are many data definition SQL statements that we have not yet described. Two of the most useful are the SQL DROP TABLE and ALTER TABLE statements.

### The DROP TABLE and ALTER TABLE Statements

The **DROP TABLE statement** is also one of the most dangerous SQL statements because it drops the table's structure along with all of the table's data. For example, to drop the ASSIGNMENT table and all its data, you use the following SQL statement:

```
DROP TABLE ASSIGNMENT;
```

The DROP TABLE statement does not work if the table contains or could contain values needed to fulfill referential integrity constraints. EMPLOYEE, for example, contains values of EmployeeNumber needed by the foreign key constraint ASSIGN_EMP_FK. In this case, an attempt to issue the statement DROP TABLE EMPLOYEE fails, and an error message is generated.

### The ALTER TABLE Statement

To drop the EMPLOYEE table, you must first drop the ASSIGNMENT table, or at least delete the foreign key constraint ASSIGN_EMP_FK. This is one place where the ALTER TABLE command is useful. You use the **ALTER TABLE statement** to add, modify, and drop columns and constraints. For example, you can use it to drop the ASSIGN_EMP_FK constraint with the statement:

```
ALTER TABLE ASSIGNMENT
    DROP CONSTRAINT ASSIGN_EMP_FK;
```

After either dropping the ASSIGNMENT table or the ASSIGN_EMP_FK foreign key constraint, you can then successfully drop the EMPLOYEE table.

---

**B T W**

Now you know why it is an advantage to control constraint names by using the CONSTRAINT syntax. Because we created the foreign key constraint name ASSIGN_EMP_FK ourselves, we know what it is. This makes it easy to use when we need it.

---

### The CHECK Constraint

We can also use the ALTER statement to add a constraint. For example, consider the PROJECT table, which has the columns StartDate and EndDate. Obviously, the StartDate must be earlier than the EndDate, but there is currently nothing in the table definition to enforce this. This is a perfect place to use a CHECK constraint. CHECK constraints are similar to WHERE clauses in SQL queries. They can contain the keywords IN, NOT IN, and LIKE (for the specification of decimal places), and they can use less than (<) and greater than (>) signs for range checks.

> ### Does Not Work with Microsoft Access ANSI-89 SQL
>
> **As discussed earlier, Microsoft Access does not support the CHECK column constraints.**
>
> **Solution:** **An equivalent constraint can be set in the table Design view. See the discussion in this chapter's section of "The Access Workbench."**

To modify the PROJECT table with the needed constraint, we use the following SQL statement:

```
ALTER TABLE PROJECT
     ADD CONSTRAINT PROJECT_Check_Dates
          CHECK (StartDate < EndDate);
```

The ALTER TABLE statement is handy when you need to add or drop columns. For example, suppose that you want to add a column to PROJECT to track how many hours have actually been worked on a project. If the name of this column is CurrentTotalHours, you can add it to the table with the SQL statement (note that the keyword COLUMN is *not* used in this command):

```
ALTER TABLE PROJECT
     ADD CurrentTotalHours Numeric(8,2) NULL;
```

Note that because you are adding a column to an existing table that contains data you cannot add a NOT NULL column; the constraint would immediately be violated because there would be missing data in each row. If you want a column to be NOT NULL, you must create it as NULL, insert the needed data, and then modify the column to NOT NULL. For example, you can put data into CurrentTotalHours column for the existing rows and then convert the column to NOT NULL by using the SQL statements:

```
UPDATE PROJECT SET CurrentTotalHours = 0;

ALTER TABLE PROJECT
     ALTER COLUMN CurrentTotalHours Numeric(8,2) NOT NULL;
```

If you decided that this column was not needed, you could drop it from the PROJECT table by using the SQL statement:

```
ALTER TABLE PROJECT
     DROP COLUMN CurrentTotalHours;
```

We can also use the ALTER TABLE statement to modify data types, but you have to be careful because this can result in a loss of data. Check your DBMS documentation carefully before attempting to modify data types.[4]

 ## SQL VIEWS

SQL contains a powerful tool known as an SQL view. An **SQL view** is a virtual table created by a DBMS-stored SELECT statement. Such views can combine access to data in multiple tables and even in other views. SQL views are discussed in Chapter 3A.

---

[4]Also see David M. Kroenke and David J. Auer, *Database Processing: Fundamentals, Design, and Implementation*, 11th edition (Upper Saddle River, NJ: Prentice Hall, 2010), Chapter 8.

## THE ACCESS WORKBENCH

### Section 3

### Working with Queries in Microsoft Access

In the previous sections of "The Access Workbench," you learned how to create Microsoft Access databases, tables, forms, and reports in multiple-table databases. In this section, you will:

- Learn how to use Microsoft Access SQL
- Learn how to run queries in single and multiple tables, using both SQL and Query by Example (QBE)
- Learn how to manually set table and relationship properties that Microsoft Access SQL does not support

In this section, we will continue to use the WMCRM database we have been using. At this point, we have created and populated (that is, inserted the data into) the CUSTOMER and CONTACT tables and set the referential integrity constraint between them.

#### Working with Microsoft Access SQL

You work with Microsoft Access SQL in the SQL view of a query window. The following simple query shows how this works:

```
SELECT * FROM CUSTOMER;
```

#### *Opening a Microsoft Access Query Window in Design View*

1. Start Microsoft Access 2010.
2. Click the **File** command tab to display the Backstage view and then click the **WMCRM.accdb** database file name in the quick access list to open the database.
3. Click the **Create** command tab to display the Create command groups, as shown in Figure AW-3-1.
4. Click the **Query Design** button.
5. The Query1 tabbed document window is displayed in Design view, along with the Show Table dialog box, as shown in Figure AW-3-2.
6. Click the **Close** button on the Show Table dialog box. The Query1 document window now looks as shown in Figure AW-3-3. This window is used for creating and editing Microsoft Access queries in Design view and is used with Microsoft Access QBE, as discussed later in this section.

Note that in Figure AW-3-3 the Select button is selected in the Query Type group on the Design tab. You can tell this is so because active or selected buttons are always shown in color on the Ribbon. This indicates that we are creating a query that is the equivalent of an SQL SELECT statement.

Also note that in Figure AW-3-3 the View gallery is available in the Results group of the Design tab. We can use this gallery to switch between Design view and SQL view. However, we can also just use the displayed SQL View button to switch to SQL view, which is being displayed because Microsoft Access considers that to be the view you would most likely choose in the gallery if you used it. Microsoft Access always presents a "most likely needed" view choice as a button above the View gallery.

FIGURE AW-3-1

The Create Command Tab

The **Create** command tab

The **Query Design** button

FIGURE AW-3-2

The Show Table Dialog Box

The **Query1** tabbed document window

The **Show Table** dialog box

Click the **Close** button

*(Continued)*

## FIGURE AW-3-3

### The Query Tools Contextual Command Tab

The **Query Tools** command tab

The **SQL View** button

The **View gallery** drop-down arrow button

The **Select** Query Type button

The **Query Type** command group

The **Query1** tabbed document window in Design view

The **Design** tab command tab

*Opening a Microsoft Access SQL Query Window and Running a Microsoft Access SQL Query*

1. Click the **SQL View** button in the Results group on the Design tab. The Query1 window switches to the SQL view, as shown in Figure AW-3-4. Note the basic SQL command **SELECT**; that's shown in the window. This is an incomplete command, and running it will not produce any results.
2. Edit the SQL SELECT command to read **SELECT \* FROM CUSTOMER;**, as shown in Figure AW-3-5.
3. Click the **Run** button on the Design tab.

## FIGURE AW-3-4

### The Query1 Window in SQL View

The **Query1** window in SQL view

The SQL **SELECT;** statement—this is an incomplete statement and will not run as written—it is intended as the start of an SQL query

**FIGURE AW-3-5**

The SQL Query

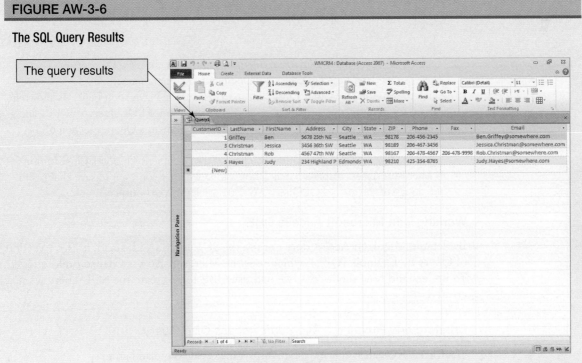

4. Click the **Shutter Bar Open/Close** button to minimize the Navigation Pane, and then click the **Query1** document tab to select the Query1 window. The query results appear, as shown in Figure AW-3-6.

Just as we can save Microsoft Access objects such as tables, forms, and reports, we can save Microsoft Access queries for future use.

### Saving a Microsoft Access SQL Query

1. To save the query, click the **Save** button on the Quick Access Toolbar. The Save As dialog box appears as shown in Figure AW-3-7.

**FIGURE AW-3-6**

The SQL Query Results

*(Continued)*

**FIGURE AW-3-7**

The Save As Dialog Box

The **Save** button

The **Save As** dialog box

Type the query name **SQLQuery-AW-3-01** here

The **OK** button

**FIGURE AW-3-8**

The Named and Saved Query

The query window is now named **SQLQuery-AW-3-01**

The **Queries** section of the Navigation Pane

The **SQLQuery-AW-3-01** query object

2. Type in the query name **SQLQuery-AW-3-01** and then click the **OK** button. The query is saved, and the window is renamed with the query name.
3. Click the **Shutter Bar Open/Close** button to expand the Navigation Pane. As shown in Figure AW-3-8, the query document window is now named SQLQuery-AW-3-01 and a newly created SQLQuery-AW-3-01 query object appears in a Queries section of the Navigation Pane.
4. Close the Query-AW-3-01 window by clicking the document window's **Close** button.
5. If Microsoft Access displays a dialog box asking whether you want to save changes to the design of the query SQLQuery-AW-3-01, click the **Yes** button.

### Working with Microsoft Access QBE

By default, Microsoft Access does not use the SQL interface. Instead, it uses a version of Query by Example (QBE), which uses the Microsoft Access GUI to build queries. To understand how this works, we will use QBE to re-create the SQL query we just created.

*Creating and Running a Microsoft Access QBE Query*

1. Click the **Create** command tab to display the Create command groups.
2. Click the **Query Design** button.

**FIGURE AW-3-9**

**The QBE Query1 Query Window**

This query is a Select query

Tables in the query appear in the top pane, together with a list of their columns (the *field list*) and an asterisk (*), meaning "all columns"

Columns in the query are called *fields* and appear in the bottom pane, together with related property values

3. The Query1 tabbed document window is displayed in Design view, along with the Show Table dialog box, as shown in Figure AW-3-2.
4. Click **CUSTOMER** to select the CUSTOMER table. Click the **Add** button to add the CUSTOMER table to the query.
5. Click the **Close** button to close the Show Table dialog box.
6. Rearrange and resize the query window objects in the Query1 query document window, using standard Windows drag-and-drop techniques. Rearrange the window elements until they look as shown in Figure AW-3-9.
7. Note the elements of the Query1 window shown in Figure AW-3-9: Tables and their associated set of columns—called a *field list*—that are included in the query are shown in the upper pane, and the columns (fields) actually included in the query are shown in the lower pane. For each included column (field), you can set whether this column's data appear in the results, how the data are sorted, and the criteria for selecting which rows of data will be shown. Note that the first entry in the table's field list is the asterisk (*), which has its standard SQL meaning of "all columns in the table."
8. Include columns in the query by dragging them from the table's field list to a field column in the lower pane. Click and drag the * in CUSTOMER to the first field column, as shown in Figure AW-3-10. Note that the column is entered as **CUSTOMER**.* from the table CUSTOMER.
9. To save the QBE query, click the **Save** button on the Quick Access Toolbar to display the Save As dialog box. Type in the query name **QBEQuery-AW-3-02**, and then click the **OK** button. The query is saved, and the window is renamed QBEQuery-AW-3-02, and a newly created QBEQuery-AW-3-02 query object appears in a Queries section of the Navigation Pane.
10. Click the **Run** button on the Query Design toolbar.
11. Click the **Shutter Bar Open/Close** button to minimize the Navigation Pane. You may need to resize column widths to see all the data. The query results appear, as shown in Figure AW-3-11. Note that these results are identical to the results shown in Figure AW-3-6.

*(Continued)*

## FIGURE AW-3-10

### Adding Columns to the QBE Query

To add a column to the query, click the column name and drag it to a cell in the **Field**: row in the lower pane

The asterisk (*) symbol was dragged and dropped here to add the **CUSTOMER.\*** field to the query

The table name is automatically added to the query to specify the source of the column—this is important if there is more than one table in the query with the same column name

## FIGURE AW-3-11

### The QBE Query Results

As expected, the query results are identical to those shown in Figure AW-3-6

The results are sorted by CustomerID

12. Click the **Shutter Bar Open/Close** button to expand the Navigation Pane and then click the query document tab to select it.
13. Close the QBEQuery-AW-3-02 query.
14. If Microsoft Access displays a dialog box asking whether you want to save changes to the layout of the query QBEQuery-AW-3-02, click the **Yes** button.

This query is about as simple as they get, but we can use QBE for more complicated queries. For example, consider a query that uses only some of the columns in the table,

FIGURE AW-3-12

The QBEQuery-AW-3-03 Query Window

The **CustomerID,
LastName,** and
**FirstName** fields are
in the query

The results will be
sorted by LastName
in descending order
(Z–A)

The results will show
only customers with a
CustomerID greater
than 2

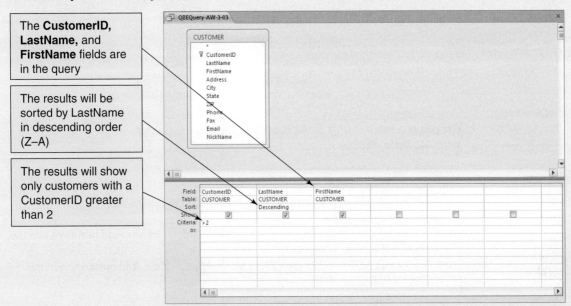

includes the SQL WHERE clause, and also sorts data using the SQL ORDER BY clause:

```
SELECT      CustomerID, LastName, FirstName
FROM        CUSTOMER
WHERE       CustomerID > 2
ORDER BY    LastName DESC;
```

This QBE query, named QBEQuery-AW-3-03, is shown in Figure AW-3-12. Note that now we have included the specific columns that we want used in the query instead of the asterisk, that we have used the Sort property for CustomerID, and that we have included row selection conditions in the Criteria property for LastName.

### Creating and Running QBEQuery-AW-3-03

1. Using the previous instructions for QBEQuery-AW-3-02, create, run, and save QBEQuery-AW-3-03. The query results are shown in Figure AW-3-13.

FIGURE AW-3-13

The QBEQuery-AW-3-03 Query Results

The results show
only customers with
a CustomerID
greater than 2, sorted
by LastName in
descending order
(Z–A)

*(Continued)*

Of course, we can use more than one table in a QBE query. Next, we will create the QBE version of this SQL query:

```
SELECT    LastName, FirstName, ContactDate, ContactType,
          Remarks
FROM      CUSTOMER, CONTACT
WHERE     CUSTOMER.CustomerID = CONTACT.CustomerID
          AND CustomerID = 3
ORDER BY  ContactDate;
```

### Creating and Running a Microsoft Access QBE Query with Multiple Tables

1. Click the **Create** command tab.
2. Click the **Query Design** button.
3. The Query1 tabbed document window is displayed in Design view, along with the Show Table dialog box.
4. Click **CUSTOMER** to select the CUSTOMER table. Click the **Add** button to add the CUSTOMER table to the query.
5. Click **CONTACT** to select the CONTACT table. Click the **Add** button to add the CUSTOMER table to the query.
6. Click the **Close** button to close the Show Table dialog box.
7. Rearrange and resize the query window objects in the Query1 query document window by using standard Windows drag-and-drop techniques. Rearrange the window elements until they look as shown in Figure AW-3-14. Note that the relationship between the two tables is already included in the diagram. This implements the SQL clause:

```
WHERE CUSTOMER.CustomerID = CONTACT.CustomerID
```

8. From the CUSTOMER table, click and drag the **CustomerID**, **LastName**, and **FirstName** column names to the first three field columns in the lower pane.

---

**FIGURE AW-3-14**

The Query Window with Two Tables

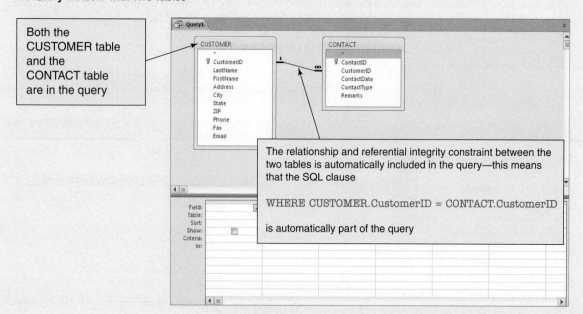

Both the CUSTOMER table and the CONTACT table are in the query

The relationship and referential integrity constraint between the two tables is automatically included in the query—this means that the SQL clause

```
WHERE CUSTOMER.CustomerID = CONTACT.CustomerID
```

is automatically part of the query

**FIGURE AW-3-15**

**The Completed Two-Table Query**

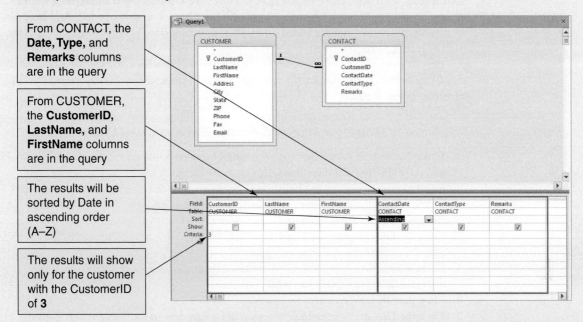

From CONTACT, the **Date, Type,** and **Remarks** columns are in the query

From CUSTOMER, the **CustomerID, LastName,** and **FirstName** columns are in the query

The results will be sorted by Date in ascending order (A–Z)

The results will show only for the customer with the CustomerID of **3**

9. From the CONTACT table, click and drag the **ContactDate**, **ContactType**, and **Remarks** column names to the next three field columns in the lower pane.
10. In the field column for CustomerID, uncheck the **Show** check box so that the data from this column is not included in the results display.
11. In the field column for CustomerID, type the number **3** in the Criteria row.
12. In the field column for ContactDate, set the Sort setting to **Ascending**. The completed QBE query appears, as shown in Figure AW-3-15.
13. To save the query, click the **Save** button on the Quick Access Toolbar to display the Save As dialog box. Type in the query name **QBEQuery-AW-3-04**, and then click the **OK** button. The query is saved, the document window is renamed with the new query name, and the QBEQuery-AW-3-04 object is added to the Queries section of the Navigation Pane.
14. Click the **Run** button. The query results appear, as shown in Figure AW-3-16.
15. Close the QBEQuery-AW-3-04 window.

**FIGURE AW-3-16**

**The Two-Table Query Results**

The results are shown for the customer with the CustomerID of 3, which is Jessica Christman

The results are sorted by Date in ascending order (earliest date to latest date)

*(Continued)*

### Working with Microsoft Access Parameter Queries

Microsoft Access allows us to construct queries that prompt the user for values to be used in the WHERE clause of the query. These are known as **parameterized queries**, where the word *parameter* refers to the column for which a value is needed. And because we can create reports that are based on queries, parameterized queries can be used as the basis of parameterized reports.

For an example of a parameterized query, we will modify QBEQuery-AW-3-04 so that CustomerID is the parameter and the user is prompted for the CustomerID value when the query is run.

#### Creating and Running a Microsoft Access Parameterized Query

1. In the Navigation Pane, right-click the **QBEQuery-AW-3-04** query object to select it and open the shortcut menu, and then click the **Design View** button in the shortcut menu to open the query in Design view. Note that the CustomerID column, which was the first column, now appears as the *last column* in Design view. This occurs because we specified that the column would *not* be displayed.
2. Click the **File** command tab, and then click the Save Object As command to display the Save As dialog box, as shown in Figure AW-3-17.
3. In the Save 'QBEQuery-AW-03-04' to: text box of the Save As dialog box, edit the query name to read **QBEQuery-AW-3-05**.
4. Click the **OK** button to save the query.
5. Click the **Design** command tab to return to Design view of the query, which is now renamed as QBEQuery-AW-3-05.
6. Click the **Shutter Bar Open/Close** button to minimize the Navigation Pane.
7. In the Criteria row of the CustomerID column, delete the number value (which is 3), and enter the text **[Enter the CustomerID Number:]** in its place. You will need to expand the CustomerID column width for all the text to be visible at the same time. The QBEQuery-AW-3-05 window now looks as shown in Figure AW-3-18.

---

### FIGURE AW-3-17

**The Query Save As Dialog Box**

The **File** command tab

The **Save Object As** command

The **Design** command tab

The **Save As** dialog box

Type the new query name **QBEQuery-AW-3-05** in this text box

The **OK** button

### FIGURE AW-3-18

**The Completed Parameterized Query**

The CustomerID column is now shown last because it is not displayed in the query results

Criteria for the CustomerID column now contains the text for a prompt to be displayed in the Enter Parameter Value dialog box that will be displayed to get a parameter value from the user

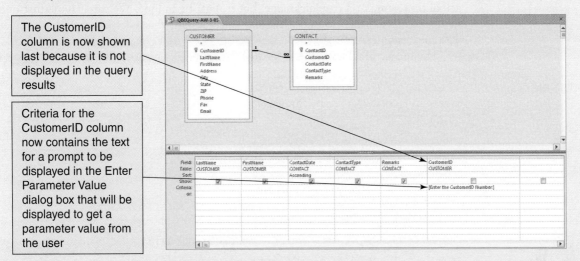

8. Click the **Save** button on the Quick Access Toolbar to save the changes to the query design.
9. Click the **Run** button. The **Enter Parameter Value** dialog box appears, as shown in Figure AW-3-19. Note that the text we entered in the Criteria row now appears as a prompt in the dialog box.
10. Enter the CustomerID number **3** as a parameter value and then click the **OK** button. The query results appear. They are identical to those shown in Figure AW-3-16.
11. Close the QBEQuery-AW-3-05 Query.
12. Click the **Shutter Bar Open/Close** button to expand the Navigation Pane.

This completes our discussion of SQL and QBE queries in Microsoft Access 2010. You should be able to run any needed query in a Microsoft Access database with the query tools we have described.

### Creating Tables with Microsoft Access SQL

In previous sections of "The Access Workbench," we created and populated Microsoft Access tables using table Design view. Now we will create and populate a table by using Microsoft Access SQL, as done in the SQL view of a query window. So far, the

### FIGURE AW-3-19

**The Enter Parameter Value Dialog Box**

The **Enter Parameter Value** dialog box

This is the text that was entered into the criteria field for CustomerID

Enter Parameter Value

Enter the CustomerID Number:

OK      Cancel

Enter the CustomerID number here

Click the **OK** button to run the query

*(Continued)*

Wallingford Motors CRM database has been constructed to be used by only a single salesperson. In this section, we will add a SALESPERSON table. Each salesperson at Wallingford Motors is identified by a nickname. The nickname may be the person's actual first name or a true nickname, but it must be unique. We can assume that one salesperson is assigned to each customer and that only that salesperson makes contact with the customer.

The full set of tables in the WMCRM database will now look like this:

SALESPERSON (<u>NickName</u>, LastName, FirstName, HireDate, WageRate, CommissionRate, Phone, Email)

CUSTOMER (<u>CustomerID</u>, LastName, FirstName, Address, City, State, ZIP, Phone, Fax, Email, *NickName*)

CONTACT (<u>ContactID</u>, *CustomerID*, Date, Type, Remarks)

The referential integrity constraints are:

NickName in CUSTOMER must exist in NickName in SALESPERSON

CustomerID in CONTACT must exist in CustomerID in CUSTOMER

The database column characteristics for SALESPERSON are shown in Figure AW-3-20, and SALESPERSON data are shown in Figure AW-3-21.

---

**FIGURE AW-3-20**

Database Column Characteristics for the SALESPERSON Table

| Column Name | Type | Key | Required | Remarks |
|---|---|---|---|---|
| NickName | Text (35) | Primary Key | Yes | |
| LastName | Text (25) | No | Yes | |
| FirstName | Text (25) | No | Yes | |
| HireDate | Date/Time | No | Yes | Medium Date |
| WageRate | Number | No | Yes | Double, Currency, Default value = $12.50 |
| CommissionRate | Number | No | Yes | Double, Percent, 3 Decimal places |
| Phone | Text (12) | No | Yes | |
| Email | Text (100) | No | Yes | Unique |

---

**FIGURE AW-3-21**

Data for the SALESPERSON Table

| Nick Name | Last Name | First Name | Hire Date | Wage Rate | Commission Rate | Phone | Email |
|---|---|---|---|---|---|---|---|
| Tina | Smith | Tina | 10-AUG-04 | $ 15.50 | 12.500% | 206-287-7010 | Tina@WM.com |
| Big Bill | Jones | William | 25-SEP-04 | $ 15.50 | 12.500% | 206-287-7020 | BigBill@WM.com |
| Billy | Jones | Bill | 17-MAY-05 | $ 12.50 | 12.000% | 206-287-7030 | Billy@WM.com |

Note that adding the SALESPERSON table will require alterations to the existing CUSTOMER table. We need a new column for the foreign key NickName, a referential integrity constraint between CUSTOMER and SALESPERSON, and new data for the NickName column.

First, we will build the SALESPERSON table. The correct SQL statement is:

```
CREATE TABLE SALESPERSON(
       NickName           Char(35)            NOT NULL,
       LastName           Char(25)            NOT NULL,
       FirstName          Char(25)            NOT NULL,
       HireDate           DateTime            NOT NULL,
       WageRate           Numeric(5,2)        NOT NULL
                                                  DEFAULT(12.50),
       CommissionRate     Numeric(5,3)        NOT NULL,
       Phone              Char(12)            NOT NULL,
       Email              VarChar(100)        NOT NULL UNIQUE,
       CONSTRAINT         SALESPERSON_PK      PRIMARY KEY
                                                  (NickName)

       );
```

This statement uses standard SQL data types (specifically SQL Server data types), but this is not a problem, because Microsoft Access will correctly read them and translate them into Microsoft Access data types. However, from the SQL discussion in this chapter we know that Microsoft Access does not support the numeric data type with the (m,n) notation (where m = total number of digits, and n = number of digits to the right of the decimal). Further, Microsoft Access does not support the UNIQUE constraint or the DEFAULT keyword. Therefore, we have to create an SQL statement without these items and then use the Microsoft Access GUI to fine-tune the table after it is created.

The SQL that will run in Microsoft Access is:

```
CREATE TABLE SALESPERSON(
       NickName           Char(35)            NOT NULL,
       LastName           Char(25)            NOT NULL,
       FirstName          Char(25)            NOT NULL,
       HireDate           DateTime            NOT NULL,
       WageRate           Numeric             NOT NULL,
       CommissionRate     Numeric             NOT NULL,
       Phone              Char(12)            NOT NULL,
       Email              VarChar(100)        NOT NULL,
       CONSTRAINT         SALESPERSON_PK      PRIMARY KEY
                                                  (NickName)

       );
```

### Creating the SALESPERSON Table Using Microsoft Access SQL

1. As described earlier in this chapter's section of "The Access Workbench," open a Microsoft Access query window in SQL view.
2. Type the SQL code into the query window. The query window now looks as shown in Figure AW-3-22.

*(Continued)*

**FIGURE AW-3-22**

**The SQL CREATE TABLE SALESPERSON Statement**

The complete SQL
CREATE TABLE
SALESPERSON
statement

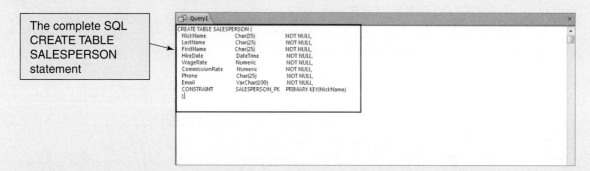

**FIGURE AW-3-23**

**The SALESPERSON Objects in the Navigation Pane**

The **SALESPERSON**
table

The **Create-Table-
SALESPERSON**
query—note the
Design icon that
identifies this as a
data definition query

3. Click the **Run** button. The statement runs, but because this statement creates a table the only immediately visible results are that the SALESPERSON table object is added to the Tables section of the Navigation Pane.
4. Save the query as **Create-Table-SALESPERSON**.
5. Close the query window. The Create-Table-SALESPERSON query object now appears in the Queries section of the Navigation Pane, as shown in Figure AW-3-23.

### Modifying Microsoft Access Tables to Add Data Requirements Not Supported by Microsoft Access SQL

To modify the SALESPERSON table to add the table requirements not supported by Microsoft Access SQL, we use the Microsoft Access table Design view.[5]

First, recall that Microsoft Access SQL does not support the numeric(m,n) syntax, where m is the number of digits stored and n is the number of digits to the right of the

---

[5]Although we do not fully discuss the matter in this book, it is important to mention that Microsoft Access SQL confounds the treatment of the SQL NOT NULL column constraint. When you use NOT NULL in defining a column, Microsoft Access properly sets the column's Required field property to Yes. (We discussed how to do this manually in Chapter 1's section of "The Access Workbench," when we created the CUSTOMER table.) However, Microsoft Access adds a second field property, the **Allow Zero Length field property**, which it sets to Yes. To truly match NOT NULL, this value should be set to *No*. For a full discussion of setting the Allow Zero Length field property, see the Microsoft Access help system.

decimal place. We can set the number of digits to some extent by setting the **Field Size field property** (which is as close as Microsoft Access gets to setting the value of m). By default, Microsoft Access sets a numeric value Field Size property to double. We could change this, but a full discussion of this field property is beyond the scope of this book—see the Microsoft Access help system discussion of the Field Size property for more information.

We can, however, easily set the number of decimal places (which is the value of n) using the **Decimal Places field property**. In addition, Microsoft Access does have the advantage of having a **Format field property** that allows us to apply formatting to a numeric value so that the data appears as currency, a percentage, or in other formats. We will leave the default Field Size setting and change the Format and Decimal Places property values.

Recall that Microsoft Access SQL does not support the SQL DEFAULT keyword, so we will have to add any needed default values. We can do this using the **Default Value field property**.

### Setting Number and Default Value Field Properties

1. To open the SALESPERSON table in Design view, right-click the **SALESPERSON** table object to select it and open the shortcut menu and then click the **Design View** button in the shortcut menu. The SALESPERSON table appears in Design view, as shown in Figure AW-3-24.
2. Select the **WageRate** field. The WageRate field properties are displayed in the General tab, as shown in Figure AW-3-25.
3. Click the **Format** text field. A drop-down list arrow appears on the right end of the text field, as shown in Figure AW-3-26. Click the drop-down list arrow to display the list and select **Currency**.
   - ▪ **NOTE:** When you do this, a small icon appears to the left of the text field. This is the Property Update Options drop-down list. Simply ignore it, and it will disappear when you take the next action. Then it will reappear for that action! In general, ignore it and keep working.

---

**FIGURE AW-3-24**

**The SALESPERSON Table in Design View**

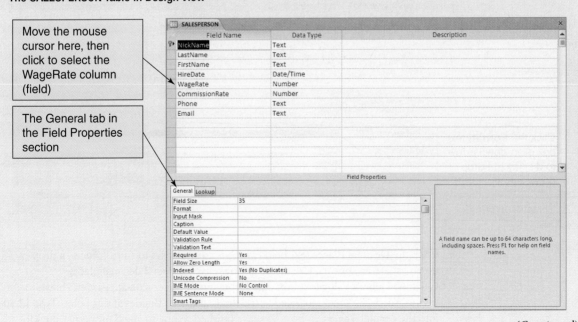

*(Continued)*

FIGURE AW-3-25

**The WageRate Field Properties**

The WageRate column is selected

The **Format** text box

The **Decimal Places** text box

The **Default Value** text box

FIGURE AW-3-26

**The Format Text Box**

Click in the **Format** text box to select it

Click the **Format** text box drop-down arrow to display the drop-down list

Select **Currency**

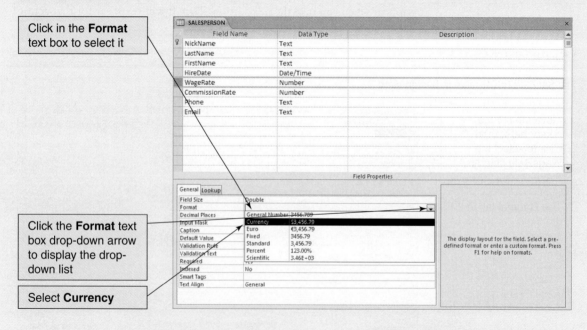

4. Click the **Decimal Places** text field (which is currently set to Auto). Again, a drop-down list arrow appears. Use the drop-down list to select **2** decimal places.
5. Click the **Default Value** text box. The Expression Builder icon appears, as shown in Figure AW-3-27. We do not need to use the Expression Builder at this point. Type **12.50** into the Default Value text box. We have finished setting the field property values for WageRate. The final values are shown in Figure AW-3-28.

FIGURE AW-3-27

The Default Value Text Box

The **Property Update Options** icon—you can simply ignore it

Click in the **Default Value** text box to select it

The **Expression Builder** icon, which we will not use at this time

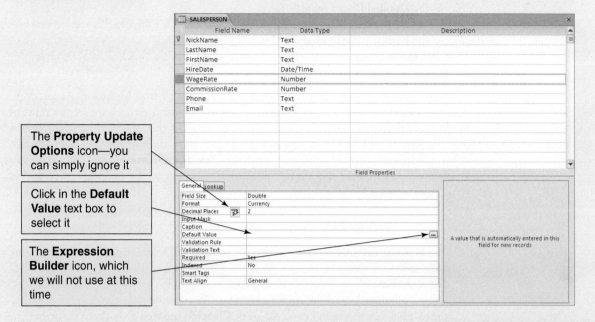

FIGURE AW-3-28

The Completed WageRate Field Properties

Data format is set to **Currency**

Number of decimal places is set to **2**

The default value is set to **12.50**

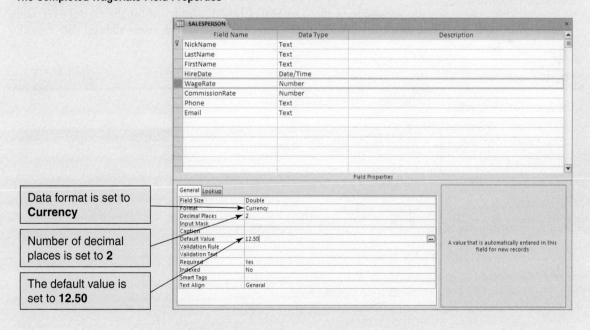

■ **NOTE:** Microsoft Access actually stores this number as 12.5, which is the same value without the trailing zero. Do not be alarmed if you look at these property values again and notice the missing zero!

6. Click the **Save** button to save the completed changes to the SALESPERSON table. Leave the SALESPERSON table in Design view.

*(Continued)*

7. Select the **CommissionRate** field. The CommissionRate field properties are displayed in the General tab.
8. Set the **Format** value to **Percentage**.
9. Set the **Decimal Places** value to **3**.
10. Select the **HireDate** field. The HireDate field properties are displayed in the General tab.
11. Set the **Format** value to **Medium Date**.
12. Click the **Save** button to save the completed changes to the SALESPERSON table.
13. Leave the SALESPERSON table open in Design view for the next set of steps.

The UNIQUE constraint is another SQL constraint that Microsoft Access SQL does not support. To set a UNIQUE constraint in Microsoft Access, we set the value of the **Indexed field property**. Microsoft Access initially sets this value to No, which means that no index (a tool for making queries more efficient) is built for this column. The two other possible values of this property are **Yes (Duplicates OK)** and **Yes (No Duplicates)**. We enforce the UNIQUE constraint by setting the property value to **Yes (No Duplicates)**.

### Setting Indexed Field Properties

1. The **SALESPERSON** table should already be open in Design view. If it is not, open the table in Design view.
2. Select the **Email** field.
3. Click the **Indexed** text field. A drop-down list arrow button appears on the right end of the text field, as shown in Figure AW-3-29. Click the **Indexed** drop-down list arrow button to display the list and select **Yes (No Duplicates)**.
4. Click the **Save** button to save the completed changes to the SALESPERSON table.
5. Close the SALESPERSON table.

Finally, we will implement an SQL CHECK constraint for the CONTACT table. When we created the CONTACT table, we noted that the only allowed data types for

---

**FIGURE AW-3-29**

**The Email Field Properties**

the ContactType column were Phone, Fax, Email, and Meeting. The correct SQL statement to add this constraint to the CONTACT table would be:

```
ALTER TABLE CONTACT
    ADD CONSTRAINT CONTACT_Check_Type
        CHECK (Type IN ('Phone', 'Fax', 'Email', 'Meeting'));
```

To implement the CHECK constraint in Microsoft Access, we set the value of the **Validation Rule field property** for the Type column.

### Creating the CHECK Constraint for the CONTACT Table

1. Open the **CONTACT** table in Design view.
2. Select the **ContactType** column.
3. Click the Validation Rule text box, and then type in the text **Phone or Fax or Email or Meeting**, as shown in Figure AW-3-30.
   - ■ **NOTE:** Do *not* enclose the allowed terms in quotation marks. Microsoft Access will add quotation marks to each term when it saves the changes to the table design. If you add your own set of quotation marks, you will end up with each word enclosed in two sets of quotes, and Microsoft Access will not consider this a match to the existing data in the table when it runs the data integrity check discussed in step 4.
4. Click the **Save** button on the Quick Access Toolbar to save the CONTACT table. As shown in Figure AW-3-31, Microsoft Access displays a dialog box, warning that existing data may not match the data integrity rule we have just established by setting a validation rule.
5. Click the **Yes** button on the dialog box
6. Close the CONTACT table.

---

**FIGURE AW-3-30**

Specifying a Validation Rule

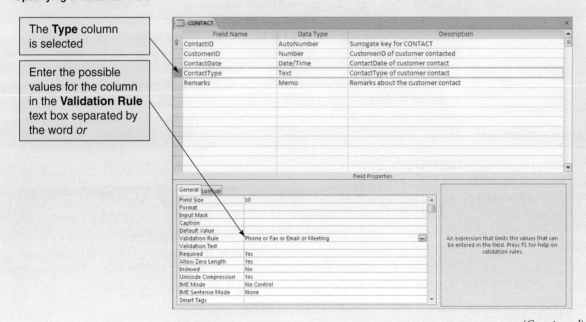

The **Type** column is selected

Enter the possible values for the column in the **Validation Rule** text box separated by the word *or*

*(Continued)*

### FIGURE AW-3-31

The Data Integrity Warning Dialog Box

The **Data Integrity** warning dialog box

Click the **Yes** button

### Inserting Data with Microsoft Access SQL

We can use Microsoft Access SQL to enter the data shown in Figure AW-3-20 into the SALESPERSON table. The only problem here is that Microsoft Access will not handle multiple SQL commands in one query, so each row of data must be input individually. The SQL commands to enter the data are:

```
INSERT INTO SALESPERSON
        VALUES('Tina', 'Smith', 'Tina', '10-AUG-06',
        '15.50', '.125', '206-287-7010', 'Tina@WM.com');
INSERT INTO SALESPERSON
        VALUES('Big Bill', 'Jones', 'William', '25-SEP-06',
        '15.50', '.125', '206-287-7020', 'BigBill@WM.com');
INSERT INTO SALESPERSON
        VALUES('Billy', 'Jones', 'Bill', '17-MAY-07',
        '12.50', '.120', '206-287-7030', 'Billy@WM.com');
```

*Inserting Data into the SALESPERSON Table Using Microsoft Access SQL*

1. As described previously, open a Microsoft Access query window in SQL view.
2. Type the SQL code for the first SQL INSERT statement into the query window.
3. Click the **Run** button. As shown in Figure AW-3-32, the query changes to Append Query and a dialog box appears, asking you to confirm that you want to insert the data.
4. Click the **Yes** button in the dialog box. The data are inserted into the table.
5. Repeat steps 2, 3, and 4 for the rest of the SQL INSERT statements for the SALESPERSON data.

### FIGURE AW-3-32

Inserting Data into the SALESPERSON Table

The SQL **INSERT** command

The dialog box confirming the INSERT

Click the **Yes** button to complete the INSERT

## FIGURE AW-3-33

### The Data in the SALESPERSON Table

The data are stored by NickName (the primary key value) in ascending order

6. Close the Query1 window. A dialog box appears, asking if you want to save the query. Click the **No** button—there is no need to save this SQL statement.
7. Open the **SALESPERSON** table in Datasheet view.
8. Click the **Shutter Bar Open/Close** button to minimize the Navigation Pane and then arrange the columns so that all column names and data are displayed correctly.
9. The table looks as shown in Figure AW-3-33. Note that the rows are sorted alphabetically, in ascending order, on the primary key (NickName) value—they do not appear in the order in which they were input.
   - **NOTE:** This is *not* typical of an SQL DBMS. Normally, if you run a SELECT * FROM SALESPERSON query on the table, the data appears in the order in which they were input, unless you added an ORDER BY clause.
10. Click the **Shutter Bar Open/Close** button to expand the Navigation Pane.
11. Click the **Save** button on the Quick Access Toolbar to save the change to the table layout.
12. Close the SALESPERSON table.

At this point, the SALESPERSON table has been created and populated. At Wallingford Motors each customer is assigned to one and only one salesperson, so now we need to create the relationship between SALESPERSON and CUSTOMER. This will require a foreign key in CUSTOMER to provide the needed link to SALESPERSON.

The problem is that the column needed for the foreign key—NickName—does not exist in CUSTOMER. Therefore, before creating the foreign key constraint we must modify the CUSTOMER table by adding the NickName column and the appropriate data values.

Figure AW-3-34 shows the column characteristics for the NickName column in the CUSTOMER table, and Figure AW-3-35 shows the data for the column.

## FIGURE AW-3-34

### Database Column Characteristics for the NickName Column

| Column Name | Type | Key | Required | Remarks |
|---|---|---|---|---|
| NickName | Text (35) | Foreign Key | Yes | |

## FIGURE AW-3-35

### CUSTOMER NickName Data

| CustomerID | LastName | FirstName | ... | NickName |
|---|---|---|---|---|
| 1 | Griffey | Ben | ... | Big Bill |
| 3 | Christman | Jessica | ... | Billy |
| 4 | Christman | Rob | ... | Tina |
| 5 | Hayes | Judy | ... | Tina |

*(Continued)*

As shown in Figure AW-3-34, NickName is constrained as NOT NULL. As discussed in this chapter, however, adding a populated NOT NULL column requires multiple steps. First, the column must be added as a NULL column. Next, the column values must be added. Finally, the column must be altered to NOT NULL. We could do this by using the Microsoft Access GUI interface, but because we are working with the Microsoft Access SQL in this section we will do these steps in SQL. The needed SQL statements are:

```
ALTER TABLE CUSTOMER
      ADD NickName Char(35) NULL;

UPDATE CUSTOMER
SET        NickName = 'Big Bill'
WHERE      CustomerID = 1;

UPDATE CUSTOMER
SET        NickName = 'Billy'
WHERE      CustomerID = 3;

UPDATE CUSTOMER
SET        NickName = 'Tina'
WHERE      CustomerID = 4;

UPDATE CUSTOMER
SET        NickName = 'Tina'
WHERE      CustomerID = 5;

ALTER TABLE CUSTOMER
      ALTER COLUMN NickName Char(35) NOT NULL;
```

### Creating and Populating the NickName Column in the CUSTOMER Table Using Microsoft Access SQL

1. As described previously, open a Microsoft Access query window in SQL view.
2. Type the SQL code for the first SQL ALTER TABLE statement into the query window.
3. Click the **Run** button.
   - **NOTE:** The only indication that the command has run successfully is the fact that *no* error message is displayed. To see the new column in the CUSTOMER table, you would have to open the CUSTOMER table—we'll do that *after* we've completed all the SQL commands in this set of steps.
4. Type the SQL code for the first SQL UPDATE statement into the query window.
5. Click the **Run** button. When the dialog box appears, asking you to confirm that you want to insert the data, click the **Yes** button in the dialog box. The data are inserted into the table.
6. Repeat steps 4 and 5 for the rest of the SQL UPDATE statements for the CUSTOMER data.
7. Type the SQL code for the second SQL ALTER TABLE statement into the query window.
8. Click the **Run** button.
   - **NOTE:** Again, the only indication that the command has run successfully is the fact that *no* error message is displayed.
9. Close the Query1 window. A dialog box appears, asking if you want to save the query. Click the **No** button—there is no need to save this SQL statement.
10. Open the **CUSTOMER** table.

FIGURE AW-3-36

The CUSTOMER Table with NickName Data

The **Design View** button

The added **NickName** column and data

11. Click the **Shutter Bar Open/Close** button to minimize the Navigation Pane and then scroll to the right so that the added NickName column and the data in it are displayed. The table looks as shown in Figure AW-3-36.
12. Click the **Shutter Bar Open/Close** button to expand the Navigation Pane and then click the Design View button to switch the **CUSTOMER** table into Design view.
13. Click the **NickName** field name to select it.
14. The table with the added NickName column looks as shown in Figure AW-3-37. Note that the data are required in the column—this is the Microsoft Access equivalent of NOT NULL.
15. Close the CUSTOMER table.

### Adding Referential Integrity Constraints Using Microsoft Access SQL

Now that the NickName column has been added and populated in the CUSTOMER table we can create the needed referential integrity constraint by adding a foreign key

FIGURE AW-3-37

The Altered CUSTOMER Table

The added **NickName** column

Data in the column are required, which is the Microsoft Access equivalent of NOT NULL

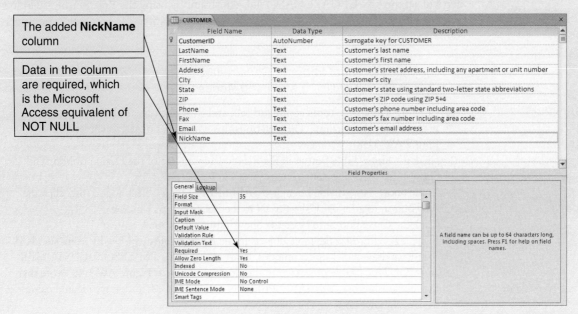

*(Continued)*

constraint between SALESPERSON and CUSTOMER. Because NickName is not a surrogate key, we will want any changed values of NickName in SALESPERSON to be updated in CUSTOMER. However, if a row is deleted from SALESPERSON we do *not* want that deletion to cause the deletion of CUSTOMER data. Therefore, the needed constraint, written as an SQL ALTER TABLE statement, is:

```
ALTER TABLE CUSTOMER
       ADD CONSTRAINT CUSTOMER_SP_FK FOREIGN KEY(NickName)
            REFERENCES SALESPERSON(NickName)
                 ON UPDATE CASCADE;
```

Unfortunately, as discussed in this chapter, Microsoft Access SQL does not support ON UPDATE and ON DELETE clauses. Therefore, we have to set ON UPDATE CASCADE manually after creating the basic constraint with the SQL statement:

```
ALTER TABLE CUSTOMER
       ADD CONSTRAINT CUSTOMER_SP_FK FOREIGN KEY(NickName)
            REFERENCES SALESPERSON(NickName);
```

### Creating the Referential Integrity Constraint Between CUSTOMER and SALESPERSON Using Microsoft Access SQL

1. As described previously, open a Microsoft Access query window in SQL view.
2. Type the SQL code for the SQL ALTER TABLE statement into the query window.
3. Click the **Run** button.
   - **NOTE:** As before, the only indication that the command has run successfully is the fact that *no* error message is displayed.
4. Close the Query1 window. A dialog box appears, asking if you want to save the query. Click the **No** button—there is no need to save this SQL statement.

### Modifying Microsoft Access Databases to Add Constraints Not Supported by Microsoft Access SQL

We will set the ON UPDATE CASCADE constraint by using the Relationships window and the Edit Relationships dialog box, as discussed in Chapter 2's section of "The Access Workbench."

### Creating a Referential Integrity Constraint Between CUSTOMER and SALESPERSON Using Microsoft Access SQL

1. Click the **Database Tools** command tab, and then click the **Relationships** button in the Show/Hide group. The Relationships window appears, as shown in Figure AW-3-38.
2. Click the **Show Table** button in the Relationships group of the Design ribbon. The Show Table dialog box appears, as shown in Figure AW-3-39.
3. In the Show Table dialog box, click **SALESPERSON** to select it, and then click the **Add** button to add SALESPERSON to the Relationships window.
4. Click the **Close** button to close the Show Table dialog box.
5. Rearrange and resize the table objects in the Relationships window by using standard Windows drag-and-drop techniques. Rearrange the SALESPERSON, CUSTOMER, and CONTACT table objects until they look as shown in Figure AW-3-40. Note that the relationship between SALESPERSON and CUSTOMER that we created using SQL is already shown in the diagram.

**FIGURE AW-3-38**

The Relationships Window with the Current Relationship Diagram

The **Show Table** button

This is the relationship diagram as we created it in Chapter 2's section of "The Access Workbench"—note that the NickName column has been added to CUSTOMER

**FIGURE AW-3-39**

Adding the SALESPERSON Table to the Relationship Diagram

The **Show Table** dialog box—click a table name and then click the **Add** button to add a table to the relationship diagram

The **Add** button

When you have added all the tables needed, click the **Close** button

6. Right-click the **relationship line** between SALESPERSON and CUSTOMER, and then click **Edit Relationship** in the shortcut menu that appears. The **Edit Relationships** dialog box appears. Note that the **Enforce Referential Integrity** check box is already checked—this was set by the SQL ALTER TABLE statement that created the relationship between the two tables.

7. Set ON UPDATE CASCADE by clicking the **Cascade Update Related Fields** check box. The Edit Relationships dialog box now looks as shown in Figure AW-3-41.

8. Click the **OK** button to close the Edit Relationships dialog box.

9. Close the Relationships window. When you do so, a Microsoft Access dialog box appears, asking whether you want to save the changes to the layout of "Relationships." Click the **Yes** button to save the changes and close Relationships.

*(Continued)*

## FIGURE AW-3-40

### The Updated Relationship Diagram

The relationship between SALESPERSON and CUSTOMER already exists—it was created using SQL—so right-click the **relationship line** and then click **Edit Relationship** in the shortcut menu that appears to display the **Edit Relationships** dialog box

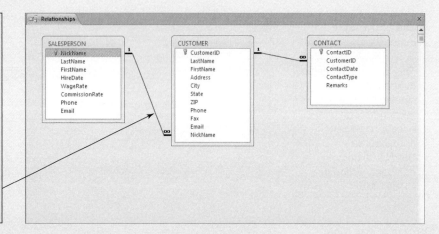

## FIGURE AW-3-41

### The Completed Edit Relationships Dialog Box

The **Enforce Referential Integrity** check box is already selected because of the SQL CONSTRAINT FOREIGN KEY statement

Check the **Cascade Update Related Fields** check box to set the equivalent of the SQL ON UPDATE CASCADE statement

Leave the **Cascade Delete Related Fields** check box *unchecked*—this is equivalent to the SQL ON DELETE NO ACTION statement

### Closing the Database and Exiting Microsoft Access

Now we are done adding the SALESPERSON table to the database. We created the SALESPERSON table, added data, altered the CUSTOMER data with a new column and foreign key values, and created the referential integrity constraint between the two tables. In the process, we saw where Microsoft Access SQL does not support the standard SQL language and learned how to use the Microsoft Access GUI to compensate for the lacking SQL language features.

That completes the work we will do in this chapter's section of "The Access Workbench." As usual, we finish by closing the database and Microsoft Access.

### Closing the WMCRM Database and Exiting Microsoft Access

1. Close the WMCRM database and exit Microsoft Access by clicking the **Close** button in the upper-right corner of the Microsoft Access window.

## SUMMARY

Structured Query Language (SQL) is a data sublanguage that has constructs for defining and processing a database. SQL has several components, two of which are discussed in this chapter: a data definition language (DDL), which is used for creating database tables and other structures, and a data manipulation language (DML), which is used to query and modify database data. SQL can be embedded into scripting languages, such as VBScript, or programming languages, such as Java and C#. In addition, SQL statements can be processed from a command window. SQL was developed by IBM and has been endorsed as a national standard by the American National Standards Institute (ANSI). There have been several versions of SQL. Our discussion is based on SQL-92. However, later versions exist that have added new features, particularly support for Extensible Markup Language (XML). Modern DBMS products provide graphic facilities for accomplishing many of the tasks that SQL does, but there are still many circumstances that require manually creating SQL statements.

Microsoft Access 2010 uses a variant of SQL known as ANSI-89 SQL, or Microsoft Jet SQL, which differs significantly from SQL-92. Not all SQL statements written in SQL-92 and later versions run in Microsoft Access ANSI-89 SQL.

You use the CREATE TABLE statement for creating relations. Each column is described in three parts: column name, data type, and optional column constraints. The following column constraints were discussed in this chapter: PRIMARY KEY, NULL, NOT NULL, and UNIQUE. The DEFAULT keyword (which may or may not be treated as a constraint depending upon the DBMS) was also considered. If no column constraint is specified, the column is set to NULL.

Standard data types are Char, VarChar, Integer, Numeric, and DateTime. These types have been supplemented by DBMS vendors. Figure 3-5 shows some of the additional data types for SQL Server, Oracle Database, and MySQL.

If a primary key has only one column, you can define it by using the primary key constraint. Another way to define a primary key is to use the table constraint. You can use such constraints to define single-column and multicolumn primary keys, and you can also implement referential integrity constraints by defining foreign keys. Foreign key definitions can specify that updates and deletions should cascade.

After the tables and constraints are created, you can add data by using the INSERT command, and you can query data by using the SELECT command. The basic format of the SQL SELECT command is SELECT (column names or the asterisk symbol [*]), FROM (table names, separated by commas if there is more than one), WHERE (conditions). You can use SELECT to obtain specific columns, specific rows, or both.

Conditions after WHERE require single quotes around values for Char and VarChar columns but no single quotes for Integer and Numeric columns. You can specify compound conditions with AND and OR. You can use sets of values with IN (match any in the set) and NOT IN (not match any in the set). You can use the wildcard symbols _ and % (? and * in Microsoft Access) with LIKE to specify a single unknown character or multiple unknown characters, respectively. You can use IS NULL to test for null values.

You can sort results by using the ORDER BY command. The five SQL built-in functions are COUNT, SUM, MAX, MIN, and AVG. SQL can also perform mathematical calculations. You can create groups by using GROUP BY, and you can limit groups by using HAVING. If the keywords WHERE and HAVING both occur in an SQL statement, WHERE is applied before HAVING.

You can query multiple tables by using either subqueries or joins. If all the result data come from a single table, then subqueries can be used. If results come from two or more tables, then joins must be used. The JOIN . . . ON syntax can be used for joins. Rows that do not match the join conditions do not appear in the results. Outer joins can be used to ensure that all rows from a table appear in the results.

You can modify data by using UPDATE and delete data by using DELETE. UPDATE and DELETE can easily cause disasters, so the commands must be used with great care.

You can remove tables (and their data) from a database by using DROP TABLE. You can remove constraints by using the ALTER TABLE DROP CONSTRAINT command. You can modify tables and constraints by using the ALTER TABLE command. Finally, you can use the CHECK constraint to validate data values.

## KEY TERMS

ALTER TABLE statement
American National Standards
   Institute (ANSI)
AND keyword
AS keyword
ASC keyword
asterisk (*)
AVG
business rule
CASCADE keyword
CHECK constraint
comparison operators
CONSTRAINT keyword
COUNT
CREATE TABLE statement
data definition language (DDL)
data manipulation language
   (DML)
data sublanguage
DEFAULT keyword
DELETE command
DESC keyword
DISTINCT keyword

DROP TABLE statement
equijoin
Extensible Markup Language
   (XML)
GROUP BY clause
HAVING clause
IDENTITY (M,N) phrase
IN keyword
inner join
INSERT statement
IS NOT NULL phrase
IS NULL keyword
join operation
JOIN . . . ON syntax
LEFT keyword
LIKE keyword
MAX
MIN
NO ACTION keyword
NOT IN phrase
NOT keyword
NOT LIKE phrase
NOT NULL constraint

NULL constraint
ON DELETE phrase
ON UPDATE phrase
OR keyword
ORDER BY clause
outer join
percent sign (%)
PRIMARY KEY constraint
Query by Example (QBE)
question mark (?)
RIGHT keyword
SQL built-in functions
SQL SELECT/FROM/WHERE
   framework
SQL view
Structured Query Language
   (SQL)
subquery
SUM
underscore symbol (_)
UNIQUE constraint
UPDATE . . . SET command
wildcard characters

## REVIEW QUESTIONS

**3.1**  What does SQL stand for?

**3.2**  Why is it important to learn SQL?

**3.3**  Explain the importance of SQL-92.

**3.4**  What is a data sublanguage?

**3.5**  Describe in your own words the purpose of the two business rules listed on page 118.

**3.6**  Why do some standard SQL-92 statements fail to run successfully in Microsoft Access?

Use the following tables for your answers to questions 3.7 through 3.50:

PET_OWNER (OwnerID, OwnerLastName, OwnerFirstName, OwnerPhone, OwnerEmail)

PET (PetID, PetName, PetType, PetBreed, PetDOB, *OwnerID*)

Sample data for these tables are shown in Figures 3-15 and 3-16. For each SQL statement you write, show the results based on these data.

If possible, run the statements you write for the questions that follow in an actual DBMS, as appropriate, to obtain results. Name your database Pet-Database. Use data types that are consistent with the DBMS you are using. If you are not using an actual DBMS, consistently represent data types by using either the SQL Server, Oracle Database, or MySQL data types shown in Figure 3.5.

**3.7**   Write an SQL CREATE TABLE statement to create the PET_OWNER table, with OwnerID as a surrogate key. Justify you choices of column properties. Write SQL Statements to insert the data in Figure 3-15 into the PET_OWNER table.

**3.8**   Write an SQL CREATE TABLE statement to create the PET table *without* a referential integrity constraint on OwnerID in PET. Justify your choices of column properties. Why not make every column NOT NULL? Write SQL Statements to insert the data in Figure 3-16 into the PET table.

**3.9**   Create a referential integrity constraint on OwnerID in PET. Assume that deletions should cascade.

The following table schema for the PET_2 table is an alternate version of the PET table:

PET_2 (PetName, PetType, PetBreed, PetDOB, *OwnerID*)

**3.10**   Create a referential integrity constraint on OwnerID in PET. Assume that deletions should not cascade.

**3.11**   Write the required SQL statements to create the PET_2 table.

**3.12**   Is PET or PET_2 a better design? Explain your rationale.

---

## FIGURE 3-15

**PET_OWNER Data**

| OwnerID | OwnerLastName | OwnerFirstName | OwnerPhone | OwnerEmail |
|---------|---------------|----------------|------------|------------|
| 1 | Downs | Marsha | 555-537-8765 | Marsha.Downs@somewhere.com |
| 2 | James | Richard | 555-537-7654 | Richard.James@somewhere.com |
| 3 | Frier | Liz | 555-537-6543 | Liz.Frier@somewhere.com |
| 4 | Trent | Miles | | Miles.Trent@somewhere.com |

---

## FIGURE 3-16

**PET Data**

| PetID | PetName | PetType | PetBreed | PetDOB | OwnerID |
|-------|---------|---------|----------|--------|---------|
| 1 | King | Dog | Std. Poodle | 27-Feb-09 | 1 |
| 2 | Teddy | Cat | Cashmere | 01-Feb-10 | 2 |
| 3 | Fido | Dog | Std. Poodle | 17-Jul-08 | 1 |
| 4 | AJ | Dog | Collie Mix | 05-May-09 | 3 |
| 5 | Cedro | Cat | Unknown | 06-Jun-07 | 2 |
| 6 | Wooley | Cat | Unknown | NULL | 2 |
| 7 | Buster | Dog | Border Collie | 11-Dec-06 | 4 |

**3.13** Write the SQL statements necessary to remove the PET_OWNER table from the database. Assume that the PET table is to be removed. *Do not run these commands in an actual database!*

**3.14** Write the SQL statements necessary to remove the PET_OWNER table from the database. Assume that the referential integrity constraint is to be removed. *Do not run these commands in an actual database!*

**3.15** Write an SQL statement to display all columns of all rows of PET. Use the asterisk (*) notation.

**3.16** Write an SQL statement to display all columns of all rows of PET. Do not use the asterisk (*) notation.

**3.17** Write an SQL statement to display the PetBreed column of PET.

**3.18** Write an SQL statement to display the PetBreed column of PET. Do not show duplicates.

**3.19** Write an SQL statement to display the PetBreed and PetType of all pets.

**3.20** Write an SQL statement to display the PetBreed, PetType, and PetDOB of all pets having the PetType of Dog.

**3.21** Write an SQL statement to display the PetID, PetName, PetBreed, and PetType for all pets having a four-character name starting with K.

**3.22** Write an SQL statement to display the PetName, PetBreed, and PetType for all pets that are not of PetType of Dog, Bird, or Fish.

**3.23** Write an SQL statement to display the PetBreed, PetType, and PetDOB of all pets having the PetType of Dog and the PetBreed of Std. Poodle.

**3.24** Write an SQL statement to display the OwnerLastName, OwnerFirstName, and OwnerEmail of all owners who have an email address ending with somewhere.com. Assume that email account names can be any number of characters.

**3.25** Write an SQL statement to display the OwnerLastName, OwnerFirstName, and OwnerEmail of any owner who has a NULL value for OwnerPhone.

**3.26** Write an SQL statement to display the PetName and PetBreed of all pets, sorted by PetName.

**3.27** Write an SQL statement to display the PetName and PetBreed of all pets, sorted by PetBreed in ascending order and by PetName in descending order within PetBreed.

**3.28** Write an SQL statement to count the number of distinct breeds.

The following table schema for the PET_3 table is another alternate version of the PET table:

PET_3 (PetID, PetName, PetBreed, PetType, PetDOB, PetWeight, *OwnerID*)

Data for PET_3 is shown in Figure 3-17. Except as specifically noted in the question itself, use the PET_3 table for your answers to all the remaining Review Questions.

**3.29** Write an SQL statement to count the number of pets.

**3.30** Write SQL Statements to create the PET_3 table, and to insert the data in Figure 3-17 into the PET_3 table. Assume that Weight is Numeric(4,1):

**3.31** Write an SQL statement to display the minimum, maximum, and average weight of dogs.

**3.32** Write an SQL statement to group the data by PetBreed and display the average weight per breed.

**3.33** Answer question 3.32 but consider only breeds for which two or more pets are included in the database.

**3.34** Answer question 3.33 but do not consider any pet having the PetBreed Unknown.

**FIGURE 3-17**

PET_3 Data

| PetID | PetName | PetType | PetBreed | PetDOB | PetWeight | OwnerID |
|-------|---------|---------|----------|--------|-----------|---------|
| 1 | King | Dog | Std. Poodle | 27-Feb-09 | 25.5 | 1 |
| 2 | Teddy | Cat | Cashmere | 01-Feb-10 | 10.5 | 2 |
| 3 | Fido | Dog | Std. Poodle | 17-Jul-08 | 28.5 | 1 |
| 4 | AJ | Dog | Collie Mix | 05-May-09 | 20.0 | 3 |
| 5 | Cedro | Cat | Unknown | 06-Jun-07 | 9.5 | 2 |
| 6 | Wooley | Cat | Unknown | NULL | 9.5 | 2 |
| 7 | Buster | Dog | Border Collie | 11-Dec-06 | 25.0 | 4 |

**3.35** Write an SQL statement to display the OwnerLastName, OwnerFirstName, and OwnerEmail of any owners of cats. Use a subquery.

**3.36** Write an SQL statement to display the OwnerLastName, OwnerFirstName, and OwnerEmail of any owners of cats with the name Teddy. Use a subquery.

The following table schema for the BREED table shows a new table to be added to the pet database:

BREED (BreedName, MinWeight, MaxWeight, AverageLifeExpectancy)

Assume that PetBreed in PET_3 is a foreign key that matches the primary key BreedName in BREED, and that PetBreed in PET_3 is now a foreign key linking the two tables with the referential integrity constraint:

PetBreed in PET_3 must exist in BreedName in BREED

(If needed, you may also assume that a similar referential integrity constraint exists between PET and BREED and between PET_2 and BREED). The BREED table data are shown in Figure 3-18.

**3.37** Write SQL Statements to (1) create the BREED table, (2) insert the data in Figure 3-18 into the BREED table, (3) alter the PET_3 table so that PetBreed is a foreign key referencing BreedName in BREED, and (4) display the OwnerLastName, OwnerFirstName, and OwnerEmail of any owner of a pet that has an AverageLifeExpectancy value greater than than 15 using a subquery.

**3.38** Answer question 3.35 but use a join.

**3.39** Write an SQL statement to display the OwnerLastName, OwnerFirstName, PetName, PetType, PetBreed and AverageLifeExpectancy for pets with a known PetBreed.

**3.40** Answer question 3.36 but use a join.

**3.41** As in question 3.37, write an SQL Statement to display the OwnerLastName, OwnerFirstName, and OwnerEmail of any owner of a pet that has an AverageLifeExpectancy value greater than 15, but use joins.

**FIGURE 3-18**

BREED Data

| BreedName | MinWeight | MaxWeight | AverageLifeExpectancy |
|-----------|-----------|-----------|------------------------|
| Border Collie | 15.0 | 22.5 | 20 |
| Cashmere | 10.0 | 15.0 | 12 |
| Collie Mix | 17.5 | 25.0 | 18 |
| Std. Poodle | 22.5 | 30.0 | 18 |
| Unknown | | | |

**FIGURE 3-19**

Additional PET_OWNER Data

| OwnerID | OwnerLastName | OwnerFirstName | OwnerPhone | OwnerEmail |
|---------|---------------|----------------|------------|------------|
| 5 | Rogers | Jim | 555-232-3456 | Jim.Rogers@somewhere.com |
| 6 | Keenan | Mary | 555-232-4567 | Mary.Keenan@somewhere.com |
| 7 | Melnik | Nigel | 555-232-5678 | Nigel.Melnik@somewhere.com |
| 8 | Mayberry | Jenny | 555-454-1243 | |
| 9 | Roberts | Ken | 555-454-2354 | |
| 10 | Taylor | Sam | 555-454-3465 | |

**3.42** Write SQL statements to add three new rows to the PET_OWNER table. Assume that OwnerID is a surrogate key and the DBMS will provide a value for it. Use the first three lines of the data provided in Figure 3-19.

**3.43** Write SQL statements to add three new rows to the PET_OWNER table. Assume that OwnerID is a surrogate key and the DBMS will provide a value for it. Assume, however, that you have only OwnerLastName, OwnerFirstName, and OwnerPhone and that OwnerEmail is NULL. Use the last three lines of the data provided in Figure 3-19.

**3.44** Write SQL statements to change the value of Std. Poodle in BreedName of BREED to Poodle, Std. When you do this, what happens to the values of PetBreed in PET_3?

**3.45** Explain what will happen if you leave the WHERE clause off your answer to question 3.44.

**3.46** Write an SQL statement to delete all rows of pets of PetType Anteater. What will happen if you forget to code the WHERE clause in this statement?

**3.47** Write an SQL statement to add a PetWeight column like the one in PET_3 to the PET table, given that this column is NULL. Again, assume that Weight is Numeric(4,1).

**3.48** Write SQL statements to insert data into the PetWeight column you created in question 3.47. Use the PetWeight from the PET_3 table as shown in Figure 3-17.

**3.49** Write SQL statements to add a PetWeight column like the one in PET_3 to the PET table, given that this column is NOT NULL. Again, assume that PetWeight is Numeric(4,1). Use the same weight data you used in question 3.48.

**3.50** Write an SQL statement to add a CHECK constraint to the PET table so that the weight data recorded in the PetWeight column you added to the table in either question 3.47 or 3.49 is less than 250.

**3.51** Write an SQL statement to drop the PetWeight column you added to the PET table in either question 3.47 or 3.49.

## EXERCISES

The following is a set of tables for the Art Course database shown in Figure 1-10. For the data for these tables, use the data shown in Figure 1-10.

CUSTOMER (<u>CustomerNumber</u>, CustomerLastName, CustomerFirstName, Phone)

COURSE (<u>CourseNumber</u>, Course, CourseDate, Fee)

ENROLLMENT (*<u>CustomerNumber</u>, <u>CourseNumber</u>*, AmountPaid)

where:

CustomerNumber in ENROLLMENT must exist in CustomerNumber in CUSTOMER

CourseNumber in ENROLLMENT must exist in CourseNumber in COURSE

CustomerNumber and CourseNumber are surrogate keys. Therefore, these numbers will never be modified, and there is no need for cascading updates. No customer data are ever deleted, so there is no need to cascade deletions. Courses can be deleted, and if there are enrollment entries for a deleted class they should also be deleted.

These tables, referential integrity constraints, and data are used as the basis for the SQL statements you will create in the exercises that follow. If possible, run these statements in an actual DBMS, as appropriate, to obtain results. Name your database Art-Course-Database. For each SQL statement you write, show the results based on these data. Use data types consistent with the DBMS you are using. If you are not using an actual DBMS, consistently represent data types using either the SQL Server, Oracle Database, or MySQL data types shown in Figure 3-5.

**3.52** Write and run the SQL statements necessary to create the tables and their referential integrity constraints.

**3.53** Populate the tables with data.

**3.54** Write and run an SQL query to list all occurrences of Adv. Pastels. Include all associated data for each occurrence of the class.

**3.55** Write and run an SQL query to list all students and courses they are registered for. Include, in this order, CustomerNumber, CustomerLastName, CustomerFirstName, Phone, CourseNumber, AmoutPaid.

**3.56** Write and run an SQL query to list all students registered in Adv. Pastels starting on October 1, 2011. Include, in this order, Course, CourseDate, Fee, CustomerLastName, CustomerFirstName, and Phone.

**3.57** Write and run an SQL query to list all students registered in Adv. Pastels starting on October 1, 2011. Include in this order, Course, CourseDate, CustomerLastName, CustomerFirstName, Phone, Fee, and AmountPaid. Use a join.

**3.58** Modify your query to include all students, regardless of whether they registered in the Adv. Pastels, starting October 1, 2011. Include, in this order, CustomerLastName, CustomerFirstName, Phone, Course, CourseDate, Fee, and AmountPaid.

**3.59** Write a set of SQL statements (*Hint:* Use the SQL ALTER TABLE command.) to add a FullFeePaid column to ENROLLMENT and populate the column, assuming that the column is NULL. The only possible values for this column are Yes and No. (Compare COURSE.Fee to ENROLLMENT.AmountPaid to determine data values.)

**3.60** Write a set of SQL statements (*Hint:* Use the SQL ALTER TABLE command.) to add a FullFeePaid column to ENROLLMENT and populate the column, assuming that the column is NOT NULL. The only possible values for this column are Yes and No. (Compare COURSE.Fee to ENROLLMENT.AmountPaid to determine data values.) What is the difference between your answer to this question and your answer to question 3.59?

**3.61** Write an ALTER TABLE statement to add a CHECK constraint to the ENROLLMENT table to ensure that the value of FullFeePaid is either Yes or No.

The following exercises are intended for use with a DBMS other than Microsoft Access. If you are using Microsoft Access, see the equivalent questions in the "Access Workbench Exercises" that follow.

**3.62** If you have not already done so, create the WPC database, tables, and relationships described in this chapter, using the SQL DBMS of your choice. Be sure to populate the tables with the data shown in Figure 3-2.

**3.63** Using the SQL DBMS of your choice, create and run queries to answer the questions in exercise AW.3.1.

**3.64** Using the SQL DBMS of your choice, complete steps A through E in exercise AW.3.3, but *exclude step F.*

## ACCESS WORKBENCH KEY TERMS

Allow Zero Length field property
Decimal Places field property
Default Value field property
Field Size field property

Format field property
Indexed field property
parameterized query

Validation Rule field property
Yes (Duplicates OK)
Yes (No Duplicates)

## ACCESS WORKBENCH EXERCISES

In the "Access Workbench Exercises" in Chapters 1 and 2, you created a database for the Wedgewood Pacific Corporation (WPC) of Seattle, Washington. In this set of exercises, you will:

- Create and run queries against the database by using Microsoft Access SQL
- Create and run queries against the database by using Microsoft Access QBE
- Create tables and relationships by using Microsoft Access SQL
- Populate tables by using Microsoft Access SQL

**AW.3.1**    Using Microsoft Access SQL, create and run queries to answer the questions that follow. Save each query using the query name format SQLQuery-AWE-3-1-##, where the ## sign is replaced by the letter designator of the question. For example, the first query will be saved as SQLQuery-AWE-3-1-A.

**A.**    What projects are in the PROJECT table? Show all information for each project.

**B.**    What are the ProjectID, ProjectName, StartDate, and EndDate values of projects in the PROJECT table?

**C.**    What projects in the PROJECT table started before August 1, 2010? Show all the information for each project.

**D.**    What projects in the PROJECT table have not been completed? Show all the information for each project.

**E.**    Who are the employees assigned to each project? Show ProjectID, EmployeeNumber, LastName, FirstName, and Phone.

**F.**    Who are the employees assigned to each project? Show ProjectID, ProjectName, and Department. Show EmployeeNumber, LastName, FirstName, and Phone.

**G.**    Who are the employees assigned to each project? Show ProjectID, ProjectName, Department, and Department Phone. Show EmployeeNumber, LastName, FirstName, and Employee Phone. Sort by ProjectID, in ascending order.

**H.**    Who are the employees assigned to projects run by the marketing department? Show ProjectID, ProjectName, Department, and Department Phone. Show EmployeeNumber, LastName, FirstName, and Employee Phone. Sort by ProjectID, in ascending order.

**I.**    How many projects are being run by the marketing department? Be sure to assign an appropriate column name to the computed results.

**J.** What is the total MaxHours of projects being run by the marketing department? Be sure to assign an appropriate column name to the computed results.

**K.** What is the average MaxHours of projects being run by the marketing department? Be sure to assign an appropriate column name to the computed results.

**L.** How many projects are being run by each department? Be sure to display each DepartmentName and to assign an appropriate column name to the computed results.

**AW.3.2** Using Microsoft Access QBE, create and run new queries to answer the questions in exercise AW.3.1. Save each query using the query name format QBEQuery-AWE-3-1-##, where the ## sign is replaced by the letter designator of the question. For example, the first query will be saved as QBEQuery-AWE-3-1-A.

**AW.3.3** WPC has decided to keep track of computers used by the employees. In order to do this, two new tables will be added to the database. The schema for these tables, as related to the existing EMPLOYEE table, is:

EMPLOYEE (EmployeeNumber, FirstName, LastName, *Department*, Phone, Email)

COMPUTER (SerialNumber, Make, Model, ProcessorType, ProcessorSpeed, MainMemory, DiskSize)

COMPUTER_ASSIGNMENT (*SerialNumber, EmployeeNumber*, DateAssigned, DateReassigned)

The referential integrity constraints are:

Serial Number in COMPUTER_ASSIGNMENT must exist in SerialNumber in COMPUTER

EmployeeNumber in COMPUTER_ASSIGNMENT must exist in EmployeeNumber in EMPLOYEE

EmployeeNumber is a surrogate key and never changes. Employee records are never deleted from the database. SerialNumber is not a surrogate key because it is not generated by the database. However, a computer's SerialNumber never changes; therefore, there is no need to cascade updates. When a computer is at its end of life, the record in COMPUTER for that computer and all associated records in COMPUTER_ASSIGNMENT are deleted from the database.

**A.** Figure 3-20 shows the column characteristics for the WPC COMPUTER table. Using the column characteristics, use Microsoft Access SQL to create the COMPUTER table and its associated constraints in the WPC database. Are there any table characteristics that cannot be created in SQL? If so, what are they? Use the Microsoft Access GUI to finish setting table characteristics, if necessary.

**B.** The data for the COMPUTER table are in Figure 3-21. Use Microsoft Access SQL to enter these data into your COMPUTER table.

**C.** Figure 3-22 shows the column characteristics for the WPC COMPUTER_ASSIGNMENT table. Using the column characteristics, use Microsoft Access SQL to create the COMPUTER_ASSIGNMENT table and the associated constraints in the WPC database. Are there any table or relationship settings or characteristics that cannot be created in SQL? If so, what are they? Use the Microsoft Access GUI to finish setting table characteristics and relationship settings, if necessary.

*(Continued)*

**FIGURE 3-20**

Database Column Characteristics for the COMPUTER Table

| Column Name | Type | Key | Required | Remarks |
|---|---|---|---|---|
| SerialNumber | Number | Primary Key | Yes | Long Integer |
| Make | Text (12) | No | Yes | Must be "Dell" or "Gateway" or "HP" or "Other" |
| Model | Text (24) | No | Yes | |
| ProcessorType | Text (24) | No | No | |
| ProcessorSpeed | Number | No | Yes | Double [3,2], Between 1.0 and 4.0 |
| MainMemory | Text (15) | No | Yes | |
| DiskSize | Text (15) | No | Yes | |

**FIGURE 3-21**

WPC COMPUTER Data

| Serial Number | Make | Model | Processor Type | Processor Speed | Main Memory | DiskSize |
|---|---|---|---|---|---|---|
| 9871234 | HP | Compaq dx7500 | Intel Core 2 Duo | 2.80 | 2.0 GBytes | 160 GBytes |
| 9871245 | HP | Compaq dx7500 | Intel Core 2 Duo | 2.80 | 2.0 GBytes | 160 GBytes |
| 9871256 | HP | Compaq dx7500 | Intel Core 2 Duo | 2.80 | 2.0 GBytes | 160 GBytes |
| 9871267 | HP | Compaq dx7500 | Intel Core 2 Duo | 2.80 | 2.0 GBytes | 160 GBytes |
| 9871278 | HP | Compaq dx7500 | Intel Core 2 Duo | 2.80 | 2.0 GBytes | 160 GBytes |
| 9871289 | HP | Compaq dx7500 | Intel Core 2 Duo | 2.80 | 2.0 GBytes | 160 GBytes |
| 6541001 | Dell | OptiPlex 960 | Intel Core 2 Quad | 3.00 | 4.0 GBytes | 320 GBytes |
| 6541002 | Dell | OptiPlex 960 | Intel Core 2 Quad | 3.00 | 4.0 GBytes | 320 GBytes |
| 6541003 | Dell | OptiPlex 960 | Intel Core 2 Quad | 3.00 | 4.0 GBytes | 320 GBytes |
| 6541004 | Dell | OptiPlex 960 | Intel Core 2 Quad | 3.00 | 4.0 GBytes | 320 GBytes |
| 6541005 | Dell | OptiPlex 960 | Intel Core 2 Quad | 3.00 | 4.0 GBytes | 320 GBytes |
| 6541006 | Dell | OptiPlex 960 | Intel Core 2 Quad | 3.00 | 4.0 GBytes | 320 GBytes |

**FIGURE 3-22**

Database Column Characteristics for the COMPUTER_ASSIGNMENT Table

| Column Name | Type | Key | Required | Remarks |
|---|---|---|---|---|
| SerialNumber | Number | Primary Key, Foreign Key | Yes | Long Integer |
| EmployeeNumber | Number | Primary Key, Foreign Key | Yes | Long Integer |
| DateAssigned | Date/Time | Primary Key | Yes | Medium Date |
| DateReassigned | Date/Time | No | No | Medium Date |

**FIGURE 3-23**

**WPC COMPUTER_ASSIGNMENT Data**

| SerialNumber | EmployeeNumber | DateAssigned | DateReassigned |
|---|---|---|---|
| 9871234 | 11 | 15-Sep-10 | 21-Oct-10 |
| 9871245 | 12 | 15-Sep-10 | 21-Oct-10 |
| 9871256 | 4 | 15-Sep-10 | |
| 9871267 | 5 | 15-Sep-10 | |
| 9871278 | 8 | 15-Sep-10 | |
| 9871289 | 9 | 15-Sep-10 | |
| 6541001 | 11 | 21-Oct-10 | |
| 6541002 | 12 | 21-Oct-10 | |
| 6541003 | 1 | 21-Oct-10 | |
| 6541004 | 2 | 21-Oct-10 | |
| 6541005 | 3 | 21-Oct-10 | |
| 6541006 | 6 | 21-Oct-10 | |
| 9871234 | 7 | 21-Oct-10 | |
| 9871245 | 10 | 21-Oct-10 | |

**D.** The data for the COMPUTER_ASSIGNMENT table are in Figure 3-23. Use Microsoft Access SQL to enter these data into your COMPUTER_ASSIGNMENT table.

**E.** Who is currently using which computer at WPC? Create an appropriate SQL query to answer this question. Show SerialNumber, Make, Model, ProcessorType, ProcessorSpeed, and DateAssigned. Show EmployeeID, LastName, FirstName, Department, and Employee Phone. Sort first by Department and then by employee LastName. Save this query using the query naming rules in exercise AW.3.1.

**F.** Who is currently using which computer at WPC? Create an appropriate QBE query to answer this question. Show SerialNumber, Make, Model, ProcessorType, ProcessorSpeed and DateAssigned. Show the EmployeeNumber, LastName, FirstName, Department, and Employee Phone. Sort first by Department and then by employee LastName. Save this query using the query naming rules in exercise AW.3.2.

## GARDEN GLORY PROJECT QUESTIONS

Assume that Garden Glory designs a database with the following tables:

OWNER (<u>OwnerID</u>, OwnerName, OwnerEmail, OwnerType)

PROPERTY (<u>PropertyID</u>, PropertyName, Street, City, State, Zip, *OwnerID*)

EMPLOYEE (<u>EmployeeID</u>, LastName, FirstName, CellPhone, ExperienceLevel)

SERVICE (*<u>PropertyID</u>, <u>EmployeeID</u>*, ServiceDate, HoursWorked)

The referential integrity constraints are:

OwnerID in PROPERTY must exist in OwnerID in OWNER

PropertyID in SERVICE must exist in PropertyID in PROPERTY

EmployeeID in SERVICE must exist in EmployeeID in EMPLOYEE

Assume that OwnerID in OWNER, PropertyID in PROPERTY, and EmployeeID in EMPLOYEE are surrogate keys with values as follows:

OwnerID      Start at 1   Increment by 1
PropertyID   Start at 1   Increment by 1
EmployeeID   Start at 1   Increment by 1

Some sample data are shown in Figure 2-29, but you need to create additional data to populate the tables. (Alternatively, your instructor may provide you with a data set.) OwnerType in OWNER is either Individual or Corporation, and set.) ExperienceLevel in EMPLOYEE is one of Junior, Senior, Master, or SuperMaster. These tables, referential integrity constraints, and data are used as the basis for the SQL statements you will create in the exercises that follow. If possible, run these statements in an actual DBMS, as appropriate, to obtain your results. Name your database Garden-Glory.

Use data types consistent with the DBMS you are using. If you are not using an actual DBMS, consistently represent data types using either the SQL Server, Oracle Database, or MySQL data types shown in Figure 3-5. For each SQL statement you write, show the results based on your data.

Write SQL statements and answer questions for this database as follows:

**A.** Write CREATE TABLE statements for each of these tables.

**B.** Write foreign key constraints for the relationships in each of these tables. Make your own assumptions regarding cascading updates and deletions and justify those assumptions. (*Hint:* You can combine the SQL for your answers to questions A and B.)

**C.** Write SQL statements to insert at least three rows of data into each of these tables. Assume that any surrogate key value will be supplied by the DBMS. Use the data in Figure 2-29, as appropriate.

**D.** Write SQL statements to list the data from all columns for all tables.

**E.** Write an SQL statement to list LastName, FirstName, and CellPhone for all employees having an experience level of Master.

**F.** Write an SQL statement to list LastName, FirstName and CellPhone for all employees having an experience level of Master and LastName that begins with the letter *J*.

**G.** Write an SQL statement to list the LastName and FirstName of employees who have worked on a property in Seattle. Use a subquery.

**H.** Answer part G but use a join.

**I.** Write an SQL statement to list the LastName and FirstName of employees who have worked on a property owned by a corporation. Use a subquery.

**J.** Answer part I but use a join.

**K.** Write an SQL statement to show the name and sum of hours worked for each employee.

**L.** Write an SQL statement to show the sum of hours worked for each ExperienceLevel of EMPLOYEE. Sort the results by ExperienceLevel, in descending order.

**M.** Write an SQL statement to show the sum of HoursWorked for each type of OWNER but exclude services of employees who have ExperienceLevel of Junior and exclude any type with less than three members.

**N.** Write an SQL statement to modify all EMPLOYEE rows with ExperienceLevel of Master to SuperMaster.

**O.** Write an SQL statement to switch the values of ExperienceLevel so that all rows currently having the value Junior will have the value Senior and all rows currently having the value Senior will have the value Junior.

**P.** Given your assumptions about cascading deletions in your answer to part B, write the fewest number of DELETE statements possible to remove all the data in your database but leave the table structures intact. Do *not* run these statements if you are using an actual database!

# JAMES RIVER JEWELRY PROJECT QUESTIONS

Assume that James River designs a database with the following tables:

CUSTOMER (<u>CustomerID</u>, LastName, FirstName, Phone, Email)
PURCHASE (<u>InvoiceNumber</u>, InvoiceDate, PreTaxAmount, *CustomerID*)
PURCHASE_ITEM (*<u>InvoiceNumber</u>, <u>ItemNumber</u>*, RetailPrice)
ITEM (<u>ItemNumber</u>, Description, Cost, ArtistName)

The referential integrity constraints are:

CustomerID in PURCHASE must exist in CustomerID in CUSTOMER
InvoiceNumber in PURCHASE_ITEM must exist in InvoiceNumber in PURCHASE
ItemNumber in PURCHASE_ITEM must exist in ItemNumber in ITEM

Assume that CustomerID of CUSTOMER, ItemNumber of ITEM, InvoiceNumber of PURCHASE, and ItemNumber of PURCHASE_ITEM are all surrogate keys with values as follows:

| | | |
|---|---|---|
| CustomerID | Start at 1 | Increment by 1 |
| InvoiceNumber | Start at 1 | Increment by 1 |
| ItemNumber | Start at 1 | Increment by 1 |

Some sample data are shown in Figure 2-30, but you need to create additional data to populate the tables. (Alternatively, your instructor may provide you with a data set.) These tables, referential integrity constraints, and data are used as the basis for the SQL statements you will create in the exercises that follow. If possible, run these statements in an actual DBMS, as appropriate, to obtain your results. Name your database James-River-Jewelry.

Use data types consistent with the DBMS you are using. If you are not using an actual DBMS, consistently represent data types using either the SQL Server, Oracle Database, or MySQL data types shown in Figure 3-5. For each SQL statement you write, show the results based on your data.

Write SQL statements and answer questions for this database as follows:

**A.** Write SQL CREATE TABLE statements for each of these tables.

**B.** Write foreign key constraints for the relationships in each of these tables. Make your own assumptions regarding cascading deletions and justify those assumptions. (*Hint:* You can combine the SQL for your answers to parts A and B.)

**C.** Write SQL statements to insert at least three rows of data into each of these tables. Assume that surrogate key column values will be supplied by the DBMS. Use the data in Figure 2-30, as appropriate.

**D.** Write SQL statements to list the data from all columns for all tables.

**E.** Write an SQL statement to list ItemNumber and Description for all items that cost more than $100.

**F.** Write an SQL statement to list ItemNumber and Description for all items that cost more than $100 and were produced by an artist with a name ending with the letters *son*.

**G.** Write an SQL statement to list LastName and FirstName of customers who have made at least one purchase with PreTaxAmount greater than $200. Use a subquery.

**H.** Answer part G but use a join.

**I.** Write an SQL statement to list LastName and FirstName of customers who have purchased an item that costs more than $50. Use a subquery.

**J.** Answer part I but use a join.

**K.** Write an SQL statement to list the LastName and FirstName of customers who have purchased an item that was created by an artist with a name that begins with the letter *J*. Use a subquery.

**L.** Answer part K but use a join.

**M.** Write an SQL statement to show the LastName, FirstName and sum of PreTaxAmount for each customer.

**N.** Write an SQL statement to show the sum of PreTaxAmount for each ArtistName. Sort the results by ArtistName, in descending order.

**O.** Write an SQL statement to show the sum of PreTaxAmount for each ArtistName but exclude any items that were part of purchases with PreTaxAmount less than or equal to $25.00.

**P.** Write an SQL statement to change all ITEM rows with a name of Baker to Rex Baker.

**Q.** Write SQL statements to switch the values of ArtistName so that all rows currently having the value Baker will have the value Baxter and all rows currently having the value Baxter will have the value Baker.

**R.** Given your assumptions about cascading deletions in your answer to part B, write the fewest number of DELETE statements possible to remove all the data in your database but leave the table structures intact. Do not run these statements if you are using an actual database!

 ## THE QUEEN ANNE CURIOSITY SHOP PROJECT QUESTIONS

Assume that The Queen Anne Curiosity Shop designs a database with the following tables:

CUSTOMER (<u>CustomerID</u>, LastName, FirstName, Address, City, State, ZIP, Phone, Email)

EMPLOYEE (<u>EmployeeID</u>, LastName, FirstName, Phone, Email)

VENDOR (<u>VendorID</u>, CompanyName, ContactLastName, ContactFirstName, Address, City, State, ZIP, Phone, Fax, Email)

ITEM (<u>ItemID</u>, ItemDescription, PurchaseDate, ItemCost, ItemPrice, *VendorID*)

SALE (<u>SaleID</u>, *CustomerID, EmployeeID*, SaleDate, SubTotal, Tax, Total)
SALE_ITEM (<u>*SaleID*</u>, <u>SaleItemID</u>, *ItemID*, ItemPrice)

The referential integrity constraints are:

VendorID in ITEM must exist in VendorID in VENDOR
CustomerID in SALE must exist in CustomerID in CUSTOMER
EmployeeID in SALE must exist in EmployeeID in EMPLOYEE
SaleID in SALE_ITEM must exist in SaleID in SALE
ItemID in SALE_ITEM must exist in ItemID in ITEM

Assume that CustomerID of CUSTOMER, EmployeeID of EMPLOYEE, ItemID of ITEM, SaleID of SALE, and SaleItemID of SALE_ITEM are all surrogate keys with values as follows:

| | | |
|---|---|---|
| CustomerID | Start at 1 | Increment by 1 |
| EmployeeID | Start at 1 | Increment by 1 |
| VendorID | Start at 1 | Increment by 1 |
| ItemID | Start at 1 | Increment by 1 |
| SaleID | Start at 1 | Increment by 1 |

A vendor may be an individual or a company. If the vendor is an individual, the CompanyName field is left blank, while the ContactLastName and ContactFirstName fields must have data values. If the vendor is a company, the company name is recorded in the CompanyName field, and the name of the primary contact at the company is recorded in the ContactLastName and ContactFirstName fields.

Some sample data are shown in Figures 2-31 and 2-32, but you need to create additional data to populate the tables. (Alternatively, your instructor may provide you with a data set.) These tables, referential integrity constraints, and data are used as the basis for the SQL statements you will create in the exercises that follow. If possible, run these statements in an actual DBMS, as appropriate, to obtain your results. Name your database QACS.

Use data types consistent with the DBMS you are using. If you are not using an actual DBMS, consistently represent data types using either the SQL Server, Oracle Database, or MySQL data types shown in Figure 3-5. For each SQL statement you write, show the results based on your data.

Write SQL statements and answer questions for this database as follows:

**A.** Write SQL CREATE TABLE statements for each of these tables.

**B.** Write foreign key constraints for the relationships in each of these tables. Make your own assumptions regarding cascading deletions and justify those assumptions. (*Hint:* You can combine the SQL for your answers to parts A and B.)

**C.** Write SQL statements to insert at least three rows of data into each of these tables. Assume that all surrogate key column values will be supplied by the DBMS. Use the data in Figures 2-31 and 2-32, as appropriate.

**D.** Write SQL statements to list the data from all columns for all tables.

**E.** Write an SQL statement to list the data from all and ItemDescription for all items that cost $1000 or more.

**F.** Write an SQL statement to list ItemID and ItemDescription for all items that cost $1000 or more and were purchased from a vendor whose CompanyName starts with the letters *New*.

**G.** Write an SQL statement to list LastName, FirstName, and Phone of the customer who made the purchase with SaleID 1. Use a subquery.

**H.** Answer part G but use a join.

**I.** Write an SQL statement to list LastName, FirstName, and Phone of the customers who made the purchase with SaleIDs 1, 2, and 3. Use a subquery.

**J.** Answer part I but use a join.

**K.** Write an SQL statement to list LastName, FirstName, and Phone of customers who have made at least one purchase with SubTotal greater than $500. Use a subquery.

**L.** Answer part K but use a join.

**M.** Write an SQL statement to list LastName, FirstName, and Phone of customers who have purchased an item that has an ItemPrice of $500 or more. Use a subquery.

**N.** Answer part M but use a join.

**O.** Write an SQL statement to list LastName, FirstName, and Phone of customers who have purchased an item that was supplied by a vendor with a CompanyName that begins with the letter *L*. Use a subquery.

**P.** Answer part O but use a join.

**Q.** Write an SQL statement to show the sum of SubTotal for each customer. List CustomerID, LastName, FirstName, Phone, and the calculated result. Name the sum of SubTotal as SumOfSubTotal and sort the results by CustomerID, in descending order.

**R.** Write an SQL statement to modify the vendor with CompanyName of *Linens and Things* to *Linens and Other Stuff*.

**S.** Write SQL statements to switch the values of vendor CompanyName so that all rows currently having the value *Linens and Things* will have the value *Lamps and Lighting* and all rows currently having the value *Lamps and Lighting* will have the value *Linens and Things*.

**T.** Given your assumptions about cascading deletions in your answer to part B, write the fewest number of DELETE statements possible to remove all the data in your database but leave the table structures intact. Do *not* run these statements if you are using an actual database!

# SQL Views

**Chapter Objectives**

> Learn basic SQL statements for creating views

> Learn basic SQL statements for using views

> Understand the reasons for using views

In Chapter 3, we discussed SQL in depth. We discussed two basic categories of SQL statements: data definition language (DDL) statements, which are used for creating tables, relationships, and other structures, and data manipulation language (DML) statements, which are used for querying and modifying data. This appendix describes and illustrates SQL views, which extend the DML capabilities of SQL.

## CREATING SQL VIEWS

An **SQL view** is a virtual table that is constructed from other tables or views. A view has no data of its own but uses data stored in tables or retrieved via other views. Views are created using SQL SELECT statements and then used in other SELECT statements just as if they were in any other table. The only limitation on the SQL statements that create the views is that they cannot contain ORDER BY clauses.[1] If the results of a query using a view need to be sorted, the sort order must be provided by the SELECT statement that processes the view.

---

### Does Not Work with Microsoft Access ANSI-89 SQL

Unfortunately, Microsoft Access does not support views. However, Microsoft Access allows you to create a query, name it, and then save it, which is not supported in a standard SQL implementation. You can then process Microsoft Access queries in the same ways that you process views in the following discussion.

**Solution:** Create Microsoft Access view-equivalent queries, as discussed in the section of "The Access Workbench" at the end of this appendix.

---

We will use the WPC database that we created in Chapter 3 as the example database for this discussion of views. You use the SQL **CREATE VIEW statement** to create view structures. The essential format of this statement is:

```
CREATE VIEW ViewName AS
       {SQL SELECT statement};
```

The following statement defines a view named EmployeePhoneView based on the EMPLOYEE table:

```
CREATE VIEW EmployeePhoneView AS
       SELECT    FirstName, LastName, Phone AS EmployeePhone
       FROM      EMPLOYEE;
```

Figure 3A-1 shows the view being created in the SQL Server Management Studio Express Edition, and Figure 3A-2 shows the view being created in the MySQL Workbench.

---

**B T W**

SQL Server 2005, SQL Server 2008, and most other DBMSs process the CREATE VIEW statements as written here without difficulty. However, SQL Server 2000 will not run such statements unless you *remove the semicolon* at the end of the CREATE VIEW statement. We have no idea why SQL Server 2000 works this way, but be aware of this peculiarity if you are using SQL Server 2000.

---

[1]This limitation appears in the SQL-92 standard. Some DBMSs modify this limitation in their implementation of SQL. For example, Oracle Database allows views to include ORDER BY, and SQL Server allows ORDER BY in very limited circumstances.

## FIGURE 3A-1

Creating a View in the Microsoft SQL Server Management Studio

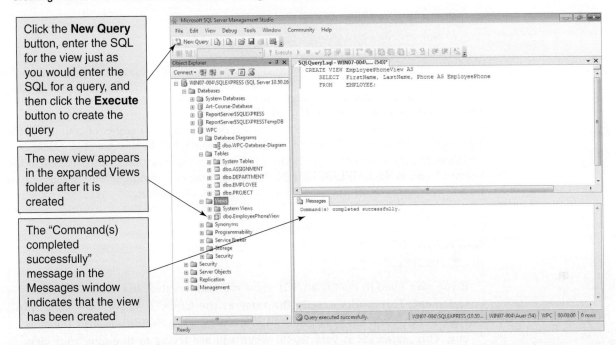

Click the **New Query** button, enter the SQL for the view just as you would enter the SQL for a query, and then click the **Execute** button to create the query

The new view appears in the expanded Views folder after it is created

The "Command(s) completed successfully" message in the Messages window indicates that the view has been created

## FIGURE 3A-2

Creating a View in the MySQL Workbench

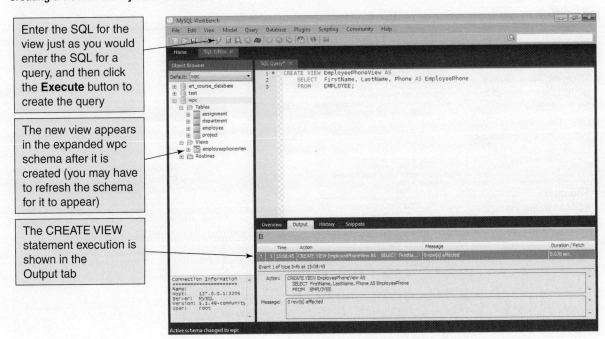

Enter the SQL for the view just as you would enter the SQL for a query, and then click the **Execute** button to create the query

The new view appears in the expanded wpc schema after it is created (you may have to refresh the schema for it to appear)

The CREATE VIEW statement execution is shown in the Output tab

After we create the view, we can use it in the FROM clause of SELECT statements just as you would use a table. The following obtains a list of employee names and phone numbers, sorted first by employee last name and then by employee first name:

```
SELECT      *
FROM        EmployeePhoneView
ORDER BY    LastName, FirstName;
```

Figure 3A-3 shows this SQL statement run in SQL Server Management Studio, and Figure 3A-4 shows it run in the MySQL Workbench.

Note that the number of columns returned depends on the number of columns in the view, not on the number of columns in the underlying table. In this example, SELECT * produces just three columns because the view has just three columns. Also notice that the column Name in the EMPLOYEE table has been renamed EmployeePhone in the view, so the DBMS uses the label EmployeePhone when producing results.

---

**B T W**

If you ever need to modify an SQL view you have created, use the **ALTER VIEW** statement. This works exactly the same as the CREATE VIEW *ViewName* AS statement except that it replaces the existing view definition with the new one. This statement is very useful when you are trying to fine-tune your view definitions.

If you ever want to delete a view, simply use the SQL **DROP VIEW** {*ViewName*} statement.

---

**FIGURE 3A-3**

Using EmployeePhoneView in the Microsoft SQL Server Management Studio

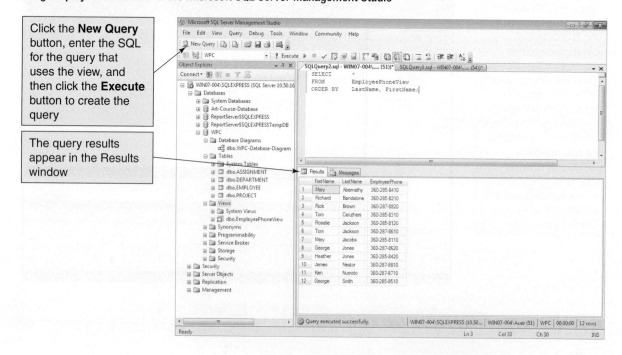

Click the **New Query** button, enter the SQL for the query that uses the view, and then click the **Execute** button to create the query

The query results appear in the Results window

**FIGURE 3A-4**

Using EmployeePhoneView in the MySQL Workbench

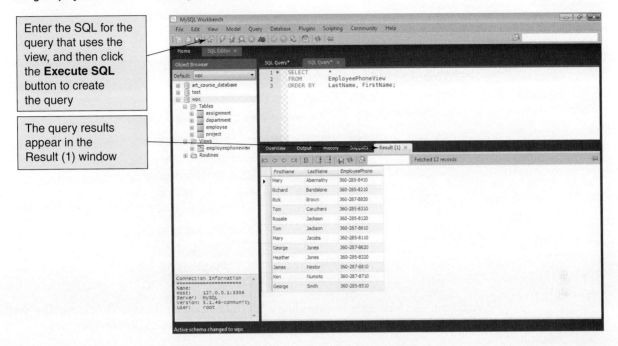

Enter the SQL for the query that uses the view, and then click the **Execute SQL** button to create the query

The query results appear in the Result (1) window

## USING SQL VIEWS

Figure 3A-5 lists some of the uses for views.[2] They can hide columns or rows. They also can be used to display the results of computed columns, to hide complicated SQL syntax, and to layer the use of built-in functions to create results that are not possible with a single SQL statement. We will give examples of each of these uses.

### Using Views to Hide Columns and Rows

Views can be used to hide columns to simplify results or to prevent the display of sensitive data. For example, suppose the users at WPC Ridge want a simplified list of departments that has just the department names and phone numbers. One use for such a view would be to populate a Web page. The following statement defines a view, BasicDepartmentDataView, that will produce that list:

```
CREATE VIEW BasicDepartmentDataView AS
    SELECT    DepartmentName, Phone AS DepartmentPhone
    FROM      DEPARTMENT;
```

**FIGURE 3A-5**

Some Uses for SQL Views

- Hide columns or rows
- Display results of computations
- Hide complicated SQL syntax
- Layer built-in functions

---

[2]Additional uses of SQL views are discussed in David M. Kroenke and David J. Auer, *Database Processing: Fundamentals, Design, and Implementation*, 11th edition (Upper Saddle River, NJ: Prentice Hall, 2010), Chapter 7.

The following SELECT statement obtains a list of department names and phone numbers sorted by the DepartmentName:

```
SELECT      *
FROM        BasicDepartmentDataView
ORDER BY    DepartmentName;
```

The results of a SELECT sorted by DepartmentName on this view are:

| | DepartmentName | DepartmentPhone |
|---|---|---|
| 1 | Accounting | 360-285-8300 |
| 2 | Administration | 360-285-8100 |
| 3 | Finance | 360-285-8400 |
| 4 | Human Resources | 360-285-8500 |
| 5 | InfoSystems | 360-287-8800 |
| 6 | Legal | 360-285-8200 |
| 7 | Marketing | 360-287-8700 |
| 8 | Production | 360-287-8600 |

Views can also hide rows by providing a WHERE clause in the view definition. The next SQL statement defines a view of WPC projects in the Marketing department:

```
CREATE VIEW MarketingDepartmentProjectView AS
      SELECT      ProjectID, ProjectName, MaxHours,
                  StartDate, EndDate
      FROM        PROJECT
      WHERE       Department = 'Marketing';
```

The following SELECT statement obtains a list of projects managed by the Marketing department, sorted by the ProjectID number:

```
SELECT      *
FROM        MarketingDepartmentProjectView
ORDER BY    ProjectID;
```

The results of a SELECT sorted by ProjectID on this view are:

| | ProjectID | ProjectName | MaxHours | StartDate | EndDate |
|---|---|---|---|---|---|
| 1 | 1000 | 2010 Q3 Product Plan | 135.00 | 2010-05-10 ... | 2010-06-15 ... |
| 2 | 1300 | 2010 Q4 Product Plan | 150.00 | 2010-08-10 ... | 2010-09-15 ... |

As desired, only the Marketing department projects are shown in this view. This limitation is not obvious from the results because Department is not included in the view. This characteristic can be good or bad, depending on the use of the view. It is good if this view is used in a setting in which only Marketing department projects matter; it is bad if the view indicates that these projects are the only WPC projects currently under way.

## Using Views to Display Results of Computed Columns

Another use of views is to show the results of computed columns without requiring the user to enter the computation expression. For example, the following view allows the user to compare the maximum hours allocated for each WPC project to the total hours worked to date on the project:

```
CREATE VIEW ProjectHoursToDateView AS
     SELECT      PROJECT.ProjectID,
                 ProjectName,
                 MaxHours AS ProjectMaxHours,
                 SUM(HoursWorked) AS ProjectHoursWorkedToDate
     FROM        PROJECT, ASSIGNMENT
     WHERE       PROJECT.ProjectID = ASSIGNMENT.ProjectID
     GROUP BY    PROJECT.ProjectID;
```

When the view user enters:

```
SELECT      *
FROM        ProjectHoursToDateView
ORDER BY    ProjectID;
```

these results are displayed:

| | ProjectID | ProjectName | ProjectMaxHours | ProjectHoursWorkedToDate |
|---|---|---|---|---|
| 1 | 1000 | 2010 Q3 Product Plan | 135.00 | 160.00 |
| 2 | 1100 | 2010 Q3 Portfolio Analysis | 120.00 | 85.00 |
| 3 | 1200 | 2010 Q3 Tax Preparation | 145.00 | 130.00 |
| 4 | 1300 | 2010 Q4 Product Plan | 150.00 | 165.00 |
| 5 | 1400 | 2010 Q4 Portfolio Analysis | 140.00 | 52.50 |

Placing computations in views has two major advantages. First, it saves users from having to know or remember how to write an expression to get the results they want. Second, it ensures consistent results. If developers who use a computation write their own SQL expressions, they may write the expression differently and obtain inconsistent results.

---

**B T W**

SQL Server requires that any column specified in the SELECT phrase be used in either an SQL built-in function or the GROUP BY phrase. The previous SQL statement is correct SLQ-92 syntax and will run in MySQL as written. However, SQL Server requires you to write:

```
CREATE VIEW ProjectHoursToDateView AS
   SELECT      PROJECT.ProjectID,
               ProjectName,
               MaxHours AS ProjectMaxHours,
               SUM(HoursWorked) AS ProjectHoursWorkedToDate
   FROM        PROJECT, ASSIGNMENT
   WHERE       PROJECT.ProjectID = ASSIGNMENT.ProjectID
   GROUP BY    PROJECT.ProjectID, ProjectName, MaxHours;
```

Note the use of the extra column names in the GROUP BY clause. These are necessary to create the view but have no practical effect on the results.

## Using Views to Hide Complicated SQL Syntax

Another use of views is to hide complicated SQL syntax. By using views, developers do not need to enter complex SQL statements when they want particular results. Also, such views allow developers who do not know how to write complicated SQL statements to enjoy the benefits of such statements. This use of views also ensures consistency.

Suppose that WPC users need to know which employees are assigned to which project and how many hours each employee has worked on that project. To get these results, two joins are necessary: one to join EMPLOYEE to ASSIGNMENT and another to join that result to PROJECT. Along with the two joins, we need an ORDER BY clause to sort the results in the desired order. You saw the SQL statement to do this in Chapter 3:

```
SELECT     ProjectName, FirstName, LastName, HoursWorked
FROM       EMPLOYEE AS E JOIN ASSIGNMENT AS A
           ON   E.EmployeeNumber = A.EmployeeNumber
              JOIN PROJECT AS P
                  ON    A.ProjectID = P.ProjectID
ORDER BY     P.ProjectID, A.EmployeeNumber;
```

Now, we need to make it into a view named EmployeeProjectHoursWorkedView. Remember that we cannot include the ORDER BY clause in the view. If we want to sort the output, we will need to do this when we use the view:

```
CREATE VIEW EmployeeProjectHoursWorkedView AS
     SELECT     ProjectName, FirstName, LastName,
                HoursWorked
     FROM       EMPLOYEE AS E JOIN ASSIGNMENT AS A
                ON  E.EmployeeNumber = A.EmployeeNumber
                   JOIN  PROJECT AS P
                       ON    A.ProjectID = P.ProjectID;
```

This is a complicated SQL statement to write, but after the view is created the results of this statement can be obtained with a simple SELECT statement. When the user uses:

```
SELECT * FROM EmployeeProjectHoursWorkedView;
```

these results will be displayed (and may be reordered as necessary by adding an ORDER BY clause to the SQL query).

| | Project Name | First Name | Last Name | Hours Worked |
|---|---|---|---|---|
| 1 | 2010 Q3 Product Plan | Mary | Jacobs | 30.00 |
| 2 | 2010 Q3 Product Plan | Tom | Jackson | 75.00 |
| 3 | 2010 Q3 Product Plan | Ken | Numoto | 55.00 |
| 4 | 2010 Q3 Portfolio Analysis | Tom | Caruthers | 40.00 |
| 5 | 2010 Q3 Portfolio Analysis | Mary | Abernathy | 45.00 |
| 6 | 2010 Q3 Tax Preparation | Mary | Jacobs | 25.00 |
| 7 | 2010 Q3 Tax Preparation | Rosalie | Jackson | 20.00 |
| 8 | 2010 Q3 Tax Preparation | Tom | Caruthers | 45.00 |
| 9 | 2010 Q3 Tax Preparation | Heather | Jones | 40.00 |
| 10 | 2010 Q4 Product Plan | Mary | Jacobs | 35.00 |
| 11 | 2010 Q4 Product Plan | Tom | Jackson | 80.00 |
| 12 | 2010 Q4 Product Plan | Ken | Numoto | 50.00 |
| 13 | 2010 Q4 Portfolio Analysis | Tom | Caruthers | 15.00 |
| 14 | 2010 Q4 Portfolio Analysis | Heather | Jones | 10.00 |
| 15 | 2010 Q4 Portfolio Analysis | Mary | Abernathy | 27.50 |

Clearly, using the view is much simpler than constructing the join syntax. Even developers who know SQL well will appreciate having a simpler view with which to work.

## Layering Computations and Built-in Functions

Recall from Chapter 3 that you cannot use a computation or a built-in function as part of a WHERE clause. You can, however, construct a view that computes a variable and then write an SQL statement on that view that uses the computed variable in a WHERE clause. To understand this, consider the ProjectHoursToDateView definition created previously:

```
CREATE VIEW ProjectHoursToDateView AS
      SELECT    PROJECT.ProjectID,
                ProjectName,
                MaxHours AS ProjectMaxHours,
                SUM(HoursWorked) AS ProjectHoursWorkedToDate
      FROM      PROJECT, ASSIGNMENT
      WHERE     PROJECT.ProjectID = ASSIGNMENT.ProjectID
      GROUP BY PROJECT.ProjectID;
```

The view definition contains the maximum allocated hours for each project and the total hours actually worked on the project to date as ProjectHoursWorkedToDate. Now we can use ProjectHoursWorkedToDate in both an additional calculation and the WHERE clause, as follows:

```
SELECT    ProjectID, ProjectName, ProjectMaxHours,
          ProjectHoursWorkedToDate
FROM      ProjectHoursToDateView
WHERE     ProjectHoursWorkedToDate > ProjectMaxHours
ORDER BY  ProjectID;
```

Here we are using the result of a computation in a WHERE clause, something that is not allowed in a single SQL statement. This allows users to determine which projects have exceeded the number of hours allocated to them by producing the result:

|   | ProjectID | ProjectName | ProjectMaxHours | ProjectHoursWorkedToDate |
|---|-----------|-------------|-----------------|--------------------------|
| 1 | 1000 | 2010 Q3 Product Plan | 135.00 | 160.00 |
| 2 | 1300 | 2010 Q4 Product Plan | 150.00 | 165.00 |

Such layering can be continued over many levels. We can turn this SELECT statement into another view named ProjectsOverAllocatedMaxHoursView (again without the ORDER BY clause):

```
CREATE VIEW ProjectsOverAllocatedMaxHoursView AS
      SELECT    ProjectID, ProjectName, ProjectMaxHours,
                ProjectHoursWorkedToDate
      FROM      ProjectHoursToDateView
      WHERE     ProjectHoursWorkedToDate > ProjectMaxHours;
```

Now, we can use ProjectsOverAllocatedMaxHoursView in a further calculation—this time to find the number of hours that each project has overrun its allocated hours:

```
SELECT      ProjectID, ProjectName, ProjectMaxHours,
            ProjectHoursWorkedToDate,
            (ProjectHoursWorkedToDate - ProjectMaxHours)
                AS HoursOverMaxAllocated
FROM        ProjectsOverAllocatedMaxHoursView
ORDER BY    ProjectID;
```

Here are the results:

| | ProjectID | ProjectName | ProjectMaxHours | ProjectHoursWorkedToDate | HoursOverMaxAllocated |
|---|---|---|---|---|---|
| 1 | 1000 | 2010 Q3 Product Plan | 135.00 | 160.00 | 25.00 |
| 2 | 1300 | 2010 Q4 Product Plan | 150.00 | 165.00 | 15.00 |

These SQL views are very useful tools for database developers and application programmers.

## THE ACCESS WORKBENCH

### Section 3A

### Working with Views in Microsoft Access

In Chapter 3's section of "The Access Workbench," you learned to work with Microsoft Access SQL and QBE. In this section, you will learn how to create the Microsoft Access equivalent of SQL views.

We will continue to use the WMCRM database we have been using. At this point, we have created and populated the CUSTOMER, CONTACT, and SALESPERSON tables, and we have set the referential integrity constraints between them.

#### Working with SQL Views in Microsoft Access

Although a view is a virtual table, it can also be represented as a stored query. Although most DBMSs do not allow queries to be saved in a database, Microsoft Access does. Microsoft Access allows us to run queries against tables or against saved queries. This gives us a way to implement a **Microsoft Access equivalent of an SQL view:** We simply save the SELECT query that would be used to create the SQL view and use it as we would an SQL view in other queries.

Here is an SQL CREATE VIEW statement that would be used to list customer data from the WMCRM database if we were creating a standard SQL view:

```
CREATE VIEW CustomerPhoneView AS
        SELECT      FirstName, LastName, Phone
        FROM        CUSTOMER;
```

In Microsoft Access, we can create a query—using either Microsoft Access SQL or QBE—based on the SELECT portion of this statement:

```
SELECT      FirstName, LastName, Phone
FROM        CUSTOMER;
```

After we create the query, we save it using a query name that indicates that this query is intended to be used as an SQL view. We can use the naming convention of putting the word *view* at the beginning of any such query name. Thus, we can name this query viewCustomerPhone.

*Opening a Microsoft Access Query Window in Design View and Creating a Microsoft Access Query as a View Equivalent*

1. Start Microsoft Access 2010.
2. Click the **File** command tab to display the Backstage view and then click the **WMCRM.accdb** database file name in the quick access list to open the database.
3. Click the **Create** command tab to display the Create command groups.
4. Click the **Query Design** button.
5. The Query1 tabbed document window is displayed in Design view, along with the Show Table dialog box.
6. Using either the SQL or QBE technique of creating queries, as described in Chapter 3's section of "The Access Workbench," create the query:

```
SELECT  FirstName, LastName, Phone
FROM    CUSTOMER;
```

7. To save the query, click the **Save** button on the Quick Access Toolbar. The Save As dialog box appears.
8. Type in the query name **viewCustomerPhone** and then click the **OK** button. The query is saved, the document window is renamed with the query name, and a newly created viewCustomerPhone query object appears in the Queries section of the Navigation Pane, as shown in Figure AW-3A-1. Note that Figure AW-3A-1 shows the query created in Microsoft Access QBE.
9. Close the viewCustomerPhone window by clicking the document window's **Close** button.

**FIGURE AW-3A-1**

The viewCustomerPhone Query in the Queries Pane

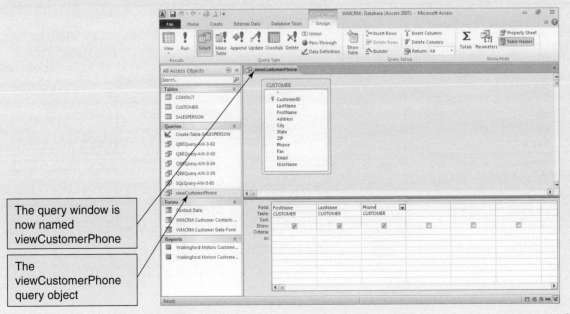

The query window is now named viewCustomerPhone

The viewCustomerPhone query object

*(Continued)*

10. If Microsoft Access displays a dialog box that asks whether you want to save changes to the design of query viewCustomerPhone, click the **Yes** button.

Now, we can use the viewCustomerPhone query just as we would any other SQL view (or Microsoft Access saved query). For example, we can implement the following SQL statement:

```
SELECT    FirstName, LastName, Phone
FROM      viewCustomerPhone
ORDER BY  LastName;
```

We will use Microsoft Access QBE in this example.

### Using a Microsoft Access Query in Another Microsoft Access Query

1. Click the **Create** command tab to display the Create command groups.
2. Click the **Query Design** button.
3. The Query1 tabbed document window is displayed in Design view, along with the Show Table dialog box.
4. In the Show Table dialog box, click the **Queries** tab to select it. The list of all saved queries appears, as shown in Figure AW-3A-2.
5. Click **viewCustomerPhone** to select the viewCustomerPhone query. Click the **Add** button to add the viewCustomerPhone query to the new query.
6. Click the **Close** button to close the Show Table dialog box.
7. From the viewCustomerPhone query, click and drag the **LastName, FirstName**, and **Phone** column names to the first three field columns in the lower pane.
8. In the field column for LastName, set the Sort setting to **Ascending**. The completed QBE query looks as shown in Figure AW-3A-3. If necessary, resize the table object and the Field columns so that complete labels are displayed.
9. Save the query as **QBEQuery-AW-3A-01**.

### FIGURE AW-3A-2

Queries Displayed in the Show Table Dialog Box

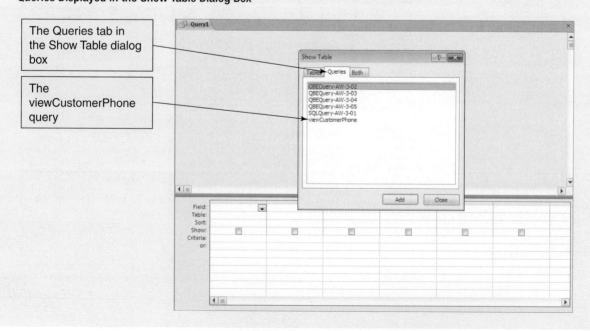

## FIGURE AW-3A-3

**The Completed Query**

The
viewCustomerPhone
query object

Object and Field
column boundaries
can be adjusted as
necessary to display
complete titles and
names

## FIGURE AW-3A-4

**The Query Results**

The data is sorted
by LastName, but *not*
by FirstName

| FirstName | LastName | Phone |
|-----------|-----------|--------------|
| Rob | Christman | 206-478-4567 |
| Jessica | Christman | 206-467-3456 |
| Ben | Griffey | 206-456-2345 |
| Judy | Hayes | 425-354-8765 |

10. Click the **Run** button on the Design command tab. The query results appear as shown in Figure AW-3A-4.
11. Close the QBEQuery-AW-3A-01 query window.

Now, we can use the equivalent of SQL views in Microsoft Access by using one query as the source for additional queries. That completes the work we will do in this section of "The Access Workbench," so we can close the database and Microsoft Access.

### Closing the WMCRM Database and Exiting Microsoft Access

1. To close the WMCRM database and exit Microsoft Access, click the **Close** button in the upper-right corner of the Microsoft Access window.

## SUMMARY

An SQL view is a virtual table that is constructed from other tables and views. An SQL SELECT statement is used as part of a CREATE VIEW *ViewName* statement to define a view. However, view definitions cannot include ORDER BY clauses. Once defined, view names are used in SELECT statements the same way table names are used.

Views have several uses. Views are used (1) to hide columns or rows, (2) to show the results of computed columns, (3) to hide complicated SQL syntax, and (4) to layer computations and built-in functions.

## KEY TERMS

ALTER VIEW statement
CREATE VIEW statement

DROP VIEW {ViewName}
  statement

SQL view

## REVIEW QUESTIONS

**3A.1**  What is an SQL view? What purposes do views serve?

**3A.2**  What SQL statements are used to create SQL views?

**3A.3**  What is the limitation on SELECT statements used in SQL views?

**3A.4**  How are views handled in Microsoft Access?

Use the following tables for your answers to questions 3A.5 through 3A.18:

PET_OWNER (OwnerID, OwnerLastName, OwnerFirstName, OwnerPhone, OwnerEmail)

PET_3 (PetID, PetName, PetType, PetBreed, PetDOB, PetWeight, OwnerID)

These are the same tables that are used in the review questions for Chapter 3, and data for these tables are shown in Chapter 3. For each SQL statement you write, show the results based on these data.

If possible, run the statements you write in the questions that follow in an actual DBMS, as appropriate, to obtain your results.

**3A.5**  Code an SQL statement to create a view named OwnerPhoneView that shows OwnerLastName, OwnerFirstName, and OwnerPhone.

**3A.6**  Code an SQL statement that displays the data in OwnerPhoneView, sorted alphabetically by OwnerLastName and OwnerFirstName.

**3A.7**  Code an SQL statement to create a view named CatBreedView that shows PetID, PetName, PetBreed, and PetDOB for cats.

**3A.8**  Code an SQL statement that displays the data in CatBreedView, sorted alphabetically by PetName.

**3A.9**  Code an SQL statement to create a view named DogBreedView that shows PetID, PetName, PetBreed, and PetDOB for dogs.

**3A.10**  Code an SQL statement that displays the data in DogBreedView, sorted alphabetically by PetName.

**3A.11**  Code an SQL statement to create a view named PetOwnerView that shows PetID, PetName, PetType, OwnerID, OwnerLastName, OwnerFirstName, OwnerPhone, and OwnerEmail.

**3A.12**  Code an SQL statement that displays the data in PetOwnerView, sorted alphabetically by OwnerLastName, OwnerFirstName, and PetName.

**3A.13**  Code an SQL statement to create a view named OwnerPetView that shows OwnerID, OwnerLastName, OwnerFirstName, PetID, PetName, PetType, PetBreed, and PetDOB.

**3A.14**  Code an SQL statement that displays the data in OwnerPetView, sorted alphabetically by OwnerLastName, OwnerFirstName, and PetName.

**3A.15**  Code an SQL statement to create a view named DogBreedCountView that shows each PetBreed of dog and the number of each PetBreed in the database.

**3A.16** Code an SQL statement that displays the data in DogBreedCountView, sorted alphabetically by PetBreed.

**3A.17** Code an SQL statement to create a view named PetCountView that shows each type (that is, dog or cat) and the number of each type (that is, how many dogs and how many cats) in the database.

**3A.18** Code an SQL statement that displays the data in PetCountView, sorted alphabetically by PetType.

## EXERCISES

If you have not created the Art Course database described in Chapter 3, create it now (by completing exercises 3.52 and 3.53). Use the Art Course database to answer exercises 3A.19 through 3A.26.

**3A.19** Code an SQL statement to create a view named CourseView that shows unique Course names and Fee.

**3A.20** Code an SQL statement that displays the data in CourseView, sorted alphabetically by Course.

**3A.21** Code an SQL statement to create a view named CourseEnrollmentView that shows CourseNumber, Course, CourseDate, CustomerNumber, CustomerLastName, CustomerFirstName, and Phone.

**3A.22** Code an SQL statement that displays the data in CourseEnrollmentView for the Advanced Pastels course starting 10/01/11. Sort the data alphabetically by CustomerLastName.

**3A.23** Code an SQL statement that displays the data in CourseEnrollmentView for the Beginning Oils course starting 10/15/11. Sort the data alphabetically by CustomerLastName.

**3A.24** Code an SQL statement to create a view named CourseFeeOwedView that shows CourseNumber, Course, CourseDate, CustomerNumber, CustomerLastName, CustomerFirstName, Phone, Fee, AmountPaid, and the calculated column (Fee – AmountPaid), renamed as AmountOwed.

**3A.25** Code an SQL statement that displays the data in CourseFeeOwedView, sorted alphabetically by CustomerLastName.

**3A.26** Code an SQL statement that displays the data in CourseFeeOwedView, sorted alphabetically by CustomerLastName for any customer who still owes money for a course fee.

### ACCESS WORKBENCH KEY TERMS

Microsoft Access equivalent of an SQL view

### ACCESS WORKBENCH EXERCISES

In Exercises AW.3A.1 and AW.3A.3, use the WMCRM database as completed in this chapter's section of "The Access Workbench."

In the "Access Workbench Exercises" sections for Chapters 1, 2, and 3, you created a database for Wedgewood Pacific Corporation (WPC) of Seattle, Washington. In this set of exercises, you will use that database, as completed in Chapter 3's section

*(Continued)*

of "The Access Workbench Exercises," to create and use Microsoft Access queries as SQL view equivalents in Exercises AW.3A.2 and AW.3A.4

**AW.3A.1**  Using Microsoft Access QBE or SQL, create and run view-equivalent queries to answer the questions that follow. Save each query using the query name format *viewViewQueryName*, as specified in the question.

**A.**  Create a Microsoft Access view-equivalent query named viewCustomerContact that shows CUSTOMER.CustomerID, LastName, FirstName, ContactDate, ContactType, and Remarks.

**B.**  Create a Microsoft Access view-equivalent query named viewSalespersonCustomerContact that shows SALESPERSON.NickName, SALESPERSON.LastName, SALESPERSON.FirstName, CUSTOMER.CustomerID, CUSTOMER.LastName, CUSTOMER.FirstName, ContactDate, ContactType, and Remarks.

**AW.3A.2**  Using Microsoft Access QBE or SQL, create and run view-equivalent queries to answer the questions that follow. Save each query using the query name format *viewViewQueryName*, as specified in the question.

**A.**  Create a Microsoft Access view-equivalent query named viewComputer that shows Make, Model, SerialNumber, ProcessorType, ProcessorSpeed, MainMemory, and DiskSize.

**B.**  Create a Microsoft Access view-equivalent query named viewEmployeeComputer that uses viewComputer for part C to show EMPLOYEE.EmployeeNumber, LastName, FirstName, and the data about the computer assigned to that employee, including Make, Model, SerialNumber, ProcessorType, ProcessorSpeed, MainMemory, and DiskSize.

**AW.3A.3**  Using Microsoft Access QBE, create and run the queries that follow. Save each query using the query name QBEQuery-AWE-3A-3-## where ## is replaced by the letter designator of the part. For example, the first query will be saved as QBEQuery-AWE-3A-3-A.

**A.**  Create a Microsoft Access QBE query to display the data in viewCustomerContact, sorted alphabetically by LastName and FirstName.

**B.**  Create a Microsoft Access QBE query to display the data in viewSalespersonCustomerContact, sorted alphabetically by SALESPERSON.LastName and SALESPERSON.FirstName.

**AW.3A.4**  Using Microsoft Access QBE, create and run the queries that follow. Save each query using the query name format QBEQuery-AWE-3A-4-##, where ## is replaced by the letter designator of the part. For example, the first query will be saved as QBEQuery-AWE-3A-4-A.

**A.**  Create a Microsoft Access QBE query to display the data in viewComputer, sorted alphabetically by Make and Model and then numerically by SerialNumber.

**B.**  Create a Microsoft Access QBE query to display the data in viewEmployeeComputer. Sort the results alphabetically by LastName, FirstName, Make, and Model and then numerically by SerialNumber.

## GARDEN GLORY PROJECT QUESTIONS

These questions are based on Chapter 3's Garden Glory project questions. Base your answers to the questions that follow on the Garden Glory database, as described there. If possible, run your SQL statements in an actual DBMS to validate your work.

**A.** Create (and run) the following SQL view statements:

1. Create an SQL view named OwnerPropertyView that shows OWNER.OwnerID, OwnerName, OwnerType, PropertyID, PropertyName, Street, City, State, and Zip.

2. Create an SQL view named PropertyServiceView that shows PROPERTY.PropertyID, PropertyName, Street, City, State, Zip, ServiceDate, and HoursWorked.

**B.** Create (and run) the following SQL queries:

1. Create an SQL statement to run OwnerPropertyView, with the results sorted alphabetically by OwnerName.

2. Create an SQL statement to run PropertyServiceView, with the results sorted alphabetically by Zip, State, and City.

## JAMES RIVER JEWELRY PROJECT QUESTIONS

These questions are based on Chapter 3's James River Jewelry project questions. Base your answers to the questions that follow on the James River Project database, as described there. If possible, run your SQL statements in an actual DBMS to validate your work.

**A.** Create (and run) the following SQL view statements:

1. Create an SQL view named CustomerPurchaseView that shows CUSTOMER.CustomerID, LastName, FirstName, InvoiceNumber, InvoiceDate and PreTaxAmount.

2. Create an SQL view named PurchaseItemItemView that shows InvoiceNumber, ItemNumber, ArtistName, Description, Cost, and RetailPrice.

**B.** Create (and run) the following SQL queries:

1. Create an SQL statement to run CustomerPurchaseView, with the results sorted alphabetically by LastName and FirstName.

2. Create an SQL statement to run PurchaseItemItemView, with the results sorted by InvoiceNumber and ItemNumber.

3. Create an SQL query that uses PurchaseItemItemView to calculate and display the sum of Cost as TotalItemCost and the sum of RetailPrice as TotalRetailSales.

# THE QUEEN ANNE CURIOSITY SHOP PROJECT QUESTIONS

These questions are based on Chapter 3's Queen Anne Curiosity Shop project questions. Base your answers to the questions that follow on the Queen Anne Curiosity Shop project database, as described there. If possible, run your SQL statements in an actual DBMS to validate your work.

**A.** Create (and run) the following SQL view statements:

    **1.** Create an SQL view named BasicCustomerView that shows each customer's CustomerID, LastName, FirstName, Phone, and Email.

    **2.** Create an SQL view named SaleItemItemView that shows SaleID, SaleItemID, SALE_ITEM.ItemID, SaleDate, ItemDescription, ItemCost, ITEM.ItemPrice as ListItemPrice, and SALE_ITEM.ItemPrice as ActualItemPrice.

**B.** Create (and run) the following SQL queries:

    **1.** Create an SQL statement to run BasicCustomerView, with the results sorted alphabetically by LastName and FirstName.

    **2.** Create an SQL statement to run SaleItemItemView, with the results sorted by SaleID and SaleItemID.

    **3.** Create an SQL query that uses SaleItemItemView to calculate and display the sum of SALE_ITEM.ItemPrice (which is relabeled as ActualItemPrice) as TotalPretaxRetailSales.

# PART II

# Database Design

In Part I, you were introduced to the fundamental concepts and techniques of relational database management. In Chapter 1, you learned that databases consist of related tables, and you learned the major components of a database system. Chapter 2 introduced you to the relational model, and you learned the basic ideas of functional dependencies and normalization. In Chapter 3, you learned how to use SQL statements to create and process a database.

All the material you have learned so far gives you a background for understanding the nature of database management and the required basic tools and techniques. However, you do not yet know how to apply all this technology to solve a business problem. Imagine, for example, that you walk into a small business—for example, a bookshop—and are asked to build a database to support a frequent buyer program. How would you proceed? So far, we have assumed that the database design already exists. How would you go about creating the design of the database?

The next two chapters address this important topic. We begin Chapter 4 with an overview of the database design process and then we describe data modeling—a technique for representing database requirements. In Chapter 5, you will learn how to transform a data model into a relational database design. After that database design is completed, you will learn about creating and managing a database in Part III.

# CHAPTER 4

# Data Modeling and the Entity-Relationship Model

**Chapter Objectives**

> Learn the basic stages of database development

> Understand the purpose and role of a data model

> Know the principal components of the E-R data model

> Understand how to interpret traditional E-R diagrams

> Understand how to interpret the Information Engineering (IE) model's Crow's Foot E-R diagrams

> Learn to construct E-R diagrams

> Know how to represent 1:1, 1:N, N:M, and binary relationships with the E-R model

> Understand two types of weak entities and know how to use them

> Understand nonidentifying and identifying relationships and know how to use them

> Know how to represent subtype entities with the E-R model

> Know how to represent recursive relationships with the E-R model

> Learn how to create an E-R diagram from source documents

The **database development process** consists of three major stages: requirements analysis, component design, and implementation. During the **requirements analysis stage**, system users are interviewed, and sample forms, reports, queries, and descriptions of update activities are obtained. These system requirements are used to create a **data model** during the **component design stage**. A data model is a representation of the content, relationships, and constraints of the data needed to support the requirements. Often, prototypes, or working demonstrations of selected portions of the future system, are created during the requirements phase. Such prototypes are used to obtain feedback from the system users.

During the **implementation stage**, the data model is transformed into a **database design**. Such a design consists of tables, relationships, and constraints. The design includes the table names and the names of all table columns. The design also includes the data types and properties of the columns, as well as a description of primary and foreign keys. Data constraints consist of limits on data values (for example, part numbers are seven-digit numbers starting with the number 3), referential integrity constraints, and business rules. An example of a business rule for a manufacturing company is that every purchased part will have a quotation from at least two suppliers.

The last stage of database development is the **implementation stage**. During this stage, the database is constructed and filled with data; queries, forms, and reports are created; application programs are written; and all these are tested. Finally, during this stage users are trained, documentation is written, and the system is installed for use.

The database development process as we describe it is a subset of the systems development life cycle (SDLC) model. The SDLC is described in detail in online Appendix C—Getting Started in Systems Analysis and Design, and if you want more information about how the database development process fits into the creation of the information systems used in businesses today you should refer to Appendix C. In this chapter we will take a look at two parts of the database development process—requirements analysis and data modeling. In Chapter 6, we will see how a data model is implemented as a database design in a DBMS.

## REQUIREMENTS ANALYSIS

Sources of user requirements are listed in Figure 4-1. As described in online Appendix C, and as you will learn in your systems development class, the general practice is to identify the users of the new information system and to interview them. During the interviews, examples of existing forms, reports, and queries are obtained. In addition, the users are asked about the need for changes to existing forms, reports, and queries and also about the need for new forms, reports, and queries.

**Use cases** are descriptions of the ways users will employ the features and functions of the new information system. A use case consists of a description of the roles users will play when utilizing the new system, together with descriptions of activities' scenarios. Inputs provided to the system and outputs generated by the system are defined. Sometimes dozens of such use cases are necessary. Use cases provide sources of requirements and also can be used to validate the data model, design, and implementation.

In addition to these requirements, you need to document characteristics of data items. For each data item in a form, report, or query, the team needs to determine its data type, properties, and limits on values.

Finally, during the process of establishing requirements system developers need to document business rules that constrain actions on database activity. Generally, such rules arise from business policy and practice. For example, the following business rules could pertain to an academic database:

- Students must declare a major before enrolling in any class.
- Graduate classes can be taken by juniors or seniors with a grade point average of 3.70 or greater.
- No adviser may have more than 25 advisees.
- Students may declare one or two majors but no more.

**FIGURE 4-1**

Sources of
Requirements for a
Database Application

> User interviews
> Forms
> Reports
> Queries
> Use cases
> Business rules

# THE ENTITY-RELATIONSHIP DATA MODEL

The system requirements described in the preceding section, although necessary and important as a first step, are not sufficient for designing a database. In addition, the requirements must be transformed into a data model. When writing application programs, program logic must first be documented in flowcharts or object diagrams; similarly, with a database, data requirements must first be documented in a data model.

A number of different techniques can be used to create data models. By far the most popular is the **entity-relationship model**, first published by Peter Chen[1] in 1976. Chen's basic model has since been extended to create the **extended entity-relationship (E-R) model**. Today, when we say *E-R model*, we mean the extended E-R model, and we use it in this text.

Several versions of the E-R model are in use today. We begin with the traditional E-R model. Later in the chapter, after the basic principles of E-R models have been examined, we will look at and use another version of the E-R model.

The most important elements of the E-R model are entities, attributes, identifiers, and relationships. We now consider each of these, in turn.

## Entities

An **entity** is something that users want to track. Examples of entities are CUSTOMER John Doe, PURCHASE 12345, PRODUCT A4200, SALES-ORDER 1000, SALESPERSON John Smith, and SHIPMENT 123400. Entities of a given type are grouped into an **entity class**. Thus, the EMPLOYEE entity class is the collection of all EMPLOYEE entities. In this text, entity classes are shown in capital letters.

An **entity instance** of an entity class is the occurrence of a particular entity, such as CUSTOMER 12345. It is important to understand the differences between an entity class and an entity instance. An entity class is a collection of entities and is described by the structure of the entities in that class. There are usually many instances of an entity in an entity class. For example, the class CUSTOMER has many instances—one for each customer represented in the database. The ITEM entity class and two of its instances are shown in Figure 4-2.

When developing a data model, the developers analyze the forms, reports, queries, and other system requirements. Entities are usually the subject of one or more forms or reports,

**FIGURE 4-2**

The ITEM Entity and
Two Entity Instances

| ITEM |
|---|
| ItemNumber<br>Description<br>Cost<br>ListPrice<br>QuantityOnHand |

Entity Class

| | |
|---|---|
| 1100<br>100 amp panel<br>$127.50<br>$170.00<br>14 | 2000<br>Door handle set<br>$52.50<br>$39.38<br>0 |

Two Entity Instances

[1]Peter P. Chen, "The Entity-Relationship Model—Towards a Unified View of Data," *ACM Transactions on Database Systems* (January 1976): 9–36.

or they are a major section in one or more forms or reports. For example, a form named PRODUCT Data Entry Form indicates the likelihood of an entity class called PRODUCT. Similarly, a report named CUSTOMER PURCHASE Summary indicates that most likely the business has CUSTOMER and PURCHASE entities.

## Attributes

Entities have **attributes**, which describe the entity's characteristics. Examples of attributes include EmployeeName, DateOfHire, and JobSkillCode. In this text, attributes are printed in a combination of uppercase and lowercase letters. The E-R model assumes that all instances of a given entity class have the same attributes. For example, in Figure 4-2 the ITEM entity has the attributes ItemNumber, Description, Cost, ListPrice, and QuantityOnHand.

An attribute has a data type (character, numeric, date, currency, and the like) and properties that are determined from the requirements. Properties specify whether the attribute is required, whether it has a default value, whether its value has limits, and any other constraint.

## Identifiers

Entity instances have **identifiers**, which are attributes that name, or identify, entity instances. For example, the ITEM entity in Figure 4-2 uses ItemNumber as an identifier. Similarly, EMPLOYEE instances could be identified by SocialSecurityNumber, by EmployeeNumber, or by EmployeeName. EMPLOYEE instances are not likely to be identified by attributes such as Salary or DateOfHire, because these attributes normally are not used in a naming role. CUSTOMER instances could be identified by CustomerNumber or CustomerName, and SALES-ORDER instances could be identified by OrderNumber.

The identifier of an entity instance consists of one or more of the entity's attributes. Identifiers that consist of two or more attributes are called **composite identifiers**. Examples are (AreaCode, LocalNumber), (ProjectName, TaskName), and (FirstName, LastName, PhoneExtension).

An identifier may be either unique or nonunique. The value of a **unique identifier** identifies one, and only one, entity instance. In contrast, the value of a **nonunique identifier** identifies a set of instances. EmployeeNumber is normally a unique identifier, but EmployeeName is most likely a nonunique identifier (for example, more than one John Smith might be employed by the company).

---

**B T W**

As you can tell from these definitions, identifiers are similar to keys in the relational model, but with two important differences. First, an identifier is a logical concept: It is one or more attributes that users think of as a name of the entity. Such identifiers might or might not be represented as keys in the database design. Second, primary and candidate keys must be unique, whereas identifiers might or might not be unique.

---

As shown in Figure 4-3, entities are portrayed in three levels of detail in a data model. Sometimes an entity and all its attributes are displayed. In such cases, the identifier of the attribute is shown at the top of the entity, and a horizontal line is drawn after the identifier, as shown in Figure 4-3(a). In a large data model, so much detail can make the data model

**FIGURE 4-3**

Levels of Entity
Attribute Display

| ITEM |
|---|
| ItemNumber |
| Description<br>Cost<br>ListPrice<br>QuantityOnHand |

(a) Entity with All
Attributes

| ITEM |
|---|
| ItemNumber |

(b) Entity with
Identifier
Attributes

| ITEM |
|---|

(c) Entity with No
Attributes

diagrams unwieldy. In those cases, the entity diagram is abbreviated by showing just the identifier, as in Figure 4-3(b), or by showing just the name of the entity in a rectangle, as shown in Figure 4-3(c).

## Relationships

Entities can be associated with one another in **relationships**. The E-R model contains relationship classes and relationship instances. **Relationship classes** are associations among entity classes, and **relationship instances** are associations among entity instances. In the original specification of the E-R model, relationships could have attributes. In modern practice, that feature is not used, and only entities have attributes.

A relationship class can involve many entity classes. The number of entity classes in the relationship is known as the **degree** of the relationship. In Figure 4-4(a), the SUPPLIER-QUOTATION relationship is of degree two because it involves two entity classes: SUPPLIER and QUOTATION. The PARENT relationship in Figure 4-4(b) is of degree three because it involves three entity classes: MOTHER, FATHER, and CHILD. Relationships of degree two, which are the most common, are called **binary relationships**. Similarly, relationships of degree three are called **ternary relationships**.

---

**B T W**

You may be wondering what the difference is between an *entity* and a *table*. They may seem like different terms for the same thing. *The principal difference between an entity and a table is that you can express a relationship between entities without using foreign keys.* In the E-R model, you can specify a relationship just by drawing a line connecting two entities. Because you are doing *logical data modeling*, and not physical database design, you need not worry about primary and foreign keys, referential integrity constraints, and the like.

This characteristic makes entities easier to work with than tables, especially early in a project when entities and relationships are fluid and uncertain. You can show relationships between entities before you even know what the identifiers are. For example, you can say that a DEPARTMENT relates to many EMPLOYEEs before you know any of the attributes of either EMPLOYEE or DEPARTMENT. This characteristic allows you to work from the general to the specific. When you are creating a data model, you first identify the entities, then you think about the relationships, and finally you determine the attributes.

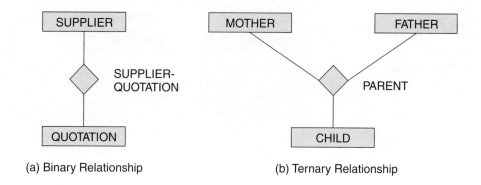

**FIGURE 4-4**

Example
Relationships

(a) Binary Relationship (b) Ternary Relationship

**Three Types of Binary Relationships** Figure 4-5 shows the three types of binary relationships:

- The one-to-one (1:1) relationship
- The one-to-many (1:N) relationship
- The many-to-many (N:M) relationship

In a 1:1 relationship, a single entity instance of one type is related to a single entity instance of another type. In Figure 4-5(a), the LOCKER-ASSIGNMENT relationship associates a single EMPLOYEE with a single LOCKER. According to this diagram, no employee has more than one locker assigned, and no locker is assigned to more than one employee.

Figure 4-5(b) shows a 1:N binary relationship. In this relationship, which is called the ITEM-QUOTE relationship, a single instance of ITEM relates to many instances of QUOTATION. According to this sketch, an item has many quotations, but a quotation has only one item.

Think of the diamond as representing the relationship. The position of the 1 indicates that the relationship has one ITEM; the position of the N indicates that it also has many QUOTATION entities. Thus, each instance of the relationship consists of one ITEM and many QUOTATIONS. Notice that if the 1 and the N were reversed and the relationship were written N:1, each instance of the relationship would have many ITEMs and one QUOTATION.

When discussing 1:N relationships, the terms *parent* and *child* are sometimes used. The **parent entity** is the entity on the one side of the relationship and the **child entity** is the entity

**FIGURE 4-5**

Three Types of Binary
Relationships

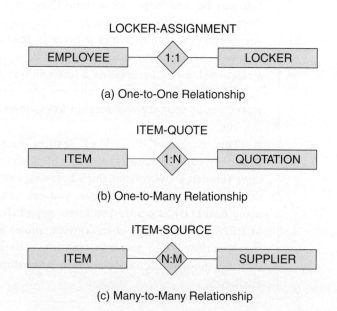

LOCKER-ASSIGNMENT

(a) One-to-One Relationship

ITEM-QUOTE

(b) One-to-Many Relationship

ITEM-SOURCE

(c) Many-to-Many Relationship

on the many side of the relationship. Thus, in the 1:N relationship between ITEM and QUOTATION, ITEM is the parent, and QUOTATION is the child.

Figure 4-5(c) shows an N:M binary relationship. This relationship is named ITEM-SOURCE, and it relates instances of ITEM to instances of SUPPLIER. In this case, an item can be supplied by many suppliers, and a supplier can supply many items.

**Maximum Cardinality**    The three types of binary relationships are named and classified by their **cardinality**, which is a word that means *count*. In each of the relationships in Figure 4-5, the numbers inside the relationship diamond show the *maximum* number of entity instances that can occur on each side of the relationship. These numbers are called the relationship's **maximum cardinality**, which is the maximum number of entity instances that can participate in a relationship instance.

The ITEM-QUOTE relationship in Figure 4-5(b), for example, is said to have a maximum cardinality of 1:N. However, the cardinalities are not restricted to the values shown here. It is possible, for example, for the maximum cardinality to be other than 1 and N. The relationship between BASKETBALL-TEAM and PLAYER, for example, could be 1:5, indicating that a basketball team has at most five players.

**Minimum Cardinality**    Relationships also have a **minimum cardinality**, which is the minimum number of entity instances that *must* participate in a relationship instance. Minimum cardinality can be shown in several different ways. One way, illustrated in Figure 4-6, is to place a *hash mark* across the relationship line to indicate that an entity must exist in the relationship and to place an *oval* across the relationship line to indicate that an entity might or might not be in the relationship.

Accordingly, Figure 4-6 shows that an ITEM must have a relationship with at least one SUPPLIER but that a SUPPLIER is not required to have a relationship with an ITEM. The complete relationship restrictions are that an ITEM has a minimum cardinality of one and a maximum cardinality of many SUPPLIER entities. A SUPPLIER has a minimum cardinality of zero and a maximum cardinality of many ITEM entities.

If the minimum cardinality is zero, the entity's participation in the relationship is **optional**. If the minimum cardinality is one, the entity's participation in the relationship is **mandatory**.

---

**B T W**

Interpreting minimum cardinalities in diagrams such as Figure 4-6 is often one of the most difficult parts of E-R models. It is very easy to become confused about which entity is optional and which is required (mandatory). An easy way to clarify this situation is to imagine that you are standing in the diamond, on the relationship line, and looking toward one of the entities. If you see an oval in that direction, then that entity is optional; if you see a hash mark, then that entity is required. Thus, in Figure 4-6, if you stand on the diamond and look toward SUPPLIER, you see a hash mark. This means that SUPPLIER is required in the relationship.

---

**FIGURE 4-6**

A Relationship with Minimum Cardinalities

## ENTITY-RELATIONSHIP DIAGRAMS

The sketches in Figures 4-5 and 4-6 are called **entity-relationship (E-R) diagrams**. Such diagrams are standardized, but only loosely. According to this standard, entity classes are shown using rectangles, relationships are shown using diamonds, the maximum cardinality of the relationship is shown inside the diamond, and the minimum cardinality is shown by the oval or hash mark next to the entity. The name of the entity is shown inside the rectangle, and the name of the relationship is shown near the diamond. You will see examples of such E-R diagrams, and it is important for you to be able to interpret them.

> ### B T W
>
> Relationships like those in Figures 4-5 and 4-6 are sometimes called **HAS-A relationships**. This term is used because each entity instance has a relationship to a second entity instance. An employee has a badge, and a badge has an employee. If the maximum cardinality is greater than one, then each entity has a set of other entities. An employee has a set of skills, for example, and a skill has a set of employees who have that skill.

For two reasons, however, this original notation is seldom used today. First, a number of different versions of the E-R model are in use, and they use different symbols. Second, data modeling software products use different techniques. For example, Computer Associates' product ERwin uses one set of symbols, and Microsoft Visio uses a different set.

### Variations of the E-R Model

At least three different versions of the E-R model are currently in use. One of them, called **Information Engineering (IE)**, was developed by James Martin in 1990. This model uses "crow's feet" to show the many side of a relationship, and it is sometimes called the **IE Crow's Foot model**. It is easy to understand, and we will use it in this text.

Other significant variations include the IDEF1X version and the Unified Modeling Language (UML) version of the E-R model.[2] In 1993, the National Institute of Standards and Technology announced that the **Integrated Definition 1, Extended (IDEF1X)**[3] version of the E-R model would be a national standard. This standard incorporates the basic ideas of the E-R model but uses different graphical symbols that, unfortunately, make it difficult to understand and use. Still, it is a national standard used in government work, and, therefore, it may be important to you. To add further complication, an object-oriented development methodology called the **Unified Modeling Language (UML)** adopted the E-R model but introduced its own symbols while putting an object-oriented programming spin on it. UML has begun to receive widespread use among object-oriented programming (OOP) practitioners, and you may encounter UML notation in systems development courses.

### E-R Variations in Data Modeling Products

In addition to differences due to different versions of the E-R model, differences also arise due to software products. For example, two products that both implement the IE Crow's Foot model may do so in different ways. Thus, when creating a data model diagram, you

---

[2]For more information on these models, see David M. Kroenke and David J. Auer, *Database Processing: Fundamentals, Design, and Implementation*, 11th edition (Upper Saddle River, NJ: Prentice Hall, 2010), Appendix B (IDEF1X) and Appendix C (UML).

[3]National Institute of Standards and Technology, *Integrated Definition for Information Modeling (DEF1X)*. Federal Information Processing Standards Publication 184, 1993.

FIGURE 4-7

Two Versions of a 1:N
Relationship

(a) Original E-R Model Version

(b) Crow's Foot Version

need to know not just the version of the E-R model you are using but also the idiosyncrasies of the data modeling product you use.

Figure 4-7 shows the same N:M optional-to-mandatory relationship in two different models. Figure 4-7(a) shows the original E-R model version. Figure 4-7(b) shows the IE Crow's Foot model using common Crow's Foot symbols. Notice that the line representing the relationship is drawn as a dashed line. (The reason for this is explained later in this chapter.) Notice the **crow's foot symbol** used to show the many side of the relationship. The IE Crow's Foot model uses the notation shown in Figure 4-8 to indicate relationship cardinality.

The symbol closest to the entity shows the maximum cardinality, and the other symbol shows the minimum cardinality. A hash mark indicates one (and therefore also mandatory), a circle indicates zero (and thus optional), and the crow's foot indicates many. Thus, the diagram in Figure 4-7(b) shows that a DEPARTMENT has one or more EMPLOYEEs (the symbol shows many and mandatory), and an EMPLOYEE belongs to zero or one DEPARTMENT (the symbol shows one and optional).

A 1:1 relationship would be drawn in a similar manner, but the line connecting to each entity would be similar to the connection shown for the one side of the 1:N relationship in Figure 4-7(b).

FIGURE 4-8

Crow's Foot Notation

| Symbol | Meaning |
|---|---|
|  | One—Mandatory |
|  | Many—Mandatory |
|  | One—Optional |
|  | Many—Optional |

**FIGURE 4-9**

Two Versions of an
N:M Relationship

(a) Original E-R Model Version

(b) Crow's Foot Version

Figure 4-9 shows the same N:M optional-to-mandatory relationship in two different models. According to the original E-R model diagram shown in Figure 4-9(a), an EMPLOYEE must have a SKILL, and may have several. At the same time, although a particular SKILL may or may not be held by any EMPLOYEE, A SKILL may also be held by several EMPLOYEES. The IE Crow's Foot version in Figure 4-9(b) shows the N:M cardinalities using the notation in Figure 4-8. The IE Crow's Foot symbols again indicate the minimum cardinalities for the relationship.

Throughout the rest of this text, we use the IE Crow's Foot model for E-R diagrams. There is no completely standard set of symbols for the IE Crow's Foot notation, but we use the symbols and notation described in this chapter. You can obtain various modeling products that will produce IE Crow's Foot models, and they are easily understood and related to the original E-R model. However, those products may use the oval, hash mark, crow's foot, and other symbols in slightly differently ways.

---

**B T W**

You can try a number of modeling products, each with its own idiosyncrasies. Computer Associates produces ERwin, a commercial data modeling product that handles both data modeling and database design tasks. You can download a free trial version from the Computer Associates Web site (**http://erwin.com/products/ detail/ca_erwin_data_modeler/**). Look for AllFusion ERwin Data Modeler r7.3. You can use ERwin to produce either IE Crow's Foot or IDEF1X diagrams. Although it is better at creating database designs (as discussed in Chapter 5) than data models, Microsoft's Visio is also a possibility. A trial version is available from the Microsoft Web site (**http://us20.trymicrosoftoffice.com/product.aspx?sku=3082928**). Finally, Oracle is continuing development of the MySQL Workbench, and a freely downloadable (but somewhat limited) version is available at the MySQL Web site (**http://dev.mysql.com/downloads/workbench/5.2.html**). Although, like Microsoft Visio, MySQL Workbench is better for database designs than data models, it is a very useful tool, and the database designs it produces can be used with any DBMS, not just MySQL. These are just a few of the many data modeling products available.

---

## Weak Entities

The E-R model defines a special type of entity called a weak entity. A **weak entity** is an entity that cannot exist in a database unless another type of entity also exists in that database. An entity that is *not* weak is called a **strong entity**.

## ID-Dependent Entities

The E-R model includes a special type of weak entity called an **ID-dependent entity**. With this type of entity, the identifier of the entity includes the identifier of another entity. Consider the entities BUILDING and APARTMENT, shown in Figure 4-10(a).

**FIGURE 4-10**

**Example ID-Dependent Entities**

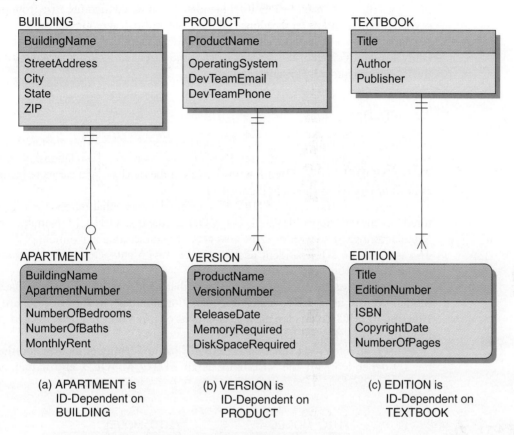

(a) APARTMENT is
ID-Dependent on
BUILDING

(b) VERSION is
ID-Dependent on
PRODUCT

(c) EDITION is
ID-Dependent on
TEXTBOOK

As you would expect, the identifier of BUILDING is a single attribute, in this case BuildingName. The identifier of APARTMENT, however, is *not* the single attribute ApartmentNumber, but rather the composite identifier (BuildingName, ApartmentNumber). This happens because logically and physically an APARTMENT simply cannot exist unless a BUILDING exists for that APARTMENT to be part of. Whenever this type of situation occurs, an ID-dependent entity exists. In this case, APARTMENT is ID-dependent on BUILDING. The identifier of an ID-dependent entity is always a composite that includes the identifier of the entity that the ID-dependent entity depends on for its existence.

As shown in Figure 4-10, in our E-R models we use an entity with rounded corners to represent the ID-dependent entity. We also use a solid line to represent the relationship between the ID-dependent entity and its parent. This type of a relationship is called an **identifying relationship**. A relationship drawn with a dashed line (refer to Figure 4-7) is used between strong entities and is called a **nonidentifying relationship** because there are no ID-dependent entities in the relationship.

ID-dependent entities are common. Another example is shown in Figure 4-10(b), where the entity VERSION is ID-dependent on the entity PRODUCT. Here, PRODUCT is a software product, and VERSION is a release of that software product. The identifier of PRODUCT is ProductName, and the identifier of VERSION is (ProductName, VersionNumber). A third example is shown in Figure 4-10(c), where EDITION is ID-dependent on TEXTBOOK. The identifier of TEXTBOOK is Title, and the identifier of EDITION is (Title, EditionNumber). In each of these cases, the ID-dependent entity cannot exist unless the parent (the entity on which it depends) also exists. Thus, the minimum cardinality from the ID-dependent entity to the parent is always one.

However, whether the parent is required to have an ID-dependent entity depends on business requirements. In Figure 4-10(a), the database can contain a BUILDING, such as a store or warehouse, so APARTMENT is optional. In Figure 4-10(b), every PRODUCT made by this company has versions (including version 1.0), so VERSION is mandatory. Similarly, in Figure 4-10(c), every TEXTBOOK has an EDITION number (including the first edition), which makes EDITION mandatory. Those restrictions arise from the nature of each business and its applications and not from any logical requirement.

Finally, notice that you cannot add an ID-dependent entity instance until the parent entity instance is created, and when you delete the parent entity instance you must delete all the ID-dependent entity instances as well.

## Non–ID-Dependent Weak Entities

All ID-dependent entities are weak entities. However, there are other entities that are weak but not ID-dependent. To understand weak entities, consider the relationship between the AUTO_MODEL and VEHICLE entity classes in the database of a car manufacturer, such as Ford or Honda, as shown in Figure 4-11.

In Figure 4-11(a), each VEHICLE is assigned a sequential number as it is manufactured. So, for the "Super SUV" AUTO_MODEL, the first VEHICLE manufactured gets a ManufacturingSeqNumber of 1, the next gets a ManufacturingSeqNumber of 2, and so on. This is clearly an ID-dependent relationship because ManufacturingSeqNumber is based on the Manufacturer and Model.

Now let us assign VEHICLE an identifier that is independent of the Manufacturer and Model. We will use a VIN (vehicle identification number), as shown in Figure 4-11(b). Now, the VEHICLE has a unique identifier of its own and does not need to be identified by its relation to AUTO_MODEL.

This is an interesting situation. VEHICLE has an identity of its own and therefore is not ID-dependent, yet the VEHICLE is an AUTO_MODEL, and if that particular

**FIGURE 4-11**

**Weak Entity Examples**

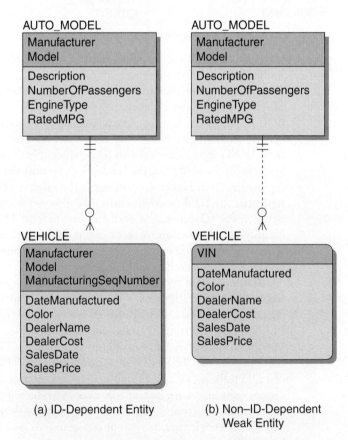

(a) ID-Dependent Entity     (b) Non–ID-Dependent Weak Entity

AUTO_MODEL did not exist the VEHICLE itself would never have existed. Therefore, VEHICLE is now a *weak but non–ID-dependent entity.*

Consider *your* car—let us say it is a Ford Mustang just for the sake of this discussion. Your individual Mustang is a VEHICLE, and it exists as a physical object and is identified by the VIN that is required for each licensed automobile. It is *not* ID-dependent on AUTO_MODEL, which in this case is Ford Mustang, for its identity. However, if the Ford Mustang had never been created as an AUTO_MODEL—a logical concept that was first designed on paper—your car would never have been built because *no* Ford Mustangs would ever have been built! Therefore, your physical individual VEHICLE would not exist without a logical AUTO_MODEL of Ford Mustang, and in a data model (which *is* what we're talking about) a VEHICLE cannot exist without a related AUTO_MODEL. This makes VEHICLE a weak but non–ID-dependent entity.

Unfortunately, an ambiguity is hidden in the definition of *weak entity*, and this ambiguity is interpreted differently by different database designers (as well as different textbook authors). The ambiguity is that, in a strict sense, if a weak entity is defined as any entity whose presence in the database depends on another entity, then any entity that participates in a relationship having a minimum cardinality of one to a second entity is a weak entity. Thus, in an academic database, if a STUDENT must have an ADVISER, then STUDENT is a weak entity because a STUDENT entity cannot be stored without an ADVISER.

This interpretation seems too broad to some people. A STUDENT is not physically dependent on an ADVISER (unlike an APARTMENT to a BUILDING), and a STUDENT is not logically dependent on an ADVISER (despite how it might appear to either the student or the adviser).Therefore, STUDENT should be considered a strong entity.

To avoid such situations, some people interpret the definition of weak entity more narrowly. They say that to be a weak entity an entity must logically depend on another entity. According to this definition, APARTMENT is a weak entity, but STUDENT is not. An APARTMENT cannot exist without a BUILDING in which it is located. However, a STUDENT can logically exist without an ADVISER, even if a business rule requires it.

To illustrate this interpretation, consider the examples shown in Figure 4-12. Suppose that a data model includes the relationship between an ORDER and a SALESPERSON

**FIGURE 4-12**

Examples of
Required Entities

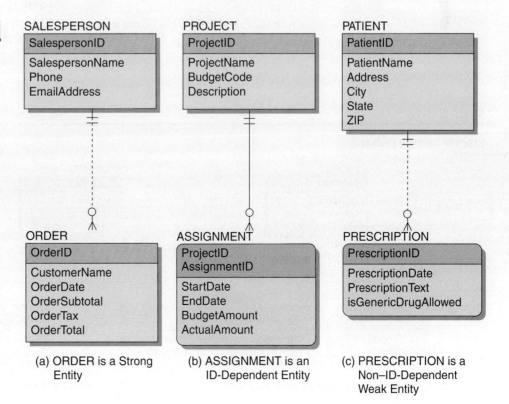

(a) ORDER is a Strong Entity

(b) ASSIGNMENT is an ID-Dependent Entity

(c) PRESCRIPTION is a Non–ID-Dependent Weak Entity

shown in Figure 4-12(a). Although you might state that an ORDER must have a SALESPERSON, it does not necessarily require one for its existence. (The ORDER could be a cash sale in which the salesperson is not recorded.) Hence, the minimum cardinality of one arises from a business rule, not from logical necessity. Thus, ORDER requires a SALESPERSON but is not existence-dependent on it. Therefore, ORDER is a strong entity.

Now, consider ASSIGNMENT in Figure 4-12(b), which is ID-dependent on PROJECT, and the identifier of ASSIGNMENT contains the identifier of PROJECT. Here, not only does ASSIGNMENT have a minimum cardinality of one, and not only is ASSIGNMENT existence-dependent on PROJECT, but ASSIGNMENT is also ID-dependent on PROJECT because its identifier requires the key of the parent entity. Thus, ASSIGNMENT is a weak entity that is ID-dependent.

Finally, consider the relationship of PATIENT and PRESCRIPTION in Figure 4-12(c). Here, a PRESCRIPTION cannot logically exist without a PATIENT. Hence, not only is the minimum cardinality one, but the PRESCRIPTION is also existence-dependent on PATIENT. Thus, PRESCRIPTION is a weak entity.

In this text, we define weak entity as an entity that logically depends on another entity. Hence, not all entities that have a minimum cardinality of one in relation to another entity are weak. Only those that are logically dependent are weak. This definition implies that all ID-dependent entities are weak. In addition, every weak entity has a minimum cardinality of one on the entity on which it depends, but every entity that has a minimum cardinality of one is not necessarily weak.

As illustrated in Figures 4-11 and 4-12, in our E-R models, we again use an entity with rounded corners to represent the non–ID-dependent entity, but we also use a dashed line to represent the nonidentifying relationship between the non–ID-dependent entity and its parent.

## Subtype Entities

The extended E-R model introduced the concept of subtypes. A **subtype entity** is a special case of another entity called the **supertype entity**. Students, for example, may be classified as undergraduate or graduate students. In this case, STUDENT is the supertype, and UNDERGRADUATE and GRADUATE are subtypes. Figure 4-13 shows these subtypes for a student database. Note that the identifier of the supertype is also the identifier of the subtypes.

**FIGURE 4-13**

**Example Subtype Entities**

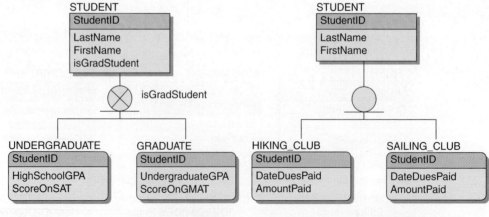

(a) Exclusive Subtypes with Discriminator   (b) Inclusive Subtypes

Alternatively, a student could be classified as a freshman, sophomore, junior, or senior. In that case, STUDENT would be the supertype, and FRESHMAN, SOPHOMORE, JUNIOR, and SENIOR would be the subtypes.

As illustrated in Figure 4-13, in our E-R models we use a circle with a line under it as a subtype symbol to indicate a supertype/subtype relationship. Think of this as a symbol for an optional (the circle) 1:1 (the line) relationship. In addition, we use a solid line to represent an ID-dependent subtype entity because each subtype is ID-dependent on the supertype. Also note that none of the line end symbols shown in Figure 4-8 are used on the connecting lines.

In some cases, an attribute of the supertype indicates which of the subtypes is appropriate for a given instance. An attribute that determines which subtype is appropriate is called a **discriminator**. In Figure 4-13, the attribute isGradStudent (which has only the values Yes and No) is the discriminator. In our E-R diagrams, the discriminator is shown next to the subtype symbol, as illustrated in Figure 4-13(a). Not all supertypes have a discriminator. Where a supertype does not have a discriminator, application code must be written to create the appropriate subtype.

Subtypes can be exclusive or inclusive. With **exclusive subtypes**, a supertype instance is related to at most one subtype. With **inclusive subtypes**, a supertype instance can relate to one or more subtypes. In Figure 4-13(a), the $X$ in the circle means that the UNDERGRADUATE and GRADUATE subtypes are exclusive. Thus, a STUDENT can be either an UNDERGRADUATE or a GRADUATE, but not both.

Figure 4-13(b) shows that a STUDENT can join either the HIKING_CLUB or the SAILING_CLUB or both. These subtypes are inclusive (note that there is no $X$ in the circle). Because a supertype may relate to more than one subtype, inclusive subtypes do not have a discriminator.

Subtypes are used in a data model to avoid inappropriate NULL values. Undergraduate students take the SAT exam and report that score, whereas graduate students take the GMAT and report their score on that exam. Thus, the SAT score would be NULL in all STUDENT entities for graduates, whereas the GMAT score would be NULL for all undergraduates. Such NULL values can be avoided by creating subtypes.

---

**B T W**

The relationships that connect supertypes and subtypes are called **IS-A relationships** because a subtype is the same entity as the supertype. Because this is so, the identifier of a supertype and all its subtypes must be the same; they all represent different aspects of the same entity. Contrast this with HAS-A relationships, in which an entity has a relationship to another entity, but the identifiers of the two entities are different.

---

## Recursive Relationships

It is possible for an entity to have a relationship to itself. Figure 4-14 shows a CUSTOMER entity in which one customer can refer to many other customers. This is called a **recursive relationship** (and because it has only one entity, it is also known as a **unary relationship**). As with binary relationships, recursive relationships can be 1:1, 1:N (shown in Figure 4-14), and N:M. We discuss each of these three types further in Chapter 5.

# DEVELOPING AN EXAMPLE E-R DIAGRAM

The best way to gain proficiency with data modeling is to do it. In this section, we examine a set of documents used by a small business and create a data model from those documents. After you have read this section, you should practice creating data models with one or more of the projects at the end of the chapter.

**FIGURE 4-14**

Example Recursive
Relationship

## Heather Sweeney Designs

Heather Sweeney is an interior designer who specializes in home kitchen design. She offers a variety of seminars at home shows, kitchen and appliance stores, and other public locations. The seminars are free; she offers them as a way of building her customer base. She earns revenue by selling books and videos that instruct people on kitchen design. She also offers custom-design consulting services.

After someone attends a seminar, Heather wants to leave no stone unturned in attempting to sell that person one of her products or services. She would therefore like to develop a database to keep track of customers, the seminars they have attended, the contacts she has made with them, and the purchases they have made. She wants to use this database to continue to contact her customers and offer them products and services.

## The Seminar Customer List

Figure 4-15 shows the seminar customer list form that Heather or her assistant fills out at seminars. This form includes basic data about the seminar as well as the name, phone, and email address of each attendee at the seminar. If we examine this list in terms of a data model, you see two potential entities: SEMINAR and CUSTOMER. From the form in

**FIGURE 4-15**

Example Seminar
Customer List

*Heather Sweeney Designs*
*Seminar Customer List*

Date:   October 11, 2010                    Location:   San Antonio Convention Center

Time:   11 AM                               Title:   Kitchen on a Budget

| Name | Phone | Email Address |
|---|---|---|
| Nancy Jacobs | 817-871-8123 | NJ@somewhere.com |
| Chantel Jacobs | 817-871-8234 | CJ@somewhere.com |
| Ralph Able | 210-281-7687 | RA@somewhere.com |
| Etc. | | |

27 names in all

## FIGURE 4-16

### Initial E-R Diagram for Heather Sweeney Designs

(a) First Version of the SEMINAR and CUSTOMER E-R Diagram

(b) Second Version of the SEMINAR and CUSTOMER E-R Diagram

(c) Third Version of the SEMINAR and CUSTOMER E-R Diagram

Figure 4-15, we can conclude that a SEMINAR relates to many CUSTOMERs, and we can make the initial E-R diagram shown in Figure 4-16(a).

However, from this single document we *cannot* determine a number of other facts. For example, we are not sure about cardinalities. Currently, we show a 1:N relationship, with both entities required in the relationship, but we are not certain about this. Neither do we know what to use for the identifier of each entity.

Having missing facts is typical during the data modeling process. We examine documents and conduct user interviews, and then we create a data model with the data we have. We also note where data are missing and supply those data later as we learn more. Thus, there is no need to stop data modeling when something is unknown; we just note that it is unknown and keep going, with the goal of supplying missing information at some later point.

Suppose we talk with Heather and determine that customers can attend as many seminars as they would like, but she would like to be able to record customers even if they have not been to a seminar. ("Frankly, I'll take a customer wherever I can find one!" was her actual response.) Also, she never offers a seminar to fewer than 10 attendees. Given this information, you can fill out more of the E-R diagram, as shown in Figure 4-16(b).

Before continuing, consider the minimum cardinality of the relationship from SEMINAR to CUSTOMER in Figure 4-16(b). The notation says that a seminar must have at least 10 customers, which is what we were told. However, this means that we cannot add a new SEMINAR to the database unless it already has 10 customers. This is incorrect. When Heather first schedules a seminar, it probably has no customers at all, but she would still like to record it in the database. Therefore, even though she has a business policy of requiring at least 10 customers at a seminar, we cannot place this limit as a constraint in the data model.

In Figure 4-16(b), neither of the entities has an identifier. For SEMINAR, the composites (Date, Time, Location) and (Date, Time, Title) are probably unique, and either could be the identifier. However, identifiers will become table keys during database design, and these will be large character keys. A surrogate key is probably a better idea here, so we should add one. Also, looking at the data and thinking about the nature of email addresses, we can reasonably suppose that EmailAddress can be the identifier of CUSTOMER. All these decisions are shown for the E-R diagram in Figure 4-16(c).

## The Customer Form Letter

Heather records every customer contact she makes. She considers customer attendance at a seminar as one type of customer contact, and Figure 4-17 shows a form letter that Sweeney Designs uses as another type of customer contact.

Heather also sends messages like this via email. We should therefore represent this form letter with an entity called CONTACT, which could be a letter, an email, or some other form

**FIGURE 4-17**

Heather Sweeney
Designs Customer
Form Letter

**Heather Sweeney Designs**
122450 Rockaway Road
Dallas, Texas 75227
972-233-6165

Ms. Nancy Jacobs
1400 West Palm Drive
Fort Worth, Texas 76110

Dear Ms. Jacobs:

Thank you for attending my seminar "Kitchen on a Budget" at the San Antonio Convention Center. I hope that you found the seminar topic interesting and helpful for your design projects.

As a seminar attendee, you are entitled to a 15 percent discount on all of my video and book products. I am enclosing a product catalog and I would also like to invite you to visit our Web site at www.Sweeney.com.

Also, as I mentioned at the seminar, I do provide customized design services to help you create that just-perfect kitchen. In fact, I have a number of clients in the Fort Worth area. Just give me a call at my personal phone number of 555-122-4873 if you'd like to schedule an appointment.

Thanks again and I look forward to hearing from you!

Best regards,

Heather Sweeney

of customer contact. Heather uses several different form letters and emails, and she refers to each one by a number (form letter 1, form letter 2, etc., and email 1, email 2, etc.). For now, we will represent the attributes of CONTACT as ContactNumber and ContactType, where ContactType can be Seminar, Email01, Email02, FormLetter01, FormLetter02, or some other type.

Reading the form letter, we see that it refers to a seminar and a customer. Therefore, we can add it to the E-R diagram with relationships to both of those entities, as shown in Figure 4-18.

As shown in the design in Figure 4-18(a), a seminar can result in many contacts, and a customer may receive many contacts, so the maximum cardinality of these relationships is N. However, neither a customer nor a seminar need generate a contact, so the minimum cardinality of these relationships is zero.

Working from CONTACT back to SEMINAR and CUSTOMER, we can determine that the contact is for a single CUSTOMER and refers to a single SEMINAR, so the maximum cardinality in that direction is one. Also, some of the form letters refer to seminars and some do not, so the minimum cardinality back to SEMINAR is zero. However, a contact must have a customer, so the minimum cardinality of that relationship is one. These cardinalities are shown in Figure 4-18(a).

Now, however, consider the identifier of CONTACT, which is shown as unknown in Figure 4-18(a). What could be the identifier? None of the attributes by themselves suffice because many contacts will have the same values for ContactNumber, ContactType, or Date. Reflect on this for a minute, and you will begin to realize that some attribute of CUSTOMER has to be part of CONTACT. That realization is a signal that something is wrong. In a data model, the same attribute should not logically need to be part of two different entities.

Could it be that CONTACT is a weak entity? Can a CONTACT logically exist without a SEMINAR? Yes, because not all CONTACTs refer to a SEMINAR. Can a CONTACT logically exist without a CUSTOMER? The answer to that question has to be no. Who would we be contacting without a CUSTOMER? Aha! That is it: CONTACT is a weak entity, depending on CUSTOMER. In fact, it is an ID-dependent entity because the identifier of CONTACT includes the identifier of CUSTOMER.

Figure 4-18(b) shows the data model with CONTACT as an ID-dependent entity on CUSTOMER. After further interviews with Heather, we determine that she never contacts a customer more than once on the same day, so (EmailAddress, Date) can be the identifier of CONTACT. (EmailAddress is the identifier of CUSTOMER.)

This E-R diagram has one other problem. The contact letter has the customer's address, but the CUSTOMER entity has no address attributes. Consequently, they need to be added, as shown in Figure 4-18(c). This adjustment is typical; as more forms and reports are obtained, new attributes and other changes will need to be made to the data model.

## The Sales Invoice

The sales invoice that Heather uses to sell books and videos is shown in Figure 4-19. The sales invoice itself needs to be an entity, and because the sales invoice has customer data, it has a relationship back to CUSTOMER. (Note that we do not duplicate the customer data because we can obtain data items via the relationship; if data items are missing, we add them to CUSTOMER.) Because Heather runs her computer with lax security, she decided that she did not want to record credit card numbers in her computer database. Instead, she records only the PaymentType value in the database and files the credit card receipts in a (locked) physical file with a notation that relates them back to an invoice number.

Figure 4-20 shows the completion of the Heather Sweeney Designs data model. Figure 4-20(a) shows a first attempt at the data model with INVOICE. This diagram is missing data about the line items on the order. Because there are multiple line items, the line item data cannot be stored in INVOICE. Instead, an ID-dependent entity, LINE_ITEM, must be defined. The need for an ID-dependent entity is typical for documents that contain a group of repeating data. If the repeating group is not logically independent, then it must be made into an ID-dependent weak entity. Figure 4-20(b) shows the adjusted design.

FIGURE 4-18

Heather Sweeney Designs Data Model with CONTACT

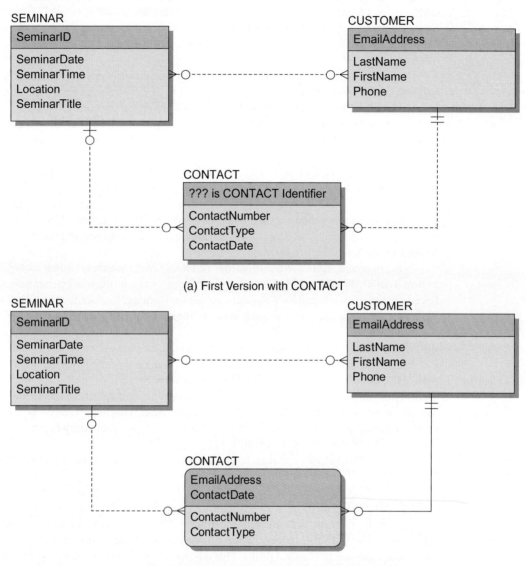

(a) First Version with CONTACT

(b) Second Version with CONTACT as a Weak Entity

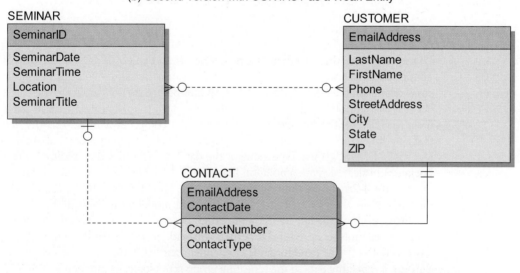

(c) Third Version with Modified CUSTOMER

**FIGURE 4-19**

Heather Sweeney Designs Sales Invoice

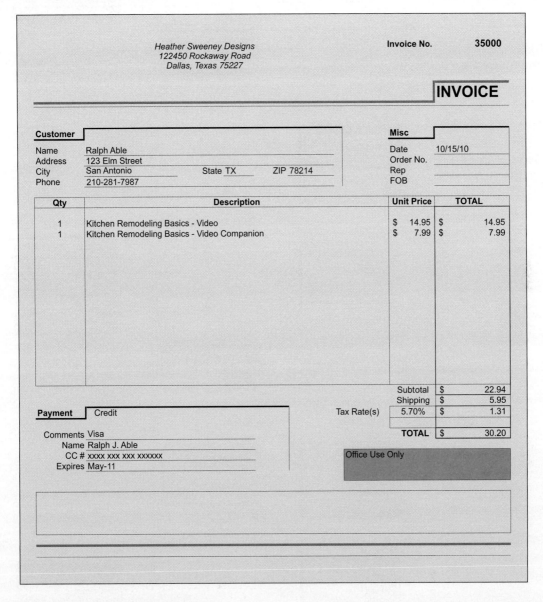

Because LINE_ITEM belongs to an identifying relationship from INVOICE, it needs an attribute that can be used to identify a particular LINE_ITEM within an INVOICE. The identifier we will use for LINE_ITEM will be the composite (InvoiceNumber, LineNumber), where InvoiceNumber is the identifier of INVOICE, and the LineNumber attribute identifies the line within the INVOICE on which an item appears.

We need to make one more correction to this data model. Heather sells standard products—that is, her books and videos have standardized names and prices. She does not want the person who fills out an order to be able to use nonstandard names or prices. We therefore need to add a PRODUCT entity and relate it to LINE_ITEM, as shown in Figure 4-20(c).

Observe that UnitPrice is an attribute of both PRODUCT and LINE_ITEM. This was done so that Heather can update UnitPrice without affecting the recorded orders. At the time a sale is made, UnitPrice in LINE_ITEM is set equal to UnitPrice in PRODUCT. The LINE_ITEM UnitPrice never changes. However, as time passes and Heather changes prices

FIGURE 4-20

The Final Data Model
for Heather Sweeney
Designs

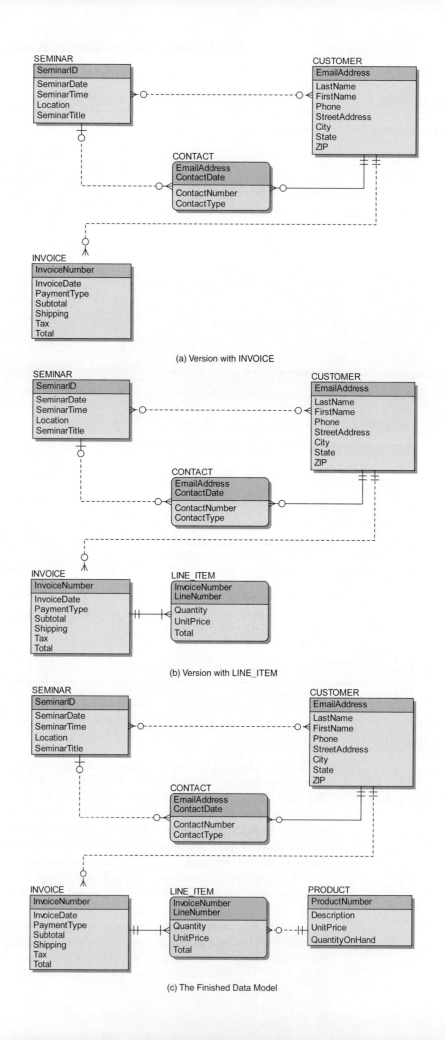

(a) Version with INVOICE

(b) Version with LINE_ITEM

(c) The Finished Data Model

for her products she can update UnitPrice in PRODUCT. If UnitPrice were not copied into LINE_ITEM, when the PRODUCT price changes, the price in already stored LINE_ITEMs would change as well, and Heather does not want this to occur. Therefore, although two attributes are named UnitPrice, they are different attributes used for different purposes.

Note in Figure 4-20(c) that based on interviews with Heather we have added ProductNumber and QuantityOnHand to PRODUCT. These attributes do not appear in any of the documents, but they are known by Heather and are important to her.

## Attribute Specifications

The data model in Figure 4-20(c) shows entities, attributes, and entity relationships, but it does not document details about attributes. To do that, we need to create a set of tables like those shown in Figure 4-21.

Figure 4-21 documents the data type, default values, and other properties of the attributes of each entity. These attributes and properties are used to create the tables in the database design, as you will see in Chapter 5.

## Business Rules

When creating a data model, we need to be on the lookout for business rules that constrain data values and the processing of the database. We encountered such a business rule with regard to CONTACT, when Heather Sweeney stated that no more than one form letter or email per day is to be sent to a customer.

## FIGURE 4-21

Heather Sweeney Designs Attribute Specifications

| Column Name | Data Type (Length) | Key | Required | Default Value | Remarks |
|---|---|---|---|---|---|
| SeminarID | AutoNumber | Primary Key | Yes | DBMS supplied | Surrogate Key: Initial value=1 Increment=1 |
| SeminarDate | Date | No | Yes | None | As: mm/dd/yy |
| SeminarTime | Time | No | Yes | None | As: ##:##(AM/PM) |
| Location | VarChar (100) | No | Yes | None | |
| SeminarTitle | VarChar (100) | No | Yes | None | |

### (a) SEMINAR

| Column Name | Data Type (Length) | Key | Required | Default Value | Remarks |
|---|---|---|---|---|---|
| EmailAddress | VarChar (100) | Primary Key | Yes | None | |
| LastName | Char (25) | No | Yes | None | |
| FirstName | Char (25) | No | Yes | None | |
| Phone | Char (12) | No | Yes | None | As: (###)###-#### |
| StreetAddress | Char (35) | No | No | None | |
| City | Char (35) | No | No | Dallas | |
| State | Char (2) | No | No | TX | As: SS |
| ZIP | Char (10) | No | No | 75201 | As: #####-#### |

### (b) CUSTOMER

*(Continued)*

**FIGURE 4-21  (Continued)**

| Column Name | Data Type (Length) | Key | Required | Default Value | Remarks |
|---|---|---|---|---|---|
| EmailAddress | VarChar (100) | Primary Key | Yes | None | REF: CUSTOMER |
| ContactDate | Date | Primary Key | Yes | None | As: mm/dd/yy |
| ContactNumber | Integer | No | Yes | None | |
| ContactType | Char (15) | No | Yes | None | |

**(c) CONTACT**

| Column Name | Data Type (Length) | Key | Required | Default Value | Remarks |
|---|---|---|---|---|---|
| InvoiceNumber | AutoNumber | Primary Key | Yes | DBMS supplied | Surrogate Key: Initial value=35000 Increment=1 |
| InvoiceDate | Date | No | Yes | None | As: mm/dd/yy |
| PaymentType | Char (25) | No | Yes | Cash | |
| Subtotal | Numeric (9,2) | No | No | None | |
| Shipping | Numeric (9,2) | No | No | None | |
| Tax | Numeric (9,2) | No | No | None | |
| Total | Numeric (9,2) | No | No | None | |

**(d) INVOICE**

| Column Name | Data Type (Length) | Key | Required | Default Value | Remarks |
|---|---|---|---|---|---|
| InvoiceNumber | Integer | Primary Key | Yes | None | REF: INVOICE |
| LineNumber | Integer | Primary Key | Yes | None | This is not quite a Surrogate Key — for *each* InvoiceNumber: Initial value=1 Increment=1 Application logic will be needed to supply the correct value |
| Quantity | Integer | No | No | None | |
| UnitPrice | Numeric (9,2) | No | No | None | |
| Total | Numeric (9,2) | No | No | None | |

**(e) LINE_ITEM**

| Column Name | Data Type (Length) | Key | Required | Default Value | Remarks |
|---|---|---|---|---|---|
| ProductNumber | AutoNumber | Primary Key | Yes | DBMS supplied | Surrogate Key: Initial value=100 Increment=1 |
| Description | VarChar (100) | No | Yes | None | |
| UnitPrice | Numeric (9,2) | No | Yes | None | |
| QuantityOnHand | Integer | No | Yes | 0 | |

**(f) PRODUCT**

In more complicated data models, many such business rules would exist. These rules are generally too specific or too complicated to be enforced by the DBMS. Rather, application programs or other forms of procedural logic need to be developed to enforce such rules.

## Validating the Data Model

After a data model has been completed, it needs to be validated. The most common way to do this is to show it to the users and obtain their feedback. However, a large, complicated data model is off-putting to many users, so often the data model needs to be broken into sections and validated piece by piece or expressed in some other terms that are more understandable.

As mentioned earlier in this chapter, prototypes are sometimes constructed for users to review. Prototypes are easier for users to understand and evaluate than data models. We can develop prototypes that show the consequences of data model design decisions without requiring the users to learn E-R modeling. For example, showing a form with room for only one customer is a way of indicating that the maximum cardinality of a relationship is one. If the users respond to such a form with the question "But where do I put the second customer?" you know that the maximum cardinality is greater than one.

It is relatively easy to create mock-ups of forms and reports by using Microsoft Access wizards. We can even develop such mock-ups in situations where Microsoft Access is not going to be used as the operational DBMS, because they are still useful for demonstrating the consequences of data modeling decisions.

Finally, a data model needs to be evaluated against all use cases. For each use case, we need to verify that all the data and relationships necessary to support the use case are present and accurately represented in the data model.

Data model validation is exceedingly important. It is far easier and less expensive to correct errors at this stage than it is to correct them after the database has been designed and implemented. Changing the cardinality in a data model is a simple adjustment to a document, but changing the cardinality later might require the construction of new tables, new relationships, new queries, new forms, new reports, and so forth. So every minute spent validating a data model will pay great dividends down the line.

## THE ACCESS WORKBENCH

### Section 4

### Prototyping Using Microsoft Access

In this chapter, when discussing data modeling concepts and techniques we talked about building a **prototype database** for users to review as a model validation technique. Prototypes are easier for users to understand and evaluate than data models. In addition, they can be used to show the consequences of data-model design decisions.

Because it is relatively easy to create mock-ups of forms and reports by using Microsoft Access wizards, mock-ups are often developed even in situations in which Microsoft Access is not going to be used as the operational DBMS. The mock-ups can be used as a prototyping tool to demonstrate the consequences of data modeling decisions. In this section, you will use Microsoft Access as a prototyping tool. We will continue to use the WMCRM database. At this point, we have created and populated the CONTACT, CUSTOMER, and SALESPERSON tables. In the preceding sections of "The Access Workbench," you also learned how to create forms, reports, and queries. And if you studied Chapter 3A's section of "The Access Workbench" together with Chapter 3, you have learned how to create and use view-equivalent queries.

*(Continued)*

---

**FIGURE AW-4-1**

The WMCRM Database as a Data Model

Let us start by considering what the WMCRM database looks like from a data modeling point of view. Figure AW-4-1 shows the WMCRM database as an IE Crow's Foot E-R model.

This model is based on the business rule that each CUSTOMER works with one and only one SALESPERSON. Therefore, we have a 1:N relationship between SALESPERSON and CUSTOMER, which shows that each SALESPERSON can work with many CUSTOMERs, but each CUSTOMER is attended to by only one SALESPERSON. Further, because there is no doubt about which SALESPERSON is involved in each CONTACT with a CUSTOMER, the connection to CONTACT is a 1:N relationship to CUSTOMER.

But all this would change if the business rule were that any CUSTOMER could work with more than one SALESPERSON. This would allow any SALESPERSON to contact the CUSTOMER as needed rather than relying on just one SALESPERSON to be available whenever needed for work with a particular CUSTOMER. Each CONTACT would now need to be linked to the CUSTOMER contacted and the SALEPERSON making the CONTACT. This results in a data model like the one shown in Figure AW-4-2.

Here we have a 1:N relationship between SALESPERSON and CONTACT instead of between SALESPERSON and CUSTOMER, while the 1:N relationship between CUSTOMER and CONTACT remains the same. CONTACTs for one CUSTOMER can now be linked to various SALESPERSONs.

Imagine that you have been hired as a consultant to create the WMCRM database. You now have two alternative data models that you need to show to management at Wallingford Motors so that they can make a decision about which model to use. But they do not understand E-R data modeling.

How can you illustrate the differences between the two data models? One way is to generate some mock-up prototype forms and reports in Microsoft Access. Users can more easily understand forms and reports than they can understand your abstract E-R model.

### Creating a Prototype Form for the Original Data Model

We will start by creating a sample form in the current version of the WMCRM database, which we are treating here as a prototype we created to illustrate the first data model. (This includes populating the database with sample data.) The database structure for this database is shown in the Relationships window in Figure AW-4-3.

You already know how to create forms that use more than one table, and the only difference in this form will be that it uses three tables instead of two. The basic table is SALESPERSON, with CUSTOMER as the second table added to the form, followed by

**The Modified WMCRM Data Model**

the CONTACT table. When you use the Form Wizard, various choices of design options will lead to different appearances of the final form. One possible design of the WMCRM Salesperson Contacts Form is shown in Figure AW-4-4.

This form has three distinct sections: The top section shows SALESPERSON data, the middle section shows selectable CUSTOMER data, and the bottom section shows the CONTACT data for the current CUSTOMER. It should be fairly easy to explain this form to the Wallingford Motors management and users.

**The Original WMCRM Database**

1:N relationship between SALESPERSON and CUSTOMER

*NickName* is a foreign key linking to SALESPERSON

*(Continued)*

**FIGURE AW-4-4**

The WMCRM Salesperson Contacts Form

- SALESPERSON data
- CUSTOMER data—use the record buttons to move between CUSTOMERs associated with the current SALESPERSON
- CONTACT data—only the data for the current CUSTOMER are shown

### Creating a Prototype Form for the Modified Data Model

Before we can create the equivalent WMCRM Salesperson Contacts Form for the second data model, we must prototype the resulting database in Microsoft Access. Fortunately, we do not need to create a new database from scratch—we can simply make a copy of the existing Microsoft Access database. One of the nice features of Microsoft Access is that each database is stored in one *.accdb file. For example, recall from Chapter 1's section of "The Access Workbench" that the original database was named WMCRM.accdb and stored in the Documents library. We can make renamed copies of this file as the basis for prototyping other data models.

#### Copying the WMCRM.accdb Database

1. Select **Start | Documents** to open the My Documents library.
2. Right-click the **WMCRM.accdb** file object to display the shortcut menu, and then click **Copy**.
3. Right-click anywhere in the empty area of the Documents library window to display the shortcut menu and then click **Paste**. A file object named **WMCRM - Copy.accdb** appears in the Documents library window.
4. Right-click the **WMCRM - Copy.accdb** file object to display the shortcut menu, and then click **Rename**.
5. Edit the file name to read **WMCRM-AW04-v02.accdb**, and then press the **Enter** key.

Now we need to modify this database file. The goal is the set of database relationships shown in Figure AW-4-5.

The modifications are straightforward, and we have done most of the steps in previous sections. We need to:

- Remove the relationship between SALESPERSON and CUSTOMER (this is new).
- Delete the NickName field in CUSTOMER (this is new).
- Add the NickName field to CONTACT as NULL.
- Populate the NickName field in CONTACT.
- Modify the NickName field in CONTACT to NOT NULL.
- Create the relationship between SALESPERSON and CONTACT.

## FIGURE AW-4-5

### The Modified WMCRM Database

The only new steps are deleting a relationship and deleting a field from a table.

### Deleting the SALESPERSON-to-CUSTOMER Relationship

1. Start Microsoft Access 2010.
2. If the File command tab is not selected, click the **File** command tab to display the Backstage view, and then click the **Open** button. The Open dialog box appears. Browse to the **WMCRM-AW04-v02.accdb** file, click the file name to highlight it, and then click the **Open** button.
3. The **Security Warning** bar appears with the database. Click the Security Warning bar's **Enable Content** button.
4. Click the **Database Tools** command tab.
5. Click the **Relationships** button in the Relationships command group. The Relationships tabbed document window appears. Note that along with the Relationships window a contextual tab named Relationship Tools is displayed and that this tab adds a new command tab named Design to the set of command tabs displayed.
6. Right-click the **relationship line** between SALESPERSON and CUSTOMER to display the shortcut menu, and then click **Delete**.
7. A dialog box appears with the message "Are you sure you want to permanently delete the selected relationship from your database?" Click the **Yes** button.
8. Click the Relationships window's **Close** button to close the window.
9. If a dialog box appears with the message "Do you want to save the changes to the layout of 'Relationships'?", click the **Yes** button.

### Deleting a Column (Field) in a Microsoft Access Table

1. Open the **CUSTOMER** table in Design view.

*(Continued)*

2. Select the **NickName** column (field).
3. Right-click anywhere in the selected row to display the shortcut menu. Click **Delete Rows**.
   - **NOTE:** A Delete Rows button is also included in the Tools group on the Design command tab of the Table Tools contextual command tab. You can use this button instead of the shortcut menu if you want to.
4. A dialog box appears with the message "Do you want to permanently delete the selected field(s) and all the data in the field(s)?" To permanently delete the column, click the **Yes** button.
5. Click the **Save** button on the Quick Access Toolbar to save the changes to the table design.
6. Close the **CUSTOMER** table.

The other steps needed to modify the database are the same ones we used when we added the SALESPERSON table to the database in Chapter 3's section of "The Access Workbench." Following the instructions in that section, we can add the NickName column to CONTACT, populate it, and create the relationship between SALESPERSON and CONTACT. In Chapter 3's section of "The Access Workbench," we used Microsoft Access SQL to accomplish these tasks. In this section, we will walk through similar steps with Microsoft Access QBE. Note that Figure AW-4-5 shows NickName inserted as the third column (field) in the table—it could just as easily be added as the last column in the table. In a relational table, the column order does not matter: We use the one that makes it easier for database developers to read!

Figure AW-4-6 shows the NickName column as it is initially added to the CONTACT table. Note that the data type is Text(35), but currently the column is *not* required. This is the Microsoft Access equivalent of the SQL NULL constraint.

Figure AW-4-7 shows the NickName column data added to the CONTACT table. Now each CONTACT record contains the name of the salesperson making the contact.

After the NickName column data have been added to the CONTACT table, we need to set the NickName column's Required field property to Yes, as shown in Figure AW-4-8.

---

**FIGURE AW-4-6**

The NickName Column in CONTACT

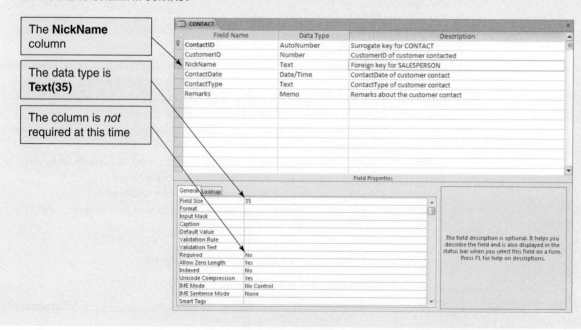

FIGURE AW-4-7

### The NickName Data in CONTACT

The **NickName** column

The **SALESPERSON NickName** is entered for every CONTACT record

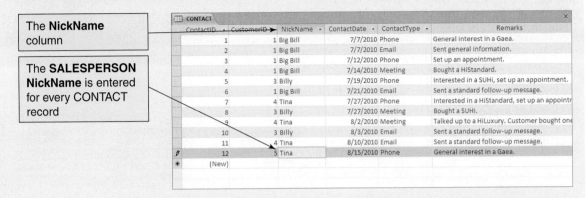

This is the equivalent of the SQL NOT NULL constraint, and because NickName is a foreign key linking to SALESPERSON the NickName column in CONTACT must be NOT NULL.

With the CONTACT table modifications done, we need to build the new relationship between the SALESPERSON and CONTACT tables. This relationship is shown in Figure AW-4-5, with the Edit Relationships dialog box showing that referential integrity is being enforced for the relationship.

With these modifications done, we now create another version of the WMCRM Salesperson Contacts Form. This version is shown in Figure AW-4-9.

This form has two distinct sections: The top section shows SALESPERSON data, and the bottom section shows that the data for each CUSTOMER are combined with

FIGURE AW-4-8

### The Required NickName Column in CONTACT

The **NickName** column

The column is required—this is the equivalent of the SQL NOT NULL constraint

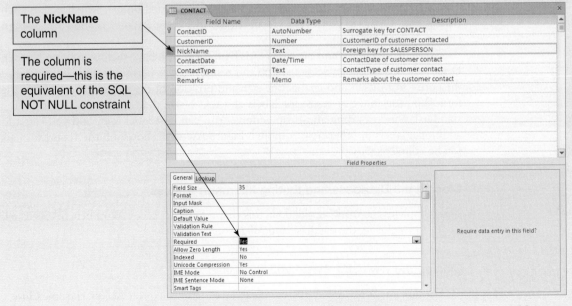

*(Continued)*

---

**FIGURE AW-4-9**

The WMCRM Salesperson Contacts Form for the Modified Database

SALESPERSON data

The Customer Contact data area now includes CUSTOMER data as well as the CONTACT data—each contact record shows which customer was contacted

---

the CONTACT data for each customer contact. This form is distinctively different from the form based on the first data model, but, again, it should be fairly easy to explain this form to Wallingford Motors' management and users. Based on the two forms, management and users will be able to decide how they want the data presented, and this decision will then determine which data model should be used.

### The Microsoft Access Banded Form and Report Editors

The form in Figure AW-4-9 has extensively rearranged labels and data text boxes in the Customer Contact section of the form. Microsoft Access uses **banded form editors** and **banded report editors**, where each element of the form or report is displayed in its own band (for example, Header, Detail, or Footer), which makes such rearranging very easy to do. The form shown in Figure AW-4-9 is shown in Design view in Figure AW-4-10.

Note that the form and the CONTACT subform each have their own Form Header, Detail, and Form Footer sections. You can resize these as necessary, and you can resize the entire form itself and change the size and position of the subform area within the form. You can move or resize the labels and text boxes that display the data by using standard Windows drag-and-drop actions. You can edit label text, and you can add additional labels or other text. Although Figure AW-4-10 shows a form, report formats can be edited exactly the same way.

### Closing the Database and Exiting Microsoft Access

This completes the work we will do in this chapter's "The Access Workbench." As usual, we finish by closing the database and Microsoft Access.

#### Closing the WMCRM-AW04-v02 Database

1. To close the WMCRM-AW04-v02 database and exit Microsoft Access, click the **Close** button in the upper-right corner of the Microsoft Access window.

**FIGURE AW-4-10**

The Microsoft Access 2010 Banded Form Editor

SALESPERSON portion of the form—note the Form Header and Detail bands

Customer Contact subform—again note the Form Header and Detail bands

Labels and data text boxes can be moved and resized as necessary

The size of the form and the subform within the form can be adjusted as needed

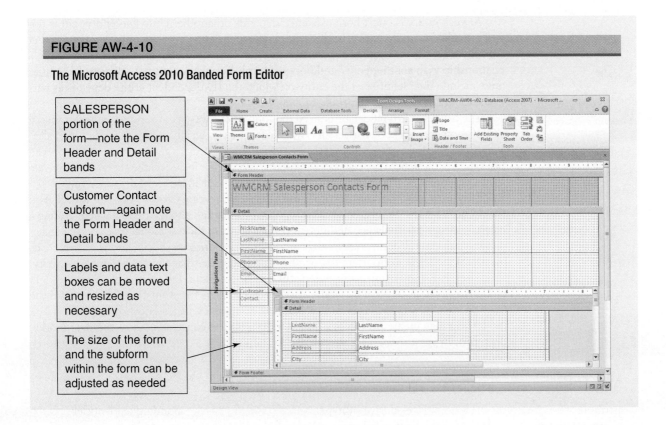

## SUMMARY

The process of developing a database system consists of three stages: requirements analysis, component design and implementation. During the requirements analysis stage, you interview users, document systems requirements, and construct a data model. Oftentimes, you will create prototypes of selected portions of the future system. During the component design stage, you transform the data model into a relational database design. During the implementation stage, you construct the database and fill it with data and you create queries, forms, reports, and application programs.

In addition to creating a data model, you must also determine data-item data types, properties, and limits on data values. You also need to document business rules that constrain database activity.

The entity-relationship (E-R) model is the most popular tool used to develop a data model. With the E-R model, entities, which are identifiable things of importance to the users, are defined. All the entities of a given type form an entity class. A particular entity is called an instance. Attributes describe the characteristics of entities, and one or more attributes identify an entity. Identifiers can be unique or nonunique.

Relationships are associations among entities. The E-R model explicitly defines relationships. Each relationship has a name, and there are relationship classes as well as relationship instances. According to the original specification of the E-R model, relationships may have attributes; however, this is not common in contemporary data models.

The degree of a relationship is the number of entities participating in the relationship. Most relationships are binary. The three types of binary relationships are 1:1, 1:N, and N:M. A recursive relationship occurs when an entity has a relationship to itself.

In traditional E-R diagrams, such as the traditional E-R model, entities are shown in rectangles, and relationships are shown in diamonds. The maximum cardinality of a relationship is shown inside the diamond. The minimum cardinality is indicated by a hash mark or an oval.

A weak entity is one whose existence depends on another entity; an entity that is not weak is called a strong entity. In this text, we further define a weak entity as an entity that logically depends on another entity. An entity can have a minimum cardinality of one in a relationship with another entity and not necessarily be a weak entity. ID-dependent entities must include the identifier of the entity on which the ID-dependent entity depends as part of the identifier of the ID-dependent entity.

The extended E-R model introduced the concept of subtypes. A subtype entity is a special case of another entity known as its supertype. In some cases, an attribute of the supertype, called a discriminator, indicates which of the subtypes is appropriate for a given instance. Subtypes can be exclusive (the supertype relates to at most one subtype) or inclusive (the supertype can relate to one or more subtypes). The identifier of the subtype is the identifier of the supertype.

This text's E-R diagrams use the Information Engineering Crow's Foot E-R model. You should be familiar with diagrams of that style, but you should also realize that when creating a database design no fundamental difference exists between the traditional style and this style.

In addition to E-R diagrams, a data model includes attribute specifications. When creating a data model, it is important to document business rules that constrain database activity.

After E-R models are completed, they must be evaluated. You can show the data model, or portions of the data model, directly to the users for evaluation. This requires the users to learn how to interpret an E-R diagram. Sometimes, instead of showing users a data model you may create prototypes that demonstrate the consequences of the data model. Such prototypes are easier for users to understand.

## KEY TERMS

attribute
binary relationship
cardinality
child entity
component design stage
composite identifier
crow's foot symbol
data model
database design
database development process
degree
design stage
discriminator
entity
entity class
entity instance
entity-relationship (E-R) diagram
entity-relationship model

exclusive subtype
extended entity-relationship
   (E-R) model
HAS-A relationship
ID-dependent entity
identifier
identifying relationship
IE Crow's Foot model
implementation stage
inclusive subtype
Information Engineering (IE) model
Integrated Definition 1, Extended
   (IDEF1X)
IS-A relationship
mandatory
maximum cardinality
minimum cardinality
nonidentifying relationship

nonunique identifier
optional
parent entity
recursive relationship
relationship
relationship class
relationship instance
requirements analysis stage
strong entity
subtype entity
supertype entity
ternary relationship
unary relationship
Unified Modeling Language
   (UML)
unique identifier
use case
weak entity

## REVIEW QUESTIONS

**4.1**   Name the three stages in the process of developing database systems. Summarize the tasks in each.

**4.2**   What is a data model, and what is its purpose?

**4.3**   What is a use case, and what is its purpose?

**4.4**   What is a prototype, and what is its purpose?

**4.5**   Give an example of a business rule that would need to be documented in a database development project.

**4.6**   Give an example of a data constraint.

**4.7** Define the term *entity* and give an example other than those used in this book.

**4.8** Explain the difference between an entity class and an entity instance.

**4.9** Define the term *attribute* and give examples for the entity you described in question 4.7.

**4.10** Define the term *identifier* and indicate which attribute defined in your answer to question 4.9 identifies the entity.

**4.11** Define the term *composite identifier* and give an example other than those used in this book.

**4.12** Define the term *relationship* and give an example other than those used in this book.

**4.13** Explain the difference between a relationship class and a relationship instance.

**4.14** Define the term *degree of relationship*. Give an example, other than one used in this text, of a relationship greater than degree two.

**4.15** List and give an example of the three types of binary relationships other than the ones used in this book. Draw both a traditional E-R diagram and an IE Crow's Foot E-R diagram for each.

**4.16** Define the terms *maximum cardinality* and *minimum cardinality*.

**4.17** Draw an IE Crow's Foot E-R diagram for the entities DEPARTMENT and EMPLOYEE and the 1:N relationship between them. Assume that a DEPARTMENT does not need to have an EMPLOYEE, but that every EMPLOYEE is assigned to a DEPARTMENT. Include appropriate identifiers and attributes for each entity.

**4.18** Define the term *ID-dependent entity* and give an example other than one used in this text. Draw an IE Crow's Foot E-R diagram for your example.

**4.19** Define the term *weak entity* and give an example other than one used in this text. Draw an IE Crow's Foot E-R diagram for your example.

**4.20** Explain the ambiguity in the definition of the term *weak entity*. Explain how this book interprets this term.

**4.21** Define the terms *supertype*, *subtype*, and *discriminator*.

**4.22** What is an inclusive subtype relationship? Give an example other than one shown in this chapter. Draw an IE Crow's Foot E-R diagram for your example.

**4.23** What is an exclusive subtype relationship? Give an example other than one shown in this book. Draw an IE Crow's Foot E-R diagram for your example.

**4.24** Give an example of a recursive relationship other than the one shown in this chapter. Draw an IE Crow's Foot E-R diagram for your example.

**4.25** List important attribute properties that need to be developed as part of a data model.

**4.26** Create sample properties for the attributes in your E-R diagram for DEPARTMENT and EMPLOYEE in question 4.17.

**4.27** Give an example of a business rule for your work for question 4.17.

**4.28** Summarize one technique for evaluating a data model and explain how that technique could be used to evaluate the data model in Figure 4-20.

**4.29** Describe why it is important to evaluate a data model.

## EXERCISES

**4.30** Suppose that Heather Sweeney wants to include records of her consulting services in her database. Extend the data model in Figure 4-20(c) to include CONSULTING_PROJECT and DAILY_PROJECT_HOURS entities. CONSULTING_PROJECT contains data about a particular project for one of Heather's customers, and DAILY_PROJECT_HOURS contains data about the hours spent and a description of the work accomplished on a particular day for a particular project. Use strong and/or weak entities as appropriate. Specify minimum and maximum cardinalities. Use the IE Crow's Foot E-R model for your E-R diagrams.

**4.31** Extend your work for question 4.30 to include supplies that Heather uses on a project. Assume that she wants to track the description, price, and amount used of each supply. Supplies are used on multiple days of a project. Use the IE Crow's Foot E-R model for your E-R diagrams.

**4.32** Develop a data model of a genealogical diagram. Model only biological parents; do not model stepparents. Use the IE Crow's Foot E-R model for your E-R diagrams.

**4.33** Develop a data model of a genealogical diagram. Model all parents, including stepparents. Use the IE Crow's Foot E-R model for your E-R diagrams.

**4.34** Using recursive relationships, as appropriate, develop a data model of the boxcars on a railway train. Use the IE Crow's Foot E-R model for your E-R diagrams.

## ACCESS WORKBENCH KEY TERMS

banded form editor                     banded report editor                     prototype database

## ACCESS WORKBENCH EXERCISES

"The Access Workbench" section in this chapter describes how to create two prototype databases and sample forms. That section details some steps that are new, but you have done most of the needed steps before. In the following set of exercises, you will:

- Create prototype forms
- Create prototype reports

**AW.4.1**    You have built an extensive database for the Wedgewood Pacific Corporation (**WPC.accdb**). You will now use it to build some prototype forms and reports so that the users at WPC can evaluate the proposed database. In this case, there is no need to restructure the database.

**A.**    Create a form that allows users to view and edit employee data. The form should show information about the employee, the department that he or she works for, and which projects the employee is assigned to.

**B.**    Create a report that displays the employee information shown on the form you created in part A. The report should show this information for all users, sorted alphabetically in ascending order by LastName.

**C.**    Create a form that allows users to view and edit project data. The form should show information about the project and the department that is responsible for the project, and it should list all employees who are assigned to work on that project.

**D.**    Create a report that displays the project information shown on the form you created in part C. The report should show this information for all projects, sorted in ascending order by ProjectID.

## GARDEN GLORY PROJECT QUESTIONS

Garden Glory wants to expand its database applications beyond the recording of property services. The company still wants to maintain data on owners, properties, employees, and services, but it wants to include other data as well. Specifically, Garden Glory wants to track equipment, how it is used during services, and equipment repairs. In addition, employees need to be trained before they use certain equipment, and management wants to be able to determine who has obtained training on which equipment.

With regard to properties, Garden Glory has determined that most of the properties it services are too large and complex to be described in one record. The company wants the database to allow for many subproperty descriptions of a property. Thus, a particular property might have subproperty descriptions such as Front Garden, Back Garden, Second-Level Courtyard, and so on. For better accounting to the customers, services are to be related to the subproperties rather than to the overall property.

   **A.** Draw an E-R data model for the Garden Glory database schema shown in Chapter 3's "Garden Glory Project Questions." Use the IE Crow's Foot E-R model for your E-R diagrams. Justify the decisions you make regarding minimum and maximum cardinality.

   **B.** Extend and modify the E-R data model to meet Garden Glory's new requirements. Use the IE Crow's Foot E-R model for your E-R diagrams. Create appropriate identifiers and attributes for each entity. Justify the decisions you make regarding minimum and maximum cardinality.

   **C.** Specify data properties for the attributes in your E-R diagram in part B.

   **D.** Describe how you would go about validating the model in part B.

## JAMES RIVER JEWELRY PROJECT QUESTIONS

James River Jewelry wants to expand its database applications beyond the recording of purchases and purchase awards. (See the description of the award program in Chapter 1's "James River Jewelry Project Questions.") The company still wants to maintain data on customers, purchases, and awards, but it wants to include other data as well. Specifically, James River Jewelry wants to record artists and styles and keep track of which customers are interested in which artists and styles.

James River Jewelry sells most of its jewelry on consignment, so the company does not pay the artist of a piece of jewelry until it is sold. Typically, the company pays artists 60 percent of the sales price, but the terms are negotiated separately for each item. For some items, the artists earn a larger percentage and for others they earn less. Artists and James River Jewelry personnel agree on the initial sales price at the time the item is brought to the shop. When an item has been in the shop for some time, James River Jewelry may reduce the price; sometimes it renegotiates the sales percentage.

   **A.** Draw an E-R data model for the James River Jewelry database schema shown in Chapter 3's "James River Jewelry Project Questions." Use the IE Crow's Foot E-R model for your E-R diagrams. Justify the decisions you make regarding minimum and maximum cardinality.

   **B.** Extend and modify the E-R data model to show James River Jewelry's award program. Use the IE Crow's Foot E-R model for your E-R diagrams. Create appropriate identifiers and attributes for each entity. Justify the decisions you make regarding minimum and maximum cardinality.

**C.** Extend and modify the E-R data model in part B to meet James River Jewelry's new requirements. Use the IE Crow's Foot E-R model for your E-R diagrams. Create appropriate identifiers and attributes for each entity. Justify the decisions you make regarding minimum and maximum cardinality.

**D.** Specify data properties for the attributes in your E-R diagram in part C.

**E.** Describe how you would go about validating the data model in part C.

 ## THE QUEEN ANNE CURIOSITY SHOP PROJECT QUESTIONS

The Queen Anne Curiosity Shop wants to expand its database applications beyond the current recording of sales. The company still wants to maintain data on customers, employees, vendors, sales, and items, but it wants to (a) modify the way it handles inventory and (b) simplify the storage of customer and employee data.

Currently, each item is considered unique, which means the item must be sold as a whole, and multiple units of the item in stock must be treated as separate items in the ITEM table. The Queen Anne Curiosity Shop management wants the database modified to include an inventory system that will allow multiple units of an item to be stored under one ItemID. The system should allow for a quantity on hand, a quantity on order, and an order due date. If the identical item is stocked by multiple vendors, the item should be orderable from any of these vendors. The SALE_ITEM table should then include Quantity and ExtendedPrice columns to allow for sales of multiple units of an item.

Queen Anne Curiosity Shop management has noticed that some of the fields in CUSTOMER and EMPLOYEE store similar data. Under the current system, when an employee buys something at the store, his or her data has to be reentered in the CUSTOMER table. The managers would like to have the CUSTOMER and EMPLOYEE tables redesigned using subtypes.

**A.** Draw an E-R data model for the Queen Anne Curiosity Shop database schema shown in Chapter 3's "Queen Anne Curiosity Shop Project Questions." Use the IE Crow's Foot E-R model for your E-R diagrams. Justify the decisions you make regarding minimum and maximum cardinality.

**B.** Extend and modify the E-R data model by adding *only* the Queen Anne Curiosity Shop's inventory system requirements. Use the IE Crow's Foot E-R model for your E-R diagrams. Create appropriate identifiers and attributes for each entity. Justify the decisions you make regarding minimum and maximum cardinality.

**C.** Extend and modify the E-R data model by adding *only* the Queen Anne Curiosity Shop's need for more efficient storage of CUSTOMER and EMPLOYEE data. Use the IE Crow's Foot E-R model for your E-R diagrams. Create appropriate identifiers and attributes for each entity. Justify the decisions you make regarding minimum and maximum cardinality.

**D.** Combine the E-R data models from parts B and C to meet all of the Queen Anne Curiosity Shop's new requirements, making additional modifications if any are needed. Use the IE Crow's Foot E-R model for your E-R diagrams.

**E.** Specify data properties for the attributes in your E-R diagram in question D.

**F.** Describe how you would go about validating your data model in part D.

# CHAPTER 5

# Database Design

## Chapter Objectives

> Learn how to transform E-R data models into relational designs

> Practice applying the normalization process

> Understand the need for denormalization

> Learn how to represent weak entities with the relational model

> Know how to represent 1:1, 1:N, and N:M binary relationships

> Know how to represent 1:1, 1:N, and N:M recursive relationships

> Learn SQL statements for creating joins over binary and recursive relationships

> Understand the nature and background of normalization theory

This chapter describes a process for converting E-R data models into relational designs. We begin by explaining how entities are expressed as relations (or tables). We then apply the role of the normalization process that you learned in Chapter 2 and describe normalization in more detail. Next, we show how to represent relationships using foreign keys, including how to use these techniques for representing recursive relationships. Finally, we apply all these techniques to design a database for the data model of Heather Sweeney Designs that we developed in Chapter 4.

# TRANSFORMING A DATA MODEL INTO A DATABASE DESIGN

The steps for transforming a data model into a **database design** are shown in Figure 5-1. First, we create a table for each entity in the data model. Then, we make sure that each of the tables is properly normalized. Finally, we create the relationships between the tables.[1]

---

**B T W**

As you learned in Chapter 2, the technically correct term for the representation of an entity in a relational model is **relation**. However, the use of the synonym **table** is common, and we use it in the chapter. Just remember that the two terms mean the same thing when used to discuss databases.

---

# REPRESENTING ENTITIES WITH THE RELATIONAL MODEL

The representation of entities using the relational model is direct and straightforward. First, you define a table for each entity and give that table the same name as the entity. You make the primary key of the relation the identifier of the entity. Then, you create a column in the relation for each attribute in the entity. Finally, you apply the normalization process described in Chapter 2 to remove any normalization problems. To understand this process, we will consider three examples.

## Representing the ITEM Entity

Consider the ITEM entity shown in Figure 5-2(a), which contains the attributes ItemNumber, Description, Cost, ListPrice, and QuantityOnHand. To represent this entity with a table, we define a table named ITEM and place the attributes in it as columns in the relation. ItemNumber is the identifier of the entity and becomes the primary key of the

**FIGURE 5-1**

The Steps for Transforming a Data Model into a Database Design

1. Create a table for each entity:
   - Specify primary key (consider surrogate keys as appropriate)
   - Specify properties for each column:
     - Data type
     - Null status
     - Default value (if any)
     - Specify data constraints (if any)
   - Verify normalization

2. Create relationships by placing foreign keys:
   - Strong entity relationships (1:1, 1:N, N:M)
   - ID-dependent and non–ID-dependent weak entity relationships
   - Subtypes
   - Recursive (1:1, 1:N, N:M)

---

[1]The transformation is actually a bit more complex than this when you consider the need to enforce minimum cardinalities. Although the referential integrity constraints (with ON UPDATE and ON DELETE) handle some parts of this, application logic is required to handle other parts, and that is beyond the scope of this book. See David M. Kroenke and David J. Auer, *Database Processing: Fundamentals, Design, and Implementation*, 11th edition (Upper Saddle River, NJ: Prentice Hall, 2010), Chapter 6.

**FIGURE 5-2**

The ITEM Entity
and Table

(a) The ITEM Entity

(b) The ITEM Table

table. The result is shown in Figure 5-2(b), where a key symbol identifies the primary key. The ITEM table can also be written as:

ITEM (ItemNumber, Description, Cost, ListPrice, QuantityOnHand)

Note that in this notation the primary key of the table is underlined.

**Surrogate Keys**   The ideal primary key is short, numeric, and nonchanging. ItemNumber meets these criteria. However, if the primary key does not meet these criteria, a DBMS-generated **surrogate key** should be used. Surrogate key values are numeric, unique within a table, and never change. These keys are assigned when a row is created and deleted when the row is deleted—the numbers are never reused. Surrogate keys would be ideal primary keys except for a couple of considerations.

First, the numbers generated have no intrinsic meaning. For example, if surrogate key values are used as the values of ItemNumber in the ITEM table, you cannot interpret them in a meaningful way. Second, although the surrogate key values may not be duplicated within a table, they may not be unique between two databases. Consider two databases, each of which has an ITEM table with the surrogate ID of ItemNumber. If the data from these databases is ever shared, this may present a problem. Nonetheless, surrogate keys are very useful and are commonly used as ID numbers in tables.

**Column Properties**   Note that each attribute in the ITEM entity has become a column in the ITEM table. You need to specify certain **column properties** for each column, as mentioned in the discussion of attributes at the end of Chapter 4. These include data types, null status, default values, and any constraints on the values.

**Data Types**   Each DBMS supports certain **data types**. (Data Types for SQL Server 2008, Oracle Database 11g, and MySQL 5.1 were discussed in Chapter 3, while data types for Microsoft Access 2010 were discussed in Chapter 1.) For each column, you indicate exactly what type of data will be stored in that column. Data types are usually set when the table is actually created in the database, as discussed in Chapter 3.

**NULL Status**   Next, you need to decide which column must have data values entered when a new row is created in the table. If a column *must* have a data value entered, then this column will be designated NOT NULL. If the value can be left empty, then the column will be designated NULL. The **NULL status**—NULL or NOT NULL—of the column is usually set when the table is actually created in the database, as discussed in Chapter 3.

You have to be careful here: If you specify columns as NOT NULL when you do not know the data value at the time the row is being created, you will not be able to create the row. For this reason, some columns that may appear to you as needing to be NOT NULL must actually be specified as NULL. This data will be entered, but not at the exact moment the row is created in the table.

For the ITEM table, you set only ListPrice as NULL. This is a number that may not have been determined by management at the time data on an ITEM is entered into the database. All other columns should have known values at the time a row is created and are NOT NULL.

**Default Values**   A **default value** is a value that the DBMS automatically supplies when a new row is created. The default value may be a static value or one calculated by application logic. In this book, we deal with only static values. Default values are usually set when the table is actually created in the database, as discussed in Chapter 3. In the ITEM table, you should specify a default of 0 for QuantityOnHand. This will indicate that the ITEM is out of stock until this value is updated.

***Data Constraints*** The data values in some columns may be subject to restrictions on the values that can exist in those columns. Such limitations are called **data constraints**. An example we have already seen is the referential integrity constraint, which states that the only values allowed in a foreign key column are values already existing in the corresponding primary key column in the related table. Data constraints are usually set when the table is actually created in the database, as discussed in Chapter 3. In the ITEM table, one needed data constraint is (ListPrice > Cost), to ensure that you do not inadvertently sell an ITEM for less than you paid for it.

**Verifying Normalization** Finally, you need to verify that the ITEM table is properly normalized because the table results from converting an entity sometimes have normalization problems. Therefore, the next step is to apply the normalization process from Chapter 2. In the case of ITEM, the only candidate key is the primary key, which is ItemNumber, and no other functional dependencies exist. Therefore, the ITEM table is normalized to Boyce-Codd Normal Form (BCNF). The final ITEM table, with column types, surrogate key indicator, and NULL/NOT NULL constraints indicated, is shown in Figure 5-3. Generally, we do not show this much detail in the illustrations of the tables in this chapter, but note that these types of details are available in commercial database design programs and can usually be displayed, as needed.

## Representing the CUSTOMER Entity

To understand an entity that gives rise to normalization problems, consider the CUSTOMER entity in Figure 5-4(a). If you transform the entity as just described, you obtain the table shown in Figure 5-4(b):

CUSTOMER (<u>CustomerNumber</u>, CustomerName, StreetAddress, City, State, ZIP, ContactName, Phone)

CustomerNumber is the key of the relation, and you can assume that you have done all the necessary work on column definition.

**FIGURE 5-3**

**The Final ITEM Table**

ITEM

| ITEM |
| --- |
| 🔑 ItemNumber: int IDENTITY(10000,1) |
| Description: varchar(100) NOT NULL<br>Cost: numeric(9,2) NOT NULL<br>ListPrice: numeric(9,2) NULL<br>QuantityOnHand: int NOT NULL |

**FIGURE 5-4**

**The CUSTOMER Entity and Table**

CUSTOMER

| CUSTOMER |
| --- |
| CustomerNumber |
| CustomerName<br>StreetAddress<br>City<br>State<br>ZIP<br>ContactName<br>Phone |

CUSTOMER

| CUSTOMER |
| --- |
| 🔑 CustomerNumber |
| CustomerName<br>StreetAddress<br>City<br>State<br>ZIP<br>ContactName<br>Phone |

(a) The CUSTOMER Entity        (b) The CUSTOMER Table

According to the normalization process (see page 84), you need to check for functional dependencies besides those involving the primary key. At least one exists:

ZIP → (City, State)

The only candidate key in CUSTOMER is CustomerNumber. ZIP is *not* a candidate key for this relation; therefore, this relation is not normalized. Furthermore, another possible functional dependency involves Phone. Is Phone the phone number of the CUSTOMER, or is it the phone number of the contact? If PhoneNumber is the phone number of the CUSTOMER, then:

CustomerNumber → Phone

and no additional normalization problem exists. However, if the PhoneNumber is that of the contact, then:

ContactName → Phone

and because ContactName is not a candidate key, there are normalization problems here as well.

You can determine whose phone number it is by asking the users. Assume that you do that, and the users say that indeed it is the phone number of the contact. Thus:

ContactName → Phone

Given these facts, you can proceed to normalize the CUSTOMER table. According to the normalization process, you pull the attributes of the functional dependencies out of the tables while leaving a copy of their determinants in the original relation as foreign keys. The result is the three relations shown in Figure 5-5:

CUSTOMER (<u>CustomerNumber</u>, CustomerName, StreetAddress,
   *ZIP, ContactName*)
ZIP (<u>ZIP</u>, City, State)
CONTACT (<u>ContactName</u>, Phone)

with the referential integrity constraints:

ZIP in CUSTOMER must exist in ZIP in ZIP
ContactName in CUSTOMER must exist in ContactName in CONTACT

---

**FIGURE 5-5**

**The Normalized CUSTOMER and Associated Tables**

ZIP

| ZIP |
| --- |
| City |
| State |

CUSTOMER

| CustomerNumber |
| --- |
| CustomerName |
| StreetAddress |
| ZIP |
| ContactName |

CONTACT

| ContactName |
| --- |
| Phone |

ZIP
is a foreign key referencing
ZIP in ZIP

ContactName
is a foreign key referencing
ContactName in CONTACT

These three relations are now normalized, and you can continue with the design process. However, let us first consider another perspective on normalization.

## Denormalization

It is possible to take normalization too far. Most practitioners would consider the construction of a separate ZIP table to be going too far. People are accustomed to writing their city, state, and ZIP as a group, and breaking City and State away from ZIP will make the design difficult to use. It will also mean that the DBMS has to read two separate tables just to get the customer's address. Therefore, even though it results in normalization problems, a better overall design would result by leaving ZIP, City, and State in the CUSTOMER relation. This is an example of **denormalization**.

What are the consequences of this decision to denormalize? Consider the three basic operations: insert, update, and delete. If you leave ZIP, City, and State in CUSTOMER, then you will not be able to insert data for a new zip code until a customer has that zip code. However, you will never want to do that. You only care about ZIP code data when one of the customers has that ZIP code. Therefore, leaving the ZIP data in CUSTOMER does not pose problems when inserting.

What about modifications? If a city changes its ZIP code, then you might have to change multiple rows in CUSTOMER. How frequently do cities change their ZIP codes, though? Because the answer is almost never, updates in the denormalized relation are not a problem. Finally, what about deletes? If only one customer has the ZIP data (80210, Denver, Colorado), then if you delete that customer you will lose the fact that 80210 is in Denver. This does not really matter, because when another customer with this ZIP code is inserted that customer also will provide the city and state.

Therefore, denormalizing CUSTOMER by leaving the attributes ZIP, City, and State in the relation will make the design easier to use and not cause modification problems. The denormalized design is better, and it is shown in Figure 5-6:

CUSTOMER (<u>CustomerNumber</u>, CustomerName, StreetAddress, City, State, ZIP, *ContactName*)

CONTACT (<u>ContactName</u>, Phone)

with the referential integrity constraints:

ContactName in CUSTOMER must exist in ContactName in CONTACT

The need for denormalization can also arise for reasons such as security and performance. If the cost of modification problems is low (as for zip codes), and if other factors cause denormalized relations to be preferred, then denormalizing is a good idea.

**FIGURE 5-6**

The Denormalized CUSTOMER and Associated CONTACT Tables

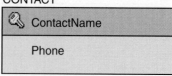

CUSTOMER

| 🔑 CustomerNumber |
| CustomerName |
| StreetAddress |
| City |
| State |
| ZIP |
| ContactName |

CONTACT

| 🔑 ContactName |
| Phone |

ContactName
is a foreign key referencing
ContactName in CONTACT

## A Relational Design for the SALES_COMMISSION Entity

To summarize the discussion so far, when representing an entity with the relational model the first step is to construct a table that has all the entity's attributes as columns. The identifier of the entity becomes the primary key of the table, and we define the column constraints. Then, the table is normalized. A reason might exist for leaving parts of a table denormalized.

By proceeding in this way, we always consider the normalized design. If we make a decision to denormalize, we then do so from a position of knowledge and not from ignorance.

To reinforce these ideas, let us consider a third example—the SALES_COMMISSION entity in Figure 5-7(a). First, you create a relation that has all the attributes as columns, as shown in Figure 5-7(b):

SALES_COMMISSION (SalespersonNumber, SalespersonLastName, SalespersonFirstName, Phone, <u>CheckNumber</u>, CheckDate, CommissionPeriod, TotalCommissionSales, CommissionAmount, BudgetCategory)

As shown, the primary key of the table is CheckNumber, the identifier of the entity. The attributes of the relation have three additional functional dependencies:

SalespersonNumber →
(SalespersonLastName, SalespersonFirstName, Phone, BudgetCategory)

CheckNumber → CheckDate

(SalespersonNumber, CommissionPeriod) →
(TotalCommissionSales, CommissionAmount, CheckNumber, CheckDate)

According to the normalization process, you extract the attributes of these functional dependencies from the original table and make the determinants the primary keys of the new tables. You also leave a copy of the determinants in the original table as foreign keys. The only complication in this case is that the name of the original table actually makes more sense when used for one of the new tables that has been created! The original table, given the primary key CheckNumber, should actually be called COMMISSION_CHECK, and it has been renamed as such in the normalization results shown in Figure 5-8:

SALESPERSON (<u>SalespersonNumber</u>, SalespersonLastName, SalespersonFirstName, Phone, BudgetCategory)
SALES_COMMISSION (*<u>SalespersonNumber</u>*, <u>CommissionPeriod</u>, TotalCommissionSales, CommissionAmount, *CheckNumber*)
COMMISSION_CHECK (<u>CheckNumber</u>, CheckDate)

**FIGURE 5-7**

The
SALES_COMMISSION
Entity and Table

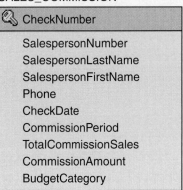

(a) The SALES_COMMISSION Entity          (b) The SALES_COMMISSION Table

**FIGURE 5-8**

The Normalized SALES_COMMISSION and Associated Tables

SalespersonNumber is a foreign key referencing
SalespersonNumber in SALESPERSON

SALES_COMMISSION is ID-dependent on SALESPERSON

CheckNumber is a foreign key referencing CheckNumber
in COMMISSION_CHECK

with the referential integrity constraints:

SalespersonNumber in SALES_COMMISSION must exist in SalespersonNumber
in SALESPERSON

CheckNumber in SALES_COMMISSION must exist in CheckNumber
in COMMISSION_CHECK

Now consider denormalization. Is there any reason not to create these new relations? Is the design better if you leave them in the COMMISSION_CHECK relation (the renamed SALES_COMMISSION relation)? In this case, there is no reason to denormalize, so you leave the normalized relations alone.

## Representing Weak Entities

The process described so far works for all entity types, but weak entities sometimes require special treatment. Recall that a weak entity logically depends on another entity. In Figure 5-8, SALES_COMMISSION is an ID-dependent weak entity that depends on SALESPERSON for its existence. In this model, there cannot be a SALES_COMMISSION without a SALESPERSON. Also note that in Figure 5-8, we consider that COMMISSION_CHECK is a strong entity because once the check is written is has a separate, physical existence of its own, just like a SALESPERSON (an alternate conceptualization would require an additional CHECKING_ACCOUNT entity as the strong entity with CHECK as an ID-dependent weak entity, in which case the composite primary key of CHECK would be used as the foreign key in SALES_COMMISSION).

If a weak entity is not ID-dependent, it can be represented as a table, using the techniques just described. The dependency needs to be recorded in the relational design so that no application will create a weak entity without its proper parent (the entity on which the weak entity depends). Finally, a business rule will need to be implemented so that when the parent is deleted the weak entity is also deleted. These rules are part of the relational design, and, in this case, take the form of an ON DELETE CASCADE constraint on the weak, non–ID-dependent table.

The situation is slightly different if a weak entity is also ID-dependent. This is the case in the dependence of SALES_COMMISSION on SALESPERSON, because each SALES_COMMISSION is identified by the SALESPERSON who made the sale. When creating a table for an ID-dependent entity, we must ensure that the identifier of the parent and the identifier of the ID-dependent weak entity itself appear in the table. For example, consider what would happen if you established the table for SALES_COMMISSION without including the key of SALESPERSON. What would be the key of this table? It would be just

**FIGURE 5-9**

Relational Representation of a Weak Entity

| (a) Weak Entity Example | (b) The LINE_ITEM Table with the Correct Primary Key |

CommissionPeriod, but because SALES_COMMISSION is ID-dependent this is not a complete key. In fact, without the needed reference to SALESPERSON included, CommissionPeriod by itself cannot be the primary key because this table would likely have duplicate rows. (This would happen if two occurrences of a specific CommissionPeriod had the same TotalCommissionSales in the same BudgetCategory, which could happen because this table records data for more than one SALESPERSON.) Thus, for an ID-dependent weak entity it is necessary to add the primary key of the parent entity to the weak entity's table, and this added attribute becomes part of that table's key. In Figure 5-8, note that SALES_COMMISSION has the correct composite primary key (SalespersonNumber, CommissionPeriod).

As another example, consider Figure 5-9(a), where LINE_ITEM is an ID-dependent weak entity. It is weak because its logical existence depends on INVOICE, and it is ID-dependent because its identifier contains the identifier of INVOICE. Again, consider what would happen if you established a relation for LINE_ITEM without including the key of INVOICE. What would be the key of this relation? It would be just LineNumber, but because LINE_ITEM is ID-dependent that cannot be a complete key. Without the needed reference to ITEM included, LINE_ITEM, like SALESPERSON_SALES in the previous example, would likely have duplicate rows. (This would happen if two invoices had the same quantity of the same item on the same line.) Figure 5-9(b) shows LINE_ITEM with the correct composite primary key (InvoiceNumber, LineNumber).

## NORMAL FORMS

A table and a spreadsheet are very similar to one another in that we can think of both as having rows, columns, and cells. Edgar Frank (E. F.) Codd, the father of the relational model, defined three normal forms in an early paper on the relational model. He defined any table that meets the definition of a relation (see Figure 2-1 on page 69) as being in **first normal form (1NF)**.

Codd pointed out that such tables can have anomalies (which are referred to elsewhere in the text as *normalization problems*), and he defined a **second normal form (2NF)** that eliminated some of those anomalies. A relation is in 2NF if and only if (1) it is in 1NF and (2) all nonkey attributes are determined by the entire primary key. This means that if the primary key is a composite primary key, no nonkey attribute can be determined by an attribute or attributes that make up only part of the key. Thus, if you have a relation (**A**, **B**, **N**, **O**, **P**) with the composite key (**A**, **B**), then none of the nonkey attributes **N**, **O**, or **P** can be determined by *just* **A** or *just* **B**.

*(Continued)*

However, the conditions of 2NF did not eliminate all the anomalies, so Codd defined **third normal form (3NF)**. A relation is in 3NF if and only if (1) it is in 2NF and (2) there are no nonkey attributes determined by another nonkey attribute. Technically, the situation described by the preceding condition is called a **transitive dependency**. Thus, in our relation (**A, B, N, O, P**) *none* of the nonkey attributes—**N, O,** or **P**—can be determined by **N, O,** or **P** or any combination of them.

Not long after Codd published his paper on normal forms, it was pointed out to him that even relations in 3NF could have anomalies. As a result, he and R. Boyce defined **Boyce-Codd Normal Form (BCNF)**, which eliminated the anomalies that had been found with 3NF. As stated in Chapter 2, a relation is in BCNF if and only if every determinant is a candidate key. This is summed up in a widely known phrase:

I swear to construct my tables so that all nonkey columns are dependent on the key, the whole key, and nothing but the key, so help me Codd!

All these definitions were made in such a way that a relation in a higher normal form is defined to be in all lower normal forms. Thus, a relation in BCNF is automatically in 3NF, a relation in 3NF is automatically in 2NF, and a relation in 2NF is automatically in 1NF.

There the matter rested until others discovered another kind of dependency, called a **multivalued dependency**. (Such dependencies are illustrated in Exercises 2-40 and 2-41 at the end of Chapter 2.) To eliminate multivalued dependencies, **fourth normal form (4NF)** was defined. To put tables into 4NF, the initial table must be split into tables such that the multiple values of any multivalued attribute are moved into the new tables. These are then accessed via 1:N relationships between the original table and the tables holding the multiple values.

A little later, another kind of anomaly involving tables that can be split apart but not correctly joined back together was identified, and **fifth normal form (5NF)** was defined to eliminate that type of anomaly.

You can see how the knowledge evolved: None of these normal forms were perfect—each one eliminated certain anomalies, and none asserted that it was vulnerable to no anomaly at all. At this stage, in 1981, R. Fagin took a different approach and asked why, rather than just chipping away at anomalies, we do not look for conditions that would have to exist in order for a relation to have no anomalies at all. He did just that and, in the process, defined **domain/key normal form (DK/NF)**. Fagin proved that a relation in DK/NF can have no anomalies, and he further proved that a relation that has no anomalies is also in DK/NF.

For some reason, DK/NF never caught the fancy of the general database population, but it should have. As you can tell, no one should brag that their relations are in 3NF; instead, we should all brag that our relations are in DK/NF. But for some reason (perhaps because there is fashion in database theory, just as there is fashion in clothes), it just is not done.

You are probably wondering what the conditions of DK/NF are. Basically, DK/NF requires that all the constraints on data values be logical implications of the definition of domains and keys. To the level of detail of this text, and to the level of detail experienced by 99 percent of all database practitioners, this can be restated as follows: Every determinant of a functional dependency must be a candidate key. This is exactly where we started and what we have defined as BCNF.

You can broaden this statement a bit to include multivalued dependencies and say that every determinant of a functional or multivalued dependency must be a candidate key. The trouble with this is that as soon as we constrain a multivalued dependency in this way it is transformed into a functional dependency. Our original statement is fine. It is like saying that good health comes to overweight people who lose weight until they are of an appropriate weight. As soon as they lose their excess weight, they are no longer overweight. Hence, good health comes to people who have appropriate weight.

So, as Paul Harvey says, now you know the rest of the story. Just ensure that every determinant of a functional dependency is a candidate key (BCNF), and you can claim that your relations are fully normalized. You do not want to say they are in DK/NF until you learn more about it, though, because someone might ask you what that means. However, for most practical purposes your relations are in DK/NF as well.

**Note:** For more information on normal forms, see David M. Kroenke and David J. Auer, *Database Processing: Fundamentals, Design, and Implementation*, 11th edition (Upper Saddle River, NJ: Prentice Hall, 2010): 106–121.

# REPRESENTING RELATIONSHIPS

So far, you have learned how to create a relational design for the entities in an E-R model. However, to convert a data model to a relational design, we must also represent the relationships.

The techniques used to represent E-R relationships depend on the maximum cardinality of the relationships. As you saw in Chapter 4, three relationship possibilities exist: one-to-one (1:1), one-to-many (1:N), and many-to-many (M:N). A fourth possibility, many-to-one (N:1), is represented in the same way as 1:N, so we need not consider it as a separate case. In general, we create relationships by placing foreign keys in tables. The following sections consider various types of relationships.

## Relationships Among Strong Entities

The easiest relationships to work with are relationships among strong entities. We will start with these and then consider other types of relationships.

### Representing 1:1 Strong Entity Relationships
The simplest form of binary relationship is a 1:1 relationship, in which an entity of one type is related to at most one entity of another type. In Figure 5-10(a), the same 1:1 relationship that was used in Figure 4-5(a) between EMPLOYEE and LOCKER is shown in IE Crow's Foot notation. According to this diagram, an employee is assigned at most one locker, and a locker is assigned to at most one employee.

Representing a 1:1 relationship with the relational model is straightforward. First, each entity is represented with a table as just described, and then the key of one of the tables is placed in the other as a foreign key. In Figure 5-10(b), the key of LOCKER is stored in EMPLOYEE as a foreign key, and you create the referential integrity constraint:

LockerNumber in EMPLOYEE must exist in LockerNumber in LOCKER

**FIGURE 5-10**

**1:1 Strong Entity Relationships**

(a) Example 1:1 Strong Entity Relationship

(b) Placing the Primary Key of LOCKER into EMPLOYEE

(c) Placing the Primary Key of EMPLOYEE into LOCKER

In Figure 5-10(c), the key of EMPLOYEE is stored in LOCKER as a foreign key, and you create the referential integrity constraint:

EmployeeNumber in LOCKER must exist in EmployeeNumber in EMPLOYEE

In general, for a 1:1 relationship the key of either table can be placed as a foreign key in the other table. To verify that this is so, consider both cases in Figure 5-10. Suppose that for the design in Figure 5-10(b) you have an employee and want the locker assigned to that employee. To get the employee data, you use EmployeeNumber to obtain the employee's row in EMPLOYEE. From this row, you obtain the LockerNumber of the locker assigned to that employee. You then use that number to look up the locker data in LOCKER.

Now consider the other direction. Assume that you have a locker and want to know which employee is assigned to that locker. Using the design in Figure 5-10(b), you access the EMPLOYEE table and look up the row that has the given LockerNumber. The data of the employee who has been assigned that locker appears in that row.

You take similar actions to travel in either direction for the alternative design in which the foreign key of EmployeeNumber is placed in LOCKER, as shown in Figure 5-10(c). Using this design, to go from EMPLOYEE to LOCKER, you go directly to the LOCKER table and look up the row in LOCKER that has the given employee's number as its value of EmployeeNumber. To travel from LOCKER to EMPLOYEE, you look up the row in LOCKER that has a given LockerNumber. From this row, you extract the EmployeeNumber and use it to access the employee data in EMPLOYEE.

In this situation, we are using the term *look up* to mean "to find a row given a value of one of its columns." Another way to view this is in terms of joins. For the relations in Figure 5-10(b), you can form the following join:

```
SELECT      *
FROM        EMPLOYEE, LOCKER
WHERE       EMPLOYEE.LockerNumber = LOCKER.LockerNumber;
```

Because the relationship is 1:1, the result of this join will have a single row for a given combination of employee and locker. The row will have all columns from both tables.

For the relations in Figure 5-10(c), you can join the two tables on EmployeeNumber as follows:

```
SELECT      *
FROM        EMPLOYEE, LOCKER
WHERE       EMPLOYEE.EmployeeNumber = LOCKER.EmployeeNumber;
```

Again, one row will be found for each combination of employee and locker. In both of these joins, neither unassigned employees nor unassigned lockers will appear.

Although the two designs in Figures 5-10(b) and 5-10(c) are equivalent in concept, they may differ in performance. For instance, if a query in one direction is more common than a query in the other, we might prefer one design to the other. Also, depending on underlying structures, if an index for EmployeeNumber is in both tables but no index on LockerNumber is in either table, then the first design is better. In addition, considering the join operation, if one table is much larger than the other, then one of these joins might be faster to perform than the other.

Another example of a 1:1 strong entity relationship is the relationship between the CUSTOMER and CONTACT tables shown in Figure 5-6. For each CUSTOMER, there is one and only one CONTACT, and based on the normalization we did we have used the primary key of CONTACT as the foreign key in CUSTOMER. The resulting relationship is shown in Figure 5-11.

**FIGURE 5-11**

1:1 Strong Entity Relationship Between CUSTOMER and CONTACT

To actually implement a 1:1 relationship in a database, we must constrain the values of the designated foreign key as UNIQUE. This can be done in the SQL CREATE TABLE statement that is used to build the table containing the foreign key, or it can be done by altering the table structure after the table is created using the SQL ALTER TABLE statement. Consider the EMPLOYEE-to-LOCKER relationships. If, for example, we decide that to place the foreign key EmployeeNumber in the LOCKER table to create the relationship, we will need to constrain EmployeeNumber in LOCKER as UNIQUE. To do this we will use the SQL statement:

```
CONSTRAINT   UniqueEmployeeNumber  UNIQUE(EmployeeNumber)
```

as a line of SQL code either in the original CREATE TABLE LOCKER command or in the following ALTER TABLE LOCKER command (which assumes that any data already in LOCKER will not violate the UNIQUE constraint),

```
ALTER TABLE LOCKER
    ADD CONSTRAINT UniqueEmployeeNumber
        UNIQUE (EmployeeNumber);
```

**Representing 1:N Strong Entity Relationships**  The second type of binary relationship, known as 1:N, is a relationship in which an entity of one type can be related to many entities of another type. In Figure 5-12(a), the 1:N relationship that was used in Figure 4-5(b) between ITEM and QUOTATION is shown in IE Crow's Foot notation. According to this diagram, we have received from zero to several quotations for each item in the database.

The terms **parent** and **child** are sometimes applied to relations in 1:N relationships. The parent relation is on the one side of the relationship, and the child relation is on the many side. In Figure 5-12(a), ITEM is the parent entity and QUOTATION is the child entity.

**FIGURE 5-12**

1:N Strong Entity Relationships

(a) 1:N Strong Entity Relationship Example

(b) Placing the Primary Key of ITEM into QUOTATION

Representing 1:N relationships is simple and straightforward. First, each entity is represented by a table, as described, and then the key of the table representing the *parent entity* is placed in the table representing the *child entity* as a foreign key. Thus, to represent the relationship in Figure 5-12(a) you place the primary key of ITEM, which is ItemNumber, into the QUOTATION table as shown in Figure 5-12(b), and you create the referential integrity constraint:

ItemNumber in QUOTATION must exist in ItemNumber in ITEM

Notice that with ItemNumber stored as a foreign key in QUOTATION you can process the relationship in both directions. Given a QuoteNumber, you can look up the appropriate row in QUOTATION and get the ItemNumber of the item from the row data. To obtain the rest of the ITEM data, you use the ItemNumber obtained from QUOTATION to look up the appropriate row in ITEM. To determine all the quotes associated with a particular item, you look up all rows in QUOTATION that have the item's ItemNumber as a value for ItemNumber. Quotation data are then taken from those rows.

In terms of joins, you can obtain the item and quote data in one table with the following:

```
SELECT      *
FROM        ITEM, QUOTATION
WHERE       ITEM.ItemNumber = QUOTATION.ItemNumber;
```

Contrast this 1:N relationship design strategy with that for 1:1 relationships. In both cases, we store the key of one relation as a foreign key in the second relation. In a 1:1 relationship, we can place the key of either relation in the other. In a 1:N relationship, however, the key of the parent relation *must* be placed in the child relation.

To understand this better, notice what would happen if you tried to put the key of the child into the parent relation (that is, put QuoteNumber in ITEM). Because attributes in a relation can have only a single value, each ITEM record has room for only one QuoteNumber. Consequently, such a structure cannot be used to represent the many side of the 1:N relationship. Hence, to represent a 1:N relationship we must always place the key of the parent relation in the child relation.

To actually implement a 1:N relationship in a database, we only need to add the foreign key column to the table holding the foreign key. Because this column will normally be unconstrained in terms of how many times a value can occur, a 1:N relationship is established by default. In fact, this is the reason that we must use a column constraint to create a 1:1 relationship, as discussed early in this chapter. We will illustrate this point in this chapter's section of "The Access Workbench."

### Representing N:M Strong Entity Relationships

The third and final type of binary relationship is N:M, in which an entity of one type corresponds to many entities of the second type and an entity of the second type corresponds to many entities of the first type.

Figure 5-13(a) shows an E-R diagram of the N:M relationship between students and classes. A STUDENT entity can correspond to many CLASS entities, and a CLASS entity can correspond to many STUDENT entities. Notice that both participants in the relationship are optional: A student does not need to be enrolled in a class, and a class is not required to have any students. Figure 5-13(b) gives sample data.

N:M relationships cannot be represented directly by relations in the same way that 1:1 and 1:N relationships are represented. To understand why this is so, try using the same strategy as for 1:1 and 1:N relationships—placing the key of one relation as a foreign key into the other relation. First, define a relation for each of the entities; call them STUDENT and CLASS. Then, try to put the primary key of STUDENT, which is SID, into CLASS. Because multiple values are not allowed in the cells of a relation, you have room for only one StudentNumber, so you have no place to record the StudentNumber of the second and subsequent students.

A similar problem occurs if you try to put the primary key of CLASS, which is ClassNumber, into STUDENT. You can readily store the identifier of the first class in which a student is enrolled, but you have no place to store the identifier of additional classes.

**FIGURE 5-13**

**N:M Strong Entity Relationships**

(a) N:M Strong Entity Relationship Example

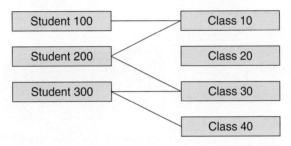

(b) Sample Data for the STUDENT-to-CLASS Relationship

Figure 5-14 shows another (but incorrect) strategy. In this case, a row is stored in the CLASS relation for each STUDENT enrolled in one class, so you have two records for Class 10 and two for Class 30. The problem with this scheme is that it duplicates the class data and creates modification anomalies. Many rows will need to be changed if, for example, the schedule for Class 10 is modified. Also, consider the insertion and deletion anomalies: How can you schedule a new class until a student has enrolled? In addition, what will happen if Student 300 drops out of Class 40? This strategy is unworkable.

The solution to this problem is to create a third table, called an **intersection table**, that represents the relationship itself. We define a table named STUDENT_CLASS, as shown in Figure 5-15(a):

STUDENT (<u>SID</u>, StudentName, Phone, EmailAddress)

CLASS (<u>ClassNumber</u>, ClassTime, ClassName, Description)

STUDENT_CLASS (<u>*SID*</u>, <u>*ClassNumber*</u>)

with the referential integrity constraints:

SID in STUDENT_CLASS must exist in SID in STUDENT

ClassNumber in STUDENT_CLASS must exist in ClassNumber in CLASS

Some instances of this relation are shown in Figure 5-15(b). Such relations are called intersection tables because each row documents the intersection of a particular student with a

**FIGURE 5-14**

**Incorrect Representation of an N:M Relationship**

| SID | Other STUDENT Data |
|-----|--------------------|
| 100 | . . . |
| 200 | . . . |
| 300 | . . . |

STUDENT

| ClassNumber | ClassTime | Other CLASS Data | SID |
|-------------|-----------|------------------|-----|
| 10 | 10:00 MWF | . . . | 100 |
| 10 | 10:00 MWF | . . . | 200 |
| 30 | 3:00 TH | . . . | 200 |
| 30 | 3:00 TH | . . . | 300 |
| 40 | 8:00 MWF | . . . | 300 |

CLASS

**FIGURE 5-15**

Representing an N:M Strong Entity Relationship

(a) The STUDENT_CLASS Intersection Table

(b) Sample Data for the STUDENT-to-CLASS Relationship

particular class. Notice in Figure 5-15(b) that the intersection relation has one row for each line between STUDENT and CLASS, as in Figure 5-13(b).

In Figure 5-15(a), notice that the relationship from STUDENT to STUDENT_CLASS is 1:N, and the relationship from CLASS to STUDENT_CLASS is also 1:N. In essence, we have decomposed the M:N relationship into two 1:N relationships. The key of STUDENT_CLASS is (SID, ClassNumber), which is the combination of the primary keys of both of its parents. The key for an intersection table is *always* the combination of parent keys. Note that the parent relations are *both* required because a parent must now exist for each key value in the intersection relation.

Finally, notice that STUDENT_CLASS is an ID-dependent weak entity, which is ID-dependent on both STUDENT and CLASS. In order to create a database design for an N:M *strong entity* relationship we have had to introduce an ID-dependent *weak entity*! (We will have more to say about relationships with weak entities in the next section.)

To summarize the above discussion, to actually implement an N:M relationship in a database, we must create a new intersection table, to which we add foreign key columns linking to the two tables in the N:M relationship. These foreign key columns will be the corresponding primary keys of the two tables, and together will form a composite primary key in the intersection table. The relationship between each table and the intersection table will be a 1:N relationship, and thus we implement an N:M relation by creating two 1:N relationships. And because each primary key in the original tables appears as in the primary key of the intersection table, the intersection table is ID-dependent on both original tables.

You can obtain data about students and classes by using the following SQL statement:

```
SELECT      *
FROM        STUDENT, CLASS, STUDENT_CLASS
WHERE       STUDENT.SID = STUDENT_CLASS.SID
AND         STUDENT_CLASS.ClassNumber = CLASS.ClassNumber;
```

The result of this SQL statement is a table with all columns for a student and the classes the student takes. The student data will be repeated in the table for as many classes as the student takes, and the class data will be repeated in the relation for as many students as are taking the class.

---

**B T W**

Now that you know that an N:M relationship in a data model is transformed into two 1:N relationships in a database design let us revisit the topic of data modeling and database design software products discussed in Chapter 4. Some products, such as Computer Associates' ERwin Data Modeler, can create true data models with correctly drawn N:M relationships. These products are also capable of correctly transforming the data models into database designs with intersection tables. However, this is exactly the point where some other good products fall short. Neither Microsoft Visio (when using its database design component, not just its basic drawing mode) nor Oracle's MySQL Workbench (even though it displays an N:M relationship as an option) can correctly draw a data model N:M relationship. Instead, they immediately create a database design intersection table and two 1:N relationships. Nonetheless, creating database designs in Microsoft Visio and MySQL Workbench can be helpful in modeling, designing, and building a database. For example, Figure 5-16 shows database design for the Wedgewood Pacific Corporation database used in Chapter 3 in MySQL Workbench, and Figure 5-17 shows just the resulting database design. Note that MySQL Workbench uses the same symbols for line ends and line types (solid or dashed) as are used in Chapters 4 and 5. See online Appendix B for more information on using MySQL Workbench, and see online Appendix D for more information on using Microsoft Visio 2010.

---

**FIGURE 5-16**

A Database Design in MySQL Workbench

The E-R diagram using Crow's Foot notation

The table editor—column characteristics are specified here

## FIGURE 5-17

**The WPC Database Design**

The E-R diagram using Crow's Foot notation

## Relationships Using Weak Entities

Because weak entities exist, they are bound to end up as tables in relationships! We have just seen one place where this occurs: An ID-dependent entity becomes the table that represents an N:M relationship. Note that the intersection table that is formed in this case has only the columns that make up its composite primary key. In the STUDENT_CLASS table, this key is (SID, ClassNumber).

Another ID-dependent weak entity occurs when we take an intersection table and add entity attributes (table columns) beyond those in the composite primary key. For example, Figure 5-18 shows the table and relationship structure of Figure 5-15(a) but with one new attribute (column)—Grade—added to STUDENT_CLASS.

STUDENT_CLASS as an entity is now called an **association entity**, and this entity has been converted into the new STUDENT_CLASS table. Note that although it stills connects STUDENT and CLASS (and is still ID-dependent on both of these tables), it now has data that are uniquely its own. This pattern is called an **association relationship**.

Finally, let us take another look at the tables shown in Figure 5-8, where you normalized SALES_COMMISSION into three related tables. Figure 5-19 shows these tables with their correct relationships.

Note the 1:N identifying relationship between SALESPERSON and the ID-dependent table SALES_COMMISSION, which correctly uses the primary key of SALESPERSON as part of the composite primary key of SALES_COMMISSION. Also note the 1:1 relationship between

## FIGURE 5-18

**The Association Relationship**

**FIGURE 5-19**

Mixed Entity
Relationship Example

SALES_COMMISSION and COMMISSION_CHECK. Because COMMISSION_CHECK is a strong entity and has its own unique primary key, this is a nonidentifying relationship. This set of tables and relationships illustrates a **mixed entity pattern**.[2]

## Relationships with Subtypes

Because the identifier of a subtype entity is the identifier of the associated supertype entity, creating relationships between the SALES_COMMISSION and COMMISSION_CHECK tables is simple. The identifier of the subtype becomes the primary key of the subtype *and* the foreign key linking the subtype to the supertype. Figure 5-20(a) shows the E-R model in Figure 4-13(a), and Figure 5-20(b) shows the equivalent database design.

**FIGURE 5-20**

**Representing Subtypes**

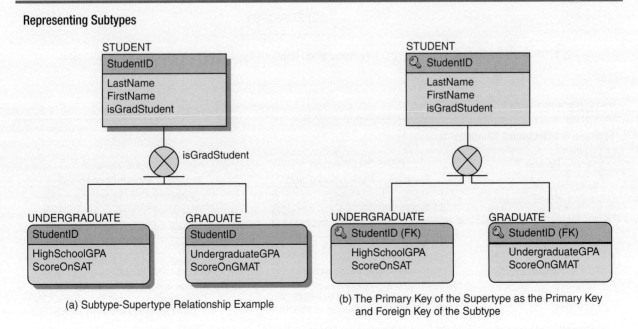

(a) Subtype-Supertype Relationship Example

(b) The Primary Key of the Supertype as the Primary Key and Foreign Key of the Subtype

[2]For more information on mixed entity patterns, see David Kroenke and David J. Auer, *Database Processing: Fundamentals, Design, and Implementation*, 11th edition (Upper Saddle River, NJ: Prentice Hall, 2010): 168–171, 206–207.

## Representing Recursive Relationships

A recursive relationship is a relationship among entities of the same class. Recursive relationships are not fundamentally different from other relationships and can be represented using the same techniques. As with nonrecursive relationships, three types of recursive relationships are possible: 1:1, 1:N, and N:M. Figure 5-21 shows an example of each of these three types.

Let us start by considering the 1:1 recursive SPONSORED_BY relationship in Figure 5-21(a). As with a regular 1:1 relationship, one person can sponsor another person, and each person is sponsored by no more than one person. Figure 5-22(a) shows sample data for this relationship.

To represent 1:1 recursive relationships, we take an approach nearly identical to that for regular 1:1 relationships; that is, we can place the key of the person being sponsored in the row of the sponsor, or we can place the key of the sponsor in the row of the person being sponsored. Figure 5-22(b) shows the first alternative, and Figure 5-22(c) shows the second. Both work.

---

**FIGURE 5-21**

**Example Recursive Relationships**

(a) 1:1 Recursive Relationship  (b) 1:N Recursive Relationship  (c) N:M Recursive Relationship

---

**FIGURE 5-22**

**Example 1:1 Recursive Relationship**

| Person | | PERSON1 Relation | | | PERSON2 Relation | |
|---|---|---|---|---|---|---|
| | | Person | PersonSponsored | | Person | PersonSponsoredBy |
| Jones | | Jones | Smith | | Jones | null |
| Smith | | Smith | Parks | | Smith | Jones |
| Parks | | Parks | null | | Parks | Smith |
| Myrtle | | Myrtle | Pines | | Myrtle | null |
| Pines | | Pines | null | | Pines | Myrtle |

| | Referential integrity constraint: | Referential integrity constraint: |
|---|---|---|
| | PersonSponsored in PERSON1 must exist in Person in PERSON1 | PersonSponsoredBy in PERSON2 must exist in Person in PERSON2 |

(a) Sample Data for a 1:1 Recursive Relationship  (b) First Alternative for Representing a 1:1 Recursive Relationship  (c) Second Alternative for Representing a 1:1 Recursive Relationship

This technique is identical to that for nonrecursive 1:1 relationships except that the child and parent rows reside in the same table. You can think of the process as follows: Pretend that the relationship is between two different tables. Determine where the key goes and then combine the two tables into a single one.

We also can use SQL joins to process recursive relationships; to do so, however, we need to introduce additional SQL syntax. In the FROM clause, it is possible to assign a synonym for a table name. For example, the expression FROM CUSTOMER A assigns the synonym A to the table CUSTOMER. Using this syntax, you can create a join on a recursive relationship for the design in Figure 5-22(b) as follows:

```
SELECT      *
FROM        PERSON1 A, PERSON1 B
WHERE       A.Person = B.PersonSponsored;
```

The result is a table with one row for each person that has all the columns of the person and also of the person he or she sponsors.

Similarly, to create a join of the recursive relationship shown in Figure 5-22(c), you would use:

```
SELECT      *
FROM        PERSON2 A, PERSON2 B
WHERE       A.Person = B.PersonSponsoredBy;
```

The result is a table with a row for each person that has all the columns of the person and also of the sponsoring person.

Now consider the 1:N recursive relationship REFERRED-BY in Figure 5-21(b). This is a 1:N relationship, as shown in the sample data in Figure 5-23(a).

When these data are placed in a table, one row represents the referrer, and the other rows represent those who have been referred. The referrer row takes the role of the parent, and the referred rows take the role of the child. As with all 1:N relationships, you place the key of the parent in the child. In Figure 5-21(b), you place the CustomerNumber of the referrer in all the rows for people who have been referred.

## FIGURE 5-23

**Example 1:N Recursive Relationship**

| Customer Number | Referred These Customers |
|---|---|
| 100 | 200, 400 |
| 300 | 500 |
| 400 | 600, 700 |

CUSTOMER Relation

| CustomerNumber | CustomerData | ReferredBy |
|---|---|---|
| 100 | . . . | null |
| 200 | . . . | 100 |
| 300 | . . . | null |
| 400 | . . . | 100 |
| 500 | . . . | 300 |
| 600 | . . . | 400 |
| 700 | . . . | 400 |

Referential integrity constraint:
ReferredBy in CUSTOMER must exist in
CustomerNumber in CUSTOMER

(a) Sample Data for a 1:N Recursive Relationship

(b) Representing a 1:N Recursive Relationship Within a Table

You can join the 1:N recursive relationship with:

```
SELECT      *
FROM        CUSTOMER A, CUSTOMER B
WHERE       A.CustomerNumber = B.ReferredBy;
```

The result is a row for each customer that is joined to the data for the customer who referred the person.

Finally, let us consider N:M recursive relationships. The TREATED-BY relationship in Figure 5-21(c) represents a situation in which doctors give treatments to each other. Sample data are shown in Figure 5-24(a).

As with other N:M relationships, you must create an intersection table that shows pairs of related rows. The name of the doctor in the first column is the one who provided the treatment, and the name of the doctor in the second column is the one who received the treatment. This structure is shown in Figure 5-24(b). You can join the N:M relationship with:

```
SELECT      *
FROM        DOCTOR A, TREATMENT-INTERSECTION, DOCTOR B
WHERE       A.Name = TREATMENT-INTERSECTION.Physician
AND         TREATMENT-INTERSECTION.Patient = B.Name;
```

The result of this is a table that has rows of doctor (as treatment provider) joined to doctor (as patient). The doctor data will be repeated once for every patient treated and once for every time the doctor was treated.

Recursive relationships are thus represented in the same way as are other relationships; however, the rows of the tables can take two different roles. Some are parent rows, and others are child rows. If a key is supposed to be a parent key and the row has no parent, its value is NULL. If a key is supposed to be a child key and the row has no child, its value is NULL.

**FIGURE 5-24**

**Example N:M Recursive Relationship**

Provider 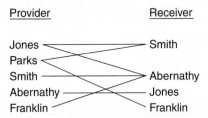 Receiver

| Provider | Receiver |
|----------|----------|
| Jones | Smith |
| Parks | |
| Smith | Abernathy |
| Abernathy | Jones |
| Franklin | Franklin |

DOCTOR Relation

| Name | Other Attributes |
|------|------------------|
| Jones | . . . |
| Parks | . . . |
| Smith | . . . |
| Abernathy | . . . |
| O'Leary | . . . |
| Franklin | . . . |

TREATMENT-INTERSECTION Relation

| Physician | Patient |
|-----------|---------|
| Jones | Smith |
| Parks | Smith |
| Smith | Abernathy |
| Abernathy | Jones |
| Parks | Franklin |
| Franklin | Abernathy |
| Jones | Abernathy |

Referential integrity constraints:
Physician in TREATMENT-INTERSECTION must exist in Name in DOCTOR

Patient in TREATMENT-INTERSECTION must exist in Name in DOCTOR

(a) Sample Data for an N:M Recursive Relationship

(b) Representing an N:M Recursive Relationship Using Tables

# DATABASE DESIGN AT HEATHER SWEENEY DESIGNS

Figure 5-25 shows the final E-R diagram for Heather Sweeney Designs, the database example discussed in Chapter 4. To transform this E-R diagram into a relational design, we follow the process described in the preceding sections. First, represent each entity with a relation of its own:

SEMINAR (<u>SeminarID</u>, SeminarDate, SeminarTime, Location, SeminarTitle)

CUSTOMER (<u>EmailAddress</u>, LastName, FirstName, Phone, StreetAddress, City, State, ZIP)

CONTACT (*<u>EmailAddress</u>*, <u>ContactDate</u>, ContactNumber, ContactType)

PRODUCT (<u>ProductNumber</u>, Description, UnitPrice, QuantityOnHand)

INVOICE (<u>InvoiceNumber</u>, InvoiceDate, PaymentType, SubTotal, Shipping, Tax, Total)

LINE_ITEM (*<u>InvoiceNumber</u>*, <u>LineNumber</u>, Quantity, UnitPrice, Total)

Next, apply the normalization process to each of these tables. Do any of them have a functional dependency that does not involve the primary key? From what we know so far, the only such functional dependency is:

ZIP → (City, State)

However, for the reasons explained earlier, we choose not to place ZIP in its own table.

One possible functional dependency concerns locations, dates, times, or titles. If, for example, Heather offers seminars only at certain times in some locations, or if she only gives certain seminar titles in some locations, then a functional dependency would exist with

## FIGURE 5-25

The Final Data Model for Heather Sweeney Designs

Location as its determinant. It would be important for the design team to check this out, but for now assume that no such dependency exists.

## Weak Entities

This model has two weak entities, and they are both ID-dependent. CONTACT is a weak entity, and its identifier depends, in part, on the identifier of CUSTOMER. Thus, we have placed the key of CUSTOMER, which is EmailAddress, into CONTACT. Similarly, LINE_ITEM is a weak entity, and its identifier depends on the identifier of INVOICE. Consequently, we have placed the key of INVOICE in LINE_ITEM. Note that in the preceding schema text both CONTACT.EmailAddress and LINE_ITEM.InvoiceNumber are underlined and italicized because they are part of a primary key and also a foreign key.

## Relationships

Now, considering the relationships in this diagram, 1:N relationships exist between SEMINAR and CONTACT, between CUSTOMER and INVOICE, and between PRODUCT and LINE_ITEM. For each of these, we place the key of the parent in the child as a foreign key. Thus, we place the key of SEMINAR in CONTACT, the key of CUSTOMER in INVOICE, and the key of PRODUCT in LINE_ITEM. The relations are now as follows:

SEMINAR (<u>SeminarID</u>, SeminarDate, SeminarTime, Location, SeminarTitle)

CUSTOMER (<u>EmailAddress</u>, LastName, FirstName, Phone, StreetAddress, City, State, ZIP)

CONTACT (<u>*EmailAddress*</u>, <u>ContactDate</u>, ContactNumber, ContactType, *SeminarID*)

PRODUCT (<u>ProductNumber</u>, Description, UnitPrice, QuantityOnHand)

INVOICE (<u>InvoiceNumber</u>, InvoiceDate, PaymentType, SubTotal, Tax, Total, *EmailAddress*)

LINE_ITEM (<u>*InvoiceNumber*</u>, <u>LineNumber</u>, Quantity, UnitPrice, Total, *ProductNumber*)

Finally, one N:M relationship exists between SEMINAR and CUSTOMER. To represent it, we create an intersection table, which we name SEMINAR_CUSTOMER. As with all intersection tables, its columns are the keys of the two tables involved in the N:M relationship. The final set of tables is:

SEMINAR (<u>SeminarID</u>, SeminarDate, SeminarTime, Location, SeminarTitle)

CUSTOMER (<u>EmailAddress</u>, LastName, FirstName, Phone, StreetAddress, City, State, ZIP)

SEMINAR_CUSTOMER (<u>*SeminarID*</u>, <u>*EmailAddress*</u>)

CONTACT (<u>*EmailAddress*</u>, <u>ContactDate</u>, ContactNumber, ContactType, *SeminarID*)

PRODUCT (<u>ProductNumber</u>, Description, UnitPrice, QuantityOnHand)

INVOICE (<u>InvoiceNumber</u>, InvoiceDate, PaymentType, SubTotal, Tax, Total, *EmailAddress*)

LINE_ITEM (<u>*InvoiceNumber*</u>, <u>LineNumber</u>, Quantity, UnitPrice, Total, *ProductNumber*)

The set of referential integrity constraints will be discussed in the next section.

Now, to express the minimum cardinalities of children back to their parents, we need to decide whether foreign keys are required. In Figure 5-23, we see that an INVOICE is required to have a CUSTOMER and that LINE_ITEM is required to have a PRODUCT. Thus, we will make INVOICE.EmailAddress and LINE_ITEM.ProductNumber required.

**FIGURE 5-26**

Database Design for Heather Sweeney Designs

CONTACT.SeminarID will not be required because a contact is not required to refer to a seminar. The final design is shown in the data structure diagram in Figure 5-26.

## Enforcing Referential Integrity

Figure 5-27 summarizes the relationship enforcement for Heather Sweeney Designs. SeminarID is a surrogate key, so no cascading update behavior will be necessary for any of the relationships that it carries. Similarly, InvoiceNumber in INVOICE is an unchanging value, so its relationships do not need cascading updates. However, updates of EmailAddress and ProductNumber do need to cascade through their relationships.

With regard to cascading deletions, rows in the intersection table require a SEMINAR and a CUSTOMER parent. Therefore, when a user attempts to cancel a seminar or to remove a customer record the deletion must either cascade or be prohibited. We must discuss this issue with Heather and her employees and determine whether users should be able to remove seminars that have customers enrolled or to remove customers who have enrolled in a seminar. We decide that neither seminars nor customers are *ever* deleted from the database (Heather *never* cancels a seminar even if no customers show up, and once Heather has a customer record she *never* lets go of it!). Hence, as shown in Figure 5-27, neither of these relationships have cascading deletions.

Figure 5-27 shows other decisions reached in the example. Because of the need to keep historic information about seminar attendance and contacts, we cannot delete a customer record. Doing so would distort seminar attendance data and data about contacts such as email messages and regular mail letters, which need to be accounted for. Foreign key constraints thus prohibit deleting the primary key record in CUSTOMER.

## FIGURE 5-27

**Referential Integrity Constraint Enforcement for Heather Sweeney Designs**

| RELATIONSHIP | | REFERENTIAL INTEGRITY CONSTRAINT | CASCADING BEHAVIOR | |
|---|---|---|---|---|
| PARENT | CHILD | | ON UPDATE | ON DELETE |
| SEMINAR | SEMINAR_CUSTOMER | SeminarID in SEMINAR_CUSTOMER must exist in SeminarID in SEMINAR | No | No |
| CUSTOMER | SEMINAR_CUSTOMER | EmailAddress in SEMINAR_CUSTOMER must exist in EmailAddress in CUSTOMER | Yes | No |
| SEMINAR | CONTACT | SeminarID in CONTACT must exist in SeminarID in SEMINAR | No | No |
| CUSTOMER | CONTACT | EmailAddress in CONTACT must exist in EmailAddress in CUSTOMER | Yes | No |
| CUSTOMER | INVOICE | EmailAddress in INVOICE must exist in EmailAddress in CUSTOMER | Yes | No |
| INVOICE | LINE_ITEM | InvoiceNumber in LINE_ITEM must exist in InvoiceNumber in INVOICE | No | Yes |
| PRODUCT | LINE_ITEM | ProductNumber in LINE_ITEM must exist in ProductNumber in PRODUCT | Yes | No |

As shown in Figure 5-27, the deletion of an INVOICE will cause the deletion of related LINE_ITEMs. Finally, an attempt to delete a PRODUCT that is related to one or more LINE_ITEMs will fail; cascading the deletion here would cause LINE_ITEMs to disappear out of ORDERs, a situation that cannot be allowed.

At this point, the design of the database for Heather Sweeney is complete enough to create tables, columns, relationships, and referential integrity constraints using a DBMS. Before going on, we would need to document any additional business rules to be enforced by application programs or other DBMS techniques. After this, the database can be created, using the SQL statements discussed in Chapter 3.

 ## THE ACCESS WORKBENCH

### Section 5

#### Relationships in Microsoft Access

At this point, we have created and populated the CONTACT, CUSTOMER, and SALESPERSON tables in the Wallingford Motors CRM database. You have also learned how to create forms, reports, and queries in the preceding sections. If you have worked through Chapter 3A's section of "The Access Workbench," you have learned more about how to create and use view equivalent queries.

All the tables you have used so far have had 1:N relationships. But how are 1:1 and N:M relationships managed in Microsoft Access? In this section, you will:

- Understand 1:1 relationships in Microsoft Access
- Understand N:M relationships in Microsoft Access

### N:M Relationships in Microsoft Access

We will start by discussing N:M relationships. This is actually a nonissue, because pure N:M relationships only occur in data modeling. Remember that when a data model is transformed into a database design an N:M relationship is broken down into two 1:N relationships. Each 1:N relationship is between a table resulting from one of the original entities in the N:M relationship and a new intersection table. If this does not make sense to you, then review the chapter section "Representing N:M Strong Entity Relationships" and see Figures 5-13 and 5-15 for an illustration of how N:M relationships are converted to two 1:N relationships.

Because databases are built in DBMSs, such as Microsoft Access, from the database design, Microsoft Access only deals with the resulting 1:N relationships. As far as Microsoft Access is concerned, there are no N:M relationships!

### 1:1 Relationships in Microsoft Access

Unlike N:M relationships, 1:1 relationships definitely exist in Microsoft Access. At this point the WMCRM database does not contain a 1:1 relationship, and here we will add one. We will let each SALESPERSON use one and only one car from the Wallingford Motors inventory as a demo vehicle. The database design with this addition is shown in Figure AW-5-1.

Note that both SALESPERSON and VEHICLE are optional in this relationship. First, a VEHICLE does not have to be assigned to a SALESPERSON, which makes sense because there will be a lot of cars in inventory and only a few SALESPERSONs. Second, a SALESPERSON does not have to take a demo car and may choose not to (yeah, right!). Also note that we have chosen to put the foreign key in SALESPERSON. In this case, there is an advantage to putting the foreign key in one table or the other

---

**FIGURE AW-5-1**

**The WMCRM Database Design with VEHICLE**

**FIGURE AW-5-2**

Database Column Characteristics for the VEHICLE Table

| Column Name | Type | Key | Required | Remarks |
|---|---|---|---|---|
| InventoryID | AutoNumber | Primary Key | Yes | Surrogate Key |
| Model | Text(25) | No | Yes | |
| VIN | Text(35) | No | Yes | |

**FIGURE AW-5-3**

Wallingford Motors VEHICLE Data

| InventoryID | Model | VIN |
|---|---|---|
| [AutoNumber] | HiStandard | G11HS123400001 |
| [AutoNumber] | HiStandard | G11HS123400002 |
| [AutoNumber] | HiStandard | G11HS123400003 |
| [AutoNumber] | HiLuxury | G11HL234500001 |
| [AutoNumber] | HiLuxury | G11HL234500002 |
| [AutoNumber] | HiLuxury | G11HL234500003 |
| [AutoNumber] | SUHi | G11HU345600001 |
| [AutoNumber] | SUHi | G11HU345600002 |
| [AutoNumber] | SUHi | G11HU345600003 |
| [AutoNumber] | HiElectra | G11HE456700001 |

because if we put it in VEHICLE the foreign key column (which would have been NickName) would be NULL for every car except the few used as demo vehicles. Finally, note that we are using this table just to illustrate a 1:1 relationship—a functional VEHICLE table would have a lot more columns.

The column characteristics for the VEHICLE table are shown in Figure AW-5-2, and the data for the table are shown in Figure AW-5-3.

Let us open the WMCRM.accdb database.

### Opening the WMCRM.accdb Database

1. Start Microsoft Access.
2. If necessary, click the **File** command tab, and then click the **WMCRM.accdb** file name in the quick access list of recently opened databases to open the database.

We already know how to create a table and populate it with data, so we will go ahead and add the VEHICLE table and its data to the WMCRM.accdb database. Next, we need to modify SALESPERSON by adding the InventoryID column and populating it with data. The column characteristics for the new InventoryID column in the SALESPERSON table are shown in Figure AW-5-4, and the data for the column are shown in Figure AW-5-5. (Tina and Big Bill are driving the HiLuxury model, while Billy opted for a SUHi.)

There is nothing here that you do not know how to do—you altered the CUSTOMER table in a similar way in Chapter 3's section of "The Access Workbench"—so you can go ahead and add the InventoryID column and its data to the SALESPERSON table. This is an easier table alteration to make than the one we made to CUSTOMER

### FIGURE AW-5-4

Database Column Characteristics for the InventoryID Column

| Column Name | Type | Key | Required | Remarks |
|---|---|---|---|---|
| InventoryID | Long Integer | Foreign Key | No | |

### FIGURE AW-5-5

SALESPERSON InventoryID Data

| NickName | LastName | FirstName | . . . | InventoryID |
|---|---|---|---|---|
| Tina | Smith | Tina | . . . | 4 |
| Big Bill | Jones | William | . . . | 5 |
| Billy | Jones | Bill | . . . | 7 |

because the InventoryID column in SALESPERSON is NOT NULL, so you do not have to set it to NULL after entering the data.

Now, we are ready to establish the relationship between the two tables.

#### Creating the Relationship Between SALESPERSON and VEHICLE

1. Click the **Database Tools** command tab.
2. Click the **Shutter Bar Open/Close** button to minimize the Navigation Pane.
3. Click the **Relationships** button in the Relationships group. The Relationships tabbed document window appears.
    - **NOTE: Warning!** The next steps lead to a peculiarity of Microsoft Access, not the final outcome that we want. Remember that we want a 1:1 relationship. See if you can figure out what is happening as we go along.
4. Click the **Show Table** button in the Relationships group of the Design ribbon.
5. In the Show Table dialog box, click **VEHICLE** to select it, and then click the **Add** button to add VEHICLE to the Relationships window.
6. In the Show Table dialog box, click the **Close** button to close the dialog box.
7. Rearrange and resize the table objects in the Relationships window by using standard Windows drag-and-drop techniques. Rearrange the SALESPERSON, CUSTOMER, CONTACT, and VEHICLE table objects until they look as shown in Figure AW-5-6.

### FIGURE AW-5-6

The Relationships Window with the Current Relationship Diagram

The new **VEHICLE** table

*(Continued)*

■ **NOTE:** Remember that we create a relationship between two tables in the Relationships window by dragging a *primary key* column and dropping it on top of the *corresponding foreign key* column.

8. Click and hold the column name **InventoryID** in the VEHICLE table object, then drag it over the column name **InventoryID** in the **SALESPERSON** table, and then release the mouse button. The Edit Relationships dialog box appears.

9. Click the **Enforce Referential Integrity** check box.

10. Click the **Create** button to create the relationship between VEHICLE and SALESPERSON.

11. Right-click the **relationship line** between VEHICLE and SALESPERSON, and then click **Edit Relationship** in the shortcut menu that appears. The **Edit Relationships** dialog box appears.

12. The relationship between the tables now appears in the Relationships window, as shown in Figure AW-5-7.

But now we have a serious problem: The relationship that was created is a 1:N relationship, not the 1:1 relationship that we wanted. It seems like there should be a way to fix the relationship somewhere on the Edit Relationships dialog box. Unfortunately, there is not. Go ahead and try everything you can think of, but it will not work. This is the peculiarity of Microsoft Access that was mentioned earlier.

So what is the trick to creating a 1:1 relationship in Microsoft Access? As discussed in this chapter, the trick is to create a UNIQUE constraint on the foreign key column. To do this in Microsoft Access, we set the **Indexed field property** of the foreign key column (InventoryID in SALESPERSON in this case) to **Yes (No Duplicates)**, as shown in Figure AW-5-8. As long as the same value can occur more than once in the foreign key column Microsoft Access will create a 1:N relationship instead of the desired 1:1 relationship.

To create the 1:1 relationship, we need to delete the existing relationship, modify the InventoryID property in SALESPERSON, and create a new relationship between the tables. First, we will delete the existing 1:N relationship.

*Deleting the Incorrect Relationship Between SALESPERSON and VEHICLE*

1. Click the **OK** button on the Edit Relationships dialog box.

2. Right-click the **relationship line** between VEHICLE and SALESPERSON to display the shortcut menu, and then click **Delete**.

**FIGURE AW-5-7**

**The Completed VEHICLE-to-SALESPERSON Relationship**

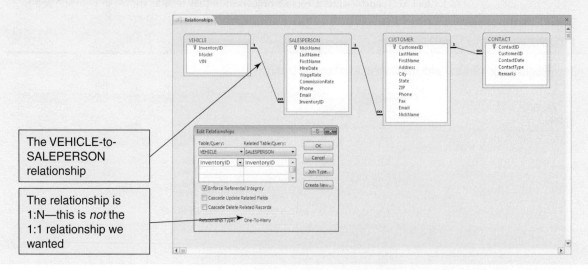

The VEHICLE-to-SALEPERSON relationship

The relationship is 1:N—this is *not* the 1:1 relationship we wanted

**FIGURE AW-5-8**

Setting the Indexed Property Value in the SALESPERSON Table

Select the **InventoryID** column

Set the Indexed property to **Yes (No Duplicates)**

3. A dialog box appears asking whether you are sure you want to permanently delete the selected relationship from your database. Click the **Yes** button.
4. Close the Relationships window.
5. A dialog box appears asking whether you want to save the changes to the layout of Relationships. Click the **Yes** button.
6. Click the **Shutter Bar Open/Close** button to expand the Navigation Pane.

Next, we will modify the SALESPSERSON table.

*Setting the Indexed Property of the InventoryID Column in SALESPERSON*

1. Open the **SALESPERSON** table in Design view.
2. Select the **InventoryID** field. The InventoryID field properties are displayed in the General tab.
3. Click the **Indexed** text field. A drop-down list arrow appears on the right end of the text field. Click the drop-down list arrow to display the list and select **Yes (No Duplicates)**. The result appears as shown in Figure AW-5-8.
4. Click the **Save** button to save the completed changes to the SALESPERSON table.
5. Close the SALESPERSON table.

Finally, we create the 1:1 relationship that we want between the SALESPERSON and VEHICLE tables.

*Creating the Correct 1:1 Relationship Between SALESPERSON and VEHICLE*

1. Click the **Database Tools** command tab.
2. Click the **Shutter Bar Open/Close** button to minimize the Navigation Pane.
3. Click the **Relationships** button in the Relationships group. The Relationships tabbed document window appears.

*(Continued)*

---

### FIGURE AW-5-9

The Correct 1:1 VEHICLE-to-SALESPERSON Relationship

The VEHICLE-to-SALEPERSON relationship

The relationship is now the correct 1:1 relationship

4. Click and hold the column name **InventoryID** in the **VEHICLE** table object, then drag it over the column name **InventoryID** in the **SALESPERSON** table, and then release the mouse button. The Edit Relationships dialog box appears.

5. Click the **Enforce Referential Integrity** check box.

6. Click the **Create** button to create the relationship between VEHICLE and SALESPERSON.

7. Right-click the **relationship line** between SALESPERSON and VEHICLE, and then click **Edit Relationship** in the shortcut menu that appears. The **Edit Relationships** dialog box appears.

8. Note that the correct one-to-one relationship between the tables now appears in the Relationships window, as shown in Figure AW-5-9.

9. Click the **Cancel** button on the Edit Relationships dialog box.

10. Close the Relationships window.

11. If a dialog box appears, asking whether you want to save the changes to the layout of Relationships window, then click the **Yes** button.

12. Click the **Shutter Bar Open/Close** button to expand the Navigation Pane.

We have successfully created the 1:1 relationship that we wanted. We just had to learn the Microsoft Access way of doing it.

### Closing the Database and Exiting Microsoft Access

That completes the work we will do in this chapter's section of "The Access Workbench." As usual, we finish by closing the database and Microsoft Access.

*Closing the WMCRM Database and Exiting Microsoft Access*

1. To close the WMCRM database and exit Microsoft Access, click the Microsoft Access **Close** button in the upper-right corner of the Microsoft Access window.

## SUMMARY

To transform an E-R data model into a relational database design, you create a table for each entity. The attributes of the entity become the columns of the table, and the identifier of the entity becomes the primary key of the table. For each column, you must define data types, null status, any default values, and any data constraints. You then apply the normalization process to each table and create additional tables, if necessary. In some cases, you need to denormalize a table. When you do, the table will have insertion, update, and deletion problems.

Denormalization makes sense if the benefit of not normalizing outweighs the possible problems that could be caused by such modifications.

Weak entities are represented by a table. ID-dependent entities must include the key columns of the tables on which they depend, as well as of the identifiers of the entities themselves. Non–ID-dependent entities must have their existence dependence recorded as business rules.

Supertypes and subtypes are each represented by separate tables. The identifier of the supertype entity becomes the primary key of the supertype table, and the identifiers of the subtype entities become the primary keys of the subtype tables. The primary key of each subtype is also the same primary key that is used for the supertype, and the primary key of each subtype serves as a foreign key that links the subtype back to the supertype.

The E-R model has three types of binary relationships: 1:1, 1:N, and N:M. To represent a 1:1 relationship, you place the key of one table into the other table. To implement the 1:1 relationship, the specified foreign key must be constrained as UNIQUE. To represent a 1:N relationship, you place the key of the parent table in the child table. Finally, to represent an M:N relationship, you create an intersection table that contains the keys of the other two tables.

Recursive relationships are relationships in which the participants in the relationship arise from the same entity class. The three types of recursive relationships are 1:1, 1:N, and N:M. These types of relationships are represented in the same way as are their equivalent nonrecursive relationships. For 1:1 and 1:N relationships, you add a foreign key to the relation that represents the entity. For an N:M recursion, you create an intersection table that represents the M:N relationship.

## KEY TERMS

| | | |
|---|---|---|
| association entity | default value | multivalued dependency |
| association relationship | denormalization | NULL status |
| Boyce-Codd Normal Form (BCNF) | domain/key normal form (DK/NF) | parent |
| | | relation |
| child | fifth normal form (5NF) | second normal form (2NF) |
| column property | first normal form (1NF) | surrogate key |
| data constraint | fourth normal form (4NF) | table |
| data type | intersection table | third normal form (3NF) |
| database design | mixed entity pattern | transitive dependency |

## REVIEW QUESTIONS

**5.1**   Explain how entities are transformed into tables.

**5.2**   Why is it necessary to apply the normalization process to the tables created according to your answer to question 5.1?

**5.3**   What is denormalization?

**5.4**   Explain how attributes are transformed into columns. What column properties do you take into account when making the transformations?

**5.5** Explain how the representation of weak entities differs from the representation of strong entities.

**5.6** Explain how supertype and subtype entities are transformed into tables.

**5.7** When is denormalization justified?

**5.8** Explain the problems that unnormalized tables have for insert, update, and delete actions.

**5.9** List the three types of binary relationships and give an example of each. Do not use the examples given in this text.

**5.10** Define the term *foreign key* and give an example.

**5.11** Show two different ways to represent the 1:1 relationship in your answer to question 5.9. Use IE Crow's Foot E-R diagrams.

**5.12** For your answers to question 5.11, describe a method for obtaining data about one of the entities, given the key of the other. Describe a method for obtaining data about the second entity, given the key of the first. Describe methods for both of your alternatives in question 5.11.

**5.13** Code SQL statements to create a join that has all data about both tables from your work for question 5.11.

**5.14** Define the terms *parent* and *child* as they apply to tables in a database design and give an example of each.

**5.15** Show how to represent the 1:N relationship in your answer to question 5.9. Use an IE Crow's Foot E-R diagram.

**5.16** For your answer to question 5.15, describe a method for obtaining data for all the children, given the key of the parent. Describe a method for obtaining data for the parent, given a key of the child.

**5.17** For your answer to question 5.15, code an SQL statement that creates a table that has all data from both tables.

**5.18** Give examples of binary 1:N relationships, other than those in this text, for (a) an optional-to-optional relationship, (b) an optional-to-mandatory relationship, (c) a mandatory-to-optional relationship, and (d) a mandatory-to-mandatory relationship. Illustrate your answer by using IE Crow's Foot E-R diagrams.

**5.19** For a 1:N relationship, explain why you must place the key of the parent table in the child table rather than place the key of the child table in the parent table.

**5.20** Show how to represent the N:M relationship in your answer to question 5.9. Use an IE Crow's Foot E-R diagram.

**5.21** Explain the meaning of the term *intersection table.*

**5.22** Explain how the terms *parent table* and *child table* relate to the tables in your answer to question 5.20.

**5.23** For your answers to questions 5.20, 5.21, and 5.22, describe a method for obtaining the children for one of the entities in the original data model, given the primary key of the table based on the second entity. Also, describe a method for obtaining the children for the second entity, given the primary key of the table based on the first entity.

**5.24** For your answer to question 5.20, code an SQL statement that creates a relation that has all data from all tables.

**5.25** What is an associative entity? What is an association relationship? Give an example of an association relationship other than one shown in this text. Illustrate your answer using an IE Crow's Foot E-R diagram.

**5.26** Give an example of a 1:N relationship with an ID-dependent weak entity, other than one shown in this text. Illustrate your answer using an IE Crow's Foot E-R diagram.

**5.27** Why is it not possible to represent N:M relationships with the same strategy used to represent 1:N relationships?

**5.28**  Give an example of a supertype–subtype relationship, other than one shown in this text. Illustrate your answer using an IE Crow's Foot E-R diagram.

**5.29**  Define the three types of recursive binary relationships and give an example of each, other than the ones shown in this text.

**5.30**  Show how to represent the 1:1 recursive relationship in your answer to question 5.29. How does this differ from the representation of 1:1 nonrecursive relationships?

**5.31**  Code an SQL statement that creates a table with all columns from the parent and child tables in your answer to question 5.30.

**5.32**  Show how to represent a 1:N recursive relationship in your answer to question 5.29. How does this differ from the representation of 1:N nonrecursive relationships?

**5.33**  Code an SQL statement that creates a table with all columns from the parent and child tables in your answer to question 5.32.

**5.34**  Show how to represent the M:N recursive relationship in your answer to question 5.29. How does this differ from the representation of M:N nonrecursive relationships?

**5.35**  Code an SQL statement that creates a table with all columns from the parent and child tables in your answer to question 5.34. Code an SQL statement using a left outer join that creates a table with all columns from the parent and child tables. Explain the difference between these two SQL statements.

## EXERCISES

**5.36**  Consider the following table, which holds data about employee project assignments:

ASSIGNMENT (<u>EmployeeNumber</u>, <u>ProjectNumber</u>, ProjectName, HoursWorked)

Assume that ProjectNumber determines ProjectName and explain why this relation is not normalized. Demonstrate an insertion anomaly, a modification anomaly, and a deletion anomaly. Apply the normalization process to this relation. State the referential integrity constraint.

**5.37**  Consider the following relation that holds data about employee assignments:

ASSIGNMENT (<u>EmployeeNumber</u>, ProjectNumber, ProjectName, HoursWorked)

Assume that ProjectNumber determines ProjectName and explain why this relation is not normalized. Demonstrate an insertion anomaly, a modification anomaly, and a deletion anomaly. Apply the normalization process to this relation. State the referential integrity constraint.

**5.38**  Explain the difference between the two ASSIGNMENT tables in questions 5.36 and 5.37. Under what circumstances is the table in question 5.36 more correct? Under what circumstances is the table in question 5.37 more correct?

**5.39**  Create a relational database design for the data model you developed for question 4.30.

**5.40**  Create a relational database design for the data model you developed for question 4.31.

**5.41**  Create a relational database design for the data model you developed for question 4.32.

**5.42**  Create a relational database design for the data model you developed for question 4.33.

**5.43**  Create a relational database design for the data model you developed for question 4.34.

## ACCESS WORKBENCH KEY TERMS

Indexed field property

## ACCESS WORKBENCH EXERCISES

**AW.5.1** Using an IE Crow's Foot E-R diagram, draw a database design for the Wedgewood Pacific Corporation (WPC) database completed at the end of Chapter 3's section of "The Access Workbench."

**AW.5.2** This chapter's section of "The Access Workbench" describes how to create 1:1 relationships in Microsoft Access. In particular, we added the business rule that each salesperson at Wallingford Motors can have one and only one vehicle as a demo car. Suppose that the rule has been changed so that each salesperson can have one or more cars as demo vehicles.

  **A.** Using an IE Crow's Foot E-R diagram, redraw the database design in Figure AW-5-1 to show the new relationship between VEHICLE and SALESPERSON. Which table(s) is (are) the parent(s) in the relationship? Which table(s) is (are) the child(ren)? In which table(s) do you place a foreign key?

  **B.** Start with the Wallingford Motors database that you have created so far (**WMCRM.accdb**) as it exists after working through all the steps in this chapter's section of "The Access Workbench." (If you have not completed those actions, do so now.) Copy the **WMCRM.accdb** database and rename the copy **WMCRM-AW05-v02.accdb**. Modify the WMCRM-AW05-v02.accdb database to implement the new relationship between VEHICLE and SALESPERSON. (*Note:* Copying a Microsoft Access database is discussed in Chapter 4's section of "The Access Workbench.")

**AW.5.3** This chapter's section of "The Access Workbench" describes how to create 1:1 relationships in Microsoft Access. In particular, we added the business rule that each salesperson at Wallingford Motors can have one and only one vehicle as a demo car. Suppose that the rule has been changed so that (1) each salesperson can have one or more cars as demo vehicles and (2) each demo vehicle can be shared by two or more salespersons.

  **A.** Using an IE Crow's Foot E-R diagram, redraw the database design in Figure AW-5-1 to show the new relationship between VEHICLE and SALESPERSON. Which table(s) is (are) the parent(s) in the relationship? Which table(s) is (are) the child(ren)? In which table(s) do you place a foreign key?

  **B.** Start with the Wallingford Motors database that you have created so far (**WMCRM.accdb**) as it exists after working through all the steps in this chapter's section of "The Access Workbench." (If you have not completed those actions, do so now.) Copy the **WMCRM.accdb** database and rename the copy **WMCRM-AW05-v03.accdb**. Modify the WMCRM-AW05-v03.accdb database to implement the new relationship between VEHICLE and SALESPERSON. (*Note:* Copying a Microsoft Access database is discussed in Chapter 4's section of "The Access Workbench.")

**GARDEN GLORY PROJECT QUESTIONS**

Convert the data model you constructed for Garden Glory in part B at the end of Chapter 4 (or an equivalent data model that your instructor provides for you to use) into a relational database design for Garden Glory. Document your database design as follows.

**A.** Specify tables, primary keys, and foreign keys.

**B.** Describe how you have represented weak entities, if any exist.

**C.** Describe how you have represented supertype and subtype entities, if any exist.

**D.** Create an IE Crow's Foot E-R diagram similar to the one in Figure 5-26.

**E.** Document referential integrity constraint enforcement, using Figure 5-27 as a guide.

**F.** Document any business rules that you think might be important.

**G.** Describe how you would validate that your design is a good representation of the data model on which it is based.

 **JAMES RIVER JEWELRY PROJECT QUESTIONS**

Convert the data model you constructed for James River Jewelry in part C at the end of Chapter 4 (or an equivalent data model that your instructor provides for you to use) into a relational database design for James River Jewelry. Document your database design as follows.

**A.** Specify tables, primary keys, and foreign keys.

**B.** Describe how you have represented weak entities, if any exist.

**C.** Describe how you have represented supertype and subtype entities, if any exist.

**D.** Create an IE Crow's Foot E-R diagram similar to the one in Figure 5-26.

**E.** Document referential integrity constraint enforcement, using Figure 5-27 as a guide.

**F.** Document any business rules that you think might be important.

**G.** Describe how you would validate that your design is a good representation of the data model on which it is based.

 **THE QUEEN ANNE CURIOSITY SHOP PROJECT QUESTIONS**

Convert the data model you constructed for The Queen Anne Curiosity Shop in part D at the end of Chapter 4 (or an equivalent data model that your instructor provides for you to use) into a relational database design for The Queen Anne Curiosity Shop. Document your database design as follows.

**A.** Specify tables, primary keys, and foreign keys.

**B.** Describe how you have represented weak entities, if any exist.

**C.** Describe how you have represented supertype and subtype entities, if any exist.

**D.** Create an IE Crow's Foot E-R diagram similar to the one in Figure 5-26.

**E.** Document referential integrity constraint enforcement, using Figure 5-27 as a guide.

**F.** Document any business rules that you think might be important.

**G.** Describe how you would validate that your design is a good representation of the data model on which it is based.

# PART III

# Database Management

So far, you have been introduced to the fundamental concepts and techniques of relational database management and database design. In Chapter 1, you learned about databases and the major components of a database system. Chapter 2 introduced you to the relational model, functional dependencies, and normalization. In Chapter 3, you learned how to use SQL statements to create and process a database. Chapter 4 gave you an overview of the database design process and a detailed introduction to data modeling. In Chapter 5, you learned how to transform a data model into a relational database design. Now that you know how to design, create, and query databases, it is time to learn how to manage databases and use them to solve business problems.

In Chapter 6, you will learn about database management and some of the problems that occur when a database is concurrently processed by more than one user. In Chapter 7, you will learn how to create Web database applications, which use databases to support Web sites. Finally, in Chapter 8 you will learn how databases support modern business intelligence (BI) systems. After completing these chapters, you will have surveyed all the basics of database technology.

# CHAPTER 6

# Database Administration

## Chapter Objectives

> Understand the need for and importance of database administration

> Learn different ways of processing a database

> Understand the need for concurrency control, security, and backup and recovery

> Learn about typical problems that can occur when multiple users process a database concurrently

> Understand the use of locking and the problem of deadlock

> Learn the difference between optimistic and pessimistic locking

> Know the meaning of ACID transaction

> Learn the four 1992 ANSI standard isolation levels

> Understand the need for security and specific tasks for improving database security

> Know the difference between recovery via reprocessing and recovery via rollback/rollforward

> Understand the nature of the tasks required for recovery using rollback/rollforward

> Know basic administrative and managerial DBA functions

> Understand distributed database processing

> Understand the concept of object-relational databases

This chapter describes the major tasks of an important business function called *database administration*. This function involves managing a database in order to maximize its value to an organization. Usually, database administration involves balancing the conflicting goals of protecting the database and maximizing its availability and benefit to users. Both the terms *data administration* and *database administration* are used in the industry. In some cases, the terms are considered synonymous; in other cases, they have different meanings. Most commonly, the term **data administration** refers to a function that applies to an entire organization; it is a management-oriented function that concerns corporate data privacy and security issues. The term **database administration** refers to a more technical function that is specific to a particular database, including the applications that process that database. This chapter addresses database administration.

Databases vary considerably in size and scope, from single-user personal databases to large interorganizational databases, such as airline reservation systems. All databases have a need for database administration, although the tasks to be accomplished vary in complexity. For a personal database, for example, individuals follow simple procedures for backing up their data, and they keep minimal records for documentation. In this case, the person who uses the database also performs the DBA functions, even though he or she is probably unaware of it.

For multiuser database applications, database administration becomes both more important and more difficult. Consequently, it generally has formal recognition. For some applications, one or two people are given this function on a part-time basis. For large Internet or intranet databases, database administration responsibilities are often too time-consuming and too varied to be handled even by a single full-time person. Supporting a database with dozens or hundreds of users requires considerable time as well as both technical knowledge and diplomatic skill, and it is usually handled by an office of database administration. The manager of the office is often known as the **database administrator**. In this case, **DBA** refers to either the office or the manager.

The overall responsibility of a DBA is to facilitate the development and use of a database. Usually, this means balancing the conflicting goals of protecting the database and maximizing its availability and benefit to users. The DBA is responsible for the development, operation, and maintenance of the database and its applications.

In this chapter, we examine three important database administration functions: concurrency control, security, and backup and recovery. Then, we discuss the need for configuration change management. Finally, we look at two advanced database topics: distributed databases and object-oriented database systems. But before you learn about any of this, we will create the Heather Sweeney Designs database discussed in the previous chapters; you'll use it as an example database for the discussion in this chapter and in Chapters 7 and 8.

## THE HEATHER SWEENEY DESIGNS DATABASE

The SQL statements to create the Heather Sweeney Designs (HSD) database are shown in Figure 6-1, in SQL Server syntax. The SQL statements are built from the HSD database design in Figure 5-26, and the column constraints follow the attribute specifications in Figure 4-21 and the referential integrity constraint specifications outlined in Figure 5-27.

The SQL statements to populate the HSD database are shown in Figure 6-2, again in SQL Server syntax. Finally, the completed HSD database is shown in SQL Server in Figure 6-3.

## THE NEED FOR CONTROL, SECURITY, AND RELIABILITY

Databases come in a variety of sizes and scopes, from single-user databases to huge, interorganizational databases, such as inventory management systems. As shown in Figure 6-4, databases also vary in the way they are processed.

We will define and discuss the various pieces of the environment shown in Figure 6-4 in detail in Chapter 7 when we discuss database processing applications. For now, just realize that it is possible for every one of the application elements in Figure 6-4 to be operating at the same time. Queries, forms, and reports can be generated while Web pages [using Active Server Pages (ASP) and Java Server Pages (JSP)] access the database, possibly invoking stored procedures. Traditional application programs running in Visual Basic, C#,

FIGURE 6-1

SQL Statements to Create the HSD Database

```
CREATE TABLE SEMINAR(
      SeminarID        Int               NOT NULL IDENTITY (1, 1),
      SeminarDate      DateTime          NOT NULL,
      SeminarTime      DateTime          NOT NULL,
      Location         VarChar(100)      NOT NULL,
      SeminarTitle     VarChar(100)      NOT NULL,
      CONSTRAINT       SEMINAR_PK        PRIMARY KEY(SeminarID)
      );


CREATE TABLE CUSTOMER(
      EmailAddress     VarChar(100)      NOT NULL,
      LastName         Char(25)          NOT NULL,
      FirstName        Char(25)          NOT NULL,
      Phone            Char(12)          NOT NULL,
      StreetAddress    Char(35)          NULL,
      City             Char(35)          NULL DEFAULT 'Dallas',
      [State]          Char(2)           NULL DEFAULT 'TX',
      ZIP              Char(10)          NULL DEFAULT '75201',
      CONSTRAINT       CUSTOMER_PK       PRIMARY KEY(EmailAddress)
      );


CREATE TABLE SEMINAR_CUSTOMER(
      SeminarID        Int               NOT NULL,
      EmailAddress     VarChar(100)      NOT NULL,
      CONSTRAINT       S_C_PK PRIMARY KEY(SeminarID,EmailAddress),
      CONSTRAINT       S_C_SEMINAR_FK   FOREIGN KEY(SeminarID)
                           REFERENCES SEMINAR(SeminarID)
                               ON UPDATE NO ACTION
                               ON DELETE NO ACTION
      CONSTRAINT       S_C_CUSTOMER_FK FOREIGN KEY(EmailAddress)
                           REFERENCES CUSTOMER(EmailAddress)
                               ON UPDATE CASCADE
                               ON DELETE NO ACTION
      );


CREATE TABLE CONTACT(
      EmailAddress     VarChar(100)      NOT NULL,
      ContactDate      DateTime          NOT NULL,
      ContactNumber    Int               NOT NULL,
      ContactType      Char(15)          NOT NULL,
      SeminarID        Int               NULL,
      CONSTRAINT       CONTACT_PK        PRIMARY KEY(EmailAddress, ContactDate),
      CONSTRAINT       CONTACT_SEMINAR_FK FOREIGN KEY(SeminarID)
                           REFERENCES SEMINAR(SeminarID)
                               ON UPDATE NO ACTION
                               ON DELETE NO ACTION,
      CONSTRAINT       CONTACT_CUSTOMER_FK FOREIGN KEY(EmailAddress)
                           REFERENCES CUSTOMER(EmailAddress)
                               ON UPDATE CASCADE
                               ON DELETE NO ACTION
      );
```

*(Continued)*

**FIGURE 6-1** *(Continued)*

```
CREATE TABLE PRODUCT(
      ProductNumber      Char(35)         NOT NULL,
      [Description]      VarChar(100)     NOT NULL,
      UnitPrice          Numeric(9,2)     NOT NULL,
      QuantityOnHand     Int              NOT NULL DEFAULT 0,
      CONSTRAINT         PRODUCT_PK       PRIMARY KEY(ProductNumber)
      );


CREATE TABLE INVOICE(
      InvoiceNumber      Int              NOT NULL IDENTITY (35000, 1),
      InvoiceDate        DateTime         NOT NULL,
      PaymentType        Char(25)         NOT NULL DEFAULT 'Cash',
      SubTotal           Numeric(9,2)     NULL,
      Shipping           Numeric(9,2)     NULL,
      Tax                Numeric(9,2)     NULL,
      Total              Numeric(9,2)     NULL,
      EmailAddress       VarChar(100)     NOT NULL,
      CONSTRAINT         INVOICE_PK       PRIMARY KEY (InvoiceNumber),
      CONSTRAINT         INVOICE_CUSTOMER_FK FOREIGN KEY(EmailAddress)
                            REFERENCES Customer(EmailAddress)
                               ON UPDATE CASCADE
                               ON DELETE NO ACTION
      );


CREATE TABLE LINE_ITEM(
      InvoiceNumber      Int              NOT NULL,
      LineNumber         Int              NOT NULL,
      Quantity           Int              NOT NULL,
      UnitPrice          Numeric(9,2)     NOT NULL,
      Total              Numeric(9,2)     NULL,
      ProductNumber      Char(35)         NOT NULL,
      CONSTRAINT         LINE_ITEM_PK PRIMARY KEY(InvoiceNumber, LineNumber),
      CONSTRAINT         L_I_INVOICE_FK   FOREIGN KEY(InvoiceNumber)
                            REFERENCES INVOICE(InvoiceNumber)
                               ON UPDATE NO ACTION
                               ON DELETE CASCADE,
      CONSTRAINT         L_I_PRODUCT_FK   FOREIGN KEY(ProductNumber)
                            REFERENCES PRODUCT(ProductNumber)
                               ON UPDATE CASCADE
                               ON DELETE NO ACTION
      );
```

**FIGURE 6-2**

SQL Statements to Populate the HSD Database

```
/*****    SEMINAR DATA    ****************************************************/

INSERT INTO SEMINAR VALUES(
   '11-OCT-2009', '11:00 AM', 'San Antonio Convention Center',
   'Kitchen on a Budget');
INSERT INTO SEMINAR VALUES(
   '25-OCT-2009', '04:00 PM', 'Dallas Convention Center',
   'Kitchen on a Big D Budget');
INSERT INTO SEMINAR VALUES(
   '01-NOV-2009', '08:30 AM', 'Austin Convention Center',
   'Kitchen on a Budget');
```

FIGURE 6-2   (*Continued*)

```
INSERT INTO SEMINAR VALUES(
    '22-MAR-2010', '11:00 AM', 'Dallas Convention Center',
    'Kitchen on a Big D Budget');


/*****   CUSTOMER DATA   *****************************************************/


INSERT INTO CUSTOMER VALUES(
    'Nancy.Jacobs@somewhere.com', 'Jacobs', 'Nancy', '817-871-8123',
    '1440 West Palm Drive', 'Fort Worth', 'TX', '76110');
INSERT INTO CUSTOMER VALUES(
    'Chantel.Jacobs@somewhere.com', 'Jacobs', 'Chantel', '817-871-8234',
    '1550 East Palm Drive', 'Fort Worth', 'TX', '76112');
INSERT INTO CUSTOMER VALUES(
    'Ralph.Able@somewhere.com', 'Able', 'Ralph', '210-281-7987',
    '123 Elm Street', 'San Antonio', 'TX', '78214');
INSERT INTO CUSTOMER VALUES(
    'Susan.Baker@elsewhere.com', 'Baker', 'Susan', '210-281-7876',
    '456 Oak Street', 'San Antonio', 'TX', '78216');
INSERT INTO CUSTOMER VALUES(
    'Sam.Eagleton@elsewhere.com', 'Eagleton', 'Sam', '210-281-7765',
    '789 Pine Street', 'San Antonio', 'TX', '78218');
INSERT INTO CUSTOMER VALUES(
    'Kathy.Foxtrot@somewhere.com', 'Foxtrot', 'Kathy', '972-233-6234',
    '11023 Elm Street', 'Dallas', 'TX', '75220');
INSERT INTO CUSTOMER VALUES(
    'Sally.George@somewhere.com', 'George', 'Sally', '972-233-6345',
    '12034 San Jacinto', 'Dallas', 'TX', '75223');
INSERT INTO CUSTOMER VALUES(
    'Shawn.Hullett@elsewhere.com', 'Hullett', 'Shawn', '972-233-6456',
    '13045 Flora', 'Dallas', 'TX', '75224');
INSERT INTO CUSTOMER VALUES(
    'Bobbi.Pearson@elsewhere.com', 'Pearson', 'Bobbi', '512-974-3344',
    '43 West 23rd Street', 'Austin', 'TX', '78710');
INSERT INTO CUSTOMER VALUES(
    'Terry.Ranger@somewhere.com', 'Ranger', 'Terry', '512-974-4455',
    '56 East 18th Street', 'Austin', 'TX', '78712');
INSERT INTO CUSTOMER VALUES(
    'Jenny.Tyler@somewhere.com', 'Tyler', 'Jenny', '972-233-6567',
    '14056 South Ervay Street', 'Dallas', 'TX', '75225');
INSERT INTO CUSTOMER VALUES(
    'Joan.Wayne@elsewhere.com', 'Wayne', 'Joan', '817-871-8245',
    '1660 South Aspen Drive', 'Fort Worth', 'TX', '76115');


/*****   SEMINAR_CUSTOMER DATA   *********************************************/

INSERT INTO SEMINAR_CUSTOMER VALUES(1, 'Nancy.Jacobs@somewhere.com');
INSERT INTO SEMINAR_CUSTOMER VALUES(1, 'Chantel.Jacobs@somewhere.com');
INSERT INTO SEMINAR_CUSTOMER VALUES(1, 'Ralph.Able@somewhere.com');
INSERT INTO SEMINAR_CUSTOMER VALUES(1, 'Susan.Baker@elsewhere.com');
INSERT INTO SEMINAR_CUSTOMER VALUES(1, 'Sam.Eagleton@elsewhere.com');
INSERT INTO SEMINAR_CUSTOMER VALUES(2, 'Kathy.Foxtrot@somewhere.com');
INSERT INTO SEMINAR_CUSTOMER VALUES(2, 'Sally.George@somewhere.com');
INSERT INTO SEMINAR_CUSTOMER VALUES(2, 'Shawn.Hullett@elsewhere.com');
INSERT INTO SEMINAR_CUSTOMER VALUES(3, 'Bobbi.Pearson@elsewhere.com');
```

(*Continued*)

FIGURE 6-2 *(Continued)*

```
INSERT INTO SEMINAR_CUSTOMER VALUES(3, 'Terry.Ranger@somewhere.com');
INSERT INTO SEMINAR_CUSTOMER VALUES(4, 'Kathy.Foxtrot@somewhere.com');
INSERT INTO SEMINAR_CUSTOMER VALUES(4, 'Sally.George@somewhere.com');
INSERT INTO SEMINAR_CUSTOMER VALUES(4, 'Jenny.Tyler@somewhere.com');
INSERT INTO SEMINAR_CUSTOMER VALUES(4, 'Joan.Wayne@elsewhere.com');


/*****    CONTACT DATA    **************************************************/


INSERT INTO CONTACT VALUES(
     'Nancy.Jacobs@somewhere.com', '11-OCT-2009', 1, 'Seminar', 1);
INSERT INTO CONTACT VALUES(
     'Chantel.Jacobs@somewhere.com', '11-OCT-2009', 1, 'Seminar', 1);
INSERT INTO CONTACT VALUES(
     'Ralph.Able@somewhere.com', '11-OCT-2009', 1, 'Seminar', 1);
INSERT INTO CONTACT VALUES(
     'Susan.Baker@elsewhere.com', '11-OCT-2009', 1, 'Seminar', 1);
INSERT INTO CONTACT VALUES(
     'Sam.Eagleton@elsewhere.com', '11-OCT-2009', 1, 'Seminar', 1);

INSERT INTO CONTACT (EmailAddress, ContactDate, ContactNumber, ContactType)
     VALUES(
     'Nancy.Jacobs@somewhere.com', '16-OCT-2009', 2, 'FormLetter01');
INSERT INTO CONTACT (EmailAddress, ContactDate, ContactNumber, ContactType)
     VALUES(
     'Chantel.Jacobs@somewhere.com', '16-OCT-2009', 2, 'FormLetter01');
INSERT INTO CONTACT (EmailAddress, ContactDate, ContactNumber, ContactType)
     VALUES(
     'Ralph.Able@somewhere.com', '16-OCT-2009', 2, 'FormLetter01');
INSERT INTO CONTACT (EmailAddress, ContactDate, ContactNumber, ContactType)
     VALUES(
     'Susan.Baker@elsewhere.com', '16-OCT-2009', 2, 'FormLetter01');
INSERT INTO CONTACT (EmailAddress, ContactDate, ContactNumber, ContactType)
     VALUES(
     'Sam.Eagleton@elsewhere.com', '16-OCT-2009', 2, 'FormLetter01');


INSERT INTO CONTACT VALUES(
     'Kathy.Foxtrot@somewhere.com', '25-OCT-2009', 1, 'Seminar', 2);
INSERT INTO CONTACT VALUES(
     'Sally.George@somewhere.com', '25-OCT-2009', 1, 'Seminar', 2);
INSERT INTO CONTACT VALUES(
     'Shawn.Hullett@elsewhere.com', '25-OCT-2009', 1, 'Seminar', 2);


INSERT INTO CONTACT (EmailAddress, ContactDate, ContactNumber, ContactType)
     VALUES(
     'Kathy.Foxtrot@somewhere.com', '30-OCT-2009', 2, 'FormLetter01');
INSERT INTO CONTACT (EmailAddress, ContactDate, ContactNumber, ContactType)
     VALUES(
     'Sally.George@somewhere.com', '30-OCT-2009', 2, 'FormLetter01');
INSERT INTO CONTACT (EmailAddress, ContactDate, ContactNumber, ContactType)
     VALUES(
     'Shawn.Hullett@elsewhere.com', '30-OCT-2009', 2, 'FormLetter01');
```

FIGURE 6-2   (*Continued*)

```
INSERT INTO CONTACT VALUES(
       'Bobbi.Pearson@elsewhere.com', '01-NOV-2009', 1, 'Seminar', 3);
INSERT INTO CONTACT VALUES(
       'Terry.Ranger@somewhere.com', '01-NOV-2009', 1, 'Seminar', 3);
INSERT INTO CONTACT (EmailAddress, ContactDate, ContactNumber, ContactType)
     VALUES(
       'Bobbi.Pearson@elsewhere.com', '06-NOV-2009', 2, 'FormLetter01');
INSERT INTO CONTACT (EmailAddress, ContactDate, ContactNumber, ContactType)
     VALUES(
       'Terry.Ranger@somewhere.com', '06-NOV-2009', 2, 'FormLetter01');
INSERT INTO CONTACT (EmailAddress, ContactDate, ContactNumber, ContactType)
     VALUES(
       'Kathy.Foxtrot@somewhere.com', '20-FEB-2010', 3, 'FormLetter02');
INSERT INTO CONTACT (EmailAddress, ContactDate, ContactNumber, ContactType)
     VALUES(
       'Sally.George@somewhere.com', '20-FEB-2010', 3, 'FormLetter02');
INSERT INTO CONTACT (EmailAddress, ContactDate, ContactNumber, ContactType)
     VALUES(
       'Shawn.Hullett@elsewhere.com', '20-FEB-2010', 3, 'FormLetter02');

INSERT INTO CONTACT VALUES(
       'Kathy.Foxtrot@somewhere.com', '22-MAR-2010', 4, 'Seminar', 4);
INSERT INTO CONTACT VALUES(
       'Sally.George@somewhere.com', '22-MAR-2010', 4, 'Seminar', 4);
INSERT INTO CONTACT VALUES(
       'Jenny.Tyler@somewhere.com', '22-MAR-2010', 1, 'Seminar', 4);
INSERT INTO CONTACT VALUES(
       'Joan.Wayne@elsewhere.com', '22-MAR-2010', 1, 'Seminar', 4);


/*****    PRODUCT DATA    *************************************************/

INSERT INTO PRODUCT VALUES(
       'VK001', 'Kitchen Remodeling Basics - Video', 14.95, 50);
INSERT INTO PRODUCT VALUES(
       'VK002', 'Advanced Kitchen Remodeling - Video', 14.95, 35);
INSERT INTO PRODUCT VALUES(
       'VK003', 'Kitchen Remodeling Dallas Style - Video', 19.95, 25);
INSERT INTO PRODUCT VALUES(
       'VK004', 'Heather Sweeney Seminar Live in Dallas on 25-OCT-07 - Video',
       24.95, 20);
INSERT INTO PRODUCT VALUES(
       'VB001', 'Kitchen Remodeling Basics - Video Companion', 7.99, 50);
INSERT INTO PRODUCT VALUES(
       'VB002', 'Advanced Kitchen Remodeling - Video Companion', 7.99, 35);
INSERT INTO PRODUCT VALUES(
       'VB003', 'Kitchen Remodeling Dallas Style - Video Companion',
       9.99, 25);
INSERT INTO PRODUCT VALUES(
       'BK001', 'Kitchen Remodeling Basics For Everyone - Book', 24.95, 75);
INSERT INTO PRODUCT VALUES(
       'BK002', 'Advanced Kitchen Remodeling For Everyone - Book', 24.95, 75);
```

(*Continued*)

**FIGURE 6-2**   *(Continued)*

```
/*****     INVOICE DATA      *************************************************/

/*****     Invoice 35000     *************************************************/
INSERT INTO INVOICE VALUES(
      '15-Oct-09', 'VISA', 22.94, 5.95, 1.31, 30.20,
      'Ralph.Able@somewhere.com');
INSERT INTO LINE_ITEM VALUES(35000, 1, 1, 14.95, 14.95, 'VK001');
INSERT INTO LINE_ITEM VALUES(35000, 2, 1, 7.99, 7.99, 'VB001');


/*****     Invoice 35001     *************************************************/
INSERT INTO INVOICE VALUES(
      '25-Oct-09', 'MasterCard', 47.89, 5.95, 2.73, 56.57,
      'Susan.Baker@elsewhere.com');
INSERT INTO LINE_ITEM VALUES(35001, 1, 1, 14.95, 14.95, 'VK001');
INSERT INTO LINE_ITEM VALUES(35001, 2, 1, 7.99, 7.99, 'VB001');
INSERT INTO LINE_ITEM VALUES(35001, 3, 1, 24.95, 24.95, 'BK001');


/*****     Invoice 35002     *************************************************/
INSERT INTO INVOICE VALUES(
      '20-Dec-09', 'VISA', 24.95, 5.95, 1.42, 32.32,
      'Sally.George@somewhere.com');
INSERT INTO LINE_ITEM VALUES(35002, 1, 1, 24.95, 24.95, 'VK004');


/*****     Invoice 35003     *************************************************/
INSERT INTO INVOICE VALUES(
      '25-Mar-10', 'MasterCard', 64.85, 5.95, 3.70, 74.50,
      'Susan.Baker@elsewhere.com');
INSERT INTO LINE_ITEM VALUES(35003, 1, 1, 14.95, 14.95, 'VK002');
INSERT INTO LINE_ITEM VALUES(35003, 2, 1, 24.95, 24.95, 'BK002');
INSERT INTO LINE_ITEM VALUES(35003, 3, 1, 24.95, 24.95, 'VK004');


/*****     Invoice 35004     *************************************************/
INSERT INTO INVOICE VALUES(
      '27-Mar-10', 'MasterCard', 94.79, 5.95, 5.40, 106.14,
      'Kathy.Foxtrot@somewhere.com');
INSERT INTO LINE_ITEM VALUES(35004, 1, 1, 14.95, 14.95, 'VK002');
INSERT INTO LINE_ITEM VALUES(35004, 2, 1, 24.95, 24.95, 'BK002');
INSERT INTO LINE_ITEM VALUES(35004, 3, 1, 19.95, 19.95, 'VK003');
INSERT INTO LINE_ITEM VALUES(35004, 4, 1, 9.99, 9.99, 'VB003');
INSERT INTO LINE_ITEM VALUES(35004, 5, 1, 24.95, 24.95, 'VK004');


/*****     Invoice 35005     *************************************************/
INSERT INTO INVOICE VALUES(
      '27-Mar-10', 'MasterCard', 94.80, 5.95, 5.40, 106.15,
      'Sally.George@somewhere.com');
INSERT INTO LINE_ITEM VALUES(35005, 1, 1, 24.95, 24.95, 'BK001');
INSERT INTO LINE_ITEM VALUES(35005, 2, 1, 24.95, 24.95, 'BK002');
INSERT INTO LINE_ITEM VALUES(35005, 3, 1, 19.95, 19.95, 'VK003');
INSERT INTO LINE_ITEM VALUES(35005, 4, 1, 24.95, 24.95, 'VK004');


/*****     Invoice 35006     *************************************************/
INSERT INTO INVOICE VALUES(
      '31-Mar-10', 'VISA', 47.89,   5.95, 2.73, 56.57,
      'Bobbi.Pearson@elsewhere.com');
INSERT INTO LINE_ITEM VALUES(35006, 1, 1, 24.95, 24.95, 'BK001');
INSERT INTO LINE_ITEM VALUES(35006, 2, 1, 14.95, 14.95, 'VK001');
INSERT INTO LINE_ITEM VALUES(35006, 3, 1, 7.99, 7.99, 'VB001');
```

FIGURE 6-2   *(Continued)*

```
/*****   Invoice 35007   ***************************************************/
INSERT INTO INVOICE VALUES(
      '03-Apr-10', 'MasterCard', 109.78, 5.95, 6.26, 121.99,
      'Jenny.Tyler@somewhere.com');
INSERT INTO LINE_ITEM VALUES(35007, 1, 2, 19.95, 39.90, 'VK003');
INSERT INTO LINE_ITEM VALUES(35007, 2, 2, 9.99, 19.98, 'VB003');
INSERT INTO LINE_ITEM VALUES(35007, 3, 2, 24.95, 49.90, 'VK004');


/*****   Invoice 35008   ***************************************************/
INSERT INTO INVOICE VALUES(
      '08-Apr-10', 'MasterCard', 47.89,   5.95, 2.73, 56.57,
      'Sam.Eagleton@elsewhere.com');
INSERT INTO LINE_ITEM VALUES(35008, 1, 1, 24.95, 24.95, 'BK001');
INSERT INTO LINE_ITEM VALUES(35008, 2, 1, 14.95, 14.95, 'VK001');
INSERT INTO LINE_ITEM VALUES(35008, 3, 1, 7.99, 7.99, 'VB001');


/*****   Invoice 35009   ***************************************************/
INSERT INTO INVOICE VALUES(
      '08-Apr-10', 'VISA', 47.89,   5.95, 2.73, 56.57,
      'Nancy.Jacobs@somewhere.com');
INSERT INTO LINE_ITEM VALUES(35009, 1, 1, 24.95, 24.95, 'BK001');
INSERT INTO LINE_ITEM VALUES(35009, 2, 1, 14.95, 14.95, 'VK001');
INSERT INTO LINE_ITEM VALUES(35009, 3, 1, 7.99, 7.99, 'VB001');


/*****   Invoice 35010   ***************************************************/
INSERT INTO INVOICE VALUES(
      '23-Apr-10', 'VISA', 24.95,   5.95, 1.42, 32.32,
      'Ralph.Able@somewhere.com');
INSERT INTO LINE_ITEM VALUES(35010, 1, 1, 24.95, 24.95, 'BK001');


/*****   Invoice 35011   ***************************************************/
INSERT INTO INVOICE VALUES(
      '07-May-10', 'VISA', 22.94,   5.95, 1.31, 30.20,
      'Bobbi.Pearson@elsewhere.com');
INSERT INTO LINE_ITEM VALUES(35011, 1, 1, 14.95, 14.95, 'VK002');
INSERT INTO LINE_ITEM VALUES(35011, 2, 1, 7.99, 7.99, 'VB002');


/*****   Invoice 35012   ***************************************************/
INSERT INTO INVOICE VALUES(
      '21-May-10', 'MasterCard', 54.89, 5.95, 3.13, 63.97,
      'Shawn.Hullett@elsewhere.com');
INSERT INTO LINE_ITEM VALUES(35012, 1, 1, 19.95, 19.95, 'VK003');
INSERT INTO LINE_ITEM VALUES(35012, 2, 1, 9.99, 9.99, 'VB003');
INSERT INTO LINE_ITEM VALUES(35012, 3, 1, 24.95, 24.95, 'VK004');


/*****   Invoice 35013   ***************************************************/
INSERT INTO INVOICE VALUES(
      '05-Jun-10', 'VISA', 47.89,   5.95, 2.73, 56.57,
      'Ralph.Able@somewhere.com');
INSERT INTO LINE_ITEM VALUES(35013, 1, 1, 14.95, 14.95, 'VK002');
INSERT INTO LINE_ITEM VALUES(35013, 2, 1, 7.99, 7.99, 'VB002');
INSERT INTO LINE_ITEM VALUES(35013, 3, 1, 24.95, 24.95, 'BK002');


/*****   Invoice 35014   ***************************************************/
INSERT INTO INVOICE VALUES(
      '05-Jun-10', 'MasterCard', 45.88, 5.95, 2.62, 54.45,
      'Jenny.Tyler@somewhere.com');
INSERT INTO LINE_ITEM VALUES(35014, 1, 2, 14.95, 29.90, 'VK002');
INSERT INTO LINE_ITEM VALUES(35014, 2, 2, 7.99, 15.98, 'VB002');
```

*(Continued)*

**FIGURE 6-2** *(Continued)*

```
/*****    Invoice 35015    ***********************************************/
INSERT INTO INVOICE VALUES(
        '05-Jun-10', 'MasterCard', 94.79, 5.95, 5.40, 106.14,
        'Joan.Wayne@elsewhere.com');
INSERT INTO LINE_ITEM VALUES(35015, 1, 1, 14.95, 14.95, 'VK002');
INSERT INTO LINE_ITEM VALUES(35015, 2, 1, 24.95, 24.95, 'BK002');
INSERT INTO LINE_ITEM VALUES(35015, 3, 1, 19.95, 19.95, 'VK003');
INSERT INTO LINE_ITEM VALUES(35015, 4, 1, 9.99, 9.99, 'VB003');
INSERT INTO LINE_ITEM VALUES(35015, 5, 1, 24.95, 24.95, 'VK004');

/*****    Invoice 35016    ***********************************************/
INSERT INTO INVOICE VALUES(
        '05-Jun-10', 'VISA', 45.88,   5.95, 2.62, 54.45,
        'Ralph.Able@somewhere.com');
INSERT INTO LINE_ITEM VALUES(35016, 1, 1, 14.95, 14.95, 'VK001');
INSERT INTO LINE_ITEM VALUES(35016, 2, 1, 7.99, 7.99, 'VB001');
INSERT INTO LINE_ITEM VALUES(35016, 3, 1, 14.95, 14.95, 'VK002');
INSERT INTO LINE_ITEM VALUES(35016, 4, 1, 7.99, 7.99, 'VB002');

/*********************************************************************/
```

**FIGURE 6-3**

The HSD Database in SQL Server

The HSD database object

The HSD table objects—*dbo* stands for *database owner*

The data in the CUSTOMER table

Java, and other programming languages can be processing transactions on the database. All this activity can cause pieces of programming code stored in the DBMS—which are known as *triggers* and *stored procedures* and are discussed in Chapter 7—to be invoked. While all this is occurring, constraints, such as those on referential integrity, must be enforced. Finally, hundreds, or even thousands, of people might be using the system, and they might want to process the database 24 hours a day, 7 days a week.

Three database administration functions are necessary to bring order to this potential chaos. First, the actions of concurrent users must be controlled to ensure that results are consistent with what is expected. Second,

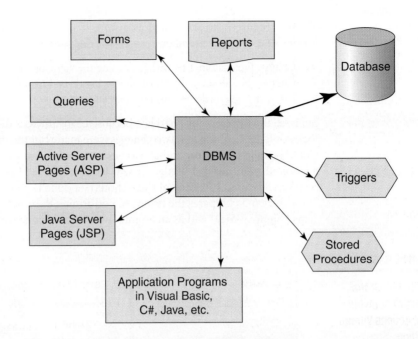

**FIGURE 6-4**

The Database
Processing
Environment

security measures must be in place and enforced so that only authorized users can take authorized actions at appropriate times. Finally, backup and recovery techniques and procedures must be operating to protect the database in case of failure and to recover it as quickly and accurately as possible when necessary. We will consider each of these, in turn, and we will see some of them in use in Chapter 7 when we use Web applications to access databases.

## CONCURRENCY CONTROL

The purpose of concurrency control is to ensure that one user's work does not inappropriately influence another user's work. In some cases, these measures ensure that a user gets the same result when processing with other users as that person would have received if processing alone. In other cases, it means that the user's work is influenced by other users but in an anticipated way.

For example, in an order-entry system, a user should be able to enter an order and get the same result, whether there are no other users or hundreds of other users. However, a user who is printing a report of the most current inventory status might want to obtain in-process data changes from other users, even if those changes might later be canceled.

Unfortunately, no concurrency control technique or mechanism is ideal for all circumstances; they all involve trade-offs. For example, a user can obtain strict concurrency control by locking the entire database, but while that person is processing no other user will be able to do anything. This is robust protection, but it comes at a high cost. As you will see, other measures are available that are more difficult to program and enforce but that allow more throughput. Still other measures are available that maximize throughput but for a low level of concurrency control. When designing multiuser database applications, developers need to choose among these trade-offs.

### The Need for Atomic Transactions

In most database applications, users submit work in the form of **transactions**, also known as **logical units of work (LUWs)**. A transaction (or LUW) is a series of actions to be taken on a database such that all of them are performed successfully or none of them are performed at all, in which case the database remains unchanged. Such a transaction is sometimes called *atomic* because it is performed as a unit. Consider the following sequence of database actions that could occur when recording a new order:

1. Change the customer record, increasing the value of Amount Owed.
2. Change the salesperson record, increasing the value of Commission Due.
3. Insert the new-order record into the database.

Suppose the last step fails, perhaps because of insufficient file space. Imagine the confusion that would ensue if the first two changes were made but the third one was not. The customer would be billed for an order that was never received, and a salesperson would receive a commission on an order that was never sent to the customer. Clearly, these three actions need to be taken as a unit: Either all of them should be done or none of them should be done.

Figure 6-5 compares the results of performing these activities as a series of independent steps [Figure 6-5(a)] and as an atomic transaction [Figure 6-5(b)].

**FIGURE 6-5**

**Comparison of the Results of Applying Serial Actions Versus a Multiple-Step Transaction**

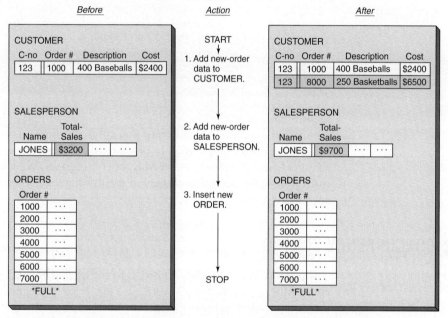

(a) Two of Three Activities Successfully Completed, Resulting in Database Anomalies

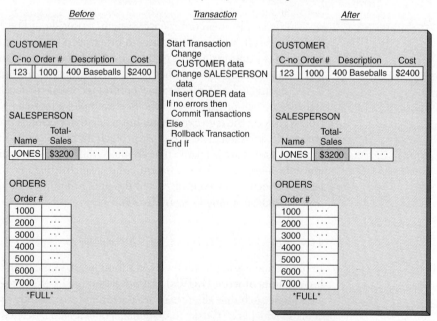

(b) No Change Made Because Entire Transaction Not Successful

Notice that when the steps are carried out atomically and one fails no changes are made in the database. Also note that the application program must issue the commands equivalent to Start Transaction, Commit Transaction, and Rollback Transaction to mark the boundaries of the transaction logic. The particular form of these commands varies from one DBMS product to another.

## Concurrent Transaction Processing

When two transactions are being processed against a database at the same time, they are termed **concurrent transactions**. Although it might appear to the users that concurrent transactions are being processed simultaneously, this cannot be true because the central processing unit (CPU) of the machine processing the database can execute only one instruction at a time. Usually transactions are interleaved, which means the operating system switches CPU services among tasks so that some portion of each of them is carried out in a given interval. This switching among tasks is done so quickly that two people seated at browsers side by side, processing against the same database, might believe that their two transactions are completed simultaneously. However, in reality, the two transactions are interleaved.

Figure 6-6 shows two concurrent transactions. User A's transaction reads Item 100, changes it, and rewrites it in the database. User B's transaction takes the same actions but on Item 200. The CPU processes User A's transaction until the CPU must wait for a read or write operation to complete or for some other action to finish. The operating system then shifts control to User B. The CPU processes User B's transaction until a similar interruption in the transaction processing occurs, at which point the operating system passes control back to User A. Again, to the users, the processing appears to be simultaneous, but in reality it is interleaved, or concurrent.

## The Lost Update Problem

The concurrent processing illustrated in Figure 6-6 poses no problems because the users are processing different data. Now suppose both users want to process Item 100. For example, User A wants to order 5 units of Item 100, and User B wants to order 3 units of Item 100. Figure 6-7 illustrates this problem.

User A reads Item 100's record, which is transferred into a user work area. According to the record, 10 items are in inventory. Then, User B reads Item 100's record, and it goes into another user work area. Again, according to the record, 10 items are in inventory. Now, User A takes 5 of them, decrements the count of items in its user work area to 5, and

**FIGURE 6-6**

Example of Concurrent Processing of Two Users' Tasks

User A
1. Read Item 100.
2. Change Item 100.
3. Write Item 100.

User B
1. Read Item 200.
2. Change Item 200.
3. Write Item 200.

Order of processing at database server
1. Read Item 100 for A.
2. Read Item 200 for B.
3. Change Item 100 for A.
4. Write Item 100 for A.
5. Change Item 200 for B.
6. Write Item 200 for B.

**FIGURE 6-7**

Example of the Lost Update Problem

User A

1. Read Item 100
   (assume item count is 10).
2. Reduce count of items by 5.
3. Write Item 100.

User B

1. Read Item 100
   (assume item count is 10).
2. Reduce count of items by 3.
3. Write Item 100.

Order of processing at database server

1. Read Item 100 (for A).
2. Read Item 100 (for B).
3. Set item count to 5 (for A).
4. Write Item 100 for A.
5. Set item count to 7 (for B).
6. Write Item 100 for B.

Note: The change and write in steps 3 and 4 are lost.

rewrites the record for Item 100. Then, User B takes 3, decrements the count in its user work area to 7, and rewrites the record for Item 100. The database now shows, incorrectly, that 7 units of Item 100 remain in inventory. To review, the inventory started at 10, then User A took 5, User B took 3, and the database wound up showing that 7 were left in inventory. Clearly, this is a problem.

Both users obtained data that were correct at the time they obtained the data. However, when User B read the record, User A already had a copy that it was about to update. This situation is called the **lost update problem**, or the **concurrent update problem**. Another similar problem is called the **inconsistent read problem**. In this situation, User A reads data that have been processed by only a portion of a transaction from User B. As a result, User A reads incorrect data.

## Concurrency Problems: Dirty Reads, Nonrepeatable Reads, and Phantom Reads

The problems that can occur due to concurrent processing have standardized names: dirty read, nonrepeatable read, and phantom read. A **dirty read** occurs when one transaction reads a changed record that has not been committed to the database. This can occur, for example, if one transaction reads a row changed by a second transaction and the second transaction later cancels its changes. A **nonrepeatable read** occurs when a transaction rereads data it has previously read and finds modifications or deletions caused by another transaction. A **phantom read** occurs when a transaction rereads data and finds new rows that were inserted by a different transaction after the prior read.

## Resource Locking

One remedy for the inconsistencies caused by concurrent processing is to prevent multiple applications from obtaining copies of the same rows or tables when those rows or tables are about to be changed. This remedy, called **resource locking**, prevents concurrent processing problems by disallowing sharing by locking data that are retrieved for update. Figure 6-8 shows the order of processing using a lock command.

Because of the lock, User B's transaction must wait until User A is finished with the Item 100 data. Using this strategy, User B can read Item 100's record only after User A has completed the modification. In this case, the final item count stored in the database is 2, which is what it should be. (It started with 10, then A took 5 and B took 3, leaving 2.)

**FIGURE 6-8**

Example of
Concurrent
Processing with
Resource Locking

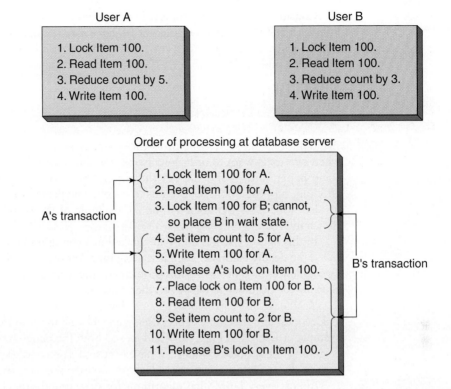

Locks can be placed automatically by the DBMS or by a command issued to the DBMS from the application program or query user. Locks placed by the DBMS are called **implicit locks**; those placed by command are called **explicit locks**.

In the preceding example, the locks were applied to rows of data; however, not all locks are applied at this level. Some DBMS products lock at the page level, some at the table level, and some at the database level. The size of a lock is referred to as the **lock granularity**. Locks with large granularity are easy for the DBMS to administer but frequently cause conflicts. Locks with small granularity are difficult to administer (the DBMS has many more details to keep track of and check), but conflicts are less common.

Locks also vary by type. An **exclusive lock** locks an item from access of any type. No other transaction can read or change the data. A **shared lock** locks an item from being changed but not from being read—that is, other transactions can read the item as long as they do not attempt to alter it.

## Serializable Transactions

When two or more transactions are processed concurrently, the results in the database should be logically consistent with the results that would have been achieved had the transactions been processed in an arbitrary serial fashion. A scheme for processing concurrent transactions in this way is said to be **serializable**.

Serializability can be achieved through a number of different means. One way is to process the transaction by using **two-phase locking**. With this strategy, transactions are allowed to obtain locks as necessary, but when the first lock is released, no other lock can be obtained. Transactions have a growing phase in which the locks are obtained and a shrinking phase in which the locks are released.

A special case of two-phase locking is used with a number of DBMS products. With it, locks are obtained throughout the transaction, but no lock is released until the COMMIT or ROLLBACK command is issued. This strategy is more restrictive than two-phase locking requires, but it is easier to implement.

Consider an order-entry transaction that involves processing data in the CUSTOMER, SALESPERSON, and ORDER table. To make sure the database will suffer no anomalies due to concurrency, the order-entry transaction issues locks on CUSTOMER, SALES-PERSON, and ORDER, as needed; makes all the database changes; and then releases all its locks.

## Deadlock

Although locking solves one problem, it causes another. Consider what might happen when two users want to order two items from inventory. Suppose User A wants to order some paper, and, if she can get the paper, she also wants to order some pencils. In addition, suppose that User B wants to order some pencils, and, if he can get the pencils, he also wants to order some paper. An example of the possible order of processing is shown in Figure 6-9.

In this figure, Users A and B are locked in a condition known as **deadlock**, sometimes called the **deadly embrace**. Each is waiting for a resource that the other person has locked. Two common ways of solving this problem are preventing the deadlock from occurring and allowing the deadlock to occur and then breaking it.

Deadlock can be prevented in several ways. One way is to allow users to issue only one lock request at a time; in essence, users must lock all the resources they want at once. For example, if User A in Figure 6-9 had locked both the paper and the pencil records at the beginning, the deadlock would not have occurred. A second way to prevent deadlock is to require all application programs to lock resources in the same order.

Almost every DBMS has algorithms for detecting deadlock. When deadlock occurs, the normal solution is to roll back one of the transactions to remove its changes from the database.

## Optimistic Versus Pessimistic Locking

Locks can be invoked in two basic styles. With **optimistic locking**, the assumption is made that no conflict will occur. Data are read, the transaction is processed, updates are issued, and then a check is made to see if conflict occurred. If there was no conflict, the transaction finishes. If there was conflict, the transaction is repeated until it processes with no conflict. With **pessimistic locking**, the assumption is made that conflict will occur. Locks are issued, the transaction is processed, and then the locks are freed.

**FIGURE 6-9**

**Example of Deadlock**

User A

1. Lock paper.
2. Take paper.
3. Lock pencils.

User B

1. Lock pencils.
2. Take pencils.
3. Lock paper.

Order of processing at database server

1. Lock paper for User A.
2. Lock pencils for User B.
3. Process A's requests; write paper record.
4. Process B's requests; write pencil record.
5. Put A in wait state for pencils.
6. Put B in wait state for paper.
** Locked **

**FIGURE 6-10**

Example of
Optimistic Locking

```
SELECT      PRODUCT.Name, PRODUCT.Quantity
FROM        PRODUCT
WHERE       PRODUCT.Name = 'Pencil'

OldQuantity = PRODUCT.Quantity

Set NewQuantity = PRODUCT.Quantity – 5

{process transaction – take exception action if NewQuantity < 0, etc.

Assuming all is OK: }

LOCK PRODUCT {at some level of granularity}

UPDATE      PRODUCT
SET         PRODUCT.Quantity = NewQuantity
WHERE       PRODUCT.Name = 'Pencil'
       AND  PRODUCT.Quantity = OldQuantity

UNLOCK   PRODUCT

{check to see if update was successful;
if not, repeat transaction}
```

**FIGURE 6-10**

Example of
Optimistic Locking

Figures 6-10 and 6-11 show examples of both styles of locking for a transaction that is reducing the quantity of the pencil row in the PRODUCT table by 5. Figure 6-10 shows optimistic locking. First, the data are read and the current value of Quantity of pencils is saved in the variable OldQuantity. The transaction is then processed, and, if everything is okay, a lock is obtained on PRODUCT. The lock might be only for the pencil row, or it might be at a larger level of granularity. In any case, an SQL statement is issued to update the pencil row with a WHERE condition that the current value of Quantity equals OldQuantity. If no other transaction has changed the Quantity of the pencil row, then this UPDATE will be successful. If another transaction has changed the Quantity of the pencil row, the UPDATE will fail, and the transaction will need to be repeated.

**FIGURE 6-11**

Example of
Pessimistic Locking

```
LOCK        PRODUCT {at some level of granularity}

SELECT      PRODUCT.Name, PRODUCT.Quantity
FROM        PRODUCT
WHERE       PRODUCT.Name = 'Pencil'

Set NewQuantity = PRODUCT.Quantity – 5

{process transaction – take exception action if NewQuantity < 0, etc.

Assuming all is OK: }

UPDATE      PRODUCT
SET         PRODUCT.Quantity = NewQuantity
WHERE       PRODUCT.Name = 'Pencil'

UNLOCK   PRODUCT

{no need to check if update was successful}
```

Figure 6-11 shows the logic for the same transaction using pessimistic locking. In this case, a lock is obtained on PRODUCT (at some level of granularity) before any work is begun. Then, values are read, the transaction is processed, the UPDATE occurs, and PRODUCT is unlocked.

The advantage of optimistic locking is that the lock is obtained only after the transaction has been processed. Thus, the lock is held for less time than with pessimistic locking. If the transaction is complicated or if the client is slow (due to transmission delays or to the user doing other work, getting a cup of coffee, or shutting down without exiting the application), the lock will be held for considerably less time. This advantage is especially important if the lock granularity is large (for example, the entire PRODUCT table).

The disadvantage of optimistic locking is that if a lot of activity occurs on the pencil row the transaction might have to be repeated many times. Thus, transactions that involve a lot of activity on a given row (purchasing a popular stock, for example) are poorly suited for optimistic locking.

## Declaring Lock Characteristics

Concurrency control is a complicated subject; some of the decisions about lock types and strategy have to be made on the basis of trial and error. For this and other reasons, database application programs generally do not explicitly issue locks. Instead, the programs mark transaction boundaries and then declare the type of locking behavior they want the DBMS to use. If the locking behavior needs to be changed, the application need not be rewritten to place locks in different locations in the transaction. Instead, the lock declaration is changed.

Figure 6-12 shows the pencil transaction with transaction boundaries marked with **SQL transaction control statements**, including the BEGIN TRANSACTION, COMMIT

**FIGURE 6-12**

**Example of Marking Transaction Boundaries**

```
BEGIN TRANSACTION:

SELECT       PRODUCT.Name, PRODUCT.Quantity
FROM         PRODUCT
WHERE        PRODUCT.Name = 'Pencil'

Old Quantity = PRODUCT.Quantity

Set NewQuantity = PRODUCT.Quantity – 5

{process part of transaction – take exception action if NewQuantity < 0, etc.}

UPDATE       PRODUCT
SET          PRODUCT.Quantity = NewQuantity
WHERE        PRODUCT.Name = 'Pencil'

{continue processing transaction} . . .



IF transaction has completed normally       THEN

       COMMIT TRANSACTION

ELSE

       ROLLBACK TRANSACTION

END IF

Continue processing other actions not part of this transaction . . .
```

TRANSACTION, and ROLLBACK TRANSACTION statements. These boundaries provide the essential information that the DBMS needs in order to enforce different locking strategies. If the developer later declares (via a system parameter or similar means) a desire for optimistic locking, the DBMS will implicitly set the locks in the correct place for that locking style. If the developer changes tactics again and requests pessimistic locking, then the DBMS will implicitly set the locks in a different place.

## Consistent Transactions

Sometimes the acronym *ACID* is applied to transactions. An **ACID transaction** is one that is *atomic*, *consistent*, *isolated*, and *durable.* Atomic and durable are easy to define. As mentioned earlier in this chapter, an **atomic** transaction is one in which all the database actions occur or none of them do. A **durable** transaction is one in which all committed changes are permanent. The DBMS will not remove such changes, even in the case of failure. If the transaction is durable, the DBMS will provide facilities to recover the changes of all committed actions when necessary.

The terms *consistent* and *isolated* are not as definitive as the terms *atomic* and *durable.* Consider the following SQL UPDATE command:

```
UPDATE      CUSTOMER
  SET       AreaCode = '425'
  WHERE     ZipCode = '98050';
```

Suppose the CUSTOMER table has 500,000 rows, and 500 of them have a ZipCode value equal to 98050. It will take some time for the DBMS to find all 500 rows. During that time, will other transactions be allowed to update the AreaCode or ZipCode fields of CUSTOMER? If the SQL statement is **consistent**, such updates will be disallowed. The update will apply to the set of rows as they existed at the time the SQL statement started. Such consistency is called **statement-level consistency**.

Now consider a transaction that contains two SQL UPDATE statements:

```
BEGIN TRANSACTION
UPDATE      CUSTOMER
  SET       AreaCode = '425'
  WHERE     ZipCode = '98050';
. . .
{other transaction work}
. . .

UPDATE      CUSTOMER
  SET       Discount = 0.05
  WHERE     AreaCode = '425';
. . .
{other transaction work}
. . .
COMMIT TRANSACTION
```

In this context, what does *consistent* mean? Statement-level consistency means that each statement independently processes consistent rows, but changes from other users to those rows might be allowed during the interval between the two SQL statements. **Transaction-level consistency** means that all rows affected by either of the SQL statements are protected from changes during the entire transaction.

**FIGURE 6-13**

Summary of Isolation Levels

| | | Isolation Level | | | |
|---|---|---|---|---|---|
| | | Read Uncommitted | Read Committed | Repeatable Read | Serializable |
| Problem Type | Dirty Read | Possible | Not possible | Not possible | Not possible |
| | Nonrepeatable Read | Possible | Possible | Not possible | Not possible |
| | Phantom Read | Possible | Possible | Possible | Not possible |

However, for some implementations of transaction-level consistency, a transaction will not see its own changes. In this example, the second SQL statement might not see rows changed by the first SQL statement.

Thus, when you hear the term *consistent* look further to determine which type of consistency is intended. Be aware as well of the potential trap of transaction-level consistency. The situation is even more complicated for the term *isolated*, which we consider next.

## Transaction Isolation Level

The 1992 ANSI SQL standard defined four isolation levels that specify which of the concurrency control problems are allowed to occur. These isolation levels are shown in Figure 6-13.

The goal of having four isolation levels is to allow the application programmer to declare the type of isolation level desired and then to have the DBMS manage locks to achieve that level of isolation. As shown in Figure 6-13, **read uncommitted isolation** allows dirty reads, nonrepeatable reads, and phantom reads to occur. With **read committed isolation**, dirty reads are disallowed. The **repeatable reads isolation** level disallows both dirty reads and nonrepeatable reads. The **serializable isolation level** does not allow any of these three.

Generally, the more restrictive the isolation level, the less throughput occurs, although much depends on the workload and how the application programs were written. Moreover, not all DBMS products support all these levels. Products also vary in the manner in which they are supported and in the burden they place on the application programmer.

## CURSOR TYPES

A cursor is a pointer into a set of rows that are the result set from an SQL SELECT statement, and cursors are usually defined using SELECT statements. For example, the following statement defines a cursor named TransCursor that operates over the set of rows indicated by this SELECT statement:

```
DECLARE CURSOR TransCursor AS
    SELECT  *
    FROM    [TRANSACTION]
    WHERE   PurchasePrice > '10000';
```

After an application program opens a cursor, it can place the cursor somewhere in the result set. Most commonly, the cursor is placed on the first or last row, but other possibilities exist.

A transaction can open several cursors—either sequentially or simultaneously. In addition, two or more cursors may be open on the same table, either directly on the table or through an SQL view on that table. Because cursors require considerable memory, having many cursors open at the same time (for example, for a thousand concurrent transactions) consumes considerable memory. One way to reduce cursor burden is to define reduced-capability cursors and use them when a full-capability cursor is not needed.

Figure 6-14 lists three cursor types supported by SQL Server 2008 R2. In SQL Server 2008 R2, cursors may be either forward-only cursors or scrollable cursors. With a **forward-only cursor**, the application can only move forward through the records, and changes made by other cursors in this transaction and other transactions will visible only if they occur to rows ahead of the cursor. With a **scrollable cursor**, the application can scroll forward and backward through the records.

There are three types of cursors, each of which can be implemented as either a forward-only or scrollable cursor. A **static cursor** takes a snapshot of a relation and processes that snapshot. Changes made using this cursor are visible; changes form other sources are not visible.

A **dynamic cursor** is a fully featured cursor. All inserts, updates, deletions, and changes in row order are visible to a dynamic cursor. Unless the isolation level of the transaction is a dirty read, only committed changes are visible.

**Keyset cursors** combine some features of static cursors with some features of dynamic cursors. When the cursor is opened, a primary key value is saved for each row. When the application positions the cursor on a row, the DBMS uses the key value to read the current value of the row. Inserts of new rows by other cursors (in this transaction or in other transactions) are not visible. If the application issues an update on a row that has been

**FIGURE 6-14**

Summary of Cursor Types

| CursorType | Description | Comments |
|---|---|---|
| Static | Application sees the data as they were at the time the cursor was opened. | Changes made by this cursor are visible. Changes from other sources are not visible. Backward and forward scrolling are allowed. |
| Keyset | When the cursor is opened, a primary key value is saved for each row in the recordset. When the application accesses a row, the key is used to fetch the current values for the row. | Updates from any source are visible. Inserts from sources outside this cursor are not visible (there is no key for them in the keyset). Inserts from this cursor appear at the bottom of the recordset. Deletions from any source are visible. Changes in row order are not visible. If the isolation level is dirty read, then committed updates and deletions are visible; otherwise, only committed updates and deletions are visible. |
| Dynamic | Changes of any type and from any source are visible. | All inserts, updates, deletions, and changes in recordset order are visible. If the isolation level is dirty read, then uncommitted changes are visible. Otherwise, only committed changes are visible. |

deleted by a different cursor, the DBMS creates a new row with the old key value and places the updated values in the new row (assuming that all required fields are present). As with dynamic cursors, unless the isolation level of the transaction is a dirty read, only committed updates and deletions are visible to the cursor.

Cursor types for DBMSs besides SQL Server 2008 R2 are similar, except that the forward-only cursor is sometimes implemented as a fourth cursor type. In this case, the static, keyset, and dynamic cursors will be strictly scrollable cursors.

The amount of overhead and processing required to support a cursor is different for each type. In general, the cost goes up as you move down the cursor types shown in Figure 6-14. In order to improve DBMS performance, therefore, an application developer should create cursors that are just powerful enough to do the job. It is also very important to understand how a particular DBMS implements cursors and whether cursors are located on the server or on the client. In some cases, it might be better to place a dynamic cursor on the client than to have a static cursor on the server. No general rule can be stated because performance depends on the implementation used by the DBMS product and the application requirements.

---

**B T W**

A word of caution: If you do *not* specify the isolation level of a transaction or do not specify the type of cursors you open, the DBMS will use a default level and types. These defaults may be perfect for your application, but they also may be terrible. Thus, even though you can ignore these issues, you cannot avoid their consequences. You must learn the capabilities of your DBMS product.

---

## DATABASE SECURITY

The goal of database security is to ensure that only authorized users can perform authorized activities at authorized times. This goal is usually broken into two parts: **authentication**, which makes sure the user has the basic right to use the system in the first place, and **authorization**, which assigns the authenticated user specific rights or **permissions** to do specific activities on the system. As shown in Figure 6-15, user authentication is achieved by requiring the user to log in to the system with a password (or other means of positive identification, such as a biometric scan of a fingerprint), whereas user authorization is achieved by granting DBMS-specific permissions.

Note that authentication (when the user logs in to the system) by itself is not sufficient for use of the database—unless the user has been granted permissions, he or she cannot access the database or take any actions that use it.

The goal of database security is difficult to achieve, and to make any progress at all the database development team must determine (1) which users should be able to use the database (authentication) and (2) the processing rights and responsibilities of each user. These security requirements can then be enforced using the security features of the DBMS, as well as additions to those features that are written into the application programs.

**FIGURE 6-15**

Database Security Authentication and Authorization

---

**FIGURE 6-16**

**Creating the Database Server Login**

The user's DBMS login name

The user's DBMS password

Uncheck this checkbox

The Logins folder

The HSD database

## User Accounts

Consider, for example, the database security needs of Heather Sweeney Designs. There must be some means of controlling which employees can have access to the database. There is: You can create a **user account** for each of the employees. Figure 6-16 shows the creation of the user login HSD-User at the DBMS security level in SQL Server.

This step creates the initial user account in the DBMS—*not* a specific database. The password being assigned is HSD-User+password, which we will also need for the HSD Web pages in Chapter 7. Note that in the Windows environment there are two choices for controlling authentication: We can use the Windows operating system to control authentication, or we can create an SQL Server internal user account with its own login name and password. For other DBMS products that are not as operating system specific as SQL Server, only the second option of internal user accounts can be used.

User accounts and passwords need to be managed carefully. The exact terminology, features, and functions of DBMS account and password security depend on the DBMS product used.

## User Processing Rights and Responsibilities

All major DBMS products provide security tools that limit certain actions on certain objects to certain users. A general model of DBMS security is shown in Figure 6-17.

According to Figure 6-17, a user can be assigned to one or more roles (groups), and a role can have one or more users. Users, roles, and objects (used in a generic sense) have many permissions. Each permission is assigned to one user or role and one object. Once a user is authenticated by the DBMS, the DBMS limits the person's actions to the defined permissions for that user and to the permissions for roles to which that user has been assigned.

Now, let's consider user authorization at Heather Sweeney Designs. The company has three types of users: administrative assistants, management (Heather and others), and a

**FIGURE 6-17**

**A Model of DBMS Security**

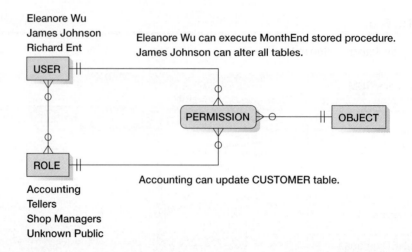

system administrator (Heather's consultant). Figure 6-18 summarizes the processing rights that Heather determined were appropriate for her business.

Administrative assistants can read, insert, and change data in all tables. However, they can delete data only from SEMINAR_CUSTOMER and LINE_ITEM. This means that administrative assistants can disenroll customers from seminars and can remove items from an order. Management can take all actions on all tables except delete CUSTOMER data. Heather believes that for as hard as she works to get a customer, she does not want to ever run the risk of accidentally deleting one.

Finally, the system administrator can modify the database structure and grant rights (assign permissions) to other users but can take no action on data. The system administrator is not a user and so should not be allowed access to user data. This limitation might seem weak. After all, if the system administrator can assign permissions, he or she can get around the security system by changing the permissions to take whatever action is desired, make the data changes, and then change the permissions back. This is true, but it would leave an audit trail in the DBMS logs. That, coupled with the need to make the security system changes, will dissuade the administrator from unauthorized activity. It is certainly better than allowing the administrator to have user data access permissions with no effort.

**FIGURE 6-18**

**Processing Rights at Heather Sweeney Designs**

### DATABASE RIGHTS GRANTED

| Table | Administrative Assistants | Management | System Administrator |
|---|---|---|---|
| SEMINAR | Read, Insert, Change | Read, Insert, Change, Delete | Grant Rights, Modify Structure |
| CUSTOMER | Read, Insert, Change | Read, Insert, Change | Grant Rights, Modify Structure |
| SEMINAR_ CUSTOMER | Read, Insert, Change, Delete | Read, Insert, Change, Delete | Grant Rights, Modify Structure |
| CONTACT | Read, Insert, Change | Read, Insert, Change, Delete | Grant Rights, Modify Structure |
| INVOICE | Read, Insert, Change | Read, Insert, Change, Delete | Grant Rights, Modify Structure |
| LINE_ITEM | Read, Insert, Change, Delete | Read, Insert, Change, Delete | Grant Rights, Modify Structure |
| PRODUCT | Read, Insert, Change | Read, Insert, Change, Delete | Grant Rights, Modify Structure |

A very important principle of database security administration (and of network administration) is that the types of permissions shown in Figure 6-18 are given to user *groups* (also known as user *roles*) and *not* to individual users, unless absolutely necessary. There may be some cases in which specific users need to be assigned permissions within the database, but we want to avoid this whenever possible. Note that because groups or roles are used, it is necessary to have a means for assigning users to groups or roles. When Heather Sweeney signs onto the computer, some means must be available to determine which group or groups she belongs to.

Now, we need to make role and permission assignments in the HSD database. HSD-User is one of Heather's administrative assistants and, therefore, needs the ability to read, insert, and change data in all tables. First, we need to grant HSD-User permission to use the HSD database within the DBMS. Figure 6-19 shows the creation of the *database-level user* named *HSD-Database-User* at the HSD database security level in SQL Server. Note that this user is being created specifically for the HSD database but is based on the already created DBMS login name. Also note that in SQL Server, no password is assigned at the database security level, only at the DBMS security level.

Figure 6-20 shows the fixed database roles in SQL Server and their associated permissions. Because HSD-Database-User needs to be able to read, insert, and change data in all tables in the HSD database, we should assign HSD-Database-User to the roles db_datareader and db_datawriter. Figure 6-21 shows HSD Database User being added to the db_datareader role. (We cover this further in the next section.)

In this discussion, we have used the phrase *processing rights and responsibilities*. As this phrase implies, responsibilities go with processing rights. If, for example, the system administrator deletes CUSTOMER data, it is that person's responsibility to ensure that those deletions do not adversely affect the company's operation, accounting, and so forth.

Processing responsibilities cannot be enforced by the DBMS or the database applications. Responsibilities are, instead, encoded in manual procedures and explained to users during systems training. These are topics for a systems development book, and we do not

**FIGURE 6-19**

**Creating the Database User Name**

The user name for the HSD database

The user's DBMS login name

The Users folder

The Logins folder

FIGURE 6-20

SQL Server Fixed Database Roles

| Fixed Database Role | Database-Specific Permissions | DBMS Server Permissions |
|---|---|---|
| db_accessadmin | Permissions granted: ALTER ANY USER, CREATE SCHEMA<br>Permissions granted with GRANT option: CONNECT | Permissions granted: VIEW ANY DATABASE |
| db_backupoperator | Permissions granted: BACKUP DATABASE, BACKUP LOG, CHECKPOINT | Permissions granted: VIEW ANY DATABASE |
| db_datareader | Permissions granted: SELECT | Permissions granted: VIEW ANY DATABASE |
| db_datawriter | Permissions granted: DELETE, INSERT, UPDATE | Permissions granted: VIEW ANY DATABASE |
| db_ddladmin | Permissions granted: *See SQL Server documentation* | Permissions granted: VIEW ANY DATABASE |
| db_denydatareader | Permissions *denied:* SELECT | Permissions granted: VIEW ANY DATABASE |
| db_denydatawriter | Permissions *denied:* DELETE, INSERT, UPDATE | Permissions granted: VIEW ANY DATABASE |
| db_owner | Permissions granted with GRANT option: CONTROL | Permissions granted: VIEW ANY DATABASE |
| db_securityadmin | Permissions granted: ALTER ANY APPLICATION ROLE, ALTER ANY ROLE, CREATE SCHEMA, VIEW DEFINITION | Permissions granted: VIEW ANY DATABASE |

**Note:** For the definitions of each of the SQL Server permissions shown in the table, consult the SQL Server documentation.

FIGURE 6-21

Assigning HSD-Database-User to the db_datareader Role

The Database **Role Properties – db_datawriter** dialog box

The HSD database user name HSD-Database-User

The Database Role db_datareader

The Database Role db_datawriter

consider them further here except to reiterate that responsibilities go with rights. Such responsibilities must be documented and enforced.

The DBA has the task of managing processing rights and responsibilities, which change over time. As the database is used and as changes are made to the applications and to the DBMS's structure, the need for new or different rights and responsibilities will arise. The DBA is a focal point for the discussion of such changes and for their implementation.

After processing rights have been defined, they can be implemented at many levels: operating system, network directory service, Web server, DBMS, and application. The next two sections consider the DBMS and application aspects. The other aspects are beyond the scope of this book.

## DBMS-Level Security

Security guidelines for a DBMS are shown in Figure 6-22. First, the DBMS should be run behind a firewall. In most cases, no communication with the DBMS or database applications should be allowed to be initiated from outside the organization's network. For example, the company's Web site should be hosted on a separate, dedicated Web server. While the Web server will have to communicate through the firewall, the DBMS server should be protected behind it.

Second, service packs and fixes for the operating system and the DBMS must be applied as soon as possible. In spring 2003, the slammer worm exploited a security hole in SQL Server, bringing major organizational database applications to their knees. Microsoft had published a patch that eliminated the hole prior to the release of the slammer worm, so any organization that had applied that patch was not affected by the worm.

A third protection is to limit the capabilities of the DBMS to only those features and functions that the applications need. For example, Oracle can support many different communications protocols. To improve security, any Oracle-supported protocol that is not used should be removed or disabled. Similarly, every DBMS ships with hundreds of system-stored procedures. Any procedure that is not used should be removed from operational databases.

Another important security measure is to protect the computer that runs the DBMS. No users should be allowed to work on the DBMS computer, and that computer should reside in a separate facility, behind locked doors. Visits to the room housing the DBMS should be logged with date and time. Further, since people can login to DBMS servers via remote control software (such as Microsoft Remote Desktop Connection in the Windows environment), there must be control of who has (and who can grant) remote access.

A user can enter a name and password; in some applications, the name and password are entered on behalf of the user. For example, as we saw in Figure 6-16, the Windows operating system user name and password can be passed directly to SQL Server. In other cases, an application program provides the user name and password.

The security systems used by SQL Server 2008 R2, Oracle Database 11g, and MySQL 5.1 are variations on the model shown in Figure 6-17. The terminology used might vary, but the essence of their security systems is the same.

**FIGURE 6-22**

DBMS Security
Guidelines

- Run the DBMS behind a firewall
- Apply the latest operating system and DBMS service packs and fixes
- Limit DBMS functionality to needed features
- Protect the computer that runs the DBMS
- Manage accounts and passwords
- Encryption of sensitive data transmitted across the network
- Encryption of sensitive data stored in databases

## Application-Level Security

Although DBMS products, such as SQL Server 2008 R2, Oracle Database 11g, and MySQL 5.1 provide substantial database security capabilities, they are generic by their very nature. If an application requires specific security measures—such as disallowing users to view a row of a table or a join of a table that has an employee name other than the user's own—the DBMS facilities will not be adequate. In these cases, the security system must be augmented by features in database applications.

For example, application security in Internet applications is often provided on the Web server computer. When application security is executed on this server, sensitive security data do not need to be transmitted over the network. To understand this better, suppose an application is written such that when users click a particular button on a browser page the following query is sent to the Web server and then to the DBMS:

```
SELECT      *
FROM        EMPLOYEE;
```

This statement returns all EMPLOYEE rows. If the application security allows employees to access only their own data, then a Web server could add the following WHERE clause to this query:

```
SELECT      *
FROM        EMPLOYEE
WHERE       EMPLOYEE.Name = '<%SESSION("EmployeeName")%>';
```

An expression like this causes the Web server to fill in the employee's name for the WHERE clause. For a user signed on under the name Benjamin Franklin, the following statement results from this expression:

```
SELECT      *
FROM        EMPLOYEE
WHERE       EMPLOYEE.Name = 'Benjamin Franklin';
```

Because the name is inserted by a program on the Web server, the browser user does not know it is occurring and cannot interfere with it. Such security processing can be done as shown here on a Web server, and it can also be done within the application programs themselves, or written as code stored within the DBMS to be executed by the DBMS at the appropriate times.

You can also store additional data in a security database that is accessed by the Web server as well as by stored DBMS code. That security database could contain, for example, the identities of users paired with additional values of WHERE clauses. For example, suppose the users in the personnel department can access more than just their own data. The predicates for appropriate WHERE clauses could be stored in the security database, read by the application program, and appended to SQL SELECT statements, as necessary.

Many other possibilities exist for extending DBMS security with application processing. In general, you should use the DBMS security features first. Only if they are inadequate for the requirements should you add to them with application code. The closer the security enforcement is to the data, the lower the chance for infiltration. Also, using the DBMS security features is faster, less expensive, and likely to produce higher-quality results than if you develop your own.

## DATABASE BACKUP AND RECOVERY

Computer systems fail. Hardware breaks. Programs have bugs. Procedures written by humans contain errors. People make mistakes. All these failures can and do occur in database applications. Because a database is shared by many people, and because it often is a key element of an organization's operations, it is important to recover it as soon as possible.

Several problems must be addressed. First, from a business standpoint, business functions must continue. For example, customer orders, financial transactions, and packing lists must be completed manually. Later, when the database application is operational again, the new data can be entered. Second, computer operations personnel must restore the system to a usable state as quickly as possible and as close as possible to what it was when the system crashed. Third, users must know what to do when the system becomes available again. Some work might need to be reentered, and users must know how far back they need to go.

When failures occur, it is impossible simply to fix the problem and resume processing. Even if no data are lost during a failure (which assumes that all types of memory are nonvolatile—an unrealistic assumption), the timing and scheduling of computer processing are too complex to be accurately re-created. Enormous amounts of overhead data and processing would be required for the operating system to be able to restart processing precisely where it was interrupted. It is simply not possible to roll back the clock and put all the electrons in the same configuration they were in at the time of the failure. However, two other approaches are possible: **recovery via reprocessing** and **recovery via rollback/rollforward**.

## Recovery via Reprocessing

Because processing cannot be resumed at a precise point, the next-best alternative is to go back to a known point and reprocess the workload from there. The simplest form of this type of recovery involves periodically making a copy of the database (called a *database save*) and keeping a record of all transactions processed since the save. Then, when failure occurs, the operations staff can restore the database from the save and reprocess all the transactions.

Unfortunately, this simple strategy normally is not feasible. First, reprocessing transactions takes the same amount of time as processing them in the first place. If the computer is heavily scheduled, the system might never catch up. Second, when transactions are processed concurrently, events are asynchronous. Slight variations in human activity, such as a user reading an email message before responding to an application prompt, could change the order of the execution of concurrent transactions. Therefore, whereas Customer A got the last seat on a flight during the original processing, Customer B might get the last seat during reprocessing. For these reasons, reprocessing is normally not a viable form of recovery from failure in multiuser systems.

## Recovery via Rollback and Rollforward

A second approach to database recovery involves periodically making a copy of the database (the database save) and keeping a log of the changes made by transactions against the database since the save. Then, when a failure occurs, one of two methods can be used. With the first method, called **rollforward**, the database is restored using the saved data and all valid transactions since the save are reapplied. Note that we are not reprocessing the transactions, because the application programs are not involved in the rollforward. Instead, the processed changes, as recorded in the log, are reapplied.

With the second method, **rollback**, we correct mistakes caused by erroneous or partially processed transactions by undoing the changes they made in the database. Then, the valid transactions that were in process at the time of the failure are restarted.

As stated, both of these methods require that a **log** of the transaction results be kept. This log contains records of the data changes in chronological order. Note that transactions must be written to the log before they are applied to the database. That way, if the system crashes between the time a transaction is logged and the time it is applied, at worst, there is a record of an unapplied transaction. If transactions were applied before being logged, it would be possible (and undesirable) to change the database without having a record of the change. If this happens, an unwary user might reenter an already completed transaction.

**FIGURE 6-23**

Undo and Redo
Transactions

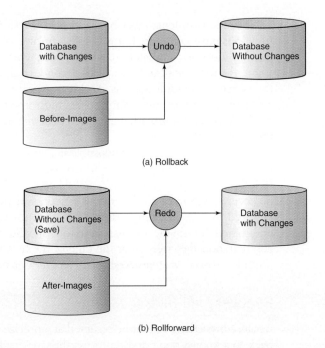

(a) Rollback

(b) Rollforward

In the event of a failure, we use the log to undo and redo transactions, as shown in Figure 6-23. To undo a transaction as shown in Figure 6-23(a), the log must contain a copy of every database record before it was changed. Such records are called **before-images**. A transaction is undone by applying before-images of all its changes to the database.

To redo a transaction as shown in Figure 6-23(b), the log must contain a copy of every database record (or page) after it was changed. These records are called **after-images**. A transaction is redone by applying after-images of all its changes to the database. Possible data items of a transaction log are shown in Figure 6-24.

For this example transaction log, each transaction has a unique name for identification purposes. Furthermore, all images for a given transaction are linked together with pointers. One pointer points to the previous change made by this transaction (the reverse pointer), and the other points to the next change made by this transaction (the forward

**FIGURE 6-24**

Transaction Log
Example

| Relative Record Number | Transaction ID | Reverse Pointer | Forward Pointer | Time | Type of Operation | Object | Before-Image | After-Image |
|---|---|---|---|---|---|---|---|---|
| 1 | OT1 | 0 | 2 | 11:42 | START | | | |
| 2 | OT1 | 1 | 4 | 11:43 | MODIFY | CUST 100 | (old value) | (new value) |
| 3 | OT2 | 0 | 8 | 11:46 | START | | | |
| 4 | OT1 | 2 | 5 | 11:47 | MODIFY | SP AA | (old value) | (new value) |
| 5 | OT1 | 4 | 7 | 11:47 | INSERT | ORDER 11 | | (value) |
| 6 | CT1 | 0 | 9 | 11:48 | START | | | |
| 7 | OT1 | 5 | 0 | 11:49 | COMMIT | | | |
| 8 | OT2 | 3 | 0 | 11:50 | COMMIT | | | |
| 9 | CT1 | 6 | 10 | 11:51 | MODIFY | SP BB | (old value) | (new value) |
| 10 | CT1 | 9 | 0 | 11:51 | COMMIT | | | |

pointer). A zero in the pointer field means that this is the end of the list. The DBMS recovery subsystem uses these pointers to locate all records for a particular transaction. Figure 6-24 shows an example of the linking of log records.

Other data items in the log are:

- The time of the action
- The type of operation (START marks the beginning of a transaction, and COMMIT terminates a transaction, releasing all locks that were in place)
- The object acted upon, such as record type and identifier
- The before-images and after-images.

Given a log with before-images and after-images, the undo and redo actions are straightforward. Figure 6-25 shows how recovery for a system crash is accomplished.

To undo the transaction in Figure 6-25(a), the recovery processor simply replaces each changed record with its before-image, as shown in Figure 6-25(b). When all before-images have been restored, the transaction is undone. To redo a transaction, the recovery processor starts with the version of the database at the time the transaction started and applies all after-images. This action assumes that an earlier version of the database is available from a database save.

Restoring a database to its most recent save and reapplying all transactions might require considerable processing. To reduce the delay, DBMS products sometimes use checkpoints. A **checkpoint** is a point of synchronization between the database and the transaction log. To perform a checkpoint, the DBMS refuses new requests, finishes processing outstanding requests, and writes its buffers to disk. The DBMS then waits until the operating system notifies it that all outstanding write requests to the database and to the log have been completed successfully. At this point, the log and the database are synchronized. A checkpoint record is then written to the log. Later, the database can be recovered from the checkpoint, and only after-images for transactions that started after the checkpoint need to be applied.

Checkpoints are inexpensive operations, and it is feasible to make three or four (or more) per hour. This way, no more than 15 or 20 minutes of processing needs to be recovered. Most DBMS products perform automatic checkpoints, making human intervention unnecessary.

## FIGURE 6-25

**Recovery Example**

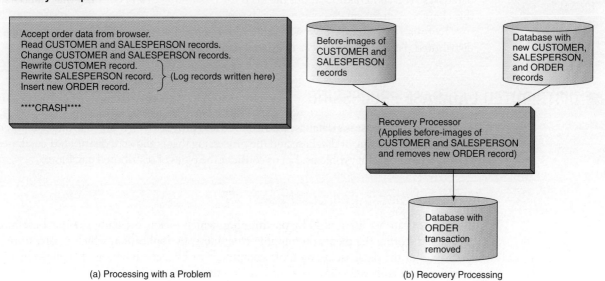

(a) Processing with a Problem                    (b) Recovery Processing

You will need to learn more about backup and recovery if you work in database administration using products such as SQL Server 2008 R2, Oracle Database 11g, or MySQL 5.1. For now, you just need to understand the basic ideas and to realize that it is the responsibility of the DBA to ensure that adequate backup and recovery plans have been developed and that database saves and logs are generated as required.

## ADDITIONAL DBA RESPONSIBILITIES

Concurrency control, security, and reliability are the three major concerns of database administration. However, other administrative and managerial DBA functions are also important.

For one, a DBA needs to ensure that a system exists to gather and record user-reported errors and other problems. A means needs to be devised to prioritize those errors and problems and to ensure that they are corrected accordingly. In this regard, the DBA works with the development team not only to resolve these problems but also to evaluate features and functions of new releases of the DBMS.

As the database is used and as new requirements develop and are implemented, requests for changes to the structure of the database will occur. Changes to an operational database need to be made with great care and thoughtful planning. Because databases are shared resources, a change to the structure of a database to implement features desired by one user or group can be detrimental to the needs of other users or groups.

Therefore, a DBA needs to create and manage a process for controlling the database configuration. Such a process includes procedures for recording change requests, conducting user and developer reviews of such requests, and creating projects and tasks for implementing changes that are approved. All these activities need to be conducted with a community-wide view.

Finally, a DBA is responsible for ensuring that appropriate documentation is maintained about database structure, concurrency control, security, backup and recovery, applications use, and a myriad of other details that concern the management and use of the database. Some vendors provide tools for recording such documentation. At a minimum, a DBMS will have its own metadata that it uses to process the database. Some products augment these metadata with facilities for storing and reporting application metadata, as well as operational procedures.

A DBA has significant responsibilities in the management and administration of a database. These responsibilities vary with the database type and size, the number of users, and the complexity of the applications. However, the responsibilities are important for all databases. You should know about the need for DBA services and consider the material in this chapter even for small, personal databases.

To finish this chapter, we will take a look at two advanced types of databases—distributed databases and object-relational databases.

## DISTRIBUTED DATABASE PROCESSING

A **distributed database** is a database that is stored and processed on more than one computer. Depending on the type of database and the processing that is allowed, distributed databases can present significant problems. Let us consider the types of distributed databases.

### Types of Distributed Databases

A database can be distributed by **partitioning**, which means breaking the database into pieces and storing the pieces on multiple computers; by **replication**, which means storing the copies of the database on multiple computers; or by a combination of replication and partitioning. Figure 6-26 illustrates these alternatives.

## FIGURE 6-26

Types of Distributed Databases

(a) Nonpartitioned, Nonreplicated Alternative

(b) Partitioned, Nonreplicated Alternative

(c) Nonpartitioned, Replicated Alternative

(d) Partitioned, Replicated Alternative

Figure 6-26(a) shows a nondistributed database with four pieces labeled W, X, Y, and Z. In Figure 6-26(b), the database has been partitioned but not replicated. Portions W and X are stored and processed on Computer 1, and portions Y and Z are stored and processed on Computer 2. Figure 6-26(c) shows a database that has been replicated but not partitioned. The entire database is stored and processed on Computers 1 and 2. Finally, Figure 6-26(d) shows a database that is partitioned and replicated. Portion Y of the database is stored and processed on Computers 1 and 2.

The portions to be partitioned or replicated can be defined in many different ways. A database that has five tables (for example, CUSTOMER, SALESPERSON, INVOICE, LINE_ITEM, and PART) could be partitioned by assigning CUSTOMER to portion W, SALESPERSON to portion X, INVOICE and LINE_ITEM to portion Y, and PART to portion Z. Alternatively, different rows of each of these five tables could be assigned to different computers, or different columns of each of these tables could be assigned to different computers.

Databases are distributed for two major reasons: performance and control. Having a database on multiple computers can improve throughput, either because multiple computers are sharing the workload or because communications delays can be reduced by placing the computers closer to their users. Distributing the database can improve control by segregating different portions of the database to different computers, each of which can have its own set of authorized users and permissions.

## Challenges of Distributed Databases

Significant challenges must be overcome when distributing a database, and those challenges depend on the type of distributed database and the activity that is allowed. In the case of a fully replicated database, if only one computer is allowed to make updates on one of the copies, then the challenges are not too great. All update activity occurs on that single computer, and copies of that database are periodically sent to the replication sites. The challenge is to ensure that only a logically consistent copy of the database is distributed (no partial or uncommitted transactions, for example) and to ensure that the sites understand that they are processing data that might not be current because changes could have been made to the updated database after the local copy was made.

If multiple computers can make updates to a replicated database, then difficult problems arise. Specifically, if two computers are allowed to process the same row at the same time, they can cause three types of error: They can make inconsistent changes, one computer can delete a row that another computer is updating, or the two computers can make changes that violate uniqueness constraints.

To prevent these problems, some type of record locking is required. Because multiple computers are involved, standard record locking does not work. Instead, a far more complicated locking scheme, called **distributed two-phase locking**, must be used. The specifics of the scheme are beyond the scope of this discussion; for now, just know that implementing this algorithm is difficult and expensive. If multiple computers can process multiple replications of a distributed database, then significant problems must be solved.

If the database is partitioned but not replicated [Figure 6-26(b)], then problems will occur if any transaction updates data that span two or more distributed partitions. For example, suppose the CUSTOMER and SALESPERSON tables are placed on a partition on one computer and that INVOICE, LINE_ITEM, and PART tables are placed on a second computer. Further suppose that when recording a sale all five tables are updated in an atomic transaction. In this case, a transaction must be started on both computers, and it can be allowed to commit on one computer only if it can be allowed to commit on both computers. In this case, distributed two-phase locking also must be used.

If the data are partitioned in such a way that no transaction requires data from both partitions, then regular locking will work. However, in this case the databases are actually two separate databases, and some would argue that they should not be considered a distributed database.

If the data are partitioned in such a way that no transaction updates data from both partitions but that one or more transactions read data from one partition and update data on a second partition, then problems might or might not result with regular locking. If dirty reads are possible, then some form of distributed locking is required; otherwise, regular locking should work.

If a database is partitioned and at least one of those partitions is replicated, then locking requirements are a combination of those just described. If the replicated portion is updated, if transactions span the partitions, or if dirty reads are possible, then distributed two-phase locking is required; otherwise, regular locking might suffice.

Distributed processing is complicated and can create substantial problems. Except in the case of replicated, read-only databases, only experienced teams with a substantial budget and significant time to invest should attempt distributed databases. Such databases also require data communications expertise. Distributed databases are not for the faint of heart.

## OBJECT-RELATIONAL DATABASES

**Object-oriented programming (OOP)** is a technique for designing and writing computer programs. Today, most new program development is done using OOP techniques. Java, C++, C#, and Visual Basic.NET are object-oriented programming languages.

**Objects** are data structures that have both **methods**, which are computer programs that perform some task, and **properties**, which are data items particular to an object. All objects of a given class have the same methods, but each has its own set of data items. When using an OOP, the properties of the object are created and stored in main memory. Storing the values of properties of an object is called **object persistence**. Many different techniques have been used for object persistence. One of them is to use some variation of database technology.

Although relational databases can be used for object persistence, using this method requires substantial work on the part of the programmer. The problem is that, in general, object data structures are more complicated than the row of a table. Typically, several, or even many, rows of several different tables are required to store object data. This means the OOP programmer must design a mini-database just to store objects. Usually, many objects are involved in an information system, so many different mini-databases need to be designed and processed. This method is so undesirable that it is seldom used.

In the early 1990s, several vendors developed special-purpose DBMS products for storing object data. These products, which were called **object-oriented DBMSs (OODBMSs)**, never achieved commercial success. The problem was that by the time they were introduced, billions of bytes of data were already stored in relational DBMS format, and no organization wanted to convert their data to OODBMS format to be able to use an OODBMS. Consequently, such products failed in the marketplace.

However, the need for object persistence did not disappear. Some vendors, most notably Oracle, added features and functions to their relational database DBMS products to create **object-relational databases**. These features and functions are basically add-ons to a relational DBMS that facilitate object persistence. With these features, object data can be stored more readily than with a purely relational database. However, an object-relational database can still process relational data at the same time. To learn more about object-relational databases, search for OODBMS and ODBMS on the Web.

## THE ACCESS WORKBENCH

### Section 6

#### Database Administration in Microsoft Access

At this point, we have created and populated the CONTACT, CUSTOMER, SALESPERSON, and VEHICLE tables in the Wallingford Motors' CRM database. We have learned how to create forms, reports, and queries in the preceding sections of "The Access Workbench," and how to create and use view-equivalent queries in Chapter 3A. We have also studied how 1:1. 1:N, and N:M relationships are created and managed in Microsoft Access.

This chapter deals with database administration topics, and in this section of "The Access Workbench" we will look at database security in Microsoft Access. In this section, you will:

- Understand database security in Microsoft Access 2010
- Understand user-level database security in Microsoft Access 2003 databases
- Understand the role of the workgroup information file in Microsoft Access 2003 security

#### Database Security in Microsoft Access

Until Microsoft Access 2007, Microsoft Access had a user-level security system that allowed a DBA to grant specific database permissions to individual users or groups of users on a basis similar to that discussed in this chapter. Starting with Microsoft Access 2007, however, a very different security model has been implemented. This model is based on

*(Continued)*

whether the entire database itself is trustworthy, and it seems like Microsoft is saying that Microsoft Access really is for personal (or small workgroup) databases, and that if you need user-level security you should be using SQL Server 2008 R2 (especially because the SQL Server 2008 R2 Express edition is a free download). At the same time, Microsoft Access 2010 (and the earlier Microsoft Access 2007) will still work with the earlier user-level security system for Microsoft Access databases in the Microsoft Access 2003 (and earlier) *.mdb file format.

In this section of "The Access Workbench," we will focus on the current Microsoft Access security system. We will take a brief look at the user-level security concepts discussed in this chapter by examining Microsoft Access 2003–style user-level security, but we will not go into detail.

First, however, we need to make a copy of our WMCRM.accdb database file. This is necessary because we have already enabled all features of that database. In earlier sections of "The Access Workbench," we learned how to make copies of Microsoft Access 2010 databases—we simply make a copy the **WMCRM.accdb** database file in the My Documents folder in the Documents library and rename this new file **WMCRM-AW06-01.accdb**.

### Database Security in Microsoft Access 2010

You can secure Microsoft Access 2010 files in three basic ways:

- By creating trusted locations for Microsoft Access database storage
- By password encrypting and decrypting Microsoft Access databases
- By deploying databases packaged with digital signatures

Let us look at each of these in turn.

### *Trusted Locations*

Up until now, whenever we have opened a Microsoft Access database for the first time during our work in "The Access Workbench" the **Security Warning message bar** has been displayed, as shown in Figure AW-6-1 where we have just opened the WMCRM-AW06-01.accdb database for the first time.

Thus far, we have always clicked the **Enable Content** button to enable the disabled content. Note that we only need to do this once for each database—the first time we open the database after it has been created. We have done this so we could use Microsoft Access features that are otherwise disabled and unavailable to us, including:

- Microsoft Access database queries (either SQL or QBE) that add, update, or delete data
- Data definition language (DDL) (either SQL or QBE) actions that create or alter database objects, such as tables

### FIGURE AW-6-1

The Security Warning Message Bar

The **Security Warning** Message Bar

Click this link to see more options

The **Enable Content** button

- SQL commands being sent from a Microsoft Access application to a database server, such as Microsoft SQL Server 2008 R2, that support the Open Database Connectivity (ODBC) standard
- ActiveX controls

We obviously need the first of these features if we are going to build Microsoft Access 2010 databases. The third feature is important if we are using a Microsoft Access 2010 database as an application front end (containing the application forms, queries, and reports) for data stored in an SQL Server 2008 database. (This use of Microsoft Access and the ODBC standard is discussed in Chapter 7.) Finally, **ActiveX controls** are software code written to Microsoft's **ActiveX specification**, and they are often used as Web browser plug-ins. The problem here is that Microsoft Access 2010 databases can be targeted by code written in ActiveX-compliant programming languages that can manipulate the databases just as Microsoft Access itself would.

Although we can simply click the **Enable Content** button to activate these features, note that Microsoft Access 2010 also provides other options for dealing with this security problem. If we click the link labeled *Some active content has been disabled. Click for more details* shown in Figure AW-6-1, we are switched to the Info page in the Backstage view, and specifically to the Security Warning section of that page, as shown in Figure AW-6-2.

Clicking the Enable Content button displays two options as shown in Figure AW-6-3—*Enable All Content* and *Advanced Options.* Clicking the **Enable All Content** button produces the same results as clicking the Enable Content button on the Security Warning toolbar, and all features of the database will always be available to us. Clicking the **Advanced Options** button displays the Microsoft Office Security Options dialog box, as shown in Figure AW-6-4.

The Microsoft Office Security Options dialog box provides the final two options. The first option is to allow Microsoft Access to continue to disable the possible

---

**FIGURE AW-6-2**

The Security Warning Section of the Info Page in the Backstage View

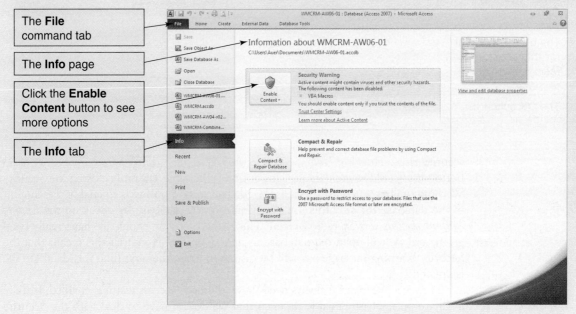

*(Continued)*

**FIGURE AW-6-3**

The Enable Content Options

Clicking **Enable All Content** is the same as clicking the *Enable Content* button on the Security Warning toolbar

Click **Advanced Options** to display the *Microsoft Office Security Options* dialog box

**FIGURE AW-6-4**

The Microsoft Office Security Options Dialog Box

The **Microsoft Office Security Options** dialog box

The **Enable content for this session** radio button

The **OK** button

security risks. Thus the *Help protect me from unknown content (recommended)* radio button is selected as the default. This option is the same as simply closing the Security Warning toolbar when it is first displayed. The second option is to enable the content in the database for *only* this use ("session") of the database by checking the *Enable content for this session* radio button. This is the first new choice we have really been given, and we will open the database using this option. Note that this means that the Security Warning message bar will be displayed again the next time this database file is opened!

However, we (nearly) always need these Microsoft Access features enabled. Is there a way to permanently enable them so that we do not have to deal with the Security Warning bar every time we open a new Microsoft Access database? Yes, there is.

The word Microsoft uses to describe our situation is *trust*: Do we *trust the content* of our database? If so, we can create a **trusted location** in which to store our trusted databases. And databases we use from the trusted location are opened *without* the security warning but *with* all features enabled.

### Creating a Trusted Location

1. Start Microsoft Access.
2. If necessary, click the **File** command tab to display the Backstage view.
3. Click the **Options** command on the Backstage view. The Microsoft Access Options dialog box appears.
4. Click the **Trust Center** button to display the Trust Center page, as shown in Figure AW-6-5.
5. Click the **Trust Center Settings** button to display the Trust Center dialog box, shown in Figure AW-6-6. Note that the Message Bar Settings for all Office Applications page is currently displayed and that the setting that enables the display of the Security Options message bar is currently selected.
6. Click the **Trusted Locations** button to display the Trusted Locations page, as shown in Figure AW-6-7. Note that the only currently trusted location is the folder that stores the Microsoft Access wizard databases. Also note that we have the ability to disable all trusted locations if we choose to do so.
7. Click the **Add new location** button to display the Microsoft Office Trusted Location dialog box, as shown in Figure AW-6-8.
8. Click the **Browse** button. The Browse dialog box appears, as shown in Figure AW-6-9.
9. Expand the **Documents** library to display the My Documents folder, and then click the **My Documents** folder to select it.
10. Click the **New Folder** button to create a new folder named New Folder in edit mode.

---

**FIGURE AW-6-5**

The Access Options Trust Center Page

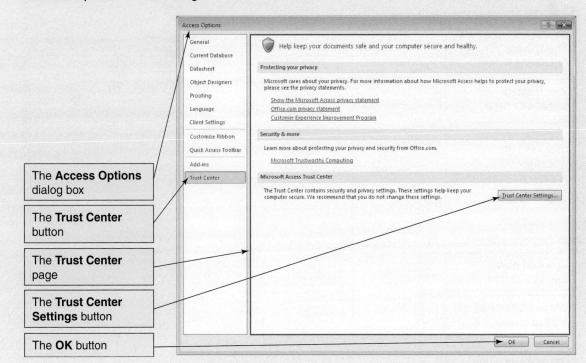

The **Access Options** dialog box

The **Trust Center** button

The **Trust Center** page

The **Trust Center Settings** button

The **OK** button

*(Continued)*

## FIGURE AW-6-6

### The Trust Center Dialog Box

The **Trust Center** dialog box

The **Trusted Locations** button

The **Message Bar** button

The **Message Bar Settings for all Office Applications** page

The **OK** button

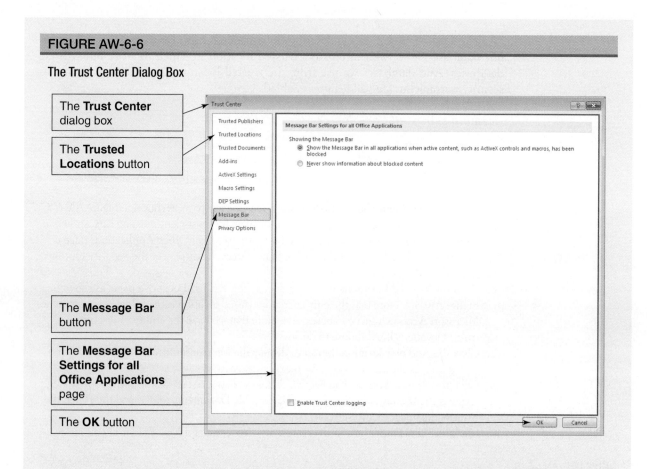

## FIGURE AW-6-7

### The Trusted Locations Page

The **Trusted Locations** button

The **Trusted Locations** page

Currently the only trusted location is where Microsoft Access wizards are stored

The **Add new location** button

We can disable all trusted locations if necessary

The **OK** button

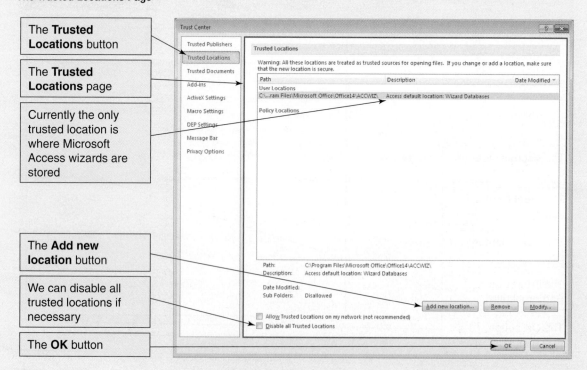

**FIGURE AW-6-8**

The Microsoft Office Trusted Location Dialog Box

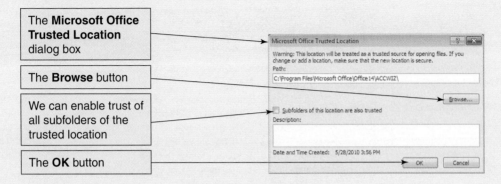

The **Microsoft Office Trusted Location** dialog box

The **Browse** button

We can enable trust of all subfolders of the trusted location

The **OK** button

**FIGURE AW-6-9**

The Browse Dialog Box

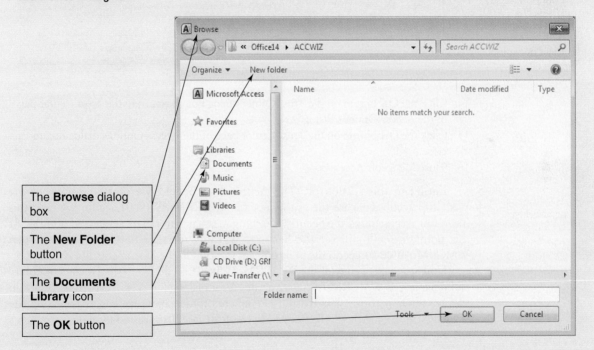

The **Browse** dialog box

The **New Folder** button

The **Documents Library** icon

The **OK** button

11. Rename the new folder as **My-Trusted-Location**. When you have finished typing in the folder name My-Trusted-Location, press the **Enter** key. The My-Trusted-Location folder now appears as shown in Figure AW-6-10.

12. Click the **OK** button on the Browse dialog box. The Microsoft Office Trusted Location dialog box appears, with the new trusted location in the Path text box.

13. Click the **OK** button on the Microsoft Office Trusted Location dialog box. The Trust Center dialog box appears, with the new path added to the User Locations section of the Trusted Locations list.

*(Continued)*

**FIGURE AW-6-10**

The My-Trusted-Location Folder

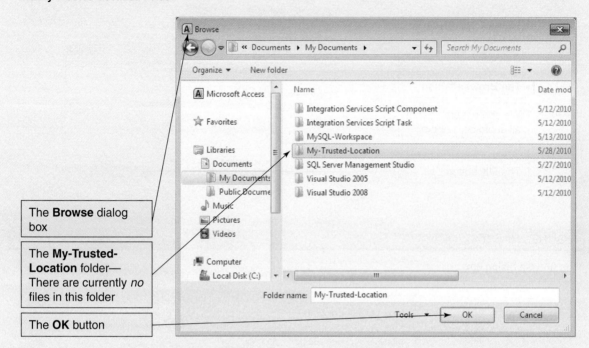

The **Browse** dialog box

The **My-Trusted-Location** folder— There are currently *no* files in this folder

The **OK** button

14. Click the **OK** button on the Trust Center dialog box to return to the Trust Center page of the Access Options dialog box.
15. Click the **OK** button on the Trust Center page of the Access Options dialog box to close it.
16. Close Microsoft Access.

Earlier in this section of "The Access Workbench" we created a copy of the WMCRM.accdb database file as the new file WMCRM-AW06-01.accdb. We used this file in our discussion of the Security Warning message bar and its associated options. At this point, we will still see the Security Warning message bar whenever we open WMCRM-AW06-01.accdb file in its current location in the Documents library.

Now we make a copy of the **WMCRM-AW06-01.accdb** file in the Document library and rename it as **WMCRM-AW06-02.accdb**. After making the WMCRM-AW06-02.accdb file, we move it to the My-Trusted-Documents folder. Now we can try opening the WMCRM-AW06-02.accdb file from a Microsoft Access 2010 trusted location.

*Opening a Microsoft Access Database from a Trusted Location*

1. Start Microsoft Access.
2. If necessary, click the **File** command tab to display the Backstage view.
3. Click the **Open** button. The Microsoft Access Open dialog box is displayed.
4. Browse to the **WMCRM-AW06-02.accdb** file in the My-Trusted-Location folder, as shown in Figure AW-6-11.
5. Click the file name to highlight it and then click the **Open** button.
6. The Microsoft Access 2010 application window appears, with the WMCRM-AW06-02 database open in it. Note that the Security Warning bar does *not* appear when the database is opened.
7. Close Microsoft Access 2010 and the WMCRM-AW06-02 database.

**FIGURE AW-6-11**

The WMCRM-AW06-02 File in the Open Dialog Box

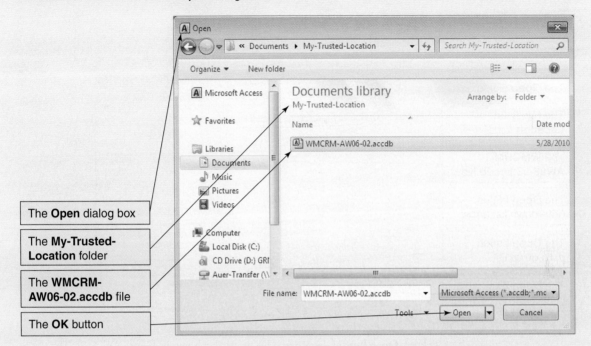

The **Open** dialog box

The **My-Trusted-Location** folder

The **WMCRM-AW06-02.accdb** file

The **OK** button

### Database Encryption with Passwords

Next, let us look at database encryption. In this case, Microsoft Access will encrypt the database, which will convert it into a secure, unreadable file format. To be able to use the encrypted database, a Microsoft Access user must enter a password to prove that he or she has the right to use the database. After the password is entered, Microsoft Access will decrypt the database and allow the user to work with it.

Each password should be a **strong password**—a password that includes lowercase letters, uppercase letters, numbers, and special characters (symbols) and that is at least 15 characters in length. Be sure to remember or record your password in a safe place—lost or forgotten passwords cannot be recovered!

For this example, we want to use a new copy of the **WMCRM.accdb** database file so that our encryption actions apply only to that file. Specifically, make a copy of **WMCRM-AW06-02.accdb** in the My-Trusted-Documents folder and name this new file **WMCRM-AW06-03.accdb**.

In order to encrypt a Microsoft Access database file, the file must be opened in **Exclusive mode.** This gives us exclusive use of the database and prevents any other users who have rights to use the database from opening it or using it. We start by opening WMCRM-AW06-03.accdb for our exclusive use.

### Opening a Microsoft Access Database in Exclusive Mode

1. Start Microsoft Access.
2. If necessary, click the **File** command tab to display the Backstage view.
3. Click the **Open** button. The Microsoft Access Open dialog box appears.
4. Browse to the **WMCRM-AW06-03.accdb** file in the My-Trusted-Location folder. Click the file object *once* to select it, but *not* twice, which would open the file in Microsoft Access.

*(Continued)*

**FIGURE AW-6-12**

The Open Exclusive Button

The **Open** dialog box

The **My-Trusted-Location** folder

The **WMCRM-AW06-03.accdb** file

The **Open** button drop-down list arrow

The **Open** button drop-down list

The **Open Exclusive** button

5.  Click the **Open** button drop-down list arrow, as shown in Figure AW-6-12. The Open button drop-down list appears.
6.  Click the **Open Exclusive** button in the Open button drop-down list to open the WMCRM-AW06-03 database in Microsoft Access 2010.
    - **NOTE:** The Security Warning bar does *not* appear when the database is opened because you are opening it from a trusted location.
    - **NOTE:** The Open button mode options shown in Figure AW-6-12 are always available when you open a Microsoft Access database. Normally, you use just Open mode because you want complete read and write permission in the database. Open Read-Only mode prevents the user from making changes to the database. Exclusive mode, as you have seen, stops other users from using the database while you are using it. Exclusive Read-Only mode, as the name implies, combines Exclusive and Read-Only modes.

Now that the database is open in Exclusive mode, we can encrypt the database and set the database password.

*Encrypting a Microsoft Access Database*

1.  Click the **File** command tab to display the Backstage view.
2.  The Info page should be displayed. If it is not, click the **Info** button to display the Info page, as shown in Figure AW-6-13.
3.  In the Encrypt with Password section of the Info page, click the **Encrypt with Password** button. The Set Database Password dialog box appears, as shown in Figure AW-6-14.
4.  In the **Password** text box of the Set Database Password dialog box, type in the password **AW06+password**.
5.  In the **Verify** text box of the Set Database Password dialog box, again type in the password **AW06+password**.
6.  Click the **OK** button of the Set Database Password dialog box to set the database password and encrypt the database file.

**FIGURE AW-6-13**

The Info Page in the Backstage View

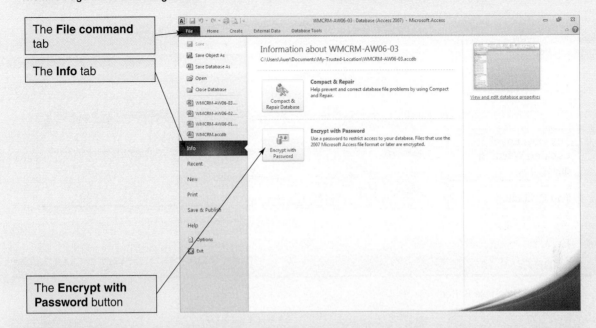

The **File command** tab

The **Info** tab

The **Encrypt with Password** button

**FIGURE AW-6-14**

The Set Database Password Dialog Box

The **Set Database Password** dialog box

The **Password** text box

The **Verify** text box

The **OK** button

7. Microsoft Access displays the warning dialog box shown in Figure AW-6-15 regarding the effect of encrypting on row level locking. Click the **OK** button to clear the warning.

8. You can check that the encryption action has been accomplished by clicking the File command tab and the Info button. After the database is encrypted, the Encrypt with Password button changes to a Decrypt Database button, as shown in Figure AW-6-16.

   ■ **NOTE:** As the Decrypt Database button name implies, if we wanted to change the database file back to its original unencrypted form we can do so using that button.

9. Click the **File** command tab and then click the **Close Database** button to close the WMCRM-AW06-03 database while leaving Microsoft Access 2010 open.

Now we can open the now-encrypted WMCRM-AW06-03.accdb database file.

### *Opening an Encrypted Microsoft Access Database*

1. Microsoft Access should still be open. If it is not, start Microsoft Access.
2. If necessary, click the **File** command tab to display the Backstage view.

*(Continued)*

FIGURE AW-6-15

The Row Level Locking Warning Dialog Box

The **Row Level Locking Warning** dialog box

The **OK** button

FIGURE AW-6-16

The Decrypt Database Button

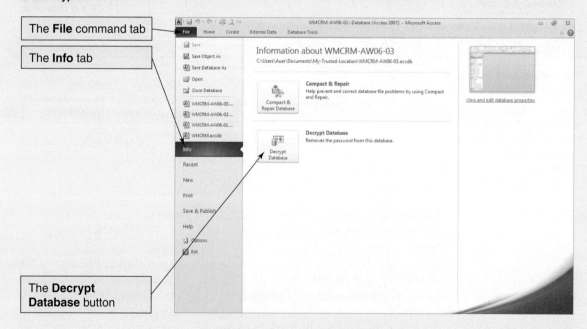

The **File** command tab

The **Info** tab

The **Decrypt Database** button

3. Click the **WMCRM-AW06-03.accdb** file name in the quick access list of recent databases As shown in Figure AW-6-17, the **Password Required** dialog box appears.

4. In the **Enter database password** text box, type in the password **AW06+password**, and then click the **OK** button. The Microsoft Access 2010 application window appears, with the WMCRM-AW06-03 database open in it.

■ **NOTE:** The Security Warning bar does *not* appear when the database is opened because you are opening it from a trusted location.

5. Close the WMCRM-AW06-03 database and exit Microsoft Access 2010.

---

**FIGURE AW-6-17**

The Password Required Dialog Box

| The **Password Required** dialog box | |
| The **Enter database password** text box | |

Password Required
Enter database password:

OK      Cancel

The **OK** button

---

### Packaging and Signing a Microsoft Access Database

Microsoft has included some tools in Microsoft Access 2010 to help us distribute secured copies of Microsoft Access databases to users. Let us look at how to use them.

**Compiling Microsoft Visual Basic for Applications (VBA) Code**   Microsoft **Visual Basic for Applications (VBA)** is included in Microsoft Access. VBA is a version of the Microsoft Visual Basic programming language that is intended to help users add specific programmed actions to Microsoft Access applications. How to use VBA is beyond the scope of this section of "The Access Workbench," but we need to know how to secure VBA code if it is included in a Microsoft Access database.

Microsoft Access 2010 includes a **Make ACCDE command** to compile and hide VBA code so that although the VBA programming still functions correctly, the user can no longer see or modify the VBA code. When we use this tool, Microsoft Access creates a version of the database file with an **\*.accde file extension.**

In the next set of steps, we well use another copy of the **WMCRM.accdb** database file so that our actions apply only to that file. Specifically, make a copy of **WMCRM-AW06-02.accdb** in the My-Trusted-Documents folder and name this new file **WMCRM-AW06-04.accdb**. We start by opening the WMCRM-AW06-04.accdb database file.

### Creating a Microsoft Access *.accde Database

1. Open Microsoft Access.
2. If necessary, click the **File** command tab to display the Backstage view.
3. Click the **Open** button. The Microsoft Access Open dialog box appears.
4. Browse to the **WMCRM-AW06-04.accdb** file in the My-Trusted-Location folder. Double-click the file object to open it.
   - **NOTE:** The Security Warning bar does *not* appear when the database is opened because you are opening it from a trusted location.
5. Click the **File** command tab to display the Backstage view.
6. Click the **Save & Publish** tab to display the Save & Publish page, as shown in Figure AW-6-18.
7. Click the **Make ACCDE** button in the Advanced group in the Save Database As section, and then click the **Save As** button. The Save As dialog box appears, as shown in Figure AW-6-19.
8. Click the **Save** button in the Save As dialog box. The WMCRM-AW06-04.accde file is created.
   - **NOTE:** The displayed database name does *not* change. The only sign that this action has been completed is that the WMCRM-AW06-04.accde object will now be displayed in the list of Microsoft Access files in the Open dialog box (and other file system tools, such as Windows Explorer).
9. Close the WMCRM-AW06-04 database, and exit Microsoft Access.

To see the new database, we open it as we would any other Microsoft Access database.

*(Continued)*

**FIGURE AW-6-18**

The Save & Publish Page—Make ACCDE

The **File** command tab

The **Save & Publish** tab

The **Make ACCDE** command

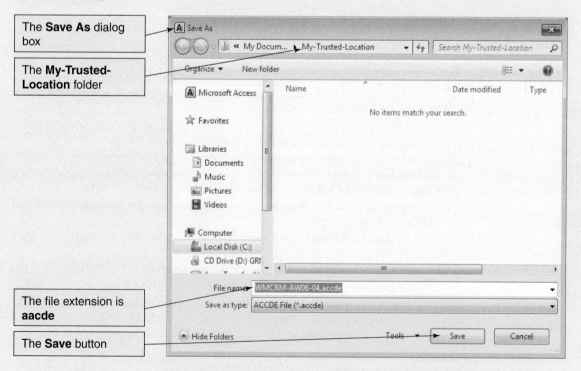

**FIGURE AW-6-19**

The Save As Dialog Box

The **Save As** dialog box

The **My-Trusted-Location** folder

The file extension is **aacde**

The **Save** button

**FIGURE AW-6-20**

The WMCRM-AW06-04.accde File

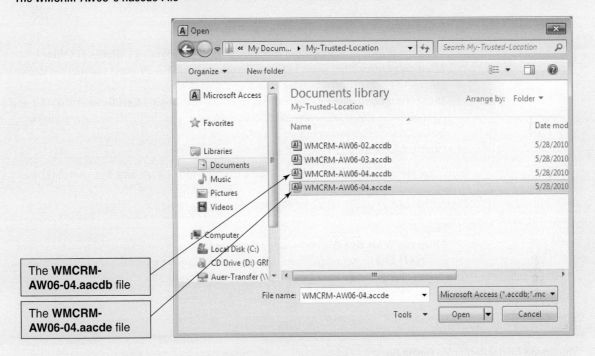

The **WMCRM-AW06-04.aacdb** file

The **WMCRM-AW06-04.aacde** file

*Opening a Microsoft Access *.accde Database*

1. Start Microsoft Access.
2. If necessary, click the **File** command tab to display the Backstage view.
3. Click the **Open** button. The Microsoft Access Open dialog box appears.
4. Browse to the **WMCRM-AW06-04.accde** file in the My-Trusted-Location folder, as shown in Figure AW-6-20.
5. Click the **Open** button. The Microsoft Access 2010 application window appears, with the WMCRM-AW06-04.accde database open in it.
   - **NOTE:** The Security Warning bar does *not* appear when the database is opened because you are opening it from a trusted location.
   - **NOTE:** While any previously existing VBA modules have been compiled and all editable source code for them has been removed, the functionality of this code is still in the database. Further note that VBA itself is still functional in the database—it has *not* been disabled.
6. Close the WMCRM-AW06-04 database and exit Microsoft Access.

**Creating a Signed Package in Microsoft Access** A **digital signature scheme** is a type of **public-key cryptography** (also known as **asymmetric cryptography**), which uses two encryption keys (a **private key** and a **public key**) to encode documents and files to protect them. Although fascinating and important topics in their own right, cryptography in general and public-key cryptography in particular are beyond the scope of this section of "The Access Workbench."[1] For our purposes, a **digital signature** is a means of guaranteeing another user of a database that the database is, indeed, from us and that it is safe to use.

---

[1]For more information, see the following Wikipedia articles: "Public-Key Cryptography" (**http://en. wikipedia.org/wiki/Asymmetric_key_algorithm**), "Digital Signature" (**http://en.wikipedia.org/wiki/ Digital_signature**), and "Public Key Certificate" (**http://en.wikipedia.org/wiki/Public_key_certificate**).

*(Continued)*

To use a digital signature, of course, we have to have one, so the first thing we have to do is to create one. This is not done in Microsoft Access, but rather with the Digital Certificate for VBA Projects utility provided with Microsoft Office 2010.

### Creating a Digital Signature

1. Click the Windows **Start** button and then select **All Programs | Microsoft Office | Microsoft Office 2010 Tools | Digital Certificate for VBA Projects** to open the Create Digital Certificate dialog box, as shown in Figure AW-6-21.
2. In the **Your certificate's name** text box, type the text **Digital-Certificate-AW06-001** and then click the **OK** button. The certificate is created, and the SelfCert Success dialog box appears, as shown in Figure AW-6-22.
3. Click the **OK** button in the SelfCert Success dialog box.

Now that we have a digital certificate, we can use it to package and sign our database.

### Creating a Microsoft Access Signed Package

1. Start Microsoft Access.
2. Open the **WMCRM-AW06-04.accde** database file.
   - **NOTE:** The Security Warning bar does *not* appear when the database is opened because you are opening it from a trusted location.

---

**FIGURE AW-6-21**

The Create Digital Certificate Dialog Box

---

**FIGURE AW-6-22**

The SelfCert Success Dialog Box

**FIGURE AW-6-23**

The Save & Publish Page—Package and Sign

The **File** command tab

The **Save & Publish** tab

The **Package and Sign** command

**FIGURE AW-6-24**

The Windows Security Confirm Certificate Dialog Box

The **Windows Security Confirm Certificate** dialog box

The **Digital-Certificate-AW06-001** digital certificate

The **Click here to view certificate properties** link

The **OK** button

3. Click the **File** command tab to display the Backstage view.
4. Click the **Save & Publish** tab to display the Save & Publish page, as shown in Figure AW-6-23.
5. Click the **Package and Sign** button to select the Package and Sign option, and then click the **Save As** button. The Windows Security Confirm Certificate dialog box appears, as shown in Figure AW-6-24.
6. Only one certificate is shown, and, although the full name is not visible, it is the one we created and want to use. However, to verify this, click the **Click here to view certificate properties** link. The Certificate Details dialog box appears, as shown in Figure AW-6-25, and our certificate name is clearly visible in the dialog box.
7. Click the **OK** button in the Certificate Details dialog box to close the dialog box.
8. Click the **OK** button in the Microsoft Security Confirm Certificate dialog box to close the dialog box. The Create Microsoft Office Access Signed Package dialog box appears, as shown in Figure AW-6-26.

*(Continued)*

FIGURE AW-6-25

The Certificate Details Dialog Box

The **Certificate Details** dialog box

The **Digital-Certificate-AW06-001** digital certificate name is displayed here

The **OK** button

FIGURE AW-6-26

The Create Microsoft Access Signed Package Dialog Box

The **Create Microsoft Access Signed Package** dialog box

The **WMCRM-AW06-04.aacdc** file name

The **Create** button

9. Click the **Create** button to create the signed package.
10. Close the WMCRM-AW06-04 database and Microsoft Access 2010.

We now have a signed package, which uses the **\*.accdc file extension,** ready to distribute to other users. To simulate this, in the My Documents folder of the Documents library create a new folder named **My-Distributed-Databases** and then copy the WMCRM-AW06-04.accdc file into it. Now we can open the signed package from this location.

### Opening a Microsoft Access *.accdc Database

1. Start Microsoft Access.
2. If necessary, click the File command tab to display the Backstage view.
3. Click the **Open** button. The Open dialog box appears.
4. Browse to the **WMCRM-AW06-04.accdc** file in the My-Distributed-Databases folder, as shown in Figure AW-6-27. Note that you must change file type in order to see any of the *.accdc files.
5. Click the **WMCRM-AW06-04.accdc** file to select it and then click the **Open** button. The Microsoft Access Security Notice dialog box appears, as shown in Figure AW-6-28.
6. Click the **Trust all from publisher** button. The **Extract Database To** dialog box appears. This dialog box is essentially the same as a Save To dialog box, so browse to the My-Distributed-Databases folder and then click the **OK** button.
7. Another **Microsoft Access Security Notice** dialog box similar to the one shown in Figure AW-6-28 appears. Click the **Open** button.

---

### FIGURE AW-6-27

The WMCRM-AW06-04.accdc File

### FIGURE AW-6-28

The Microsoft Access Security Notice Dialog Box

*(Continued)*

8. The **WMCRM-AW06-04.accde** database is opened in Microsoft Access.
   - **NOTE:** The Security Warning bar does *not* appear when the database is opened because you have chosen to trust the source of the database as documented in the digital certificate rather than open it from a trusted location.
9. Close the WMCRM-AW06-04 database and Microsoft Access 2010.

Using Windows Explorer, look at the contents of the Libraries\Documents\My Documents\My-Distributed-Databases folder. Notice that the WMCRM-AW06-04.accde file has been extracted from the WMCRM-AW06-04.accdc package and is now available for use. This is the database file that the user will open when he or she uses the database. Also note that when users open the database they will see the Microsoft Access Security Notice dialog box just discussed. But we chose *Trust all from publisher* in step 6, so why is this happening? The reason has to do with the *location* where the digital certificate has been stored on the workstation. This is a technical matter beyond the scope of this discussion, but we can at least see exactly what the problem is by following the next set of steps.

### Viewing the Certification Path in the Certificate Dialog Box

1. Start Microsoft Access 2010.
2. Open the **WMCRM-AW06-04.accde** file in the My-Distributed-Databases folder.
3. When the Microsoft Access Security Notice dialog box appears, click the **Open** button.
4. Click the **File** command tab.
5. Click the **Options** command. The Access Options dialog box appears.
6. Click the **Trust Center** button to display the Trust Center page.
7. Click the **Trust Center Settings** button to display the Trust Center dialog box.
8. Click the **Trusted Publishers** button to display the Trusted Publishers page.
9. Click the trusted publisher name **Digital-Certificate-AW06-001** to select it and then click the **View** button. The Certificate dialog box appears.
10. Click the **Certification Path** tab in the Certificate dialog box. The Certification Path page appears, as shown in Figure AW-6-29.
11. Note the **Certificate status** area, which reads "This CA Root certificate is not trusted because it is not in the Trusted Root Certification Authorities store." This is the problem that needs to be resolved before the database will open without the Microsoft Access Security Notice dialog box being displayed every time the database is opened.
12. Click the **OK** button to close the Certificate dialog box.
13. Click the **OK** button to close the Trust Center dialog box.
14. Click the **OK** button to close the Access Options dialog box.
15. Close the WMCRM-AW06-04 database and exit Microsoft Access.

This completes our discussion of how Microsoft Access 2010 handles database security for Microsoft Access 2010 *.accdb files.

### Database Security in Microsoft Access 2003.mdb Database Files

Microsoft Access 2003 *.mdb database files have a built-in user-level database security system. Microsoft Access stores the *.mdb default security settings in a **workgroup information file** named **system.mdw.** A separate copy of this file is created for each user on the workstation.

In the Windows XP operating system, this file is stored as C:\Documents and Settings\{*UserName*}\Application Data\Microsoft\Access\system.mdw.[2] Note that in

---

[2]This is a major change of location. For Microsoft Access 2003 and previous versions of Microsoft Access, the system.mdw file was stored as C:\WINDOWS\system32\system.mdw in the Windows XP operating system.

**FIGURE AW-6-29**

The Certification Path Page

The **Certificate** dialog box

The **Certificate Path** page

The **Certificate status** message

The **OK** button

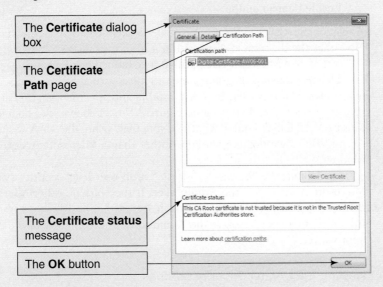

order to see the \Application Data folder and subfolders in Windows Explorer you must enable the Show hidden files and folders setting on the View tab of the Folder Options dialog box, which you open by selecting **Tools | Folder Options**.

In the Windows Vista and Windows 7 operating systems, the file is stored as C:\Documents\{UserName}\AppData\Roaming\Microsoft\Access\System.mdw. In order to see the AppData folder and subfolders in Windows Explorer, you must enable the Show hidden files and folders setting on the View tab of the Folder Options dialog box. In the version of Windows Explorer used in the Windows Vista and Windows 7 operating systems, you open this dialog box by selecting **Organize | Folder and Search Options**. Further, note that with Windows Vista and Windows 7 operating systems the system.mdw is not created until the first *.mdb database file is created or opened in Access 2010. The instructions that follow for making a backup copy of the system.mdw file cannot be completed until *after* we've opened the *.mdb file we will use in this section of "The Access Workbench" if you are using Windows Vista or Windows 7, but be sure to make a backup copy then.

Other workgroup information files (*.mdw files) can be created to secure individual databases or groups of databases, but before this is done you should make a backup copy of the original system.mdw file. Otherwise, if this file gets corrupted in some way, you will have real problems using Microsoft Access. To prevent these problems, you just need to copy the system.mdw file to your My Documents folder.

At this point, we will use the WM-Sales-System.mdb file, which contains the database that Wallingford Motors uses to record vehicle sales. You open Microsoft Access *.mdb files exactly the same way you open the Microsoft Access *.accdb files you have been using. Now we can open the WM-Sales-System.mdb file and take a look at the database.

*Opening the WM-Sales-System.mdb Database*

1. Start Microsoft Access.
2. If necessary, click the **File** command tab to open the Backstage view, and then click the **Open** button to display the Open dialog box.

*(Continued)*

3. Browse to the **WM-Sales-System.mdb** file in the My Documents folder, click the file name to highlight it, and then click the **Open** button.
4. The **Security Warning** bar appears with the database. Click the Security Warning bar's **Enable Content** button.

A relationship diagram for the WM-Sales-System database is shown in Figure AW-6-30. Note that the diagram is displayed in a Microsoft Access 2003 style floating window, rather than in a Microsoft Access 2010 style tabbed window.

The relationship diagram shows a typical structure for a sales database, with the main sales data recorded in a SALE table and specific data on each item in the sale recorded in a SALE_ITEM table. Figure AW-6-31 shows sales data in the Wallingford-Motors-Vehicle-Sales query window. Note that, again, the window shown is a Microsoft Access 2003 style floating window, rather than a Microsoft Access 2010 style tabbed window.

By default, the Microsoft Access *.mdb user-level security system has only one Microsoft Access user: the **Admin user**. If there are no other Microsoft Access users defined, then when you use Microsoft Access *.mdb files, you use them as the user Admin. Let us take a look at the Admin user in the context of the default workgroup information.

### Viewing the Default Security Settings

1. If necessary, click the **File** command tab to display the Backstage view, and the click the **Info** tab to display the information about WM-Sales-System page.
2. Click the **Users and Permissions** button to display the Users and Permissions drop-down list, as shown in Figure AW-6-32.
3. Click the **User and Group Accounts** button in the Users and Permissions drop-down list. The User and Group Accounts dialog box appears, as shown in Figure AW-6-33.
4. Click the **Name** text box drop-down list arrow. Note that there is only one user account in the system—Admin.

---

**FIGURE AW-6-30**

The WM-Sales-System Relationship Diagram

The **Relationships** window

The **WM-Sales-System** relationship diagram

Note that this is Microsoft Access 2003 style floating window, rather than a Microsoft Access 2010 style tabbed window

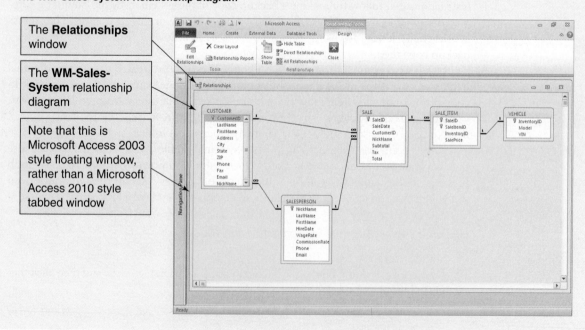

---

**FIGURE AW-6-31**

The WM-Vehicle-Sales Query Window

The **WM-Vehicle Sales** query results

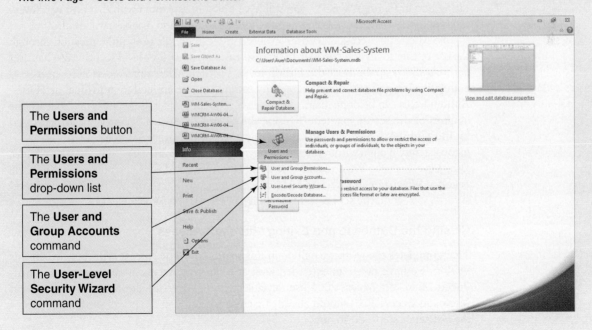

---

**FIGURE AW-6-32**

The Info Page—Users and Permissions Button

The **Users and Permissions** button

The **Users and Permissions** drop-down list

The **User and Group Accounts** command

The **User-Level Security Wizard** command

*(Continued)*

**FIGURE AW-6-33**

The User and Group Accounts Dialog Box

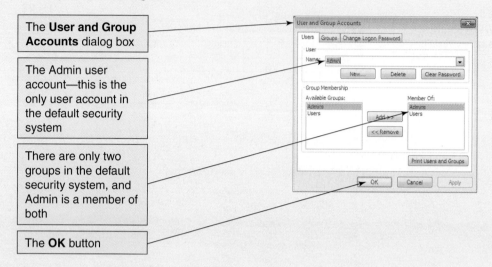

The **User and Group Accounts** dialog box

The Admin user account—this is the only user account in the default security system

There are only two groups in the default security system, and Admin is a member of both

The **OK** button

5. Note that there are two groups—Admins and Users—and that Admin is already a member of both.
6. Click the **OK** button to close the dialog box.
7. Close the WM-Sales-System database and Microsoft Access.

When we use Microsoft Access *.mdb files, we run Microsoft Access as Admin *with no password* and, thus, have full administrator privileges in Microsoft Access. Because the Admin account has not had a password, a login has not been required. If you assign Admin a password at this point (note the Change Logon Password tab in the User and Group Accounts dialog box in Figure AW-6-33), you will have to log in as Admin with that password every time you open a Microsoft Access *.mdb file, and every *.mdb database will be affected.

So Microsoft Access 2003 user-level security can handle user authentication through the use of user login and password. Microsoft Access 2003 user-level security also has user authorization capability at the DBMS level. Further, Microsoft Access 2003 user-level authentication and authorization security settings can be applied to individual databases. Although this can be done manually, it is easier to set up database security and to learn the abilities of the security system by using the Microsoft Access Security Wizard accessed by the User-level Security Wizard button shown in Figure AW-6-32. (This wizard is inconsistently named within Microsoft Access, and the wizard calls itself Security Wizard, User-Level Security Wizard, and One-step Security Wizard. We generally refer to it as the Security Wizard or just Wizard.) However, setting up Microsoft Access 2003 user-level security is beyond the scope of this section of "The Access Workbench."

### Closing the Database and Exiting Microsoft Access

That completes the work we will do in this section of "The Access Workbench." In this section, we have taken an extended look at Microsoft Access 2010 security and introduced Microsoft Access 2003 user-level security. The WM-Sales-System database and Microsoft Access 2010 should already be closed, but if you did not close them as part of the last set of steps, do so now.

#### *Closing the WM-Sales-System Database*

1. If the WM-Sales-System database is still open, click the **Close** button in the upper-right corner of the Microsoft Access window to close the database and Microsoft Access.

# SUMMARY

Database administration is a business function that involves managing a database in order to maximize its value to an organization. The conflicting goals of protecting the database and maximizing its availability and benefit to users must be balanced using good administration.

All databases need database administration. The database administration for small, personal databases is informal; database administration for large, multiuser databases can involve an office and many people. DBA can stand for *database administration* or *database administrator.* Three basic database administration functions are necessary: concurrency control, security, and backup and recovery.

The goal of concurrency control is to ensure that one user's work does not inappropriately influence another user's work. No single concurrency control technique is ideal for all circumstances. Trade-offs need to be made between the level of protection and data throughput.

A transaction, or logical unit of work, is a series of actions taken against a database that occur as an atomic unit; either all of them occur or none of them do. The activity of concurrent transactions is interleaved on the database server. In some cases, updates can be lost if concurrent transactions are not controlled. Another concurrency problem concerns inconsistent reads.

A dirty read occurs when one transaction reads a changed record that has not been committed to the database. A nonrepeatable read occurs when one transaction rereads data it has previously read and finds modifications or deletions caused by another transaction. A phantom read occurs when a transaction rereads data and finds new rows that were inserted by a different transaction.

To avoid concurrency problems, database elements are locked. Implicit locks are placed by the DBMS; explicit locks are issued by the application program. The size of a locked resource is called lock granularity. An exclusive lock prohibits other users from reading the locked resource; a shared lock allows other users to read the locked resource but not to update it.

Two transactions that run concurrently and generate results that are consistent with the results that would have occurred if the transactions had run separately are referred to as serializable transactions. Two-phase locking, in which locks are acquired in a growing phase and released in a shrinking phase, is one scheme for serializability. A special case of two-phase locking is to acquire locks throughout the transaction but not to free any lock until the transaction is finished.

Deadlock, or the deadly embrace, occurs when two transactions are each waiting on a resource that the other transaction holds. Deadlock can be prevented by requiring transactions to acquire all locks at the same time. When deadlock occurs, the only way to cure it is to abort one of the transactions and back out of partially completed work.

Optimistic locking assumes that no transaction conflict will occur and then deals with the consequences if it does. Pessimistic locking assumes that conflict will occur and so prevents it ahead of time with locks. In general, optimistic locking is preferred for the Internet and for many intranet applications.

Most application programs do not explicitly declare locks. Instead, they mark transaction boundaries with SQL transaction control statements—such as BEGIN, COMMIT, and ROLLBACK statements—and declare the concurrent behavior they want. The DBMS then places locks for the application that will result in the desired behavior. An ACID transaction is one that is atomic, consistent, isolated, and durable. Durable means that database changes are permanent. Consistency can refer to either statement-level or transaction-level consistency. With transaction-level consistency, a transaction may not see its own changes.

The 1992 SQL standard defines four transaction isolation levels: read uncommitted, read committed, repeatable read, and serializable. The characteristics of each are summarized in Figure 6-13.

A cursor is a pointer into a set of records. Four cursor types are prevalent: forward only, static, keyset, and dynamic. Developers should select isolation levels and cursor types that are appropriate for their application workload and for the DBMS product in use.

The goal of database security is to ensure that only authorized users can perform authorized activities at authorized times. To develop effective database security, the processing rights and responsibilities of all users must be determined.

DBMS products provide security facilities. Most involve the declaration of users, groups, objects to be protected, and permissions or privileges on those objects. Almost all DBMS products use some form of user name and password security. DBMS security can be augmented by application security.

In the event of system failure, the database must be restored to a usable state as soon as possible. Transactions in process at the time of the failure must be reapplied or restarted. Although in some cases recovery can be done by reprocessing, the use of logs and before-images and after-images with rollback and rollforward is almost always preferred. Checkpoints can be made to reduce the amount of work that needs to be done after a failure.

In addition to concurrency control, security, and backup and recovery, a DBA needs to ensure that a system exists to gather and record errors and problems. The DBA works with the development team to resolve such problems on a prioritized basis and also to evaluate features and functions of new releases of the DBMS. In addition, the DBA needs to create and manage a process for controlling the database configuration so that changes to the database structure are made with a community-wide view. Finally, the DBA is responsible for ensuring that appropriate documentation is maintained about database structure, concurrency control, security, backup and recovery, and other details that concern the management and use of the database.

A distributed database is a database that is stored and processed on more than one computer. A replicated database is one in which multiple copies of some or all of the database are stored on different computers. A partitioned database is one in which different pieces of the database are stored on different computers. A distributed database can be replicated and distributed.

Distributed databases pose processing challenges. If a database is updated on a single computer, then the challenge is simply to ensure that the copies of the database are logically consistent when they are distributed. However, if updates are to be made on more than one computer, the challenges become significant. If the database is partitioned and not replicated, then challenges occur if transactions span data on more than one computer. If the database is replicated and if updates occur to the replicated portions, then a special locking algorithm called distributed two-phase locking is required. Implementing this algorithm can be difficult and expensive.

Objects consist of methods and properties or data values. All objects of a given class have the same methods, but they have different property values. Object persistence is the process of storing object property values. Relational databases are difficult to use for object persistence. Some specialized products called object-oriented DBMSs were developed in the 1990s but never received commercial acceptance. Oracle and others have extended the capabilities of their relational DBMS products to provide support for object persistence. Such databases are referred to as object-relational databases.

## KEY TERMS

| | | |
|---|---|---|
| ACID transaction | checkpoint | database administrator |
| after-image | concurrent transactions | DBA |
| atomic | concurrent update problem | deadlock |
| authentication | consistent | deadly embrace |
| authorization | data administration | dirty read |
| before-image | database administration | distributed database |

distributed two-phase locking
durable
dynamic cursor
exclusive lock
explicit lock
forward-only cursor
implicit lock
inconsistent read problem
keyset cursor
lock granularity
log
logical unit of work (LUW)
lost update problem
methods
nonrepeatable read
object persistence

object-oriented DBMS (OODBMS)
object-oriented programming
  (OOP)
object-relational database
objects
optimistic locking
partitioning
permissions
pessimistic locking
phantom read
properties
read committed isolation
read uncommitted isolation
recovery via reprocessing
recovery via rollback/rollforward
repeatable reads isolation

replication
resource locking
rollback
rollforward
scrollable cursor
serializable
serializable isolation level
shared lock
SQL transaction control
  statements
statement-level consistency
static cursor
transaction
transaction-level consistency
two-phase locking
user account

## REVIEW QUESTIONS

**6.1**  What is the purpose of database administration?

**6.2**  Explain how database administration tasks vary with the size and complexity of the database.

**6.3**  What is the goal of a database security system?

**6.4**  Explain the meaning of the word *inappropriately* in the phrase "one user's work does not inappropriately influence another user's work."

**6.5**  What are two interpretations of the abbreviation *DBA*?

**6.6**  What is the purpose of concurrency control?

**6.7**  Explain the trade-off that exists in concurrency control.

**6.8**  Explain the difference between concurrent transactions and simultaneous transactions. How many CPUs are required for simultaneous transactions?

**6.9**  Describe what an atomic transaction is and explain why atomicity is important.

**6.10**  Give an example, other than the one in this text, of the lost update problem.

**6.11**  Define the terms *dirty read*, *nonrepeatable read*, and *phantom read.*

**6.12**  Explain the difference between an explicit lock and an implicit lock.

**6.13**  Explain the difference between an exclusive lock and a shared lock.

**6.14**  What is lock granularity?

**6.15**  Explain two-phase locking.

**6.16**  How does releasing all locks at the end of a transaction relate to two-phase locking?

**6.17**  What is deadlock? How can it be avoided? How can it be resolved when it occurs?

**6.18**  Explain the difference between optimistic and pessimistic locking.

**6.19**  Explain the benefits of marking transaction boundaries, declaring lock characteristics, and letting a DBMS place locks.

**6.20**  Explain the use of the SQL transaction control statements BEGIN TRANSACTION, COMMIT TRANSACTION, and ROLLBACK TRANSACTION.

**6.21**  Explain the meaning of the expression *ACID transaction.*

**6.22**  Describe statement-level consistency.

**6.23**  Describe transaction-level consistency. What disadvantage can exist with it?

**6.24**  What is the purpose of transaction isolation levels?

**6.25**  Explain what read uncommitted isolation level is. Give an example of its use.

**6.26**  Explain what read committed isolation level is. Give an example of its use.

**6.27**  Explain what repeatable read isolation level is. Give an example of its use.

**6.28**  Explain what serializable isolation level is. Give an example of its use.

**6.29**  Explain the term *cursor.*

**6.30**  Explain why a transaction may have many cursors. Also, how is it possible that a transaction may have more than one cursor on a given table?

**6.31**  What is the advantage of using different types of cursors?

**6.32**  Explain keyset cursors. Give an example of their use.

**6.33**  Explain dynamic cursors. Give an example of their use.

**6.34**  Explain forward-only cursors. Give an example of their use.

**6.35**  Explain static cursors. Give an example of their use.

**6.36**  What happens if you do not declare transaction isolation level and cursor type to a DBMS? Is not declaring the isolation level and cursor type good or bad?

**6.37**  Explain the necessity of defining processing rights and responsibilities. How are such responsibilities enforced?

**6.38**  Explain the relationships of users, groups, permission, and objects for a generic database security system.

**6.39**  Describe the advantages and disadvantages of application-provided security.

**6.40**  Describe the advantages and disadvantages of DBMS-provided security.

**6.41**  Explain how a database could be recovered via reprocessing. Why is this generally not feasible?

**6.42**  Define the terms *rollback* and *rollforward.*

**6.43**  Describe the rollback process. Under what conditions should rollback be used?

**6.44**  Describe the rollforward process. Under what conditions should rollforward be used?

**6.45**  Why is it important to write to a log before changing the database values?

**6.46**  What is the advantage of making frequent checkpoints of a database?

**6.47**  Summarize a DBA's responsibilities for configuration control.

**6.48**  Summarize a DBA's responsibilities for documentation.

**6.49**  Summarize a DBA's responsibilities for managing database user problems.

**6.50**  Define *distributed database.*

**6.51**  Explain one way to partition a database that has three tables: T1, T2, and T3.

**6.52**  Explain one way to replicate a database that has three tables: T1, T2, and T3.

**6.53**  Explain what must be done when fully replicating a database but allowing only one computer to process updates.

**6.54**  If more than one computer can update a replicated database, what three problems can occur?

**6.55**  What solution is used to prevent the problems in question 6.54?

**6.56**  Explain what problems can occur in a distributed database that is partitioned but not replicated.

**6.57**  What organizations should consider using a distributed database?

**6.58**  Explain the meaning of the term *object persistence.*

**6.59**  In general terms, explain why relational databases are difficult to use for object persistence.

**6.60**  What does *OODBMS* stand for, and what is its purpose?

**6.61**  According to this chapter, why were OODBMSs not successful?

**6.62**  What is an object-relational database?

## EXERCISES

**6.63** If you have access to SQL Server, search its help system to answer the following questions.

   **A.** Does SQL Server support both optimistic and pessimistic locking?

   **B.** What levels of transaction isolation are available?

   **C.** What types of cursors, if any, does SQL Server use?

   **D.** How does the security model for SQL Server differ from that shown in Figure 6-17?

   **E.** Summarize the types of SQL Server backup.

   **F.** Summarize the SQL Server recovery models.

**6.64** If you have access to MySQL, search its help system to answer the following questions.

   **A.** How does MySQL use read locks and write locks?

   **B.** What, if any, levels of transaction isolation are available in MySQL?

   **C.** What types of cursors, if any, does MySQL use?

   **D.** How does the security model for MySQL differ from that shown in Figure 6-17?

   **E.** Summarize the backup capabilities of MySQL.

   **F.** Summarize the recovery capabilities of MySQL.

**6.65** Search the Web for the term *distributed two-phase locking.* Find a tutorial on that topic and explain, in general terms, how this locking algorithm works.

## ACCESS WORKBENCH KEY TERMS

| | | |
|---|---|---|
| *.accdc file extension | digital signature scheme | strong password |
| *.accde file extension | Exclusive mode | system.mdw |
| ActiveX control | Make ACCDE command | trusted location |
| ActiveX specification | private key | Visual Basic for Applications |
| Admin user | public key | (VBA) |
| asymmetric cryptography | public-key cryptography | workgroup information file |
| digital signature | Security Warning message bar | |

## ACCESS WORKBENCH EXERCISES

**AW.6.1** Using the Wedgewood Pacific Corporation (WPC) database developed in previous sections of "The Access Workbench," answer the following questions.

   **A.** Analyze the data in the WPC database tables (particularly DEPARTMENT and EMPLOYEE) and create a database security plan, using Figure 6-18 as an example.

*(Continued)*

**B.** If you have not already created a My-Trusted-Location folder, follow the steps in this chapter's section of "The Access Workbench" to do so now.

**C.** Make a copy of the WPC.accdb file in the My-Trusted-Location folder and name it WPC-AW06-01.accdb. Open the WPC-AW06-01.accdb database to confirm that it opens without displaying the Security Warning bar, and then close the database.

**D.** Make a copy of the WPC.accdb file in the My-Trusted-Location folder and name it WPC-AW06-02.accdb. Encrypt the WPC-AW06-02.accdb database with the password AW06EX+password. Close the WPC-AW06-02.accdb database and then reopen it to confirm that it opens properly using the password. Close the WPC-AW06-02.accdb database.

**E.** If you have not already created the Digital-Certificate-AW06-001 digital certificate, follow the steps in this chapter's section of "The Access Workbench" to do so now.

**F.** Make a copy of the WPC.accdb file in the My-Trusted-Location folder and name it WPC-AW06-03.accdb. Create an AACDE version of the WPC-AW06-03.accdb database. Create a signed package using the WPC-AW06-03.accde database and the Digital-Certificate-AW06-001 digital certificate.

**G.** If you have not already created a My-Distributed-Databases folder, follow the steps in this chapter's section of "The Access Workbench" to do so now.

**H.** Make a copy of the WPC-AW06-03.accdc file in the My-Distributed-Databases folder. Extract the WPC-AW06-03.accde file into the folder and then open it to confirm that the database opens properly. Close the database.

## GARDEN GLORY PROJECT QUESTIONS

The following Garden Glory database design is used in Chapter 3:

OWNER (<u>OwnerID</u>, OwnerName, OwnerEmail, OwnerType)

PROPERTY (<u>PropertyID</u>, PropertyName, Street, City, State, Zip, *OwnerID*)

EMPLOYEE (<u>EmployeeID</u>, LastName, FirstName, CellPhone, ExperienceLevel)

SERVICE (*<u>PropertyID</u>*, *<u>EmployeeID</u>*, <u>SeviceDate</u>, HoursWorked)

The referential integrity constraints are:

OwnerID in PROPERTY must exist in OwnerID in OWNER

PropertyID in SERVICE must exist in PropertyID in PROPERTY

EmployeeID in SERVICE must exist in EmployeeID in EMPLOYEE

Garden Glory has modified the EMPLOYEE table by adding a TotalHoursWorked column:

EMPLOYEE (<u>EmployeeID</u>, LastName, FirstName, CellPhone, ExperienceLevel, TotalHoursWorked)

The office personnel at Garden Glory use a database application to record services and related data changes in this database. For a new service, the service-recording application reads a row from the PROPERTY table to get the PropertyID. It then creates a new row in SERVICE and updates TotalHoursWorked in EMPLOYEE by adding the HoursWorked value in the new SERVICE record to TotalHoursWorked. This operation is referred to as a Service Update Transaction.

In some cases, the employee record does not exist before the service is recorded. In such a case, a new EMPLOYEE row is created, and then the service is recorded. This is called a Service Update for New Employee Transaction.

**A.** Explain why it is important for the changes made by the Service Update Transaction to be atomic.

**B.** Describe a scenario in which an update of TotalHoursWorked could be lost during a Service Update Transaction.

**C.** Assume that many Service Update Transactions and many Service Update for New Employee Transactions are processed concurrently. Describe a scenario for a nonrepeatable read and a scenario for a phantom read.

**D.** Explain how locking could be used to prevent the lost update in your answer to part B.

**E.** Is it possible for deadlock to occur between two Service Update Transactions? Why or why not? Is it possible for deadlock to occur between a Service Update Transaction and a Service Update for New Employee Transaction? Why or why not?

**F.** Do you think optimistic or pessimistic locking would be better for the Service Update Transactions?

**G.** Suppose Garden Glory identifies three groups of users: managers, administrative personnel, and system administrators. Suppose further that the only job of administrative personnel is to make Service Update Transactions. Managers can make Service Update Transactions and Service Updates for New Employee Transactions. System administrators have unrestricted access to the tables. Describe processing rights that you think would be appropriate for this situation. Use Figure 6-18 as an example. What problems might this security system have?

**H.** Garden Glory has developed the following procedure for backup and recovery. The company backs up the database from the server to a second computer on its network each night. Once a month, it copies the database to a CD and stores it at a manager's house. It keeps paper records of all services provided for an entire year. If it ever loses its database, it plans to restore it from a backup and reprocess all service requests. Do you think this backup and recovery program is sufficient for Garden Glory? What problems might occur? What alternatives exist? Describe any changes you think the company should make to this system.

# JAMES RIVER JEWELRY PROJECT QUESTIONS

The James River Jewelry database design that was used in Chapter 3 was:

> CUSTOMER (<u>CustomerID</u>, LastName, FirstName, Phone, Email)
> PURCHASE (<u>InvoiceNumber</u>, InvoiceDate, PreTaxAmount, *CustomerID*)
> PURCHASE_ITEM (*<u>InvoiceNumber</u>*, <u>*ItemNumber*</u>, RetailPrice)
> ITEM (<u>ItemNumber</u>, Description, Cost, ArtistName)

The referential integrity constraints are:

> CustomerID in PURCHASE must exist in CustomerID in CUSTOMER
> InvoiceNumber in PURCHASE_ITEM must exist in InvoiceNumber in PURCHASE
> ItemNumber in PURCHASE_ITEM must exist in ItemNumber in ITEM

James River Jewelry has modified the database by adding two tables—OWNER and JEWELRY_ITEM—as shown below:

OWNER (<u>OwnerID</u>, LastName, FirstName, Phone, Email, AmountOwed)

JEWELRY_ITEM (<u>*ItemNumber*</u>, DateReceived, DateSold, NegotiatedSalesPrice, ActualSalesPrice, CommissionPercentage, *OwnerID*)

where

OwnerID in JEWELRY_ITEM must exist in OwnerID in OWNER

ItemNumber in JEWELRY_ITEM must exist in ItemNumber in ITEM

The tables are used to record data and maintain owner data about jewelry accepted on consignment. JEWELRY_ITEM (which is a subtype of ITEM—note the referential integrity constraint) is used to record the negotiated sales price, the commission percentage, and the actual sales price for each item of consigned jewelry.

Assume that office personnel at James River Jewelry use a database application to record consignment data. When an item is received on consignment, owner data are stored in OWNER if the owner is new; otherwise existing owner data are used. New ITEM and JEWELRY_ITEM rows are created. In ITEM, ItemNumber and Description are recorded, Cost is set to $0.00, and if there is an artist associated with the piece, ArtistName is entered. For JEWELRY_ITEM, data are stored for all columns except DateSold and ActualSalesPrice. James River Jewelry personnel refer to these actions as an Acceptance Transaction. Later, if the jewelry item does not sell, the NegotiatedSalesPrice and CommissionPercentage values may be reduced. This is called a Price Adjustment Transaction. Finally, when an item sells, the DateSold and ActualSalesPrice fields for the item are given values, and the AmountOwed value in OWNER is updated by increasing AmountOwed by the owner's percentage of the ActualSalesPrice value. This third transaction is called a Sales Transaction.

- **A.** Explain why it is important for the changes made by each of these transactions to be atomic.

- **B.** Describe a scenario in which an update of AmountOwed could be lost.

- **C.** Describe a scenario for a nonrepeatable read and a scenario for a phantom read.

- **D.** Explain how locking could be used to prevent the lost update in your answer to part B.

- **E.** Is it possible for deadlock to occur between two Acceptance Transactions? Why or why not? Is it possible for deadlock to occur between two Sales Transactions? Why or why not? Is it possible for deadlock to occur between an Acceptance Transaction and a Sales Transaction? Why or why not?

- **F.** For each of these three types of transaction, describe whether you think optimistic or pessimistic locking would be better. Explain the reasons for your answer.

- **G.** Suppose James River Jewelry identifies three groups of users: managers, administrative personnel, and system administrators. Suppose further that managers and administrative personnel can perform Acceptance Transactions and Sales Transactions, but only managers can perform Price Adjustment Transactions. Describe processing rights that you think would be appropriate for this situation. Use Figure 6-18 as an example.

- **H.** James River Jewelry has developed the following procedure for backup and recovery. The company backs up the database from the server to a second computer on its network each night. Once a month, it copies the database to a CD and stores it at a manager's house. It keeps paper records of all purchase and sales transactions for an entire year. If it ever loses its database, it plans to restore it from a backup and unrecorded transactions. Do you think this backup and recovery program is sufficient for James River Jewelry? What problems might occur? What alternatives exist? Describe any changes you think the company should make to this system.

 ## THE QUEEN ANNE CURIOSITY SHOP PROJECT QUESTIONS

The Queen Anne Curiosity Shop database design used in Chapter 3 was:

CUSTOMER (<u>CustomerID</u>, LastName, FirstName, Address, City, State, ZIP, Phone, Email)

EMPLOYEE (<u>EmployeeID</u>, LastName, FirstName, Phone, Email)

VENDOR (<u>VendorID</u>, CompanyName, ContactLastName, ContactFirstName, Address, City, State, ZIP, Phone, Fax, Email)

ITEM (<u>ItemID</u>, ItemDescription, PurchaseDate, ItemCost, ItemPrice, *VendorID*)

SALE (<u>SaleID</u>, *CustomerID*, *EmployeeID*, SaleDate, SubTotal, Tax, Total)

SALE_ITEM (*<u>SaleID</u>*, <u>SaleItemID</u>, *ItemID*, ItemPrice)

The referential integrity constraints are:

VendorID in ITEM must exist in VendorID in VENDOR

CustomerID in SALE must exist in CustomerID in CUSTOMER

EmployeeID in SALE must exist in EmployeeID in EMPLOYEE

SaleID in SALE_ITEM must exist in SaleID in SALE

ItemID in SALE_ITEM must exist in ItemID in ITEM

The Queen Anne Curiosity Shop has modified the ITEM and SALE_ITEM tables as follows:

ITEM (<u>ItemID</u>, ItemDescription, UnitCost, UnitPrice, QuantityOnHand, *VendorID*)

SALE_ITEM (*<u>SaleID</u>*, <u>SaleItemID</u>, *ItemID*, Quantity, ItemPrice, Extended Price)

These changes allow the sales system to handle nonunique items that can be bought and sold in quantity. When new items from vendors arrive at the Queen Anne Curiosity Shop, the office personnel unpack the items, put them in the stockroom, and run an Item Quantity Received Transaction that adds the quantity received to QuantityOnHand. At the same time, another transaction, called an Item Price Adjustment Transaction is run, if necessary, to adjust UnitCost and UnitPrice. Sales may occur at any time, and when a sale occurs the Sale Transaction is run. Every time a SALE_ITEM line is entered, the input Quantity is subtracted from QuantityOnHand in ITEM, and the ItemPrice is set to the UnitPrice.

**A.** Explain why it is important for the changes made by each of these transactions to be atomic.

**B.** Describe a scenario in which an update of QuantityOnHand could be lost.

**C.** Describe a scenario for a nonrepeatable read and a scenario for a phantom read.

**D.** Explain how locking could be used to prevent the lost update in your answer to part B.

**E.** Is it possible for deadlock to occur between two Sale Transactions? Why or why not? Is it possible for deadlock to occur between a Sale Transaction and an Item Quantity Received Transaction? Why or why not?

**F.** For each of the three types of transaction, describe whether you think optimistic or pessimistic locking would be better. Explain the reasons for your answer.

**G.** Suppose that the Queen Anne Curiosity Shop identifies four groups of users: sales personnel, managers, administrative personnel, and system administrators. Suppose further that managers and administrative personnel can perform Item Quantity Received Transactions, but only managers can perform Item Price Adjustment Transactions. Describe processing rights that you think would be appropriate for this situation. Use Figure 6-18 as an example.

**H.** The Queen Anne Curiosity Shop has developed the following procedure for backup and recovery. The company backs up the entire database from the server to tape every Saturday night. The tapes are taken to a safety deposit box at a local bank on the following Thursday. Printed paper records of all sales are kept for 5 years. If the database is ever lost, the plan is to restore the database from the last full backup and reprocess all the sales records. Do you think this backup and recovery program is sufficient for the Queen Anne Curiosity Shop? What problems might occur? What alternatives exist? Describe any changes you think the company should make to this system.

# CHAPTER 7

# Database Processing Applications

## Chapter Objectives

> Understand and be able to set up Web database processing

> Learn the basic concepts of Extensible Markup Language (XML)

This chapter introduces topics that build on the fundamentals you have learned in the first six chapters of this book. Now that you have designed and built a database, you are ready to put it to work. In this chapter, we will look at some of the various applications that use database processing, with a primary focus on Web-based database processing. We will also look at Extensible Markup Language (XML), which is rapidly expanding what can be done with Web-based applications.

In this chapter, we will continue to use the Heather Sweeney Designs (HSD) database that we modeled in Chapter 4, designed in Chapter 5, and created in Chapter 6. The name of the database is HSD, and an SQL Server database diagram for the HSD database is shown in Figure 7-1.

**FIGURE 7-1**

The HSD Database
Diagram

## THE DATABASE PROCESSING ENVIRONMENT

Databases vary considerably in size and scope, from single-user databases to large, interorganizational databases, such as airline reservation systems. As shown in Figure 7-2, which repeats Figure 6-4, they also vary in the way they are processed.

Some databases have only a few forms and reports. Others are processed by applications using Internet technology such as **Active Server Pages .NET (ASP.NET)** and **Java Server Pages (JSP)**. Still others are processed by application programs coded in Visual Basic .NET, Java, C#, or another language. Still other databases are processed by stored procedures and triggers. We will consider each of these types of database processing in this chapter.

### Queries, Forms, and Reports

This book has focused on the use of a DBMS to build and process databases. For example, it has covered the need to specify rules, such as cascading updates or deletions. Applications are built to use the databases managed by a DBMS. Queries, forms, and reports are the basis of applications. Query, form, and report generators can be built into a database product, such as Microsoft Access, or they can be run as separate products. It is possible to use Microsoft Access for its query, form, and report features while connecting to a database in another

**FIGURE 7-2**

The Database
Processing
Environment

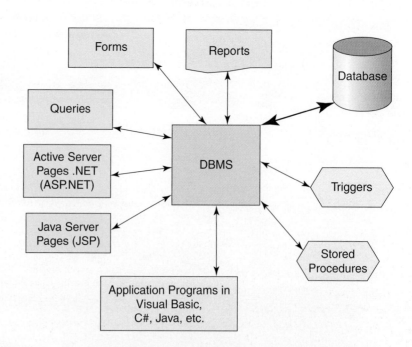

## FIGURE 7-3

### The HSD Application in Microsoft Access 2010

The linked HSD database tables in SQL Server 2008 R2 Express

DBMS, such as SQL Server. In this way, the Microsoft Access "database" actually runs as an application that uses an attached, but distinct, database. Figure 7-3 shows a Microsoft Access 2010 database designed to run as an application running against the HSD database in SQL Server, shown in Figure 6-3 and diagrammed in Figure 7-1.[1] In the application shown in Figure 7-3, Microsoft Access 2010 is connecting to SQL Server by using an Open Database Connectivity (ODBC) driver; we discuss ODBC connections later in this chapter.

Note that in Figure 7-3 the HSD tables stored in SQL Server are shown in the Tables section of the Navigation Pane and that the Customer data input form named HSD Customer Data Input Form has been created and stored in the Forms section of the Navigation Pane. This form allows users to work with data in the CUSTOMER table. Of course, this application could also contain queries and reports.

Now, let us think about some of the tasks that the DBMS—for example, Microsoft Access—needs to do in the background to implement the database processing commands. Suppose, for example, that you create a delete query on a table that has a 1:N relationship to a second table that has On Delete Cascade. Suppose further that the second table has a 1:N relationship to a third table, which has Enforce Referential Integrity but not On Delete Cascade. When running your delete query, Microsoft Access needs to delete rows from the first and second tables consistent with these relationship properties.

---

[1]Before you can connect a Microsoft Access 2010 project to an SQL Server 2008 R2 database, you must be sure that the SQL Server Browser is running. In Windows XP, select **Start | Programs | Microsoft SQL Server 2008 R2 | Configuration Tools | SQL Server Configuration Manager** to run the SQL Server Configuration Manager. In Microsoft Vista and Windows 7, select **Start | Programs | Microsoft SQL Server 2008 R2 | Configuration Tools | SQL Server Configuration Manager**. Look under SQL Server Services to find the SQL Server Browser, and make sure that it is running (State = Running) and that it automatically starts when the computer is booted (Start Mode = Automatic). If not, right-click the **SQL Server Browser** icon to display a short-cut menu, and then click **Properties** to display the SQL Server Browser Properties dialog box. On the Log On properties page, click the **Start** button, and then click the **Apply** button. Click the **Service** tab to display the Service properties page. Click the **Start Mode** line to select it, and then select **Automatic** in the Start Mode drop-down list. Click the **Apply** button, and then click the **OK** button to close the SQL Server Browser Properties dialog box. In addition, users must have appropriate permissions for database use, as discussed in Chapter 6.

The situation is even more complicated if a second user is creating a report on these three tables as your delete query is operating. What should Microsoft Access do? Should it show the report with whatever data remain as your query runs? Or should Microsoft Access protect the report from your deletions and not make any of them until the report is finished? Should it deny your query or do something else completely?

As a simpler example, suppose you create a form that has data from one table in the main section and data from a second table in a subform. Now, suppose a user makes changes in five rows in the subform, makes changes to some of the data in the first form, and then presses the Escape key. Which of these changes will actually be made to the database? None? Changes to the subform data only? Or some other option?

Even in the case of simple queries, forms, and reports, management of the background functions is complex. You can change properties in your database to govern some of Microsoft Access' behavior in these cases, but you need to know the implications of such changes. Enterprise-class DBMS products, such as SQL Server, Oracle Database, and MySQL, provide many more features and functions that let the developer change DBMS behavior for such cases. (Many of these are discussed in Chapter 6.)

## Client/Server and Traditional Application Processing

Organizational database processing began in the early 1970s. Since then, thousands, if not millions, of databases have been processed by application programs written in such programming languages as Visual Basic, C, C++, C#, and Java. All these languages embed SQL statements or their equivalent into programs written in these standard languages.

For example, to process an online order for Heather Sweeney Designs, an application needs to perform the following functions:

1. Communicate with a user to obtain the customer identifier.
2. Read CUSTOMER data.
3. Present an order entry form to a user.
4. Obtain PRODUCT and quantity data from the customer.
5. Verify stock levels for PRODUCTs.
6. Remove PRODUCTs from inventory.
7. Schedule back orders as necessary.
8. Schedule inventory picking and shipping.
9. Update CUSTOMER, INVOICE, and LINE_ITEM data (and if a sale is considered a type of customer contact, then update CONTACT).

The application will be written to respond to exceptions, such as data not present, data in error, communication failure, and dozens of other potential problems.

In addition, an order-processing application program will be written so that it can be used by many users concurrently—it is possible that 50 to 100 users might be trying to run such an application at the same time.

## Stored Procedures and Triggers

Enterprise-class DBMS products, such as SQL Server, Oracle, MySQL, and DB2, include features that allow developers to create modules of logic and database actions called *triggers* and *stored procedures*. Triggers and stored procedures are written in languages provided by the DBMS.[2] For example, SQL Server has a language called Transact-SQL (T-SQL), and Oracle has developed a language called PL/SQL. Programmers can embed SQL statements into these programming languages.

A **trigger** is a program stored within the database that is executed by the DBMS when specific events occur. The events are typically SQL commands that use the INSERT,

---

[2]For more information on triggers, stored procedures, and their uses, see David M. Kroenke and David J. Auer, *Database Processing: Fundamentals, Design, and Implementation*, 11th edition (Upper Saddle River, NJ: Prentice Hall, 2010): Chapters 7, 10, 10A, and 10B.

UPDATE, or DELETE statements. These events are then handled with BEFORE, AFTER, or INSTEAD OF trigger logic. Thus, you find such trigger combinations as BEFORE DELETE, INSTEAD OF UPDATE, and AFTER INSERT. (Note that these are only some examples—there are nine possible combinations of trigger logic and SQL statements.)

Different DBMS products support different sets of triggers. For example, Oracle Database 11g supports BEFORE, AFTER, and INSTEAD OF triggers. MySQL 5.1 supports only BEFORE and AFTER triggers. Of the nine trigger combinations listed, SQL Server 2008 R2 supports AFTER and INSTEAD OF triggers, but combines this support with additional SQL Server specific trigger types which we will not discuss in this book.

A **stored procedure** is similar to a computer program subroutine or function, but it is stored within the database that performs database activity. An example for the HSD database would be a stored procedure to update the columns of INVOICE for a particular InvoiceNumber as LINE_ITEMs are added to the INVOICE. Application programs, Web applications, and interactive query users can invoke the stored procedure, pass parameters to it, and receive results.

## WEB DATABASE PROCESSING

The environment in which today's Internet technology database applications reside is rich and complicated. As shown in Figure 7-4, a typical Web server needs to publish applications that involve data of many different data types. In this text, we have considered only relational databases, but there are many other data types as well.

Several standard interfaces have been developed for accessing database servers. Every DBMS product has an **Application Programming Interface (API)**. An API is a collection of objects, methods, and properties for executing DBMS functions from program code. Unfortunately, each DBMS has its own API, and APIs vary from one DBMS product to another. To save programmers from having to learn to use many different interfaces, the computer industry has developed standards for database access.

The **Open Database Connectivity (ODBC)** standard, mentioned earlier as the means for connecting a Microsoft Access 2010 application to an SQL Server database, was developed in the early 1990s to provide a DBMS-independent means for processing relational

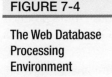

**FIGURE 7-4**

The Web Database Processing Environment

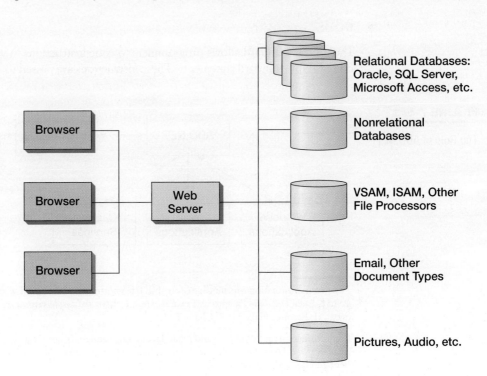

database data. In the mid-1990s, Microsoft announced **OLE DB**, which is an object-oriented interface that encapsulates data-server functionality. OLE DB was designed not just for access to relational databases but also for accessing many other types of data as well. OLE DB is readily accessible to programmers, using such programming languages as C, C#, and Java. However, OLE DB is not as accessible to users of Visual Basic (VB) and scripting languages. Therefore, Microsoft developed **Active Data Objects (ADO)**, which is a set of objects for utilizing OLE DB that is designed for use by any language, including Visual Basic (VB), VBScript, and JScript. ADO has now been followed by **ADO.NET** (pronounced "A-D-O-dot-NET"), which is an improved version of ADO developed as part of Microsoft's **.NET** (pronounced "dot-NET") initiative.

ASP.NET is used in Web pages to create Web-based database applications. Shown in Figure 7-2 as part of the database processing environment, ASP.NET uses Hypertext Markup Language (HTML) and the Microsoft .NET languages to create Web pages that can read and write database data and transmit it over public and private networks, using Internet protocols. ASP.NET runs on Microsoft's Web server product, Internet Information Services (IIS). ASP.NET is part of the Microsoft .NET Framework and relies upon ADO.NET. The use of ADO.NET is illustrated in Figure 7-5.[3]

Also shown in Figure 7-2 is JSP technology. JSP is a combination of HTML and Java that accomplishes the same function as ASP by compiling pages into Java servlets. JSPs are often used on the open-source **Apache** Web server. Another favorite combination of Web developers is the Apache Web server with the MySQL database and either the Pearl or PHP language. This combination is called **AMP** (Apache–MySQL–PHP/Pearl). When running on the Linux operating system, it is referred to as **LAMP**; when running on the Windows operating system, it is referred to as **WAMP**.[4]

In a Web-based database processing environment, if the Web server and the DBMS can run on the same computer, the system has **two-tier architecture**. (One tier is for the browsers, and one is for the Web server/DBMS computer.) Alternatively, the Web server and DBMS can run on different computers, in which case the system has **three-tier architecture**. High-performance applications might use many Web server computers, and in some systems several computers can run the DBMS as well. In the latter case, if the DBMS computers are processing the same databases, the system is referred to as a *distributed database*. (Distributed databases were discussed in Chapter 6.)

## ODBC

The ODBC standard allows programmers to code instructions to various DBMS products using ODBC standard statements. These instructions are passed to an ODBC driver, which

**FIGURE 7-5**

**The Role of ADO.NET**

---

[3]For more information on the Microsoft .NET framework and ADO.NET, see David M. Kroenke and David J. Auer, *Database Processing: Fundamentals, Design, and Implementation*, 11th edition (Upper Saddle River, NJ: Prentice Hall, 2010): Chapter 11.

[4]For information on JSP, JDBC, and related technology and tools, see David M. Kroenke and David J. Auer, *Database Processing: Fundamentals, Design, and Implementation*, 11th edition (Upper Saddle River, NJ: Prentice Hall, 2010): Chapter 11.

**FIGURE 7-6**

ODBC Three-Tier Web Server Architecture

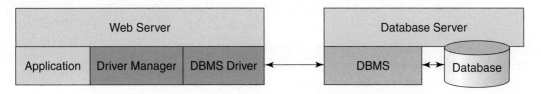

SQL Commands

translates them into the API of the particular DBMS in use. The driver receives results back from the DBMS and translates those results into a form that is part of the ODBC standard.

**ODBC Architecture**  The basic **ODBC architecture** in a three-tier Web server environment—*but before OLE DB and ADO*—is shown in Figure 7-6. The application program, the **OBDC driver manager**, and the **OBDC DBMS driver** (a multiple-tier driver in this case) all reside on the Web server. The DBMS driver sends requests to data sources, which reside on the database server. According to the ODBC standard, a **data source** is the database and its associated DBMS, operating system, and network platform.

The application issues requests to create a connection with a data source; to issue SQL statements and receive results; to process errors; and to start, commit, and roll back transactions. ODBC provides a standard means for each of these requests, and it defines a standard set of error codes and messages.

The driver manager serves as an intermediary between the application and the DBMS drivers. When the application requests a connection, the driver determines the type of DBMS that processes a given ODBC data source and loads that driver in memory (if it is not already loaded).

A **driver** processes ODBC requests and submits specific SQL statements to a given type of data source. There is a different driver for each data source type. It is the responsibility of the driver to ensure that standard ODBC commands execute correctly. The driver also converts data source error codes and messages into the ODBC standard codes and messages.

ODBC identifies two types of drivers: single tier and multiple tier. A **single-tier driver** processes both ODBC calls and SQL statements. A **multiple-tier driver** processes ODBC calls but passes the SQL requests directly to the database server. Although it may reformat an SQL request to conform to the dialect of a particular data source, it does not process the SQL.

**Establishing an ODBC Data Source Name**  A data source is an ODBC data structure that identifies a database and the DBMS that processes it. The three types of data sources are file, system, and user. A **file data source** is a file that can be shared among database users. The only requirement is that the users have the same DBMS driver and privilege to access the database. A **system data source** is local to a single computer. The operating system and any user on that system (with proper permissions) can use a system data source. A **user data source** is available only to the user who created it. Each created data source is given a **data source name (DSN)** that is used to reference the data source.

In general, the best choice for Internet applications is to create a system data source on the Web server. Browser users then access the Web server, which in turn uses a system data source to set up a connection with the DBMS and the database.

We need a system data source for the Heather Sweeney Designs HSD database so that we can use it in a Web database processing application. We created the HSD database in SQL Server 2008, and the system data source will have to provide a connection to the SQL Server 2008 DBMS. To create a system data source in the Windows operating system, you use the **ODBC Data Source Administrator**.

In Windows 7, you open the ODBC Data Source Administrator[5] as follows:

1. Open the Windows Control Panel by clicking the **Start** button and then clicking **Control Panel**.
2. In the Control Panel window, click **System and Security**.
3. In the System and Security window, click **Administrative Tools**.
4. In the Administrative Tools window, double-click the **Data Sources (ODBC)** shortcut icon.

Here is how you create a system data source named HSD for use with the Heather Sweeney Designs HSD database on a Microsoft SQL Server 2008 R2 DBMS:

1. In the ODBC Data Source Administrator, click the **System DSN** tab and then click the **Add** button.
2. In the Create New Data Source dialog box, we need to connect to SQL Server 2008 so we select the **SQL Server Native Client 10**, as shown in Windows 7 in Figure 7-7.
3. Click the **Finish** button. The Create New Data Source to SQL Server dialog box appears.
4. In the Create New Data Source to SQL Server dialog box, enter the information for the HSD database shown in Figure 7-8 (note that the database server is selected from the Server drop-down list), and then click the **Next** button.
   - **NOTE:** If the SQL server does not appear in the Server drop-down list, enter it manually as **ComputerName\SQLServerName**.
5. Click the radio button that selects **SQL Server authentication**, and then enter the Login ID of **HSD-User** and the Password of **HSD-User + password** that we created in Chapter 6. After this data has been entered, click then **Next** button.
   - **NOTE:** If the Login ID and Password are not correct, an error message is displayed at this point. Make sure you have correctly created the SQL Server login as discussed in Chapter 6, and that you have entered the correct data here.
6. Click the check box to change the default database, set the default database to **HSD**, and then click the **Next** button.
7. Click the **Finish** button. The ODBC Microsoft SQL Server Setup dialog box is displayed.
8. In the Microsoft SQL Server Setup dialog box, click the **Test Data Source** button to test the connection.
9. The SQL Server ODBC Data Source Test dialog box appears, showing that the tests completed successfully. Click the **OK** button.

---

**FIGURE 7-7**

The Create New Data Source Dialog Box

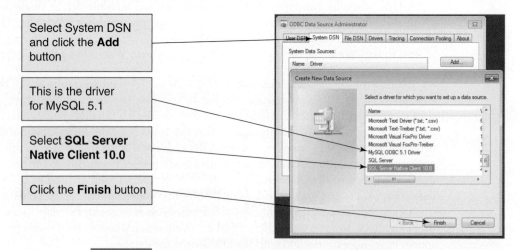

---

[5]WARNING: There are actually *multiple versions* of the OBDC Data Source Administrator in the 64-bit versions of Microsoft Vista and Microsoft Windows 7. You must use the correct version depending on whether the DBMS you are using is a 32-bit or 64-bit version. To make matters worse, all the versions use the same file name of *odbcad32.exe*! The instructions on this page open the 32-bit version, which works with 32-bit programs. If you are using ODBC to connect to a 64-bit version of Microsoft Access 2010, Microsoft SQL Server 2008 R2, or MySQL 5.1, then you must use the version of the OBDC Data Source Administrator located at **C:\Windows\SysWOW64\odbcad32.exe**.

**FIGURE 7-8**

The Create New Data Source to SQL Server Dialog Box

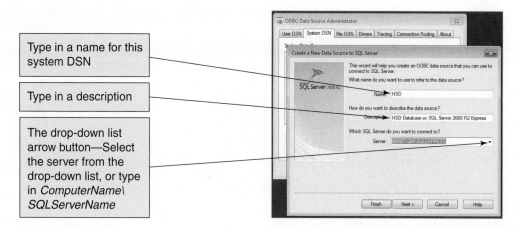

**FIGURE 7-9**

The Completed HSD System Data Source

10. Click the **OK** button in the ODBC Microsoft SQL Server Setup dialog box.
11. The completed HSD system data source is shown in Figure 7-9. Click the **OK** button to close the ODBC Data Source Administrator.

## Web Processing with the Microsoft IIS

Now that we have created our OBDC data source, let us take a look at Web database processing. To do this, we will need a Web server to store the Web pages that we will build and use. We could use the Apache HTTP Server (available from the Apache Software Foundation at **www.apache.org**). This is the most widely used Web server, and there is a version that will run on just about every operating system in existence. However, because we have been using the Windows operating system and Microsoft Access 2010 in "The Access Workbench" sections, we will build a Web site using the Microsoft IIS Web server. One advantage of using this Web server for users of the Windows XP Professional, Windows Vista, and Windows 7 operating systems is that IIS is included with the operating system: IIS version 5.1 is included with Windows XP, IIS version 7.0 is included with Windows Vista, and IIS Version 7.5 is included with Windows 7. IIS is not installed by default, but it can be easily installed at any time. This means that any user can practice creating and using Web pages on his or her own Windows workstation.

Complete instructions for setting up IIS 7.5 on Windows 7, including installing and setting up both PHP and the Eclipse PHP Development Tools (PDT) (which are discussed later in this chapter), are in the Online Appendix E—"Getting Started with Web Servers, PHP and the

## FIGURE 7-10

The IIS wwwroot Folder

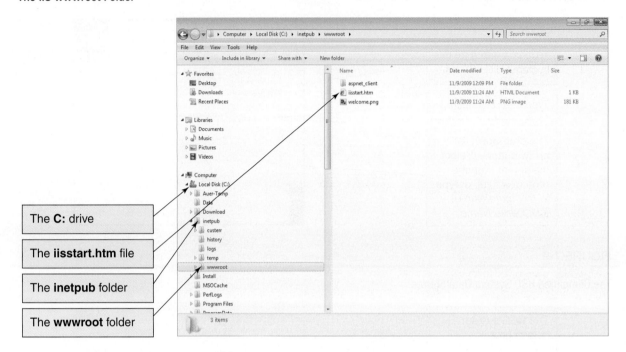

The **C:** drive

The **iisstart.htm** file

The **inetpub** folder

The **wwwroot** folder

---

**B T W**

This discussion of Web database processing has been written to be as widely applicable as possible. With minor adjustments to the following steps, you should be able to use the Apache Web server if you have it available. Whenever possible, we have chosen to use products and technologies that are available for many operating systems.

---

Eclipse PDT." We strongly recommend that you read that appendix at this point, and make sure your computer is correctly set up before continuing with the material in this chapter.

When IIS is installed, it creates an **inetpub folder** on the C: drive as C:\inetpub. Within the inetpub folder is the **wwwroot folder**, which is where IIS stores the most basic Web pages used by the Web server. Figure 7-10 shows this directory structure after IIS has been installed, with the files in the wwwroot folder displayed in the file pane. Note that the wwwroot folder security properties need to be set correctly to allow users access to this folder. As discussed in detail in the online Appendix E, we need to give the Windows Users group *Modify* and *Write* permissions to the wwwroot folder.

IIS is managed using a program called **Internet Information Services** in Windows XP and **Internet Information Services Manager** in Windows Vista and Windows 7. To open either program, open **Control Panel** and then open **Administrative Tools**. The shortcut icon for Internet Information Services/Internet Information Services Manager is located in Administrative Tools. Figure 7-11 shows the Internet Information Services Manager window.

Note that the files shown in the **Default Web Site folder** in Figure 7-11 are the same files that are in the wwwroot folder in Figure 7-10—they are the default files created by IIS when it is installed. In Windows XP, the file **iisstart.asp** generates the Web page that Internet Explorer (or any other Web browser) contacting this Web server over the Internet will see displayed. When you contact the Web from the workstation running IIS, the iisstart.asp file calls the file **localstart.asp**, which provides a special Web page for the Web server administrator. Windows Vista and Windows 7 work similarly but use just the file iisstart.htm.

## FIGURE 7-11

### Managing IIS

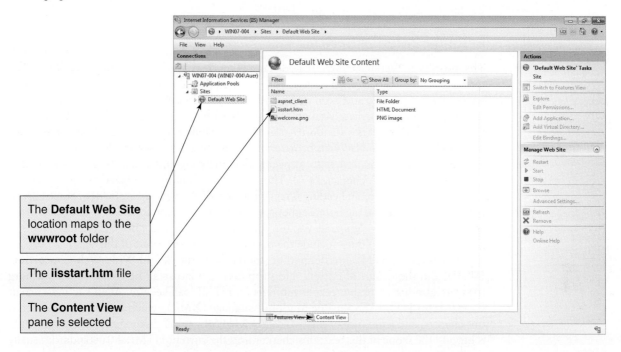

The **Default Web Site** location maps to the **wwwroot** folder

The **iisstart.htm** file

The **Content View** pane is selected

To test the Web server installation, open your Web browser, type in the URL **http://localhost**, and press the **Enter** key. For Windows 7, the Web page shown in Figure 7-12 appears. If the appropriate Web page is not displayed in your Web browser, your Web server is not installed properly.

Now, let us set up a small Web site that can be used for Web database processing of the HSD database. First, we will create a new folder named DBC (database concepts) under

## FIGURE 7-12

### The Default IIS Web Page

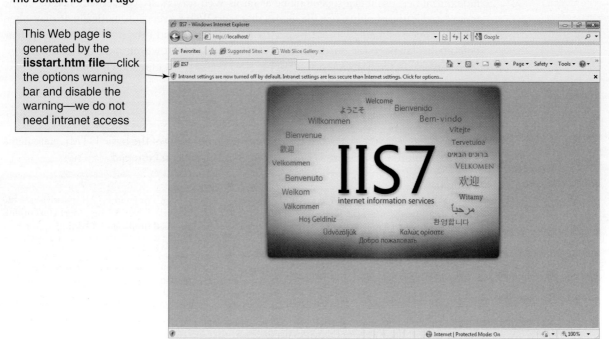

This Web page is generated by the **iisstart.htm file**—click the options warning bar and disable the warning—we do not need intranet access

the wwwroot folder. This new folder will be used to hold all the Web pages developed in discussions and exercises in this book. Second, we will create a subfolder of DBC named HSD. This folder will hold the HSD Web site. You create these folders using Windows Explorer, which is shown in Figure 7-10.

## Getting Started with HTML Web Pages

The most basic Web pages are created using **Hypertext Markup Language (HTML)**. The term *hypertext* refers to the fact that you can include links to other objects, such as Web pages, maps, pictures, and even audio and video files in a Web page, and when you click the link you are immediately taken to that other object and it is displayed in your Web browser. HTML itself is a standard set of **HTML syntax rules** and **HTML document tags** that can be interpreted by Web browsers to create specific onscreen displays.

Tags are usually paired, with a specific beginning tag and a matching ending tag that includes the backslash character ( / ). Thus, a paragraph of text is tagged as <p>{*paragraph text here*}</p>, and a main heading is tagged as <h1>{*heading text here*}</h1>. Some tags do not need a separate end tag because they are essentially self-contained. For example, to insert a horizontal line on a Web page, you use the horizontal rule tag, <hr/>. Note that such single, self-contained tags must include the backslash character as part of the tag.

The rules of HTML are defined as standards by the **World Wide Web Consortium (W3C)**, and the details of current and proposed standards can be found at **www.w3.org** (this site also has several excellent tutorials on HTML[6]). The W3C Web site has current standards for HTML; **Extensible Markup Language (XML)**, which we will discuss later in this chapter; and a mixture of the two called **XHTML**. A full discussion of these standards is beyond the scope of this text; this chapter uses the current HTML 4.01 standard (usually in what is called the "strict" form).

In this chapter, we will create a simple HTML home page for the Heather Sweeney Designs Web site and place it in the HSD folder. We will discuss some of the numerous available Web page editors shortly, but all you need really to create Web pages is a simple text editor. For this first Web page, we will use the Microsoft Notepad ASCII text editor, which has the advantage of being supplied with every version of the Windows operating system.

## The index.html Web Page

The name for the file we are going to create is **index.html**. We need to use the name index.html because it is a special name as far as Web servers are concerned. The file name index.html is one of only a few file names that *most* Web servers automatically display when a URL request is made without a specific file reference, and thus it will become the new default display page for our Web database application. However, note the phrase "*most* Web servers" in the last sentence. Apache, IIS 7.0 and IIS 7.5 (as shown in Figure 7-13) are configured to recognize index.html; however, IIS 5.1 is not.[7]

## Creating the index.html Web Page

Now we can create the index.html Web page, which consists of the basic HTML statements shown in Figure 7-14. Figure 7-15 shows the HTML code in Notepad.

---

[6]To learn more about HTML, go to the W3C Web site at **www.w3.org**. For good HTML tutorials, see the following tutorials by David Raggett: "Getting Started with HTML" (**www.w3.org/MarkUp/Guide**), "More Advanced Features" (**www.w3.org/MarkUp/Guide/Advanced.html**), and "Adding a Touch of Style" (**www.w3.org/MarkUp/Guide/Style.html**).

[7]If you are using Windows XP and IIS 5.1, you need to add index.html to the list of recognized files. You do this by using Internet Information Services. In the Internet Information Services window, you right-click the **Web Sites** object to display the shortcut menu and then click **Properties** to display the Web Sites Properties dialog box. You then click the **Documents** tab and the **Add** button to display the Add Default Document dialog box. Then enter the document name (file name) **index.html** and click the **OK** button. Finally, we close the Web Sites Properties dialog box.

**FIGURE 7-13**

The index.html File in Windows 7 IIS Manager

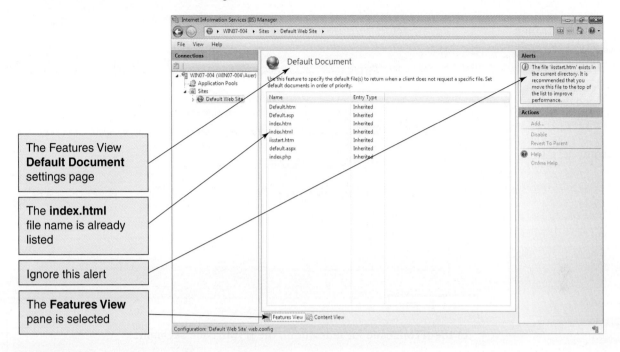

The Features View **Default Document** settings page

The **index.html** file name is already listed

Ignore this alert

The **Features View** pane is selected

**FIGURE 7-14**

The HTML Code for the index.html File in the *HSD* Folder

```html
<!DOCTYPE html PUBLIC "-//W3C//DTD HTML 4.01 Strict//EN"
"http://www.w3.org/TR/html4/strict.dtd">
<html>
    <head>
        <meta http-equiv="Content-Type" content="text/html; charset=ISO-8859-1" />
        <title>Heather Sweeney Designs Demonstration Pages Home Page</title>
    </head>
    <body>
        <h1 style="text-align: center; color: blue">
            Database Concepts (5th Edition)
        </h1>
        <p style="text-align: center; font-weight: bold">
            David M. Kroenke
        </p>
        <p style="text-align: center; font-weight: bold">
            David J. Auer
        </p>
        <hr />
        <h2 style="text-align: center; color: blue">
            Welcome to the Heather Sweeney Designs Home Page
        </h2>
        <hr />
        <p>Chapter 7 Demonstration Pages From Figures in the Text:</p>
        <p>Example 1:   
            <a href="ReadSeminar.php">
                Display the SEMINAR Table (No surrogate key)
            </a>
        </p>
        <hr />
    </body>
</html>
```

## FIGURE 7-15

The HTML Code for the index.html File in Notepad

The **index.html** HTML code—note how indentation is used to keep the code organized and readable

```
index.html - Notepad
File  Edit  Format  View  Help
<!DOCTYPE html PUBLIC "-//W3C//DTD HTML 4.01 Strict//EN" "http://www.w3.org/TR/html4/strict.dtd">
<html>
        <head>
                <meta http-equiv="Content-Type" content="text/html; charset=ISO-8859-1" />
                <title>Heather Sweeney Designs Demonstration Pages Home Page</title>
        </head>
        <body>
                <h1 style="text-align: center; color: blue">
                        Database Concepts (5th Edition)
                </h1>
                <p style="text-align: center; font-weight: bold">
                        David M. Kroenke
                </p>
                <p style="text-align: center; font-weight: bold">
                        David J. Auer
                </p>
                <hr />
                <h2 style="text-align: center; color: blue">
                        Welcome to the Heather Sweeney Designs Home Page
                </h2>
                <hr />
                <p>Chapter 7 Demonstration Pages From Figures in the Text:</p>
                <p>Example 1:   
                        <a href="ReadSeminar.php">
                                Display the SEMINAR Table (No surrogate key)
                        </a>
                </p>
                <hr />
        </body>
</html>
```

---

**B T W**

In the HTML code for index.html, the HTML code segment:

```
<!DOCTYPE html PUBLIC "-//W3C//DTD HTML 4.01 Strict//EN"
"http://www.w3.org/TR/html4/strict.dtd">
```

is an **HTML/XML document type declaration (DTD),** which is used to check and validate the contents of the code that you write. DTDs are discussed later in this chapter. For right now, just include the code as it is written.

---

If we now use the URL **http://localhost/DBC/HSD**, we get the Web page shown in Figure 7-16.

## Web Database Processing Using PHP

Now that we have our basic Web site set up, we will expand its capabilities with a Web development environment that allows us to connect Web pages to our database. Several technologies allow us to do this. Developers using Microsoft products usually work with the .NET framework and use ASP.NET technology. Developers who use the Apache Web server may prefer creating JSP files in the JavaScript scripting language or using the Java programming language in the Java Enterprise Edition (Java EE) environment.

**The PHP Scripting Language**    In this chapter, we will use the scripting language **PHP**. PHP, which is an abbreviation for **PHP: Hypertext Processor** (and which was previously known as the *Personal Hypertext Processor*), is a scripting language that can be embedded in Web pages. PHP is extremely popular. In the summer of 2007, more than 2 million Internet domains had servers running PHP,[8] and the May 2010 TIOBE Programming Community Index ranked PHP as the fourth most popular programming language (following, in order, C, Java, and C++).[9] In 2008, PHP had ranked fourth (also trailing

---

[8]See **www.php.net/usage.php**.

[9]See **www.tiobe.com/index.php/content/paperinfo/tpci/index.html**.

**FIGURE 7-16**

The index.html Web
Page in HSD

Visual Basic), while in 2010 PHP held down third place for a while. PHP appears to be maintaining or gaining in popularity among programmers and Web page designers. PHP is easy to learn and can be used in most Web server environments and with most databases. It is also an open-source product that is freely downloadable from the PHP Web site (**www.php.net**).

**The Eclipse Integrated Development Environment (IDE)**   Although a simple text editor such as Notepad is fine for simple Web pages, as we start creating more complex pages we will move to an **Integrated Development Environment (IDE)**. An IDE gives you the most robust and user-friendly means of creating and maintaining your Web pages. If you are working with Microsoft products, you will likely use Visual Studio (or the freely downloadable Visual Studio 2008 Express Edition, available at **www.microsoft.com/express/**). If you are working with JavaScript or Java, you might prefer the NetBeans IDE (available at **www.netbeans.org**).

For this chapter, we will again turn to the open-source development community and use the **Eclipse IDE**. Eclipse provides a framework that can be modified by add-in modules for many purposes. For PHP, we can use Eclipse as modified for the **Eclipse PDT (PHP Development Tools) Project**, which is specifically intended to provide a PHP development environment in Eclipse (see **www.eclipse.org/pdt/** for general information and **http://download.eclipse.org/tools/pdt/downloads/** for downloadable files—download the current stable build for your operating system).[10]

For more information on installing and using PHP and Eclipse, see Online Appendix E "Getting Started with Web Servers, PHP and the Eclipse PDT." Figure 7-17 shows the index.html file as created in the Eclipse IDE. Compare this version with the Notepad version in Figure 7-16.

Now that we have our basic Web site set up, we will start to integrate PHP into the Web pages. First, we will create a page to read data from a database table and display the results in a Web page. Specifically, we will create a Web page in the HSD folder named ReadSeminar.php to run the SQL query:

```
SELECT * FROM SEMINAR;
```

---

[10]As noted on the PDT download page, you also need to install the Java Runtime Environment (as of this writing, it is JRE 6 Update 20 from Oracle), at **http://java.com/en/download/manual.jsp**). Also note that the Windows version of Eclipse does not install like most Windows programs: You need to create a folder named EclipsePDT in the Program Files folder on your C: drive (the full path name will be C:\Program Files\EclipsePDT), unzip the Eclipse PDT files in that directory, and create a desktop shortcut to eclipse.exe. For full for instructions, see the Online Appendix E.

## FIGURE 7-17

### The HTML Code for the index.html File in the Eclipse IDE

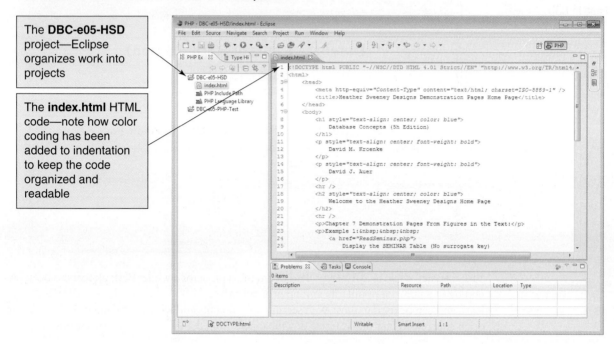

The **DBC-e05-HSD** project—Eclipse organizes work into projects

The **index.html** HTML code—note how color coding has been added to indentation to keep the code organized and readable

This page displays the result of the query, without the table's surrogate key of SeminarID, in a Web page. The HTML and PHP code for ReadSeminar.php is shown in Figure 7-18, and the same code is shown in Eclipse in Figure 7-19.

## FIGURE 7-18

### The HTML and PHP Code for ReadSeminar.php

```
<!DOCTYPE HTML PUBLIC "-//W3C//DTD HTML 4.01 Frameset//EN">
<html>
    <head>
        <meta http-equiv="Content-Type" content="text/html; charset=UTF-8">
        <title>ReadSeminar PHP Page</title>
        <style type="text/css">
            h1 {text-align: center; color: blue}
            h2 {font-family: Ariel, sans-serif; text-align: left; color: blue}
            p.footer {text-align: center}
            table.output {font-family: Ariel, sans-serif}
        </style>
    </head>
    <body>
    <?php
        // Get connection
        $Conn = odbc_connect('HSD', 'HSD-User','HSD-User+password');

        // Test connection
        if (!$Conn)
        {
            exit ("ODBC Connection Failed: " . $Conn);
        }
        // Create SQL statement
        $SQL = "SELECT * FROM SEMINAR";
```

**FIGURE 7-18** *(Continued)*

```php
        // Execute SQL statement
        $RecordSet = odbc_exec($Conn,$SQL);

        // Test existence of recordset
        if (!$RecordSet)
            {
                exit ("SQL Statement Error: " . $SQL);
            }
?>
        <!-- Page Headers -->
        <h1>
            The Heather Sweeney Designs SEMINAR Table
        </h1>
        <hr />
        <h2>
            SEMINAR
        </h2>
<?php

        // Table headers
        echo "<table class='output' border='1'>
            <tr>
                <th>SeminarDate</th>
                <th>SeminarTime</th>
                <th>Location</th>
                <th>SeminarTitle</th>
            </tr>";


        // Table data
        while($RecordSetRow = odbc_fetch_array($RecordSet))
            {
            echo "<tr>";
            echo "<td>" . $RecordSetRow['SeminarDate'] . "</td>";
            echo "<td>" . $RecordSetRow['SeminarTime'] . "</td>";
            echo "<td>" . $RecordSetRow['Location'] . "</td>";
            echo "<td>" . $RecordSetRow['SeminarTitle'] . "</td>";
            echo "</tr>";
            }
        echo "</table>";

        // Close connection
        odbc_close($Conn);
?>
        <br />
        <hr />
        <p class="footer">
            <a href="../HSD/index.html">
                Return to Heather Sweeney Designs Home Page
            </a>
        </p>
        <hr />
    </body>
</html>
```

If you use the URL **http://localhost/DBC/HSD** in your Web browser and then click the **Example 1: Display the SEMINAR Table (No surrogate key)** link on that page, the Web page shown in Figure 7-20 is displayed.

The ReadSeminar.php code blends HTML (executed on the user's workstation) and PHP statements (executed on the Web server). In Figure 7-18, the statements included

**FIGURE 7-19**

The HTML and PHP Code for ReadSeminar.php in Eclipse

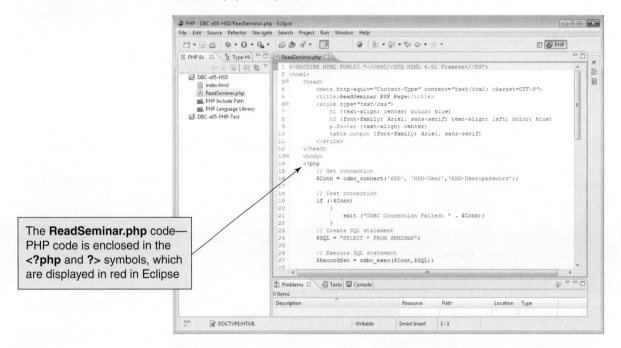

The **ReadSeminar.php** code—PHP code is enclosed in the **<?php** and **?>** symbols, which are displayed in red in Eclipse

**FIGURE 7-20**

The Results of ReadSeminar.php

**The Heather Sweeney Designs SEMINAR Table**

**SEMINAR**

| SeminarDate | SeminarTime | Location | SeminarTitle |
|---|---|---|---|
| 2009-10-11 00:00:00.000 | 1900-01-01 11:00:00.000 | San Antonio Convention Center | Kitchen on a Budget |
| 2009-10-25 00:00:00.000 | 1900-01-01 16:00:00.000 | Dallas Convention Center | Kitchen on a Big D Budget |
| 2009-11-01 00:00:00.000 | 1900-01-01 08:30:00.000 | Austin Convention Center | Kitchen on a Budget |
| 2010-03-22 00:00:00.000 | 1900-01-01 11:00:00.000 | Dallas Convention Center | Kitchen on a Big D Budget |

Return to Heather Sweeney Designs Home Page

between **<?php** and **?>** is program code that is to be executed on the Web server computer. All the rest of the code is HTML that is generated and sent to the browser client. In Figure 7-18, the statements:

```
<!DOCTYPE HTML PUBLIC "-//W3C//DTD HTML 4.01 Frameset//EN">
<html>
      <head>
            <meta http-equiv="Content-Type" content="text/
                  html; charset=UTF-8">
            <title>ReadSeminar PHP Page</title>
            <style type="text/css">
```

```
            h1 {text-align: center; color: blue}
            h2 {font-family: Ariel, sans-serif;
                   text-align: left; color: blue}
            p.footer {text-align: center}
            table.output {font-family: Ariel, sans-serif}
        </style>
    </head>
<body>
```

are normal HTML code. When sent to the browser, these statements set the title of the browser window to ReadSeminar PHP Page; define styles to be used by the headings,[11] the results table, and the footer; and cause other HTML-related actions. The next group of statements are included between <?php and ?> and, thus, are PHP code that will be executed on the Web server. Also note that all PHP statements, like SQL statements, must end with a semicolon (;).

**Creating a Connection to the Database**  In the HTML and PHP code in Figure 7-18, the following PHP code is embedded in the HTML code to create and test a connection to the database:

```php
<?php
        // Get connection
        $Conn = odbc_connect('HSD', 'HSD-User',
        'HSD-User+password');
        // Test connection
        if (!$Conn)
        {
             exit ("ODBC Connection Failed: " . $Conn);
        }
```

After it runs, the variable $Conn can be used to connect to the ODBC data source HSD. Note that all PHP variables start with the dollar sign symbol ($).

---

**B T W**

Be sure to use comments to document your Web pages. PHP code segments with two forward slashes (//) in front of them are comments. This symbol is used to define single-line comments. In PHP, comments can also be inserted in blocks between the symbols /* and */, whereas in HTML comments *must* be inserted between the symbols <!— and —>.

---

The connection is used to open the HSD ODBC data source. Here, the user ID of HSD-User and the password of HSD-User+password that we created in Chapter 6 are being used to authenticate to the DBMS.

The test of the connection is contained in the code segment:

```php
        // Test connection
        if (!$Conn)
        {
             exit ("ODBC Connection Failed: " . $Conn);
        }
```

---

[11]Styles are used to control the visual presentation of the Web page and are defined in the HTML section between the <style> and </style> tags. For more information about styles, see David Raggett's tutorial "Adding a Touch of Style" at **www.w3.org/MarkUp/Guide/Style.html**.

In English, this statement says, "IF the connection Conn does not exist, THEN print the error message 'OBDC Connection Failed' followed by the contents of the variable $Conn." Note that the code (!Conn) means NOT Conn—in PHP the exclamation point symbol (!) means NOT.

At this point, a connection has been established to the DBMS via the ODBC data source, and the database is open. The $Conn variable can be used whenever a connection to the database is needed.

**Creating a Recordset**   Given the connection with an open database, the following code segment from Figure 7-18 will store an SQL statement in the variable $SQL and then use the PHP odbc_exec command to run that SQL statement against the database to retrieve the query results and store them in the variable $RecordSet:

```
// Create SQL statement
$SQL = "SELECT * FROM SEMINAR";
// Execute SQL statement
$RecordSet = odbc_exec($Conn, $SQL);
// Test existence of recordset
if (!$objRecordSet)
{
        exit ("SQL Statement Error: " . $SQL);
}
?>
```

Note that again you need to test the results to be sure the PHP command executed correctly.

**Displaying the Results**   Now that the recordset has been created and populated, we can process the recordset collection with the following code:

```
<!- Page Headers ->
<h1>
        The Heather Sweeney Designs SEMINAR Table
</h1>
<hr />
<h2>
        SEMINAR
</h2>
<?php
// Table headers
echo "<table class='output' border='1'>
        <tr>
                <th>SeminarDate</th>
                <th>SeminarTime</th>
                <th>Location</th>
                <th>SeminarTitle</th>
        </tr>";
```

```
// Table data
while($RecordSetRow = odbc_fetch_array($RecordSet))
    {
    echo "<tr>";
    echo "<td>" . $RecordSetRow['SeminarDate'] . "</td>";
    echo "<td>" . $RecordSetRow['SeminarTime'] . "</td>";
    echo "<td>" . $RecordSetRow['Location'] . "</td>";
    echo "<td>" . $RecordSetRow['SeminarTitle'] . "</td>";
    echo "</tr>";
    }
echo "</table>";
```

The HTML section defines the page headers, and the PHP section defines how to display the SQL results in a table format. Note the use of the PHP command echo to allow PHP to use HTML syntax within the PHP code section. Also note that a loop is executed to iterate through the rows of the recordset using the PHP variable $RecordSetRow.

**Disconnecting from the Database**   Now that we have finished running the SQL statement and displaying the results, we can end our ODBC connection to the database with the code:

```
// Close connection
odbc_close($Conn);
?>
```

The basic page we have created here illustrates the basic concepts of using ODBC and PHP to connect to a database and process data from that database in a Web database processing application. You can build on this foundation by studying PHP command syntax and incorporating additional PHP features into your Web pages. For more information on PHP, see the PHP documentation at **www.php.net/docs.php**.

## Challenges for Web Database Processing

Web database application processing is complicated by an important characteristic of HTTP. Specifically, HTTP is stateless; it has no provision for maintaining sessions between requests. Using HTTP, a client at a browser makes a request of a Web server. The server services the client request, sends results back to the browser, and forgets about the interaction with that client. A second request from that same client is treated as a new request from a new client. No data are kept to maintain a session or connection with the client.

This characteristic poses no problem for serving content, either static Web pages or responses to queries of a database. However, it is not acceptable for applications that require multiple database actions in an atomic transaction. Recall from Chapter 6 that in some cases a group of database actions needs to be grouped into a transaction, with all of them committed to the database or none of them committed to the database. In this case, the Web server or other program must augment the base capabilities of HTTP.

For example, IIS provides features and functions for maintaining data about sessions between multiple HTTP requests and responses. Using these features and functions, the application program on the Web server can save data to and from the browser. A particular session will be associated with a particular set of data. In this way, the application program can start a transaction, conduct multiple interactions with the user at the browser, make intermediate changes to the database, and commit or roll back all changes when ending the transaction. Other means are used to provide for sessions and session data with Apache.

In some cases, the application programs must create their own methods for tracking session data. PHP does include support for sessions—see the PHP documentation for more information.

The particulars of session management are beyond the scope of this chapter. However, you should be aware that HTTP is stateless, and, regardless of the Web server, additional code must be added to database applications to enable transaction processing.

### SQL Injection Attacks

Our example of a Web page for a Web database application was a read-only example. To make a Web database application truly useful, we would have to have Web pages that allow us to input data as well as read it.

When we do this, however, we must use care in creating input Web pages, or we may create a vulnerability that allows an **SQL injection attack**. An SQL injection attack is similar to the application-level security example we discussed in Chapter 6, and attempts to issue SQL commands to the DBMS. For example, suppose that a Web page is used to update a user's phone number and thus requires the user to input the new phone number. The Web application would then use PHP code to create and run an SQL statement such as:

```
// Create SQL statement
$varSQL = "UPDATE CUSTOMER SET PHONE = '$NewPhone' ";
$varSQL .= "WHERE CustomerID = '$CustomerID'";
// Execute SQL statement
   $RecordSet = odbc_exec($Conn, $varSQL);
```

If the input value of NewPhone is not carefully checked, it may be possible for an attacker to use an input value such as:

```
678-345-1234; DELETE FROM CUSTOMER;
```

If this input value is accepted and the SQL statement is run, we may lose all data in the CUSTOMER table if the Web application has DELETE permissions on the CUS-TOMER table. Therefore, Web database applications must be very carefully constructed to provide for data checking and to ensure that only necessary database permissions are granted.

## DATABASE PROCESSING AND XML

XML is becoming a standard means for defining the structure of documents and for transmitting documents from one computer to another. XML is important for database processing because it provides a standardized means of submitting data to a database and for receiving results back from the database. XML is a large, complicated subject that requires several books to explain fully. Here, we touch on the fundamentals and further explain why XML is important for database processing.

### The Importance of XML

Database processing and document processing need each other. Database processing needs document processing for transmitting database views, and document processing needs database processing for storing and manipulating data. In the early 1990s, the Web development and database communities began to meet, and the result of their work became XML.

XML provides a standardized yet customizable way to describe the content of documents. It can therefore be used to describe any database view but in a standardized way. As you will learn, unlike SQL views (discussed in Chapter 3A), XML views are not limited to one multivalued path. In addition, when used with the XML Schema standard XML documents can automatically be generated from database data. Further, database data can automatically be extracted from XML documents. And there are standardized ways of defining how document components are mapped to database schema components and vice versa.

Other standards associated with XML have developed. For example, **SOAP**, which originally meant **Simple Object Access Protocol**, was defined as an XML-based standard for providing remote procedure calls over the Internet. Initially, SOAP assumed the use of HTTP as a transport mechanism, but now SOAP has been generalized as a standard protocol for sending messages of any type using any transport protocol. With this change, SOAP no longer means Simple Object Access Protocol, so now SOAP is just a name, and not an acronym.

Today, XML is used for many purposes. One of the most important is its use as a standardized means to define and communicate documents for processing over the Internet. We will begin our discussion of XML by describing its use for displaying Web pages. As you will learn, however, XML uses go far beyond Web page display. In fact, Web page display is one of the least important applications of XML. We will begin with page display only because it is an easy way to introduce XML documents. After that, we will explain the XML Schema standard and discuss its use for database processing.

## XML as a Markup Language

As a markup language, XML is significantly better than HTML in several ways. First, XML provides a clean separation between document structure, content, and materialization. XML has facilities for dealing with each, and they cannot be confounded, as they can with HTML.

Second, XML is standardized, but as its name implies, the standards allow for extension by developers. With XML, you are not limited to a fixed set of elements with tags such as <h1> . . . </h1> and <p> . . . </p>. Instead, you can create your own tags.

Third, XML forces consistent tag use. HTML tags can be used for different purposes. For example, consider the following HTML:

```
<h2>HSD Seminar Data</h2>
```

Although the <h2> tag can be used to structurally mark a level-two heading in a Web page, it can be used for other purposes, too, such as causing "HSD Seminar Data" to be displayed in a particular font size, weight, and color. Because an HTML tag has potentially many purposes, you cannot rely on HTML tags to describe the structure of an HTML page.

In contrast, the structure of an XML document is formally defined. Tags are defined in relationship to one another. If you find the XML tag <city> . . . </city>, you know exactly what data you have, where that data belong in the document, and how that tag relates to other tags.

## XML Document Type Declarations

Figure 7-21 shows a sample XML document. Notice that the document has two sections. The first section defines the structure of the document; it is referred to as the *DTD*. The second part is the document data. Figure 7-21 shows an example of an XML document with an internal DTD.

The DTD begins with the word DOCTYPE and specifies the name of this type of document, which is Seminar. Then, it specifies the content of the Seminar document: SeminarID,

**FIGURE 7-21**

**Example XML Document with an Internal DTD**

```
<?xml version="1.0" encoding="UTF-8"?>
<!DOCTYPE Seminar [
    <!ELEMENT Seminar (SeminarID, Date, Time, Location, Title)>
    <!ELEMENT SeminarID (#PCDATA)>
    <!ELEMENT SeminarDate (#PCDATA)>
    <!ELEMENT SeminarTime (#PCDATA)>
    <!ELEMENT Location (#PCDATA)>
    <!ELEMENT SeminarTitle (#PCDATA)>
]>
<Seminar>
    <SeminarID>1</SeminarID>
    <SeminarDate>10/11/2009</SeminarDate>
    <SeminarTime>11:00</SeminarTime>
    <Location>San Antonio Convention Center</Location>
    <SeminarTitle>Kitchen on a Budget</SeminarTitle>
</Seminar>
```

SeminarDate, SeminarTime, Location, and SeminarTitle. Each element is defined as #PCDATA, which means that each is a string of character data.

The data instance of Seminar shown in Figure 7-21 conforms to the DTD. Therefore, this document is said to be a **type-valid document**. If it did not conform to the DTD, it would be a **not-type-valid document**. Documents that are not type valid can still be perfectly good XML—they just do not conform to their type description. For example, if the document in Figure 7-21 had two SeminarTitle elements, it would be valid XML, but it would not be type valid.

Although DTDs are almost always desirable, they are not required in XML documents. Documents that have no DTD are by definition not type valid because there is no type against which to validate them.

The DTD does not need to be contained inside the document. Figure 7-22 shows a Seminar XML document in which the DTD is obtained from the file C:\DBC-e05\ Seminar.dtd. In this case, the DTD is located on the same computer that stores the document, but DTDs can also be referenced by URL Web addresses. The advantage of storing the DTD externally is that many documents can be validated against the same DTD. The W3C, at **www.w3.org**, stores DTD based on W3C standards for easily accessible external validation. The DOCTYPE lines shown in Figures 7-14 and 7-18 illustrate using external validation with the W3C.

Note that the creator of a DTD is free to choose any elements he or she wants. Hence, XML documents can be extended, but in a standardized and controlled way.

**FIGURE 7-22**

**Example XML Document with an External DTD**

```
<?xml version="1.0" encoding="UTF-8"?>
<!DOCTYPE Seminar SYSTEM "C:\DBC-e05\Seminar.dtd">
<Seminar>
    <SeminarID>1</SeminarID>
    <SeminarDate>10/11/2009</SeminarDate>
    <SeminarTime>11:00</SeminarTime>
    <Location>San Antonio Convention Center</Location>
    <SeminarTitle>Kitchen on a Budget</SeminarTitle>
</Seminar>
```

## Materializing XML Documents with XSLT

The XML document in Figure 7-21 shows both the document's structure and content. Nothing in the document, however, indicates how it is to be materialized. The designers of XML created a clean separation among structure, content, and format. The most popular way to materialize XML documents is to use **Extensible Style Language: Transformations (XSLT)**. XSLT is a powerful and robust transformation language. It can be used to materialize XML documents into HTML to produce Web pages, and it can be used for many other purposes as well. See the W3C Web site (**www.w3.org**) for more information.[12]

## XML Schema

DTDs were the XML community's first attempt at developing a document structure–specification language. DTDs work, but they have some limitations, and, embarrassingly, DTD documents are not XML documents. To correct these problems, the W3C defined another specification language called **XML Schema**. Today, using XML Schema is the preferred method for defining document structure.

XML Schema documents are XML documents. This means that you use the same language to define an XML Schema document as you would use to define any other XML document. It also means you can validate an XML Schema document against its schema, just as you would any other XML document.

If you are following this discussion, then you realize that there is a chicken-and-the-egg problem here: If XML Schema documents are themselves XML documents, what document is used to validate them? What is the schema of all the schemas? There is such a document: The mother of all schemas is located at the W3C site (**www.w3.org**). *All* XML Schema documents are validated against that document.

XML Schema validation involves "meta thinking." Recall that metadata is data about data. For example, the statement CUSTOMER contains column CustomerName Char(25) is metadata. Extending this idea, the statement that SQL has a data type Char(n) for defining character data of length *n* is data about metadata, or meta-metadata.

XML has the same meta levels. An XML document has a structure that is defined by an XML Schema document. The XML Schema document contains metadata because it is data about the structure of other XML documents. However, an XML Schema document has its own structure that is defined by another XML Schema document. That XML Schema document is data about metadata, or meta-metadata.

The XML case is elegant. When you use an IDE that can validate an XML document (such as the Eclipse IDE[13]), you can validate any XML document against its XML Schema document. The process is exactly the same, regardless of whether you are validating an XML document, an XML Schema document, or a document at any other level.

XML Schema is a broad and complex topic. We cannot discuss even the major topics of XML Schema within this chapter, but we will focus on a few basic terms and concepts and show how those terms and concepts are used with database processing.

**XML Schema Validation**   Figure 7-23 shows a simple XML Schema document that can be used to represent a single row from the SEMINAR table at Heather Sweeney Designs. The first line indicates what schema is to be used to validate this document.

---

[12]For more information on XSLT, see David M. Kroenke and David J. Auer, *Database Processing: Fundamentals, Design, and Implementation*, 11th edition (Upper Saddle River, NJ: Prentice Hall, 2010).

[13]Another excellent XML IDE is Altova's XMLSpy, which is available at **www.altova.com**. Altova previously provided a free XMLSpy Home Edition, but currently only a trial version of its commercial product is available for short-term student use. XMLSpy is an excellent product; all the XML examples in this book were prepared using it.

---

**FIGURE 7-23**

---

Example XML Schema Document

```
<?xml version="1.0" encoding="UTF-8"?>
<xsd:schema xmlns:xsd="http://www.w3.org/2001/XMLSchema" elementFormDefault="qualified"
attributeFormDefault="unqualified">
    <xsd:element name="Seminar">
        <xsd:annotation>
            <xsd:documentation>
                This is an XML Schema describing a Seminar at Heather Sweeney Designs.
            </xsd:documentation>
        </xsd:annotation>
        <xsd:complexType>
            <xsd:sequence>
                <xsd:element name="SeminarID" type="xsd:integer"/>
                <xsd:element name="SeminarDate" type="xsd:string"/>
                <xsd:element name="SeminarTime" type="xsd:string"/>
                <xsd:element name="Location" type="xsd:string"/>
                <xsd:element name="SeminarTitle" type="xsd:string"/>
            </xsd:sequence>
        </xsd:complexType>
    </xsd:element>
</xsd:schema>
```

(a) XML Schema

(b) Graphical Representation of XML Schema

---

**B T W**

Because this is an XML Schema document, it is to be validated against the mother of all schemas, the one at **www.w3.org**. However, this reference address is used only for identification purposes. Because this schema is so widely used, most schema validation programs have and use their own built-in copy of it.

---

This first statement in Figure 7-23(a) not only defines the document that is to be used for validation but also establishes a labeled namespace. **Namespaces** are a complicated topic in their own right, and we do not discuss them in this chapter except to explain the use of labels. In this first statement, xsd is defined by the expression xmlns:xsd. The first part of that expression stands for *XML namespace*, and the second part defines the label xsd. Notice that all the other lines in the document use the label xsd. The expression xsd:complexType simply tells the validating program to look into the namespace called xsd (here, the one defined by **www.w3.org/2001/XMLSchema**) to find the definition of the term complexType.

---

**B T W**

The designer of the document can change the name of the label. You could change xmlns:xsd to xmlns:mynamespace and then set mynamespace to point to the W3C document. Documents can also have multiple namespaces, but that topic is beyond the scope of this discussion.

---

**Elements and Attributes**   As shown in Figure 7-23(a), XML Schemas consist of elements and attributes. **Elements** are either simple or complex. A **simple element** has a single data item. In Figure 7-23(a), the elements SeminarID, SeminarDate, SeminarTime, Location, and SeminarTitle are all simple elements.

A **complex element** can contain other elements that can be either simple or complex. In Figure 7-23(a), Seminar is a complex element and is followed by (after the annotations section) a section with <xsd:complexType> . . . </xsd:complexType> tags. It contains a sequence of the five simple elements SeminarID, SeminarDate, SeminarTime, Location, and SeminarTitle. Later you will see examples of complex types that contain other complex types.

Data types can be specified in simple elements. In Figure 7-23(a), the element SeminarID is typed as xsd:integer and the element Title is typed as xsd:string.

By default, the cardinality of both simple and complex elements is 1.1, meaning that a single value is required, and no more than a single value can be specified. This is similar to a NOT NULL constraint in SQL schema definitions. If an element did not have a required value, we would add minOccurs="0" to the element definition. This is similar to the NULL statement in SQL schema definitions.

Complex elements can have attributes. An **attribute** is used to specify a characteristic about a complex element. As a general rule, for database/XML applications, elements are used to store data, and attributes are used to store metadata. However, a detailed discussion of attributes is beyond the scope of this book—note that Figure 7-23(a) does *not* use any attributes, only elements.[14]

As shown in Figure 7-23(b), XML Schema can be represented graphically. Figure 7-24 shows an XML document that is valid on the XML Schema shown in Figure 7-23. Note

---

**FIGURE 7-24**

**Example Schema-Valid XML Document**

```
<?xml version="1.0" encoding="UTF-8"?>
<Seminar xmlns:xsi="http://www.w3.org/2001/XMLSchema-instance"
    xsi:noNamespaceSchemaLocation="C:\DBC-e05\Figure-07-24.xsd">
        <SeminarID>1</SeminarID>
        <SeminarDate>10/11/2009</SeminarDate>
        <SeminarTime>11:00</SeminarTime>
        <Location>San Antonio Convention Center</Location>
        <SeminarTitle>Kitchen on a Budget</SeminarTitle>
</Seminar>
```

---

[14]For more information on the use of attributes, see David M. Kroenke and David J. Auer, *Database Processing: Fundamentals, Design, and Implementation*, 11th edition (Upper Saddle River, NJ: Prentice Hall, 2010).

that the namespace xsi is defined. This namespace is used just once—for the noNamespaceSchemaLocation attribute. Do not be concerned about the name of this attribute—this is simply a means of telling the XML parser where to find the XML Schema for this document. The focus here is on the relationship of the structure of the document and the description in the XML Schema.

## XML and Database Processing

What does everything we have been discussing have to do with database processing? How are the XML documents to be generated in the first place? In addition, after a company has received and validated a document, how does it place the data from that document into its database?

The answer is to use database applications. Such applications can be written to generate XML documents that conform to an XML Schema, and they can be written to accept such XML documents and extract the data for storage in the database. The means by which this is done is currently under development. One way is to extend SQL to cause the results from an SQL statement to be produced in XML format. For example, Figure 7-25 shows the following SQL statement, which uses the **SQL FOR XML clause**, run on SQL Server:

```
SELECT   *
FROM     SEMINAR
         FOR XML AUTO, ELEMENTS;
```

Note that in Figure 7-25, the output (which is all in one cell in this format) in the Messages window is a hyperlink. Clicking the hyperlink produces the XML output shown in Figure 7-26.

This output is saved as a file named SEMINAR.XML and edited (with added <MyData> . . . </MyData> tags) into the text output shown in Figure 7-27.

---

**FIGURE 7-25**

**An SQL FOR XML Query**

SQL query with **FOR XML** clause

The query results are one cell containing the entire XML output—click the results to display them in full

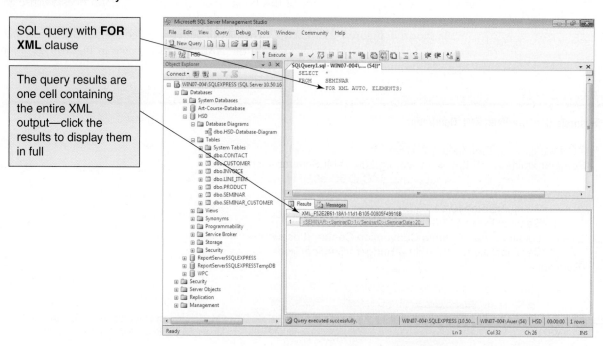

**FIGURE 7-26**

Results of the SQL FOR XML Query

The query results are now displayed in full—note the XML tags and data content

**FIGURE 7-27**

Text Output from the SQL FOR XML Query

```
<MyData>
    <SEMINAR>
        <SeminarID>1</SeminarID>
        <SeminarDate>2009-10-11T00:00:00</SeminarDate>
        <SeminarTime>1900-01-01T11:00:00</SeminarTime>
        <Location>San Antonio Convention Center</Location>
        <SeminarTitle>Kitchen on a Budget</SeminarTitle>
    </SEMINAR>
    <SEMINAR>
        <SeminarID>2</SeminarID>
        <SeminarDate>2009-10-25T00:00:00</SeminarDate>
        <SeminarTime>1900-01-01T16:00:00</SeminarTime>
        <Location>Dallas Convention Center</Location>
        <SeminarTitle>Kitchen on a Big D Budget</SeminarTitle>
    </SEMINAR>
    <SEMINAR>
        <SeminarID>3</SeminarID>
        <SeminarDate>2009-11-01T00:00:00</SeminarDate>
        <SeminarTime>1900-01-01T08:30:00</SeminarTime>
        <SeminarLocation>Austin Convention Center</Location>
        <SeminarTitle>Kitchen on a Budget</SeminarTitle>
    </SEMINAR>
    <SEMINAR>
        <SeminarID>4</SeminarID>
        <SeminarDate>2010-03-22T00:00:00</SeminarDate>
        <SeminarTime>1900-01-01T11:00:00</SeminarTime>
        <Location>Dallas Convention Center</Location>
        <SeminarTitle>Kitchen on a Big D Budget</SeminarTitle>
    </SEMINAR>
<MyData>
```

This solution is not satisfactory for a number of reasons. It works for certain data structures but not for all. Other means are currently being or have already been developed by Oracle, Microsoft, and additional companies.

## XML Web Services

The use of XML for the transmission of database data is especially important because of the development of a new standard called XML Web Services. **XML Web Services** (or just **Web Services**) involves several standards, including XML, and SOAP. XML is used for its ability to create data tags, and XML Web Services is a means for sharing elements of program functionality over the Web.

For example, suppose you have created a database application that converts currencies. Your program will receive the amount of money stated in one currency and convert it to a second currency. You can convert U.S. dollars into Mexican pesos, Japanese yen into euros, and so on. Using XML Web Services, you can publish your database application over the Web in such a way that other programs can consume your program as if it were on their own machine. It will appear to them as if they are using a local program, even though your program might be on the other side of the world.

Perhaps you have heard the statement "The Internet is the computer." That statement becomes a reality when different computers, connected via Internet plumbing, can share programs as if they were all on the same machine.

When database applications are written as XML Web Services, any computer in the world can access the database applications using standard interfaces, and it appears as if the applications are local to the machine that uses those applications. Thus, a business with a Web presence such as Costco or Best Buy can publish its ordering application as XML Web Services, and its vendors can write programs to consume that ordering application. The particulars are beyond the scope of this discussion, but Web Services are now pervasive in the Web environment.

## The NoSQL Movement

We have used the relational database model and SQL throughout this book. However, there is another school of thought that has led to what is known as the **NoSQL movement**,[15] although it has been noted that since most, but not all, associated DBMSs are also non-relational DBMSs and are often known as **structured storage**.[16]

A NoSQL DBMS is typically a distributed, replicated database as described Chapter 6, and used where this type of a DBMS is needed to support large datasets. For example, both Facebook and Twitter use the Apache Software Foundation's Cassandra database (available at **http://cassandra.apache.org/**).

Another type of implementation of a NoSQL database is one based on the use of the XML document structures we have just discussed for data storage. An example is the open source dbXML (available at **http://www.dbxml.com/**). XML databases typically support the W3C XQuery (**http://www.w3.org/TR/xquery/** and XPath (**http://www.w3.org/TR/xpath/**)standards.

The usefulness and importance of these non-relational DBMSs to organizations such as Facebook demonstrate that we can look forward to the development of not only improvements to the relational DBMSs but also to a very different approach to data storage and information processing.

---

[15]For a good overview, see the Wikipedia article on NoSQL available at **http://en.wikipedia.org/wiki/NoSQL**.

[16]See the Wikipedia article on Structured Storage at **http://en.wikipedia.org/wiki/Structured_storage**.

## THE ACCESS WORKBENCH

### Section 7

### Web Database Processing Using Microsoft Access

Now that we have built the Wallingford Motors CRM database, it is time to develop a Web application to allow Wallingford Motors' sales staff to access it over the Web. In this section, you will:

- Build a Web home page for Wallingford Motors
- Create an ODBC data source to access the WMCRM database
- Build a Web page to display data about customer contacts

#### Creating the Customer Contacts View

We want to display a list of customer contacts in a Web page. The list will contain a combination of data from the CONTACT and CUSTOMER tables. To simplify the process, we will define a view named viewCustomerContacts. SQL views are discussed in Chapter 3A; if you have not studied that material, take a few minutes to read it and work through Chapter 3A's section of "The Access Workbench." As discussed there, in Microsoft Access, a view is simply a saved query. Figure AW-7-1 shows the details of the viewCustomerContacts query.

There is nothing new here. You know how to create Microsoft Access QBE queries, so go ahead and create and save the viewCustomerContacts query. When you are done, close both the WMCRM database and Microsoft Access.

#### A Web Home Page for Wallingford Motors

The actions we need to take to create a Web page for Wallingford Motors (WM) are the same actions discussed for Heather Sweeney Designs in this chapter. We will create a

### FIGURE AW-7-1

The viewCustomerContacts Query

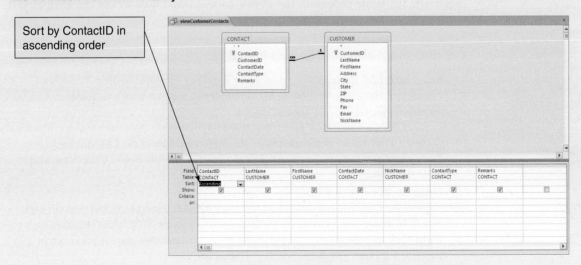

*(Continued)*

**FIGURE AW-7-2**

The HTML Code for the index.html File in the WM Folder

```html
<!DOCTYPE html PUBLIC "-//W3C//DTD HTML 4.01 Strict//EN"
      "http://www.w3.org/TR/html4/strict.dtd">
<html>
      <head>
            <meta http-equiv="Content-Type" content="text/html; charset=ISO-8859-1">
            <title>Wallingford Motors CRM Demonstration Pages Home Page</title>
      </head>
      <body>
            <h1 style="text-align: center; color: blue">
                Database Concepts (5th Edition)
            </h1>
            <h2 style="font-family: Ariel, sans-serif; text-align: center">
                The Access Workbench
            </h2>
            <hr />
            <h2 style="text-align: center; color: blue">
                Welcome to the Wallingford Motors Home Page
            </h2>
            <hr />
            <p>The Access Workbench Section 7 Web Pages:</p>
            <p>Report 1:   
                <a href="CustomerContacts.php">
                    Display the Customer Contacts List (viewCustomerContacts)
                </a>
            </p>
            <hr />
      </body>
</html>
```

folder to hold the Web site files and build a home page named index.html in that folder. The HTML code for the WM index.html page is shown in Figure AW-7-2.[17]

The code in Figure AW-7-2 can be used in any text editor or Web page editor, but the simplest editor to use for our purposes is the Microsoft Notepad ASCII text editor. Notepad is not fancy, but it does the job, produces clean HTML (what you type in and only what you type in), and comes with Windows. The following steps describe how to create the file using Notepad, but if you have learned how to use the Eclipse IDE described in the chapter, you can use it instead.

### Creating the Wallingford Motors Web Site

1. Select **Start | All Programs | Accessories | Windows Explorer** to open Windows Explorer. Expand the **C:** drive in **My Computer** so that the wwwroot folder is displayed. See Figure 7-10 for this display.
2. Expand the **wwwroot** folder to display the DBC folder.
3. Click the **DBC** folder object to display the folder and files in the DBC folder.
4. Right-click anywhere in the file pane to display the shortcut menu. Click **New**, and then click **Folder**.
5. Name the new folder **WM**.
6. Expand the DBC folder in the folder tree pane (the left hand pane), and then click the new **WM folder** object to display the folder and files in the WM folder (which is empty).
7. Right-click anywhere in the file pane (the right hand pane) to display the shortcut menu. Click **New**, and then click **Text Document**.

---

[17]If you are using IIS 5.1 on Windows XP and you haven't already added index.html to the list of default documents for the Web server, follow the steps in footnote 6 on page 388 to do so now.

## FIGURE AW-7-3

### The index.html File in Notepad

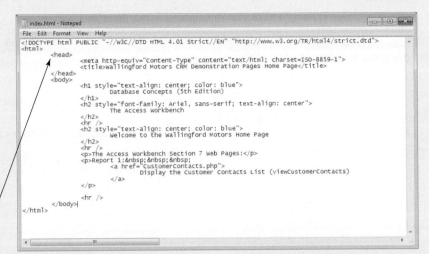

Note the indentation scheme used to identify and match HTML elements

8. Name the new text document **index.html.** When you complete renaming the file, a Rename dialog box will appear warning you that you are changing the file name extension. Click the **Yes** button in the Rename dialog box.
9. Right-click the **index.html** file to display the shortcut menu. Click **Open With**, and then click **Notepad**.
10. In Notepad, enter the text shown in Figure AW-7-2 into the open index.html.
11. Use the Notepad **File | Save** menu command to save the index.html file.
12. Close Notepad.

Notepad is a good, basic text editor that is available on every workstation running the Windows operating system. Dedicated Web page editors, however, do a superior job of working with HTML and PHP text. Figure AW-7-4 shows the index.html file being edited in Eclipse.

## FIGURE AW-7-4

### The index.html File in Eclipse

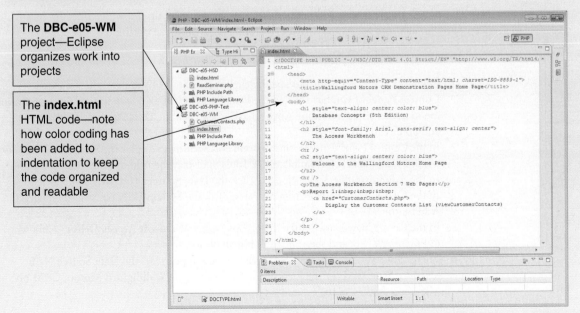

The **DBC-e05-WM** project—Eclipse organizes work into projects

The **index.html** HTML code—note how color coding has been added to indentation to keep the code organized and readable

*(Continued)*

**FIGURE AW-7-5**

The Wallingford Motors Home Page

Type the URL text here and then press the **Enter** key

Wallingford Motors CRM Demonstration Pages Home Page - Windows Internet Explorer

http://localhost/DBC/WM/ ▾ Google

Favorites Suggested Sites ▾ Web Slice Gallery ▾

Wallingford Motors CRM Demonstration Pages H... ▾ ▾ ▾ Page ▾ Safety ▾ Tools ▾ ▾

### Database Concepts (5th Edition)

#### The Access Workbench

#### Welcome to the Wallingford Motors Home Page

The Access Workbench Section 7 Web Pages:

Report 1: Display the Customer Contacts List (viewCustomerContacts)

Done  Internet | Protected Mode: On  100%

### Viewing the Wallingford Motors Web Site

1. Open Windows Internet Explorer or whatever Web browser you use.
2. Type the URL **http://localhost/DBC/WM** into the Address text box and press the **Enter** key. The WM home page appears in the Web browser, as shown in Figure AW-7-5.
3. Close the Web browser.

### Selecting the Database File

You will be working with the Wallingford Motors CRM database, so put a copy of the **WMCRM.accdb** file from your My Documents folder—which already contains the viewCustomerContacts query—in the WM Web site folder.

### Creating an ODBC Data Source

We now have the basic Wallingford Motors Web site set up. Now, we need to create an OBDC data source. Again, we follow steps similar to those outlined in the chapter.

### Creating the WM System Data Source

1. Open the Windows Control Panel by clicking the **Start** button, and then clicking **Control Panel** (if you have added the Data Sources (ODBC) icon to the Windows Start menu as described in Online Appendix E, then click the **Data sources (ODBC)** icon, and go directly to step 4).
2. In the Control Panel window, click **System and Security** to display the System and Security window, and then click **Administrative Tools** to display the Administrative Tools window.
3. In the Administrative Tools window, click the **Data Sources (ODBC)** shortcut icon.
4. In the ODBC Data Source Administrator, click the **System DSN** tab, and then click the **Add** button.
5. In the Create New Data Source dialog box, select **Microsoft Access Driver**, as shown in Figure AW-7-6, and then click the **Finish** button.
6. The ODBC Microsoft Access Setup dialog box appears. In the Data Source Name text box, type **WM**. In the Description text box, type **Wallingford Motors CRM on Microsoft Access 2010**.

**FIGURE AW-7-6**

Selecting the Microsoft Access Driver

Select this Microsoft Access driver

Click the **Finish** button

7. Click the **Database: Select** button, and then browse to the **WMCRM.accdb** database in the Select Database dialog box, as shown in Figure AW-7-7.
8. Click the **OK** button to close the Select Database dialog box.
9. Click the **OK** button to close the ODBC Microsoft Access Setup dialog box.
10. Click the **OK** button to close the ODBC Data Source Administrator.

### Creating the PHP Page

Now we need to create a PHP that we will name CustomerContacts.php. This is the Web page that will query the database and display the returned data. The code for the CustomerContacts.php is shown in Figure AW-7-8.

**FIGURE AW-7-7**

Selecting the WMCRM.accdb Database

Browse to the **c:\Inetpub\wwwroot\DBC\WM** folder (directory)

Select the **WMCRM.accdb** database

*(Continued)*

---

**FIGURE AW-7-8**

The PHP Code for CustomerContacts.php

```php
<!DOCTYPE HTML PUBLIC "-//W3C//DTD HTML 4.01 Frameset//EN">
<html>
    <head>
        <meta http-equiv="Content-Type" content="text/html; charset=UTF-8">
        <title>CustomerContacts PHP Page</title>
        <style type="text/css">
            h1 {text-align: center; color: blue}
            h2 {font-family: Ariel, sans-serif; text-align: left; color: blue}
            p.footer {text-align: center}
            table.output {font-family: Ariel, sans-serif}
        </style>
    </head>
    <body>
    <?php
        // Get connection
        $Conn = odbc_connect('WM', '', '');

        // Test connection
        if (!$Conn)
            {
                exit ("ODBC Connection Failed: " . $Conn);
            }
        // Create SQL statement
        $SQL = "SELECT * FROM viewCustomerContacts";

        // Execute SQL statement
        $RecordSet = odbc_exec($Conn,$SQL);

        // Test existence of recordset
        if (!$RecordSet)
            {
            exit ("SQL Statement Error: " . $SQL);
            }
    ?>
        <!-- Page Headers -->
        <h1>
            The Wallingford Motors CRM Customer Contacts List
        </h1>
        <hr />
        <h2>
            viewCustomerContacts
        </h2>
    <?php
        // Table headers
        echo "<table class='output' border='1'>
            <tr>
                <th>ContactID</th>
                <th>LastName</th>
                <th>FirstName</th>
                <th>ContactDate</th>
                <th>NickName</th>
                <th>ContactType</th>
                <th>Remarks</th>
            </tr>";
```

**FIGURE AW-7-8** *(Continued)*

```php
        // Table data
        while($RecordSetRow = odbc_fetch_array($RecordSet))
            {
            echo "<tr>";
            echo "<td>" . $RecordSetRow['ContactID'] . "</td>";
            echo "<td>" . $RecordSetRow['LastName'] . "</td>";
            echo "<td>" . $RecordSetRow['FirstName'] . "</td>";
            echo "<td>" . $RecordSetRow['ContactDate'] . "</td>";
            echo "<td>" . $RecordSetRow['NickName'] . "</td>";
            echo "<td>" . $RecordSetRow['ContactType'] . "</td>";
            echo "<td>" . $RecordSetRow['Remarks'] . "</td>";
            echo "</tr>";
            }
        echo "</table>";

        // Close connection
        odbc_close($Conn);
    ?>

    <br />
    <hr />
    <p class="footer">
        <a href="../WM/index.html">Return to Wallingford Motors Home Page</a>
    </p>
    <hr />
    </body>
</html>
```

We will create the CustomerContact.php file in the Eclipse IDE, but you could instead do this using Microsoft Notepad ASCII. We'll store the file in the WM folder. Figure AW-7-9 shows the CustomerContacts.php file being edited in Eclipse.

**FIGURE AW-7-9**

The CustomerContacts.php File in Eclipse

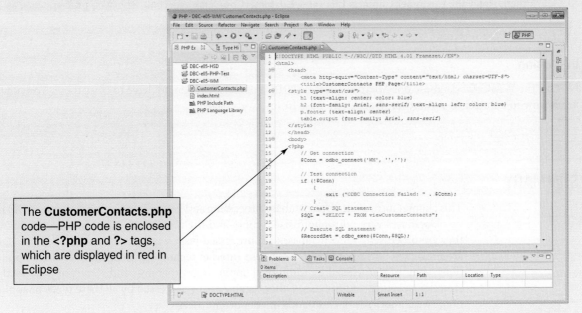

The **CustomerContacts.php** code—PHP code is enclosed in the **<?php** and **?>** tags, which are displayed in red in Eclipse

*(Continued)*

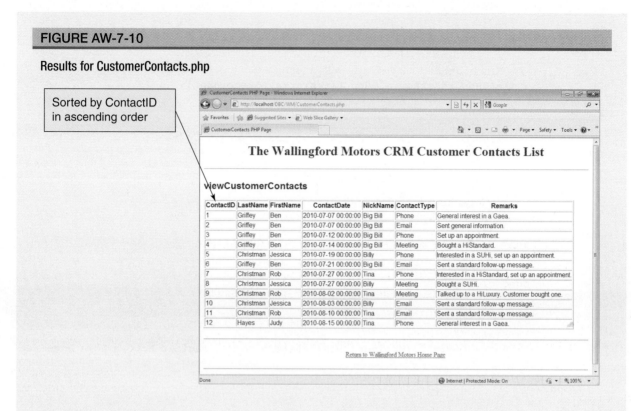

**FIGURE AW-7-10**

Results for CustomerContacts.php

Sorted by ContactID in ascending order

### Running the PHP Page

Now you can try out the CustomerContacts.php file.

### *Using the CustomerContacts.php File*

1. Open Internet Explorer or another Web browser.
2. Type the URL **http://localhost/DBC/WM** into the Address text box and press the **Enter** key. The WM home page appears in the Web browser.
3. Click the **Display the Customer Contacts List (viewCustomerContacts)** hyperlink. The Web page appears, as shown in Figure AW-7-10.
4. Close the Web browser.

### In Closing

Neither the WMCRM database nor Microsoft Access 2010 is open, so you do not have to close them. You now know how to connect to a Microsoft Access database from a Web page.

## SUMMARY

This chapter introduces Web database processing and Extensible Markup Language (XML). Databases vary not only in size, scope, and the number of users, but also in the way they are processed. Some databases are processed just by queries, forms, and reports; some are processed by ASP and JSP, which use Internet technology to publish database applications; some are processed by traditional application programs; and some are processed by stored procedures and triggers. Other databases are processed by all these types of applications, with hundreds or thousands of concurrent users.

Web database processing systems consist of users who use browsers that connect via HTTP to a Web server that processes communications and database applications. The database applications process the database via the DBMS. In a two-tiered system, the Web server and the DBMS reside on the same computer, but this is not a good configuration for performance and security reasons. Better is a three-tiered system, where the Web server and DBMS reside on different computers. Higher-capacity systems use more than one Web server, and may use multiple database servers in clusters.

If the Web server host runs Windows, the Web server software is usually IIS. IIS processes HTTP and ASP. ASP is a blend of HTML and scripting code. Database application logic is often processed using such scripts. If the Web server host runs Linux or Unix, the Web server software is normally Apache.

Every DBMS has its own API. The Open Database Connectivity (ODBC) standard provides an interface by which database applications can access and process relational data sources in a DBMS-independent manner. ODBC involves an applications program, a driver manager, a DBMS driver, and data source components. Single-tier and multiple-tier drivers are defined. The three types of data source names are file, system, and user. System data sources are recommended for Web servers. The process of defining a system data source name involves specifying the type of driver and the identity of the database to be processed.

Microsoft's latest Web server offering is ASP.NET. With it, object-oriented programming languages such as Visual Basic .NET, C#, and C++ can be used. ASP.NET pages are compiled and not interpreted.

Web database processing is complicated by the fact that HTTP is stateless. When processing atomic transactions, application programs must include logic to provide for session state. The means by which this is done depends on the Web server and language in use.

PHP (PHP: Hypertext Processor) is a scripting language that can be embedded in Web pages. PHP is extremely popular and easy to learn, and it can be used in most Web server environments and with most databases.

For creating complex pages, you need an Integrated Development Environment (IDE). An IDE gives you the most robust and user-friendly means of creating and maintaining Web pages. Microsoft Visual Studio, NetBeans for Java users, and the open-source Eclipse IDE are all good IDEs. Microsoft Visual Studio and Eclipse both provide a framework that can be modified by add-in modules. For PHP, a modification of Eclipse called the Eclipse PDT Project is specifically intended to provide a PHP development environment.

Using XML is becoming the standard means for defining documents and transmitting them from one computer to another. Increasingly, it is being used to transmit data to and from database applications. XML tags are not fixed but can be extended by document designers.

Although XML can be used to materialize Web pages, more important is its use for describing, representing, and materializing database views. XML is a better markup language than HTML primarily because XML provides a clear separation between document structure, content, and materialization. Also, XML tags are not ambiguous.

The content of XML documents can be described by document type definitions (DTDs) and by XML Schema documents. An XML document that conforms to its DTD is called type valid. A document can be well formed and not be type valid either because it violates the structure of its DTD or because it has no DTD.

XML documents are transformed when an XSLT processor applies an XSL document to the XML document.

XML Schema is a standard for describing the structure of an XML document. XML Schema can be used to define custom vocabularies. Documents that conform to XML Schema are called schema valid. Unlike DTDs, XML Schema documents are themselves XML documents and can be validated against their schema, which is maintained by W3C.

XML Schemas of elements and attributes. There are two types of elements: simple and complex. Simple elements have one data value. Complex elements can have multiple elements nested within them. Complex elements can also have attributes. The elements contained in a complex element can be simple or other complex elements. Complex elements can also define element sequences. Elements are generally used to represent data, and attributes are generally used to store metadata.

SQL Server, Oracle, and MySQL can produce XML documents from database data. SQL Server supports an add-on expression to the SQL SELECT statement, the FOR XML expression. FOR XML can be used to produce XML documents in which all data are expressed as attributes or as elements.

XML is important because it facilitates the sharing of XML documents (and hence database data) among organizations. After an XML Schema has been defined, organizations can ensure that they are receiving and sending only schema-valid documents. In addition, XSLT documents can be coded to transform any schema-valid XML document, from any source, into other standardized formats.

XML Web Services includes several standards that enable program functionality to be published, or consumed, over the Web. Thanks to XML Web Services, computer programs can use a database application across the Web as if that application were on the local machine. XML Web Services enables the Internet to become one large computer.

## KEY TERMS

.NET
?>
<?php
Active Data Objects (ADO)
Active Server Pages .NET (ASP.NET)
ADO.NET
AMP
Apache
Application Programming Interface (API)
attribute
complex element
data source
data source name (DSN)
Default Web Site folder
document type definitions (DTD)
driver
Eclipse IDE
Eclipse PDT (PHP Development Tools) Project
element
Extensible Markup Language (XML)
Extensible Style Language: Transformations (XSLT)

file data source
HTML document tags
HTML syntax rules
http://localhost
Hypertext Markup Language (HTML)
iisstart.asp
index.html
inetpub folder
Integrated Development Environment (IDE)
Internet Information Services (IIS)
Internet Information Services Manager
Java Server Pages (JSP)
LAMP
localstart.asp
multiple-tier driver
namespace
NoSQL
not-type-valid document
ODBC architecture
ODBC Data Source Administrator
ODBC DBMS driver
ODBC driver manager
OLE DB

Open Database Connectivity (ODBC)
PHP
PHP: Hypertext Processor
simple element
Simple Object Access Protocol
single-tier driver
SOAP
SQL FOR XML clause
SQL injection attack
stored procedure
structured storage
system data source
three-tier architecture
trigger
two-tier architecture
type-valid document
user data source
WAMP
Web Services
World Wide Web Consortium (W3C)
wwroot folder
XHTML
XML Schema
XML Web Services

## REVIEW QUESTIONS

**7.1** Describe five different ways databases can be processed (use Figure 7-2).

**7.2** What is a trigger, and how is it used?

**7.3** Name three types of triggers.

**7.4** Summarize the issues involved in processing a form, as described in this chapter.

**7.5** Describe, in your own words, the nature of traditional database processing applications.

**7.6**  Name the three major components of a Web database application.

**7.7**  What is a stored procedure, and how is it used?

**7.8**  Describe why the data environment is complicated.

**7.9**  As explained in this chapter, what are the two major functions of a Web server?

**7.10**  Explain the difference between two-tier and three-tier architecture.

**7.11**  What is IIS, and what functions does it serve?

**7.12**  What is Apache, and what function does it serve?

**7.13**  What do the abbreviations ASP and JSP stand for?

**7.14**  What is ASP.NET?

**7.15**  What are AMP, LAMP, and WAMP?

**7.16**  Explain the relationship among ODBC, OLE DB, and ADO.

**7.17**  Name the components of the ODBC standard.

**7.18**  What role does the DBMS driver serve?

**7.19**  What role does the driver manager serve?

**7.20**  What is a single-tier driver?

**7.21**  What is a multiple-tier driver?

**7.22**  Explain the differences between the three types of ODBC data sources.

**7.23**  Which ODBC data source type is recommended for Web servers?

**7.24**  What is Hypertext Markup Language (HTML), and what function does it serve?

**7.25**  What are HTML document tags, and how are they used?

**7.26**  What is an API, and what function does it serve?

**7.27**  What is the World Wide Web Consortium (W3C)?

**7.28**  Why is index.html a significant file name?

**7.29**  What is PHP, and what function does it serve?

**7.30**  How is PHP code designated in a Web page?

**7.31**  How are comments designated in PHP code?

**7.32**  How are comments designated in HTML code?

**7.33**  What is an Integrated Development Environment (IDE), and how is it used?

**7.34**  What is the Eclipse IDE?

**7.35**  What is the Eclipse PDT Project?

**7.36**  Show a snippet of PHP code for creating a connection to a database. Explain the meaning of the code.

**7.37**  Show a snippet of PHP code for creating a recordset. Explain the meaning of the code.

**7.38**  Show a snippet of PHP code for displaying the contents of a recordset. Explain the meaning of the code.

**7.39**  Show a snippet of PHP code for disconnecting from the database. Explain the meaning of the code.

**7.40**  In general terms, how are sessions managed by database applications when using HTTP?

**7.41**  With respect to HTTP, what does *stateless* mean?

**7.42**  Under what circumstances does statelessness pose a problem for database processing?

**7.43**  What are the problems in interpreting tags such as <h1> . . . </h1> in HTML?

**7.44**  What does *XML* stand for?

**7.45**  How does XML differ from HTML?

**7.46** Explain why XML is extensible.

**7.47** What is a DTD, and what purpose does it serve?

**7.48** What is the difference between a well-formed XML document and a type-valid XML document?

**7.49** What is the purpose of an XML Schema document?

**7.50** How does an XML Schema document differ from a DTD?

**7.51** What is a schema-valid document?

**7.52** How is an XML document validated?

**7.53** How is an XML Schema document validated?

**7.54** Explain an advantage of automated schema validation.

**7.55** Explain the difference between elements and attributes.

**7.56** Explain the difference between simple and complex elements.

**7.57** What is a general rule for using elements and attributes to represent database data?

**7.58** In general terms, explain why XML is important for database processing.

**7.59** What is the purpose of the FOR XML expression in an SQL statement?

**7.60** What is the purpose of XML Web Services?

## EXERCISES

**7.61** In this exercise, you will create a Web page in the DBC folder and link it to the HSD Web page in the HSD folder.

**A.** Figure 7-28 shows the HTML code for a Web page for the DBC folder. Note that the page is called index.html, the same name as the Web page in the HSD folder. This is not a problem because the files are in different folders. Create the index.html Web page in the DBC folder.

**B.** Figure 7-29 shows some additional HTML to be added near the end of the code for the HSD Web page in the file index.html in the HSD folder. Update the HSD index.html file with the code.

**C.** Try out the pages. Type **http://localhost/DBC** into your Web browser to display the DBC home page. From there, you should be able to move back and forth between the two pages by using the hyperlinks on each page. *Note:* You may need to click the Refresh button on your Web browser when using the HSD home page to get the hyperlink back to the DBC home page to work properly.

**7.62** Create a Web page for Heather Sweeney Designs to display all the data in the CUSTOMER table. Add a hyperlink to the HSD home page to access the page.

**7.63** Create a Web page for Heather Sweeney Designs to display the EmailAddress, LastName, FirstName, and Phone of customers in the CUSTOMER table. Add a hyperlink to the HSD home page to access the page.

**7.64** Create a Web page for Heather Sweeney Designs to display the data in the SEMINAR_CUSTOMER table. Add a hyperlink to the HSD home page to access the page.

**7.65** Create a Web page for Heather Sweeney Designs to display the data in the SEMINAR_CUSTOMER table for the SEMINAR with SeminarID = 3. Add a hyperlink to the HSD home page to access the page.

**FIGURE 7-28**

**The HTML Code for the index.html File in the DBC Folder**

```html
<!DOCTYPE html PUBLIC "-//W3C//DTD HTML 4.01 Strict//EN"
"http://www.w3.org/TR/html4/strict.dtd">
<html>
    <head>
            <meta http-equiv="Content-Type" content="text/html; charset=ISO-8859-1" />
            <title>DBC-e05 Home Page</title>
    </head>
    <body>
            <h1 style="text-align: center; color: blue">
                Database Concepts (5th Edition) Home Page
            </h1>
            <hr />
            <h3 style="text-align: center">
                Use this page to access Web-based materials from Chapter 7 of:
            </h3>
            <h2 style="text-align: center; color: blue">
                Database Concepts (5th Edition)
            </h2>
            <p style="text-align: center; font-weight: bold">
                David M. Kroenke
            </p>
            <p style="text-align: center; font-weight: bold">
                David J. Auer
            </p>
            <hr />
            <h3>Chapter 7 Demonstration Pages From Figures in the Text:</h3>
            <p>
                    <a href="HSD/index.html">
                            Heather Sweeney Designs Demonstration Pages
                    </a>
            </p>
            <p>
                    <a href="WM/index.html">
                            Wallingford Motors CRM Demonstration Pages
                    </a>
            </p>
            <hr />
    </body>
</html>
```

**7.66** Create a Web page for Heather Sweeney Designs to display data in the SEMINAR, SEMINAR_CUSTOMER, and CUSTOMER tables to list the SEMINAR data and the EmailAddress, LastName, FirstName, and Phone of any CUSTOMER who attended the SEMINAR with SeminarID = 3. Add a hyperlink to the HSD home page to access the page.

**7.67** Develop an XML Schema for a document that uses the data in the HSD SEMINAR, SEMINAR_CUSTOMER, and CUSTOMER tables. If you need more information about XML Schema, go to **www.w3.org** and read tutorials on XML and XML Schema. Create an example of an XML document for your schema. Use Internet Explorer (or any other program you find) to validate your three XML documents against your schema document.[18]

---

[18]A trial version of Altova's XMLSpy is available at **www.altova.com/xmlspy.html**. This is an excellent program for XML work.

**FIGURE 7-29**

The HTML Modifications for the index.html File in the DBC Folder

```
        <p>Chapter 7 Demonstration Pages From Figures in the Text:</p>
        <p>Example 1:   
            <a href="ReadSeminar.php">
                Display the SEMINAR Table (No surrogate key)
            </a>
        </p>
        <hr />
<!-- NEW CODE STARTS HERE -->
        <p style="text-align: center">
            <a href="../index.html">
                Return to the Database Concepts Home Page
            </a>
        </p>
        <hr />
<!-- NEW CODE ENDS HERE -->
        </body>
</html>
```

## ACCESS WORKBENCH EXERCISES

**AW.7.1**   If you haven't completed exercise 7.61, do it now.

**AW.7.2**   Link the WM Web page to the DBC Web page.

**AW.7.3**   Using the WMCRM database, code a PHP Web page to display the data in SALESPERSON. Add a hyperlink on the WM Web page to access the page. Using your database, demonstrate that your page works.

**AW.7.4**   Using the WMCRM database, code a PHP Web page to display the data in VEHICLE. Add a hyperlink on the WM Web page to access the page. Using your database, demonstrate that your page works.

**AW.7.5**   Using the WMCRM database, create a view named viewSalespersonVehicle and include in it all the columns in both the SALESPERSON and VEHICLE tables. Code a PHP Web page to display viewSalespersonVehicle. Add a hyperlink on the WM Web page to access the page. Using your database, demonstrate that your page works.

## GARDEN GLORY PROJECT QUESTIONS

If you have not already implemented the Garden Glory database shown in Chapter 3 in a DBMS product, create and populate the Garden-Glory database now in the DBMS of your choice (or as assigned by your instructor).

**A.**   Create a user named GG-User with the password GG-User+password. Assign this user to database roles so that the user can read, insert, delete, and modify data.

**B.**   If you haven't completed exercise 7.61, do it now.

**C.**   Add a new folder to the DBC Web site named GG. Create a Web page for Garden Glory in this folder—using the file name index.html. Link this page to the DBC Web page.

**D.** Create an appropriate ODBC data source for your database.

**E.** Code a Web page using PHP to display the data in PROPERTY. Add a hyperlink on the GG Web page to access the page. Using your database, demonstrate that your page works.

**F.** Code a Web page using PHP to display the data in SERVICE. Add a hyperlink on the GG Web page to access the page. Using your database, demonstrate that your page works.

**G.** Create a view named Property_Service_View that displays PROPERTY. PropertyID, PropertyName, SERVICE.EmployeeID, ServiceDate, and HoursWorked. Code a Web page using PHP to display the data in Property Service_View. Add a hyperlink to the GG Web page to access the page. Using your database, demonstrate that your page works.

## JAMES RIVER JEWELRY PROJECT QUESTIONS

If you have not already implemented the James River Jewelry database shown in Chapter 3 in a DBMS product, create and populate the James-River-Jewerly database now in the DBMS of your choice (or as assigned by your instructor).

**A.** Create a user named JRJ-User with the password JRJ-User+password. Assign this user to database roles so that the user can read, insert, delete, and modify data.

**B.** If you haven't completed exercise 7.61, do it now.

**C.** Add a new folder to the DBC Web site named JRJ. Create a Web page for James River Jewelry in this folder—use the file name index.html. Link this page to the DBC Web page.

**D.** Create an appropriate ODBC data source for your database.

**E.** Code a Web page using PHP to display the data in PURCHASE. Add a hyperlink on the JRJ Web page to access the page. Using your database, demonstrate that your page works.

**F.** Code a Web page using PHP to display the data in ITEM. Add a hyperlink on the JRJ Web page to access the page. Using your database, demonstrate that your page works.

**G.** Create a view named Purchase_Item_Item_View that displays PURCHASE. InvoiceNumber, PURCHASE_ITEM.ItemNumber, PURCHASE.InvoiceDate, ITEM. Description, and PURCHASE_ITEM.RetailPrice. Code a Web page using PHP to display the data in Purchase_Item_Item_View. Add a hyperlink to the JRJ Web page to access the page. Using your database, demonstrate that your page works.

## THE QUEEN ANNE CURIOSITY SHOP PROJECT QUESTIONS

If you have not already implemented the Queen Anne Curiosity Shop database shown in Chapter 3 in a DBMS product, create and populate the QACS database now in the DBMS of your choice (or as assigned by your instructor).

**A.** Create a user named QACS-User with the password QACS-User+password. Assign this user to database roles so that the user can read, insert, delete, and modify data.

**B.** If you haven't completed exercise 7.61, do it now.

C. Add a new folder to the DBC Web site named QACS. Create a Web page for the Queen Anne Curiosity Shop in this folder—use the file name index.html. Link this page to the DBC Web page.

D. Create an appropriate ODBC data source for your database.

E. Code a Web page using PHP to display the data in SALE. Add a hyperlink on the QACS Web page to access the page. Using your database, demonstrate that your page works.

F. Code a Web page using PHP to display the data in ITEM. Add a hyperlink on the QACS Web page to access the page. Using your database, demonstrate that your page works.

G. Create a view named Sale_Item_Item_View that displays SALE.SaleID, SALE_ITEM.SaleItemID, SALE.SaleDate, ITEM.ItemDescription, and SALE_ITEM.ItemPrice. Code a Web page using PHP to display the data in Sale_Item_Item_View. Add a hyperlink to the QACS Web page to access the page. Using your database, demonstrate that your page works.

# CHAPTER 8

# Database Processing for Business Intelligence Systems

## Chapter Objectives

> Learn the basic concepts of data warehouses and data marts

> Learn the basic concepts of dimensional databases

> Learn the basic concepts of business intelligence (BI) systems

> Learn the basic concepts of Online Analytical Processing (OLAP) and data mining

This chapter introduces topics that build on the fundamentals you have learned in the first seven chapters of this book. Now that we have designed and built a database, we are ready to put it to work. In Chapter 7, we built a Web database application. This chapter looks briefly at business intelligence (BI) applications, particularly Online Analytical Processing (OLAP) and data mining, and the data warehouse structures that they use.

In this chapter, we will continue to use the Heather Sweeney Designs database that we modeled in Chapter 4, designed in Chapter 5, created in Chapter 6, and built a Web database application for in Chapter 7. The name of the database is HSD, and an SQL Server database diagram for the HSD database is shown in Figure 8-1.

**FIGURE 8-1**

The HSD Database Diagram

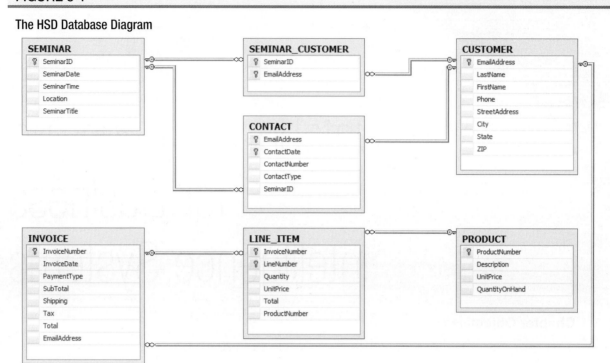

## BUSINESS INTELLIGENCE SYSTEMS

**Business intelligence (BI) systems** [also referred to as **decision support systems (DSSs)**] are information systems that assist managers and other professionals in the analysis of current and past activities and in the prediction of future events. Unlike transaction processing systems, they do not support operational activities, such as the recording and processing of orders. Instead, BI systems are used to support management assessment, analysis, planning, control, and, ultimately, decision making.

## THE RELATIONSHIP BETWEEN OPERATIONAL AND BI SYSTEMS

Figure 8-2 summarizes the relationship between operational and business intelligence systems. **Operational systems**—such as sales, purchasing, and inventory control systems—support primary business activities. They use a DBMS to both read data from and store data in the operational database. They are also known as **transactional systems** or **online transaction processing (OLTP) systems** because they record the ongoing stream of business transactions.

Instead of supporting the primary business activities, BI systems support management's analysis and decision-making activities. BI systems obtain data from three possible sources. First, they read and process data existing in the operational database—they use the operational DBMS to obtain such data, but they do not insert, modify, or delete operational data. Second, BI systems process data that are extracted from operational databases. In this situation, they manage the extracted database using a BI DBMS, which may be the same as or different from the operational DBMS. Finally, BI systems read data purchased from data vendors.

FIGURE 8-2

The Relationships Between Operational and BI Systems

## REPORTING SYSTEMS AND DATA MINING APPLICATIONS

BI systems fall into two broad categories: reporting systems and data mining applications. **Reporting systems** sort, filter, group, and make elementary calculations on operational data. **Data mining applications**, in contrast, perform sophisticated analyses on data, analyses that usually involve complex statistical and mathematical processing. The characteristics of BI applications are summarized in Figure 8-3.

### Reporting Systems

Reporting systems filter, sort, group, and make simple calculations. All reporting analyses can be performed using standard SQL, although extensions to SQL, such as those used for **Online Analytical Processing (OLAP)**, are sometimes used to ease the task of report production.

FIGURE 8-3

Characteristics of BI Applications

- Reporting
    - Filter, sort, group, and make simple calculations
    - Summarize current status
    - Compare current status to past or predicted status
    - Classify entities (customers, products, employees, etc.)
    - Report delivery crucial
- Data Mining
    - Often employ sophisticated statistical and mathematical techniques
    - Used for:
        - What-if analyses
        - Predictions
        - Decisions
    - Results often incorporated into some other report or system

Reporting systems summarize the current status of business activities and compare that status with past or predicted future activities. Report delivery is crucial. Reports must be delivered to the proper users on a timely basis, in the appropriate format. For example, reports may be delivered on paper, via a Web browser, or in some other format.

## Data Mining Applications

Data mining applications use sophisticated statistical and mathematical techniques to perform what-if analyses, to make predictions, and to facilitate decision making. For example, data mining techniques can analyze past cell phone usage and predict which customers are likely to switch to a competing phone company. Or, data mining can be used to analyze past loan behavior to determine which customers are most (or least) likely to default on a loan.

Report delivery is not as important for data mining systems as it is for reporting systems. First, most data mining applications have only a few users, and those users have sophisticated computer skills. Second, the results of a data mining analysis are usually incorporated into some other report, analysis, or information system. In the case of cell phone usage, the characteristics of customers who are in danger of switching to another company may be given to the sales department for action. Or, the parameters of an equation for determining the likelihood of a loan default may be incorporated into a loan approval application.

## DATA WAREHOUSES AND DATA MARTS

As shown in Figure 8-2, some BI applications read and process operational data directly from the operational database. Although this is possible for simple reporting systems and small databases, such direct reading of operational data is not feasible for more complex applications or larger databases. Operational data are difficult to use for several reasons:

- Querying data for BI applications can place a substantial burden on the DBMS and unacceptably slow the performance of operational applications.
- The creation and maintenance of BI systems requires application programs, facilities, and expertise that are not normally available from operations.
- Operational data have problems that limit their use for BI applications.

Therefore, larger organizations usually process a separate database constructed from an extract of the operational database.

### The Components of a Data Warehouse

A **data warehouse** is a database system that has data, programs, and personnel that specialize in the preparation of data for BI processing. Figure 8-4 shows the components of the basic data warehouse architecture. Data are read from operational databases by the **Extract, Transform, and Load (ETL) system**. The ETL system then cleans and prepares the data for BI processing. This can be a complex process.

First, operational data often cannot be directly loaded into BI applications. Some of the problems of using operational data for BI processing include:

- "Dirty data" (for example, problematic data such as value of "G" for customer gender, a value of "213" for customer age, a value of "999-999-9999" for a U.S. phone number, or a part color of "gren")

FIGURE 8-4

Components of a Data Warehouse

- Missing values
- Inconsistent data (for example, data that have changed, such as a customer's phone number or address)
- Nonintegrated data (for example, data from two or more sources that need to be combined for BI use)
- Incorrect format (for example, data that are gathered such that there are either too many data or not enough data, such as time measures in either seconds or hours when they are needed in minutes for BI use)
- Too much data (for example, an excess of columns [attributes], rows [records], or both)

Second, data may need to be changed or transformed for use in a data warehouse. For example, the operational systems may store data about countries using standard two-letter country codes, such as US (United States) and CA (Canada). However, applications using the data warehouse may need to use the country names in full. Thus, the data transformation {**CountryCode → CountryName**} will be needed before the data can be loaded into the data warehouse.

When the data are prepared for use, the ETL system loads the data into the data warehouse database. The extracted data are stored in a data warehouse database, using a data warehouse DBMS, which may be from a different vendor than the organization's operational DBMS. For example, an organization might use Oracle for its operational processing but use SQL Server for its data warehouse.

**B T W**

**Problematic operational data that have been cleaned in the ETL system can also be used to update the operational system to fix the original data problems.**

Metadata concerning the data's source, format, assumptions and constraints, and other facts is kept in a **data warehouse metadata database**. The data warehouse DBMS provides extracts of its data to BI tools, such as data mining programs.

## Data Warehouses Versus Data Marts

You can think of a data warehouse as a distributor in a supply chain. The data warehouse takes data from the data manufacturers (operational systems and purchased data), cleans and processes them, and locates the data on the shelves, so to speak, of the data warehouse. The people who work in a data warehouse are experts at data management, data cleaning, data transformation, and the like. However, they are not usually experts in a given business function.

A **data mart** is a collection of data that is smaller than that in the data warehouse and that addresses a particular component or functional area of the business. A data mart is like a retail store in a supply chain. Users in the data mart obtain from the data warehouse data that pertain to a particular business function. Such users do not have the data management expertise that data warehouse employees have, but they are knowledgeable analysts for a given business function.

Figure 8-5 illustrates these relationships. The data warehouse takes data from the data producers and distributes the data to three data marts. One data mart analyzes **click-stream data** for the purpose of designing Web pages. A second data mart analyzes store sales data and determines which products tend to be purchased together for the purpose of training sales staff. A third data mart analyzes customer order data for the purpose of reducing labor when picking up items at the warehouse. (Companies such as Amazon.com go to great lengths to organize their warehouses to reduce picking expenses.)

When the data mart structure shown in Figure 8-4 is combined with the data warehouse architecture shown in Figure 8-5, the combined system is known as an **enterprise data warehouse (EDW) architecture**. In this configuration, the data warehouse maintains all enterprise BI data and acts as the authoritative source for data extracts provided to the data marts. The data marts receive all their data from the data warehouse—they do not add or maintain any additional data.

### FIGURE 8-5

**Data Warehouses and Data Marts**

**FIGURE 8-6**

Characteristics of Operational and Dimensional Databases

| Operational Database | Dimensional Database |
|---|---|
| Used for structured transaction data processing | Used for unstructured analytical data processing |
| Current data are used | Current and historical data are used |
| Data are inserted, updated, and deleted by users | Data are loaded and updated systematically, not by users |

Of course, it is expensive to create, staff, and operate data warehouses and data marts, and only large organizations with deep pockets can afford to operate a system such as an EDW. Smaller organizations operate subsets of such systems. For example, they may have just a single data mart for analyzing marketing and promotion data.

## Dimensional Databases

The databases in a data warehouse or data mart are built to a different type of database design than the normalized relational databases used for operational systems. The data warehouse databases are built in a design called a **dimensional database** that is designed for efficient data queries and analysis. A dimensional database is used to store historical data rather than just the current data stored in an operational database. Figure 8-6 compares operational databases and dimensional databases.

Because dimensional databases are used for the analysis of historical data, they must be designed to handle data that change over time. For example, a customer may have moved from one residence to another in the same city or may have moved to a completely different city and state. This type of data arrangement is call a **slowly changing dimension**, and in order to track such changes a dimensional database must have a **date dimension** or **time dimension** as well.

**The Star Schema**   Rather than using the normalized database designs used in operational databases, a dimensional database uses a star schema. A **star schema**, so named because, as shown in Figure 8-7, it visually resembles a star, with a **fact table** at the center of the star and **dimension tables** radiating out from the center. The fact table is always fully normalized, but dimension tables may be non-normalized.

There is a more complex version of the star schema call the *snowflake schema*. In the snowflake schema, each dimension table is normalized, which may create additional tables attached to the dimension tables.

**FIGURE 8-7**

The Star Schema

A star schema for a dimensional database named HSD-DW for BI use by Heather Sweeney Designs is shown in Figure 8-8. The SQL statements needed to create the tables in the HSD-DW database are shown in Figure 8-9, and the data in the HSD-DW database are shown in Figure 8-10. Compare this model to the HSD database diagram shown in Figure 8-1 and note how data in the HSD database have been used in the HSD-DW schema.

---

**FIGURE 8-8**

The HSD-DW Star Schema

---

**FIGURE 8-9**

The HSD-DW SQL Statements

```
CREATE TABLE TIMELINE(
    TimeID          Int             NOT NULL,
    [Date]          DateTime        NOT NULL,
    MonthID         Int             NOT NULL,
    MonthText       Char(15)        NOT NULL,
    QuarterID       Int             NOT NULL,
    QuarterText     Char(10)        NOT NULL,
    [Year]          Char(10)        NOT NULL,
    CONSTRAINT      TIMELINE_PK     PRIMARY KEY(TimeID)
    );
```

FIGURE 8-9   *(Continued)*

```
CREATE TABLE CUSTOMER(
      CustomerID        Int             NOT NULL,
      CustomerName      Char(75)        NOT NULL,
      EmailDomain       VarChar(100)    NOT NULL,
      PhoneAreaCode     Char(6)         NOT NULL,
      City              Char(35)        NULL,
      [State]           Char(2)         NULL,
      ZIP               Char(10)        NULL,
      CONSTRAINT        CUSTOMER_PK     PRIMARY KEY(CustomerID)
      );

CREATE TABLE PRODUCT(
      ProductNumber     Char(35)        NOT NULL,
      ProductType       Char(25)        NOT NULL,
      ProductName       VarChar(75)     NOT NULL,
      CONSTRAINT        PRODUCT_PK      PRIMARY KEY(ProductNumber)
      );

CREATE TABLE PRODUCT_SALES(
      TimeID            Int             NOT NULL,
      CustomerID        Int             NOT NULL,
      ProductNumber     Char(35)        NOT NULL,
      Quantity          Int             NOT NULL,
      UnitPrice         Numeric(9,2)    NOT NULL,
      Total             Numeric(9,2)    NULL,
      CONSTRAINT        PRODUCT_SALES_PK
                        PRIMARY KEY (TimeID,CustomerID,ProductNumber),
      CONSTRAINT        PS_TIMELINE_FK FOREIGN KEY(TimeID)
                        REFERENCES TIMELINE(TimeID)
                            ON UPDATE NO ACTION
                            ON DELETE NO ACTION,
      CONSTRAINT        PS_CUSTOMER_FK FOREIGN KEY(CustomerID)
                        REFERENCES CUSTOMER(CustomerID)
                            ON UPDATE NO ACTION
                            ON DELETE NO ACTION,
      CONSTRAINT        PS_PRODUCT_FK FOREIGN KEY(ProductNumber)
                        REFERENCES PRODUCT(ProductNumber)
                            ON UPDATE NO ACTION
                            ON DELETE NO ACTION,
      );
```

**B T W**

Note that in the HSD-DW database the CUSTOMER table now has a surrogate primary key named CustomerID, which has an integer value. There are two reasons for this. First, the primary key EmailAddress used in the HSD database is simply too cumbersome for a data warehouse, so we switched to the preferable small and numeric surrogate key. Second, we do not use individual EmailAddress values in the HSD-DW database, only values of EmailDomain, which is not unique and cannot be used as a primary key.

**FIGURE 8-10**

**The HSD-DW Table Data**

| | TimeID | Date | MonthID | MonthText | QuarterID | QuarterText | Year |
|---|---|---|---|---|---|---|---|
| 1 | 40101 | 2009-10-15 ... | 10 | October | 3 | Qtr3 | 2009 |
| 2 | 40111 | 2009-10-25 ... | 10 | October | 3 | Qtr3 | 2009 |
| 3 | 40157 | 2009-12-20 ... | 12 | December | 3 | Qtr3 | 2009 |
| 4 | 40252 | 2010-03-25 ... | 3 | March | 1 | Qtr1 | 2010 |
| 5 | 40264 | 2010-03-27 ... | 3 | March | 1 | Qtr1 | 2010 |
| 6 | 40268 | 2010-03-31 ... | 3 | March | 1 | Qtr1 | 2010 |
| 7 | 40271 | 2010-04-03 ... | 4 | April | 2 | Qtr2 | 2010 |
| 8 | 40276 | 2010-04-08 ... | 4 | April | 2 | Qtr2 | 2010 |
| 9 | 40291 | 2010-04-23 ... | 4 | April | 2 | Qtr2 | 2010 |
| 10 | 40305 | 2010-05-07 ... | 5 | May | 2 | Qtr2 | 2010 |
| 11 | 40319 | 2010-05-21 ... | 5 | May | 2 | Qtr2 | 2010 |
| 12 | 40334 | 2010-06-05 ... | 6 | June | 2 | Qtr2 | 2010 |

(a) TIMELINE Dimension Table

| | CustomerID | CustomerName | EmailDomain | PhoneAreaCode | City | State | ZIP |
|---|---|---|---|---|---|---|---|
| 1 | 1 | Jacobs, Nancy | somewhere.com | 817 | Fort Worth | TX | 76110 |
| 2 | 2 | Jacobs, Chantel | somewhere.com | 817 | Fort Worth | TX | 76112 |
| 3 | 3 | Able, Ralph | somewhere.com | 210 | San Antonio | TX | 78214 |
| 4 | 4 | Baker, Susan | elsewhere.com | 210 | San Antonio | TX | 78216 |
| 5 | 5 | Eagleton, Sam | elsewhere.com | 210 | San Antonio | TX | 78218 |
| 6 | 6 | Foxtrot, Kathy | somewhere.com | 972 | Dallas | TX | 75220 |
| 7 | 7 | George, Sally | somewhere.com | 972 | Dallas | TX | 75223 |
| 8 | 8 | Hullett, Shawn | elsewhere.com | 972 | Dallas | TX | 75224 |
| 9 | 9 | Pearson, Bobbi | elsewhere.com | 512 | Austin | TX | 78710 |
| 10 | 10 | Ranger, Terry | somewhere.com | 512 | Austin | TX | 78712 |
| 11 | 11 | Tyler, Jenny | somewhere.com | 972 | Dallas | TX | 75225 |
| 12 | 12 | Wayne, Joan | elsewhere.com | 817 | Fort Worth | TX | 76115 |

(b) CUSTOMER Dimension Table

| | ProductNumber | ProductType | ProductName |
|---|---|---|---|
| 1 | BK001 | Book | Kitchen Remodeling Basics For Everyone |
| 2 | BK002 | Book | Advanced Kitchen Remodeling For Everyone |
| 3 | VB001 | Video Companion | Kitchen Remodeling Basics Video Companion |
| 4 | VB002 | Video Companion | Advanced Kitchen Remodeling Video Companion |
| 5 | VB003 | Video Companion | Kitchen Remodeling Dallas Style Video Companion |
| 6 | VK001 | DVD Video | Kitchen Remodeling Basics |
| 7 | VK002 | DVD Video | Advanced Kitchen Remodeling |
| 8 | VK003 | DVD Video | Kitchen Remodeling Dallas Style |
| 9 | VK004 | DVD Video | Heather Sweeney Seminar Live in Dallas on 25-OCT-07 |

(c) PRODUCT Dimension Table

| | TimeID | CustomerID | ProductNumber | Quantity | UnitPrice | Total |
|---|---|---|---|---|---|---|
| 1 | 40101 | 3 | VB001 | 1 | 7.99 | 7.99 |
| 2 | 40101 | 3 | VK001 | 1 | 14.95 | 14.95 |
| 3 | 40111 | 4 | BK001 | 1 | 24.95 | 24.95 |
| 4 | 40111 | 4 | VB001 | 1 | 7.99 | 7.99 |
| 5 | 40111 | 4 | VK001 | 1 | 14.95 | 14.95 |
| 6 | 40157 | 7 | VK004 | 1 | 24.95 | 24.95 |
| 7 | 40262 | 4 | BK002 | 1 | 24.95 | 24.95 |
| 8 | 40262 | 4 | VK002 | 1 | 14.95 | 14.95 |
| 9 | 40262 | 4 | VK004 | 1 | 24.95 | 24.95 |
| 10 | 40264 | 6 | BK002 | 1 | 24.95 | 24.95 |
| 11 | 40264 | 6 | VB003 | 1 | 9.99 | 9.99 |
| 12 | 40264 | 6 | VK002 | 1 | 14.95 | 14.95 |
| 13 | 40264 | 6 | VK003 | 1 | 19.95 | 19.95 |
| 14 | 40264 | 6 | VK004 | 1 | 24.95 | 24.95 |
| 15 | 40264 | 7 | BK001 | 1 | 24.95 | 24.95 |
| 16 | 40264 | 7 | BK002 | 1 | 24.95 | 24.95 |
| 17 | 40264 | 7 | VK003 | 1 | 19.95 | 19.95 |
| 18 | 40264 | 7 | VK004 | 1 | 24.95 | 24.95 |
| 19 | 40268 | 9 | BK001 | 1 | 24.95 | 24.95 |
| 20 | 40268 | 9 | VB001 | 1 | 7.99 | 7.99 |
| 21 | 40268 | 9 | VK001 | 1 | 14.95 | 14.95 |
| 22 | 40271 | 11 | VB003 | 2 | 9.99 | 19.98 |
| 23 | 40271 | 11 | VK003 | 2 | 19.95 | 39.90 |
| 24 | 40271 | 11 | VK004 | 2 | 24.95 | 49.90 |
| 25 | 40276 | 1 | BK001 | 1 | 24.95 | 24.95 |
| 26 | 40276 | 1 | VB001 | 1 | 7.99 | 7.99 |
| 27 | 40276 | 1 | VK001 | 1 | 14.95 | 14.95 |
| 28 | 40276 | 5 | BK001 | 1 | 24.95 | 24.95 |
| 29 | 40276 | 5 | VB001 | 1 | 7.99 | 7.99 |
| 30 | 40276 | 5 | VK001 | 1 | 14.95 | 14.95 |
| 31 | 40291 | 3 | BK001 | 1 | 24.95 | 24.95 |
| 32 | 40305 | 9 | VB002 | 1 | 7.99 | 7.99 |
| 33 | 40305 | 9 | VK002 | 1 | 14.95 | 14.95 |
| 34 | 40319 | 8 | VB003 | 1 | 9.99 | 9.99 |
| 35 | 40319 | 8 | VK003 | 1 | 19.95 | 19.95 |
| 36 | 40319 | 8 | VK004 | 1 | 24.95 | 24.95 |
| 37 | 40334 | 3 | BK002 | 1 | 24.95 | 24.95 |
| 38 | 40334 | 3 | VB001 | 1 | 7.99 | 7.99 |
| 39 | 40334 | 3 | VB002 | 2 | 7.99 | 15.98 |
| 40 | 40334 | 3 | VK001 | 1 | 14.95 | 14.95 |
| 41 | 40334 | 3 | VK002 | 2 | 14.95 | 29.90 |
| 42 | 40334 | 11 | VB002 | 2 | 7.99 | 15.98 |
| 43 | 40334 | 11 | VK002 | 2 | 14.95 | 29.90 |
| 44 | 40334 | 12 | BK002 | 1 | 24.95 | 24.95 |
| 45 | 40334 | 12 | VB003 | 1 | 9.99 | 9.99 |
| 46 | 40334 | 12 | VK002 | 1 | 14.95 | 14.95 |
| 47 | 40334 | 12 | VK003 | 1 | 19.95 | 19.95 |
| 48 | 40334 | 12 | VK004 | 1 | 24.95 | 24.95 |

(d) PRODUCT_SALES Fact Table

A fact table is used to store **measures** of business activity, which are quantitative or factual data about the entity represented by the fact table. For example, in the HSD-DW database, the fact table is PRODUCT_SALES:

PRODUCT_SALES (<u>TimeID</u>, <u>CustomerID</u>, <u>ProductNumber</u>, Quantity, UnitPrice, Total)

In this table:

- Quantity is quantitative data that record how many of the item were sold.
- UnitPrice is quantitative data that record the dollar price of each item sold.
- Total (= Quantity * UnitPrice) is quantitative data that record the total dollar value of the sale of this item.

The measures in the PRODUCT_SALES table are for *units of product per day.* We do not use individual sale data (which would be based on InvoiceNumber), but rather data summed for each customer for each day. For example, if you compare the HSD database INVOICE data in Figure 6-2 for Ralph Able for 6/5/10, you will see that Ralph made two purchases on that date (InvoiceNumber 35013 and InvoiceNumber 35016). In the HSD-DW database, however, these two purchases are summed into the PRODUCT_SALES data for Ralph (CustomerID = 3) for 6/5/10 (TimeID = 40334).

> **B T W**
>
> The TimeID values are the sequential *serial values* used in Microsoft Excel to represent dates. Starting with 01-JAN-1900 as date value 1, the date value is increased by 1 for each calendar day. Thus, 05-JUN-2010 = 40334. For more information, search "Date formats" in the Microsoft Excel help system.

A dimension table is used to record values of attributes that describe the fact measures in the fact table, and these attributes are used in queries to select and group the measures in the fact table. Thus, CUSTOMER records data about the customers referenced by CustomerID in the SALES table, TIMELINE provides data that can be used to interpret the SALES event in time (which month? which quarter?), and so on. A query to summarize product units sold by Customer (CustomerName) and Product (ProductName) would be:

```
SELECT      C.CustomerID, C.CustomerName,
            P.ProductNumber, P.ProductName,
            SUM(PS.Quantity) AS TotalQuantity
FROM        CUSTOMER C, PRODUCT_SALES PS, PRODUCT P
WHERE       C.CustomerID = PS.CustomerID
    AND     P.ProductNumber = PS.ProductNumber
GROUP BY    C.CustomerID, C.CustomerName,
            P.ProductNumber, P.ProductName
ORDER BY    C.CustomerID, P.ProductNumber;
```

The results of this query are shown in Figure 8-11.

In Chapter 5, we discussed how an N:M relationship is created in a database as two 1:N relationships by use of an intersection table. We also discussed how additional attributes can be added to the intersection table in an association relationship. Similarly, the fact table is an intersection table for the relationships between the dimension tables with additional measures also stored in it. And, as with all other intersection tables, the key of the fact table is a composite key made up of all the foreign keys to the dimension tables.

**Illustrating the Dimensional Model**   When you think of the word *dimension*, you might think of "two dimensional" or "three dimensional." The dimensional models can be illustrated by using a two-dimensional matrix and a three-dimensional cube. Figure 8-12 shows the SQL query results from Figure 8-11 displayed as a two-dimensional matrix of Product (using ProductNumber) and Customer (using CustomerID), with each cell showing the number of units of each product purchased by each customer. Note how ProductNumber and CustomerID define the two dimensions of the matrix CustomerID labels what would be the *x*-axis and ProductNumber labels the *y*-axis of the chart.

Figure 8-13 shows a three-dimensional cube with the same ProductNumber and CustomerID dimensions, but now with the added Time dimension on the *z*-axis. Now, instead of occupying a two-dimensional box, the total quantity of products purchased by each customer on each day occupies a small three-dimensional cube, and all these small cubes are combined to form a large cube.

**FIGURE 8-11**

**The HSD-DW Query Results**

| | CustomerID | CustomerName | ProductNumber | ProductName | TotalQuantity |
|---|---|---|---|---|---|
| 1 | 1 | Jacobs, Nancy | BK001 | Kitchen Remodeling Basics For Everyone | 1 |
| 2 | 1 | Jacobs, Nancy | VB001 | Kitchen Remodeling Basics Video Companion | 1 |
| 3 | 1 | Jacobs, Nancy | VK001 | Kitchen Remodeling Basics | 1 |
| 4 | 3 | Able, Ralph | BK001 | Kitchen Remodeling Basics For Everyone | 1 |
| 5 | 3 | Able, Ralph | BK002 | Advanced Kitchen Remodeling For Everyone | 1 |
| 6 | 3 | Able, Ralph | VB001 | Kitchen Remodeling Basics Video Companion | 1 |
| 7 | 3 | Able, Ralph | VB002 | Advanced Kitchen Remodeling Video Companion | 2 |
| 8 | 3 | Able, Ralph | VK001 | Kitchen Remodeling Basics | 2 |
| 9 | 3 | Able, Ralph | VK002 | Advanced Kitchen Remodeling | 2 |
| 10 | 4 | Baker, Susan | BK001 | Kitchen Remodeling Basics For Everyone | 1 |
| 11 | 4 | Baker, Susan | BK002 | Advanced Kitchen Remodeling For Everyone | 1 |
| 12 | 4 | Baker, Susan | VB001 | Kitchen Remodeling Basics Video Companion | 1 |
| 13 | 4 | Baker, Susan | VK001 | Kitchen Remodeling Basics | 1 |
| 14 | 4 | Baker, Susan | VK002 | Advanced Kitchen Remodeling | 1 |
| 15 | 4 | Baker, Susan | VK004 | Heather Sweeney Seminar Live in Dallas on 25-OCT-07 | 1 |
| 16 | 5 | Eagleton, Sam | BK001 | Kitchen Remodeling Basics For Everyone | 1 |
| 17 | 5 | Eagleton, Sam | VB001 | Kitchen Remodeling Basics Video Companion | 1 |
| 18 | 5 | Eagleton, Sam | VK001 | Kitchen Remodeling Basics | 1 |
| 19 | 6 | Foxtrot, Kathy | BK002 | Advanced Kitchen Remodeling For Everyone | 1 |
| 20 | 6 | Foxtrot, Kathy | VB003 | Kitchen Remodeling Dallas Style Video Companion | 1 |
| 21 | 6 | Foxtrot, Kathy | VK002 | Advanced Kitchen Remodeling | 1 |
| 22 | 6 | Foxtrot, Kathy | VK003 | Kitchen Remodeling Dallas Style | 1 |
| 23 | 6 | Foxtrot, Kathy | VK004 | Heather Sweeney Seminar Live in Dallas on 25-OCT-07 | 1 |
| 24 | 7 | George, Sally | BK001 | Kitchen Remodeling Basics For Everyone | 1 |
| 25 | 7 | George, Sally | BK002 | Advanced Kitchen Remodeling For Everyone | 1 |
| 26 | 7 | George, Sally | VK003 | Kitchen Remodeling Dallas Style | 1 |
| 27 | 7 | George, Sally | VK004 | Heather Sweeney Seminar Live in Dallas on 25-OCT-07 | 2 |
| 28 | 8 | Hullett, Shawn | VB003 | Kitchen Remodeling Dallas Style Video Companion | 1 |
| 29 | 8 | Hullett, Shawn | VK003 | Kitchen Remodeling Dallas Style | 1 |
| 30 | 8 | Hullett, Shawn | VK004 | Heather Sweeney Seminar Live in Dallas on 25-OCT-07 | 1 |
| 31 | 9 | Pearson, Bobbi | BK001 | Kitchen Remodeling Basics For Everyone | 1 |
| 32 | 9 | Pearson, Bobbi | VB001 | Kitchen Remodeling Basics Video Companion | 1 |
| 33 | 9 | Pearson, Bobbi | VB002 | Advanced Kitchen Remodeling Video Companion | 1 |
| 34 | 9 | Pearson, Bobbi | VK001 | Kitchen Remodeling Basics | 1 |
| 35 | 9 | Pearson, Bobbi | VK002 | Advanced Kitchen Remodeling | 1 |
| 36 | 11 | Tyler, Jenny | VB002 | Advanced Kitchen Remodeling Video Companion | 2 |
| 37 | 11 | Tyler, Jenny | VB003 | Kitchen Remodeling Dallas Style Video Companion | 2 |
| 38 | 11 | Tyler, Jenny | VK002 | Advanced Kitchen Remodeling | 2 |
| 39 | 11 | Tyler, Jenny | VK003 | Kitchen Remodeling Dallas Style | 2 |
| 40 | 11 | Tyler, Jenny | VK004 | Heather Sweeney Seminar Live in Dallas on 25-OCT-07 | 2 |
| 41 | 12 | Wayne, Joan | BK002 | Advanced Kitchen Remodeling For Everyone | 1 |
| 42 | 12 | Wayne, Joan | VB003 | Kitchen Remodeling Dallas Style Video Companion | 1 |
| 43 | 12 | Wayne, Joan | VK002 | Advanced Kitchen Remodeling | 1 |
| 44 | 12 | Wayne, Joan | VK003 | Kitchen Remodeling Dallas Style | 1 |
| 45 | 12 | Wayne, Joan | VK004 | Heather Sweeney Seminar Live in Dallas on 25-OCT-07 | 1 |

**FIGURE 8-12**

**The Two-Dimensional ProductNumber–CustomerID Matrix**

Each cell shows the total quantity of each product that has been purchased by each customer

| ProductNumber | CustomerID 1 | 2 | 3 | 4 | 5 | 6 | 7 | 8 | 9 | 10 | 11 | 12 |
|---|---|---|---|---|---|---|---|---|---|---|---|---|
| BK001 | 1 | | 1 | 1 | | | 1 | | 1 | | | |
| BK002 | | | 1 | 1 | | 1 | 1 | | | | | 1 |
| VB001 | 1 | | 2 | 1 | 1 | | | | 1 | | | |
| VB002 | | | 2 | | | | | | 1 | | 2 | |
| VB003 | | | | | | 1 | | 1 | | | 2 | 1 |
| VK001 | 1 | | 2 | 1 | 1 | | | | 1 | | | |
| VK002 | | | 2 | 1 | | 1 | | | 1 | | 2 | 1 |
| VK003 | | | | | | 1 | 1 | 1 | | | 2 | 1 |
| VK004 | | | | 1 | | 1 | 2 | 1 | | | 2 | 1 |

As human beings, we can visualize two-dimensional matrices and three-dimensional cubes. Although we cannot picture models with four, five, and more dimensions, BI systems and dimensional databases can handle such models.

**Multiple Fact Tables and Conformed Dimensions**   Data warehouse systems build dimensional models, as needed, to analyze BI questions, and the HSD-DW star schema in Figure 8-8 would be just one schema in a set of schemas. Figure 8-14 shows an extended HSD-DW schema.

In Figure 8-14, a second fact table named SALES_FOR_RFM has been added:

SALES_FOR_RFM (<u>TimeID</u>, <u>CustomerID</u>, <u>InvoiceNumber</u>, PreTaxTotalSale)

## FIGURE 8-13

The Three-Dimensional Time–ProductNumber–CustomerID Cube

Each cell will show the total quantity of each product that has been purchased by each customer on a specific date

This table shows that fact table primary keys do not need to be composed solely of foreign keys that link to dimension tables. In SALES_FOR_RFM, the primary key includes the InvoiceNumber attribute. This attribute is necessary because the composite key (TimeID, CustomerID) will not be unique and cannot be the primary key. Note

## FIGURE 8-14

The Extended HSD-DW Star Schema

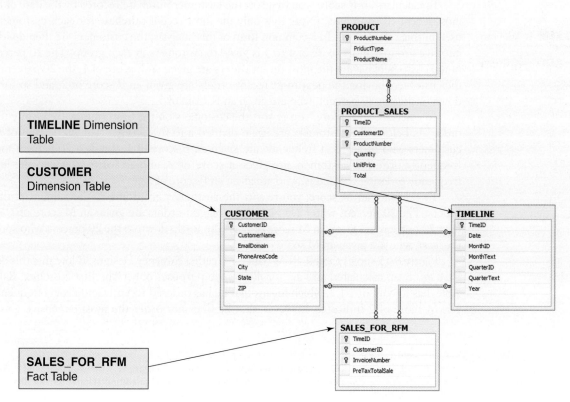

that SALES_FOR_RFM links to the same CUSTOMER and TIMELINE dimension tables as PRODUCT_SALES. This is done to maintain consistency within the data warehouse. When a dimension table links to two or more fact tables, it is called a **conformed dimension**.

Why would we add a fact table named SALES_FOR_RFM? To explain that, we need to move on to a discussion of reporting systems.

# REPORTING SYSTEMS

The purpose of a reporting system is to create meaningful information from disparate data sources and to deliver that information to the proper users on a timely basis. Unlike data mining, which uses sophisticated statistical techniques, reporting systems create information by using the simple operations of sorting, filtering, grouping, and making simple calculations.

It is easier to understand reporting systems if you are familiar with a typical report, so let us take a look at a typical reporting problem: RFM analysis.

## RFM Analysis

**RFM analysis** analyzes and ranks customers according to their purchasing patterns. It is a simple customer classification technique that considers how *recently* (**R**) a customer orders, how *frequently* (**F**) a customer orders, and *how much money* (**M**) the customer spends per order.

To produce an RFM score, we need only two things: customer data and sales data for each purchase (the date of the sale and the total amount of the sale) made by each customer. If you look at the SALES_FOR_RFM table and its associated CUSTOMER and TIMELINE dimension tables in Figure 8-14, you see that we have exactly those data: The SALES_FOR_RFM table is the starting point for RFM analysis in the HSD-DW BI system. Although we will not do it here, RFM analysis can be done using SQL statements and a table such as SALES_FOR_RFM.[1]

To calculate an **R score**, you first sort the customer purchase records by the date of the most recent (R) purchase. (Note that only the most recent purchase for each customer is used in this calculation.) In a common form of this analysis, the customers are then divided into five groups, and a score of 1 to 5 is given to customers in each group. The 20 percent of the customers having the most recent orders are given an R score of 1, the 20 percent of the customers having the next most recent orders are given an R score of 2, and so forth, down to the last 20 percent, who are given an R score of 5.

To calculate an **F score**, you re-sort the customers on the basis of how frequently they order. As before, the customers are again divided into five groups. The 20 percent of the customers who order most frequently are given an F score of 1, the next 20 percent most frequently ordering customers are given a score of 2, and so forth, down to the least frequently ordering customers, who are given an F score of 5.

To calculate an **M score**, you re-sort the customers according to the amount of their orders. The 20 percent who have placed the biggest orders are given an M score of 1, the next 20 percent are given an M score of 2, and so forth, down to the 20 percent who spend the least, who are given an M score of 5.

Figure 8-15 shows sample RFM data for Heather Sweeney Designs. (Note that this data have *not* been calculated and are for illustrative purposes only.) The first customer, Ralph Able, has a score of 1 1 2, which means that he has ordered recently and orders frequently. His M score of 2 indicates, however, that he does not order the most expensive goods.

---

[1]For a full discussion of RFM analysis using SQL statements, see David M. Kroenke and David J. Auer, *Database Processing: Fundamentals, Design, and Implementation*, 11th edition (Upper Saddle River, NJ: Prentice Hall, 2010).

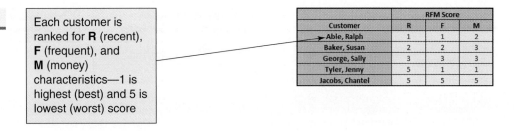

Each customer is ranked for **R** (recent), **F** (frequent), and **M** (money) characteristics—1 is highest (best) and 5 is lowest (worst) score

| Customer | RFM Score | | |
|---|---|---|---|
| | R | F | M |
| Able, Ralph | 1 | 1 | 2 |
| Baker, Susan | 2 | 2 | 3 |
| George, Sally | 3 | 3 | 3 |
| Tyler, Jenny | 5 | 1 | 1 |
| Jacobs, Chantel | 5 | 5 | 5 |

From these scores, the salespeople can surmise that Ralph is a good customer but that they should attempt to up-sell Ralph to more expensive goods.

Susan Baker is above average in terms of how frequently she shops and how recently she shops, but her purchases are average in value. Sally George is truly in the middle. Jenny Tyler could be a problem. Jenny has not ordered in some time, but in the past, when she did order, she ordered frequently, and her orders were of the highest monetary value. These data suggest that Jenny may be going to another vendor. Someone from the sales team should contact her immediately. However, no one on the sales team should be talking to Chantel Jacobs. She has not ordered for some time, she does not order frequently, and, when she does order, she only buys inexpensive items and not many of them.

## Reporting System Components

Figure 8-16 shows the major components of a reporting system. Data from disparate data sources are read and processed. As shown, reporting systems can obtain data from operational databases, data warehouses, and data marts.

A reporting system maintains a database of reporting metadata. The metadata describes reports, users, groups, roles, events, and other entities involved in the reporting activity. The reporting system uses the metadata to prepare and deliver appropriate reports to the proper users in the correct format on a timely basis.

As shown in Figure 8-16, reports can be prepared in a variety of media or formats. Figure 8-17 lists report characteristics.

**Report Types**  Some reports are **static reports**. They are prepared once from the underlying data, and they do not change. A report of the past year's sales, for example, is a static report. Other reports are **dynamic reports**; at the time of their creation, the reporting

**FIGURE 8-17**

Report
Characteristics

| Report Type | Report Media | Report Mode |
| --- | --- | --- |
| Static | Paper | Push |
| Dynamic | Web Portal | Pull |
| Query | Digital Dashboard | |
| OLAP | Email Alert | |
| | XML Web Service and Application Specific | |

system reads the latest, most current data and generates the report using those fresh data. Reports on today's sales and on current stock prices are dynamic reports.

**Query reports** are prepared in response to information entered by users. Google is an example of a reporting system that uses query reports: You enter the keywords you want to search for, and Google's reporting system searches its database and generates a response that is particular to your query. Within a specific organization, such as Heather Sweeney Designs, a query report could be generated to show current inventory levels. The user would enter item numbers, and the reporting system would respond with inventory levels of those items.

In terms of the reporting system, OLAP reports enable the user to dynamically change the report grouping structures. We will discuss OLAP later in this chapter.

**Report Media**   As illustrated in Figure 8-16 and summarized in Figure 8-17, reports are delivered via many different channels. Some reports are printed on paper, or its electronic equivalents, such as in PDF format. Other reports are delivered via **Web portals**. An organization might place a sales report on the sales department's Web portal and a report on customers serviced on the customer service department's Web portal.

A **digital dashboard** is an electronic display that is customized for a particular user. Companies such as Google, MSN, and Yahoo! offer digital dashboard services that you might have seen or used. Users can define the content they want to see—say, a local weather forecast, a list of stock prices, and a list of news sources—and the vendor constructs a customized display for each user. Such pages are called, for example, iGoogle, My MSN, and My Yahoo!. Other dashboards are designed specifically for organizations. Executives at a manufacturing organization, for example, might have a dashboard that shows up-to-the-minute production and sales activities.

Reports can also be delivered via **alerts**. Users can indicate that they want to be notified of news and events by email or cell phone. (Some cell phones are even capable of displaying Web pages and can use digital dashboards.)

Finally, reports can be delivered to other information systems. The modern way to do this is to publish reports via XML Web Services, as discussed in Chapter 7. This style of reporting is particularly useful for interorganizational information systems, such as supply chain management.

**Report Modes**   The final report characteristic summarized in Figure 8-17 is report mode. A **push report** is sent to users based on a predetermined schedule. Users receive the report without any activity on their part. In contrast, users must request a **pull report**. To obtain a pull report, a user goes to a Web portal or digital dashboard and clicks a link or button to cause the reporting system to produce and deliver the report.

## Report System Functions

As shown in Figure 8-16, report systems serve three functions: report management, report authoring, and report delivery. **Report management** consists of defining who receives what reports, when, and by what means. Most report management systems enable the report system administrator to define user accounts and user groups and to assign particular users to particular groups. For example, all the salespeople would be assigned to the Sales group, all upper-level management would be assigned to the Executive group, and so forth. All these objects and assignments are stored in the reporting system metadata shown in Figure 8-16.

**Report authoring** involves connecting to the required data sources, creating the report structure, and formatting the report. Reports created using a report authoring system are then assigned to groups and users. Assigning reports to groups saves the administrator work; when a report is created, changed, or removed, the administrator need only change the report assignments of the group, and all the users in the group will inherit the changes. The report assignment metadata not only includes the user or group and the reports assigned but also indicates the format of the report that should be sent to the user, the channel by which the report will be delivered, and whether the report is to be pushed or pulled. If it is to be pushed, the administrator declares whether the report is to be generated on a regular schedule or as an alert.

The **report delivery** function of a reporting system pushes reports or allows them to be pulled based on the report management metadata. Reports can be delivered via an email server, a Web portal, XML Web Services, or by other program-specific means. The report delivery system uses the operating system and other program security components to ensure that only authorized users receive authorized reports, and it also ensures that push reports are produced at appropriate times.

For query reports, the report delivery system serves as an intermediary between the user and the report generator. It receives a user query request, such as the item numbers in an inventory query, passes the query request to the report generator, receives the resulting report, and delivers the report to the user.

## OLAP

OLAP provides the ability to sum, count, average, and perform other simple arithmetic operations on groups of data. OLAP systems produce **OLAP reports**. An OLAP report is also called an **OLAP cube**. This is a reference to the dimensional data model, and some OLAP products show OLAP displays using three axes, like a geometric cube. The remarkable characteristic of an OLAP report is that it is dynamic: The format of an OLAP report can be changed by the viewer, hence the term *online* in the name Online Analytical Processing.

OLAP uses the dimensional database model discussed earlier in this chapter, so it is not surprising to learn that an OLAP report has measures and dimensions. A measure is a dimensional model *fact*—the data item of interest that is to be summed or averaged or otherwise processed in the OLAP report. For example, sales data may be summed to produce Total Sales or averaged to produce Average Sales. The term *measure* is used because you are dealing with quantities that have been or can be measured and recorded. A dimension, as you have already learned, is an attribute or a characteristic of a measure. Purchase date (TimeID), customer location (City), and sales region (ZIP or State) are all examples of dimensions, and in the HSD-DW database you saw how the time dimension is important.

In this section, we will generate an OLAP report by using an SQL query from the HSD-DW database and a Microsoft Excel **PivotTable**.

---

**B T W**

We use Microsoft SQL Server and Microsoft Excel to illustrate this discussion of OLAP reports and PivotTables. For other DBMS products, such as MySQL, you can use the DataPilot feature of the Calc spreadsheet application in the OpenOffice.org product suite (see **www.openoffice.org**).

---

Now we:

*Either:*
- Create an Microsoft Excel formatted table in an Microsoft Excel worksheet:
  - Copy the SQL query results into an Microsoft Excel worksheet.
  - Add column names to the results.

- Format the query results as an Microsoft Excel table (optional).
- Select the Microsoft Excel range containing the results with column names.

*or:*

- Connect to a DBMS data source.

*Then:*

- Click the PivotTable button in the Tables group of the Insert ribbon.
- Specify that the PivotTable should be in a new worksheet.
- Select the column variables (Column Labels), row variables (Row Labels), and the measure to be displayed (Values).

We can use an SQL query if we copy the data into an Microsoft Excel worksheet. The SQL query, as used in SQL Server, is:

```
SELECT      C.CustomerID, CustomerName, C.City,
            P.ProductNumber, P.ProductName,
            T.[Year], T.QuarterText,
            SUM(PS.Quantity) AS TotalQuantity
FROM        CUSTOMER C, PRODUCT_SALES PS, PRODUCT P,
            TIMELINE T
WHERE       C.CustomerID = PS.CustomerID
     AND    P.ProductNumber = PS.ProductNumber
     AND    T.TimeID = PS.TimeID
GROUP BY    C.CustomerID, C.CustomerName, C.City,
            P.ProductNumber, P.ProductName,
            T.QuarterText, T.[Year]
ORDER BY    C.CustomerName, T.[Year], T.QuarterText;
```

However, because SQL Server (and other SQL-based DBMS products, such as Oracle and MySQL) can store views but not queries, we need to create and use an SQL view if we are going to use an Microsoft Excel data connection. The SQL query to create the HSDDWProductSalesView, as used in SQL Server, is:

```
CREATE VIEW HSDDWProductSalesView AS
SELECT      C.CustomerID, C.CustomerName, C.City,
            P.ProductNumber, P.ProductName,
            T.[Year], T.QuarterText,
            SUM(PS.Quantity) AS TotalQuantity
FROM        CUSTOMER C, PRODUCT_SALES PS, PRODUCT P, TIMELINE T
WHERE       C.CustomerID = PS.CustomerID
     AND    P.ProductNumber = PS.ProductNumber
     AND    T.TimeID = PS.TimeID
GROUP BY    C.CustomerID, C.CustomerName, C.City,
            P.ProductNumber, P.ProductName,
            T.QuarterText, T.[Year];
```

Figure 8-18 shows the OLAP report as an Microsoft Excel PivotTable. Here, the measure is quantity sold, and the dimensions are ProductNumber and City. This report shows how quantity varies by product and city. For example, four copies of VB003 (Kitchen Remodeling Dallas Style Video Companion) were sold in Dallas, but none were sold in Austin.

**FIGURE 8-18**

OLAP ProductNumber by City Report

The **PivotTable** button

The **PivotTable Field List** pane—select the report elements to be displayed here

The **PivotTable report**

The PivotTable is in the **HSD-DW-Pivot-Table** worksheet

The data table is in the **SQL-Query-Results** worksheet

We have generated the OLAP report in Figure 8-18 by using a simple SQL query and Microsoft Excel, but many DBMS and BI products include more powerful and sophisticated tools. For example, SQL Server includes SQL Server Analysis Services.[2] It is possible to display OLAP cubes in many ways besides with Microsoft Excel. Some third-party vendors provide more sophisticated graphical displays, and OLAP reports can be delivered just like any of the other reports described for report management systems.

The distinguishing characteristic of an OLAP report is that the user can alter the format of the report. Figure 8-19 shows an alteration in which the user added two additional

**FIGURE 8-19**

OLAP ProductNumber by City, Customer, and Year Report

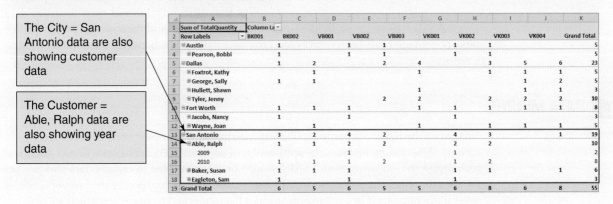

The City = San Antonio data are also showing customer data

The Customer = Able, Ralph data are also showing year data

| | A | B | C | D | E | F | G | H | I | J | K |
|---|---|---|---|---|---|---|---|---|---|---|---|
| 1 | Sum of TotalQuantity | Column La ▼ | | | | | | | | | |
| 2 | Row Labels ▼ | BK001 | BK002 | VB001 | VB002 | VB003 | VK001 | VK002 | VK003 | VK004 | Grand Total |
| 3 | ⊟Austin | 1 | | | 1 | 1 | | 1 | 1 | | 5 |
| 4 | ⊞Pearson, Bobbi | 1 | | | 1 | 1 | | 1 | 1 | | 5 |
| 5 | ⊟Dallas | 1 | 2 | | | 2 | 4 | | 3 | 5 | 6 | 23 |
| 6 | ⊞Foxtrot, Kathy | | | 1 | | | 1 | | 1 | 1 | 1 | 5 |
| 7 | ⊞George, Sally | 1 | 1 | | | | | | 1 | 2 | 5 |
| 8 | ⊞Hullett, Shawn | | | | | | 1 | | 1 | 1 | 3 |
| 9 | ⊞Tyler, Jenny | | | | 2 | 2 | | 2 | 2 | 2 | 10 |
| 10 | ⊟Fort Worth | 1 | | 1 | 1 | | 1 | 1 | 1 | 1 | 8 |
| 11 | ⊞Jacobs, Nancy | 1 | | | 1 | | | 1 | | | 3 |
| 12 | ⊞Wayne, Joan | | | 1 | | | 1 | | 1 | 1 | 1 | 5 |
| 13 | ⊟San Antonio | 3 | 2 | 4 | 2 | | 4 | 3 | | 1 | 19 |
| 14 | ⊟Able, Ralph | 1 | 1 | 2 | 2 | | 2 | 2 | | | 10 |
| 15 | 2009 | | | 1 | | | 1 | | | | 2 |
| 16 | 2010 | 1 | 1 | 1 | 2 | | 1 | 2 | | | 8 |
| 17 | ⊞Baker, Susan | 1 | 1 | 1 | | | 1 | 1 | | 1 | 6 |
| 18 | ⊞Eagleton, Sam | 1 | | 1 | | | 1 | | | | 3 |
| 19 | Grand Total | 6 | 5 | 6 | 5 | 5 | 6 | 8 | 6 | 8 | 55 |

[2]Up to this point in this book, we have been using SQL Server 2008 Express, and we have been able to do all the tasks discussed on that version of SQL Server. Unfortunately, SQL Server 2008 Express does not include SQL Server Analysis Services, so you will have to use the SQL Server Standard Edition or better if you want to use the SQL Server Analysis Services. Although OLAP reports *can* be done without SQL Server Analysis Services, Analysis Service adds a lot of functionality, and the Microsoft SQL Server 2008 Data Mining Add-ins for Microsoft Office 2007 (used in this text) will not function without it. Search the Microsoft Web site (www.microsoft.com) for more information. Also note that as this book goes to press, the Microsoft SQL Server 2008 R2 Data Mining Add-ins for Office 2010 have *not* been released, but we expect that they will be released soon.

## FIGURE 8-20

**OLAP City by ProductNumber, Customer, and Year Report**

The City variable is on the column designator

The ProductID variable is on the primary row designator

The ProductID = VB001 data are also showing **Customer** data

The Customer = Able, Ralph data are also showing year data

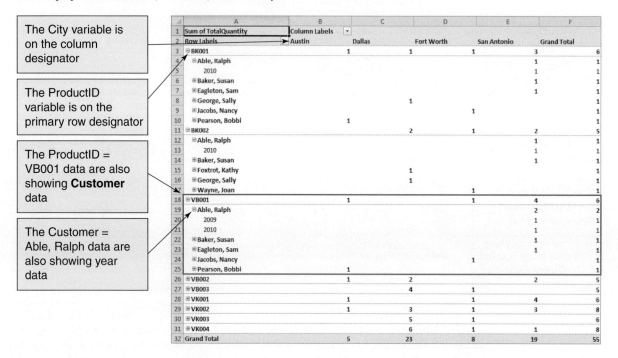

dimensions, customer and year, to the horizontal display. Quantity sold is now broken out by customer and, in one case, by year. With an OLAP report, it is possible to **drill down** into the data—that is, to further divide the data into more detail. In Figure 8-19, for example, the user has drilled down into the San Antonio data to display all customer data for that city and to display year sales data for Ralph Able.

In an OLAP report, it is also possible to change the order of the dimensions. Figure 8-20 shows city quantities as vertical data, and ProductID quantities as horizontal data. This OLAP report shows quantity sold by city, by product, customer, and year.

Both displays are valid and useful, depending on the user's perspective. A product manager might like to see product families first (ProductID) and then location data (city). A sales manager might like to see location data first and then product data. OLAP reports provide both perspectives, and the user can switch between them while viewing a report.

## DATA MINING

Instead of the basic calculations, filtering, sorting, and grouping used in reporting applications, data mining involves the application of sophisticated mathematical and statistical techniques to find patterns and relationships that can be used to classify data and predict future outcomes. As shown in Figure 8-21, data mining represents the convergence of several phenomena. Data mining techniques have emerged from the statistical and mathematics disciplines and from the artificial intelligence and machine-learning communities. In fact, data mining terminology is an odd combination of terms used by these different disciplines.

Data mining techniques take advantage of developments for processing enormous databases that have emerged in the past dozen or so years. Of course, all these data would not have been generated were it not for fast and inexpensive computers, and, without such computers, the new techniques would be impossible to compute.

**FIGURE 8-21**

Convergence of
Disciplines for Data
Mining

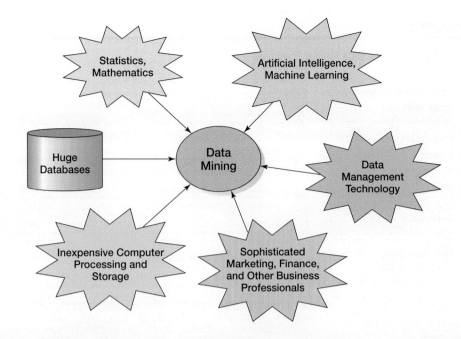

Most data mining techniques are sophisticated and difficult to use. However, such techniques are valuable to organizations, and some business professionals, especially those in finance and marketing, have developed expertise in their use. Almost all data mining techniques require specialized software. Popular data mining products are Enterprise Miner from SAS Corporation, Clementine from SPSS, and Insightful Miner from Insightful Corporation. However, there is a movement to make data mining available to more users. For example, Microsoft has created the Microsoft SQL Server 2008 Data Mining Add-ins for Office 2007.[3] As this book goes to press, Microsoft has not released data mining add-ins specifically for SQL Server 2008 R2 and Microsoft Office 2010. However, the current data mining add-ins seem to work with both products, and Figure 8-22 shows Microsoft Excel 2010 with the Data Mining command tab and command groups. With this add-in, data stored in Microsoft Excel are sent to SQL Server Analysis Services for processing, and the results are returned to Microsoft Excel for display.

Data mining techniques fall into two broad categories: unsupervised and supervised.

## Unsupervised Data Mining

When using **unsupervised data mining** techniques, analysts do not create a model or hypothesis prior to beginning the analysis. Instead, the data mining technique is applied to the data, and results are observed. After the analysis, explanations and hypotheses are created to explain the patterns found.

One commonly used unsupervised technique is **cluster analysis**. With cluster analysis, statistical techniques are used to identify groups of entities that have similar characteristics. A common use for cluster analysis is to find customer groups in order and customer demographic data. For example, Heather Sweeney Designs could use cluster analysis to determine which groups of customers are associated with the purchase of specific

---

[3]The Microsoft SQL Server 2008 Data Mining Add-ins for Office 2007 are available as part of the Microsoft SQL Server 2008 Feature Pack available at **www.microsoft.com/downloads/details.aspx?displaylang=en&FamilyID= ceb4346f-657f-4d28-83f5-aae0c5c83d52**. Note, however, that these add-ins will not work with SQL Server Express Edition. You have to have a version of SQL Server with SQL Server Analysis Services. Also note that as this book goes to press, the Microsoft SQL Server 2008 R2 Data Mining Add-ins for Office 2010 have *not* been released, but we expect that they will be released soon.

**FIGURE 8-22**

The Microsoft Excel Data Mining Command Tab

The **Data Mining** command tab

The **Cluster Analysis** button

The connection to SQL Server 2008 R2 Analysis Services

The data table is in the SQL-Query-Results worksheet

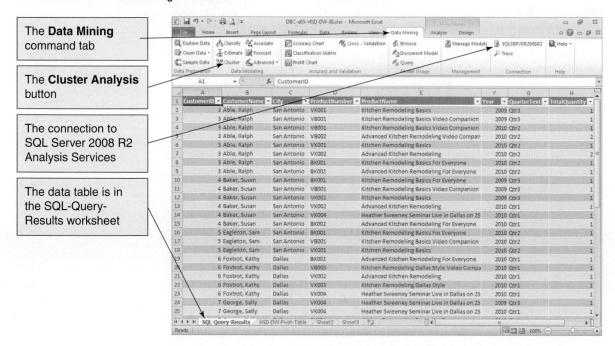

products. Figure 8-23 shows part of the results of a cluster analysis using the same HSD-DW data table in Microsoft Excel that we used to create the OLAP reports. In this case, the cluster analysis tool was asked to generate exactly two clusters based on the ProductID and City variables. Based on the analysis, it is clear that there are different sales patterns for the Dallas area and the non–Dallas area (primarily San Antonio).

**FIGURE 8-23**

The Cluster Analysis Results

The **Cluster Diagram** tab

The Shading Variable is City and the cluster with **City = Dallas** is shaded

**Cluster 2** is based on **City = Dallas**

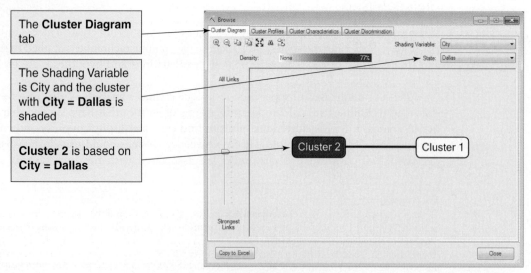

(a) The Cluster Diagram

**FIGURE 8-23**  *(Continued)*

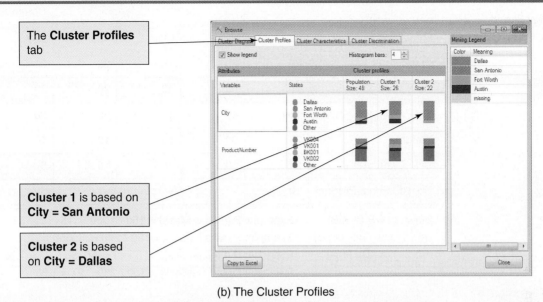

The **Cluster Profiles** tab

**Cluster 1** is based on **City = San Antonio**

**Cluster 2** is based on **City = Dallas**

(b) The Cluster Profiles

## Supervised Data Mining

When using **supervised data mining** techniques, data miners develop a model prior to the analysis and then apply statistical techniques to the data to estimate parameters of the model. For example, suppose that marketing experts at a communications company believe that the use of cell phone weekend minutes is determined by the age of the customer and the number of months the customer has had the cell phone account. A data mining analyst would then run a statistical analysis technique known as **regression analysis** to determine the coefficients of the equation of that model.

Three other popular data mining techniques are decision tree analysis, logistic regression, and neural networks. **Decision tree analysis** classifies customers or other entities of interest into two or more groups, according to history. **Logistic regression** produces equations that offer probabilities that particular events will occur. Common applications of logistic regression are using donor characteristics to predict the likelihood of a donation in a given period and using customer characteristics to predict the likelihood that customers will switch to another vendor. **Neural networks** are complex statistical prediction techniques. The name is actually a misnomer—although there is some loose similarity between the structure of a neural network and a network of biological neurons, the similarity is only superficial. Using data mining neural networks is just a technique for creating very complex mathematical functions for making predictions.

## Market Basket Analysis

Data mining techniques are usually complex. However, **market basket analysis** is a data mining technique that can be readily implemented with pure SQL. All the major data mining products have features and functions to perform market basket analysis.

Suppose that you run a diving shop, and one day you realize that one of your salespeople is much better than others at up-selling your customers. Any of your sales associates can fill a customer's order, but this particular salesperson is especially able to sell customers items in addition to those for which they ask. One day you ask him how he does it.

"It's simple," he says. "I just ask myself 'What is the next product they'll want to buy?' If someone buys a dive computer, I don't try to sell her fins. If she's buying a dive computer, she's already a diver, and she already has fins. But, look, these dive computer displays are

**FIGURE 8-24**

A Market Basket
Example

| 1,000 Transactions | Mask | Tank | Fins | Weights | Dive Computer |
|---|---|---|---|---|---|
| | 270 | 200 | 280 | 130 | 120 |
| Mask | 20 | 20 | 150 | 20 | 50 |
| Tank | 20 | 80 | 40 | 30 | 30 |
| Fins | 150 | 40 | 10 | 60 | 20 |
| Weights | 20 | 30 | 60 | 10 | 10 |
| Dive Computer | 50 | 30 | 20 | 10 | 5 |
| No Additional Product | 10 | — | — | — | 5 |

Support = P (A & B)       Example: P (Fins & Mask) = 150 / 1000 = .15

Confidence = P (A | B)       Example: P (Fins | Mask) = 150 / 270 = .55556

Lift = P (A | B)/ P (A)       Example: P (Fins | Mask) / P (Fins) = .55556 / .28 = 1.98

Note:       P (Mask | Fins) / P (Mask) = 150 / 280 / .27 = 1.98

hard to read. A better mask makes it easier to read the display and get the full benefits from the dive computer."

Market basket analysis is a data mining technique for determining such patterns. A market basket analysis shows the products that customers tend to purchase at the same time. Several different statistical techniques can be used to generate a market basket analysis. Here we discuss a technique that involves conditional probabilities.

Figure 8-24 shows hypothetical data from 1,000 transactions at a dive shop. The first row of numbers under each column is the total number of transactions that include the product in that column. For example, the 270 in the first row of Mask means that 270 of the 1,000 transactions include the purchase of a mask. The 120 under Dive Computer means that 120 of the 1,000 purchase transactions included a dive computer.

You can use the numbers in the first row to estimate the probability that a customer will purchase an item. Because 270 out of 1,000 transactions included a mask, you can estimate the likelihood that a customer will buy a mask to be 270/1,000, or .27. Similarly, the likelihood of a tank purchase is 200/1,000, or .2, and the likelihood of a fins purchase is 280/1,000, or .28.

The remaining rows in this table show the occurrences of transactions that involve two items. For example, the last column indicates that 50 transactions included both a dive computer and a mask, 30 transactions included a dive computer and a tank, 20 included a dive computer and fins, 10 included a dive computer and weights, 5 included a dive computer and another dive computer (meaning the customer bought two dive computers), and 5 transactions had a dive computer and no other product.

These data are interesting, but you can refine the analysis by computing additional factors. Marketing professionals define **support** as the probability that two items will be purchased together. From these data, the support for fins and mask is 150 out of 1,000, or .15.

**Confidence** is defined as the probability of a customer buying one product, given that he or she purchased another product. The confidence of fins, given that the customer has already purchased a mask, is the number of purchases of fins and masks out of the number of purchases of masks. Thus, in this example, the confidence is 150 out of 270, or .55556. The confidence that a customer purchases a tank, given that the customer has purchased fins, is 40 out of 280, or .14286.

**Lift** is defined as the ratio of confidence divided by the base probability of an item purchase. The lift for fins, given a mask, is the probability that a customer buys fins, given that the customer has purchased a mask, divided by the overall probability that the customer buys fins. If the lift is greater than 1, then the probability of buying fins goes up when a customer buys a mask; if the lift is less than 1, the probability of buying fins goes down when a customer buys a mask.

For the data in Figure 8-24, the lift for fins, given a mask purchase, is .55556/.28 or 1.98. This means that when someone purchases a mask, the likelihood he or she will also purchase fins almost doubles. The lift for fins, given a dive computer purchase, is 20/120 (the confidence of fins, given a dive computer) divided by .28, the probability that someone buys fins (280 of the 1,000 transactions involved fins). Therefore, 20/120 is .16667, and .16667/.28 is .59525. So the lift for fins, given purchase of a dive computer, is just under .6, meaning that when a customer buys a dive computer the likelihood that he or she will buy fins decreases.

Note that, as shown in the last line of Figure 8-24, lift is symmetrical. If the lift of fins, given purchase of a mask, is 1.98, then the lift of mask, given purchase of fins, is also 1.98.

## THE ACCESS WORKBENCH

### Section 8

### Business Intelligence Systems Using Microsoft Access

In Chapter 7's section of "The Access Workbench," we built a Web site and a Web database application for the Wallingford Motors CRM. This Web site is part of a reporting system for Wallingford Motors, and updating Web pages directly from Web-based database queries is one way to deliver such reports.

In this section, we will explore how to produce an OLAP report by using the Microsoft Excel 2010 PivotTable feature. We will build an OLAP report in Microsoft Excel 2010 based on data in a Microsoft Access 2010 database. We will start by creating an OLAP report for the WMCRM database. We will continue to use the copy of the WMCRM.accdb database file that we placed in the C:\Inetpub\wwwroot\DBC\WM folder in Chapter 7's section of "The Access Workbench." This will make anything we add to the database easily available for possible use on the Wallingford Motors Web site.

#### Creating a View Query for an OLAP Report

To create an OLAP report, we need to create a new view, one that is a slight variant of the view named viewCustomerContacts that we created earlier in Chapter 3A's section of "The Access Workbench." In the new view, we need to concatenate the customer's first and last names into a single customer name, and we need to add a quantitative measure so that we can easily analyze the number of contacts made by the Wallingford Motors sales staff. We will call the new view viewCustomerContactCount.

##### *Creating the viewCustomerContactCount Query*

1. Start Microsoft Access 2010 and open the copy of the **WMCRM.accdb** database file in the **C:\Inetpub\wwwroot\DBC\WM** folder.
2. Open the **viewCustomerContacts** query. The query is displayed.
3. Click the **File** command tab, click the **Save As** button, and then click the **Save Object As** button. The Save As dialog box appears.
4. As shown in Figure AW-8-1, in the Save As dialog box change the new object name to **viewCustomerContactCount**.
5. Click the **OK** button in the Save As dialog box. As shown in Figure AW-8-2, the new object is created and displayed in Datasheet view.
6. Click the **Design View** button in the Views group of the Home ribbon to switch the query to Design view.
7. Click the **Totals** button in the Show/Hide group of the Query Tools Design ribbon to display the Total row in the fields pane.

*(Continued)*

---

**FIGURE AW-8-1**

The Save As Dialog Box

8. Right-click the LastName field name in the LastName column to display the shortcut menu, as shown in Figure AW-8-3.
9. Click the **Build** button in the shortcut menu to display the Expression Builder.
10. Create an expression that concatenates LastName and FirstName data into a combined attribute named CustomerName as:

**CustomerName:[CUSTOMER]![LastName]&", "&[CUSTOMER]![FistName]**

Figure AW-8-4 shows the completed expression.

---

**FIGURE AW-8-2**

The Unmodified viewCustomerContactCounts Query

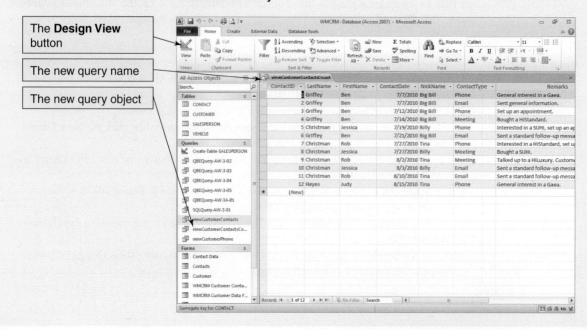

## FIGURE AW-8-3

### The Shortcut Menu

The **Totals** button

The **shortcut** menu

The **Build** button

The **Total** row

11. Create the expression in Expression Builder as shown in Figure AW-8-4, and then click the **OK** button in the Expression Builder.
12. Delete the **FirstName** column from the query design.
13. Delete the **Remarks** column from the query design.
14. Add a column named **ContactCount** to the query, as shown in Figure AW-8-5.
15. Save the changes to the query and then run it. The query results are shown in Figure AW-8-6.
16. Close the viewCustomerContactCount query.
17. Close the WMCRM database and Microsoft Access.

### Creating a Microsoft Excel Worksheet for an OLAP Report

Because the OLAP report will be in an Microsoft Excel 2010 workbook, we need to create a new workbook to hold the OLAP report. We will continue to use the Wallingford Motors

## FIGURE AW-8-4

### The Completed Expression in the Expression Builder

The **Expression Builder**

The completed expression to create **CustomerName**

Select tables from this pane

Select column names from this pane

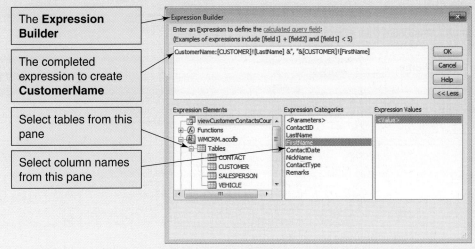

*(Continued)*

The ContactCount Column

The **ContactCount** expression

Set the Total setting to **Count**

C:\Inetpub\wwwroot\DBC\WM Web site folder as the storage location, and now we need to create a Microsoft Excel 2010 workbook named WM-DW-BI.xlsx in that folder.

*Creating the Microsoft Excel 2010 WM-DW-BI.xlsx Workbook*

1. Start Windows Explorer.
2. Browse to the **C:\Inetpub\wwwroot\DBC\WM** folder.
3. Right-click anywhere in the right-hand folder and file pane to open the shortcut menu.
4. In the shortcut menu, click the **New** command.
5. In the list of new objects, click the **Microsoft Excel Worksheet** command.
6. A new Microsoft Excel 2010 workbook object is created, with the file name highlighted in Edit mode.
7. Edit the file name to read **WM-DW-BI.xlsx**, and then press the **Enter** key.

Now you can open the WM-DW-BI.xlsx workbook.

*Opening the Microsoft Excel 2010 WM-DW-BI.xlsx Workbook*

1. Start Microsoft Excel 2010.
2. Click the **File** command tab, and then click the **Open** button.
3. In the Open dialog box, browse to the **C:\inetpub\wwwroot\DBC\WM** folder and open the **WM-DW-BI.xlsx** file. The **WM-DW-BI.xlsx** workbook is displayed, as shown in Figure AW-8-7.

### Creating a Basic OLAP Report

We can now create an OLAP report in the Microsoft Excel 2010 WM-DW-BI.xlsx workbook. Fortunately, Microsoft has made it possible to link directly to Microsoft Access 2010

viewCustomerContactCount Query Results

The **CustomerName** data

The **ContactCount** data

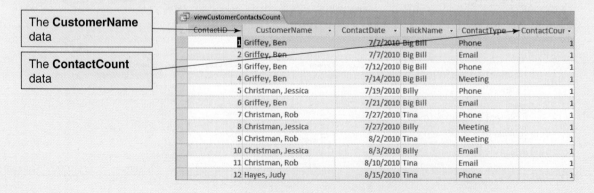

## FIGURE AW-8-7

### The WM-DW-BI.xlsx Workbook

The **Data** command tab

The **WM-DW-BI.xlsx** workbook file

to obtain the data needed for the report. We will connect the Microsoft Excel workbook to the Microsoft Access database and create the basic, blank OLAP report PivotTable.

> **B T W**
>
> Microsoft Excel 2010 uses the same Microsoft Office fluent user interface that you have learned to use in Microsoft Access 2010. Because you should already be familiar with the Microsoft Office fluent user interface, we do not discuss the Microsoft Excel variant of this interface.

### Creating the Basic OLAP Report PivotTable

1. In the WM-DW-BI.xlsx workbook, click the **Data** command tab to display the Data command groups, as shown in Figure AW-8-8.

## FIGURE AW-8-8

### The Microsoft Excel Data Command Tab

The **From Access** button

*(Continued)*

2. Click the **From Access** button in the Get External Data group of the Data ribbon. The Select Data Source dialog box appears.

3. In the Select Data Source dialog box, which functions just like an Open dialog box, browse to the **C:\inetpub\wwwroot\DBC\WM** folder. Select the Microsoft Access **WMCRM.accdb** database file, and then click the **Open** button.

4. At this point, the **Data Link Properties** dialog box *may* appear. If it does, you do not need to change anything in the dialog box, so just click the **OK** button.

5. At this point, the **Please Enter Microsoft Access Database Engine OLE DB Initialization Information** dialog box *may* appear. If it does, you do not need to change anything in the dialog box, so just click the **OK** button.

6. As shown in Figure AW-8-9, the Select Table dialog box appears.

7. In the Select Table dialog box, select the new **viewCustomerContactCount** query and then click the **OK** button.

8. As shown in Figure AW-8-10, the Import Data dialog box appears.

9. In the Import Data dialog box, select the **PivotTable Report**, and then click the **OK** button.

10. As shown in Figure AW-8-11, the basic PivotTable report structure is displayed in the Microsoft Excel worksheet.

11. Click the Save button on Microsoft Excel Quick Access Toolbar to save your work to this point.

- **NOTE:** From now on, when you open the WM-DW-BI.xlsx workbook a Security Warning bar will appear, warning that data connections have been disabled. This is similar to the Microsoft Access 2010 Security Warning bar you have already learned to use, and essentially the same action is necessary: Click the **Enable Options** button.

### Structuring an OLAP Report

We can now create the structure of the OLAP report. We do this by using the Microsoft Excel PivotTable Field List pane, shown in Figure AW-8-11 and Figure AW-8-12. To

---

**FIGURE AW-8-9**

The Select Table Dialog Box

Select the **viewCustomerContacts Count** object

---

**FIGURE AW-8-10**

The Import Data Dialog Box

Select **PivotTable Report**

## FIGURE AW-8-11

**The Basic PivotTable Report Structure**

The **Save** button

The **PivotTable Tools** command tab

The initial **PivotTable** area

The **PivotTable Field List** pane—the structure of the PivotTable is built using these controls

## FIGURE AW-8-12

**The PivotTable Field List Pane**

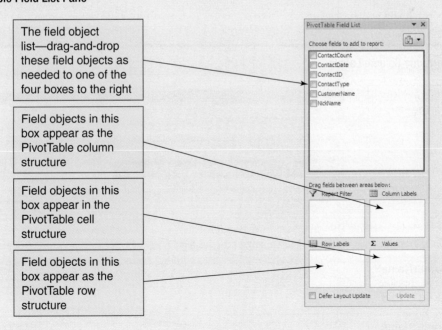

The field object list—drag-and-drop these field objects as needed to one of the four boxes to the right

Field objects in this box appear as the PivotTable column structure

Field objects in this box appear in the PivotTable cell structure

Field objects in this box appear as the PivotTable row structure

*(Continued)*

build the structure of the PivotTable, we drag and drop the field objects from the field object list. We drag the measures we want displayed to the Values box. We drag the dimension attributes we want as column structure to the Column Labels box, and we drag the dimension attributes we want as row structure to the Row Labels box.

For the Wallingford Motors Customer Contact PivotTable, we will use ContactCount as the measure, so it needs to go in the Values box. The column structure will have customer attributes, in this case only CustomerName. Finally, the row structure will have contact attributes—NickName (for SalesPerson) first, followed by ContactType and then Contact Date.

### Creating the OLAP Report's PivotTable Structure

1. Click-and-hold the **CustomerName** field object, drag it to the Column Labels box, and drop it there. As shown in Figure AW-8-13, the CustomerName labels and a GrandTotal label are added to the worksheet columns, the CustomerName field object in the field objects list is checked and displayed in bold, and the field object CustomerName is listed in the Column Labels box.
2. Click-and-hold the **ContactCount** field object, drag it to the Values box, and drop it there. As shown in Figure AW-8-14, the sum of the CustomerCount values is added to the worksheet, the CustomerCount field object in the field objects list is checked and displayed in bold, and the field object Sum of CustomerCount is listed in the Column Labels box.
3. Click-and-hold the **NickName** field object, drag it to the Row Labels box, and drop it there. As shown in Figure AW-8-15, the sum of the NickName row labels is added to the worksheet, the NickName field object in the field objects list is checked and displayed in bold, and the field object NickName is listed in the Row Labels box. In addition, the values in the report are starting to show up.

---

### FIGURE AW-8-13

**The CustomerName Column Labels**

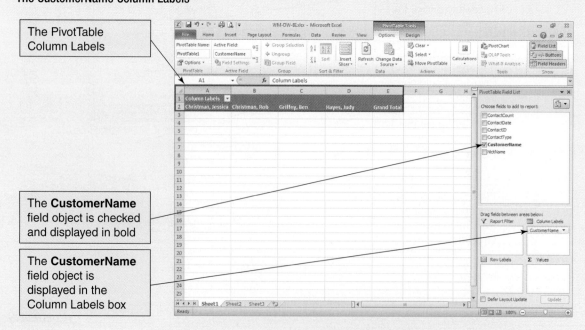

The **PivotTable** Column Labels

The **CustomerName** field object is checked and displayed in bold

The **CustomerName** field object is displayed in the Column Labels box

**FIGURE AW-8-14**

**The CustomerCount Values**

The PivotTable cell values are now displayed—at this point only the sum for each column is shown

The **ContactCount** object is checked and displayed in bold

The **Sum of ContactCount** object is displayed in the Values box

4. Click-and-hold the **ContactType** field object, drag it to the Row Labels box, and drop it there, *below* NickName. As shown in Figure AW-8-16, the sum of the NickName row labels is divided into contact type, the Type field object in the field objects list is checked and displayed in bold, and the field object Type is listed in the Row Labels

**FIGURE AW-8-15**

**The NickName Row Labels**

The NickName row labels are displayed, and now the PivotTable cell values are displayed

The **NickName** field object is checked and displayed in bold

The **NickName** field object is displayed in the Row Labels box

*(Continued)*

## FIGURE AW-8-16

### The ContactType Row Labels

The NickName row labels are divided by Type

The **ContactType field** object is checked and displayed in bold

The **ContactType field** object is displayed in the Row Labels box

box. In addition, the values in the report are now distributed according to salesperson (NickName) and type of contact (ContactType).

5. Click-and-hold the **ContactDate** field object, drag it to the Row Labels box, and drop it there, *below* ContactType. As shown in Figure AW-8-17, the sum of the NickName row labels is divided into contact type and date, the ContactDate field object in the field

## FIGURE AW-8-17

### The ContactDate Row Labels

The NickName row labels are divided by Type, and Type is divided by Date

The **ContactDate field** object is checked and displayed in bold

The **ContactDate field** object is displayed in the Row Labels box

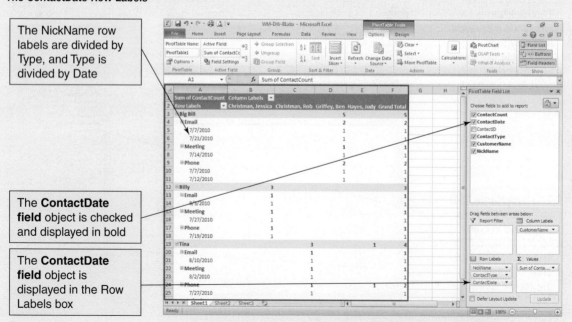

objects list is checked and displayed in bold, and the field object ContactDate is listed in the Row Labels box. In addition, the values in the report are now distributed according to salesperson (NickName), type of contact (Type), and date of contact (ContactDate).

6. Click the **Save** button on the Microsoft Excel Quick Access Toolbar to save your work to this point.

### Modifying an OLAP Report

We have finished building our OLAP report. We can modify it as needed by moving the field objects in the PivotTable Field List pane. We can also format the OLAP report to make it look the way we want it.

#### Modifying the OLAP Report PivotTable Structure

1. Click-and-hold the **ContactDate** field object in the Row Labels box, drag it within the box to between the NickName and Type field objects' Column Labels box, and drop it there. As shown in Figure AW-8-18, the order of the row labels in the OLAP report changes, and the data move, too.
2. As shown in Figure AW-8-18, you can contract and expand various portions of the OLAP report. In that figure, the data for Big Bill are shown fully expanded, while Billy's data are completely contracted. The data for Tina are shown at the Date level of detail, but without Type detail.

#### Formatting the OLAP Report

1. Click the PivotTable Tools **Design** command tab to display the Design command groups, as shown in Figure AW-8-19.
2. Click the **Banded Columns** check box in the PivotTable Style Options command group.
3. Click the **PivotTable Styles Gallery** drop-down arrow button to display the PivotTable Styles Gallery, as shown in Figure AW-8-20.
4. Select the PivotTable style shown in Figure AW-8-20 to format the OLAP report.

---

**FIGURE AW-8-18**

**The Rearranged Row Labels**

The NickName row labels are divided by Date, and Date is divided by Type

Big Bill's data fully expanded, Billy's data fully contracted, and Tina's data displayed at the Date level of detail

The **ContactDate field** object is now displayed between the NickName and ContactType field objects

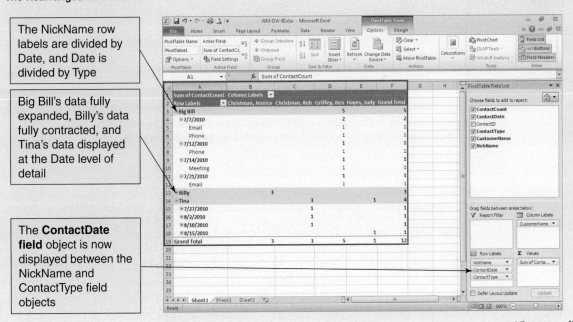

*(Continued)*

FIGURE AW-8-19

The Microsoft Excel PivotTable Tools Design Command Tab

The **Banded Columns** checkbox

The **PivotTable Styles** gallery drop-down arrow button

FIGURE AW-8-20

The Microsoft Excel PivotTable Styles Gallery

The columns in the OLAP report now have borders

The **PivotTable Styles** gallery

Click this style to format the OLAP report

5. Adjust the column widths of columns B, C, D, E, and F so that they are uniform and the entire table is visible on the worksheet when the PivotTable Field List pane is visible.
6. The final, formatted PivotTable OLAP report is shown in Figure AW-8-21.
7. Click the **Save** button on the Microsoft Excel Quick Access Toolbar.
8. Close the WM-DW-BI.xlsx workbook.
9. Close Microsoft Excel.

### In Closing

Our work is done. In "The Access Workbench," you have learned the essentials of working with Microsoft Access (and just a bit about working with Microsoft Excel). You have not learned everything there is to know, but now you know how to create and populate Microsoft Access databases; build and use Microsoft Access queries (including view-equivalent queries), forms, and reports; secure a Microsoft Access database; connect to a Microsoft Access database from a Web page; and create a PivotTable OLAP report. You now have a solid foundation to build on, which was, after all, the overall goal of "The Access Workbench."

**FIGURE AW-8-21**

**The Final PivotTable OLAP Report**

Big Bill's data fully expanded, Billy's data fully contracted, and Tina's data displayed at the Date level of detail

| | A | B | C | D | E | F |
|---|---|---|---|---|---|---|
| 1 | Sum of ContactCount | Column Labels | | | | |
| 2 | Row Labels | Christman, Jessica | Christman, Rob | Griffey, Ben | Hayes, Judy | Grand Total |
| 3 | Big Bill | | | 5 | | 5 |
| 4 | 7/7/2010 | | | 2 | | 2 |
| 5 | Email | | | 1 | | 1 |
| 6 | Phone | | | 1 | | 1 |
| 7 | 7/12/2010 | | | 1 | | 1 |
| 8 | Phone | | | 1 | | 1 |
| 9 | 7/14/2010 | | | 1 | | 1 |
| 10 | Meeting | | | 1 | | 1 |
| 11 | 7/21/2010 | | | 1 | | 1 |
| 12 | Email | | | 1 | | 1 |
| 13 | Billy | 3 | | | | 3 |
| 14 | Tina | | 3 | | 1 | 4 |
| 15 | 7/27/2010 | | 1 | | | 1 |
| 16 | 8/2/2010 | | 1 | | | 1 |
| 17 | 8/10/2010 | | 1 | | | 1 |
| 18 | 8/15/2010 | | | | 1 | 1 |
| 19 | Grand Total | 3 | 3 | 5 | 1 | 12 |

## SUMMARY

Business intelligence (BI) systems assist managers and other professionals in the analysis of current and past activities and in the prediction of future events. BI applications are of two major types: reporting applications and data mining applications. Reporting applications make elementary calculations on data; data mining applications use sophisticated mathematical and statistical techniques.

BI applications obtain data from three sources: operational databases, extracts of operational databases, and purchased data. A BI system sometimes has its own DBMS, which may or not be the operational DBMS. Characteristics of reporting and data mining applications are listed in Figure 8-4.

Direct reading of operational databases is not feasible for any but the smallest and simplest BI applications and databases—for several reasons. Querying operational data can unacceptably slow the performance of operational systems, operational data have problems that limit their usefulness for BI applications, and BI system creation and maintenance require programs, facilities, and expertise that are normally not available for an operational database.

Operational data may have problems. Because of the problems with operational data, many organizations have chosen to create and staff data warehouses and data marts. Extract, Transform, and Load (ETL) systems are used to extract data from operational systems; transform the data and load them into data warehouses; and maintain metadata that describes the source, format, assumptions, and constraints about the data. A data mart is a collection of data that is smaller than that held in a data warehouse and that addresses a particular component or functional area of the business. In Figure 8-5, the enterprise data warehouse distributes data to three smaller data marts, each of which services the needs of a different aspect of the business.

Operational databases and dimensional databases have different characteristics, as shown in Figure 8-6. Dimensional databases use a star schema with a fully normalized fact table that connects to dimension tables that may be non-normalized. Dimensional databases must deal with slowly changing dimensions, and therefore a time dimension is important in a dimensional database. Fact tables hold measures of interest, and dimension tables hold attribute values used in queries. The star schema can be extended with additional fact tables, dimension tables, and conformed dimensions.

The purpose of a reporting system is to create meaningful information from disparate data sources and to deliver that information to the proper users on a timely basis. Reports are produced by sorting, filtering, grouping, and making simple calculations on the data. RFM analysis is a typical reporting application. Customers are grouped and classified according to how recently they have placed an order (R), how frequently they order (F), and how much money (M) they spend on orders. The result of an RFM analysis is three scores. In a typical analysis, the scores range from 1 to 5. An RFM score of 1 1 4 indicates that the customer has purchased recently, purchases frequently, and does not purchase large-dollar items. An RFM report can be produced using SQL statements.

For RFM data to add value to an organization, an RFM report must be prepared and delivered to the appropriate users. The components of a modern reporting system are shown in Figure 8-16. Reporting systems maintain metadata that supports the three basic report functions: authoring, managing, and delivering reports. The metadata includes information about users, user groups, and reports and data about which users are to receive which reports, in what medium, and when. As shown in Figure 8-17, reports vary by type, media, and mode.

Online Analytical Processing (OLAP) reporting applications enable users to dynamically restructure reports. A measure is a data item of interest. A dimension is a characteristic of a measure. An OLAP report, or OLAP cube, is an arrangement of measures and dimensions. With OLAP, users can drill down and exchange the order of dimensions.

Data mining is the application of mathematical and statistical techniques to find patterns and relationships and to classify and predict. Data mining has arisen in recent years because of the confluence of factors shown in Figure 8-21.

With unsupervised data mining, analysts do not create models or hypotheses prior to the analysis. Rather, results are explained after the analysis is performed. With supervised techniques, hypotheses are formed and tested before the analysis. Five popular data mining techniques are cluster analysis, regression analysis, decision tree analysis, logistic regression, and neural networks.

Market basket analysis is used to determine which sets of products are likely to be sold at the same time. According to market basket analysis terminology, the support for two products is the frequency with which they appear together in transactions. Confidence is the conditional probability that one item will be purchased, given that another item has already been purchased. Lift is confidence divided by the base probability that an item will be purchased.

## KEY TERMS

alert
business intelligence (BI) system
click-stream data
cluster analysis
confidence
conformed dimension
data mart
data mining application
data warehouse
data warehouse metadata database
date dimension
decision support system (DSS)
decision tree analysis
digital dashboard
dimension table
dimensional database
drill down
dynamic report
enterprise data warehouse (EDW)
    architecture

Extract, Transform, and Load
    (ETL) System
F score
fact table
lift
logistic regression
M score
market basket analysis
measure
neural network
OLAP cube
OLAP report
Online Analytical Processing
    (OLAP)
online transaction processing
    (OLTP) systems
operational system
PivotTable
pull report

push report
query report
R score
regression analysis
report authoring
report delivery
report management
reporting system
RFM analysis
slowly changing dimension
star schema
static report
supervised data mining
support
time dimension
transactional system
unsupervised data mining
Web portal

## REVIEW QUESTIONS

**8.1** What are BI systems?

**8.2** Name and describe the two main categories of BI systems.

**8.3** What are the three sources of data for BI systems?

**8.4** How do BI systems differ from transaction processing systems?

**8.5** Summarize the problems with operational databases that limit their usefulness for BI applications.

**8.6** What is an ETL system, and what functions does it perform?

**8.7** Why are data warehouses necessary?

**8.8** What problems in operational data create the need to clean data before loading the data into a data warehouse?

**8.9** What does it mean to transform data? Give an example other than the ones used in this book.

**8.10** Give examples of data warehouse metadata.

**8.11** Explain the difference between a data warehouse and a data mart. Give an example other than the ones used in this book.

**8.12** What is the enterprise data warehouse (EDW) architecture?

**8.13** Describe the differences between operational databases and dimensional databases.

**8.14** What is a star schema?

**8.15** What is a measure?

**8.16** What is a fact table? What type of data are stored in fact tables?

**8.17** What is a dimension table? What type of data are stored in dimension tables?

**8.18** What is a slowly changing dimension?

**8.19** What is a conformed dimension?

**8.20** Why is the time dimension important in a dimensional model?

**8.21** State the purpose of a reporting system.

**8.22** Name and describe the purpose of the major components of a reporting system.

**8.23** What are the major functions of a reporting system?

**8.24** In RFM analysis, what do the letters *RFM* stand for?

**8.25** Describe, in general terms, how to perform an RFM analysis.

**8.26** Explain the characteristics of customers that have the following RFM scores:

{1 1 5}, {1 5 1}, {5 5 5}, {2 5 5}, {5 1 2}, {1 1 3}

**8.27** Summarize the types of reports described in this chapter.

**8.28** Describe the various media used to deliver reports.

**8.29** Summarize the modes of reports described in this chapter.

**8.30** Describe the major tasks in report management. Explain the role of report metadata in report management.

**8.31** Name three tasks of report authoring.

**8.32** Describe the major tasks in report delivery.

**8.33** What does OLAP stand for?

**8.34** What is the distinguishing characteristic of OLAP reports?

**8.35** Define *measure*, *dimension*, and *cube.*

**8.36** Give an example, other than ones in this text, of a measure, two dimensions related to your measure, and a cube.

**8.37** What is drill down?

**8.38** Explain two ways that the OLAP report in Figure 8-20 differs from that in Figure 8-19.

**8.39** Define *data mining*.

**8.40** Explain the difference between unsupervised and supervised data mining.

**8.41** For the HSD-DW cluster analysis results shown in Figure 8-23, give an explanation for the two clusters. Use the report data and data descriptions for the HSD-DW data in the text to describe which cities and products are primarily associated with each cluster. [Hint: Study the City and ProductNumber results in Figure 8-23(b).]

**8.42** Name five popular data mining techniques. Use the data in Figure 8-24 to answer questions 8.43 through 8.48.

**8.43** What is the probability that someone will buy a tank?

**8.44** What is the support for buying a tank and fins? What is the support for buying two tanks?

**8.45** What is the confidence for fins, given that a tank has been purchased?

**8.46** What is the confidence for a second tank, given that a tank has been purchased?

**8.47** What is the lift for fins, given that a tank has been purchased?

**8.48** What is the lift for a second tank, given that a tank has been purchased?

# EXERCISES

**8.49** Based on the discussion of the Heather Sweeney Designs operational database (HSD) and dimensional database (HSD-DW) in the text, answer the following questions.

**A.** Using the SQL statements shown in Figure 8-9, create the HSD-DW database in a DBMS.

**B.** What transformations of data were made before HSD-DW was loaded with data? List all the transformations, showing the original format of the HSD data and how they appear in the HSD-DW database.

**C.** Write the complete set of SQL statements necessary to load the transformed data into the HSD-DW database.

**D.** Populate the HSD-DW database, using the SQL statements you wrote to answer part C.

**E.** Figure 8-25 shows the SQL code to create the SALES_FOR_RFM fact table shown in Figure 8-14. Using those statements, add the SALES_FOR_RFM table to your HSD-DW database.

**F.** What transformations of data are necessary to load the SALES_FOR_RFM table? List any needed transformations, showing the original format of the HSD data and how they appear in the HSD-DW database.

**G.** What data will be used to load the SALES_FOR_RFM fact table? Write the complete set of SQL statements necessary to load this data.

**H.** Populate the SALES_FOR_RFM fact table, using the SQL statements you wrote to answer part G.

**FIGURE 8-25**

The HSD-DW SALES_FOR_RFM SQL Statements

```
CREATE TABLE SALES_FOR_RFM(
        TimeID              Int                 NOT NULL,
        CustomerID          Int                 NOT NULL,
        InvoiceNumber       Int                 NOT NULL,
        PreTaxTotalSale     Numeric(9,2)        NOT NULL,
        CONSTRAINT          SALES_FOR_RFM_PK
                            PRIMARY KEY (TimeID, CustomerID, InvoiceNumber),
        CONSTRAINT          SRFM_TIMELINE_FK FOREIGN KEY(TimeID)
                                REFERENCES TIMELINE(TimeID)
                                    ON UPDATE NO ACTION
                                    ON DELETE NO ACTION,
        CONSTRAINT          SRFM_CUSTOMER_FK FOREIGN KEY(CustomerID)
                                REFERENCES CUSTOMER(CustomerID)
                                    ON UPDATE NO ACTION
                                    ON DELETE NO ACTION,
);
```

**I.** Write an SQL query similar to the one shown on page 433 that uses the total dollar amount of each day's product sales as the measure (instead of the number of products sold each day).

**J.** Write the SQL view equivalent of the SQL query you wrote to answer part I.

**K.** Create the SQL view you wrote to answer part J in your HSD-DW database.

**L.** Create a Microsoft Excel 2010 workbook named HSD-DW-BI-Exercises.xlsx.

**M.** Using either the results of your SQL query from part K (copy the results of the query into a worksheet in the HSD-DW-BI.xlsx workbook and then format this range as a worksheet table) or your SQL view from part L (create a Microsoft Excel data connection to the view), create an OLAP report similar to the OLAP report shown in Figure 8-19. (*Hint:* If you need help with the needed Microsoft Excel actions, search in the Microsoft Excel help system for more information.)

**N.** Using Figure 8-24 as a model, create a market basket analysis matrix for Heather Sweeney Designs. Use your matrix to answer the following questions.

**(1)** What is the probability that someone will buy VK003 (Kitchen Remodeling Dallas Style)?

**(2)** What is the probability that someone will buy VB003 (Kitchen Remodeling Dallas Style Video Companion)?

**(3)** What is the probability that someone will buy VK004 (Heather Sweeney Seminar Live in Dallas on 25-OCT-07)?

**(4)** What is the support for buying VK003 and VB003?

**(5)** What is the support for buying VK003 and VK004?

**(6)** What is the confidence for VB003, given that VK003 has been purchased?

**(7)** What is the confidence for VK004, given that VK003 has been purchased?

**(8)** What is the lift for VB003, given that VK003 has been purchased?

**(9)** What is the lift for VK004, given that VK003 has been purchased?

**O.** Heather Sweeney is interested in the effects of payment type on sales in dollars.

**(1)** Modify the design of the HSD-DW dimensional database to include a PAYMENT_TYPE dimension table.

**(2)** Modify the HSD-DW database to include the PAYMENT_TYPE dimension table.

**(3)** What data will be used to load the PAYMENT_TYPE dimension table? What data will be used to load foreign key data into the PRODUCT_SALES fact table? Write the complete set of SQL statements necessary to load these data.

**(4)** Populate the PAYMENT_TYPE and PRODUCT_SALES tables, using the SQL statements you wrote to answer part 3.

**(5)** Create the SQL queries or SQL views needed to incorporate the PaymentType attribute.

**(6)** Create a Microsoft Excel 2010 OLAP report to show the effect of payment type on product sales in dollars.

**8.50** The following questions require that you have completed question 8.49 and that you have a version of SQL Server 2008 that includes SQL Server Analysis Services.

**A.** Download and install the Microsoft SQL Server 2008 Data Mining add-ins for Microsoft Office 2010.

**B.** Use the data mining add-in in Microsoft Excel 2010 to do a cluster analysis of the HSD-DW data results from your SQL query results from question 8.49, part I, or SQL view from questions 8.49, part J, and 8.49, part K. Use only the City and ProductNumber attributes in your analysis. Interpret you results.

## ACCESS WORKBENCH EXERCISES

**AW.8.1**    Using the discussion of dimensional models and OLAP reports in the text and the specific discussion of OLAP reports based on a Microsoft Access 2010 database in this chapter's section of "The Access Workbench" as your reference, complete exercise 8.49 (excluding part N) for Heather Sweeney Designs. Create your HSD-DW database in Microsoft Access 2010 and your OLAP report in Microsoft Excel 2010.

**AW.8.2**    Using the discussion of dimensional models and OLAP reports in the text and the specific discussion of OLAP reports based on a Microsoft Access 2010 database in this chapter's section of "The Access Workbench" as your reference, complete exercise 8.49, part O, for Heather Sweeney Designs. Modify your HSD-DW database in Microsoft Access 2010 and produce your OLAP report in the Microsoft Excel 2010.

## GARDEN GLORY PROJECT QUESTIONS

If you have not already implemented the Garden Glory database shown in Chapter 3 in a DBMS product, create and populate the Garden-Glory database now in the DBMS of your choice (or as assigned by your instructor).

**A.** You need about 20 SERVICE transactions in the database. Write the needed SQL statements for any needed additional SERVICE transactions and insert the data into your database.

**B.** Design a data warehouse star schema for a dimensional database named GG-DW. The fact table measure will be HoursWorked.

**C.** Create the GG-DW database in a DBMS product.

**D.** What transformations of data will need to be made before the GG-DW database can be loaded with data? List all the transformations, showing the original format of the GARDEN_GLORY data and how it appears in the GG-DW database.

**E.** Write the complete set of SQL statements necessary to load the transformed data into the GG-DW database.

**F.** Populate the GG-DW database, using the SQL statements you wrote to answer part A.

**G.** Write an SQL query similar to the one shown in the text on page 433 that uses the hours worked per day as the measure.

**H.** Write the SQL view equivalent of the SQL query you wrote to answer part G.

**I.** Create the SQL view you wrote to answer part H in your GG-DW database.

**J.** Create the Microsoft Excel 2010 workbook named GG-DW-BI-Exercises.xlsx.

**K.** Using either the results of your SQL query from part G (copy the results of the query into a worksheet in the GG-DW-BI.xlsx workbook and then format this range as a worksheet table) or your SQL view from part I (create a Microsoft Excel data connection to the view), create an OLAP report similar to the OLAP report shown in Figure 8-18. (*Hint:* If you need help with the needed Microsoft Excel actions, search in the Microsoft Excel help system for more information.)

 # JAMES RIVER JEWELRY PROJECT QUESTIONS

If you have not already implemented the James River Jewelry database shown in Chapter 3 in a DBMS product, create and populate the James-River-Jewerly database now in the DBMS of your choice (or as assigned by your instructor).

**A.** You need about 20 PURCHASE transactions in the database. Write the needed SQL statements for any needed additional PURCHASE transactions and insert the data into your database.

**B.** Design a data warehouse star schema for a dimensional database named JRJ-DW. The fact table measure will be RetailPrice.

**C.** Create the JRJ-DW database in a DBMS product.

**D.** What transformations of data will need to be made before the JRJ-DW database can be loaded with data? List all the transformations, showing the original format of the JAMES_RIVER_JEWELRY data and how it appears in the JRJ-DW database.

**E.** Write the complete set of SQL statements necessary to load the transformed data into the JRJ-DW database.

**F.** Populate the JRJ-DW database, using the SQL statements you wrote to answer part A.

G.   Write an SQL query similar to the one shown in the text on page 433 that uses retail price as the measure.

H.   Write the SQL view equivalent of the SQL query you wrote to answer part G.

I.   Create the SQL view you wrote to answer part H in your JRJ-DW database.

J.   Create a Microsoft Excel 2010 workbook named JRJ-DW-BI-Exercises.xlsx.

K.   Using either the results of your SQL query from part G (copy the results of the query into a worksheet in the JRJ-DW-BI.xlsx workbook and then format this range as a worksheet table) or your SQL view from part I (create a Microsoft Excel data connection to the view), create an OLAP report similar to the OLAP report shown in Figure 8-18. (*Hint:* If you need help with the needed Microsoft Excel actions, search in the Microsoft Excel help system for more information.)

 ## THE QUEEN ANNE CURIOSITY SHOP PROJECT QUESTIONS

If you have not already implemented the Queen Anne Curiosity Shop database shown in Chapter 3 in a DBMS product, create and populate the QACS database now in the DBMS of your choice (or as assigned by your instructor).

A.   You need about 30 PURCHASE transactions in the database. Write the needed SQL statements for any needed additional PURCHASE transactions and insert the data into your database.

B.   Design a data warehouse star schema for a dimensional database named QACS-DW. The fact table measure will be ItemPrice.

C.   Create the QACS-DW database in a DBMS product.

D.   What transformations of data will need to be made before the QACS-DW database can be loaded with data? List all the transformations, showing the original format of the QACS and how it appears in the QACS-DW database.

E.   Write the complete set of SQL statements necessary to load the transformed data into the QACS-DW database.

F.   Populate the QACS-DW database, using the SQL statements you wrote to answer part A.

G.   Write an SQL query similar to the one shown in the text on page 433 that uses retail price as the measure.

H.   Write the SQL view equivalent of the SQL query you wrote to answer part G.

I.   Create the SQL view you wrote to answer part H in your QACS-DW database.

J.   Create a Microsoft Excel 2010 workbook named QACS-DW-BI-Exercises.xlsx.

K.   Using either the results of your SQL query from part G (copy the results of the query into a worksheet in the QACS-DW-BI.xlsx workbook and then format this range as a worksheet table) or your SQL view from part I (create a Microsoft Excel data connection to the view), create an OLAP report similar to the OLAP report shown in Figure 8-18. (*Hint:* If you need help with the needed Microsoft Excel actions, search in the Microsoft Excel help system for more information.)

# Online Appendices

Complete versions of these appendices are available on the textbook's Web site www.pearsonhighered.com/kroenke

## Appendix A

Getting Started with Microsoft SQL Server 2008 R2 Express Edition

## Appendix B

Getting Started with Oracle MySQL Community Server 5.1

## Appendix C

Getting Started in Systems Analysis and Design

## Appendix D

Getting Started with Microsoft Visio 2010

## Appendix E

Getting Started with Web Servers, PHP and the Eclipse PDT

# Glossary

While this section defines many of the key terms in the book, it is not meant to be exhaustive. Terms related to a specific DBMS product, for example, should be referenced in the chapter or appendix dedicated to that product. These references can be found in the index. Similarly, SQL concepts are included, but details of SQL commands and syntax should be referenced in the chapter that discusses those details, and Microsoft Access 2010 terms should be referenced in the sections of "The Access Workbench."

**.NET Framework (.NET):**  Microsoft's comprehensive application development platform. It includes such components as ADO.NET and ASP.NET.

**<?php and ?>:**  The symbols used to indicate blocks of PHP code in Web pages.

**ACID transaction:**  A transaction that is *atomic, consistent, isolated*, and *durable*. An atomic transaction is one in which a set of database changes are committed as a unit; either all of them are completed or none of them are. A consistent transaction is one in which all actions are taken against rows in the same logical state. An isolated transaction is one that is protected from changes by other users. A durable transaction is one that, once committed to a database, is permanent regardless of subsequent failure. There are different levels of consistency and isolation. *See* **transaction-level consistency** and **statement-level consistency**. *See also* **transaction isolation level**.

**Active Server Pages (ASP):**  A combination of HTML and scripting language statements. Any statement included in <% ... %> is processed on the server. Used with Internet Information Server (IIS).

**Active Data Objects (ADO):**  An implementation of OLE DB that is accessible via object- and non-object-oriented languages. It is used primarily as a scripting-language (JScript, VBScript) interface to OLE DB.

**ADO.NET:**  A data access technology that is part of Microsoft's .NET initiative. ADO.NET provides the capabilities of ADO, but with a different object structure. ADO.NET also includes new capabilities for the processing of datasets.

**After-image:**  A record of a database entity (normally a row or a page) after a change. Used in recovery to perform rollforward.

**Alert:**  In reporting systems, a type of report that is triggered by an event.

**American National Standards Institute (ANSI):**  The American standards organization that creates and publishes the SQL standards.

**AMP:**  An abbreviation for Apache, MySQL, and PHP/Pearl/Python. *See* Apache Web Server, PHP.

**Anomaly:**  In normalization, an undesirable consequence of a data modification. With an insertion anomaly, facts about two or more different themes must be added to a single row of a relation. With a deletion anomaly, facts about two or more themes are lost when a single row is deleted.

**Apache:**  A popular Web server that runs on most operating systems, particularly Windows and Linux.

**Application program interface (API):**  The set of objects, methods, and properties that is used to access the functionality of a program such as a DBMS.

**Association entity:**  An entity that represents the combination of at least two other objects and that contains data about that combination. It is often used in contracting and assignment applications.

**Association relationship:**  In database design, a table pattern where an intersection table contains additional attributes beyond the attributes that make up the composite primary key.

**Asterisk (*):**  A wildcard character used in Microsoft Access queries to represent one or more unspecified characters. *See* SQL percent sign (%) wildcard character.

**Atomic transaction:**  A group of logically related database operations that are performed as a unit. Either all the operations are performed or none of them are.

**Attribute:**  (1) A value that represents a characteristic of an entity. (2) A column of a relation.

**Before-image:**  A record of a database entity (normally a row or a page) before a change. Used in recovery to perform rollback.

**Binary relationship:**  A relationship between exactly two entities or tables.

**Boyce-Codd Normal Form (BCNF):**  A relation in third normal form in which every determinant is a candidate key.

**Business intelligence (BI) systems:**  Information systems that assist managers and other professionals in analyzing current and past activities and in predicting future events. Two major categories of BI systems are reporting systems and data mining systems.

**Business rule:**  A statement of a policy in a business that restricts the ways in which data can be inserted, updated, or deleted in the database.

**Candidate key:**  An attribute or a group of attributes that identifies a unique row in a relation. One of the candidate keys is chosen to be the primary key.

**Cardinality:**  In a binary relationship, the maximum or minimum number of elements allowed on each side of the relationship. The maximum cardinality can be 1:1, 1:N, N:1, or N:M. The minimum cardinality can be optional/optional, optional/mandatory, mandatory/optional, or mandatory/mandatory.

**Cascading deletion:**  A property of a relationship that indicates that when one row is deleted, related rows should be deleted as well.

**Cascading update:**  A referential integrity action specifying that when the key of a parent row is updated, the foreign keys of matching child rows should be updated as well.

**Checkpoint:**  The point of synchronization between a database and a transaction log. At the checkpoint, all buffers are written to external storage. (This is the standard definition of *checkpoint*, but DBMS vendors sometimes use this term in other ways.)

**Child:**  A row, record, or node on the many side of a one-to-many relationship. *See also* **parent**.

**Click-stream data:**  Data about a customer's clicking behavior on a Web page; such data are often analyzed by e-commerce companies.

**Cluster analysis:**  A form of data mining that uses statistical techniques to identify groups of similar data.

**Column:** A logical group of bytes in a row of a relation or a table. The meaning of a column is the same for every row of the relation.

**Commit:** A command issued to a DBMS to make database modifications permanent. After the command has been processed, the changes are written to the database and to a log in such a way that they will survive system crashes and other failures. A commit is usually used at the end of an atomic transaction. Contrast this with **rollback**.

**Composite identifier:** An identifier of an entity that consists of two or more attributes.

**Composite key:** A key of a relation that consists of two or more columns.

**Computed value:** A column of a table that is computed from other column values. Values are not stored but are computed when they are to be displayed.

**Concurrent transactions:** A condition in which two or more transactions are processed against a database at the same time. In a single-CPU system, the changes are interleaved; in a multi-CPU system, the transactions can be processed simultaneously, and the changes on the database server are interleaved.

**Concurrent update problem:** An error condition in which one user's data changes are overwritten by another user's data changes. Also called lost update problem.

**Confidence:** In market basket analysis, the probability of a customer's buying one product, given that the customer has purchased another product.

**Conformed dimension:** In a dimensional database design, a dimension table that has relationships to two or more fact tables.

**Consistent:** In an ACID transaction, either statement-level or transaction-level consistency. *See* ACID transaction, Consistency, Statement-level consistency, and Transaction-level consistency.

**Consistency:** Two or more concurrent transactions are consistent if the result of their being processed is the same as it would have been had they been processed in some sequential order.

**COUNT:** In SQL, a function that counts the number of rows in a query result. *See* SQL built-in functions.

**Cube:** *See* **OLAP cube**.

**Data administration:** An enterprisewide function that concerns the effective use and control of an organization's data assets. A person can perform it but more often it is performed by a group. Specific functions include setting data standards and policies and providing a forum for conflict resolution. *See also* **database administration**.

**Data definition language (DDL):** A language used to describe the structure of a database.

**Data manipulation language (DML):** A language used to describe the processing of a database.

**Data mart:** A facility similar to a data warehouse, but with a restricted domain. Often, the data are restricted to particular types, business functions, or business units.

**Data mining application:** The use of statistical and mathematical techniques to find patterns in database data.

**Data model:** (1) A model of users' data requirements, usually expressed in terms of the entity-relationship model. It is sometimes called a users' data model. (2) A language for describing the structure and processing of a database.

**Data sublanguage:** A language for defining and processing a database intended to be embedded in programs written in another language—in most cases, a procedural language such as COBOL, C#, or Visual Basic. A data sublanguage is an incomplete programming language because it contains only constructs for data definition and processing.

**Data warehouse:** A store of enterprise data that is designed to facilitate management decision making. A data warehouse includes not only data, but also metadata, tools, procedures, training, personnel information, and other resources that make access to the data easier and more relevant to decision makers.

**Data warehouse metadata database:** The database used to store the data warehouse metadata.

**Database:** A self-describing collection of related records, or, for relational databases, of related tables.

**Database administration (DBA):** A function that concerns the effective use and control of a particular database and its related applications.

**Database administrator (DBA):** A person or group responsible for establishing policies and procedures to control and protect a database. They work within guidelines set by data administration to control the database structure, manage data changes, and maintain DBMS programs.

**Database backup:** A copy of database files that can be used to restore a database to some previous, consistent state.

**Database design:** A graphical display of tables (files) and their relationships. The tables are shown in rectangles, and the relationships are shown using lines. A many relationship is shown with a crow's foot on the end of the line, an optional relationship is depicted by an oval, and a mandatory relationship is shown with hash marks.

**Database management system (DBMS):** A set of programs used to define, administer, and process a database and its applications.

**Database schema:** A complete logical view of a database.

**Deadlock:** A condition that can occur during concurrent processing in which each of two (or more) transactions is waiting to access data that the other transaction has locked. It also is called the **deadly embrace**.

**Deadly embrace:** *See* **deadlock**.

**Decision support system (DSS):** One or more applications designed to help managers make decisions. An earlier name for business intelligence (BI).

**Decision tree analysis:** A form of unsupervised data mining that classifies entities of interest into two or more groups according to values of attributes that measure the entities' past history.

**Degree:** In the entity-relationship model, the number of entities participating in a relationship.

**Deletion anomaly:** In a relation, the situation in which the removal of one row of a table deletes facts about two or more themes.

**Denormalization:** The process of intentionally designing a relation that is not normalized. Denormalization is done to improve performance or security.

**Determinant:** One or more attributes that functionally determine another attribute or attributes. In the functional dependency $(A, B) \rightarrow D, C$, the attributes $(A, B)$ are the determinant.

**Digital dashboard:** In reporting systems, a display that is customized for a particular user. Typically, a digital dashboard has links to many different reports.

**Dimension table:** In a star schema dimensional database, the tables that connect to the central fact table. Dimension tables hold attributes used in the organizing queries in analyses such as those of OLAP cubes.

**Dimensional database:** A database design that is used for data warehouses and is designed for efficient queries and analysis. It contains a central fact table connected to one or more dimension tables.

**Dirty read:** A read of data that have been changed but not yet committed to a database. Such changes may later be rolled back and removed from the database.

**Discriminator:** In the entity-relationship model, an attribute of a supertype entity that determines which subtype pertains to the supertype.

**Distributed database:** A database that is stored and processed on two or more computers.

**Distributed two-phase locking:** A sophisticated form of record locking that must be used when database transactions are processed on two or more machines.

**Document type declaration (DTD):** A set of markup elements that defines the structure of an XML document.

**Domain:** (1) The set of all possible values an attribute can have. (2) A description of the format (data type, length) and the semantics (meaning) of an attribute.

**Domain key/normal form (DK/NF):** A relation in which all constraints are logical consequences of domains and keys. In this text, this definition has been simplified to a relation in which the determinants of all functional dependencies are candidate keys.

**Drill down:** User-directed disaggregation of data used to break higher-level totals into components.

**Durable:** In an ACID transaction, the database changes are permanent. *See* ACID transaction.

**Dynamic cursor:** A fully featured cursor. All inserts, updates, deletions, and changes in row order are visible to a dynamic cursor.

**Dynamic report:** In reporting systems, a report that reads the most current data at the time of the report's creation. Contrast with static report.

**Eclipse IDE:** A popular open-source integrated development environment.

**Eclipse PDT (PHP Development Tools) Project:** A version of the Eclipse IDE customized for use with PHP. *See* Eclipse IDE, PHP.

**Enterprise-class database system:** A DBMS product capable of supporting the operating requirement of large organizations.

**Enterprise data warehouse (EDW) architecture:** A data warehouse architecture that links specialized data marts to a central data warehouse for data consistency and efficient operations.

**Entity:** Something of importance to a user that needs to be represented in a database. In the entity-relationship model, entities are restricted to things that can be represented by a single table. *See also* **strong entity** and **weak entity**.

**Entity class:** A set of entities of the same type; two examples are EMPLOYEE and DEPARTMENT.

**Entity instance:** A particular occurrence of an entity; for example, Employee 100 (an EMPLOYEE) and Accounting Department (a DEPARTMENT).

**Entity-relationship diagram (E-R diagram):** A graphic used to represent entities and their relationships. Entities are normally shown in squares or rectangles, and relationships are shown in diamonds. The cardinality of the relationship is shown inside the diamond.

**Entity-relationship model (E-R model):** The constructs and conventions used to create a model of users' data. The things in the users' world are represented by entities, and the associations among those things are represented by relationships. The results are usually documented in an entity-relationship diagram. *See also* **data model**.

**Exclusive lock:** A lock on a data resource that no other transaction can read or update.

**Explicit lock:** A lock requested by a command from an application program.

**Export:** A function of a DBMS that writes a file of data in bulk. The file is intended to be read by another DBMS or program.

**Extended entity-relationship (E-R) model:** A set of constructs and conventions used to create data models. The things in the users' world are represented by entities, and the associations among those things are represented by relationships. The results are usually documented in an entity-relationship (E-R) diagram.

**Extensible Markup Language (XML):** A markup language whose tags can be extended by document designers. *See also* **XML Schema document**.

**Extract, Transform, and Load (ETL) system:** The portion of a data warehouse that converts operation data to data warehouse data.

**F score:** In RFM analysis, the "how frequently" score, which reflects how often a customer makes a purchase. *See* RFM Analysis.

**Fact table:** The central table in a dimensional database. Its attributes are called measures. *See also* **measure**.

**Field:** (1) A logical group of bytes in a record used with file processing. (2) In the context of the relational model, a synonym for *attribute*.

**Fifth normal form (5NF):** A normal form necessary to eliminate an anomaly where a table can be split apart but not correctly joined back together. Also known as Project-Join Normal Form (PJ/NF)

**File data source:** An ODBC data source stored in a file that can be emailed or otherwise distributed among users.

**First normal form (1NF):** Any table that fits the definition of a relation.

**Foreign key:** An attribute that is a key of one or more relations other than the one in which it appears.

**Form:** A structured on-screen presentation of selected data from a database. Forms are used for both data input and data reading. A form is part of a database application. Compare this with a report.

**Fourth normal form (4NF):** A relation in BCNF in which every multivalue dependency is a functional dependency.

**Functional dependency:** A relationship between attributes in which one attribute or group of attributes determines the value of another. The expressions $X \rightarrow Y$, "X determines Y," and "Y is functionally dependent on X" mean that given a value of X, we can determine the value of Y.

**HAS-A relationship:** A relationship between two entities or objects that are of different logical types; for example, EMPLOYEE HAS-A(n) AUTO. Contrast this with an IS-A relationship.

**HTML document tags:** The tags in HTML documents that indicate the structure of the document.

**HTML syntax rules:** The standards that are used to create HTML documents.

**Http://localhost:** For a Web server, a reference to the user's computer.

**Hypertext Markup Language (HTML):** A standardized set of text tags for formatting text, locating images and other nontext files, and placing links or references to other documents.

**Hypertext Transfer Protocol (HTTP):** A standardized means for using TCP/IP to communicate over the Internet.

**ID-dependent entity:** An entity that cannot logically exist without the existence of another entity. APPOINTMENT, for example, cannot exist without CLIENT to make the appointment. To be an ID-dependent entity, the identifier of the entity must contain the identifier of the entity on which it depends. Such entities are a subset of a weak entity. *See also* **existence-dependent entity**, **strong entity**, and **weak entity**.

**Identifier:** In an entity, a group of one or more attributes that determine entity instances. *See also* **nonunique identifier** and **unique identifier**.

**Identifying relationship:** A relationship that is used when the child entity is ID-dependent upon the parent entity.

**IE Crow's Foot model:** Formally known as the Information Engineering (IE) Crow's Foot model, it is a system of symbology used to construct E-R diagrams in data modeling and database design.

**Implicit lock:** A lock that is placed automatically by a DBMS.

**Inconsistent backup:** A backup file that contains uncommitted changes.

**Inconsistent read problem:** An anomaly that occurs in concurrent processing in which transactions execute a series of reads that are inconsistent with one another. This problem can be prevented by using two-phase locking and other strategies.

**Index.html:** A default Web page name provided by most Web servers.

**Inetpub folder:** In Windows operating systems, the root folder for the IIS Web server.

**Information:** (1) Knowledge derived from data, (2) data presented in a meaningful context, or (3) data processed by summing, ordering, averaging, grouping, comparing, or other similar operations.

**Information Engineering (IE) model:** An E-R model developed by James Martin.

**Inner join:** *See* **join**.

**Integrated Definition 1, Extended (IDEF1X):** A version of the entity-relationship model, adopted as a national standard, but difficult to understand and use. Most organizations use a simpler E-R version like the crow's foot model.

**Integrated Development Environment (IDE):** An application that provides a programmer or application developer with a complete set of development tools in one package.

**Insertion anomaly:** In a relation, a condition that exists when, to add a complete row to a table, one must add facts about two or more logically different themes.

**Internet Information Server (IIS):** A Windows Web server product that processes Active Server Pages (ASP).

**Intersection table:** A table (also called a relation) used to represent a many-to-many relationship. It contains the keys of the relations in the relationship. When used to represent entities having a many-to-many relationship, it may have non-key data if the relationship contains data.

**IS-A relationship:** A relationship between a supertype and a subtype. For example, EMPLOYEE and ENGINEER have an IS-A relationship.

**Isolation level:** *See* **transaction isolation level**.

**Java Database Connectivity (JDBC):** A standard means for accessing DBMS products from Java. With JDBC, the unique API of a DBMS is hidden, and the programmer writes to the standard JDBC interface.

**Java Server Pages (JSP):** A combination of HTML and Java that is compiled into a servlet.

**Join operation:** A relational algebra operation on two relations, A and B, that produces a third relation, C. A row of A is concatenated with a row of B to form a new row in C if the rows in A and B meet restrictions concerning their values. For example, A1 is an attribute in A, and B1 is an attribute in B. The join of A with B in which (A1 = B1) will result in a relation, C, having the concatenation

of rows in A and B in which the value of A1 is equal to the value of B1. In theory, restrictions other than equality are allowed—a join could be made in which A1 < B1. However, such non-equal joins are not used in practice. Also known as inner join. *See also* **natural join**.

**Key:** (1) A group of one or more attributes that identify a unique row in a relation. Because relations cannot have duplicate rows, every relation must have at least one key that is the composite of all the attributes in the relation. A key is sometimes called a logical key. (2) With some relational DBMS products, an index on a column used to improve access and sorting speed. It is sometimes called a physical key. *See also* **nonunique key**, **unique key**, and **physical key**.

**LAMP:** A version of AMP that runs on Linux. *See* AMP.

**Lift:** In market basket analysis, confidence divided by the base probability of an item purchase.

**Lock:** To allocate a database resource to a particular transaction in a concurrent-processing system. The size at which the resource can be locked is known as the lock granularity. *See also* **exclusive lock** and **shared lock**.

**Lock granularity:** The detail possible with a lock.

**Log:** A file that contains a record of database changes. The log contains before-images and after-images.

**Logical unit of work (LUW):** An equivalent term for transaction. *See* Transaction.

**Logistic regression:** A form of supervised data mining that estimates the parameters of an equation to calculate the odds that a given event will occur.

**Lost update problem:** Same as concurrent update problem.

**M score:** In RFM analysis, the "how much money" score, which reflects how much a customer spends per purchase. *See* RFM Analysis.

**Market basket analysis:** A type of data mining that estimates the correlations of items that are purchased together. *See also* confidence and lift.

**MAX:** In SQL, a function that determines the largest value in a set of numbers. *See* SQL built-in functions.

**Maximum cardinality:** (1) The maximum number of values that an attribute can have within a semantic object. (2) In a relationship between tables, the maximum number of rows to which a row of one table can relate in the other table.

**Measure:** In OLAP, a data value that is summed, averaged, or processed in some simple arithmetic manner.

**Metadata:** Data concerning the structure of data in a database stored in the data dictionary. Metadata are used to describe tables, columns, constraints, indexes, and so forth. *See also* **application metadata**.

**MIN:** In SQL, a function that determines the smallest value in a set of numbers. *See* SQL built-in functions.

**Minimum cardinality:** In a relationship between tables, the minimum number of rows to which a row of one table can relate in the other table.

**Modification anomaly:** A situation that exists when the storing of one row in a table records facts about two themes or the deletion of a row removes facts about two themes, or when a data change must be made in multiple rows for consistency.

**Multiple-tier driver:** In ODBC, a two-part driver, usually for a client-server database system. One part of the driver resides on the client and interfaces with the application; the second part resides on the server and interfaces with the DBMS.

**Multivalued dependency:** A condition in a relation with three or more attributes in which independent attributes appear to have relationships they do not have. Formally, in a relation R (A, B, C), having key (A, B, C) where A is matched with multiple values of B (or of C or of both), B does not determine C, and C does not determine B. An example is the relation EMPLOYEE (EmpNumber, EmpSkill, DependentName), where an employee can have multiple values of Emp-skill and Dependent-name. Emp-skill and Dependent-name do not have any relationship, but they do appear to in the relation.

**N:M:** An abbreviation for a many-to-many relationship between the rows of two tables.

**Natural join:** A join of a relation A having attribute A1 with relation B having attribute B1, where A1 = B1. The joined relation, C, contains either column A1 or B1 but not both.

**Neural network:** A form of supervised data mining that estimates complex mathematical functions for making predictions. The name is a misnomer. Although there is some loose similarity between the structure of a neural network and a network of biological neurons, the similarity is only superficial.

**Nonidentifying relationship:** In data modeling, a relationship between two entities such that one is *not* ID-dependent on the other. *See* Identifying relationship.

**Nonrepeatable reads:** A situation that occurs when a transaction reads data it has previously read and finds modifications or deletions caused by a committed transaction.

**Nonunique identifier:** An identifier that determines a group of entity instances. *See also* **unique identifier**.

**Nonunique key:** A key that potentially identifies more than one row.

**Normal form:** A rule or set of rules governing the allowed structure of relations. The rules apply to attributes, functional dependencies, multivalue dependencies, domains, and constraints. The most important normal forms are 1NF, 2NF, 3NF, BCNF, 4NF, 5NF, and DK/NF.

**Normalization process:** The process of evaluating a relation to determine whether it is in a specified normal form and, if necessary, of converting it to relations in that specified normal form.

**Not-type-valid document:** An XML document that either does not conform to its Document Type Declaration (DTD) or does not have a DTD. *See also* type-valid document and schema-valid document.

**Null value:** An attribute value that has never been supplied. Such values are ambiguous and can mean the value is unknown, the value is not appropriate, or the value is known to be blank.

**Object persistence:** The storage of object data values.

**Object-oriented DBMS (OODBMS):** A type of DBMS that provides object persistence. OODBMSs have not received commercial acceptance.

**Object-oriented programming (OOP):** A programming methodology that defines objects and the interactions between them to create application programs.

**Object-relational database:** A database created by a DBMS that provides a relational model interface as well as structures for object persistence. Oracle is the leading object-relational DBMS.

**ODBC conformance level:** In ODBC, definitions of the features and functions that are made available through the driver's application program interface (API). A driver API is a set of functions that the application can call to receive services. There are three conformance levels: Core API, Level 1 API, and Level 2 API.

**ODBC data source:** In the ODBC standard, a database and its associated DBMS, operating system, and network platform.

**ODBC Data Source Administrator:** The application used to create ODBC data sources.

**ODBC Driver:** In ODBC, a program that serves as an interface between the ODBC driver manager and a particular DBMS product. Runs on the client machines in a client-server architecture.

**ODBC Driver Manager:** In ODBC, a program that serves as an interface between an application program and an ODBC driver. It determines the required driver, loads it into memory, and coordinates activity between the application and the driver. On Windows systems, it is provided by Microsoft.

**OLAP cube:** In OLAP, a set of measures and dimensions arranged, normally, in the format of a table.

**OLAP report:** The output of an OLAP analysis in tabular format. For example, this can be a Microsoft Excel PivotTable. *See* OLAP Cube.

**OLE DB:** The COM-based foundation of data access in the Microsoft world. OLE DB objects support the OLE object standard. ADO is based on OLE DB.

**1:1:** An abbreviation for a one-to-one relationship between the rows of two tables.

**1:N:** An abbreviation for a one-to-many relationship between the rows of two tables.

**Online Analytical Processing (OLAP):** A technique for analyzing data values, called measures, against characteristics associated with those data values, called dimensions.

**Online Transaction processing (OLTP) system:** An operational database system available for, and dedicated to, transaction processing.

**Open Database Connectivity (ODBC):** A standard means for accessing DBMS products. Using ODBC, the unique API of a DBMS is hidden, and the programmer writes to the standard ODBC interface.

**Operational system:** A database system in use for the operations of the enterprise, typically a OLTP system. *See* Online Transaction processing (OLTP) system.

**Optimistic locking:** A locking strategy that assumes no conflict will occur, processes a transaction, and then checks to determine whether conflict did occur. If so, the transaction is aborted. *See also* **deadlock** and **pessimistic locking**.

**Outer join:** A join in which all the rows of a table appear in the resulting relation, regardless of whether they have a match in the join condition. In a left outer join, all the rows in the left-hand relation appear; in a right outer join, all the rows in the right-hand relation appear.

**Parent:** A row, record, or node on the one side of a one-to-many relationship. *See also* **child**.

**Parent mandatory and child mandatory (M-M):** A relationship where the minimum cardinality of the parent is 1 and the minimum cardinality of the child is 1.

**Parent mandatory and child optional (M-O):** A relationship where the minimum cardinality of the parent is 1 and the minimum cardinality of the child is 0.

**Parent optional and child mandatory (O-M):** A relationship where the minimum cardinality of the parent is 0 and the minimum cardinality of the child is 1.

**Parent optional and child optional (O-O):** A relationship where the minimum cardinality of the parent is 0 and the minimum cardinality of the child is 0.

**Partitioned database:** A database in which portions of the database are distributed to two or more computers.

**Personal database system:** A DBMS product intended for use by an individual or small workgroup. Such products typically include application development tools such as form and report generators in addition to the DBMS. For example, Microsoft Access 2010.

**Pessimistic locking:** A locking strategy that prevents conflict by placing locks before processing database read and write requests. *See also* **deadlock** and **optimistic locking**.

**Phantom read:** A situation that occurs when a transaction reads data it has previously read and then finds new rows that were inserted by a committed transaction.

**PHP:** *See* PHP: Hypertext Processor.

**PHP: Hypertext Processor:** A Web page scripting language used to create dynamic Web pages. It now includes an object-oriented programming component and PHP Data Objects (PDO). *See* PHP Data Objects (PDO).

**Primary key:** A candidate key selected to be the key of a relation.

**Processing rights and responsibilities:** Organizational policies regarding which groups can take which actions on specified data items or other collections of data.

**Properties:** Same as attributes.

**Pull report:** In reporting systems, a report that must be requested by users.

**Push report:** In reporting systems, a report that is sent to users according to a schedule.

**Query by Example (QBE):** A style of query interface, first developed by IBM but now used by other vendors, that enables users to express queries by providing examples of the results they seek.

**Question mark (?) wildcard character:** A character used in Access 2010 queries to represent a single unspecified character. *See* SQL underscore (_) wildcard character.

**R score:** In RFM analysis, the "how recently" score, which reflects how recently a customer made a purchase. *See* RFM Analysis.

**Read committed isolation:** A level of transaction isolation that prohibits dirty reads but allows nonrepeatable reads and phantom reads.

**Read uncommitted isolation:** A level of transaction isolation that allows dirty reads, nonrepeatable reads, and phantom reads to occur.

**Record:** (1) A group of fields pertaining to the same entity; used in file-processing systems. (2) In the relational model, a synonym for row and tuple. *See also* **row**.

**Recovery via reprocessing:** Recovering a database by restoring the last full backup, and then recreating each transaction since the backup.

**Recovery via rollback/rollforward:** Recovering a database by restoring the last full backup, and then using data stored in a transaction log to modify the database as needed by either adding transactions (roll forward) or removing erroneous transactions (rollback).

**Recursive relationship:** A relationship among entities, objects, or rows of the same type. For example, if CUSTOMERs refer other CUSTOMERs, the relationship is recursive.

**Referential integrity constraint:** A relationship constraint on foreign key values. A referential integrity constraint specifies that the values of a foreign key must be a proper subset of the values of the primary key to which it refers.

**Regression analysis:** A form of supervised data mining in which the parameters of equations are estimated by data analysis.

**Relation:** A two-dimensional array that contains single-value entries and no duplicate rows. The meaning of the columns is the same in every row. The order of the rows and columns is immaterial.

**Relational model:** A data model in which data are stored in relations and relationships between rows are represented by data values.

**Relational database:** A database that consists of relations. In practice, relational databases contain relations with duplicate rows. Most DBMS products include a feature that removes duplicate rows when necessary and appropriate. Such removal is not done as a matter of course because it can be time-consuming and expensive.

**Relational schema:** A set of relations with referential integrity constraints.

**Relationship:** An association between two entities, objects, or rows of relations.

**Relationship cardinality constraint:** A constraint on the number of rows that can participate in a relationship. Minimum cardinality constraints determine the number of rows that must participate; maximum cardinality constraints specify the largest number of rows that can participate.

**Relationship class:** An association between entity classes.

**Relationship instance:** (1) An association between entity instances, (2) a specific relationship between two tables in a database.

**Repeatable reads isolation:** A level of transaction isolation that disallows dirty reads and nonrepeatable reads. Phantom reads can occur.

**Replicated database:** A database in which portions of the database are copied to two or more computers.

**Report:** A formatted set of information created to meet a user's need.

**Report authoring:** In a reporting system, connecting to the data source, creating the report structure, and formatting the report.

**Report delivery:** In a reporting system, pushing the reports to users, or allowing them to pull the reports as needed.

**Report management:** In a reporting system, defining who receives which reports, when, and by what means.

**Reporting systems:** Business intelligence (BI) systems that process data by filtering, sorting, and making simple calculations. OLAP is a type of reporting system.

**Resource locking:** *See* **lock**.

**RFM analysis:** A type of reporting system in which customers are classified according to how recently (R), how frequently (F), and how much money (M) they spend on their orders.

**Rollback:** A process that involves recovering a database in which before-images are applied to the database to return to an earlier checkpoint or other point at which the database is logically consistent.

**Rollforward:** A process that involves recovering a database by applying after-images to a saved copy of the database to bring it to a checkpoint or other point at which the database is logically consistent.

**Row:** A group of columns in a table. All the columns in a row pertain to the same entity. Also known as tuple or record.

**Schema-valid document:** An XML document that conforms to XML Schema.

**Scrollable cursor:** A cursor type that enables forward and backward movement through a recordset. Three scrollable cursor types discussed in this text are snapshot, keyset, and dynamic.

**Second normal form (2NF):** A relation in first normal form in which all non-key attributes are dependent on all the keys.

**Serializable isolation level:** A level of transaction isolation that disallows dirty reads, nonrepeatable reads, and phantom reads.

**Shared lock:**  A lock against a data resource in which only one transaction can update the data but many transactions can concurrently read those data.

**Simple Object Access Protocol (SOAP):**  A standard used for remote procedure calls. It uses XML for definition of the data and HTTP for transport.

**SQL:**  *See* Structured Query Language.

**SQL AND operator:**  The SQL operator used to combine conditions in an SQL WHERE clause.

**SQL built-in function:**  In SQL, any of the functions COUNT, SUM, AVG, MAX, or MIN.

**SQL CREATE TABLE statement:**  The SQL command used to create a database table.

**SQL CREATE VIEW statement:**  The SQL command used to create a database view.

**SQL FROM clause:**  The part of an SQL SELECT statement that specifies conditions used to determine which tables are used in a query.

**SQL GROUP BY clause:**  The part of an SQL SELECT statement that specifies conditions for grouping rows when determining the query results.

**SQL HAVING clause:**  The part of an SQL SELECT statement that specifies conditions used to determine which rows are in the groupings in GROUP BY clause.

**SQL OR operator:**  The SQL operator used to specify alternate conditions in an SQL WHERE clause.

**SQL ORDER BY clause:**  The part of an SQL SELECT statement that specifies how the query results should be sorted when they are displayed.

**SQL percent sign (%) wildcard character:**  The standard SQL wildcard character used to specify multiple characters. Microsoft Access uses an asterisk (*) character instead of the underscore character.

**SQL SELECT clause:**  The part of an SQL SELECT statement that specifies which columns are in the query results.

**SQL SELECT/FROM/WHERE framework:**  The basic structure of an SQL query. *See* SQL SELECT clause, SQL FROM clause, SQL WHERE clause, SQL ORDER BY clause, SQL GROUP BY clause, SQL HAVING clause, SQL AND operator, and SQL OR operator.

**SQL SELECT * statement:**  A variant of an SQL SELECT query that returns all columns for all tables in the query.

**SQL SELECT . . . FOR XML statement:**  A variant of an SQL SELECT query that returns the query results in XML format.

**SQL underscore (_) wildcard character:**  The standard SQL wildcard character used to specify a single character. Microsoft Access uses a question mark (?) character instead of the underscore character.

**SQL view:**  A relation that is constructed from a single SQL SELECT statement. SQL views have at most one multivalued path. The term *view* in most DBMS products, including Microsoft Access, SQL Server, Oracle Database, and MySQL, means SQL view.

**SQL WHERE clause:**  The part of an SQL SELECT statement that specifies conditions used to determine which rows are in the query results.

**Star schema:**  In a dimensional database and as used in an OLAP database, the structure of a central fact table linked to dimension tables.

**Statement-level consistency:**  A situation in which all rows affected by a single SQL statement are protected from changes made by other users during the execution of the statement. *See also* **transaction-level consistency**.

**Static cursor:**  A cursor that takes a snapshot of a relation and processes that snapshot.

**Static report:**  In reporting systems, a report that is prepared once from underlying data and does not change when the underlying data change. Contrast with dynamic report.

**Stored procedure:**  A collection of SQL statements stored as a file that can be invoked by a single command. Usually, DBMS products provide a language for creating stored procedures that augments SQL with programming language constructs. Oracle provides PL/SQL for this purpose, and SQL Server provides Transact-SQL (T-SQL). With some products, stored procedures can be written in a standard language such as Java. Stored procedures are often stored within the database.

**Strong entity:**  In the entity-relationship model, any entity whose existence in the database does not depend on the existence of any other entity. *See also* **ID-dependent entity** and **weak entity**.

**Structured Query Language (SQL):**  A language for defining the structure and processing of a relational database. It can be used as a stand-alone query language, or it can be embedded in application programs. SQL was developed by IBM and is accepted as a national standard by the American National Standards Institute.

**Subquery:**  A SELECT statement that appears in the WHERE clause of an SQL statement. Subqueries can be nested within each other.

**Subtype entity:**  In generalization hierarchies, an entity or object that is a subspecies or subcategory of a higher-level type, called a supertype. For example, ENGINEER is a subtype of EMPLOYEE.

**Surrogate key:**  A unique, system-supplied identifier used as the primary key of a relation. The values of a surrogate key have no meaning to the users and usually are hidden on forms and reports.

**SUM:**  In SQL, a function that adds up a set of numbers. *See* SQL built-in functions.

**Supertype entity:**  In generalization hierarchies, an entity or object that logically contains subtypes. For example, EMPLOYEE is a supertype of ENGINEER, ACCOUNTANT, and MANAGER.

**Supervised data mining:**  A form of data mining in which an analyst creates a prior model or hypothesis and then uses the data to test that model or hypothesis.

**Support:**  In market basket analysis, the probability that two items will be purchased together.

**Table:**  A database structure of rows and columns to create cells that hold data values. Also known as a *relation* in a relational database, although strictly only tables that meet specific conditions can be called relations. *See* Relation.

**Ternary relationship:**  A relationship between three entities.

**Third normal form (3NF):**  A relation in second normal form that has no transitive dependencies.

**Three-tier architecture:**  A Web database processing architecture in which the DBMS and the Web server reside on separate computers.

**Time dimension:**  A required dimension table in a dimensional database. The time dimension allows the data to be analyzed over time.

**Transaction:**  (1) A group of actions that is performed on the database atomically; either all actions are committed to the database, or none of them are. (2) In the business world, the record of an event. *See also* **ACID transaction** and **atomic transaction**.

**Transaction isolation level:**  The degree to which a database transaction is protected from actions by other transactions. The 1992 SQL standard specifies four isolation levels: read uncommitted, read committed, repeatable read, and serializable.

**Transaction-level consistency:** A situation in which all rows affected by any of the SQL statements in a transaction are protected from changes during the entire transaction. This level of consistency is expensive to enforce and is likely to reduce throughput. It might also prevent a transaction from seeing its own changes. *See also* **statement-level consistency**.

**Transactional system:** A database dedicated to processing transactions such as product sales and orders. It is designed to make sure that only complete transactions are recorded in the database.

**Transitive dependency:** In a relation having at least three attributes, such as R (A, B, C), the situation in which A determines B and B determines C, but B does not determine A.

**Trigger:** A special type of stored procedure that is invoked by the DBMS when a specified condition occurs. BEFORE triggers are executed before a specified database action, AFTER triggers are executed after a specified database action, and INSTEAD OF triggers are executed in place of a specified database action. INSTEAD OF triggers are normally used to update data in SQL views.

**Tuple:** *See* **row**.

**Two-phase locking:** A procedure in which locks are obtained and released in two phases. During the growing phase, the locks are obtained; during the shrinking phase, the locks are released. After a lock is released, no other lock will be granted that transaction. Such a procedure ensures consistency in database updates in a concurrent-processing environment.

**Two-tier architecture:** A Web database processing architecture in which the DBMS and the Web server reside on the same computer.

**Type-valid document:** An XML document that conforms to its Document Type Declaration (DTD). Contrast with not-type-valid document.

**UML:** *See* Unified Modeling Language.

**Unified Modeling Language (UML):** A set of structures and techniques for modeling and designing object-oriented programs and applications. UML is a methodology and a set of tools for such development. UML incorporates the entity-relationship model for data modeling.

**Unique identifier:** An identifier that determines exactly one entity instance. *See also* **nonunique identifier**.

**Unique key:** A key that identifies a unique row.

**Unsupervised data mining:** A form of data mining in which analysts do not create a prior model or hypothesis, but rather let the data analysis reveal a model.

**User:** A person using an application.

**User data source:** An ODBC data source that is available only to the user who created it.

**User group:** A group of users. *See* User.

**WAMP:** AMP running on a Windows operating system. *See* AMP.

**Weak entity:** In the entity-relationship model, an entity whose logical existence in a database depends on the existence of another entity. *See also* **ID-dependent entity** and **strong entity**.

**Web portal:** A Web page designed to be an entrance point for a Web site. It may display information from several sources, and may require authentication to access.

**Web Services:** A set of XML standards that enable applications to consume each other's services using Internet technology.

**World Wide Web Consortium (W3C):** The group that creates, maintains, revises and publishes standards for the World Wide Web including HTML, XML, and XHMTL.

**wwwroot folder:** The root folder or directory of a Web site on a Microsoft IIS Web server.

**XHTML:** The Extensible Hypertext Markup Language. A reformulation of HTML to XML standards of well-formed documents.

**XML Schema:** An XML document that describes the structure of a class of XML documents by defining the tags and the valid relationship of those tags.

# Index